THE RECOVERY OF MAINTENANCE IN THE EU AND WORLDWIDE

This book grew out of a major European Union (EU) funded project on the Hague Maintenance Convention of 2007 and on the EU Maintenance Regulation of 2009. The project involved carrying out analytical research on the implementation into national law of the EU Regulation and empirical research on the first year of its operation in practice. The project also engaged international experts in a major conference on recovery of maintenance in the EU and worldwide in Heidelberg in March 2013. The contributions in this book are the revised, refereed and edited versions of the best papers that were given at the conference. The book is divided into four parts: (i) comparative context; (ii) international, looking at national and non-European regional practice and how the Hague Convention could change things; (iii) international and the EU, looking at issues covered by both the Hague Convention and the EU Regulation; and (iv) the EU—looking at the Maintenance Regulation. This is the first study to look carefully at both of the new cross-border maintenance regimes globally and in Europe and to begin the examination of the practical operation of the latter regime. The approval of the Hague Convention by the EU on 9 April 2014 is a major step forward for its practical significance in enabling the recovery of child and spousal support, as from 1 August 2014 all of the 28 EU Member States apart from Denmark will be bound by the Convention.

Volume 15 in the series Studies in Private International Law

Studies in Private International Law

Volume 1: Electronic Consumer Contracts in the Conflict of Laws
Sophia Tang

Volume 2: Foreign Currency Claims in the Conflict of Laws
Vaughan Black

Volume 3: Jurisdiction and Judgments in Relation to EU Competition Law Claims
Mihail Danov

Volume 4: Cases and Materials on EU Private International Law
Stefania Bariatti

Volume 5: International Commercial Disputes: Commercial Conflict of Laws in English Courts
Jonathan Hill and Adeline Chong

Volume 6: International Child Abduction: The Inadequacies of the Law
Thalia Kruger

Volume 7: Mediating International Child Abduction Cases
Sarah Vigers

Volume 8: International Antitrust Litigation: Conflict of Laws and Coordination
Edited by Jürgen Basedow, Stéphanie Francq and Laurence Idot

Volume 9: The Governing Law of Companies in EU Law
Justin Borg-Barthet

Volume 10: Intellectual Property and Private International Law: Comparative Perspectives
Edited by Toshiyuki Kono

Volume 11: Child Abduction within the European Union
Katarina Trimmings

Volume 12: International Surrogacy Arrangements: Legal Regulation at the International Level
Edited by Katarina Trimmings and Paul Beaumont

Volume 13: The Hague Child Abduction Convention: A Critical Analysis
Rhona Schuz

Volume 14: Interregional Recognition and Enforcement of Civil and Commercial Judgments: Lessons for China from the US and EU Law
Jie Huang

The Recovery of Maintenance in the EU and Worldwide

Edited by

Paul Beaumont
Burkhard Hess
Lara Walker
and
Stefanie Spancken

• HART •
PUBLISHING
OXFORD AND PORTLAND, OREGON
2016

Published in the United Kingdom by Hart Publishing Ltd
16C Worcester Place, Oxford, OX1 2JW
Telephone: +44 (0)1865 517530
Fax: +44 (0)1865 510710
E-mail: mail@hartpub.co.uk
Website: http://www.hartpub.co.uk

Published in North America (US and Canada) by
Hart Publishing
c/o International Specialized Book Services
920 NE 58th Avenue, Suite 300
Portland, OR 97213-3786
USA
Tel: +1 503 287 3093 or toll-free: (1) 800 944 6190
Fax: +1 503 280 8832
E-mail: orders@isbs.com
Website: http://www.isbs.com

First published in hardback 2014
Paperback edition, 2016

Hart Publishing is an imprint of Bloomsbury Publishing plc.

British Library Cataloguing in Publication Data
Data Available

ISBN: HB: 978-1-84946-573-1
PB: 978-1-50990-928-5

Typeset by Compuscript Ltd, Shannon
Printed and bound in Great Britain by
Lightning Source UK Ltd

FOREWORD

by

William Duncan CMG, LLD, former Deputy Secretary General of the Hague Conference on Private International Law

This book is a worthy testament to the extraordinary efforts which are currently being undertaken nationally, regionally and internationally to improve cross-border systems for the recovery of maintenance, and in particular, child support. These efforts have a long history beginning, at the multinational level, with work on a preliminary draft Convention undertaken by UNIDROIT in 1929, on the initiative of the League of Nations. Later, under the United Nations, this culminated in the ground-breaking New York Convention of 1956 on the Recovery Abroad of Maintenance. This Convention, with its novel provisions for cooperation between national transmitting and receiving authorities, is still benefiting families in different parts of the globe.

The Hague Conference on Private International Law began playing its part in the 1950s with two Conventions on maintenance obligations towards children, the first (1956) dealing with applicable law, and the second (1958) dealing with recognition and enforcement of foreign orders. These were followed in 1973 with two further Conventions dealing with maintenance obligations arising from family relationships more broadly. The latest product of the Hague Conference, the 2007 Convention on the International Recovery of Child Support and Other Forms of Family Maintenance (together with its Protocol on the Law Applicable to Maintenance Obligations), which is one of the focuses of the book, was very much influenced by all of these earlier instruments, drawing from their successes and shortcomings, combining simplified rules on recognition and enforcement with detailed provision for administrative cooperation, confronting the crucial issue of costs in child support cases, and containing new provisions designed to promote effective enforcement by national authorities.

Work at the multilateral level has both influenced and benefitted from national and regional developments. The European Union Maintenance Regulation of 2009, which is another principal focus of the book, is an example of a regional instrument which has been influenced by international instruments, particularly the 2007 Hague Convention, but which has been able to achieve a higher degree of integration, illustrated by its inclusion of uniform direct rules of jurisdiction and the partial abolition of '*exequatur*'. The implementation of the Regulation in Member States of the European Union is subject to careful analysis in the book. The book also includes the results of a pioneering empirical study of the Regulation's first year in operation.

Other early efforts at the regional level mentioned in the book include, for South America, the Bustamante Code of 1928 and the 1989 Inter American Convention on Child and Family Maintenance. There is also the Commonwealth system, which in some countries (for example in Africa) still provides the principal basis for cross-border cooperation.

National Child Support Systems

One of the benefits of the negotiations on the 2007 Hague Convention was the cross-fertilization of ideas concerning national systems for the recovery of child support and other family maintenance. A great deal of information was exchanged during the negotiations and this process continues as more information is made available through the Country Profiles. It is also clear that, if the ambition expressed in the Preamble for procedures '*which produce results and are accessible, prompt, efficient, cost-effective, responsive and fair*' is to be met, implementation of the 2007 Hague Convention in many countries will need to be accompanied by reforms and efficiencies within national systems.

Some of the Chapters of the book contain critiques or provide examples of improvements in national systems, or of models which bear examination in other countries. It is noticeable that while many of the reforms are about improving efficiency in maintenance recovery systems, there are also concerns about other matters such as the use of alternative methods of dispute resolution or making efforts to prevent maintenance defaults from occurring. Notable too are the concerns that remain in some countries about the interaction of child support and custody or access disputes. It may be recalled that at an early stage in the negotiations on the 2007 Hague Convention there were also concerns about the interplay between child support and abduction cases.

The matter of enforcement under national law is another important theme. During the negotiations on the 2007 Hague Convention there was real concern that carefully crafted procedures for recognition and enforcement could be frustrated by inadequate enforcement at national level. On the other hand there was concern among some delegations that there should not be excessive intrusion into national law. The result is the compromise which appears in Chapter VI of the Convention. Enforcement is to be 'prompt'and the enforcement measures made available must be 'effective'. While there is an illustrative list of possible enforcement measures, none are made mandatory.

Keep it Simple

The decision to work on the new Hague Convention began with the Special Commission meetings of 1995 and 1999 which reviewed the practical operation of the existing Hague Conventions on Maintenance Obligations, as well as the *New York Convention of 20 June 1956 on the Recovery Abroad of Maintenance* (the 1956 New York Convention). The mandate for the second of these Special Commissions was broader, including an examination of the desirability of revising the Hague Conventions and including in a new instrument, rules on judicial and administrative co-operation.

The 1999 meeting began with a recognition of the complications which then surrounded (and still do) international maintenance recovery, with the large and confusing configuration of instruments operating at bilateral, regional and global levels. There was a general sense that the international system was not working well, that it suffered from lack of integration, that it was underutilized, often slow in its operation and not cost-effective. As against this there was an understandable reluctance to embark on yet another international instrument, with the considerable investment of time and resources that would be involved. Better, some thought, to concentrate on improving the functioning of the existing instruments. In the end frustration with the existing set-up overcame this reluctance, and the mandate for the 2007 Hague Convention was framed in the conclusions of the 1999 Special Commission, later to be endorsed, with some additions, by the Council on General Affairs and Policy of the Hague Conference.

One important question is how to prevent the new systems introduced by the 2007 Hague Convention from appearing or becoming too complex in their operation. Compared with other Hague Conventions, the 2007 Hague Convention is unusually long and detailed. Together with the *Protocol of 23 November 2007 on the Law Applicable to Maintenance Obligations*, it takes up 77 pages in the Hague Conference's *Collection of Conventions (1951–2009)*. It is in marked contrast with, for example, the *Hague Convention of 25 October 1980 on the Civil Aspects of International Child Abduction*, which is not only a much shorter instrument, but also contains less detail concerning procedural and other requirements.

There are good reasons why the 2007 Hague Convention contains the detail that it does. The rather precise rules on the applications available and on the processing of applications and requests are designed to avoid the uncertainties and ambiguities which can arise from more generalised provisions, as occurred with the 1956 New York Convention. The rules on effective access to procedures, including the provisions on free legal assistance for child support applications, are precise because negotiating States wanted a clear idea of the obligations they would be undertaking, and because they are designed to accommodate different national procedures.

The provisions of Article 20 (bases for recognition and enforcement) are complex because they are designed to capture the widest range of existing orders that consensus would permit. Similarly the provisions on scope are designed to bring within the 2007 Hague Convention framework the broadest possible range of maintenance obligations, also allowing States to expand on a reciprocal basis their definitions of what constitute maintenance obligations arising from a family relationship, parentage, marriage or affinity, including obligations in respect of vulnerable persons.

These and other complexities are therefore explicable. At the same time they give rise to the need to provide very clear and straightforward explanations of how the 2007 Hague Convention is intended to operate, especially for States that have less experience in the operation of child support and family maintenance systems. The work carried out by the Hague Conference and others to explain and simplify the workings of the Convention is already substantial. There is first the *Explanatory Report* drawn up by Alegria Borras and Jennifer Degeling which, among other things, explains the underlying purposes and objectives of the Convention as a whole, as well as its component parts. There is the *Practical Handbook for Caseworkers* on the operation of the Convention, drawn up and reviewed by experienced case workers, which, together with *standardised forms* and *country profiles*, should provide those who handle individual cases with the guidance they need to operate efficiently. Their work will be made even more efficient if carried out with the aid of the *electronic case management and communication system* currently being developed by the Permanent Bureau, as described in the book. Also, we should not underestimate the great need for education and training if the 2007 Hague Convention is to achieve its full global potential.

Simplicity should also be a guiding principle for those who, in courts, Central Authorities or agencies, are called upon to interpret the provisions of the 2007 Hague Convention. The sometimes complex language of the 2007 Hague Convention should not mask its basically simple objectives which are described in Article 1 and explained further in the Preamble. With regard to child support there are also the clear fundamental principles set out in the

UN Convention and repeated in the Preamble to the 2007 Hague Convention. And with regard to any danger of conflicting interpretation in different countries, the wording in Article 53 is crucial,

> In the interpretation of this Convention, regard should be had to its international character and to the need to promote uniformity in its application.

It is important too that the basics of the 2007 Hague Convention be understandable, not only to the professionals concerned with its implementation and operation, but also to others, including in particular Parliamentarians, whose role in advocating for ratification or accession is crucial. This book will play an important role in spreading knowledge of, and interest in, both the Hague Convention and the European Regulation.

Administrative Co-operation

It was the wisdom of the creators of the 1956 New York Convention to recognise the central importance of international co-operation at the administrative level between transmitting and receiving agencies. With the advantage of hindsight and several decades of experience in operating systems of administrative co-operation in other Hague Conventions (concerned with both legal co-operation and child protection), together with the experience gained in operating various bilateral and regional arrangements, it was possible in the 2007 Hague Convention to define a much broader and more comprehensive set of general and case-specific functions for Central Authorities. The functions include: to assist applicants in the recovery of maintenance abroad by the exchange and the provision of relevant information concerning procedures and services available in the different legal systems, to facilitate the proceedings for the establishment and enforcement of new orders or the recognition and enforcement of existing orders, to provide various ancillary services, such as the location of the debtor. There is no need to say more because the 2007 Hague Convention in Articles 5 and 6 provides a comprehensive list of services.

The 1956 New York Convention only partly achieved its pioneering objectives. It provided and still provides a useful cooperative mechanism among the limited number of States which furnish the resources needed to make it effective. The reasons for its limited success are worth recalling in the light of the efforts which are now being made to implement the 2007 Hague Convention and the 2009 Regulation successfully.

The open texture of the 1956 New York Convention, combined with the absence of a system of monitoring and review, contributed to the development of divergent interpretations and practices, which themselves undermined the sense of reciprocity and fairness needed to attract the full commitment of all the Contracting States. Some of the most basic aspects of treaty administration were absent. It was, for example, left to the Hague Conference to maintain an updated list of authorities appointed under the Convention, and it was the Hague Conference which with the agreement of the UN, carried out the review of the operation of the Convention in the two Special Commissions in the 1990s.

Building an International Child Support Community

The best examples of cross-border legal and administrative co-operation are those which, despite geographical distances, generate a sense of community among those charged with the responsibility of co-operation in the different participating States. Success is more likely if the formal system of co-operation established by a Convention is cemented by persons who work with a common purpose, a common understanding of the Convention's requirements and objectives, a common commitment to the development of best practices, a common willingness to understand that implementation cannot be achieved at the same level or the same speed in all countries, a common concern in addressing shared problems, and most of all a common commitment to improving the lives of the children and families who are the beneficiaries of the international system.

In short, what is needed is the development of an international community, devoted to the issue of family maintenance, and in particular child support. It is through the building of such a community of experts in child support that the 2007 Hague Convention is most likely to succeed, to spread to all parts of the globe and even to adapt to a changing environment.

It should be remembered that the 2007 Hague Convention, like the other Hague Children's Conventions but in contrast with the European Regulation, does not have the benefit of a single authoritative body to resolve differences in interpretation which will arise at the national level, nor does it contain a mechanism for the investigation and resolution of complaints concerning State compliance with Convention obligations. Mechanisms for amending the Convention, though they exist, are complicated and more difficult to negotiate than changes within national systems. The 2007 Hague Convention will therefore rely very much on the consensual development of good practices—something which can best be achieved if those who are responsible for implementing and operating the 2007 Hague Convention perceive themselves as a community with a common purpose.

In fact the process of community building began long before the 2007 Hague Convention came into force. The negotiating process itself, based on the principle of consensus, helped to unify the participating States around a common goal. The work of the Administrative Co-operation Working Group (ACWG), which continued to meet largely through conference calls in between negotiating sessions, not only helped to find solutions to some of the practical issues surrounding the processing of cases—it also began the process of community building and helped to focus attention on the necessary post-Convention work. The process continued with the convening of the Special Commission meeting on the implementation of the 2007 Hague Convention, which took place in November 2009.

At the regional level too, much work is being done to support the development of the networks on which the health of the 2007 Hague Convention will depend. This has been particularly the case within Europe and in the Americas. Therefore, already there exists a certain momentum towards the formation of a global child support community, but it will be important to see that this momentum is not lost through the frustrations which inevitably accompany the implementing process, and to ensure that it is not confined to the countries with better developed national systems of child support. Already much has been done to generate this sense of a global community. The publication of this book, together with the earlier convening in March 2013 of the Heidelberg Conference on which the book is based, will help to cement that vital community-building process.

Congratulations are due, not only to the editors and contributors, but also to the Organiser of the Heidelberg Conference, the German Institute for Youth Human Services, and its principal partners, the Universities of Aberdeen and of Heidelberg, as well as to the associate partners, the German Federal Ministry of Justice, the National Child Support Enforcement Association (USA), the Hague Conference on Private International Law and the University of Lyon.

The Hague
March 2014

EDITORS' PREFACE

This book grew out of a research project which was funded by the European Commission that had at its heart the Conference 'International Recovery of Maintenance in the EU and Worldwide' held in Heidelberg in 2013, but also included the empirical research carried out by the editors and reported on in two chapters in this book. The Conclusions and Recommendations of the Conference can be found on the conference website, and these are intended to be the starting point for a global network on the international recovery of maintenance.[1] The editors would like to take this opportunity to thank Richard Hart for having faith in this endeavour. He has published many excellent English language law books particularly, for our interests, within the series 'Studies in Private International Law'. It is very sad that he will no longer be working in this role and we are sorry to see him go.

The book contains a collection of the papers that were originally presented at the Conference. The chapters provide a wide range of perspectives on the international recovery of maintenance as they are written by policy makers, practitioners and academics from a variety of jurisdictions. The book begins with an excellent paper written by Professor Jayme, derived from his inspirational keynote speech at the Conference, which provides an essential introduction to the topic of this book. The editors greatly appreciate his contribution and his participation in the conference as a truly outstanding Professor of Private International Law. He has the breadth of knowledge—culturally, legally and intellectually—to set the scene for the whole volume. As always he is a great credit to the University of Heidelberg. The remainder of the book is divided up into three Parts (International, International and European Union, and European Union) with a brief introduction from two of the editors to the first two of these Parts and from the other two editors to the third Part. The editors would like to thank all the authors for their contributions and their interest in the project without which there would be no book. We would also like to thank the anonymous referees for their very helpful comments and assistance.

William Duncan has kindly agreed to take the time to write a Foreword for this book. We are extremely grateful that he is willing to do this given his key role in piloting the creation of the 2007 Convention as the then Deputy Secretary General of the Hague Conference on Private International Law.

The editors would especially like to thank Céline Camara, Research Fellow at the Max Planck Institute Luxembourg for International, European and Regulatory Procedural Law for her support.

[1] Available at www.heidelberg-conference2013.de/conference.html (accessed January 2014).

Finally we would like to express our gratitude to Thomas Meysen, Elisabeth Unger,[2] and all their excellent colleagues at DIJuF for all their efforts to coordinate the EU funded research project and to organise the Conference in a way that made it a great success.

Paul Beaumont, Burkhard Hess, Stefanie Spancken, Lara Walker

2 April 2014

[2] Elisabeth Unger has recently published a detailed report on the conference. See E Unger, 'Internationale Unterhaltsrealisierung in der EU und weltweit, Fachübergreifende internationale Konferenz in Heidelberg—Ein Tagungsbericht' (2013) *Zeitschrift für das gesamte Familienrecht* 1941–46.

CONTENTS

LIST OF CONTRIBUTORS

Matthias Abendroth
Research assistant at the Institute for Private Law and Civil Procedure / Chair for Civil Law, Civil Procedure, Medical Law and Comparative Law of Prof Dr Volker Lipp, Georgia Augusta University Göttingen, Germany.

Nadia de Araujo
Professor of Private International Law, Law Department, Pontificia Universidade Catolica do Rio de Janeiro, Brazil.

Paul Beaumont
Professor of European Union and Private International Law and Director of the Centre for Private International Law, University of Aberdeen, Scotland, UK.

Ana-Sabine Boehm, Natalie Faetan and Isabelle Jäger-Maillet
The German Institute for Youth Human Services and Family Law (DIJuF), Heidelberg, Germany.

James Ding
Deputy Principal Government Counsel in the International Law Division, Department of Justice of the Hong Kong Special Administrative Region of the People's Republic of China.

Ann Laquer Estin
Aliber Family Chair in Law, The University of Iowa College of Law, USA.

Maja Groff
Senior Legal Officer at the Permanent Bureau of the Hague Conference on Private International Law, The Hague, The Netherlands.

Burkhard Hess
Director of the Max Planck Institute Luxembourg for International, European and Regulatory Procedural Law and Professor of Law at the Universities of Heidelberg and Luxembourg.

Jayne Holliday
PhD Student in Private International Law, Research Assistant, Secretary of the Centre for Private International Law, University of Aberdeen, Scotland, UK.

Erik Jayme
Emeritus Professor, Institut für auslandisches und internationales Privat-und Wirtschaftsrecht, der Ruprecht-Karls-Universität Heidelberg, Germany.

Floor de Jongh Bekkali
Head of the child support section at NAV (National Office for Social Insurance Abroad), Norwegian Central Authority for the Hague Maintenance Convention 2007, Oslo, Norway.

Milana Karayanidi
Ph.D. Candidate, School of Law, Trinity College Dublin, Ireland.

Robert Keith
Chief Counsel for Children, Families and Aging programmes in the Office of the General Counsel, US Department of Health and Human Services, USA.

Inez Lopes
Professor of Public and Private International Law, Faculty of Law, University of Brasilia, Brazil. Former Coordinator General of International Legal Cooperation in Civil Matters of the Department of Recovery Assets and International Legal Cooperation (DRCI)—Ministry of Justice, Brazil.

Philippe Lortie
First Secretary, Hague Conference on Private International Law, The Hague, The Netherlands.

Dieter Martiny
Emeritus Professor at Europa-Universität Viadrina in Frankfurt/Oder, Germany

Csongor István Nagy
Associate Professor, University of Szeged, Hungary.

Olanike Adelakun-Odewale
Lecturer, Department of International Law, Lead City University, Ibadan, Nigeria.

Richard Frimpong Oppong
Assistant Professor of Law, Thompson Rivers University, Faculty of Law, British Columbia, Canada.

Hannah Roots
Managing Director, Family Maintenance Enforcement Programme, British Columbia, Canada.

Nieve Rubaja
Professor of Private International Family Law and researcher, University of Buenos Aires, Argentina.

Jorid Saue
Senior advisor and Britt Rustad Head of Insurance Collection Section at the Norwegian Collection Agency of the Labour and Welfare Administration, Oslo, Norway.

Elisabeth Sœttem
Senior adviser at the Norwegian Ministry of Labour- and Social Affairs, Oslo, Norway.

Stefanie Spancken
Legal Trainee at the District Court of Münster, Germany.

Mark Takayesu and Steven Eldred
Orange County Department of Child Support Services, California, USA.

Maarja Torga
Lecturer of Civil Law, University of Tartu, Estonia.

Katarina Trimmings
Lecturer in Law and Deputy Director of the Centre for Private International Law, University of Aberdeen, Scotland, UK.

Ilaria Viarengo
Professor of International Law at the University of Milan (Università degli Studi di Milano), Italy.

Lara Walker
Lecturer in Law, University of Sussex, England, UK.

Mirela Župan
Assistant Professor of Private International Law, Faculty of Law, J J Strossmayer University of Osijek, Croatia.

Part One

Comparative Context

1

Cultural Dimensions of Maintenance Law from a Private International Law Perspective

ERIK JAYME

I. Introduction

A. Legal Culture

i. Family Law and Social Security Law

The question of the cultural dimension of law can be interpreted in different ways. First, legal norms and legal institutions are embedded in their legal culture of origin. This legal culture is based primarily on a certain legal tradition. This holds true for the legal system as such, but also for the administration of justice and, in particular, the professional practice. It is clear that the current law of maintenance is embedded in such an environment of customs and habits. In Germany, for example, courts decide on maintenance obligations, while in many other countries, in principle, it is social authorities who decide. This also affects the structure of maintenance law. The New Zealand Child Support Act 1991, section 128 (under the heading 'Debt due to the Crown') provides:

> Any amount of financial support payable under this Act (including penalty or interest imposed thereon) is a debt due to the Crown.

ii. Maintenance Tables

Different jurisdictions have found different solutions for the demarcation of family law and social security law, that is, private law and public law, including criminal penalties for the failure to pay maintenance. German courts decide on the basis of maintenance tables that show the amount of maintenance due to the exact cent. These tables exist for every higher Regional Courts district. The best known of these is the so-called Düsseldorf Maintenance Table.

Other countries manage their maintenance cases almost completely without such tables; the focus is on the individual case. A maintenance law based on tables aims to foster equality in society. In a law without tables, the focus of attention lies on the individual and his or her needs. These differences again correspond to the sense of justice that prevails in a society. In Germany, the individual only seems to be satisfied if he or she is treated in the same way as all others. In other societies, citizens are convinced of the uniqueness of their cases and demand appropriate justice in each individual case. Apart from that, tables take the pressure off from those in charge to decide on the maintenance claim, be it a judge or a social authority. The structure of the law of maintenance also affects private international and international procedural law. The similarity of the law of maintenance in New Zealand and Australia has led to a bilateral agreement that guarantees the mutual cross-border enforcement of maintenance claims.

iii. History and Science

Moreover, the legal system as such, which has evolved over time, forms part of the legal culture. In this sense, the French Civil Code is part of the country's cultural heritage, a monument of rationality and precise legal language. Further, legal science is of crucial importance: We may recall, for example, the concept of *Anspruch* (material claim). Only the German *Pandektistik* in the nineteenth century separated the *Anspruch* from the procedural action.

In countries that adopted this distinction, other legal issues related to the recovery of maintenance claims arose. There could be a conflict between a maintenance claim and a party's legal standing, for example, in cases of child maintenance. Section 1629(3) sentence 1 of the German Civil Code reads:

> If the parents of the child are married to each other, then one parent, as long as the parents live apart or a matrimonial matter between them is pending before a court, may assert maintenance claims of the child against the other parent only in his own name.

This situation is called *Prozessstandschaft*: One parent is entitled to bring the legal action in his or her own name while the holder of the maintenance claim remains the child.

In other jurisdictions, these questions do not arise and therefore these issues do not need to be addressed by the legislature—the material claim and the legal standing coincide; a distinction is not necessary. That is, for example, the case in English law. Under the Children Act 1989, section 1(1), Schedule 1 (which concerns orders for financial relief against parents) the court may, at the request of one parent, require the other parent to make periodical payments for the benefit of the child, either directly to the latter or to the applicant. English law does not distinguish between the claim itself and its procedural enforcement; in other words, substantive claim and procedural action merge in the application.

iv. Language

Language forms an important part of the legal culture, especially as regards the concept of 'maintenance'. From a comparative law perspective, there is a lack of a uniform, transnational concept. Italian law, for example, distinguishes between *mantenimento* and *alimenti*. The latter concerns maintenance obligations towards other people than immediate family members: the recipient of a gift may in certain cases be obliged to maintain the donor. In addition, it follows from Article 438 of the Italian Civil Code that *alimenti* are only a form of second degree maintenance, while the *mantenimento* encompasses all forms of maintenance.

v. Religion

The influence of religion also forms part of the legal culture, especially in countries where in family law matters religious law applies to members of a religious group. It is striking that numerous religious laws do not provide for provisions on maintenance. This holds true even for the laws of the various Christian churches. In States with Islamic legal traditions, spousal maintenance in particular is determined by such traditions. A post-marital maintenance obligation does not exist. The Jewish Talmudic law also does not provide for spousal maintenance obligations. In Israel however, spousal maintenance follows from State Regulations (in the area of maintenance law). The States which have been influenced by Islam have created legal institutions intended to substitute the maintenance obligation.

B. Comparative Law

This briefly sketched cultural dimension of law plays a key role in cross-border situations, which are the main topic of this book. In this context, it is necessary first to examine the role of comparative law since only comparative law may provide the basis for an answer to the numerous questions arising out of cross-border situations. Postmodern comparative law focuses on the diversities between national laws rather than on the commonalities. Only as a second step are equivalences to be identified in order to allocate the legal norm in question to a hypernym, here to 'maintenance'.

An example is provided by an older decision of the Court of Justice of the European Union (CJEU) of 6 March 1980[1]: The question was whether a French ruling that ordered the spouse to make a *prestation compensatoire* according to Article 270ff of the French Civil Code could be seen as a decision on 'maintenance', since the Convention on jurisdiction and the enforcement of judgments in civil and commercial matters did not apply to rights in property arising out of a matrimonial relationship, but to maintenance obligations. The court pointed out that in French law such compensation depends on the needs and resources of the spouses and is therefore to be regarded as 'maintenance'. However, French law distinguishes clearly between *pension alimentaire* and *prestation compensatoire*.[2] The maintenance obligation—*devoir de secours*—ends with the divorce, except in cases of a divorce because of a *rupture de la vie commune* (an irretrievable breakdown in the relationship, under Article 270 of the French Civil Code). However, this illustrates that in international cases the notion of 'maintenance' in conflict of law rules may have a broader meaning than in national law.

Furthermore, by using comparative law, different types of maintenance may be identified. For instance in Germany, *Bedarfsunterhalt*, that is, maintenance to help provide for the necessities of daily life, such as clothing and housing, may be distinguished from *Ausgleichsunterhalt*, that is, maintenance which allows the creditor to benefit from the more prosperous financial situation of another family member. The boundaries between

[1] Case 120/79 *de Cavel II* [1980] ECR 731 noted in (1981) *Praxis des Internationalen Privat- und Verfahrensrechts* 19; *cf* R Hausmann, 'Zur Anerkennung von Annex-Unterhaltsentscheidungen nach dem EG-Gerichtsstands- und Vollstreckungsübereinkommen' (1981) *Praxis des Internationalen Privat- und Verfahrensrechts* 5ff.

[2] P Giron, 'Prestation compensatoire et pension alimentaire' (1994) *Dalloz chronique* 262.

maintenance and the family property regime might be blurry in many cases, particularly as regards spousal maintenance.

C. Cultural Differences

i. Extended Family or Nuclear Family

The differences between the legal systems with regard to maintenance based on cultural differences can also be due to different forms of family and home life, and different ideologies in the respective society. This becomes particularly clear when looking at the persons entitled to maintenance. The beneficiaries of maintenance in the different legal systems vary according to whether a society is based on the extended family or the nuclear family. While the legal systems in the European Union limit maintenance obligations to relatives in direct line, spouses and civil partners, Turkish law, for instance, extends maintenance obligations to siblings.

For example, the German Bundesfinanzhof (Federal Fiscal Court) had to rule on a case involving a Turkish national domiciled in Germany.[3] The claimant was subject to taxation in Germany and claimed a tax deduction for maintenance paid to relatives living in Turkey as exceptional costs, namely 8.800 DM which he had paid to his father and his step-mother and 17.608 DM paid to his sister and her three children. The Federal Fiscal Court held that the principles of maintenance obligations under German law were decisive. The second sentence of the first official case report reads as follows: 'Maintenance paid in accordance with foreign law to persons related collaterally who would not have been entitled to maintenance under German law are not tax deductible in Germany, even if the maintenance obligation arising from foreign law is to be complied with in Germany according to private international law'.

This decision has justly been criticised. The tax payer is exposed to a conflict of obligations—on the one hand, he is required to pay maintenance to his relatives living in Turkey under German private international law, while on the other hand he is obliged to pay taxes in Germany for amounts which no longer form part of his disposable income, because his taxable income is determined considering the German principles of maintenance obligations. It should be remembered that judgments given in Turkey may be enforced in Germany. In German doctrine, Wilhelm Wengler stated that avoiding conflicts of obligations was a fundamental goal of private international law. The Turkish tax payer is put in a virtually hopeless situation, stuck between the opposing claims of the German treasury and of his Turkish family.

As can be seen, extended family and nuclear family are culturally diverging concepts, and this has an effect on the law of maintenance.

ii. Non-marital Partnerships

In many legal systems, maintenance obligations are limited to relatives and spouses. However, in some legal systems the non-marital partnership is also of importance.

[3] BFH, 4 April 2002, (2004) *Praxis des Internationalen Privat- und Verfahrensrechts* 242; *cf* the critical comment by M Gebauer and U Hufeld, 'Gleichbehandlung der Unterhaltsschuldner im Steuerrecht und Art. 18 EGBGB' (2004) *Praxis des Internationalen Privat- und Verfahrensrechts* 327ff.

According to Article 1694 of the Brazilian Civil Code, it is not only relatives and spouses who are entitled to maintenance but also partners in non-marital partnerships, known as *companheiros*. Under Portuguese law, Article 2020 of the Portuguese Civil Code contains a provision addressing the *união de facto* (the factual union). The surviving partner of a factual union which has lasted for at least two years is entitled to maintenance which is to be paid from the estate of the deceased partner. The attribution of legal effects to the factual union is a characteristic of Lusophonic legal systems. However, the embodiment of the factual union in family law can also be found in the succession States of the former Yugoslavia, for instance, in Serbian law, which imposes maintenance obligations on the partners in a factual union (Article 156 of the Serbian Family Law).

D. Parent Maintenance in Particular

Traditionally, a distinction is made between spousal maintenance and child maintenance, although the two areas may overlap. This is the case if one parent is entitled to claim maintenance (*Betreuungsunterhalt*) in order to take care of a child that lives with him or her after parents have separated.

More recently however, discussion has focused on parent maintenance (maintenance claims of parents against their children).[4] This is particularly true for countries which, due to their demographic development, are facing a declining birth rate and an increasing number of elderly people in need of support. The question which arises is whether parent maintenance is subject to exceptional rules. Section 1611(1) of the German Civil Code reads as follows:

> If the person entitled to maintenance has become in need of financial support as a result of his own moral fault, if he has grossly neglected his own obligation to maintain the person who is now liable for maintenance or intentionally committed severe misconduct against the person liable for maintenance or a close relative of the person liable for maintenance, the person liable for maintenance is required to pay only such contribution to maintenance as may be deemed to be equitable. The obligation lapses completely if it would be grossly inequitable for the person liable for maintenance to be held to be so liable.

Section 1611(2) of the German Civil Code reads: 'The provisions of subsection (1) do not apply to the obligation of parents to maintain their minor unmarried children'.

Thus, it is possibility that the right to parent maintenance may be forfeited by parents, as a result of their own reprehensible behaviour.

Thus, it can be seen that parents are obliged to fulfil their maintenance obligation irrespective of the behaviour of the children, but not vice versa. Parents who have grossly neglected their obligation as parents to maintain their children, may not then claim parent maintenance from the latter. In practice, courts are mostly concerned with the question of if and how far social security authorities may recover social benefit payments for parents in need from the children. In private international law, parent maintenance has not yet been the subject of separate consideration. However, parent maintenance will be a big issue

[4] *Cf* S Casabona, *Il dovere di assistenza verso il genitore in stato di bisogno—Una indagine di diritto comparato* (Naples, Edizioni Scientifiche Italiane, 2008); M Nehmer, *Erbunwürdigkeit und Elternunterhalt im Internationalen Privatrecht* (Frankfurt am Main, Peter Lang, 2013).

in future. In this respect, *Demenztourismus* (so-called dementia tourism) should also be mentioned, that is, the placement of feeble-minded elderly people in remote countries by their children, for instance from Switzerland to Thailand, in order to reduce the costs of assistance and care.

I will come back to the cultural dimension of maintenance law and in particular private international law aspects below, and then I will re-address comparative law aspects of the cultural differences between legal orders.

II. Private International Law

A. Cultural Identity—Nationality and Habitual Residence

If one speaks about the cultural dimension in private international law, reference is made to the cultural identity of the persons concerned, rather than to the differences in the legal cultures. Private international law is based on a system of connecting factors, which determine the applicable law. In international family law those connecting factors indicate the particular personal links of a person with a specific legal order. Previously, most legal systems in continental Europe applied the nationality principle. The law of the nationality, the *lex patriae*, was considered to be the appropriate legal regime. In common law countries, the principle of domicile had a similar function. Then, however, the principle of habitual residence came into play. Regarding maintenance, the Hague Convention of 24 October 1956 on the Law Applicable to Maintenance Obligations towards Children determined a shift towards the principle of habitual residence. The needs of the person entitled to maintenance were determined according to the place of his or her habitual residence. A person's habitual residence was considered a factual notion. Nowadays, in other contexts—such as parental responsibility and child abduction—the cultural identity of those concerned is again taken into consideration, while in legal literature there is at least one academic who requires an element of intent for the establishment of the habitual residence.[5] There have been several CJEU rulings on the principle of habitual residence. In its decision of 2 April 2009[6] on Article 8(1) of the Brussels II bis Regulation, the CJEU was again required to consider cultural circumstances. According to the Court, important factors for the determination of the habitual residence are: 'In particular, the duration, regularity, conditions and reasons for the stay on the territory of a Member State and the family's move to that State, the child's nationality, the place and conditions of attendance at school, linguistic knowledge and the family and social relationships of the child in that State'.

It seems that the concept of habitual residence in European conflict of laws varies depending on the respective legal issue. It appears that for maintenance, as in the past, a factual interpretation applies, especially since the term derives from the Hague Conventions, while for the conflicts of laws with regard to parental custody, a culturally determined notion of habitual residence prevails.

[5] M-P Weller, 'Der gewöhnliche Aufenthalt' in S Leible and H Unberath (eds), *Brauchen wir eine Rom 0-VO?* (Munich, Sellier European Law Publishers, 2013) 293.

[6] Case C-523/07 *A* [2009] ECR I-2805 (2011) *Praxis des Internationalen Privat- und Verfahrensrechts* 76.

B. *Lex Fori*

However, other aspects arising from the Hague Maintenance Protocol of 2007, which recently entered into force in the European Union, also play a role. The Maintenance Protocol was ratified by the European Union on 8 April 2010 but it did not enter into force under international law until 1 August 2013.[7] However, since 18 June 2011 it has applied with binding effect in all Member States, except Denmark and the UK.

A very recent case from Germany illustrates the new legal situation; the case originates from the request for an expert opinion submitted to the Heidelberg Institute for International Law.

A couple domiciled in Germany had separated. Together with the couple's daughter the wife moved to the State of New York in the United States. The husband remained in Germany with their son. The wife brought an action against her husband in a German court claiming maintenance for their daughter. The court—rooted in a traditional way of thinking—wanted to know how much maintenance a child living in New York can claim from the father under New York law and whether the mother is entitled to make these claims on behalf of the child. The Hague Maintenance Protocol, however, shows that in such a case the relevant law is not that of New York, but of Germany. Article 4(3) sentence 1 of the Hague Maintenance Protocol reads: 'Notwithstanding Article 3, if the creditor has seised the competent authority of the State where the debtor has his habitual residence, the law of the forum shall apply'.

That means the *lex fori*, the law of the court seised, here German law, is the relevant law. That way, the establishment of the content and application of foreign law can be avoided and the workload for both the courts and the parties is lessened. This enhances the efficiency and speed of the procedure.

The new rules are not based primarily on the idea of consideration of the cultural identity of the person concerned—in this case of the child entitled to maintenance. If the child—or the mother on behalf of the child—brought an action at her own habitual residence, the *lex fori* is relevant as well.

C. *'Conflits Mobiles'*

The case in the local court led to the subsequent request for an expert opinion. In the meantime, during the proceedings, the father had moved to England with their son and now lived in London. The court held that the claims by the New York resident daughter were governed by New York law (Article 3 of the Hague Maintenance Protocol), because the debtor no longer lived in Germany. So far, this question has not been discussed in Andrea Bonomi's 'Explanatory Report to the Hague Maintenance Protocol' or in the literature. In Article 4(3) sentence 1 of the Hague Maintenance Protocol the change of habitual residence of the debtor is not regulated. It is different when the creditor's habitual residence changes, since then according to Article 3(2) of the Hague Maintenance Protocol

[7] The Hague Protocol entered into force under international law on 1 August 2013 for the European Union and Serbia and no other States have signed or ratified it, see www.hcch.net/index_en.php?act=conventions.status&cid=133 (accessed January 2014).

the applicable law changes, too; a *conflit mobile* occurs. One must assume that when the obligated party changes their habitual residence, the German *lex fori* remains applicable, resulting in the strange case of a German court retaining jurisdiction even if both parties to the claim live abroad. The court may, however, apply its own law.

D. Party Autonomy

Another principle, which has very recently started to affect the international law of maintenance, is the choice of the applicable law and of the competent court[8] by the parties. Article 8 of the Hague Maintenance Protocol is, in many ways, an interesting and original provision. The weakness of such choice of the applicable law by the parties is shown whenever the rights of third parties are involved. Thus, the choice of law is excluded if it would affect the maintenance obligations towards those persons who have not yet come of age. This means the parents cannot, on behalf of the children, choose between themselves a law that governs the applicable law for their maintenance obligations towards the children. This choice is limited to the rights mentioned in Article 8(1) of the Hague Maintenance Protocol. Here again, the nationality of one of the two parties is of paramount consideration, a classic characteristic of the—presumed—cultural identity of the person.

E. Control of Choice of Law

Article 8(5) of the Maintenance Protocol is a provision of particular originality:

> Unless at the time of the designation the parties were fully informed and aware of the consequences of their designation, the law designated by the parties shall not apply where the application of that law would lead to manifestly unfair or unreasonable consequences for any of the parties.

Maintenance arrangements between family members are diversely controlled at the substantive law level. The aim is to protect the economically weaker party. Here the choice is between control of content and subsequent control.[9] The control of content relates to adverse clauses, such as the mutual maintenance waiver, in cases where one party is in need. The subsequent control serves to establish whether a subsequent change of circumstances has rendered the maintenance agreement unjust for one of the contracting parties. However, each control also threatens legal certainty, which is the essence of all contracts.

It is interesting to see that such control has now also reached private international law, as made apparent by Article 8(5) of the Hague Maintenance Protocol, though it concerns only contracts between spouses. Here the cultural differences between the various rights can be seen clearly. In common law legal systems, such as in Australia,[10] there is no judicial review of prenuptial agreements, if each spouse had the benefit of separate legal

[8] Art 4 of Council Regulation (EC) 4/2009 of 18 December 2008 on jurisdiction, applicable law, recognition and enforcement of decisions and cooperation in matters relating to maintenance obligations [2009] OJ L7/1 (Maintenance Regulation).

[9] See also *Versorgungsausgleichsgesetz* (Pension Rights Adjustment Act), s 8(1): 'The agreement for the pension rights adjustment has to withstand a control of content and a subsequent control'.

[10] C Luhn, *Privatautonomie und Inhaltskontrolle von Eheverträgen: ein kritischer Vergleich des deutschen und des australischen Rechts mit Bezügen zum Internationalen Privatrecht* (Frankfurt am Main, Lang, 2008).

advice. In German law, the Bundesverfassungsgericht (the Federal Constitutional Court) has established a 'social control' of prenuptial agreements; there the courts decide. The common law approach has prevailed in the Hague Maintenance Protocol. In my opinion that approach is superior to the German solution because it promotes legal certainty and relieves the pressure on courts, which for more than a decade have been constantly occupied with such cases.

Article 8(5) does not address the subsequent control. In the past, there was a rule in Swiss law requiring divorce agreements concluded at the beginning of the marriage to be confirmed later in the divorce proceedings. It remains to be seen whether such a subsequent control will be implemented with regard to a choice of law, for example, by using general principles of law, such as the abuse of rights or estoppel. However, Article 8(5) of the Hague Maintenance Protocol establishes a barrier to the choice of law, which could be used as a model in other contexts as well.

III. Distinction between Spousal and Child Maintenance

A. The Hague Maintenance Convention of 2007

It is striking that spousal maintenance and child maintenance in the Hague Convention of 23 November 2007 on the International Recovery of Child Support and Other Forms of Family Maintenance are treated differently. The entire system of administrative cooperation via Central Authorities does not apply to maintenance claims between spouses and former spouses, unless the request is filed together with a request for child support.

From a comparative perspective, it can be seen that child support and spousal support follow very different principles. For spousal maintenance the borders with other legal instruments of property law, in particular rights in property arising out of the matrimonial relationship, are blurred. A number of national laws allow an 'equitable distribution' of marital property by court decision in the divorce proceedings, covering the questions of maintenance.

In addition, the way of dealing with post-marital maintenance in particular varies considerably in the different national laws. Here, again, cultural traditions and the views of society play an important role. Post-marital maintenance is unknown or only ordered for a short period in certain jurisdictions, for example, in many Islamic countries. While in these legal systems other instruments are used to improve the economic situation of the divorced spouse, such as a 'dower', in principle there is no obligation to pay post-marital maintenance. Those legal systems that emphasise the personal responsibility of spouses after divorce come to similar results. For example, in Scandinavian countries, the obligation to pay post-marital maintenance, if it exists at all, is limited in time.

Diametrically opposed principles can be found in German law. Dieter Schwab once formulated the paradox: the marriage is indissoluble only when it has been dissolved. German law used to recognise a guarantee of standard of living. That meant that even after divorce the marital standard of living constituted a major factor in calculating post-marital maintenance. That maintenance was subdivided in *Bedarfsunterhalt*, *Aufstockungsunterhalt* and *Vorsorgeunterhalt*. In 2008 however, the German legislature replaced the guarantee of standard of living with the concept of compensation for disadvantages resulting from the marriage. As a consequence, in the case law, fictitious revenues[11] such as those that could have been earned if the maintenance creditor or debtor had complied with its obligations, are of paramount importance.[12] On 1 March 2013 the amended provisions on spousal maintenance entered into force. This change in legislation accords greater importance to the duration of the marriage and may be a step back from the opinion mentioned earlier.[13]

B. Spousal Maintenance and Marital Property Regime

Similarly, since 2005 Spanish common civil law provides for compensation for economic imbalances between the spouses resulting from a divorce, involving a deterioration of their situations prior to the marriage (Article 97 of the Spanish Civil Code). It should be noted that the statutory default matrimonial regime in Spanish common civil law, for example, the *derecho común* of the Civil Code, is the community of property. This implies the participation *in rem* in the acquisitions made by the spouses during marriage. As a consequence, the situation for post-marital maintenance changes as the latter is also determined with respect to the economic conditions of the spouses. In cases where the default matrimonial regime is the separation of property, post-marital maintenance is of greater importance for the economically weaker spouse. In contrast to child support, spousal maintenance aims at compensating for disadvantages and therefore means taking into account the assets of the other spouse. There is also specific legislation illustrating that the marital property system affects the amount of marital maintenance to be paid.[14] Child support, however, focuses on the need of the child, for example, for food, clothing, housing and education.

Thus it can be seen that the marital property regime and marital maintenance law complement each other and follow different principles. An exception is the *Betreuungsunterhalt* (section 1570 of the German Civil Code), maintenance that may be granted to and for the benefit of the spouse taking care of a common child. Overall, the approach taken in the 2007 Hague Maintenance Convention to limit the central provisions to child support and a connected spousal maintenance seems comprehensible and appropriate.

Private international law has responded to this close link between marital property regimes and post-marital maintenance. Pursuant to Article 8(1)(c) of the 2007 Hague Maintenance Protocol

> the maintenance creditor and debtor may at any time designate one of the following laws as applicable to a maintenance obligation—
>
> …
>
> c) the law designated by the parties as applicable, or the law in fact applied, to their property regime;

[11] BGH, 28 November 2012 (2013) *Neue Juristische Wochenschrift* 530ff, 531: 'if the maintenance debtor is in breach of his/her duty, he/she will be treated as if he/she had performed that duty. In the case of a breach of his/her duty to earn revenues, the maintenance debtor must be held to have made that fictitious income. He/she cannot be forced to work; however, he/she has to bear the consequences of not doing so with regard to maintenance'.

[12] BGH, 3 December 2012, (2013) *Neue Juristische Wochenschrift* 528: 'If the maintenance creditor complies with his/her current duty to work, he/she cannot be held responsible for not having made efforts in the past that would result now in a compensation of the financial disadvantages resulting from the marriage'.

[13] *Cf* W Born, 'Erhöhter Stellenwert der Ehedauer im Unterhaltsrecht—Klarstellung oder "Reform der Reform"?' (2013) *Neue Juristische Wochenschrift* 561ff.

[14] *Cf* German Civil Code, ss 1583, 1604.

C. Deficiency Cases—Hierarchy of Maintenance Claims

One of the most complicated problems of the law of maintenance concerns the so-called 'deficiency cases'. If the maintenance debtor's available income does not suffice to cover all maintenance claims, a hierarchy between the claims has to be established. The main question is the relationship between the claims of the divorced spouse (post-marital maintenance) and the claims of the second, new spouse of the maintenance debtor. German law gives priority to the post-marital maintenance claim, while in many other jurisdictions the claims of both mentioned spouses are treated equally.

In conflict of laws the question arises as to which law governs such deficiency cases. This is particularly difficult to answer when the potential maintenance creditors are domiciled in different countries. Then two legal regimes following different principles apply at the same time.

The District Court of Munich I had to decide a case where the post-marital maintenance claim was governed by Bosnian law, while the maintenance claim of the new spouse of the debtor was governed by German law. The court stated:

> The conflict between the national laws in the present case can be solved by keeping the Bosnian Law's result, giving both claims the same priority order. This allows the available assets to be distributed in compliance with the needs of the maintenance creditors in the most appropriate way.[15]

D. Questions of Combined Procedures

One last issue of conflict of laws remains to be addressed: the close relationship and interplay between personal status decisions, for example, legal separation, divorce, judicial determination of paternity and maintenance orders. In recent times, as a result of private international law provisions, different national laws apply to, for example, divorce and maintenance. Different legal regimes apply although both questions are substantively and procedurally closely interlinked.

Two examples from German case law illustrate the questions that can arise. The Pankow/Weissensee District Court (28 March 2012)[16] had to decide on the following facts: a married couple from Mozambique lived in Germany. They had separated and requested a divorce with mutual consent. At that time the governing law was the national law of the spouses, namely the law of Mozambique. This requires, for a divorce with mutual consent, that the spouses agree on the essential legal consequences of their divorce. An agreement on post-marital maintenance forms part of this. In the present case such an agreement did not exist. German law, that was then applicable to the maintenance claim, does not require such an agreement. The court ordered the divorce since German procedural law provides

[15] LG München I, 5 August 2010 (2010) *Die Deutsche Rechtsprechung auf dem Gebiete des Internationalen Privatrechts* No 106, 227, 228.

[16] *Pankow/Weissensee*, 28 March 2012 (2012) *Praxis des Internationalen Privat- und Verfahrensrechts* 450 with comment by E Jayme, 'Einverständliche Scheidung und Internationales Privatrecht' in R Michaels and D Solomon (eds), *Liber Amicorum Klaus Schurig zum 70. Geburtstag* (Munich, Sellier European Law Publishers, 2012) 73.

that the court will only decide on maintenance at the request of one of the parties, and such a request was made in this case.

This decision shows that the conflict of law rules may lead to the application of different national laws to divorce and their legal consequences, in particular maintenance claims, although divorce with mutual consent may only be possible if the spouses agree on the economic consequences of divorce.

Another decision—this time from the District Court of Tettnang (29 October 2004)[17]—concerned Serbian spouses living in Germany. The husband obtained a divorce in Serbia. In the proceedings before the Serbian court the wife did not ask the court to make a maintenance order, which is required by Serbian law to obtain maintenance. She applied for post-marital maintenance in Germany. The German court dismissed the application as unfounded, and stated that the Serbian proceedings should be respected by the German courts. There are too many comments in the legal literature on the problems that arise in such contexts to respond to them all. However, the case demonstrates clearly that applying different legal regimes to questions of personal status (in this case, divorce) and of maintenance leads to conflicts since in many national laws these questions are substantively and procedurally interlinked.

IV. Concluding Remarks

Looking at the cultural dimension of maintenance law from the viewpoint of private international law, one can find various differences originating from the differences in legal cultures. The latter are themselves caused by differences in legal traditions, in religion and ideologies. In many legal systems, maintenance law forms a part of family law, while in other legal systems it is rather associated with social security law. The cultural identity of the persons concerned plays a minor role in international maintenance law, but is still of some interest. For instance, the law of the party's nationality may be chosen. Apart from that, there is a certain tendency to apply the *lex fori*. It remains an essential concern of private international law to appropriately consider the relationship and interplay between questions of personal status and maintenance, from both substantive and procedural perspectives. The current tendency to deal with interlinked legal issues separately and to address them under different legal regimes should be subject to a critical review and should—if necessary—be revised.

[17] AG Tettnang, 29 October 2004 (2005) *Praxis des Internationalen Privat- und Verfahrensrechts* 154 with comment by E Jayme.

Part Two

International Perspective

2

Introduction to Part Two (International) and Part Three (International and EU)

PAUL BEAUMONT AND LARA WALKER

I. International

The most recent development in the international recovery of child support and other forms of family maintenance is the Hague Maintenance Convention of 2007 (the 2007 Convention).[1] The 2007 Convention entered into force in January 2013 and now applies in four States.[2] It is hoped that the United States (a State that signed the Convention straight away) will ratify the 2007 Convention soon.[3] EU becoming party to the 2007 Convention from 1 August 2014 should give huge momentum to further ratifications. The 2007 Convention introduces some key features such as free legal assistance in almost all child support applications,[4] and a separate chapter on actual enforcement.[5] The 2007 Convention also contains two tracks on recognition and enforcement in order to increase flexibility and encourage wide ratification.[6] On paper the 2007 Convention appears to be a workable instrument that takes positive steps in the context of the

[1] Hague Convention of 23 November 2007 on the International Recovery of Child Support and Other Forms of Family Maintenance.

[2] Norway, Albania, Bosnia and Herzegovina and the Ukraine www.hcch.net/index_en.php?act=conventions.status&cid=131 (accessed January 2014).

[3] Ibid. In the case of the EU the necessary Council Decision permitting the EU to adopt the Convention has been adopted, Art 2 of which empowers the President of the Council to designate the person empowered to deposit on behalf of the European Union the instrument of ratification, acceptance or approval of the Convention by the EU (see Council Decision of 9 June 2011 on the approval, on behalf of the European Union, of the Hague Convention of 23 November 2007 on the International Recovery of Child Support and Other Forms of Family Maintenance [2011] OJ L192/39-70). Member States were required to give all the relevant information to the Commission by 31 December 2012 to enable the EU to become a party to the Convention. All EU Member States apart from Denmark will be bond by the Convention from 1 August 2014.

[4] See Arts 15 and 16, and A Borrás and J Degeling, 'Explanatory Report on the Convention on the International Recovery of Child Support and Other Forms of Family Maintenance' (2009, HCCH) (Borrás and Degeling Report) paras 381–401.

[5] Borrás and Degeling Report (n 4) Chapter VI, paras 570–87 and L Walker, 'The Latest Private International Law Maintenance Regime, Internationally and in Europe' (2013, PhD thesis) section 8.2. See also L Walker, *Maintenance and Child Support in Private International Law* (Oxford, Hart Publishing, forthcoming 2015 March 2015).

[6] Borrás and Degeling Report (n 4) Arts 23 and 24, paras 490–525 and Walker (n 5) section 7.5.

international recovery of maintenance,[7] and the book seeks to discover what benefits it can bring by including a range of chapters that focus specifically on certain elements of the cross-border recovery of maintenance.

Part Two of the book includes chapters focusing on specific regions and associations: Asia (with a particular emphasis on Hong Kong), South America and Commonwealth Africa.[8] It then contains chapters on specific countries, some within these regions. The countries covered are: Argentina, Brazil, Kazakhstan, Nigeria, Norway and the United States. The chapters consider the current mechanisms for the recovery of maintenance and child support within the specific States and regions before analysing the benefits and challenges that ratification of the 2007 Convention might bring. These benefits and challenges are often interlinked, such as the benefit of having prescribed mechanisms for enforcement in States where mechanisms for enforcement are limited, along with the challenge of incorporating suitable and workable enforcement mechanisms into these systems. Identifying how the Convention could be managed in national systems and highlighting the benefits it could bring are essential for marketing the Convention as a workable instrument that can be widely ratified. The fact that systems can be developed to create very efficient collection of maintenance payments, even in cross-border cases, is highlighted by the reports from Norway and the United States. Other chapters also address the benefits of having two tracks for recognition and enforcement and identify the track that would be preferable in that particular State or region. Finally, one of the chapters looks beyond the implementation of the 2007 Convention and towards the future.[9] This forward thinking approach adds an interesting dimension to the book and encourages reflection beyond the challenges that are currently faced.

These region and State specific reports are complemented by chapters analysing data on migration, remittances, recovery of maintenance and child support, the implications for the 2007 Convention and Hague Protocol 2007 for maintenance disputes arising from children born through a surrogacy arrangement, and information on when the recovery of monetary claims is most successful. This creates a comprehensive overview of systems for the recovery of maintenance, and the management of these systems, while highlighting the scale of the problem thus emphasising the benefits that the 2007 Convention can bring. The inclusion of the data serves to highlight important information such as which States have the most maintenance traffic between them, and which States have most success with enforcement of orders. The information contained in these reports also draws upon the relationship between maintenance and global poverty. Of particular significance is the fact that the book contains two chapters analysing this link, which are supplemented by a chapter providing data on the ability and likelihood of the debtor to pay child support, depending on the debtor's circumstances.

Therefore this Part of the book covers a wide range of issues that relate to the international cross-border recovery of maintenance. It analyses the current systems that are in place, if any, in selected regions and States and the effectiveness of these systems. It suggests

[7] For more information on the 2007 Convention see the Borrás and Degeling Report (n 4) and Walker (n 5), chs 2, 4, 7, 8, 9 and 10.

[8] The term association is used as the Commonwealth Charter refers to the Commonwealth as a 'voluntary association' (Charter of the Commonwealth, signed Commonwealth Day 2013 available at www.thecommonwealth.org/our-charter (accessed January 2014)).

[9] See Robert Keith, ch 3 of this volume.

what improvements there could be within these States if the 2007 Convention is ratified, provides information on the frequency of these claims and explains the importance of the effective recovery of child support in relation to combatting global poverty. As a consequence this Part of the book highlights the intercourse between maintenance as a private matter for individuals and maintenance as a public matter for governments and other public bodies.

II. International and EU

In Part Three of the book there are two chapters by two of the key partners in the research project that underpins this book: DIJuF (the German Institute for Youth Human Services and Family Law) based in Heidelberg and the Hague Conference on Private International Law. The important subject of maintenance obligations made enforceable through authentic instruments is carefully analysed in a German context taking full account of the 2007 Convention, the Hague Protocol 2007 and the EU Maintenance Regulation by three colleagues from DIJuF who are experts in the practice of authentic instruments in maintenance (especially cross-border). They give us important insights into this key consensual way of reaching a maintenance agreement. A consensual approach should be highly prized in the area of maintenance as it tends to lead to maintenance actually being paid. They also highlight the tensions that exist in the 2007 Convention and even more so in the EU Maintenance Regulation between the systems for modification of a maintenance agreement and for actual enforcement of the agreement. Finally, the Part includes a chapter by Philippe Lortie who helped William Duncan pilot the creation of the 2007 Convention and the Hague Protocol 2007. One of Philippe's passions throughout the process was to ensure that the new international maintenance regime made maximum use of information technology (IT). His chapter in this book is, not surprisingly, on effective IT systems and the benefit of these systems in relation to the cross-border enforcement of maintenance obligations internationally under the 2007 Convention and within the EU under the EU Maintenance Regulation. One very significant way forward would be the adoption of iSupport by all Hague Contracting States for the 2007 Convention and all EU Member States for the EU Maintenance Regulation. It is very encouraging indeed to see that the EU Commission is investing a lot of money to enable the Hague Conference to develop iSupport. This is an outstanding example of cooperation between the EU and the Hague Conference for their mutual benefit. The last chapter in Part Three of the book also highlights the value of cooperation between the EU and the Hague Conference in making the reform of private international law work in an optimum way consistent with the principle of reverse subsidiarity. The fact that the EU chose to use the Hague Conference as the context for developing its own applicable law rules for maintenance through the Hague Protocol 2007 is an encouraging example of true internationalism by the EU.

3

The Modern History, Evolution and Projected Future of Child Support Enforcement in the United States and Globally: 1975 to 2025

ROBERT KEITH*

I. Introduction

1975 was a bellwether year for child support enforcement in the United States. Unprecedented Federal legislation was enacted on 4 January 1975[1] creating a cooperative Federal/State programme under a new 'title IV-D' of the Social Security Act,[2] for the purpose of enforcing the support obligations owed by non-custodial parents. The IV-D programme was originally conceived as a welfare recoupment initiative, generously funded and ambitious in its scope and intended goals. Primary responsibility for establishing and enforcing support orders remained with the States, but substantial Federal resources were made available to provide technical assistance, to conduct regular audits, and even to tap Federal data banks to assist in locating absent parents.[3] The first few years were marked by

* I gratefully acknowledge the editorial assistance of Marie Coridalia Scott.

[1] See An Act to Amend the Social Security Act to Establish a Consolidated Program of Federal Financial Assistance to Encourage Provision of Services by the States, Pub L No 93-647, 88 Stat 2337 (1975). The Social Security Amendments of 1974, was enacted on 4 January 1975, but its effective date was delayed by Pub L No 94-46 until 1 August 1975. See An Act to Continue for a Temporary Period the Existing Suspension of Duty on Certain Istle, Pub L No 94-46, 89 Stat 245 (1975).

[2] The Senate Finance Committee, concerned with the rapid increase in the Aid to Families with Dependent Children (AFDC) population, noted that '2.4 million persons were receiving AFDC in 1961 because the father was absent from the home … By the beginning of 1971, 7.5 million persons were receiving AFDC because of the father's absence from the home, and by the end of June 1974 that figure had grown to almost 8.7 million.' (S Rep No 93-1356, 8146 (1974)).

[3] Most significantly, Federal funding for the programme was set at 75% of State expenditures. In addition, States shared in the collection of child support recovered in AFDC cases in proportion to their contribution towards the original public assistance payments. Consideration was given to going even further and establishing a Federal programme to nationalise the collection of child support. Many viewed this as an intrusion by the Federal government into domestic relations, traditionally the province of the States. In signing the bill, President Ford observed that 'provisions for use of the Federal courts, the tax collection procedures …, and excessive audit requirements are an undesirable and unnecessary intrusion of the Federal Government into domestic relations' (11 Weekly Comp Pres Doc 20 (13 January 1975)). Although Congress rejected complete 'Federalisation' of the programme, it envisioned 'a far more active role on the part of the Federal government in monitoring and evaluating State programs'. Direct assistance was also contemplated, using the vast resources of the US Government in the form of helping to locate absent parents and, using the Internal Revenue Service's collection capabilities, to obtain support payments from them (S Rep No 93-1356, 8150).

rapid growth throughout the country as all States rushed to hire case workers and attorneys and began to seek court orders establishing paternity and child support obligations on a massive scale. Archaic judicial systems struggled under an avalanche of new cases, which seemed to expand exponentially each year. Revolutionary changes were soon proposed as State and local governments tackled the crisis of parental failure to support families.[4] State legislatures, gradually coming to the realisation that they were addressing social rather than law enforcement problems, enacted bold progressive new laws. Public attorneys, faced with mounting pressure to handle unprecedented caseloads and achieve meaningful results, pressed the limits of the emerging law of parental responsibility to overcome legal impediments.

There were many success stories during these early years, but the pervasiveness and growing extent of the problem of rising numbers of out-of-wedlock births, deserting fathers, and the uncontrolled growth of families resorting to public assistance moved Congress to act again less than ten years later. The result, in 1984, was an extraordinary, *unanimous*, bi-partisan effort to improve efficiency and effectiveness throughout the country by enacting sweeping amendments to title IV-D of the Social Security Act. These changes were developed, in large measure, by building upon the most successful of the individual States' recent innovations, and requiring that all States enact similar legislation. The new 'mandatory State laws' were supported by a rare coalition of interest groups from across the full range of the political spectrum.[5] Further legislative enhancements, building upon the 1984 consensus, were passed in 1988. By this point, it was apparent that child support enforcement was no longer an issue that could be handled locally, but it required an interstate solution with even stronger involvement of the Federal government. It was also increasingly recognised that child support was but one element of the 'safety net' protecting families in financial straits, and that a broader approach was needed to attack what was perceived to be an institutional problem of intergenerational poverty. In 1996 Congress enacted 'Welfare Reform' legislation, which, yet again, leaned heavily upon recent State experience in furthering child support reforms to help move single-parent families off welfare and into employment and sustained self-sufficiency. Further automation of procedures, much stronger interstate enforcement mechanisms, and additional improvements in establishing paternity and enforcing support orders were key elements. Welfare Reform also promoted a new emphasis on 'Responsible Fatherhood' and 'Healthy Marriage' as the Government's focus completed its evolution from the strong law enforcement orientation of the 1970s to a more comprehensive emphasis on family well-being and financial security.

The rapid growth and success of the title IV-D programme in the United States today can largely be attributed to four principles. First, mandatory wage withholding is required from the time of entry of virtually all child support orders, ensuring regular timely payment with minimal accrual of arrearages. Second, all States are required to have automated data retrieval and case processing systems, supported by substantial government funding and access to government employment and financial information records, but carefully

[4] In order to qualify for Federal funding, each State was required to establish or designate 'a single and separate organizational unit', which, Congress noted, 'States would be free to establish ... within or outside of their welfare agencies (for example, it could be established in the State Attorney General's office)' (S Rep No 93-1356, 8150).

[5] Extensive hearings were held by Congress on how to improve the child support enforcement programme, and testimony was heard from 'a wide range of persons concerned with the child support program', even including 'both custodial and non-custodial parents and their spokesmen' (S Rep No 98-387, 27 (1984)).

monitored and safeguarded to assure privacy protections. Third, all States must have and use guidelines for setting child support awards, and must regularly review and modify orders, if there is a substantial change in circumstances of the parties, assuring equitable and reasonable orders based upon both the family's needs and the parents' respective abilities to contribute support. Lastly, the programme strives to protect children's birthrights by achieving near universal determination of paternity, through a non-adversarial, largely voluntary system supported by affordable genetic testing. These precepts, radical proposals a few short years ago, are the cornerstones of the IV-D programme; but States and local authorities continue to have broad latitude to experiment and explore countless additional variations in child support enforcement in response to their particular circumstances and needs. The basic jurisdictional and core principles of parental responsibility are, however, standardised by universal adoption in every State of the Uniform Interstate Family Support Act (UIFSA).[6] Thus, a *fifth principle* that could be included as integral to the American IV-D programme is that standardised interstate family law and expedited judicial and administrative procedures and forms have been created to handle cases which cross jurisdictional boundaries. It is submitted that these core principles are universally applicable, and may serve as basic tenets of a cohesive and effective international family support programme.

In the foreseeable future it can confidently be predicted that many, if not most, of the countries which participated in the development of the 2007 Convention on the International Recovery of Child Support and Other Forms of Family Maintenance will ratify and implement the Convention, but questions remain concerning each nation's employment of its own systems and procedures in the context of international case processing. As confidence builds amongst and between countries, it is expected that formal and informal bi-lateral arrangements will assure the use of standardised forms and uniform procedures. In the not too distant future it is even conceivable that procedures may be developed to permit international enforcement, by the country of origin, via wage withholding orders sent directly to employers in the country where the debtor resides and works. Such procedures could possibly be patterned after the United States' Office of Child Support Enforcement's Interstate Wage Withholding Order, which is used so effectively in interstate child support enforcement proceedings in the United States.[7]

The experience of the United States during the past 35 years, demonstrating that widely diverging approaches of the 50 States' child support enforcement programmes can be harmonised in the interests of efficiency, effectiveness and equitable division of responsibilities (both parental and governmental), could serve as a model for the global community. This chapter highlights the most significant lessons learned from that experience and offers suggestions for international partnerships with nations seeking to develop and improve their own child support enforcement infrastructure, practice and procedures to better respond to the new challenges anticipated as international caseloads swell.

[6] Uniform Interstate Family Support Act (2008).

[7] The Federal form can be found on the Administration for Children and Families website or at www.acf.hhs.gov/sites/default/files/ocse/omb_0970_0154.pdf (accessed December 2013), and instructions for its use are at www.acf.hhs.gov/sites/default/files/ocse/omb_0970_0154_instructions.pdf (accessed December 2013).

II. The Child Support Enforcement Programme Evolves: 1980–88

The initial years of the title IV-D programme in the United States presented a hodgepodge of approaches to addressing the child support enforcement problem. Many States viewed the programme as a quasi-law enforcement enterprise and had difficulty reconciling it with institutional biases favouring a welfare agency approach to such problems, often resulting in limited backing from State administration officials and competition for scarce resources. In some States the programme was embraced as a progressive means to address societal problems and innovative solutions were proposed for its management.[8] Nonetheless, as collections grew and new paternity adjudications were obtained, broad popular support for the programme quickly followed. Largely due to the generous 75 per cent Federal rate of reimbursement for State and local expenditures, most States generated significant revenue from their child support enforcement operations and began to lobby for increased staff and resources to grow their revenues even faster.[9] The programme was widely praised as one of the few government initiatives which served families in need of assistance while producing savings for taxpayers at the same time through recoupment of monies spent for welfare payments.

The United States Congress recognised the success of the programme, and made several notable legislative changes in the 1980s to expedite further enhancements. On 9 June 1980 a law was enacted which made Federal matching funds available to cover 90 per cent of the costs of automating child support data processing and management systems.[10] The law also provided access for State and local IV-D agencies to wage information maintained by the Social Security Administration and State employment security agencies, which could be used to locate non-custodial parents, determine income for purposes of establishing appropriate child support orders, and identify employers to assist in enforcing support obligations. In 1981 the Federal government itself directly entered into the enforcement of child support debts by enacting legislation which permitted the collection of past due child and spousal support by interception of Federal tax refunds.[11] With only a few months to implement the new tax refund interception programme, slightly over half of the States certified several hundred of their cases with large unpaid arrearages, and over half a million dollars were collected by the Internal Revenue Service in the country's first federal-level automated child support enforcement action.[12]

[8] Federal law required that each State establish or designate 'a single and separate organizational unit' responsible for its support enforcement programme, and some States made a complete break with their social services agency when they initiated IV-D operations. Massachusetts and Florida, eg, placed the IV-D programme in their Departments of Revenue.

[9] All but nine States operated in the black in 1981, generating net savings of over $230 million—Office of Child Support Enforcement, US Department of Health and Human Services, Child Support Enforcement, Sixth Annual Report to Congress for the Period Ending September 30, 1981 (1981). Part of the States' savings was attributable to incentive payments made by the Federal government for AFDC recoveries.

[10] Social Security Disability Amendments of 1980, Pub L No 96-265, 94 Stat 441 (1980) (90% funding for 'computerized matching information systems' was effective by 1 July 1981).

[11] The Omnibus Budget Reconciliation Act of 1981, Pub L No 97-35, 95 Stat 357 (1981).

[12] In the rush to take advantage of this unprecedented new initiative to use the awesome powers of the Federal Treasury to collect private debt, there was a profound failure to consider affording due process protections to taxpayers, and no pre-offset notices nor pre-attachment hearing rights were provided until the following year's tax

In 1981 there were over 8 million women in the United States raising children alone.[13] Thirty per cent were living in poverty.[14] Fewer than half of these single-parent families even had established orders providing that the absent parents of their children were required to make any payment whatsoever for child support, and, of those who had orders, most received only partial payment or no payment at all.[15] Hearings were held in early 1984 at which the Reagan Administration strongly urged Congress to reconcile its differences and pass the much needed new law. In August 1984, something happened which is almost inconceivable today. Both the House of Representatives and the United States Senate *unanimously* passed amendments to title IV-D; and, on 16 August 1984, President Reagan signed into law the Child Support Enforcement Amendments of 1984.[16]

The new law provided both fiscal incentives and the threat of expanded federal audits and possible penalties to strongly encourage States to improve the efficiency and effectiveness of their IV-D operations.[17] A much needed new emphasis was also placed on the interstate enforcement of child support obligations.[18] In the past, States were reluctant to recognise and enforce orders from other jurisdictions, sometimes ignoring the other State's request for enforcement. The 1984 law mandated that States have in effect new standardised procedures, enacting legislation if necessary, which would assure recognition and enforcement of sister States' orders, and streamline procedures for establishing new support orders. Many of the model laws and procedures had been identified in a study by the National Conference of State Legislatures and were already in effect in certain jurisdictions and had been shown to be effective. Unquestionably, the most important of these measures was the requirement for *mandatory wage withholding*. Newly issued or modified child support orders were required to include provision for wage withholding, unless limited exceptions applied.[19]

States were also required to mandate employer compliance with such withholding orders, to give child support 'priority over any other legal process under State law against the same wages', and to 'extend its withholding system … [to] include withholding from income derived within such State in cases where the applicable support orders were issued in other States, in order to assure that child support … will be collected without regard

refund offset processing. The result was almost immediate litigation and challenges to the programme on several grounds. Eg, see *Nelson v Regan* 731 F.2d 105 (2d Cir 1984) (district court held tax intercept programme violated due process by failing to provide notice and appeal procedures).

[13] See Office of Child Support Enforcement, US Department of Health and Human Services, Child Support Enforcement, Ninth Annual Report to Congress for the Period Ending September 30, 1984 (1984).

[14] Ibid.

[15] Ibid.

[16] See Child Support Enforcement Amendments of 1984, Pub L No 98-378, 98 Stat 1305 (1984).

[17] The law actually reduced the frequency of Federal audits to triennial reviews, unless a State was under penalty, and the standard was based upon 'substantial compliance,' rather than 'full compliance' with IV-D requirements (42 USCA § 603(h)(1); see also 42 USCA § 602(a)(27) (1984)). Penalties were also reduced from 5% of title IV-A (AFDC) funds to graduated penalties of between 1 and 5%, with an opportunity for corrective action to avoid progressive increases in the penalty amount. These changes signalled to States that performance mattered in all respects, not just recoupment of welfare expenditures. Penalties, in a reduced amount, were more likely to be imposed if States failed to meet the law's requirements.

[18] Interstate cases presented 'one of the most difficult areas of child support enforcement' (S Rep No 98-387, 34 (1984)). To address this growing problem Congress provided grants for State programmes to improve interstate enforcement techniques and also expanded incentive payments to both the initiating and responding States involved in interstate collection efforts. See 42 USCA §§ 655(e) and 658(d) (1984).

[19] 42 USCA § 666(b).

to the residence of the child'.[20] However, the provision suffered from one serious defect. Withholding did not take effect until the non-custodial parent fell into arrears totalling a full month's payment, so families faced the uncertainty of payments which were erratic or untimely.

Other important provisions of the 1984 amendments included a requirement for all States to adopt expedited procedures (either judicial or administrative) for establishing and enforcing support orders, procedures requiring interception of State income tax refunds (patterned after the 1981 Federal law), and enforcement measures permitting imposition of liens against property, posting bonds or other security to ensure timely payment, and reporting of child support delinquencies to consumer credit agencies. By mandating new laws and procedures for all child support cases, not just welfare families, Congress made it clear that title IV-D was no longer primarily a welfare recoupment programme, but would be oriented towards assisting all families with support orders.[21]

Congress intervened once again with the Family Support Act of 1988.[22] This law, further amending title IV-D of the Social Security Act, was intended to encompass a comprehensive overhaul of not just the mechanics of child support establishment and enforcement, but also to address some of the underlying causes of poverty contributing to the plight of families in America. In addition to strengthening child support enforcement, the law expanded opportunities for education and training of both custodial and non-custodial parents, and laid down the foundational elements for emerging programmes of transitional assistance enabling families to move from welfare into the workforce. Many of these latter initiatives would see fruition years later with 'welfare reform' initiatives, but the child support changes were effective almost immediately.

III. Mandatory Wage Withholding, Statewide Guidelines and Automated Date Processing Systems

The 1988 amendments, as the 1984 legislation had a few years earlier, continued to build upon the framework of the 1975 title IV-D enactment. Notably, it filled several gaping loopholes left by Congress in the sweeping enhancements enacted in 1984. Probably the most pervasive change was made in the very first provision of the new law, section 101, 'Immediate Income Withholding'. States were now required to have laws and procedures mandating that: 'The wages of an absent parent shall be subject to … withholding, regardless of whether support payments by such parent are in arrears' in all newly issued or

[20] 42 USCA § 666(b)(7) and (b)(9).

[21] Congress was concerned that, by measuring success 'solely in terms of welfare savings', many States were disinclined to assist non-AFDC families (HR Rep No 98-527 (1983)). The 1984 amendments to title IV-D were designed to ensure, 'through mandatory income withholding, incentive payments to States, and other improvements in the child support enforcement program, that all children in the United States who are in need of assistance in securing financial support from their parents will receive such assistance regardless of their circumstances' (Child Support Enforcement Amendments of 1984, Pub L No 98-378, preamble, 98 Stat 1305 (1984)); see also ibid § 23(a)(3) ('Congress is strengthening the program to recognize the needs of all children.').

[22] Family Support Act of 1988, Pub L No 100-485, 102 Stat 2343 (1988).

modified support orders.[23] So long as the payer had a job and steady income, child support would be deducted from wages and paid timely to the family.

Another hole left open in the 1984 amendments involved statewide guidelines to be used in setting child support awards. Whereas Congress in 1984 had seen the wisdom in requiring States to establish such guidelines, it had not taken the next obvious step of mandating that they be applied in setting all new child support orders. The 1988 law rectified that problem. Section 103 required that State guidelines would henceforth establish a 'rebuttable presumption in any judicial or administrative proceeding for the award of child support that the amount of the award which would result from the application of such guidelines is the correct amount of child support to be awarded'.[24] Compulsory statewide guidelines for setting child support awards eliminated inequity and most disputes involving determination of a fair amount of the award, resulting in substantial savings for the parties in legal fees. In convening legislative committees and seeking public input to establish the parameters for guidelines, States also placed renewed emphasis on the overall well-being of families. Guidelines often included provision for health care coverage, education and any special needs of a child.

Still another major change, which would have profound implications for the future of child support enforcement in years to come, was a requirement that all States must develop Federally approved systems to monitor child support cases being enforced under title IV-D. Congress had expanded the scope of the extremely generous 90 per cent matching funding for automated systems in the 1984 legislation,[25] but not all States had taken advantage of the opportunity to modernise, and a few were seriously lagging in efforts to automate their IV-D operations. The 1988 law required that any State which was not already operating an automated data processing and information retrieval system must submit a plan by 1 October 1991 for approval by the Secretary of the Department of Health and Human Services, and have an operational system in effect by 1 October 1995 (when 90 per cent funding would be discontinued).

Additional provisions of the 1988 law to improve child support enforcement included: mandatory provision of parents' social security numbers upon birth of a child,[26] expanded access to wage and unemployment compensation information, a requirement that States respond promptly to requests for IV-D services, and provision of monthly notices to families of the amount of support collected.[27] The 1988 legislation signalled a new Congressional attitude towards addressing broad issues of parental responsibility, and during the next few years States responded positively with further innovations and programme improvements. Within two decades the ground had shifted in child support enforcement. From a system in 1975, where child support was paid irregularly, if at all, and the most common means of enforcing payment was the threat of incarceration, the child support enforcement programme had evolved by 1995 into a system which ensured that

[23] Ibid § 101.

[24] 42 USCA § 667(b)(2); Family Support Act of 1988, Pub L No 100-485, § 103(a), 102 Stat 2343 (1988).

[25] To facilitate wage withholding and monitoring of other new provisions provided in the 1984 legislation, 90% funding was made available for 'automated data processing and information retrieval systems' (including hardware costs). See Child Support Enforcement Amendments of 1984, Pub L 98-378, § 6, 98 Stat 1305 (1984).

[26] Social Security Numbers (SSNs) are the most important data element in using automated data mechanisms to search and locate a parent's residence, place of employment and many other financial assets.

[27] Families on welfare were permitted to keep the first $50 of each monthly child support payment, and the notice helped assure that such funds were accurately distributed.

all orders would include provision for automatic and immediate withholding from wages, guidelines were employed to establish fair and equitable orders, and a unified national system was rapidly taking shape which would ensure consistent enforcement of support orders wherever the family resided or moved.

IV. 1996—Welfare Reform—Child Support, an Integral Part of a Plan for Family Self-sufficiency

In the first two decades of the cooperative Federal/State child support enforcement programme in the United States there had been a dramatic improvement in the number of cases in which a family received at least a portion of the support that was owed under an existing order. There was a 92 per cent increase in paying cases for married women separated from their spouse, a 43 per cent increase for divorced women, and, for never-married mothers, there was a 250 per cent increase in the number of cases which received at least a partial payment of the amount due.[28] But the remaining gap between what was owed and collected under existing orders, and the amount of support which potentially could be provided for families was disturbing. One study argued that if child support orders were established for all children, setting a realistic amount based upon a non-custodial parent's true ability to pay, collections would more than triple.[29] Census Bureau data for 1991 indicated that for nearly half of the families in the country with an absent parent, no child support award had even been established.[30] A primary cause of this disparity was a failure to establish paternity in many cases.

After much study by the Government and academic institutions, and considerably less accord than accompanied the 1984 legislation, Congress enacted the Personal Responsibility and Work Opportunity Reconciliation Act of 1996 (PRWORA).[31] PRWORA made profound changes in reforming the family welfare system in the United States. A maximum five-year lifetime limit on benefits was established (with some exceptions), and the new law imposed mandatory work requirements and minimum participation rates and evaluated States on their success in moving recipients into the workforce. Penalties were established for poorly performing States. A major focus of the new programme was to 'end the dependence of needy parents on government benefits by promoting job preparation, work, and marriage.'[32] An essential component of the new programme was a greatly expanded, more efficient and automated national child support enforcement programme. The drafters recognised that regular and reliable payment of child support was an integral

[28] See P Legler, 'The Coming Revolution in Child Support Policy: Implications of the 1996 Welfare Act' (1996) 30 *Family Law Quarterly* 519, 523.

[29] See E Sorenson, *Noncustodial Fathers: Can They Afford to Pay More Child Support?* (Urban Institute, 1994) http://aspe.hhs.gov/hsp/isp/13xsum.htm; *cf* Legler (n 28).

[30] See Bureau of the Census, Current Population Reports Series P60-187, Child Support for Custodial Mothers and Fathers: 1991 (1991). The study showed that, of 5.3 million families with child support orders in the US, roughly half received the full amount due, whereas 25% received only partial payment and the remaining quarter of families received nothing.

[31] Personal Responsibility and Work Opportunity Reconciliation Act of 1996, Pub L No 104-193, 110 Stat 2105 (1996).

[32] 42 USCA § 601(a)(2).

component of a family's income and that it was essential to assist the family in attaining self-sufficiency.

The changes made by PRWORA to the national child support enforcement programme were myriad, but can generally be grouped under three broad categories: (1) uniform and automated procedures to locate non-custodial parents and process cases; (2) greatly expedited and simplified means to establish paternity; and (3) broad new enforcement measures to assure that, once a child support order was established, it would be paid. Among the most significant provisions were that: all States were required to adopt, without amendment, UIFSA;[33] mass case processing was facilitated by the creation of mandatory central State and Federal registries of child support orders and new State and Federal directories of newly hired employees; and expedited enforcement procedures were required in all jurisdictions for genetic testing, automatic wage withholding, and such remedies as tax refund interception, liens, licence revocation and seizure of funds in financial institutions. In addition, to help assure that orders were set in reasonable amounts, and were adjusted periodically as circumstances changed, all States were required to establish procedures for 'review and adjustment of support orders' on, at least, a three-year cycle.[34]

A. Automated Data

The first essential requisite for efficient mass case processing is good data. Each State agency, as a condition of continued receipt of Federal funding for both its child support enforcement programme *and* the block grant for its welfare programme (Temporary Assistance for Needy Families), was required to establish a 'State Case Registry' containing standardised data elements for both custodial and non-custodial parents in child support cases, including names, social security numbers and other uniform elements such as dates of birth of the children and the State's case identification numbers. That information was sent to a Federal Case Registry for matching against national data bases maintained or accessible by the Federal Parent Locator Service (FPLS) to help locate non-custodial parents wherever they lived throughout the United States. States also were required to establish a 'State Directory of New Hires'.[35] Not later than 20 days after an employer hires a new employee (and typically much sooner depending upon State law) the employer must report the name, address and social security number of the new employee to the State Directory.[36] Automated data matches are conducted to compare the records of the State Case Registry and the State Directory of New Hires, and, if the employee owes child support, a notice is sent to the employer within two business days directing the employer to withhold an amount equal to the child support obligation (including past due support) from the employee's wages.[37] Under the new system, a wage withholding order was commonly in place within the State by the time the employee received his or her second paycheck, and the family was assured of regular and timely payment of support thereafter.

[33] As a requirement for approval of each State's title IV-D Plan, the State was required to 'have in effect the Uniform Interstate Family Support Act … together with any amendments officially adopted before January 1, 1998 by the National Conference of Commissioners on Uniform State Laws' (42 USCA § 666(f)).

[34] 42 USCA § 666(a)(10).

[35] 42 USCA § 653A(a)(1).

[36] 42 USCA § 653A(b)(2)(A).

[37] 42 USCA § 653A(g).

B. Interstate Enforcement by Administrative Wage Withholding

Historically, one of the greatest difficulties facing child support enforcement practitioners concerned interstate cases. Locating a non-custodial parent who had moved to another State, registering an order for recognition in that jurisdiction, and securing the assistance of local authorities to enforce the order was time-consuming and inefficient. To address this problem PRWORA mandated new procedures for 'Administrative Enforcement in Interstate Cases.'[38] The State seeking enforcement could transmit its request, 'by electronic or other means,' and such transmittal constituted a certification of the amount due and assurance that all due process requirements had been satisfied.[39] PRWORA went much farther, however, by laying the groundwork for a national system of reporting newly hired employees and establishing a mechanism for a State child support enforcement agency to send a wage withholding order directly to the employer in another State without recourse to any other State's assistance.[40]

The National Directory of New Hires (NDNH) receives quarterly extracts of State wage and unemployment compensation information paid to individuals in the State.[41] Within three business days after new hire information is entered into a State Directory of New Hires it must then be furnished to the NDNH. Through direct administrative wage withholding the State agency where the custodial parent and child resides can expeditiously enforce the support order within a few days after the non-custodial parent's employer is identified and without the intervention of another State's enforcement authorities.

The NDNH, a component of the Federal Parent Locator Service (FPLS), has been a boon to the interstate child support enforcement programme with vastly more expansive and current information than had previously been available from national databases. Child support obligors who change employment frequently, such as part-time and seasonal labourers, can no longer effectively avoid support enforcement efforts, and administrative costs and hurdles entailed in sending orders for registration and enforcement by another State's authorities have been practically eliminated.

C. Administrative Establishment of Paternity

The changes mandated by PRWORA for the collection and use of location information and for mass automated processing of cases, including direct administrative wage withholding, were profound, and had an almost immediate impact upon child support collection efforts. Possibly of equal significance, although the impact was noticeable over a much longer term, were the changes PRWORA made in the way paternity was established in the United States. There had been a near tripling in the rate of out-of-wedlock births

[38] Personal Responsibility and Work Opportunity Reconciliation Act of 1996, Pub L 104-193, § 323, 110 Stat 2105, 2222–23 (1996).

[39] Ibid.

[40] 42 USCA §§ 653(i), 'National Directory of New Hires' and 666(f), 'Uniform Interstate Family Support Act.' The UIFSA, which all States have adopted, provides for the direct enforcement of income-withholding orders received by an employer from any other State. See UIFSA, Art 5, Enforcement of Support Order Without Registration.

[41] 42 USCA § 653A(g)(2)(B).

in the country from 1970 to 1990.[42] Antiquated judicial processes were still commonly employed in many jurisdictions, although in-hospital voluntary paternity establishment programmes were rapidly gaining momentum.[43] It was generally recognised that far and away the most opportune time to approach the unwed father and seek a voluntary recognition of paternity was at the time of birth in the hospital.[44] PRWORA expanded and refined these programmes and took them to a new level.

A contributing factor prompting an interest in greatly expanded efforts to assure establishment of paternity for most out-of-wedlock children was the growing realisation that unwed fathers were not necessarily poor and irresponsible, but, in fact, many were older males with some regular income.[45] It was also increasingly apparent that many, perhaps most, unwed fathers continued to have a relationship with the mother at the time the child was born; they were often at the hospital at the time of birth; and most were willing, often eager, to acknowledge paternity at that time.[46]

PRWORA built upon the existing requirements that States must have in-hospital paternity establishment programmes (although they varied considerably from State to State), and addressed several lingering legal issues. All States were required to have procedures 'under which a signed voluntary acknowledgment of paternity is considered a legal finding of paternity' subject to a limited right to rescind the acknowledgment.[47] Any future challenge to the voluntary acknowledgement is permitted 'only on the basis of fraud, duress, or material mistake of fact, with the burden of proof upon the challenger.'[48] No further judicial or administrative proceedings are required. The unchallenged acknowledgment is sufficient to establish paternity for all legal purposes, and it is a simple and efficient means to clarify birth records in most situations where there is no dispute between the parties. Establishment of paternity at the time of birth also substantially eliminates the possibility of legal challenges at a later time, if the relationship sours for any reason and the father later objects to paying child support. In such instances, he would face a heavy burden of proof in attempting to rescind the acknowledgment.

Of course, in-hospital paternity establishment, as effective as it is, only works when the putative father is willing to voluntarily accept his responsibilities as a parent. PRWORA also addressed the burgeoning problem of increasingly expensive paternity litigation in contested cases. The new laws mandated several enhancements for States to expedite their administrative and judicial processes for paternity establishment, the most important of which were new mandatory procedures requiring prompt genetic testing. The key to such expedited procedures was the broad authority afforded all State child support agencies to order genetic testing 'without the necessity of obtaining an order from any other judicial

[42] In 1970 there were about 400,000 out-of-wedlock births compared to 3.7 million children born in the United States (nearly 11%), and by 1990 that rate had risen to roughly 1.2 million out-of-wedlock births for about 4 million total children born (30%). See GA Akerlof and JL Yellen, 'An Analysis of Out-of-wedlock Births in the United States, Brookings Policy Brief Series #5' (1996 Fall) *Brookings Review*.

[43] See Omnibus Budget Reconciliation Act of 1993, Pub L No 103-66, 107 Stat 312 (1993), which had required all States to implement in-hospital paternity establishment programmes.

[44] See Legler (n 28) 529–30.

[45] Ibid fnn 48–49.

[46] Ibid 529–30 and fn 54.

[47] 42 USCA § 666(a)(5)(D)(ii). The acknowledgment can be rescinded within 60 days, unless there is an earlier administrative or judicial action to which the putative father is a party.

[48] 42 USCA § 666(a)(5)(D)(iii).

or administrative tribunal'.[49] Either the mother alleging paternity, or the putative father denying paternity, can request testing.[50] The State agency pays for the tests.[51]

Paternity disputes are still a vexatious source of family discord, but DNA testing has eliminated any credible challenges to the *fact* of a parent-child relationship per se. Remaining issues concern such matters as: fraud, duress, or material mistake of fact as a basis to challenge an acknowledgment of paternity; the period during which the paternity of a child born to a presumed father (husband of the child's mother) may be challenged; paternity disestablishment based upon genetic testing; and child support owed after an order disestablishing paternity.[52]

If there is one lesson to be learned from the experience of the United States in its 45-year struggle to fairly and efficiently resolve questions of disputed paternity,it is the final recognition, in law, practice and social perspective, that the father-child relationship is, ultimately, a biological fact which can be determined with medical certainty. It should *not* generally be considered to be a legal question, subject to the inevitable uncertainty and occasionally subjective influences of a trial in a court of law.

V. Strong Fiscal Commitment Plus Accountability

The success of the cooperative Federal-State child support enforcement programme certainly must be attributed, in large part, to the generous government funding made available since the programme began. Two-thirds of all State expenditures properly attributed to title IV-D operations are reimbursed by the Federal government. In addition, incentives are paid to States based upon their effective performance. Although the public assistance caseload is diminished, and most current activity is on behalf of non-welfare families, Temporary Assistance for Needy Families (TANF) recipients still assign their support payments to the State and a portion of those collections is used to offset their benefit payments.[53] Through the years many States actually ran their IV-D programmes with net revenue gains, as Federal matching of expenditures, plus incentives and welfare recoupment, more than compensated for the State's share of expenditures. In the end, all States benefit from the immeasurable gains which must be attributed to helping families live above base poverty lines, utilising their own means and resources, without recourse to public assistance.

[49] 42 USCA § 666(c)(1).

[50] The requirement of a sworn statement by the requesting party was an essential prerequisite for permitting genetic testing to be ordered by the child support agency with no additional judicial or quasi-judicial scrutiny. Prior practice was generally to permit genetic testing to occur, but only when both parties voluntarily acquiesced or when it was ordered by a court or administrative tribunal. See Legler (n 28) 534 and fn 72.

[51] At State option, the agency could subsequently seek recoupment of such costs from the alleged father after paternity was established.

[52] See HH Clark, Jr and A Laquer Estin, *Cases and Problems on Domestic Relations*, 7th edn (St Paul, MN, Thomson/West, 2005) 285–86.

[53] Significant changes were made in 2005 to the Federal rules for assignment of support rights and State procedures for distributing child support collections. States are encouraged to pass on considerably more of the support collected each month directly to the family and to retain less for reimbursement of TANF benefits. See Deficit Reduction Act of 2005, Pub L 109-171, § 7301, 120 Stat 4, 141–44 (2006).

It should be noted that States are motivated to run efficient and effective child support enforcement programmes, not only by their potential revenue gains, but also by the risk of substantial fiscal penalties for running ineffective programmes. Performance for determining incentives is measured in five key areas, three of which are also used to determine whether or not a State may be subject to a penalty.[54] If a State does not meet the required level of performance in any of these three critical areas (paternity establishment, establishment of support orders and current collections), it must take corrective action in the 'immediately succeeding fiscal year' to achieve the appropriate level.[55] Failure to attain the required level of performance, after the one-year corrective action period, or failure to submit data that are accurate, reliable and complete, so as to determine the State's level of performance, will result in a penalty.[56] The Federal Office of Child Support Enforcement (OCSE) conducts triennial audits.[57] Incentives are paid, and penalties assessed, accordingly, based upon reports submitted by the States using the States' own data. It is thus very difficult for a State to protest that it met the performance standard and should not be penalised, when its own data reflect otherwise.[58]

There were 15.8 million cases in the IV-D programme as of the end of fiscal year 2011 (30 September 2011).[59] Collections distributed in FY 2011 in IV-D cases increased slightly over the preceding year to total $27.3 billion, and an additional $3.9 billion was collected in non-IV-D cases for a total of $31.9 billion.[60] Over two-thirds of all collections are derived from income withholding (primarily payroll-based withholding).[61] Of the balance of collections, a significant and increasing portion is attributable to Federal enforcement efforts, including tax refund interception, Social Security benefit garnishments, data matching with multi-state financial institutions, passport denial and insurance proceeds matches.[62] Administrative costs, both State and Federal expenses combined, totalled $5.7 billion and the national cost-effectiveness ratio was $5.12 collected for each dollar expended.[63] Looking purely at the numbers, it cannot be gainsaid that the title IV-D programme in the United States is monumental in size and phenomenally effective in establishing and enforcing child support orders. Another way of evaluating the programme, however, which cannot be quantified, is to consider the myriad ways in which child support enforcement

[54] 45 CFR § 305.2. The five performance measures are: paternity establishment; support order establishment; current collections; arrearage collections; and cost-effectiveness. All five measures factor into the calculation of payment of the State's share of the annual incentive payment pool. Three of these measures are used to determine whether a State may be assessed a penalty for poor performance: paternity establishment; establishment to support orders; and current collections.

[55] 45 CFR § 305.61(a).

[56] Ibid.

[57] 42 USCA § 652(a)(4)(C).

[58] When the first performance penalties were assessed against States there was litigation contending that the Federal government had failed to give States proper notice and that the corrective action year was improperly determined. Fourteen States were penalised in FY 2002 based upon 2001 data (AL, DC, DE, GU, HI, IN, KS, LA, NV, NH, NM, PR, RI and VI). Ten States appealed their penalties to the Health and Human Services Departmental Appeals Board (DAB) which affirmed the penalties in Decisions Nos 1989 and 2001 (2005). Nine States subsequently appealed the DAB decisions in the Federal District Court, and Summary Judgment was granted for the Department of HHS: *Alabama, et al v US Dep't of Health and Human Servs,* 478 F. Supp. 2d 85 (2007).

[59] Office of Child Support Enforcement, US Department of Health and Human Services, FY 2011 Preliminary Report (2012) www.acf.hhs.gov/programs/css/resource/fy2011-preliminary-report (accessed December 2013).

[60] Ibid.

[61] Ibid.

[62] Ibid.

[63] Ibid.

efforts contribute to families' overall well-being. Relationships are established and birth records clarified. Health insurance and other benefits are realised. Unemployed parents are often referred to programmes and services which benefit them as well, and the regular and timely payment of child support promotes healthy family relationships and fosters cooperation between both parents.[64]

VI. Where Will the Child Support Enforcement Programme Go from Here? Globalisation and Interoperability

A. Globalisation and Interoperability: 2025[65]

The child support enforcement programme in the United States, and in many other countries, has been remarkable for its fast-forwarding history of continuous improvement and constant modernisation, in line with advances in technology and changing social norms. From the beginning, leaders in the field have been willing to break away from traditional and archaic systems of establishing and enforcing orders, and have challenged conventional wisdom and 'this is how we have always done it' attitudes. From its underpinning as a law enforcement-oriented programme bogged down in antiquated judicial proceedings, child support enforcement has evolved into a primarily administrative, highly automated and efficient system. As more countries ratify or accede to the 2007 Maintenance Convention domestic systems will rapidly be inundated with requests for services in international cases, both transmitting and receiving applications. Automation, improvements in communication, rethinking old procedures and innovative new ideas will be essential to streamline operations to handle the influx. These changes, with the advantages of existing technological advancement, will occur internationally in a fraction of the time it took the United States to reach its present level of *interoperability* amongst 50 State programmes. Child support enforcement is now a global concern, and *globalisation* (integration of systems, communications and goals) will soon be as well established in human services as it is now in commerce, transportation and multiple other fields.

What are the administrative hurdles we must still surmount, and what practical problems are entailed in reconciling our disparate, and often bureaucratic, international systems? How will countries cope with their vastly increased volume of international child support enforcement cases once the 2007 Maintenance Convention is fully implemented and several dozen countries are parties to it? We come to the intersection of 50 years of largely failed efforts to process relatively small numbers of actions across international boundaries and a new road to the future, the 2007 Convention, with optimism and good intentions but considerable baggage. Our judicial and administrative processes remain very different,

[64] See *Vision for Children & Families*, Administration for Children and Families www.acf.hhs.gov/programs/css/about/vision (accessed December 2013).

[65] The closing sections of this chapter are conceived as a forward-thinking essay speculating on how the child support programme, in the United States and globally, may reasonably be anticipated to grow and evolve in the coming decade. The author's opinion, based upon 37 years of experience in the field, is entirely his own and does not represent the official policy nor necessarily the views of the United States Government.

and our parochial biases, inertia and resistance to change are likely to continue to be major impediments. Seeking solutions to the financial difficulties of tens of thousands of families is a daunting task; when the parents reside in different countries, all of the problems are compounded. One thing of which we can be certain is that the old way of doing things will not suffice; all of us in this new world community must recognise that progress requires innovation, creativity, and most importantly, a willingness to adapt and to try working collaboratively. You do not plough new ground by tilling the same rows over and again.

Communication will be, and has always been, the key. The difficulties faced in the United States in reconciling 50 disparate State programmes pale in comparison to the challenge of coordinating inter-governmental systems and creating a cohesive global child support enforcement system. The 2007 Maintenance Convention set the basic rules for administrative cooperation and communication, including two critical mandatory forms.[66] The Caseworker Handbook, soon to be issued, lays out the particulars, with a further emphasis upon communication between Central Authorities. Countries now must conspire to work together and make globalisation of child support services a reality. The same bold and creative thinking that spurred the child support enforcement programme in the past to break the mold and invent new solutions to age-old problems exists today. The goal is noble and unimpeachable: our children's future; what is best for them and how can we achieve it?

B. Parental Access and Visitation

To begin we might ask: What is truly 'in the best interests of the child?' Should it be obtaining the maximum amount of support? What about time spent with the child? How should we value that? The United States has done a very good job of requiring that all States use guidelines to set support orders, greatly simplifying settlement in divorce and paternity actions by removing one of its most contentious issues. This country also does a good job of assuring that child support orders are paid regularly and on time. We have not done much to assure that non-custodial parents' visitation and custody orders are enforced, and the 2007 Convention does not address this aspect of family relations at all. In 2025 there will be a programme, in its infancy still but showing promise and growing rapidly, to enforce visitation. It is, surely, to the child's advantage, and to a parent's, that they be allowed to spend time together. Child support practitioners today are already beginning to consider how to integrate access and visitation rights into support enforcement proceedings, and we may anticipate that this will eventually be an integral part of their operations.

The child support enforcement programme of 2025 will emphasise the word '*support*'. Support comes in many forms. Financial, of course, but equally important are the *personal* facets of support (emotional and inspirational) which inure in a relationship. It used to be that only time spent physically with a child provided opportunities for that kind of bonding. Today social media replaces some of the need for geographical proximity. Perhaps

[66] Convention on the International Recovery of Child Support and Other Forms of Family Maintenance, 23 November 2007, 47 ILM 257 (2007 Convention). Annex 1 to the 2007 Convention is the *Transmittal Form* required under Art 12(2) and Annex 2 is the *Acknowledgement Form* required under Art 12(3). Other recommended forms have been prepared which will greatly facilitate international communications, but these two are required to be used with all applications and there is a six-week time limit prescribed for acknowledging receipt and providing critical contact details for the person or unit responsible for responding to further inquiries.

visitation rights should incorporate an allotted hour or so several times each week to Skype with Dad (or Mum). If that distant parent is motivated to master the technology common to a teenager, and takes the time and initiative to stay connected in this way, then three cheers for the NCP (non-custodial parent)!

The United States has signed, and is moving towards ratification of the 1996 Protection of Children Convention.[67] In simplest terms the 1996 Convention addresses enforcement of visitation and custody orders and fills a gap left by the 1980 Abduction Convention (which requires prompt return of children taken to another treaty country in violation of a support order).[68] In 2025 the United States will have fully implemented the 1996 treaty and financial support and *personal* support will be on more of an equal footing.[69] Either will be enforceable using common established international rules and procedures and common forms. Government agencies, even across borders, will have appropriate access to each other's relevant records and will communicate and coordinate their actions as *interoperability* of systems and services will have become well-established.

C. Systems Automation and Better Data Analytics

We already have most of the tools we need; at least they are ready on the shelf. Some may need dusting off and many have yet to be tested in international practice. At the same time it must be recognised that it is not effective to use a six-pound hammer to drive a two-penny nail. Just because it usually works (to threaten revocation of a driver's licence for example), is no guarantee that the cookie cutter remedy will be most effective in an individual case or an international action. While automation is essential to handle mass processing of caseloads, better use of data will show that some cases will profit most from the uncommon remedial action rather than the traditional approach. Automated systems permit an efficiency of scale when it is imperative that 1,000 identical functions be accomplished as quickly as possible. Those systems fail, however, when a small percentage of those functions are wholly inappropriate and counter-productive. Research, testing and better analysis will enable caseworkers to hone in on the few cases which warrant specialised attention. We already have, for the most part, all of the data we need.[70] Case management in the future will employ better data analytics to focus resources where they

[67] The United States signed the Hague Convention of 19 October 1996 on Jurisdiction, Applicable Law, Recognition, Enforcement and Cooperation in Respect of Parental Responsibility and Measures for the Protection of Children on 22 October 2010.

[68] The Hague Convention of 25 October 1980 on the Civil Aspects of Child Abduction. The Convention was ratified by the United States in 1988.

[69] An essential intermediary step before ratification of the treaty can occur is the development of uniform domestic law in each State. The Uniform Law Commission, with the financial support of the United States Department of State and technical assistance of the United States Department of Health and Human Services, is working on proposed changes to the Uniform Child Custody Jurisdiction and Enforcement Act which will enable the United States to fulfil its obligations under the treaty when it is ratified.

[70] 'Child support agencies across the country possess treasure troves of historical data on the cases they manage. States gather such extensive case-level information as monthly support obligation, employer information, asset information, arrears information, income, prior enforcement actions taken, and so on.' Margot Bean, et al, Deloitte, Advanced analytics for child support programmes: From reactive enforcement to proactive prevention—Part I www.deloitte.com/assets/Dcom-UnitedStates/Local%20Assets/Documents/us_state_advanced_analytics_for_child_support_Programs_PART_1_83012.pdf (accessed December 2013).

are likely to be most effective, alleviating many of the complexities of dealing with the increased volume.[71]

Pro-active data analytics, for example, will target suspicious circumstances to identify the cause of a sudden change in the pattern of payment. If the debtor has suffered an injury or been laid-off from work, a temporary reduction in the amount owed should be easily obtained. At the same time the debtor will be counselled and encouraged to take advantage of subsidised work, education and vocational training opportunities, as such programmes will be commonly available. The presumption will be that non-custodial parents would willingly contribute towards their offspring's support, but may simply need assistance in acquiring the means. Responsible parenting classes too, encouraging healthier family relationships, will be available to anyone who wishes to take advantage of them as automated systems relieve the caseworker from endless repetitive work and enable more personalised and focused remedies to be employed.

D. Privacy Concerns: Have We Gone Too Far?

We already have, for a majority of families, all of the information we could possibly need. In fact, we often have more data than we can use, and, in consequence, we use it poorly. But, in some instances, maintenance of data is performed by another jurisdiction or governmental institution and the child support enforcement system is unable to acquire it. Too often it is a lack of trust which impedes sharing information, even at a government to government level. Personal data should, of course, be guarded carefully and used judiciously. Perhaps, though, the pendulum has swung too far towards protecting all personal information when a great deal of it is publicly available and no longer warrants meticulous safeguarding. Government agencies are often the worst offenders. Much of this data initially derives from government records (tax, property, licences, marriage/birth/death registries …), and our public agencies thus assume a proprietary interest in holding it closely. In fairness, they have been charged with a high standard of responsibility to ensure that personal information is not casually disclosed or potentially misused. But sometimes these institutional biases to safeguard and non-disclose persist long after their usefulness has vanished.

The truth, which any of our Millennial Generation will affirm, is that most of what their parents valued as personal and private identifying data is no longer particularly private. Spend a few minutes with a tech-savvy 23-year-old, and examine your own life through the magnifying glass of the internet. Why do some government agencies persist in jealously protecting information from disclosure which is already commonly available? At the very least, there should be more openness towards sharing data amongst those agencies which have a legitimate need for it and will use it to further accepted societal goals.

Scholars may debate whether we have compromised our personal selves as our lives are more available to public scrutiny. It is far too late to change. In actuality no one is likely to be shocked or even offended to discover that their personal identifying information is

[71] Predictive modelling and advanced analytics will enable child support agencies 'to weigh 40 or 50 predictive dimensions, not merely 4 or 5.' Margot Bean, et al, Deloitte, Advanced analytics for child support programs: From reactive enforcement to proactive prevention—Part II www.deloitte.com/assets/Dcom-UnitedStates/Local%20Assets/Documents/us_state_advanced_analytics_for_child_support_Programs_PART_%202_83012.pdf (accessed December 2013).

easily obtained and widely disseminated. What is the expectation of privacy today when, to qualify to rent a property or buy a car, you willingly disclose your social security and driver's licence numbers, email address, phone numbers, and even provide copies of your income tax returns and most recent bank statements? Do we expect the real estate broker or used car salesman to safeguard and protect all the information we have provided, or suspect it may be sold to the highest bidder? There is no real expectation of privacy anymore. Your bank, your credit card company, and anyone willing to pay a small fee to search for the information know where you live and work, your family and professional connections and much more about you. We probably do not want to know the extent to which our personal data is shared, and we do not particularly care. So long as the information is not corrupted, or used for some immoral purpose, it is generally acknowledged that our lives are no longer private, and we do not worry a great deal about it.

Some government agencies might take a page from the new book (most likely a Kindle reader) and reevaluate their data protection and proscriptive data utilisation policies, at least insofar as information is shared with other government authorities. In the United States we have largely mooted the question of whether most personal information can or should be shared by government agencies, or even made available to the parties in a child support enforcement action. Directories and registries are compared and automated matches churn out case profiles that are accessible by those who need them. The fact is that where you work, how much you earn, whether you served in the military or went to college, and far more information may already be in the public domain. In 2025 most countries that are parties to the 2007 Convention will exchange information pertinent to the establishment and enforcement of support orders as easily as child support agencies in the United States do now in interstate cases. Bilateral agreements will be common, and some countries will even establish cross-border data portals that will permit access by caseworkers in partnering jurisdictions. Information sharing will be the norm, and it will be greatly expanded. Vast amounts of personal data will be acquired, sorted, updated and analysed (with appropriate protections to assure information is not misused) to determine exactly what procedures in each case would be most efficacious. It is a Brave New World, but Big Brother is a benevolent paternal figure. He has the best interests of the child always at the centre pinnacle of his mindset.

VII. Where the 2007 Maintenance Convention Falls Short and How it May Nonetheless be Made to Work through International Cooperation and Creative Solutions

A. Paternity Acknowledgement Replaces Paternity Establishment

In the United States paternity *establishment* in judicial proceedings has been largely replaced by paternity *acknowledgment* by the parents themselves. Apprised of their rights and responsibilities, parents prefer this route to the necessity of court or administrative hearings to clarify parentage. Paternity trials, rarely warranted in this day, are pre-decided with DNA analysis. (Sadly, when trials do occur they more and more frequently involve issues of paternity disestablishment. The downside of DNA testing is that it can also be used, decisively, to prove that the long-presumed husband/father has no biological connection to the child.)[72]

Voluntary paternity acknowledgment, by written agreement of both parents, after genetic testing (if requested) should eliminate the necessity for judicial hearings or other formal procedures in many (probably most) cases where paternity has not already been determined and recorded on birth records. Cooperation between a requesting country and the Central Authority in a requested country could facilitate paternity proceedings where the child resides, where birth records likely are maintained, and where medical and education records will need to be updated. In many cases it may be sufficient for the Central Authority in the requested country to interview the putative father, apprise him of his rights and the responsibilities of parenthood, and, if he agrees, to assist the father in making his written acknowledgment of paternity. In disputed cases, or if there is uncertainty, genetic testing can be facilitated.

The 2007 Convention requires Central Authorities to accept and process applications for establishment of a decision, 'including where necessary the establishment of parentage.'[73] *Establishment* of paternity inherently connotes an official, often adversarial, proceeding where evidence is presented and the petitioning party bears a burden of proof to demonstrate a material fact. Today, it is far more common, certainly in the United States, for paternity to be *acknowledged* by both parents, in writing, after they have each been apprised of their rights and the responsibilities attendant with such voluntary attestation. A great deal more consideration should be given between countries party to the new Convention to recognise and further refine procedures permitting the parties themselves to clarify parentage and birth records and, thus, avoid potentially expensive and contentious formal legal proceedings.[74]

B. Direct Immediate Wage Withholding in International Cases

When an order to pay support is established in the United States, there is an immediate simultaneous order issued for wage or other income withholding, and the procedural paperwork and notices are generated with a few clicks of a computer keyboard.[75] Other

[72] These cases commonly occur in the context of divorce proceedings. 'Dad' may have accepted all along the chance or even near certainty that he did not father the child, until the relationship sours and child support looms. Suddenly he 'discovers' that he was deceived, the wool had been pulled over his eyes and he was led to believe he was the father, only to find out recently that the mother was a 'liar, deceiver, out to get his money'. The author finds these belated revelations to be disgusting. Being a father for even a day—many unwed men are at the birth—is of inestimable value. Should we denigrate the hospital acknowledgements executed with both parents' willing and informed signatures? The author would submit that there should never be a paternity disestablishment unless there is a simultaneous assumption of rights and responsibilities by an adoptive or duly established biological father. He would also argue for continuing rights of the disestablished dad who has loved and nurtured a child for any significant length of time and been a father *in fact* to the child. (Disclaimer: the author has three children, none of whom claim his DNA.)

[73] 2007 Convention, Art 10(1)(c).

[74] Requested countries, eg, could facilitate genetic testing where there may be, initially, a question of paternity. When that fact is no longer subject to dispute, the requested country might be asked to assist the father in preparing an acknowledgment statement which could be used in the requesting country to clarify birth and medical records of the child. These services could be provided under Art 7, Specific Measures. See discussion of Requests for Specific Measures below.

[75] Or with the touch of a finger.

enforcement measures (passport or licence denial/revocation; liens; garnishment of insurance/lottery/bank account or other assets) are similarly determined by ADP systems automatically, but automated wage withholding is always the first remedy of choice. When an income withholding order is in place immediately following entry of a support order, the obligor never risks falling behind on payments and the family has the assurance of regular timely payment of child support. The United States has refined and improved its procedures over 25 years and now it is routine practice for the State where the original order was entered to send a withholding order *directly* to an employer in another State.[76] In the very few cases where there is a dispute, an appeal is permitted and the State where the employee resides conducts a review to determine whether the action is warranted.

International direct wage withholding, when a support order has been recognised in another country, may one day eliminate the need for the requested country to monitor payments, initiate its own enforcement remedies, and assume responsibility for transmission of collections to the creditor in the requesting country. In the United States direct wage withholding, across State lines, has been institutionalised with standard forms and procedures, due protection for individuals' rights, and careful regard for the concerns of employers. We should anticipate that countries which are parties to the 2007 Convention will one day establish bi-lateral agreements, or other comity arrangements to allow the country of the creditor's residence to send a wage or income withholding order directly to the employer in the country where the debtor is employed. Possibly a *Hague Convention Seal* or other certification will be fashioned, and the debtor's employer will recognise instantly the stamp of international approval. After notice to the employee and an opportunity to appeal (locally), most requests will be honoured.

It will still be necessary to make an application for recognition of the underlying order in the requested country, but, once that order has been declared enforceable or registered for enforcement, consideration should be given in the future to allowing the requesting country to use its own enforcement mechanisms, such as direct wage withholding. As the volume of cases requiring international enforcement, and confidence in sister countries' procedures grow such solutions will become apparent. After all, the country where the creditor resides is best situated to monitor compliance, and motivated to take prompt enforcement measures. Procedural protections, priorities if there are multiple orders, laws permitting the debtor to retain at least minimum income for personal subsistence, and similar measures would continue to be the province of the country where the debtor is employed.

C. Translation, Currency Conversion and Improved Means for Transmitting Documents

Some of the most commonly touted practical problems faced in international cases will appear quaint when viewed retrospectively in 2025. That we were ever concerned with translation or conversion of currency will seem as dated in a few years as descriptions of

[76] OMB 0970-0154, Income Withholding for Support Form www.acf.hhs.gov/sites/default/files/ocse/omb_0970_0154.pdf (accessed December 2013).

the former manner of litigating disputed paternity cases.[77] Computers will 'talk' to one another.[78] Money will move instantaneously from the debtor's account to the creditor's account. Similarly, we will find more efficient ways to exchange records necessary for the establishment and enforcement of child support orders.[79] It is not too radical an idea to suggest that many of the costs and complexities of transmitting relevant information, and some countries' insistence upon the use of the Evidence Convention whenever there is a request to officially verify or supply information, could be eliminated.[80] Information of course may become evidence; and evidence, obtained incorrectly, may be challenged; but evidentiary problems are obviated when authorities have access to each other's data banks and information sources and can determine reasonable and appropriate support orders. The parties are most likely to agree when confronted with facts that are verifiable and cannot be denied; support is most likely to be paid when it is set in an amount which accurately reflects earnings and ability to pay. Rather than focus upon the risks of litigation in the difficult case where all facts are denied regardless of the evidence, we should build our interfacing systems on the assumption that facts speak clearly for themselves, and typically they never need be offered formally in an evidentiary proceeding.[81]

D. Periodic Review and Modification

One area in which the 2007 Maintenance Convention certainly falls short of addressing and providing an adequate solution to a problem which is faced, eventually, in nearly every support proceeding, is a failure to include a provision assuring simple procedures for regular

[77] Proof by clear and convincing evidence, or even beyond a reasonable doubt (before DNA testing); jury trials; requirements that the mother be present personally to testify (as in a criminal proceeding), and other archaic procedures were commonplace when the United States' child support enforcement was in its infancy.

[78] Today, even within the same country, there may be two or more 'official' languages. The 2007 Convention addresses language requirements and translation issues, and these will continue to be significant difficulties for some countries for years to come. See 2007 Convention, Arts 44 and 45. This is an area ripe for application of technology already developed to facilitate not only accurate translation of documents and written communications, but instantaneous conversion of verbal communications, vastly improving and encouraging regular direct person-to-person exchanges of case status, updates and the need for further documentation or assistance.

[79] The 2007 Convention contemplates the electronic transmission of documents. Art 13, Means of Communication, provides that documents and information furnished by a Central Authority 'may not be challenged by the respondent by reason only of the medium or means of communication employed'.

[80] See Convention on the Taking of Evidence Abroad in Civil or Commercial Matters, 18 March 1970, 23 UST 2555. The Evidence Convention is applicable where it is necessary to 'take evidence abroad' for use in a legal proceeding. An argument can be made that not all governmental exchanges of information and records constitute evidentiary transactions. In fact, most applications for establishment of an order in another country are likely to result in a settlement, obviating the necessity of an evidentiary proceeding. Unless there is a challenge to the validity of a document in a contested case, the cooperative exchange of information using Art 7, Specific Measures may often prove to be the most appropriate, convenient and least expensive means to facilitate the exchange of pertinent information.

[81] DNA analysis, for instance, has practically eliminated any need for hearings in paternity cases. If the findings are questioned, it is a simple matter to do the tests again—possibly in a different laboratory, or with greater precautions taken to ensure accurate identification of the parties and chain of custody of the genetic material to prevent any possibility of corruption or substitution. Open and free sharing of case file information pertinent to establishing and enforcing a child support order (eg employment, earnings, assets and credit history), similarly, can eliminate the need for most hearings in other cases. In the unusual disputed case, where the debtor challenges the information, it can be substantiated (at the debtor's expense); but in the standard proceeding it should be no more difficult to ascertain a reasonable support amount, based upon earnings and asset information, than it is to determine a credit limit when applying for a new Visa card.

review and adjustment of orders as circumstances of the parties change. A persuasive argument can be made that establishment of unreasonably high levels of support obligation and draconian measures taken to collect accumulated debt drive the parent into hiding or to resort to the underground economy, and add to the friction and tension of an already tenuous relationship between the parents. Periodic review and modification of orders, and even compromise of arrears in appropriate cases, are as important to the child support enforcement system as procedures to establish and enforce orders.[82] The 2007 Maintenance Convention allows applications for modification, but there is no requirement for updating orders and there is a clear bias towards creditors' applications.

An application for modification of a decision can be made, by either a creditor or a debtor, but debtors can only make an application to modify a decision in the creditor's state, if that is where the original decision was made.[83] There is no equivalent limit on proceedings based upon applications by creditors. It is also possible to charge debtors for legal assistance provided in their applications to modify, whereas creditors making applications receive free legal assistance. Finally, the Convention permits applications to seek new orders in some circumstances where that approach appears more expeditious than obtaining a modification. This will unfortunately lead to multiple orders concerning the same parties, and will result in conflict and disputes as to which order takes precedence. It is a problem of particular relevance to orders issued originally in the United States. The United States places limitations on proceedings to modify which go further than Article 18. If either of the parties, or the child, continues to reside in the original jurisdiction, that State retains continuing exclusive jurisdiction over the order and it is the *only* jurisdiction where a modification can occur. If a creditor requests establishment of a new order in another country, it is questionable whether such an order would be recognised and enforced in the United States even if there was personal jurisdiction over the debtor.

E. Requests for Specific Measures: Assistance in Making an Application under the 2007 Convention and Cases 'Having an International Element'

It may not be immediately apparent, but arguably the greatest advancement in international procedures for administrative cooperation which was incorporated into the 2007 Convention may prove to be Article 7, Requests for specific measures. There was considerable debate during the Special Sessions concerning the inclusion of a provision for largely voluntary procedures to take measures which may enable a requesting country either: to 'assist a potential applicant in making an application under Article 10 or in determining whether such an application should be initiated'; or to assist another Central Authority 'in

[82] 'In FY2011, $111.3 billion in child support arrearages was owed to families receiving CSE services, but less than 7% ($7.7 billion) of those arrearages was actually paid … One interpretation of this information is that many noncustodial parents simply have too many financial obligations (eg food and shelter for themselves) to cover with their limited incomes' (C Solomon Fears, G Falk, and AL Fernandes-Alcantara, Congressional Research Service, R 41431, 'Child Well-Being and Noncustodial Fathers' (2013) 29–30).

[83] 2007 Convention, Art 18. Exceptions are provided where the parties agree to jurisdiction in another State, the creditor submits to jurisdiction, the competent authority in the State of origin 'cannot or refuses to, exercise jurisdiction to modify,' or the decision in the State of origin cannot be recognised or declared enforceable.

relation to a case having an international element concerning the recovery of maintenance pending in the requesting State.'[84] Some countries' representatives argued against allowing for such measures, much less mandating that appropriate assistance be provided in relation to an Article 10 application (or determination whether to initiate an application).[85]

The discretionary Article 7(2) measures, 'in relation to a case having an international element concerning the recovery of maintenance pending in the requesting state,' were even more controversial. In partial compromise of various interests and concerns, Article 8 departs from the fundamental premise that there should be no charge for services provided by the Central Authorities and allows charges to be imposed for 'exceptional costs' arising under Article 7 requests.[86] Critics of the provision were particularly concerned that these very broadly defined services should not be viewed as a replacement authority for the service of documents or taking of evidence Hague Conventions.[87] The 2007 Convention specifically mentions the relationship with these prior Conventions, but the Explanatory Report unequivocally states that the legal obligations of States under the Service and Evidence Conventions are not addressed.[88] As more countries become parties to the 2007 Convention there will soon be tens of thousands of applications for recognition and enforcement of support orders, and it will be essential for countries to streamline procedures. Requesting countries seeking assistance under Article 7 will determine for themselves whether any other Convention applies, and services should be routinely provided by requested countries' Central Authorities in the interest of facilitating case processing.[89]

VIII. Conclusion

It took the United States the better part of 35 years to establish a truly integrated, largely automated, efficient and effective child support enforcement system. As the programme grew and evolved, so did its focus and the scope of its services. Today's programme bears no resemblance to the law enforcement prototype that was common in 1975. Non-custodial parents' needs (education, training, work support) are considered along with current income and ability to pay. Children's needs for *support* (emotional as well as financial)

[84] 2007 Convention, Art 7(1) and (2).

[85] A Central Authority *must* take appropriate measures necessary to assist with an application pending or being considered under Art 10. See Art 7(1).

[86] Costs may be recovered for 'exceptional costs arising from a request for a specific measure under Article 7,' but the applicant must understand what it will cost and give prior consent for the provision of services. See Art 8.

[87] Convention on the Service Abroad of Judicial and Extrajudicial Documents in Civil or Commercial Matters, 15 November 1965, 20 UST 361; Convention on the Taking of Evidence Aboard in Civil or Commercial Matters, 18 March 1970, 23 UST 2555.

[88] See A Borrás and J Degeling, 'Hague Conference on Private International Law, Convention of 23 November 2007 on the International Recovery of Child Support and Other Forms of Family Maintenance: Explanatory Report' notes 74 and 83 (2009).

[89] Requests for specific measures under Art 7(2) are made to assist the requesting State in establishing and enforcing a support order itself. Eg, State A, where the creditor and child reside, may have established personal jurisdiction over a debtor (accused debtor or putative father) in State B. State A might ask State B to: confirm the address of the debtor; explain to a putative father his rights and responsibilities, and assist him in preparing a written acknowledgment of paternity that can be used to clarify birth records; facilitate voluntary genetic testing requested by one of the parties; verify employment; provide income/earnings and other financial information; or to facilitate direct communication with the authorities in State A.

are considered as well. Review and modification of awards is required at least triennially; paternity questions are resolved scientifically by mandatory genetic testing upon request of either parent, and paid for by the State; wage withholding orders are entered automatically when a support order is established, and direct withholding across State lines is initiated with a keystroke. The 2007 Maintenance Convention does not expressly incorporate any of these procedures; nor does it prohibit them.

There are other countries with systems as well-advanced, or superior, to those in the United States. The proven effective and most innovative procedures of all countries should be shared and widely adopted. Opportunities to improve the 2007 Maintenance Convention through implementation of best practices and expansive interpretation of the Convention itself will ensure its successful implementation. Parochial domestic systems and entrenched bureaucratic processes must be set aside to permit truly global operations to take their place. Automation and better use of data through analytics, and openness to further advances in technology should be embraced. It is not too bold a prediction to suggest that the progress made in the United States since 1975 will be not only replicated, but surpassed on the international stage by 2025.

4

Recognition and Enforcement of Foreign Maintenance Orders in Commonwealth African Countries*

RICHARD FRIMPONG OPPONG

> Systemic failures to enforce maintenance orders have a negative impact on the rule of law. The courts are there to ensure that the rights of all are protected. The judiciary must endeavour to secure for vulnerable children and disempowered women their small but life sustaining legal entitlements. If court orders are habitually evaded and defied with relative impunity the justice system is discredited and the constitutional promise of human dignity and equality is seriously compromised for those dependent on the law.
>
> *S v Gawaseb* 2007 (2) NR 600, 602

I. Introduction

A maintenance order or award is a periodical money claim between two persons who are, or were, husband and wife.[1] The payments due under the claim may be for the benefit of one of the spouses or their dependant(s). In essence, a foreign maintenance order is a foreign judgment. However, for legal, historical, and pragmatic reasons, a separate regime for enforcing such orders has always existed in the 15 countries studied in this chapter. This chapter comparatively examines the recovery of foreign maintenance orders in Commonwealth African countries, with a special focus on private international law issues. It discusses the law in—Botswana, the Gambia, Ghana, Kenya, Lesotho, Malawi, Namibia,

* This research was supported by the Social Sciences and Humanities Research Council of Canada.

[1] Christopher Forsyth, *Private International Law* (Cape Town, Juta & Company, 2012) 449. Such an order may also be made in relation to two unmarried persons, eg to an unmarried mother for the support of her child from the father. In most of the countries under study, a maintenance order is statutorily defined as 'an order other than an order of affiliation for the periodical payment of sums of money towards the maintenance of the wife or other dependants of the person against whom the order is made'.

Nigeria, Sierra Leone, South Africa, Swaziland, Tanzania, Uganda, Zambia and Zimbabwe (hereafter the countries under study).[2]

There are two separate regimes for enforcing foreign maintenance orders in each of the countries under study. These are the common law and statutory regimes. Regardless of which regime one is looking at, in all the countries under study the competence to enforce a foreign maintenance order lies with a judicial authority. However, in some cases, the processes for enforcing such orders are not entirely judicial—they may be administrative, often beginning with an executive action.

II. The Common Law Regime for Enforcing Foreign Maintenance Orders

Each of the countries under study has a statutory regime for the registration of foreign money judgments.[3] However, foreign maintenance orders are expressly excluded from the statutory regimes for enforcing foreign money judgments[4] and, as discussed below, a separate statutory regime has been created for foreign maintenance orders. Operating alongside the statutory regimes for registering foreign money judgments is a common law regime.[5] The common law procedure for enforcing a foreign judgment is an action on the judgment debt. The courts will enforce the judgment if three conditions are satisfied. These entail first that the foreign court should be regarded by the enforcing state as having had jurisdiction; second, that the judgment is final and conclusive, and third, that the judgment should not be impeachable on the bases of fraud, breach of natural justice or public policy.[6]

It is difficult to use the common law regime to enforce foreign maintenance orders. As noted above, it is an essential requirement of the common law regime that the foreign judgment is final and conclusive. In many jurisdictions, a maintenance order is often subject to variation and thus would fall foul of the finality requirement of the common law regime. The Zimbabwean case of *Knight v Baldi*[7] illustrates this point. In March 1948 in Cape Town, the plaintiff instituted action for restitution of conjugal rights. Subsequent

[2] Cameroon, Mauritius, Mozambique, Rwanda and Seychelles are also part of the Commonwealth but are not examined in this chapter. Zimbabwe is currently not a member of the Commonwealth but is included in this study.

[3] See R F Oppong, *Private International Law in Commonwealth Africa* (Cambridge, Cambridge University Press, 2013) 353–96.

[4] Botswana—Judgments (International Enforcement) Act 1981; Gambia—Reciprocal Enforcement of Judgments Act 1922 and the Foreign Judgment Reciprocal Enforcement Act 1936; Ghana—Courts Act 1993; Kenya—Foreign Judgments (Reciprocal Enforcement) Act 1984; Lesotho—Reciprocal Enforcement of Judgments Act 1922; Namibia—Enforcement of Foreign Civil Judgments Act, 1994; Nigeria—Reciprocal Enforcement of Judgments Ordinance 1922 and the Foreign Judgments (Reciprocal Enforcement) Act 1961; South Africa—Enforcement of Foreign Civil Judgments Act, 1988; Tanzania—Foreign Judgments (Reciprocal Enforcement) Ordinance 1935; Uganda—Foreign Judgments (Reciprocal Enforcement) Act 1961, the Reciprocal Enforcement of Judgments Act 1922; Zambia—Foreign Judgments (Reciprocal Enforcement) Act 1937; Zimbabwe—Civil Matters (Mutual Assistance) Act 1995.

[5] Oppong (n 3) 313–52.

[6] J D McClean, *Recognition of Family Judgments in the Commonwealth* (London, Butterworths, 1983) 106.

[7] 1966 (3) SA 19.

to this, the parties signed a consent paper, which provided that, in the event of the court granting a decree of divorce, the plaintiff would have custody of their minor child and the defendant would pay maintenance for the child. In April 1948, the parties were divorced. In this action, which was brought in Zimbabwe, the plaintiff claimed arrears of maintenance. It was held that, as the order of court was an order of a foreign court which was not a final judgment, the plaintiff could not rely on it. Similarly, in the Malawian case of *Webb v Murray, ex parte Murray*,[8] it was held that:

> [A]n order for maintenance, unlike a decree of divorce to which it is ancillary and which is in rem, is no more than an order in personam … the order can be varied at any time at the discretion of the court that made it, not only with regard to future, but also with regard to past instalments, which have accrued due and are in arrears. In the result, the order in personam, not being a final judgment, could not be enforced by suing out [sic] a writ at common law.[9]

Because of this legal position, in all the countries under study, specific legislation has been enacted to regulate the enforcement of both final and provisional foreign maintenance orders. In other words, it is the failure of the common law regime to provide an adequate mechanism for the enforcement of maintenance awards that has led to the enactment of the statutory regimes. This raises the question of whether the common law regime can be reformed to accommodate the enforcement of foreign maintenance orders. This is an important question given, as we will see, the very limited scope of application for the statutory regime. Admittedly, to the extent that a judgment creditor can demonstrate that a foreign maintenance order is final and conclusive, there should be no difficulty in relying on the common law regime to enforce it. Thus, it should be relatively easy to enforce accrued or vested arrears of maintenance under the common law regime.

To date, there is no jurisprudence in any of the countries under study that leaves room for reforming this common law rule, at least in respect of maintenance orders. Comparatively, it is worth noting that the rule that a foreign order cannot be enforced at common law because it is not final and conclusive is not followed in some jurisdictions, such as Ireland. There, a foreign maintenance order which determines the issues between the parties so as to attract the principle of *res judicata* may be treated as final and conclusive even though capable of retrospective variation.[10] This approach is reasonable and is recommended to the countries under study.

Another interesting question to which there does not appear to be significant authority in the countries under study is whether, instead of fully enforcing the foreign maintenance order at common law, the court has jurisdiction to vary the order. In the Zimbabwean case of *Walls v Walls*,[11] the court doubted whether this could be done. In the words of the court:

> I find it difficult to agree that if the application had been commenced in a court in South Africa and that court had been asked to apply Zimbabwean law, it would have countenanced granting an

[8] [1961–1963] ALR Mal 205.

[9] Ibid 207. See generally *Walls v Walls* 1996 (2) ZLR 117, which involved an application to vary a maintenance award when the parties were resident abroad.

[10] See *McC v McC* [1994] IRLM 101 (cited in Lord Collins of Mapesbury et al (eds), *Dicey, Morris and Collins on the Conflict of Laws*, 15th edn (London, Sweet & Maxwell, 2012) 1095, where it is suggested a similar approach also exists in the United States).

[11] *Walls v Walls* 1996 (2) ZLR 117. Given that at common law the action is on a judgment debt, 'variation' would mean a review of the merits, which is always regarded as forbidden.

> order amending or varying an order of a Zimbabwean court. It seems to me that if one Division of the South African Supreme Court will not countenance amending or varying an order made by another Division of the South African Supreme Court, that it is most unlikely that a South African Court would consider amending or varying a decision of the Zimbabwe High Court.[12]

In contrast, as will be discussed below, the statutory regimes for registering foreign maintenance orders in some of the countries under study expressly give the courts jurisdiction to vary foreign maintenance awards.

III. Statutory Regimes for Enforcing Maintenance Orders

In addition to the common law regime for enforcing foreign maintenance orders, each of the countries under study has a statutory regime for enforcing such orders,[13] but only in respect of orders from designated countries. The following paragraphs look at some of the common provisions and issues arising under the national regimes. While an action on a debt (ie in this instance, a foreign judgment) can take time to be decided, the statutory regimes on maintenance order enforcement aim at providing a very simplified process for giving effect to such orders.

A. Nature of a Maintenance Order

In most of the countries under study, a 'maintenance order' means an order, other than an order of affiliation, for the periodical payment of sums of money towards the maintenance of the wife or other dependants of the person against whom the order is made.[14] An important feature of these definitions is that they are limited to cases where periodical payments of sums of money are ordered. Lump sum payments, settlement of

[12] Ibid 126.

[13] The principal legislation in the respective countries is: Botswana—Judgments (International Enforcement) Act 1981; Gambia—Maintenance Orders (Facilities for Enforcement) Act 1921; Ghana—Courts Act 1993; Kenya—Maintenance Orders Enforcement Act; Lesotho—Maintenance Orders Proclamation 1921; Malawi—Maintenance Orders (Enforcement) Act 1921; Namibia—Reciprocal Enforcement of Maintenance Orders Act 1995; Nigeria—Maintenance Orders Act 1921; Sierra Leone—Maintenance Orders (Facilities for Enforcement) Act 1921; South Africa—Reciprocal Enforcement of Maintenance Orders Act 1963 and Reciprocal Enforcement of Maintenance Orders (Countries in Africa) Act 1989; Swaziland—Maintenance Order Act 1920; Tanzania—Law of Marriage Act 1971; Uganda—Maintenance Orders Enforcement Act 1921; Zambia—Maintenance Orders (Enforcement) Act 1921; Zimbabwe—Maintenance Orders (Facilities for Enforcement) Act 1921. These statutes were based on the United Kingdom's Maintenance Orders (Facilities for Enforcement) Act 1920.

[14] Some, such as Botswana, Ghana and Kenya, include an order or decree for the recovery or payment of the cost of public relief or maintenance. In Namibia's Reciprocal Enforcement of Maintenance Orders Act 1995, which appears to be the most recent on the subject, a maintenance order is defined as: any order for the periodical payment by any person of sums of money towards the maintenance of any other person whom the first mentioned person is liable to maintain in accordance with the law of the country in which the order is made.

property and other types of financial relief that may be granted in foreign jurisdictions are excluded.[15]

With the increasing transformation of the nature of marriage, an important question that arises in the context of this definition is whether a party to a gay or lesbian relationship or their dependant may be deemed a 'wife or other dependant' for the purposes of this definition, so as to enable him or her to invoke the provisions of the respective Acts. At the time that most of the statutes were originally enacted, this would not have been an issue, and it is thus not surprising that the language of the statute does not directly address it. Given the provisions of South Africa's Civil Union Act 2006, and the recent decision of the court in *AS v CS*[16] to recognise an English civil partnership, it is likely that a South African court would be prepared to enforce a maintenance order granted in favour of a party to a same-sex marriage. The position in the other countries of study remains unclear. It is however worth pointing out that under the existing legislation, although 'wife' is not defined, a dependant is defined by reference to foreign law, that is, the law of the place where the maintenance order was made. Thus, the real question is whether the country where enforcement is sought would exclude the application of foreign law in cases where that foreign law treats a party to a same-sex relationship as a dependant.[17] In many of the countries under study, same sex relationships are not legally recognised. Public policy will play a significant role in determining whether an enforcing court will recognise the status of dependant acquired abroad through a same sex relationship.

Apart from Namibia, South Africa and Zimbabwe, all the other countries under study expressly exclude an 'order of affiliation' from the scope of their statutory regimes. The exclusion of orders of affiliation, which are orders that an illegitimate child be maintained by their father, could be problematic. This is because, under the constitutions and laws of some of the countries under study, every child, whether or not born in wedlock, is entitled to reasonable provision out of the estate of its parents.[18] It would be difficult to justify why a foreign maintenance order obtained against a man who fathers a child (perhaps now staying with a grandparent in one of the countries which exclude such orders) when not married to the mother, cannot be enforced against the assets of that person. It is submitted that this restriction on the definition of a maintenance order is anachronistic and should be reformed. Indeed, the exclusion of orders of affiliation is inconsistent with trends in other Commonwealth countries such as Australia, Canada and New Zealand, and also under existing international conventions on maintenance.[19]

[15] This appears not to be the case in South Africa, where both the Reciprocal Enforcement of Maintenance Orders (Countries in Africa) Act 1989 and the Reciprocal Enforcement of Maintenance Orders Act 1963 define a maintenance order as 'any order for the payment, including the periodical payment, by any person of sums of money towards the maintenance of any other person whom the first mentioned person is liable to maintain in accordance with the law of the country in which the order is made, and in Zimbabwe, where the Maintenance Orders (Facilities for Enforcement) Act define it as an order for the payment of money, whether in a lump sum or in periodical payments or otherwise, towards the maintenance of the wife or other dependants of the person against whom the order is made'.

[16] 2011 (2) SA 360.

[17] McClean (n 6) 121–22.

[18] See eg Constitution of the Republic of Ghana, Art 28(2); Namibia—Children's Status Act 2006, s 16(2); *Frans v Paschke* 2007 (2) NR 520.

[19] Hague Convention of 23 November 2007 on the International Recovery of Child Support and Other Forms of Family Maintenance, Art 2(4).

A Kenyan court has held that a maintenance order may be ancillary to a decree of divorce or made separately in a different proceeding.[20] In other words, a maintenance order need not be the only order made by the foreign court, or the sole or primary object of the proceedings before the foreign court. This is significant because in many jurisdictions a maintenance order may be made in diverse proceedings and, also, as part of a judgment dealing with other issues. For example, in Ghana an application for maintenance of a child can arise both within and outside matrimonial proceedings.[21]

B. International Jurisdiction

A national court must have jurisdiction to enforce a foreign maintenance order. As with any claim involving foreign elements, a court has to have the jurisdiction to adjudicate the action in order to enforce a foreign maintenance order. A person who seeks to enforce a foreign maintenance order must satisfy the enforcing court's rules on jurisdiction in international matters, or the courts will not be able to assume jurisdiction to hear the case.[22] In many instances, this requirement would not be difficult to meet—the defendant may have assets or may be present or ordinarily resident within the jurisdiction. In Botswana, Lesotho, Namibia, South Africa, Swaziland and Zimbabwe, assets within the jurisdiction (the object of the action) could be attached to found or confirm jurisdiction.[23] Roman Dutch law influenced the legal systems in these countries. In Gambia, Ghana, Kenya, Malawi, Nigeria, Sierra Leone, Tanzania, Uganda and Zambia, residence and the presence of a defendant in the country can be the bases of the court's jurisdiction[24]—attachment of assets within the jurisdiction is not a basis of jurisdiction in these countries.[25] This raises the question of what happens when the judgment debtor has assets within the jurisdiction, but is himself/herself neither resident in the jurisdiction nor prepared to submit to it.

[20] *In re Roderick Fountaine Antrobus Johnston* (1954) 27 KLR 94, 97–98. As part of the principle that the enforcing court will not review the foreign order on its merits, the Kenyan court in this case (at 99) declined to review whether under Zimbabwean law the child at issue was a dependant.

[21] Matrimonial Causes Act 1971, ss 16 and 22; Children's Act 1998, s 48. The provisions of the Children's Act are subject to the Matrimonial Causes Act, and no action may be brought for a maintenance order if an application for maintenance is pending in matrimonial proceedings. See Children's Act, s 58.

[22] *Cloete v Brink* 1995 BLR 275 (also reported in 1996 BLR 244). In this case, the plaintiff sought to recover from the defendant an amount due in terms of a judgment obtained against the defendant in South Africa. The defendant contested the jurisdiction of the High Court of Botswana to hear the case. The parties were *peregrines*, the cause of action arose in South Africa, and there was no clear indication of where the defendant actually resided. The court rejected the plaintiff's argument that the defendant had submitted to its jurisdiction by requesting the plaintiff to file a bond of security. In that request, the defendant expressly noted it would contest the court's jurisdiction. Accordingly, it was held that the court had no jurisdiction to hear the action to enforce the South African judgment. See also *Zwyssig v Zwyssig* 1997 (2) SA 467. This was an action to enforce a Florida judgment. The defendant challenged the jurisdiction of the South African court to hear the action on the grounds that he was neither domiciled nor resident in South Africa. The court rejected this argument and found that the defendant was in fact resident in South Africa. The defendant owned a house, was present in South Africa six months a year, maintained a telephone line at the house, and was a member of a local health club.

[23] Oppong (n 3) 68–90.

[24] Ibid 47–67.

[25] See generally R F Oppong, 'Roman-Dutch Law meets the Common Law on Jurisdiction in International Matters' (2008) *Journal of Private International Law* 311.

To illustrate the problem: Alice obtains a maintenance order in France against her former husband, Paul, in respect of their children currently resident in Ghana. Paul, who is resident in France, has a house and bank account in Ghana and visits Ghana once every seven years. In Gambia, Ghana, Kenya, Malawi, Nigeria, Sierra Leone, Tanzania, Uganda and Zambia, it is an undecided issue whether service outside the jurisdiction may be allowed in an action to enforce a foreign maintenance order at common law or, subject to the discussion below, to register a foreign maintenance order. At present, there is no specific statutory foundation for allowing service outside the jurisdiction on the basis of an action to enforce a foreign maintenance award or, indeed, any foreign judgment.[26]

It can be argued that the need to establish the jurisdiction of the court to enforce a foreign order is only relevant when action is brought to enforce the award at common law, and not when the award is being registered under the statutory regime and there are assets within the jurisdiction. Indeed, an action to enforce a foreign judgment at common law is a new action for which jurisdiction must be established through service. There is some merit in the position that in respect of registering foreign maintenance orders service is not required. The position finds support in the jurisprudence in some commonwealth countries such as England,[27] Canada[28] and Australia.[29] The position is also pragmatic—it would be a travesty of justice if assets within the jurisdiction could not be used for the benefit of the person to be maintained, purely on the basis that the judgment creditor who owns those assets is not within the jurisdiction to be served, and there is no statutory foundation for serving him or her out of the jurisdiction. The statutes in the countries under study do not expressly address this issue. Given the importance of jurisdiction to the exercise of judicial power, it is likely that some courts may be unwilling to register a foreign maintenance order unless they are satisfied they have jurisdiction over the judgment debtor. It is in this regard that an amendment to the relevant national laws to allow for service out in actions to enforce or register foreign judgments (including maintenance orders) would be appropriate.

[26] Compare England and Wales—Civil Procedure Rules, para 3.1(10) of Practice Direction 6B; *Tasarruf Mevduati Sigorta Fonu v Demirel* [2007] 1 WLR 2508, [2007] 4 All ER 1014. As noted in the 1985 'White Book' (*Supreme Court Practice 1985*, vol 1, 84, para 11.1.25): 'this paragraph blocks a small but irritating loophole in the law. The presence of assets within the jurisdiction does not in itself give the English courts jurisdiction over a person outside the jurisdiction. Accordingly a foreign judgment could not be enforced against English assets in cases not falling within the provisions for the reciprocal enforcement of judgments legislation unless the debtor could be served in England or was 'domiciled or ordinarily resident within the jurisdiction'. *Perry v Zissis* [1977] 1 Lloyd's Rep 607.

[27] See eg Lord Collins of Mapesbury et al (eds), *Dicey, Morris and Collins on the Conflict of Laws*, 15th edn (London, Sweet & Maxwell, 2012) 752, and 457 where it is noted that 'where enforcement by registration is possible the *in personam* jurisdiction of the English court over the defendant is irrelevant'. *Tasarruf Mevduati Sigorta Fonu v Demirel* [2007] 1 WLR 2508, 2513 where it was observed: 'the origin of the rule was RSC Ord 11, r 1(1)(m), which was added in 1985 to fill a gap revealed in cases where the judgment creditor wished to enforce the judgment against *assets in England but there was no reciprocal enforcement arrangement enabling the foreign judgment to be registered in England*'. The italicised words suggest that where there are assets in England and there is a reciprocal enforcement arrangement enabling the foreign judgment to be registered in England, the fact that the judgment creditor is not present in the jurisdiction to be served is immaterial.

[28] The Civil Jurisdiction and Proceedings Transfer Act which has been adopted in British Columbia, Saskatchewan and Nova Scotia expressly allows for service out of the jurisdiction in an action for enforcement of a judgment of a court made in or outside the province or an arbitral award made in or outside the province.

[29] *Hunt v BP Exploration Co (Libya) Ltd* (1980) 144 CLR 565.

C. Applicable Law

In the countries under study, the enforcement of foreign maintenance orders appears to be a subject that is governed almost entirely by the *lex fori*. The scope for the application of foreign law in such actions is very limited. Under the existing statutes, two areas where there must be recourse to foreign law lie in determining whether an order is provisional,[30] and whether someone is a dependant of the person against whom the order has been made.[31] The fact that the question of who is a dependant has to be decided by reference to foreign law is significant: it makes it irrelevant whether the forum where registration of a maintenance order is sought would treat the judgment creditor as a dependant under its own laws.

The *lex fori* in this instance is mainly a reference to the statutory regime for registering foreign maintenance orders.[32] In many of the countries under study, where the statutory regime for enforcing foreign judgments applies, it is exclusive: a judgment enforceable under the regime cannot be enforced using the common law regime. However, unlike the statutory regime for enforcing foreign judgments, the regime for enforcing foreign maintenance orders is not expressed as exclusive. Accordingly, it is possible for a maintenance order that is either within or outside the scope of the regime to be enforced, using the common law for enforcing foreign judgments. However, as noted above, because maintenance orders might be subject to variation by the foreign court—they are not final and conclusive—enforcing them at common law may be difficult. This may be the reason why no such exclusivity provision is included in the regimes for registering foreign maintenance orders.

D. Reciprocity and Designation

The statutory regimes operate on the basis of reciprocity.[33] The President or the Minister of Justice, as the case may be, is given the discretion to designate countries that shall be beneficiaries of the regimes. Some countries restrict states that can be designated solely to the Commonwealth.[34] This is an undue restraint on the scope and applicability of the statutory regime. The table below presents the countries that have been designated in the countries under study.

It is evident from the above that maintenance orders from a significant number of countries in the world cannot be enforced in the countries under study using the statutory

[30] In most cases a court will not need to refer to the foreign law to determine if an order is provisional because the order will arrive as a provisional order with the appropriate documentation. The *lex fori* will then determine whether the local court has power to confirm it.

[31] See section III (A) of this chapter.

[32] Most of the statutes were enacted in 1921 and were modelled on the United Kingdom's Maintenance Orders (Facilities for Enforcement) Act 1920.

[33] Professor McClean has discussed the concept of 'unilateral reciprocity' under which country A has legislation declaring country B to be a reciprocal country but no effective reciprocal legislation can be traced in country B. Eg, in the table displayed, Botswana designates Kenya but Kenya has not designated Botswana. Similarly, Nigeria designates Zambia (Northern Rhodesia) but Zambia has not designated Nigeria. See McClean (n 6) 199.

[34] Gambia, Lesotho, Nigeria, Sierra Leone, Uganda and Zambia.

Country	Designated countries
Botswana	England and Wales; Ireland; the Island of Jersey; Lesotho; Swaziland; Zambia; Zimbabwe; Republic of South Africa; Zanzibar; New South Wales; Malawi; Western Australia; Uganda; Queensland; Kenya; New Zealand; Tasmania; South Australia; Victoria; Commonwealth of Australia; Cook Islands; India (except the States of Jammu and Kashmir); Bailiwick of Guernsey; Pakistan and the Isle of Man.
Gambia	United Kingdom; Ireland; Sierra Leone; Nigeria; New South Wales; the Commonwealth of Australia; Island of Jersey; Bailiwick of Guernsey and the Isle of Man.
Ghana	Switzerland; United Kingdom; the following States in Australia: Queensland, Tasmania, Western Australia; the following Provinces in Canada: Alberta, British Columbia, Newfoundland, North-West Territories, Nova Scotia, Ontario and Prince Edward Island.
Kenya	United Kingdom and Ireland.
Lesotho	England; Ireland; Botswana; Swaziland; Zambia; Zimbabwe; South Africa; New South Wales; Zanzibar; Malawi; Western Australia; Uganda; Queensland; Kenya; New Zealand; Tasmania; South Australia; Victoria; the Commonwealth of Australia; the Cook Islands; the Island of Jersey; India (except the State of Jammu and Kashmir); the Bailiwick of Guernsey and Pakistan.
Malawi	England[35] or Ireland; the Seychelles; the State of New South Wales; Uganda; Zambia; Lesotho; Botswana; Swaziland; Southern Rhodesia; Kenya; the States of Victoria; South Australia; Queensland; Tasmania and Western Australia; the Territory for the seat of the Government of the Commonwealth of Australia; the Republic of India (excluding the State of Jammu and Kashmir); the Bailiwick of the Island of Guernsey; the Bailiwick of Jersey; the Isle of Man; Singapore; the Northern Territory of Australia; the Republic of South Africa and the United Republic of Tanzania.
Namibia	The Reciprocal Enforcement of Maintenance Orders Act 1995 replaced the South African Reciprocal Enforcement of Maintenance Orders Act 1963. Section 13 of the Act provides that any country designated under the 1963 Act will be deemed to be a designated country for the purposes of the Act. These will be all the countries designated by South Africa, below. South Africa has also been named as a designated country.
Nigeria	England; Ireland; the Gambia; Ghana; Sierra Leone; New South Wales; St. Vincent; Grenada; British Guiana; Victoria; the Commonwealth of Australia; Northern Rhodesia; Western Australia; the Union of South Africa; New Zealand and the Island of Jersey.
Sierra Leone	England or Ireland; the Colony of the Gambia; the Colony of the Gold Coast; Ashanti and the Northern Territories of the Gold Coast (now Ghana); Nigeria; the territory of the seat of Government of the Commonwealth of Australia and Gibraltar.

(*Continued*)

[35] The statutes in Lesotho, Malawi, Nigeria, Sierra Leone, Uganda, Zambia and Zimbabwe specifically mention only England. This raises the question whether 'England' should be read as England and Wales.

Country	Designated countries
South Africa	Australian Capital Territory; Lesotho; Botswana; Cocos (Keeling) Islands; Cyprus; United Kingdom; Fiji; Guernsey; Isle of Man; Kenya; Mauritius; New South Wales; New Zealand; Nigeria; Norfolk Island; Northern Island; Zambia; Northern Territory of Australia; Malawi; Ontario; Queensland; Sarawak; Singapore; South Australia; Zimbabwe; Namibia; St Helena; Swaziland; Victoria; Western Australia; Island of Jersey; British Columbia; Hong Kong; Northwest Territories of Canada; California and Alberta.
Swaziland	Botswana, Cook Islands, Guernsey, India, Isle of Man, Jersey, Kenya, Lesotho, Malawi, New South Wales, New Zealand, Pakistan, Queensland, South Africa, South Australia, Tasmania, Uganda, United Kingdom, Victoria, Western Australia, Zambia and Zimbabwe.
Tanzania	United Kingdom and Malawi.
Uganda	England, Northern Ireland; Republic of Ireland; the Seychelles; Sri Lanka; Mauritius; Malawi; Zambia; Lesotho; Botswana; Swaziland; New South Wales and its dependencies in the Commonwealth of Australia; Territory for the seat of Government of the Commonwealth of Australia; Kenya; Zanzibar; the Island of Jersey; India (excluding the State of Jammu and Kashmir); the State of South Australia; the Bailiwick of Guernsey; the State of Tasmania and its dependencies in the Commonwealth of Australia; the Isle of Man and New Zealand.
Zambia	England; Ireland; Northern Territory of Australia, the Australian States of Queensland; South Australia and Tasmania.
Zimbabwe	Alberta, Botswana, British Columbia, Cook Islands, England and Northern Ireland, Guernsey, India, Isle of Man, Jersey, Kenya, Lesotho, Malawi, Manitoba, New Zealand, Newfoundland, Northwest Territories of Canada, Nova Scotia, Ontario, Papua (*not* New Guinea), Prince Edward Island, Saskatchewan, Swaziland, Tanganyika, Yukon Territory and Zambia.

regimes. The only countries whose orders are enforceable in almost all the countries under study are England and Ireland.[36] The reason for this is largely historical. Given the limitations on using the common law to enforce foreign maintenance awards, this state of affairs is a significant challenge, most significant for countries outside the Commonwealth. Apart from Switzerland (designated by Ghana), Republic of Ireland (designated by Uganda); and California (designated by South Africa) and also Hong Kong (also designated by South Africa and no longer a Commonwealth territory), it appears there is no other non-Commonwealth state that has been designated in any of the countries under study.

[36] It is open to debate whether 'Ireland' is a reference to Northern Ireland or the Republic of Ireland. In general one cannot but notice that the list of designated countries contains some obsolete names and also names that raise issues as to state succession. A revision of the list of designated countries in each of the countries under study is long overdue. On the legal challenges posed by such an obsolete or outdated list see *Italframe Ltd v Mediterranean Shipping Company* [1986] KLR 54 (where the appellant obtained a judgment from the High Court in Tanzania and sought unsuccessfully to register it in Kenya. The court reasoned that the Foreign Judgment Act did not apply to the decree of the High Court of Tanzania since it referred to the High Court of Tanganyika, the former name of Tanzania); and *In re Lowenthal and Air France* 1966 (2) ALR Comm 301, [1967] EA 75 (where it was held that a judgment of a Zambian court cannot be registered in Kenya under the Foreign Judgments Enforcement Act because the application of that Act to judgments of Northern Rhodesia cannot be taken to have been extended to Zambia after independence).

There are a number of ways to overcome this challenge: the countries under study can designate many other countries as beneficiaries of their respective regimes; become parties to existing international conventions, or negotiate their own conventions to which other countries in and outside Africa can become parties. Given the highly similar content of the statutory regimes in the countries under study, it should not be difficult for them to conclude among themselves a convention for the reciprocal enforcement of maintenance orders, to which other countries may join. However, it is doubtful whether there will be the political will for such a convention, or indeed, whether it will address any pressing problem. Although I have not conducted any empirical study on the subject, I assume the number of cases in which a maintenance order from one African country is sought to be enforced in another African country is very low. The need to enforce foreign maintenance orders is likely to be more pressing for countries outside Africa. As discussed below, for these countries, the designation through diplomatic negotiations or the relevant country becoming party to an international convention would be an easier course.

E. Procedures for Enforcement

Each of the countries under study provides two distinct procedures for enforcing foreign maintenance orders. A distinction is drawn between provisional and final maintenance orders.

An order that is 'provisional only and has no effect unless and until confirmed' by the domestic court, is registered only after a hearing or an inquiry. At the hearing, which should be held after notice of the proceedings has been given to the respondent, it is open to the respondent to raise any defence that he or she could have raised in the original proceedings, had they been a party to them. Most of the statutes in the countries under study are unanimous in providing that no other defence is permissible.[37] A certificate from the foreign court, stating the grounds on which the making of the order might have been opposed if the person against whom the order was made had been a party to the proceedings, is conclusive evidence that those are grounds on which the order could have been challenged. In other words, although it is open to the respondent to raise a defence, his or her options are constrained to those that would have been available to them in the foreign court.

The fact that a respondent is limited to defences that would have been available to him or her in the foreign court is problematic. It could be argued that the respondent is not permitted to assert how enforcement of the order would contravene the enforcing country's public policy, since this is a defence he or she could not have raised in the foreign country. Many Africans emigrate to various jurisdictions with different values and legal systems. It is possible for such persons to become the objects of maintenance orders that are founded on bases which might be considered offensive to domestic public policy. The fact that such

[37] The Namibian regime is generally silent on this issue of defences. However, under s 6(6) of the Reciprocal Enforcement of Maintenance Orders Act 1995 and s 13(3) of the Maintenance Act 2003, 'the person presiding at the maintenance court must conduct the maintenance enquiry in a manner that is aimed at ensuring that substantial justice is achieved between the parties as well as the beneficiary of the maintenance claim'. In general, it is also worth noting that although the respondent at the 'confirmation' stage may only raise one of the listed defences to the very making of the order, he or she may nonetheless ask the court to exercise its power to confirm the order *with modifications* (eg as to the amount to be paid under the order as confirmed).

persons are not able to raise that defence before an enforcing court (because they definitely could not have raised it in the foreign court) is unacceptable. Indeed, the fact that affiliation orders are excluded from the scope of the majority of maintenance order enforcement regimes suggests that not all foreign maintenance orders are acceptable in the countries under study. Significantly, international conventions on the enforcement of foreign maintenance orders recognise public policy as a basis for refusing recognition and enforcement.[38] It is submitted that one defence that can be raised by a respondent in such proceedings is the foreign court's lack of jurisdiction. The enforcing court has jurisdiction to confirm or refuse to register the provisional order. In other words, registration of provisional maintenance orders is neither automatic nor mandatory.

An important aspect of the regime for enforcing provisional orders is the power given to the enforcing court to make a reference back to the foreign court, which made the order. This so called 'shuttlecock' or remission procedure is provided for in the legal regimes in the countries under study. For example, section 91(6) of Ghana's Courts Act 1993 provides that 'if the person against whom the summons was issued appears at the hearing and satisfies the court that for the purpose of any defence it is necessary to remit the case to the court which made the provisional order to take further evidence, the court may remit the case and adjourn the proceedings for that purpose'. It is however, unclear what the phrase 'for the purpose of any defence' means.[39] It is likely courts may adopt a broad interpretation of the phrase such as would allow, for example, a case in which the judgment debtor wants to produce new evidence to cast doubt on the judgment.

In contrast, the enforcement of foreign final maintenance orders is automatic and mandatory in most of the countries under study.[40] On receipt of the copy of the order, which in many of the countries under study should be transmitted through a member of the executive, such as the Minister of Justice or the President, the prescribed officer of the court is obliged to—'shall'—register the order. In other words, registration of final maintenance orders (as opposed to provisional orders) is mandatory. In a South African case, it was held that the registration of a final foreign order of maintenance is not in any way a judicial or quasi-judicial act, nor is it a civil suit or proceeding; it is 'purely an administrative act'.[41]

Registration renders the order domestically enforceable. Unlike provisional orders, the provisions applicable to orders which are not expressed as provisional assume that the foreign court has had jurisdiction—there is no provision for inquiring into or contesting the jurisdiction of the foreign court.[42] Indeed, there is no requirement for a hearing

[38] The Hague Convention on the International Recovery of Child Support and Other Forms of Family Maintenance 2007, Art 22(a); Hague Convention on the Recognition and Enforcement of Decisions Relating to Maintenance Obligations 1973, Art 5(1).

[39] McClean (n 6) 137–38.

[40] The Botswana and Ghanaian statutes use 'may be registered' instead of 'shall be registered'. This suggests that, in both countries, the registration of final foreign maintenance orders is discretionary.

[41] *Severin v Severin* 1951 (1) SA 225; *Marendaz v Marendaz* 1955 (2) SA 117. See also *Ex parte Worth* 1951 (4) SA 230, 232: 'the separation order is coupled with a maintenance order of a kind which has been recognised by the Legislature in the Maintenance Orders (Facilities for Enforcement) Act (Chap. 154). It has not yet been registered in this Colony, but if it were transmitted through the proper channels it would *automatically be registered* and become as enforceable here as though it had been made by a competent court in this Colony'.

[42] McClean (n 6) 127 where he notes that 'the legislation imposes no requirements as to the jurisdiction of the original court. The intention seems to have been that, as in cases under the Judgments Extension Act 1868, the fact that a court in a reciprocating country had made an order was sufficient basis for registration and enforcement. This may also be compared with the regimes for registering foreign money judgments, which allow for the international competence of the foreign court to be examined.'

prior to registration. However, given that proceedings may be taken on an order registering the foreign order, as if the latter was originally obtained in the court that registered it, a registered order is, arguably, open to appeal (or application to set the registration aside). However, this interpretation has been rejected in Malawi and Kenya. Courts in both jurisdictions have held that, where a foreign order which is not expressed as provisional is registered, the fact that it becomes an order of the registering court does not afford the respondent the right to appeal, either from the order itself or from the registration of it, nor is the court empowered to discharge or vary the foreign order. An application to vary the order must be made to the foreign court.[43]

It is doubtful whether, in future, courts will adopt a similar interpretation when confronted with the same issue. It could be argued that denying the respondent the right to appeal in the domestic forum amounts to a denial of the right of access to justice, even though, admittedly, giving effect to that right does not necessarily dictate litigation in any particular forum. It is worth noting here, that each of the statutory regimes for enforcing foreign judgments provide a procedure for, and grounds on which registration may be set aside. It is ironic that no similar provision exists for registered maintenance orders.

When compared to the regimes for enforcing foreign judgments, the 'privileged' status given to foreign maintenance orders is difficult to rationalise. *Re Ian Douglas Hunter*[44] rationalises this position with an argument that matrimonial jurisdiction is founded on domicile and 'as the state of matrimony in the case of divorce has come to an end, it is necessary to embalm the deceased matrimonial domicile permanently in the pronouncing court'. However, the current state of the law on jurisdiction in matrimonial causes renders this position obsolete or indefensible. At present, in most of the countries under study, domicile is not the sole basis of jurisdiction in matrimonial matters. Moreover, an action for maintenance need not necessarily be preceded by the grant of a petition of divorce—it may be instituted in respect of a child within marriage. Furthermore, there are considerations related to the inconvenience and cost of litigation in the foreign court that must be taken into account. Indeed, in Zimbabwe, the courts have jurisdiction to discharge or vary registered orders which have not been expressed as provisional, but they have the discretion to refer the matter to the foreign court.[45]

F. Receiving and Transmitting Maintenance Orders

A common feature of most of the statutory regimes is executive involvement in transmitting the foreign maintenance order to the enforcing court. The South African legislation expresses the need to do this through 'diplomatic channels' and in the other countries, the order must be transmitted by the 'appropriate authority' or the 'Secretary of State' [of the foreign country] to a named Minister (usually the Minister of Justice) for transmission to the court. In this respect, the Botswana, Gambian and Ghanaian regimes are more open in the sense that they do not mandate that transmission to the Minister should be undertaken

[43] *Webb v Murray, Ex parte Murray* [1961–63] ALR Mal 205; *In re Ian Douglas Hunter* [1955] 28 KLR 120.

[44] [1955] 28 KLR 120, 127.

[45] Maintenance Orders (Facilities for Enforcement) Act 1921, s 3(3).

through a particular channel or person.[46] In the 1920s, when most of the statutes were enacted, executive involvement in the transmission of foreign maintenance orders to courts may have been appropriate. However, under current conditions, it is submitted that this procedure is anachronistic, inappropriate and in need of reform.

Executive involvement and the use of diplomatic channels are likely to slow down the transmission of the order to the enforcing court. Indeed, the statutory regimes for the registration of foreign judgments do not envisage such a procedure: rather, armed with the requisite documents, the judgment creditor is allowed to apply directly to the court for the registration of the foreign judgment. A similar procedure is recommended for the registration of foreign maintenance awards. As Gutteridge recommended a long time ago, 'the enforcement of maintenance orders calls for a procedure which is simple, inexpensive and rapid in its operation'.[47]

A move away from the use of the executive branch to transmit maintenance orders to court for registration may, however, have an impact on the registration process, which is envisaged as an administrative, as opposed to a judicial proceeding. The use of the executive branch or diplomatic channels safeguards against fraud and other forms of interference with the content of maintenance orders. As Justice Cram once observed 'it is vital that before registering any order, such order should come through the diplomatic channel which provides a guarantee that the certified copy is, in fact, a genuine judicial order'.[48] Similar guarantees may be absent if transmission is carried out directly by the judgment creditor.

Each of the countries under study provides a regime for the transmission of domestic maintenance orders abroad.[49] The essence of the regimes is that, where a court has made a maintenance order against a person and it appears (or it is 'proved')[50] to the court that he or she is resident in a reciprocating county, the court shall send a copy of the order to a named person from the executive (usually the Minster of Justice or Foreign Affairs) for transmission to the appropriate foreign court for registration. In Botswana and Ghana, the transmission should be made 'at the request of the applicant for the order'. The limitation placed by the Botswana and Ghanaian legislation on who can make an application for transmission of the order abroad is too restrictive. A maintenance order may be for the benefit of persons (eg children) other than the applicant for the order.

G. Maintenance Orders in Foreign Currency

Although in many countries, including in all the countries under study, a judgment may be given in foreign currency, a maintenance order would often be given in the currency of the forum. When the enforcement of such an order is sought abroad, it raises the question of

[46] Botswana and Ghana's statutes provide that, 'a certified copy of the order shall in the first instance be sent to the Minister for transmission to the appropriate court for registration'. Gambian legislation simply provides that a certified copy of the order has been transmitted to the Minister.

[47] H C Gutteridge, 'The International Enforcement of Maintenance Orders' (1948) 2 *International Law Quarterly* 155, 157.

[48] *In re Roderick Fountaine Antrobus Johnston* (1954) 27 KLR 94, 97.

[49] See, eg, Botswana—Judgments (International Enforcement) Act 1961, ss 17–18; Ghana—Courts Act 1993, ss 92 and 93; Kenya—Maintenance Orders Enforcement Act 1964, ss 4 and 5; Lesotho—Maintenance Orders Proclamation 1921, ss 4 and 5; Zimbabwe—Maintenance Orders (Facilities for Enforcement) Act 1921, ss 4 and 5.

[50] In some courts, this has to be proved to the court. See, eg, Gambia, Kenya, Lesotho, Malawi, Nigeria, Sierra Leone, Tanzania, Uganda, Zambia and Zimbabwe.

whether the enforcing court can enforce it in the foreign currency. Given the relatively low values of the currencies in the countries under study, compared to some major foreign currencies, enforcement in foreign currency can offer advantages to the judgment creditor.

The statutory regimes for enforcing foreign judgments in the countries under study deal with the issue of judgments in foreign currency. Apart from Lesotho, Nigeria[51] and Zimbabwe, it is a requirement in all the countries that, where (as would often be the case) a foreign judgment is in foreign currency, it should be registered in the currency of the registering court. Kenya's statute gives courts discretion on this. Even though the countries under study are almost unanimous on the need for conversion, there is divergence on the equally important issue of when the conversion should be made. Gambia, Botswana, Ghana, Nigeria, South Africa, Tanzania, Uganda and Zambia opt for the date of the foreign judgment. Kenya and Namibia opt for the date of registration.

As noted above, the statutory regimes for registering foreign judgments do not apply to the enforcement of foreign maintenance orders. The statutory provisions on the enforcement of foreign maintenance orders in all the countries under study are silent on the foreign currency issues arising in the context of such action. It is, however, likely that in resolving these foreign currency issues, the courts will be guided by the provisions dealing with the enforcement of foreign judgments.

It is worth pointing out that courts in all the countries under study have jurisdiction to give judgment in foreign currency. Historically, courts in most of the countries under study have declined jurisdiction to give judgment in foreign currency. Where there is a need to convert the foreign currency judgment into local currency (eg for the purpose of execution), the cases decided in the countries under study reflect wide acceptance of the payment date rule. In other words, where there is the need for it, conversion of foreign currency into the national currency is carried out at the official rate of exchange prevailing on the date of actual payment.

It is submitted that, given the fact there is jurisdiction to give judgments in foreign currency, and in the absence of legislation to the contrary, courts should be prepared to register foreign maintenance orders in the foreign currency. Where there is need for conversion, the date of registration should be used.

IV. Participation in International Initiatives

None of the countries under study are party to the United Nations Convention on the Recovery Abroad of Maintenance 1956;[52] the Hague Convention Concerning the Recognition and Enforcement of Decisions Relating to Maintenance Obligations 1973, or the Hague Convention on the International Recovery of Child Support and other Forms

[51] The Reciprocal Enforcement of Judgments Ordinance 1922. Foreign Judgments (Reciprocal Enforcement Act) 1990, s 4(3), which requires currency conversion prior to registration, has not yet been extended to any country. See *Witt & Busch Ltd v Dale Power System Plc* [2007] 17 NWLR 1, 19–20, which held that, until the 1990 Act comes into force 'there is no restriction for any superior court in Nigeria to register a foreign judgment in foreign currency'; *Momah v VAB Petroleum Inc* [2000] 2 SC 142, 156–57, [2000] 4 NWLR 534, 552.

[52] The following African countries are parties to the Convention: Burkina Faso; Cape Verde; the Central African Republic; Liberia; Niger; the Seychelles and Tunisia.

of Family Maintenance 2007 (the Hague Maintenance Convention).[53] The South African Law Reform Commission has recommended that South Africa should accede to both the UN Convention on the Recovery Abroad of Maintenance and the Hague Convention on the Recognition and Enforcement of Decisions Relating to Maintenance Obligations,[54] but it appears that to date, the recommendation has not been adopted.[55]

In general, the countries under study are parties to a few international conventions that offer procedural protection to children on a reciprocal basis. They are however, party to a number of international conventions that afford substantive rights to children, especially on the subject of children's rights. It is recommended that the countries under study should consider the ratification of the Hague conventions on matters relating to children as a matter of utmost importance. This should be seen as part of fulfilling their international commitment to the protection of children and enhancing the constitutional and statutory rights guaranteed for children in their respective countries. The benefits of the protection afforded to children by the Hague conventions far outweigh any disadvantages that might result from becoming party to those conventions, including the need to change certain aspects of national law, or to adopt new legislation. Indeed, it would not be inappropriate if the countries under study (apart from South Africa, which is a member) became members of the Hague Conference on Private International Law in order to take full advantage of all the benefits that the Conference offers.

Specific to our topic, given the fact that, amongst the countries under study, only a few (and these mostly Commonwealth countries) have been designated to benefit from the statutory regimes for enforcing foreign maintenance orders if they become parties to international conventions on the subject, such action will greatly benefit the world, especially those non-Commonwealth countries that are parties to the international conventions, such as the Hague Maintenance Convention.

The Hague Maintenance Convention provides a common legal and international framework to facilitate the international recovery of maintenance orders.[56] The Convention creates a worldwide system of cooperation between national authorities, provides for free legal assistance in cross-border child support applications, and streamlines procedures for recognition and enforcement of foreign maintenance orders. Because the vast majority of maintenance orders are for the benefit of children, the Convention is first and foremost a measure to protect children. This should make it attractive to the countries under study

[53] The Convention came into force on 1 January 2013. In Africa, only Burkina Faso has signed this Convention. Albania, Bosnia and Herzegovina, Norway and Ukraine have ratified the Convention. The EU and the United States have both signed the Convention, but have not yet ratified it.

[54] The Law Reform Commission's Report, 'Consolidated Legislation Pertaining to International Co-Operation in Civil Matters' (Project 121, 2006). It is worth noting that the recommendation was made in 2006 before the Hague Maintenance Convention of 2007 was agreed. South Africa took part in negotiating the 2007 Convention.

[55] South Africa is a member of the Hague Conference on Private International Law. It has ratified the Convention of 5 October 1961 on the Conflicts of Laws Relating to the Form of Testamentary Dispositions; the Convention of 5 October 1961 on Abolishing the Requirement of Legalisation for Foreign Public Documents; the Convention of 18 March 1970 on the Taking of Evidence Abroad in Civil or Commercial Matters; the Convention of 25 October 1980 on the Civil Aspects of International Child Abduction; and the Convention of 29 May 1993 on the Protection of Children and Co-operation in Respect of Intercountry Adoption.

[56] The scope of the Convention is broader than how a maintenance order is defined under the statutory regimes for registering maintenance orders in the countries under study. See Hague Maintenance Convention, Art 2. See generally E Long, 'The New Hague Maintenance Convention' (2008) *International and Comparative Law Quarterly* 984.

because their laws emphasise the rights of children and the need to ensure the welfare or best interest of children.

Indeed, the Convention espouses a number of principles that are in line with the legal position in the countries under study. For example, under the Convention the law of the enforcing state governs recognition and enforcement.[57] But the Convention also addresses many issues currently unaddressed or uncertain under the existing legal regimes in the countries under study such as timelines for recognising and enforcing maintenance orders,[58] jurisdictional requirements for recognition and enforcement of maintenance orders,[59] grounds for refusing recognition and enforcement of maintenance orders, maintenance arrangements[60] and transfer of funds payable as maintenance.[61] How the Convention addresses these issues may offer a model in any future reform of the existing statutory regimes in the countries under study.[62]

A significant consideration for Commonwealth African countries in becoming parties to the Convention would be the cost associated with administering it, especially as regards provision of cost-free administrative services by Central Authorities[63] and free legal assistance to applicants.[64] Under the Convention each Central Authority shall bear its own cost of applying the Convention and may not impose any charge on an applicant for provision of their services under the Convention. As noted in the Explanatory Report on the Convention 'the general principle of cost-free administrative services for applicants and Central Authorities was well supported, and consistent with the Convention's aims for a simple, low cost and rapid procedure. This principle was considered to be particularly important with regard to maintenance for children. It was also considered important to ensure that access to the benefits and services of the Convention was not denied to applicants because of their limited financial circumstances.'[65]

On the face of it, cost-free administrative services for applicants and Central Authorities and free legal assistance may seem to impose significant burdens on Contracting States. It is however important to recognise that the Convention imposes limitations on the scope of operation of both principles.[66] It is also possible to find creative solutions that are not inconsistent with the Convention to reduce the burdens imposed by the operation of both principles. An example is imposing charges on a debtor who unsuccessfully opposed the

57 Hague Maintenance Convention, Arts 23(1) and 32.

58 Ibid Art 12.

59 Ibid Art 20.

60 Ibid Art 30.

61 Ibid Art 35.

62 There have been instances where African countries have incorporated aspects of Hague Conventions into their national laws without becoming parties to the relevant convention. Eg, an examination of ss 15, 16 and 17 of the Wills Act 1971 of Ghana and s 22(4) of the Wills Act 1987 of Zimbabwe reveals that apart from insignificant changes in wording, they appear to be wholly based on the UK's Wills Act 1963 which implements the Hague Convention on the Conflict of Laws relating to the Form of Testamentary Dispositions. See F S Tsikata, 'The Wills Act 1971 (Act 360)' (1972) *Review of Ghana Law* 5, 16 where he notes that the Ghanaian Act 'reproduces, with slight verbal modifications' the English Act enacted to bring English law in line with the Hague Convention of the form of Testamentary Dispositions.

63 Hague Maintenance Convention, Art 8.

64 Ibid Arts 14–17.

65 Alegría Borrás and Jennifer Degeling, *Explanatory Report on the Convention on the International Recovery of Child Support and Other Forms of Family Maintenance* (Hague Conference on Private International Law, 2013) 107.

66 Hague Maintenance Convention, Arts 8(2) and 14(2)(3).

legal proceedings to enforce the maintenance order, or the debtor's employer who refused to implement a wage withholding order.[67] A Contracting State may also seek technical assistance from the Hague Conference to establish a Central Authority, solicit financial support from external donors, and explore low-cost models for the recovery of maintenance.[68]

The statutory regimes for registering foreign maintenance orders currently in force in the countries under study need not be abrogated should they become parties to the Convention. Their statutory regime can operate concurrently with the Convention.[69] Indeed, the Convention makes a 'concession' to countries operating the Commonwealth scheme for registering maintenance orders (the regime in the countries under study) but who are not yet parties to the Convention. It allows provisional orders from such countries that have been confirmed in a Contracting State to come within the scope of the Convention and, accordingly, to be enforceable in another Contracting State.[70] For example, a provisional order from Ghana (which is currently not a party to the Convention) that is confirmed in England (assuming the UK becomes a party to the Convention) is enforceable under the Convention. This is so even though, in essence, the order is a decision of both a Contracting and Non-contracting State.

V. Conclusion

This chapter has examined the common law and statutory regimes for enforcing foreign maintenance orders in Commonwealth Africa. It is notable that the regimes are seldom engaged. There are very few cases on the subject and academic work on this topic is thin on the ground.[71] Although it is likely that not all cases go to court and get reported (indeed one can expect this to be so in the majority of cases), statistical information on the number of cases where there have been attempts to enforce such orders is not readily available.

This chapter suggests that the common law regime for enforcing foreign maintenance orders mainly exists in name only. In practice, because of the common law requirement of finality, and the reality that many foreign maintenance orders are subject to variation, it is often a challenge relying on the common law regime. There is a need for judicial reform in this area. The common law allows for the enforcement of foreign judgments, even when an appeal is pending or envisaged in the foreign country. It is submitted that it should be equally willing to enforce a foreign maintenance order, even though there is the prospect that it may be varied by the foreign court. The obligation or right created by the maintenance order vests in the judgment creditor once the order is made. The courts should be prepared to give effect to this right when it has become so.

[67] Borrás and Degeling (n 65) 109.

[68] See Hague Conference on Private International Law, Information Document No 2 of April 2007—Descriptions of low-cost systems for the recovery of maintenance (Australia, Austria, Brazil, Costa Rica, Norway and Slovakia), available at www.hcch.net/index_en.php?act=publications.details&pid=4146&dtid=28 (accessed 21 January 2014).

[69] An example of this in some of the countries under study is the operation of the statutory regime for registering foreign arbitral awards and awards made under the United Nations Convention on the Recognition and Enforcement of Foreign Arbitral Awards 1958. See Oppong (n 3) 402–05.

[70] Hague Maintenance Convention, Art 31.

[71] See generally Oppong (n 3) ch 12; Forsyth (n 1) 449–51.

At present, the statutory regimes provide the best way of enforcing maintenance awards in the countries under study. The main shortfall of the regimes is that they are currently founded on reciprocity and very few countries have been designated to benefit from them. This is especially so with non-Commonwealth countries. It would be useful for foreign governments to work more aggressively and diplomatically to ensure their respective countries are designated under the relevant statutes in the countries under study. Furthermore, becoming parties to international conventions, such as the Hague Maintenance Convention is one of the principal ways of ensuring that many more countries' maintenance orders are enforceable in Commonwealth Africa.

The current regime for transmitting foreign maintenance orders to the enforcing court is inappropriate. It is likely to be entangled in the corridors of bureaucracy, which will delay the enforcement of such orders. As is the case with the registration of foreign judgments, it would be better to allow the judgment creditor to apply directly to the enforcing court for registration. Alternatively, there should be a specific department within the executive—akin to the Central Authorities under the Hague conventions—dedicated to transmitting such orders. The transmission of maintenance orders should not be made part of the already weighty portfolio of the Attorneys General, Ministers of Foreign Affairs, or the Presidents of the respective countries.

In addition to the limitations above, there are a number of issues that merit further consideration in any future reform of the existing laws. The exclusion of affiliation orders from the scope of many of the statutory regimes; maintenance orders in the context of same-sex relationships; defences against the registration of a foreign order; currency conversion and transfer of funds payable as maintenance; the procedure for asserting jurisdiction on non-resident/non-submitting judgment debtors, and the right to appeal against a registered final maintenance order are some of the issues that merit further attention and/or legislative reform. As discussed above, in future reform of the statutory regimes legislators may borrow from provisions of the Hague Maintenance Convention, especially to the extent that it addresses issues currently unaddressed or uncertain in the statutory regimes.

5

Recovery of Child Maintenance in South America and in Mercosur's Countries

NADIA DE ARAUJO

> In the light of the aforesaid multiculturalism comprises various aspects, on the one hand the presence of foreigners who speak foreign languages and profess different religions, and on the other hand the diversity of life-styles and moral standards.
>
> As a result, the question arises as to what could and what should be the contents of private law in order to meet the needs of a multicultural society. The answer to this question will be the following: the law should provide for alternatives and flexibility. There should be options for different solutions. Party autonomy should be enhanced. In addition, minorities have to be protected against uniformity of legal rules. The legal term that emerges is 'cultural identity', a term that may adopt different meanings depending on the context in which it is used. In the field of private law it is the person's cultural identity that will have an impact on legal solutions concerning questions of personal law, including names, family law and succession. There are several elements which become essential for determining the cultural identity of a person, in particular language and religion as indicators of the person's cultural links. These factors will, therefore, provide for primary guidance in developing appropriate legal solutions.
>
> Erik Jayme[1]

I. Introduction

The family unit is a model whose joint functioning has proven to be the most effective way of providing for its sustenance, especially in respect of children. Nowadays, however, the idea that couples will remain together for their whole life is becoming increasingly less the norm. Each State regulates family law differently but there is always a legal provision dealing with the matter of child support in the case of separation of the couple. The current tendency is for the woman to be the beneficiary of maintenance only when she is a disadvantaged person rather than as a general rule. Regulating this recovery of maintenance calls for a great amount

[1] E Jayme, *Multicultural Society and Private Law German Experiences*, vol 33 (Rome, Centro di studi e ricerche di diritto comparato e straniero, 1999).

of energy and resources from the legal system and is one of the areas of judicial power most used by the general population.

There are countless problems involving the effective provision of maintenance for those in need and non-compliance is so serious that in some countries defaulting debtors may be imprisoned. In the face of real difficulties, such as the urgent need of someone who depends on maintenance receiving it, establishing and enforcing maintenance presents grave challenges to the judiciary. In some countries, a legal solution in this area must be quick, because no delay can be tolerated without this compromising the dignified survival of those who receive support. In comparative law the peculiarities of each country, based on their cultural traditions, are clearly shown in their legislative options. For example, with regard to the subject of child support on the international level, the question of the age until which maintenance is enforced varies a great deal from country to country.

It is obvious that in the light of these challenges, child maintenance on the international level demands joint action of States through international cooperation of a judicial and/or administrative nature. Thus, multilateral and bilateral treaties are of supreme importance. In studying this topic in private international law, the issue transcends the question of applicable law, since it refers to various aspects related to international jurisdiction, international administrative and judicial cooperation and transfer of funds.[2]

This chapter presents the world and regional initiatives in legal cooperation related to child support, with particular attention being paid to the countries of South America and Mercosur. There is a detailed examination of the main questions raised by the 1956 Convention on the Recovery Abroad of Maintenance, made in New York, and by the Inter-American Convention on Support Obligations, as far as Brazil's interaction with the other countries of South America is concerned.[3] The chapter closes with some reflections on maintenance obligations in the regional-integration initiative that is one of the main features of Mercosur.

II. Global and Regional Initiatives

Despite being the object of several initiatives in the nineteenth and early twentieth centuries,[4] the problem of child support on the international level was only considered on a more serious level following the Second World War, when it was discussed under the auspices of UNIDROIT.[5] The Institute's project was later forwarded to the United Nations, which resulted in a diplomatic conference in 1956 and concluded the New York

[2] On this topic, with regard to the international sphere, see D Martiny, 'Maintenance obligations in the conflicts of law' (1994) 247 *Hague Academy Collected Courses* 143.

[3] For an analysis of Brazil's interaction with South America, specifically with Argentina and Chile, see S Kleebanks, *Cooperação Jurídica por Via Diplomática: avaliação e propostas de atualização do quadro normativo* (Brasília, Instituto Rio Branco, Fundação Alexandre de Gusmão, 2004) 92–94.

[4] M Verwilghen, 'Les Obligations Alimentaires en Droit Conventionnel' *Obligations Alimentaires en Droit International Privé,* ed. CNRS, vol 2 (Paris, 1987) 187, 191.

[5] The International Institute for the Unification of Private Law (UNIDROIT) is an independent international organisation designed to promote the unification and coordination of private law among the States, whether through juridical mechanisms, rules or principles.

Convention on the Recovery Abroad of Maintenance (the New York Convention). In South America seven States have ratified the New York Convention.[6]

Almost parallel to this, the Hague Conference on Private International Law[7] standardised the question through two Conventions,[8] the Convention on the Law Applicable to Maintenance Obligations towards Children 1956, and the Convention concerning the Recognition and Enforcement of Decisions relating to Maintenance Obligations towards Children 1958, later modified in 1973.[9] None of these Conventions were adopted in South America.

New York Convention of 1956 - South America

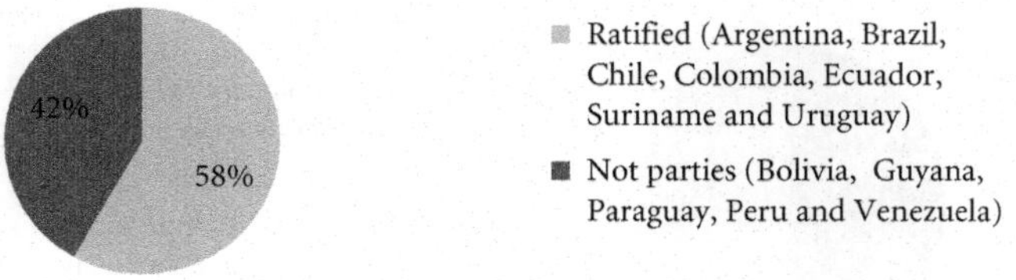

On the regional level a pioneering initiative dealing explicitly with child support was the Bustamante Code of 1928.[10] In the nineteenth century, two large Congresses involving several countries from the American continent discussed issues of private international law, which led to the Treaty of Lima in 1872 and the Treaties of Montevideo in 1888 and 1889. However, none of these treaties specifically addressed the matter of international recovery of child and family maintenance, which is why the Bustamante Code is hailed as a pioneering initiative. Despite the two Articles dealing specifically with the applicable law on maintenance,[11] there are no special norms for the questions relating to judicial

[6] Argentina adhered on 29 November 1972; Brazil ratified on 14 November 1960; Chile, on 9 January 1961; Colombia, on 10 November 1999; Ecuador, on 4 June 1974; Suriname adhered on 12 October 1979; and Uruguay, on 18 September 1995.

[7] The Hague Conference was established in 1893 to promote harmony of legislation related to private international law. Since its creation it has held numerous conferences resulting in various Conventions. The list of Conventions and attending countries can be found at www.hcch.net. At its 17th Session the Conference adopted a resolution in which it made clear that its objective was to become a world centre for judicial and administrative international cooperation on issues of private law, notably in the area of protection of children. See the paper drafted by the assistant secretary general, M Pelichet, *Note on the operation of the Hague Conventions relating to maintenance obligations and of the New York Convention on the Recovery Abroad of Maintenance*, of 1995. Document available at www.hcch.net, (last accessed on 8 April 2014).

[8] Convention of 24 October 1956 on the Law Applicable to Maintenance Obligations towards Children and Convention of 15 April 1958 Concerning the Recognition and Enforcement of Decisions Relating to Maintenance Obligations towards Children.

[9] Convention of 2 October 1973 on the Recognition and Enforcement of Decisions Relating to Maintenance Obligations and Convention of 2 October 1973 on the Law Applicable to Maintenance Obligations.

[10] The following countries ratified the Bustamante Code: Bolivia, Brazil, Chile, Ecuador, Peru and Venezuela. Argentina, together with Colombia, Paraguay and Uruguay, signed but did not ratify the Bustamante Code. Guyana and Suriname did not sign the Bustamante Code.

[11] Bustamante Code, Art 67 'The legal concept of obligatory maintenance, the nature of such provision, the manner of it being administered, and the extent of this right will be subject to the personal law of the creditor'; Art 68 'The provisions that establish the obligation to provide child and family maintenance, the amount, reduction and increase of the same, the timeframe when these are due, and the form of payment pertain to international public policy, as do those provisions that prohibit renouncing and ceding this right' (author's

and administrative cooperation. Thus execution of maintenance obligations follows the traditional methods that are generically employed for cooperation among countries.

Article 67 of the Bustamante Code subjects the entitlement to maintenance to the personal law[12] of the creditor, describes the legal concept of maintenance and the order of provision and determines the extension of this right. Articles 59 and 68[13] provide that the duty to provide maintenance, its amount, any reduction or increase therein, the time it is due and how it should be paid, as well as the rules that prohibit renouncing or ceding this right, are matters of public policy. However, our research did not manage to determine how the courts of the signatory countries have used these three Articles.

Bustamante Code

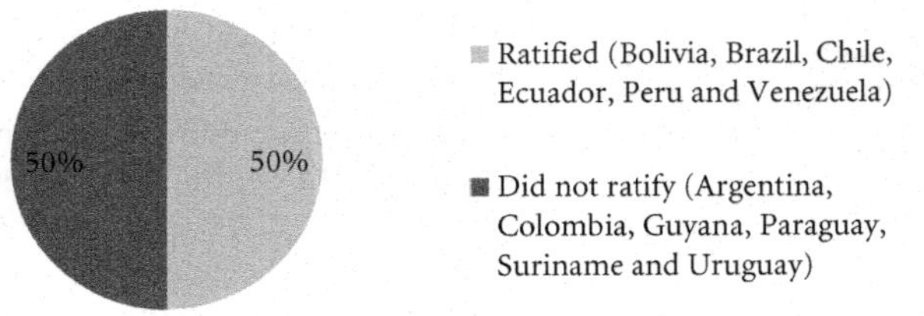

As regards the American continent, in addition to the Bustamante Code it should be noted that it was only at its fourth meeting held in Montevideo in 1989, that the Specialised Conference in Private International Law drew up the Inter-American Convention on Child Maintenance Obligations.[14]

Inter-American Convention - South America

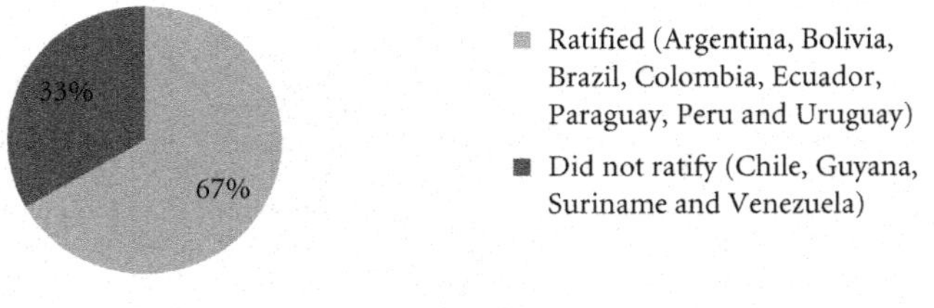

translation of Art 67 'Sujeitar-se-ão à lei pessoal do alimentado o conceito legal dos alimentos, a ordem de sua prestação, a maneira de os subministrar e a extensão desse direito'; Art 68 'São de ordem pública internacional as disposições que estabelecem o dever de prestar alimentos, seu montante, redução e aumento, a oportunidade em que são devidos e a forma do seu pagamento, assim como as que proíbem renunciar e ceder esse direito').

[12] Under the Bustamante Code, the personal law can refer to either domicile or nationality. This was a compromise to allow the Code to be adopted by Latin American countries, which used domicile, and Brazil, which at that time, used nationality as a criteria to determine the applicable law. Throughout the Code this method of compromise appears to be the solution for issues where there was no consensus.

[13] Bustamante Code, Art 59 'The rule that gives the child the right to maintenance pertains to international public policy' (author's translation of 'É de ordem pública internacional a regra que dá ao filho o direito a alimentos').

[14] Latin American countries that ratified the Inter-American Convention: Argentina, Bolivia, Brazil, Colombia, Ecuador, Paraguay, Peru and Uruguay.

III. The New York Convention and its Application in Brazil

The New York Convention was signed in 1956 and came into effect in Brazil in 1958,[15] being the first international instrument of judicial and administrative cooperation in the area of family maintenance obligations. The New York Convention introduced a complementary system to the one instituted by the Hague Conference in the 1950s. Although the New York Convention[16] does not have rules on applicable law, it has been more widely accepted and implemented in a greater number of countries than the two Hague Conventions.

The New York Convention addresses matters of an administrative nature regarding recovery of maintenance and is silent on the concept of obligation. It creates the entity of Central Authorities for the purpose of making recovery of maintenance more practical, without passing through any other diplomatic or administrative body. Some advantages are given to the creditor, such as free legal aid, waiver of collateral, free services to expedite documents, and uncomplicated transfer of funds. These features of the Convention bore a positive influence on the Inter-American document and the work undertaken by the Hague Conference in the Convention of 2007 concerning recovery of maintenance. Although it provides for the possibility of revision, as expressed in Article 20,[17] this provision has not been used.

According to the system of the New York Convention, the party can seek help in claiming maintenance from the Central Authority in the country where he or she habitually resides. This may entail bringing a claim to establish a maintenance obligation or to seek recognition and enforcement of an existing maintenance order. The main objective of the Convention is to make it easier to obtain child and family maintenance by using all possible means to attain positive results. It even concerns itself with the existing barriers to transferring funds overseas[18] (Article 10).

As far as Brazil is concerned, the New York Convention can be recognised as a successful treaty. It has been in force in Brazil for several years. The Office of the Federal Attorney General (PGR) is the Central Authority assigned to function both as an intermediary and

[15] Approved by Decree No 10, dated 1958, and promulgated by Executive Decree No 56.826.

[16] Member States: Algeria, Argentina, Australia, Austria, Barbados, Belarus, Belgium, Bosnia-Herzegovina, Brazil, Burkina Faso, Cape Verde, Central-African Republic, Chile, Colombia, Croatia, Cyprus, Czech Republic, Denmark, Ecuador, Estonia, Finland, France, Germany, Greece, Guatemala, Haiti, Holy See, Hungary, Ireland, Israel, Italy, Kazakhstan, Kyrgyzstan, Liberia, Luxembourg, Former Yugoslav Republic of Macedonia, Mexico, Monaco, Montenegro, Morocco, Netherlands, Niger, Norway, New Zealand, Pakistan, Poland, Portugal, Philippines, Republic of Moldova, Rumania, Serbia, Seychelles, Slovakia, Slovenia, Spain, Sri-Lanka, Suriname, Sweden, Switzerland, Tunisia, Turkey, Ukraine, UK, Uruguay.

[17] Art 20.1 '1. Any Contracting Party may request revision of this Convention at any time by a notification addressed to the Secretary General. 2. The Secretary General shall transmit the notification to each Contracting Party with a request that such Contracting Party reply within four months whether it desires the convening of a Conference to consider the proposed revision. If a majority of the Contracting Parties favour the convening of a Conference it shall be convened by the Secretary General.'

[18] Art 10 'A Contracting Party under whose law the transfer of funds abroad is restricted shall accord the highest priority to the transfer of funds payable as maintenance or to cover expenses in respect of proceedings under this Convention.'

as a transmitting authority. Its functions are centralised in its main office in Brasília, with the Federal Public Prosecutor's Office providing the structure necessary for its operation.[19]

There are two types of procedures: those where Brazil is the requested party and those where Brazil is the requesting party. In the first case, the Federal Public Prosecutor's Office forwards the information received to the proper entities; the case may consist of a request for recognition of a decision,[20] processing of letters rogatory, or, if need be, initiating a claim in Brazil for maintenance, via the Public Prosecutor, in the defendant's place of residence. Conversely, once in possession of the documents that originate in Brazil, the Federal Public Prosecutor's Office makes contact with the corresponding Central Authority abroad so that the petition can be processed.

The New York Convention has been the subject of several decisions in Brazilian courts. The Office of the Federal Attorney General either coordinates the requests for recognition and enforcement of foreign decisions or starts legal action directly. This is because in maintenance cases the initial petition usually settles a provisional amount for maintenance, which was very difficult to obtain at the Federal Supreme Court (STF)[21] thanks to its restrictive jurisprudence in granting execution-type measures or any effect on the petition in the course of recognition and enforcement of foreign decision procedures. The South American countries with whom Brazil cooperates most closely include Chile and Argentina.[22] As stated above, the New York Convention has been successful in achieving its objective because of its acceptance by a considerable number of countries. In Brazil, the action of the Central Authority, regulated by Law 5.478/68, which Article 26[23] expressly designates the Office of the Federal Attorney General, was one of the factors contributing to its success. On the other hand, the absence of a provision in the Inter-American Convention for cooperation of an administrative nature between Central Authorities has contributed to its lack of use in Brazil.

[19] There are very few studies on the Convention in Brazil, and none at all on the work carried out by the PGR. In the Law Department at the Pontifical Catholic University in Rio de Janeiro, the topic was the subject of several dissertations.

[20] Many decisions have been homologated by the STF. *Cf* among others, SE 4321, judgment of 5 June 1992; SE 3294, judgment of 13 June 1984; SE 3653, judgment of 16 April 1999; SE 4601, judgment of 19 December 1997; and SE 3726, judgment of 2 May 1991.

[21] The STF was the competent court to recognize foreign decisions prior to Amendment 45/06, when jurisdiction was transferred to the Superior Court of Justice (STJ).

[22] In 2013, most of the requests are shown to come from European countries, with Germany, Switzerland and Portugal presenting the highest numbers of requests (59, 34, 79, respectively). In Latin America, Chile ranks highest with 12 cases, followed by Argentina with 6 requests. In conversations with the PGR, it appears that the number of cases has grown, and the division that deals with them has increased its resources and is currently very active. For more information, visit www.sci.pgr.mpf.mp.br/ or telephone 55.(61) 3105-6228. The author extends her sincerest thanks to Secretary Vladimir Aras who kindly compiled the 2013 data on maintenance requests under the New York Convention.

[23] Art 26 'The Federal Court of the Capital of the Brazilian Federal department where the debtor resides is competent for maintenance cases resulting from application of Legislative Decree No 10, dated 13 November 1958, and Decree No 56.826, dated 2 September 1965, with the PGR being considered as an intermediary institution for the effect of these decrees' (author's translation of 'É competente para as ações de alimentos decorrentes da aplicação do Decreto Legislativo No 10, de 13 de novembro de 1958, e Decreto No 56.826, de 2 de setembro de 1965, o Juízo Federal da Capital da unidade federativa brasileira em que reside o devedor, sendo considerada instituição intermediária, para os fins dos referidos decretos, a Procuradoria-Geral da República').

IV. The Inter-American Convention

The Inter-American Convention on Child and Family Maintenance resulted from the Fourth Specialised Inter-American Conference on Private International Law held in 1989 and known as CIDIP IV. This Convention presents in a single document the two themes dealt with in the Hague Conventions of 1973,[24] namely, the issue of applicable law, and recognition and enforcement of judgments. It also includes norms of a material nature meant to ensure the functioning of private international law rules. It is in effect in a total of thirteen countries. As mentioned earlier, eight South American countries have ratified it.[25]

Among the positive features of the Convention is a norm of a material nature, a true rule of *ius cogens* that establishes the duty of States to recognise the universal right to maintenance.[26] Another material-type norm concerns the amount of maintenance,[27] which is in complete agreement with the necessity versus possibility concept, which guides Brazilian law.

The Inter-American Convention's sphere of application is restricted to child maintenance obligations and maintenance arrangements between spouses resulting from marriage or divorce; it is therefore more restrictive than the Hague Convention of 2007,[28] where children conceived out of wedlock are contemplated.

The choice of applicable law is a theme addressed by the Convention based on modern methods of private international law, which designate more than one connecting factor. The competent authority is assigned to choose the applicable law based on the rule most favourable to the creditor, to be chosen from two alternatives: the rule of the creditor's domicile or habitual residence, or that of the domicile or habitual residence of the debtor.[29] Giving the creditor the chance to recover the higher amount of maintenance available under the habitual residence of the creditor or the debtor is done in order to satisfy the overriding objective of protecting the child.[30]

[24] Convention of 2 October 1973 on the Recognition and Enforcement of Decisions Relating to Maintenance Obligations and Convention of 2 October 1973 on the Law Applicable to Maintenance Obligations.

[25] States that ratified the Convention: Argentina, Belize, Bolivia, Brazil, Colombia, Costa Rica, Ecuador, Guatemala, Mexico, Panama, Paraguay, Peru and Uruguay. The Latin America countries that ratified the Convention: Argentina, Bolivia, Brazil, Colombia, Ecuador, Paraguay, Peru and Uruguay. In Brazil the Convention was promulgated by Decree No 2.428.

[26] Art 4 'Any person, without regard to nationality, race, sex, religion, parentage, place of origin, immigration status or any other distinction, is entitled to receive support.'

[27] Art 10 'Support shall be commensurate with both the need of the creditor and the financial resources of the debtor. Should a judicial or administrative authority responsible for enforcing or securing the effectiveness of a judgment order provisional measures or provide for execution of judgment in an amount lower than requested, the rights of the creditor shall not thereby be impaired.'

[28] The Hague Convention on the International Recovery of Child Support and Other Forms of Family Maintenance entered into force on 1 January 2013. However, none of the South American countries have adhered to it yet.

[29] Art 6 'Support obligations, as well as the definition of support creditor and debtor, shall be governed by whichever of the following laws the competent authority finds the most favourable to the creditor: That of the State of domicile or habitual residence of the creditor; that of the State of domicile or habitual residence of the debtor.'

[30] C Fresnedo de Aguirre, *Curso de Derecho Internacional Privado, Parte Especial*, vol II (Montevidéu, Fundação de Cultura Universitária, 2003) 125.

There have also been innovations in the area of international jurisdiction. Three possibilities for determining the forum are admitted: the place where the creditor is domiciled or habitually resides (sub-item 'a' of Article 8);[31] the place where the debtor is domiciled or habitually resides (sub-item 'b' of the same Article); and finally sub-item 'c', the place with which the debtor maintains personal ties—such as assets, income or economic benefits—will be deemed to have jurisdiction to deal with matters relating to maintenance. The Convention also accepts the jurisdiction of the authorities in other States based on submission, provided that the debtor in the case has presented no timeous objection to that jurisdiction.

Article 8 is of special interest to Brazilian law, because the rule on concurrent jurisdiction established in Article 88 of the Code of Civil Procedure (CPC)[32] fails to take into account the interests of the Brazilian community. Since it is common for ex-wives of Brazilian nationality to return to Brazil with their children and claim maintenance there, the literal interpretation of Article 88 would not allow that jurisdiction. Thus, the alternatives presented in Article 8 of the Inter-American Convention are better-suited for this situation.

Also, the Convention, which is binding on those States that have ratified it, may be used to compensate for lacunae in the law with regard to cases with countries that are not party to the Convention.

One difference in relation to the New York Convention is the fact that no system of cooperation is set up using Central Authorities; it is a more traditional sort of Convention, with rules on applicable law and recognition and enforcement of foreign decisions.

Article 13[33] provides that foreign decisions should be complied with without delay and the judge is required to act directly on his or her own initiative.

In Brazil this Article stands in clear opposition to Brazilian internal rules, included in the Constitution, which require the recognition and enforcement of foreign decisions in the STJ before they have any effects in Brazil.[34] There are no reported cases on the operation of the Inter-American Convention in Brazil.

[31] Art 8 'At the option of the creditor, support claims may be heard by the following judicial or administrative authorities: a. Those of the State of domicile or habitual residence of the creditor; b. Those of the State of domicile or habitual residence of the debtor; or c. Those of the State to which the debtor is connected by personal links such as possessing property, receiving income or obtaining financial benefits.'

Notwithstanding the provisions of this Article, a judicial or administrative authority of another State shall also have jurisdiction if the defendant appears before it without challenging its jurisdiction.

[32] Art 88 CPC 'The Brazilian judiciary authority is competent when: I—the debtor, no matter of what nationality, is domiciled in Brazil; II—the maintenance obligation has to be enforced in Brazil; III—the action derives from a fact which occurred or an act that took place in Brazil. Sole paragraph: for the effect of the provision in I, a foreign corporation which has an agency, affiliate or branch here is held to be domiciled in Brazil' (author's translation of 'É competente a autoridade judiciária brasileira quando: I—o réu, qualquer que seja a sua nacionalidade, estiver domiciliado no Brasil; II - no Brasil tiver de ser cumprida a obrigação; III—a ação se originar de fato ocorrido ou de ato praticado no Brasil. Parágrafo único. Para o fim do disposto no No I, reputa-se domiciliada no Brasil a pessoa jurídica estrangeira que aqui tiver agência, filial ou sucursal').

[33] Art13 'Compliance with the above requirements shall be ascertained directly by the competent authority from which enforcement is sought, which shall proceed summarily, giving notice to the debtor and, where necessary, to the appropriate public agency and holding a hearing without reopening the merits. Should the enforcement decision be appealable, the appeal shall not suspend provisional measures or such collection or enforcement orders as may be in effect.'

[34] J Dolinger, *Direito Internacional Privado. A criança no Direito Internacional* (Rio de Janeiro, Renovar, 2003) 359. Dolinger's understanding is that this Article, which was not a matter of reservation, represents an exception to the Brazilian system. Nevertheless, the constitutional provision (higher in the hierarchy) leaves no doubt as to the need for recognition, and in the event of any conflict between national law and the Constitution, constitutional provisions prevail. However, there is no case law in this matter.

V. Mercosur

Mercosur, or the Common Market of the South, constitutes the response to a proposal for the regional and economic integration of the South American continent. This association was the fruit of the Treaty of Asuncion,[35] which was initially signed on 26 March 1991 by Argentina, Brazil, Paraguay and Uruguay. Later on, Venezuela became the fifth member of the regional bloc in 2012, following the promulgation of the Protocol on Adhesion of the Bolivarian Republic of Venezuela to Mercosur.

In the field of child support, it should be noted that most of the countries that are parties to the Mercosur Treaty are also parties to the Inter-American and New York Conventions. Only Venezuela belongs to neither of the two treaties. Nevertheless, experience and case law have shown that countries that are members of the bloc resort more to the New York Convention on account of the administrative structure of the designated Central Authorities, or to the classic system of international judicial cooperation of Mercosur. The Inter-American Convention is seldom used.

Mercosur's system on international cooperation is based on two Protocols. Rules are found (a) in the Protocol on Cooperation and Jurisdictional Assistance on Civil, Commercial, Labour and Administrative Matters (Protocol of Las Leñas) from 1992 and (b) in the Protocol on Provisional Measures from 1994, which deals with international juridical cooperation between members of the bloc, and can be used in maintenance cases.[36]

Moreover, there is a tendency towards harmonising material rules in respect to maintenance, which can be explained both by the fact that most Mercosur countries belong to the Conventions referred to in this chapter and by the legacy of the system of civil law that these same countries share. Nonetheless, within the framework of international legal cooperation, a specific Protocol[37] is under negotiation in Mercosur on the subject of family law, but without rules addressing the question of maintenance obligations. There is a very important innovation in this draft Protocol in comparison with the Inter-American and New York Conventions, namely the inclusion of non-matrimonial unions[38] among

[35] The Treaty of Asuncion was approved in Brazil by the National Congress by means of Legislative Decree No 197/1991, and promulgated by Executive Decree No 350/1991.

[36] On the question of maintenance in the scope of international cooperation among the Mercosur countries, see DF Arroyo (Coord), *Derecho Internacional Privado de los Estados del Mercosur* (Buenos Aires, Zavalía Editor, Bs As, 2003) 831–40.

[37] This is the Agreement between States Parties to Mercosur and Associates on Internationally Competent Jurisdiction, Applicable Law and International Legal Cooperation on Matters of Matrimony, Personal Relations among Spouses, Matrimonial Regimes of Property, Divorce, Conjugal Separation and Non-Matrimonial Unions.

[38] Maintenance in non-matrimonial unions, together with maintenance obligations for the unborn, are two topics of increasing relevance, but private international law has demurred in regulating them as far as international legal cooperation is concerned. With regard to Mercosur, only Argentina does not include a legal provision in its internal laws as to maintenance in cases of non-matrimonial union and maintenance obligations for the unborn. Notwithstanding, in the Draft Reform of the Civil Code, provisions regulating these matters have been added, eg in Art 434:

> Maintenance following divorce. Maintenance obligations may be settled even after divorce: a) in favour of those persons suffering from a serious illness prior to the divorce that disables them from supporting themselves. If the debtor dies, the maintenance obligation is transferred to his/her heirs. b) in favour of those persons without sufficient resources of their own or any reasonable possibility of obtaining such. Consideration is taken of

family relations whose effects can entail maintenance obligations on the international level.[39] Furthermore, Article 13[40] makes explicit reference to the Protocols of Las Leñas and Provisional Measures as regards the procedures of international juridical cooperation, opening the way for other regulations that are more favourable to the issue. No Central Authority is expressly designated, which leaves matters to the Protocols.[41]

paragraphs b), c) and e) of the previous article. The obligation cannot extend beyond the number of years that the marriage lasted and does not apply in favour of persons who receive the economic compensation described in article 441. In the two monetary amounts provided in this article, the obligation ceases if: the cause that motivated it disappears, or if the person benefitted marries again or lives in a non-matrimonial union, or when the creditor commits any undignified act. If the agreement that regulates the divorce refers to maintenance, the agreed rules are to be followed

The above is the author's translation of:

Alimentos posteriores al divorcio. Las prestaciones alimentarias pueden ser fijadas aun después del divorcio: a) a favor de quien padece una enfermedad grave preexistente al divorcio que le impide autosustentarse. Si el alimentante fallece, la obligación se trasmite a sus herederos. b) a favor de quien no tiene recursos propios suficientes ni posibilidad razonable de procurárselos. Se tienen en cuenta los incisos b), c) y e) del artículo anterior. La obligación no puede tener una duración superior al número de años que duró el matrimonio y no procede a favor del que recibe la compensación económica del artículo 441. En los dos supuestos previstos en este artículo, la obligación cesa si: desaparece la causa que la motivó, o si la persona beneficiada contrae matrimonio o vive en unión convivencial, o cuando el alimentado incurre en alguna de las causales de indignidad. Si el convenio regulador del divorcio se refiere a los alimentos, rigen las pautas convenidas

Art 665 'Pregnancy. Pregnant women have the right to claim maintenance from the presumed progenitor, following summary proof of the alleged filiation' (author's translation of 'Mujer embarazada. La mujer embarazada tiene derecho a reclamar alimentos al progenitor presunto con la prueba sumaria de la filiación alegada').

[39] Art 8:

The law of the place of recognition or registration of a non-matrimonial union between two persons of different or the same sex rules on the capacity of persons to constitute such unions, their form, existence and validity, as well as their dissolution. The effects derived from such non-matrimonial unions are ruled by the law of the State where they are intended to be applicable. However, recognition of non-matrimonial unions celebrated between persons of the same sex will not be obligatory for the State Party where they are intended to apply if its laws do not allow such unions.

The above is the author's translation of:

A lei do lugar de reconhecimento ou registro das uniões não matrimoniais entre duas pessoas de distinto ou mesmo sexo rege a capacidade das pessoas para constituí-las, sua forma, existência e validade, assim como a sua dissolução. Os efeitos derivados dessas uniões não matrimoniais regem-se pela lei do Estado onde se pretendam fazer valer. Entretanto, o reconhecimento das uniões não matrimoniais celebrado entre pessoas do mesmo sexo não será obrigatório para o Estado Parte onde se pretende fazê-lo valer, se seu ordenamento jurídico não o admitir.

[40] Art 13 'The international legal cooperation enabled in this instrument will proceed as provided in the Agreements for Cooperation and Jurisdictional Assistance on Civil, Commercial, Labour and Administrative Matters among the States Parties to MERCOSUR and Associated States and in the Protocol of Precautionary Measures or other more favourable norms on the matter' (the author's translation of 'A cooperação jurídica internacional a que se dá lugar neste Instrumento tramitará conforme o previsto nos Acordos de Cooperação e Assistência Jurisdicional em matéria Civil, Comercial, Trabalhista e Administrativa entre os Estados Partes do MERCOSUL e Estados Associados e no Protocolo sobre Medidas Cautelares ou outras normas mais favoráveis na material').

[41] The Las Leñas Protocol states in Art 2 'For the effects of this Agreement, the States Parties will appoint a Central Authority assigned to receive and proceed with requests for legal assistance on civil, commercial, labour and administrative matters. To this end, the Central Authorities will communicate directly with one another, allowing whenever necessary the intervention of the respective competent authorities; States Parties, by depositing the instruments of ratification of this Agreement, will inform the depositary government of this act, and the other States will also be informed; The Central Authority may at any moment be substituted, and the respective government shall communicate this fact as soon as possible to the depositary government of this Agreement so that the other States be given notice of the substitution performed'; and the Protocol on Precautionary Measures, in Art 20, 'Each State Party shall appoint a Central Authority assigned to receive and transmit petitions for precautionary cooperation'.

VI. Conclusion

In Latin America the rules that deal specifically with international maintenance obligations are based on three different international documents, namely: the Bustamante Code, the New York Convention and the Inter-American Convention. Although a pioneer in its time, the Bustamante Code has been replaced by the rules of the Inter-American Convention. The latter, despite its advances in relation to the Bustamante Code and innovative provisions in the field of applicable law and recognition of foreign decisions, is not well known by the judiciary of the participating countries and is thus seldom used. Also, the Inter-American Convention often overlaps with the New York Convention, which is the preferred regulatory system in use. Furthermore, the draft Protocol on family situations currently being discussed in Mercosur cannot be considered to be useful in child support situations because it does not specifically regulate the question of recovery of child maintenance.

Thus, from experience and from the research carried out, we believe that the New York Convention is the most important treaty in this area in Latin America. The reason for its success can be traced to the fact that it is the only treaty that has put in place an administrative structure with a system of Central Authorities. This system adds uniformity to the Latin American countries' relations not only between themselves but also with other countries outside Latin America, such as those in Europe as well.

We have no doubt, at least in Brazil, that there are many cases that would benefit from the 2007 Hague Convention, which would represent a significant step forward in the mechanisms of administrative cooperation initiated by the New York Convention. The Hague Convention has more modern mechanisms for cooperation and provides a more comprehensive role for the Central Authority that would benefit needy parties. Over the years, personal experience of lawyers indicates that it is difficult to use the New York Convention. The most recent Convention is better adapted to the modern needs of transnational families, because it allows for better cooperation between Central Authorities.

6

Enforcing Foreign Maintenance Decisions in the Hong Kong Special Administrative Region of the People's Republic of China and the Hague Convention on International Recovery of Child Support and Other Forms of Family Maintenance from an Asian Perspective

JAMES DING[1]

I. Introduction

The first part of this chapter provides a brief overview of the current situation on enforcement of foreign maintenance decisions in the Hong Kong Special Administrative Region of the People's Republic of China (the HKSAR) and the second part of the chapter aims to highlight some of the challenges and opportunities for countries particularly in Asia to become a Contracting Party to the Hague Convention of 23 November 2007 on International Recovery of Child Support and Other Forms of Family Maintenance (the 2007 Convention).

II. Current Situation in the HKSAR

While there are several international Conventions in the field of recovery of maintenance, such as the United Nations Convention of 20 June 1956 on the Recovery Abroad of Maintenance, the Hague Convention of 15 April 1958 Concerning the Recognition and Enforcement of Decisions Relating to Maintenance Obligations towards Children, or the

[1] The views expressed in this chapter are the personal views of the author.

Hague Convention of 2 October 1973 on the Recognition and Enforcement of Decisions Relating to Maintenance Obligations, none of them is applicable to the HKSAR.

The HKSAR maintains the previous mechanism on reciprocal recognition and enforcement of maintenance orders (which is often known as REMO or the Commonwealth Scheme and which will be discussed below). Through this mechanism, reciprocity is maintained between the HKSAR and a number of common law jurisdictions. Thus, the old legislative scheme on reciprocal enforcement of maintenance orders that was previously in force before reunification with China on 1 July 1997 continues to govern international recovery of maintenance orders in Hong Kong.[2]

A. Before 1 July 1997

There was a scheme for reciprocal enforcement of maintenance orders between members of the Commonwealth which applied to Hong Kong until 30 June 1997. Under the scheme, Commonwealth jurisdictions have their own domestic legislation for the enforcement of one another's maintenance orders on the basis of reciprocity. No formal treaty needs to be signed. This system is based on a model introduced by the UK, often known as the Commonwealth Scheme.[3]

Where, under a maintenance order granted in one participating jurisdiction, maintenance is payable by a person residing in another participating jurisdiction, the person to whom the maintenance is payable can apply to have that maintenance order transmitted to the other jurisdiction for enforcement. Each reciprocating jurisdiction has its own domestic legislation enabling the other maintenance orders to be enforced on the basis of reciprocity.

Until 30 June 1997, the Maintenance Orders (Reciprocal Enforcement) Ordinance, Chapter 188 of the Laws of Hong Kong (the Ordinance)[4] enabled maintenance orders granted by a court in any of the reciprocating jurisdictions to be registered and enforced in Hong Kong. The designated jurisdictions are listed in the Schedule to the Maintenance Orders (Reciprocal Enforcement) (Designation of Reciprocating Countries) Order, subsidiary legislation B in Chapter 188 of the Laws of Hong Kong.[5]

The reciprocating jurisdictions were designated by means of Orders in Gazette,[6] though most of them were designated at the time of enactment of the Ordinance in the late seventies.

[2] In accordance with Art 8 of the Basic Law of the Hong Kong Special Administrative Region of the People's Republic of China (Basic Law), the laws previously in force shall be maintained except for any that contravene the Basic Law and subject to any amendment by the legislature of the HKSAR. The Basic Law is the constitutional document for the HKSAR, which was adopted on 4 April 1990 by the Seventh National People's Congress of the People's Republic of China and came into effect on 1 July 1997. For more information about the Basic Law, see the relevant website maintained by the HKSARG Government at www.basiclaw.gov.hk/en/index/index.html (accessed December 2013).

[3] For a useful introduction to the background of the Commonwealth Scheme, see JD McClean, *Recognition of Family Judgments in the Commonwealth* (London, Butterworths, 1983) 117–48 and see Richard Frimpong Oppong, ch 4 of this volume.

[4] The full text of the Ordinance is available at www.legislation.gov.hk/blis/eng/index.html (accessed December 2013).

[5] The full text of the Order is also available at www.legislation.gov.hk/blis/eng/index.html (accessed December 2013).

[6] The Government Gazette is available at www.gld.gov.hk/egazette/english/gazette/toc.php (accessed December 2013).

At that time, the usual practice was for an official of the jurisdiction to write to the Hong Kong Government signifying that they would like to be included as a reciprocating jurisdiction by Hong Kong and that they were prepared to do the same to Hong Kong in return. The relevant legislation would be exchanged and studied. A date would then be suggested for both parties to publish the designation. No formal international agreement was signed in any of those cases.

B. Since 1 July 1997

Since 1 July 1997, Hong Kong has become a Special Administrative Region of the People's Republic of China and has ceased to be a member of the Commonwealth.[7] Notwithstanding this change, the Ordinance continues to apply to maintenance orders granted by a reciprocating jurisdiction from the Commonwealth provided that the relevant Commonwealth jurisdiction accords similar benefits to maintenance orders from the HKSAR.[8]

The jurisdictions designated under the Ordinance have not been changed. While section 3 of the Ordinance[9] gives the Chief Executive[10] the same power of designation as the Governor before, such power has never been exercised by the Chief Executive. Therefore, there has been no addition to the designated jurisdictions since 1 July 1997.

i. Legislative Framework under the Ordinance[11]

The Ordinance is primarily modelled on Part I of the UK Maintenance Orders (Reciprocal Enforcement) Act 1972. There are two types of maintenance orders under the Ordinance, a 'maintenance order' and a 'provisional maintenance order'.[12] A provisional maintenance

[7] In accordance with the Joint Declaration between the People's Republic of China and the United Kingdom of Great Britain and Northern Ireland on the Question of Hong Kong signed on 19 December 1984, China has resumed sovereignty over Hong Kong with effect from 1 July 1997. Hong Kong, with effect from that date, became a Special Administrative Region of the People's Republic of China.

[8] For instance, reciprocal benefits are accorded: by the Maintenance Orders Reciprocal Enforcement Notification 2002 in Brunei; by the Maintenance Orders (Facilities for Enforcement) Order 2003 in Malaysia; and by the Maintenance Orders (Reciprocal Enforcement) Act in Singapore.

[9] s 3(1) provides, inter alia, that 'The Chief Executive, if satisfied that, in the event of the benefits conferred by this Ordinance being applied to, or to particular classes of, maintenance orders made by the courts of any country or place other than Hong Kong, similar benefits will in that country or place be applied to, or to those classes of, maintenance order made by the courts of Hong Kong, may by order designate that country or place as a reciprocating country for the purposes of this Ordinance'.

[10] The Chief Executive is the head of the Government of the HKSAR. For more information about the current Chief Executive, see www.ceo.gov.hk/eng/index.html (accessed December 2013).

[11] In addition to the mechanism under the Ordinance, an applicant may also consider making a local application for child support under the Guardianship of Minors Ordinance (Chapter 13 of the Laws of Hong Kong), if the applicant is a parent of the child. A married person could consider issuing an application for spousal support and/or child support under s 8 of the Matrimonial Proceedings and Property Ordinance (Chapter 192 of the Laws of Hong Kong) or under the Separation and Maintenance Orders Ordinance (Chapter 16 of the Laws of Hong Kong). In an exceptional case, a person may even register a foreign order for ancillary relief to pay spousal maintenance under the Foreign Judgments (Reciprocal Enforcement) Ordinance (Chapter 319 of the Laws of Hong Kong) by way of a supplemental order: see *Lai Ling Ling v Chun Foo Keung* [2005] 3 HKC 589. The full text of the above legislation is available at www.legislation.gov.hk/blis/eng/index.html (accessed December 2013).

[12] The meaning of 'maintenance order' under the Ordinance is very wide, covering orders for periodical payment of sums of money towards the maintenance of any person whom the payer is liable to maintain according to the law in the foreign place (*CY v PYKC* [2006] 1 HKC 64, 67).

order has no effect unless and until it has been confirmed either by the court in a reciprocating country or by the Hong Kong court.[13]

A maintenance order of a reciprocating country can be registered at the District Court[14] in Hong Kong (section 7).[15] A registered order may be enforced in Hong Kong as if it is an order made by the District Court (section 9).[16] Similarly, a maintenance order of Hong Kong could be transmitted to a reciprocating country for enforcement there (section 4).[17]

It is worthy of note that a maintenance order of a reciprocating country registered in Hong Kong could be varied by a provisional order of the District Court, subject to confirmation by the court of the reciprocating country under section 10.[18] A maintenance order made in Hong Kong could also be varied by a Hong Kong court under section 6.[19]

The District Court may also make a provisional order against a person in a reciprocating country in certain circumstances under section 5.[20] This provisional order is subject to confirmation by the court of the reciprocating country. Once it has been confirmed by the court of the reciprocating country, it is to be treated as an ordinary maintenance order made by the District Court for the purpose of enforcement in the reciprocating country (section 5(6)).[21] Similarly, once a provisional order of a reciprocating country has been confirmed by the District Court under section 8,[22] it could be registered and then be enforced in Hong Kong under section 9.[23]

[13] It is worthy of note that the term 'court' is widely defined in s 2 of the Ordinance to include 'any tribunal or person having power to make, confirm, enforce, vary or revoke a maintenance order' and is not necessarily limited to a judicial authority.

[14] In the HKSAR, the family court deals with matrimonial matters including matters relating to family maintenance and is placed within the District Court.

[15] It should be noted that s 7(4) requires that 'Before registering an order under this section the Registrar shall take such steps as he thinks fit for the purpose of ascertaining whether the payer under the order is residing in Hong Kong, and if after taking those steps he is satisfied that the payer is not so residing he shall return the certified copy of the order to the Chief Executive with a statement giving such information as he possesses as to the whereabouts of the payer'.

[16] It has been held that the effect of s 9 is to presume that the District Court had jurisdiction to make the order and that even if the District Court did not have the jurisdiction to make the registered order, it would still have the jurisdiction to deal with the enforcement proceedings (*CY v PYKC* [2006] 1 HKC 64, 67–68).

[17] s 4 provides for the requirements and procedure for transmission of the order made by the court in Hong Kong for enforcement when the payer is residing in a reciprocating country.

[18] s 10 imposes certain restrictions on the court to vary or revoke a registered foreign order otherwise than by a provisional order. Eg, the District Court may only vary or revoke the registered foreign order by a provisional order if both the payer and the payee under the registered order are not for the time being residing in Hong Kong.

[19] s 6 requires the court to vary its own order by a provisional order in certain cases. Eg, s 6(3) provides that: when the variation is by increasing the rate of the payments under the order then, unless either—

(a) both the payer and the payee under the order appear in the proceedings; or

(b) the applicant appears and the appropriate process has been duly served on the other party,

the order varying the order shall be a provisional order.

[20] s 5 sets out the conditions for the making of a provisional order against a person residing in a reciprocating country and the required documentation to support the application for such an order.

[21] s 5(6) provides that 'A maintenance order made by virtue of this section which has been confirmed by a competent court in a reciprocating country shall be treated for all purposes as if the court in Hong Kong which made the order had made it in the form in which it was confirmed and as if the order had never been a provisional order, and subject to s 6, any such order may be enforced, varied or revoked accordingly'.

[22] s 8 also allows the payer to establish a defence in opposition to confirmation of the order. The grounds of defence are not limited to those certified by the court in the reciprocating country (*K v L (Reciprocal enforcement of maintenance)* [2008] HKFLR 207, 216). In fact, it has been held that the court has wide discretion in confirming a provisional order, as if the court is hearing an application made in Hong Kong for a maintenance order (ibid).

[23] s 9(3) provides that 'a sum ordered to be paid under a registered order shall be recoverable as a civil debt and if an application is made to the District Court alleging that default has been made in paying a sum ordered to be paid under a registered order, the District Court may, if it considers the circumstances require it, for the purpose of securing the presence of the person alleged to be in default, issue a warrant to arrest him and bring him before the court, whether or not a summons has been issued previously'.

ii. Designated Jurisdictions under the Ordinance

There are two categories of jurisdictions designated under the Ordinance as set out below:

For maintenance orders generally
UK
Bermuda
Manitoba
Saskatchewan
Ontario
Isle of Man

For maintenance orders other than affiliation orders[24]
The Commonwealth of Australia and its territories
Brunei
British Columbia
Malaysia
New Zealand
Singapore
The Solomon Islands
South Africa
Sri Lanka

From 2000 to 2012, there were only a total of eight outgoing cases to Australia, Singapore and the UK and 60 incoming cases from Canada, Singapore and the UK under the Ordinance. The annual number of outgoing cases ranged from zero (in 2001–04, 2006 and 2011) to just two (in 2005 and 2008) while the annual number of incoming cases ranged from zero (in 2011) to nine (in 2009). In 2012, there were merely three incoming cases from Canada and the UK respectively and one outgoing case to Australia.[25]

While it may require more thorough research to examine the effectiveness of the current mechanism in view of its very limited usage, it seems quite clear that a possible reason for such low numbers of cases may be due to the limited number of jurisdictions covered by the Ordinance as well as the inherent limitations of the current mechanism.[26] Therefore, the development of a new international instrument—the 2007 Convention—which provides a valuable alternative to the current mechanism, was a very welcome initiative by the Hague Conference on Private International Law.

[24] The Affiliation Proceedings Ordinance has been repealed and there is no longer any affiliation order in Hong Kong as parents have the same duties to maintain children born within or outside wedlock. (For more information about equal treatment of children born outside wedlock in Hong Kong, see Parents and Child Ordinance, Chapter 429 of the Laws of Hong Kong.)

[25] This statistical information is based on the information shared by the Department of Justice of the HKSAR Government at the Heidelberg Conference 2013: Recovery of Maintenance in the European Union and worldwide.

[26] For instance, the current mechanism providing for court hearings in both the jurisdictions of the maintenance creditor and maintenance debtor through the use of provisional and confirmation orders (often known as the 'shuttlecock' procedure) may not be the most time efficient or cost effective mechanism which could cause inconvenience or even deterrence to some applicants in terms of time and money. An in-depth analysis of the current mechanism and its limitations falls outside the scope of this chapter. This issue is also discussed by Richard Frimpong Oppong, ch 4 of this volume.

III. 2007 Convention

While the HKSAR does not apply any international Convention in the field of international recovery of maintenance, representatives from the HKSAR took an active role, as part of the delegation of China, in the negotiation of the 2007 Convention during all Special Commission and other meetings leading to its adoption in 2007, including participation in the Drafting Committee at the Diplomatic Session.

Drawing from the author's experience during the negotiations, some of the main features of the 2007 Convention that may be of particular interest or importance to the Asia Pacific region as well as some challenges that countries in the region may face will be discussed.

A. Some Key Features of the 2007 Convention

i. Administrative Cooperation

Recovery of maintenance abroad not only involves difficult legal issues but also many practical obstacles such as language barriers and the need for translation of the relevant documents. Given that there is no common language in the Asia Pacific region, it is not surprising that countries in the region commonly share such practical difficulties at the moment.[27]

In addition, it is also not uncommon to modify a maintenance decision from time to time, especially for children. Therefore, it could be a lengthy and recurring process since child maintenance can last for many years until a child reaches his or her adulthood, which will often require regular intervention or assistance. Thus, it would be most helpful for there to be a regular contact point in a foreign country which can be approached whenever there is a need for modification. This is particularly important for Asia Pacific as people in the region very often move from one place to another to pursue their studies or for other purposes at different stages of their lives.[28]

Chapter II of the 2007 Convention is therefore dedicated to the establishment of an effective and efficient mechanism for an administrative cooperation system to overcome these practical difficulties. A Central Authority would need to be established by each Contracting State which would undertake a wide range of functions providing different levels of services or assistance to other Contracting States, including processing of applications for recognition and enforcement of a foreign maintenance decision, locating

[27] Despite recent technological advances in translation technology which have helped to alleviate the problem, there are still many challenges ahead given the diversity of the Asian languages. For a short discussion on the technological advances and some challenges in Asia, see S Nakamura, 'Overcoming the Language Barrier with Speech Translation Technology' (2009) *Science and Technology Trends—Quarterly Review* 35–48.

[28] There are many reasons for such movements in the region; for a succinct discussion on the different types of population movement and the underlying reasons, see the articles by LL Lim and M Abella, 'The Movement of People in Asia: Internal, Intra-regional and International Migration' (1994) *Asian and Pacific Migration Journal* 209–50 and L Low, 'Population Movement in the Asia Pacific Region: Singapore Perspective' (1995) *International Migration Review* 745–64. Many of the factors referred to in these articles are still generally valid today. For a more recent discussion on the developments, see GJ Hugo, 'International Migration in the Asia-Pacific Region: Emerging Trends and Issues' in DS Massey and JE Taylor (eds), *International Migration: Prospects and Policies in a Global Market*, (Oxford, Oxford University Press, 2004) 77–103.

the debtor or creditor within the jurisdiction, and facilitating settlement and transfer of payments. The provision of such services by the Central Authority should also be free of charge, subject to a few exceptions.[29]

ii. Effective Access to Procedures

Another major practical obstacle for international recovery of maintenance is the financial costs involved. Creditors for maintenance (in particular, children) are usually in an impecunious situation and hence even very small financial obstacles could deter or prevent them from bringing an application. Given that there are quite a number of developing countries in the Asia Pacific region, many creditors in these countries have very limited resources at their disposal for recovering maintenance abroad.[30]

Chapter III of the 2007 Convention provides for a simplified and speedy system for processing applications by the Central Authorities which could significantly reduce the costs involved. Further, it also provides for a system in which effective access to procedures is guaranteed. Effective access to procedures is often related to the provision of legal assistance.

It is clear that the 2007 Convention could not work satisfactorily in practice if an applicant could not eventually seek recognition or enforcement because of the legal costs involved. During the negotiation of the 2007 Convention, it was considered that a major drawback of the existing international instruments in the area of international recovery of maintenance is the inability to provide effective cost-free services to an applicant.

However, some countries may have difficulties in providing free legal assistance in all cases. As a compromise, Article 16 of the 2007 Convention allows a State which is not ready to accept the principle of free legal assistance in all cases to make a declaration that it will apply a means test based on the means of a child. As such, the principle of free legal assistance is still the main principle while a State is free to decide whether to make such a declaration which will provide a limited exception to Article 15.[31]

iii. Recognition and Enforcement

There are many legal difficulties in recognising and enforcing a foreign decision such as the form of foreign decisions, jurisdictions of foreign courts and varying grounds for refusal, given that unlike the European Union where there are regional regulations in the area,[32]

[29] See Art 8 of the 2007 Convention.

[30] In spite of the fact that the Asia Pacific region is one of the fastest growing regions in the world, it is home to half of the world's poor and there are 14 Least Developed Countries in the region. For more information, see UNDP Report: *Leveraging Change for Better Lives: UNDP in Asia and the Pacific (2008–2012)*, published in July 2013, available at www.undp.org/content/dam/undp/library/Poverty%20Reduction/Inclusive%20development/UNDP_Asia_Pacific_Leveraging_Change.pdf (accessed December 2013).

[31] It should be noted that it is the understanding of the negotiating parties that the test in Art 16(1) should exclude only the very wealthy child from receiving free legal assistance and therefore the exception is likely to be of limited practical effect. See the *Explanatory Report on on the Convention on the International Recovery of Child Support and Other Forms of Family Maintenance* (The Hague, HCCH Publications, 2009) para 398.

[32] For instance, Council Regulation (EC) No 4/2009 on jurisdiction, applicable law, recognition and enforcement of decisions and cooperation in matters relating to maintenance obligations [2009] OJ L7, came into force on 11 June 2011 for the European Union Member States.

there is no uniform regional instrument providing for reciprocal recognition and enforcement of maintenance decision in the Asia Pacific region.

Many of these difficulties are resolved by Chapter V of the 2007 Convention. In particular, it is noted that in many jurisdictions nowadays, maintenance decisions are no longer judicial decisions but are administrative decisions decided by an authority through an established and transparent administrative procedure. In some countries, the amount of maintenance payable is also decided by private agreements or by the use of authentic instruments. The 2007 Convention is broad enough to cover all these decisions (subject to any reservation made by a Contracting State) and provides an efficient and simplified procedure for the recognition and enforcement of these decisions.

It should be noted that in the Asia Pacific region, maintenance decisions also take various forms—while some are administrative decisions like those from Australia and New Zealand, many of them are judicial decisions like those from Hong Kong, Japan, Malaysia and Singapore. Thus, the 2007 Convention is comprehensive enough to cover the reality in the region.

The 2007 Convention seeks to eliminate the costs and delay that will be incurred and reduces the need for making a fresh application because of the difficulty in recognition and enforcement of foreign decisions. It also helps to lessen the legal problem of multiple conflicting orders.

iv. Application to Public Bodies

Lastly, it should be noted that the 2007 Convention also covers public bodies as applicants. This is of particular significance to countries that have such public bodies like Australia and New Zealand.[33] Although it is understood that the primary responsibility for maintenance rests with the debtor, in some places, public bodies may be called upon to provide maintenance in place of the debtor. For example, in some places, the public body will pay the maintenance if attempts to recover maintenance from the debtor have failed. In other places, the public body will pay the maintenance to the creditor first and then seek recovery from the debtor. In many other places, the creditor will rely on public assistance or public welfare if it is not possible to obtain maintenance from the debtor.

Therefore, it is considered justified to cover public bodies as applicants under the 2007 Convention and to allow them to seek reimbursement from the debtor for the benefit paid to the creditor in lieu of maintenance. Chapter VII thus contains detailed rules for the public body in seeking the reimbursement.

B. Challenges

It is clear, therefore, that the 2007 Convention is significant in various aspects of facilitating international recovery of maintenance but it provides both opportunities and challenges for many countries in the region.

[33] In Australia, child support is administered by the Department of Human Services while child support is administered by the Inland Revenue in New Zealand. These authorities assist in the collection of payment from the paying parent and transfer of the payment to the receiving parent.

Since the purpose of the 2007 Convention is to establish an efficient system of administrative cooperation through a network of Central Authorities in order to remove the practical obstacles for international recovery of maintenance, countries that are considering becoming party to the 2007 Convention should ensure that they could identify a competent Central Authority that is capable of discharging the wide range of functions required by the 2007 Convention. Sometimes, new legislation may be required to empower an existing authority or to create a new authority to discharge those functions.

The 2007 Convention also requires provision of effective access to procedures. It is understandable that the requirement of free legal assistance may pose a big challenge for many countries, it should however be noted that there is a limited exception available under the 2007 Convention. A country may make use of the exception through a declaration under Article 16 so that it would not be necessary to provide free legal assistance in all cases.[34] A country may also change its internal procedure by creating an administrative system for maintenance recovery or by mechanical assessment based on fixed rules or formulae so that legal assistance would not necessarily be required in order to minimise the financial burden for the provision of free legal assistance.

Further, the 2007 Convention provides for a simplified and comprehensive system for recognition and enforcement of foreign maintenance decisions, as well as reimbursement of foreign public bodies (which may be a new mechanism for many countries in the region). Countries should seriously examine the compatibility of their existing systems and the need for introducing any changes to their current systems.

In spite of the possible challenges identified above, the benefits that are brought by the 2007 Convention would probably offset the additional resources required for overcoming the challenges.

An efficient system of administrative cooperation through a network of Central Authorities and effective access to procedures could help to remove most of the practical obstacles for international recovery of maintenance and save much of the associated costs currently incurred in practice. A simplified and comprehensive system for recognition and enforcement of foreign maintenance decisions would also have the effect of deterring debtors from evading their obligations, hence reducing the number of default cases, resulting in significant savings in economic and human resources. The reimbursement of public bodies from the debtor abroad would also help to reduce social welfare and public expenses. Moreover, as mentioned above, the use of a limited exception for provision of free legal assistance and improvement of internal procedures may also help to minimise costs. Most importantly, the 2007 Convention will definitely help the families and children who are in need of maintenance in the region and beyond.

[34] The exception as provided for under Art 16 allows the use of a means test based on the means of the child. While the test in Art 16(1) should exclude only the very wealthy child from receiving free legal assistance, the stringency of the test is left to the internal law of the Contracting States. See *Explanatory Report* (n 30) para 398. Given the huge divergence in gross domestic product (GDP) per capita between some developing countries in Asia and developed Western countries, this exception may provide some comfort to some poor Asian counties since a child who is considered to be reasonably wealthy in the Western countries may be regarded as a very wealthy child in those Asian countries.

IV. Conclusion

At the Fourth Asia Pacific Conference of the Hague Conference on Private International Law held in Manila in 2011, in relation to the 2007 Convention, the Conference '[r]ecognized the importance of the Convention and its Protocol as the appropriate administrative and legal framework for the recovery of child support and other forms of family maintenance and encouraged States in the Region to become Contracting States to the Convention and its Protocol; and [a]cknowledged the role of the Convention in inviting reforms to domestic systems for the recovery of child support and other forms of family maintenance in the Region'.[35]

As discussed above, the current regime in the HKSAR is very different from that under the 2007 Convention.[36] If the 2007 Convention is to be applied to the HKSAR, it will constitute a significant reform to the current regime and could significantly simplify and strengthen the regime for international recovery of maintenance.[37] In addition to the effective and speedy recovery mechanism under the 2007 Convention,[38] it also facilitates international recovery of family maintenance with any Contracting State in the world which is much broader than the currently very limited number of jurisdictions designated under the Ordinance.[39] The 2007 Convention is currently under study by the relevant authorities in the HKSAR in light of some of the challenges that have to be overcome as mentioned above.

Lastly, it is reassuring to note that the countries in the Asia Pacific region are not facing these challenges alone, since the Hague Conference on Private International Law has now established its Asia Pacific Regional Office in the HKSAR, which was officially opened on 13 December 2012.[40] Promotion of the 2007 Convention and the provision of technical assistance in relation to its implementation have been identified as being among their priority areas of work.[41]

[35] Conclusions and Recommendations adopted on 28 October 2011 by the Fourth Asia Pacific Conference of the Hague Conference on Private International Law: The Work of the Hague Conference on Private International Law (26–28 October 2011, Manila, Philippines) 4. The full text of the Conclusions and Recommendations is available at www.hcch.net/upload/ap4concl.pdf (accessed December 2013).

[36] On the other hand, it should be noted that there are also provisions in the 2007 Convention—such as Art 31 which has specifically addressed decisions produced by the combined effects of provisional and confirmation orders—which are quite compatible with the current regime of the HKSAR.

[37] For instance, administrative assistance available under the Convention, which is not currently provided for under the Ordinance, would have removed many of the practical obstacles as mentioned in Section III A (i) above.

[38] Eg, the simplified and speedy system for processing applications in Chapter III and the streamlined recognition and enforcement procedure in Chapter V of the Convention provide a welcome alternative to the current 'shuttlecock' procedure through the use of provisional and confirmation orders. See further (n 25) above.

[39] So far, the 2007 Convention is already in force in Albania, Bosnia and Herzegovina, Norway and Ukraine while Burkina Faso, the European Union and the United States have also signed the Convention (all the above have not yet been designated under the Ordinance). Following strong interest and support at the Heidelberg Conference 2013: Recovery of Maintenance in the European Union and worldwide, there is a good possibility that more countries will join the 2007 Convention in the near future. Thus, the potential coverage of the Convention will be much wider than that under the Ordinance.

[40] See the relevant press release by the Hague Conference on Private International Law, available at www.hcch.net/index_en.php?act=events.details&year=2012&varevent=294 (accessed December 2013).

[41] See the Information Document No 2 of April 2012 for the attention of the Council on General Affairs and Policy of the Conference, 6–7, available at www.hcch.net/upload/wop/gap2012info02en.pdf (accessed December

It is hoped that the Regional Office will help countries in the Asia Pacific region to become fully aware of the opportunities offered by the 2007 Convention and provide advice and assistance to those interested in becoming Contracting Parties to the 2007 Convention and help with its implementation. With this vital input from the Regional Office, it is expected that the 2007 Convention will have a significant impact on countries in the Asia Pacific region and beyond.

2013). For more information about the Regional Office, see the booklet entitled 'The Establishment of HCCH Asia-Pacific Regional Office in Hong Kong' (Department of Justice of the HKSAR Government, November 2012), also available at www.doj.gov.hk/eng/about/pdf/DOJ_HCCH_Booklet2012.pdf (accessed December 2013).

7

The Potential of the 2007 Child Support Convention: Addressing Global Poverty and Supporting Economic Rights

MAJA GROFF

I. Introduction

The recovery of child support, spousal support and other types of family maintenance from abroad has been an important international priority for some time.[1] National and international statistics have highlighted the importance of a focus on the needs of children raised in single-parent families in particular, who are often susceptible to disproportionate rates of poverty.[2] Even at the national level, the establishment and subsequent effective enforcement of maintenance obligations have been observed to be 'notoriously problematic'.[3] At the international level, the practical and legal problems are only amplified: a creditor of support seeking to obtain maintenance from a debtor abroad may be 'faced with almost insuperable legal obstacles, and the cost involved is such as to discourage most claimants from even attempting to commence proceedings in a foreign country'.[4] Speaking to the importance of finding a solution to the problem, the preamble to the 1956 United Nations Convention on the Recovery Abroad of Maintenance[5] which set up international cooperation mechanisms for the recovery of maintenance, notes 'the urgency of solving the humanitarian problem resulting from the situation of persons in need dependent for their maintenance on persons abroad'. The recognition of the need for coordinated action on this 'humanitarian' issue can be seen emanating from actors across geographic regions and across the political and philosophical spectrum: 41 States from all regions of the world participated, directly or as observers, in the negotiation of the 1956

[1] The League of Nations referred the topic to UNIDROIT in 1929. See P Contini, 'The United Nations Convention on the Recovery Abroad of Maintenance' (1956) *St. John's Law Review* 1, 2.

[2] See, eg, *Doing Better for Families* (Organisation for Economic Co-operation and Development (OECD), 27 April 2011) 41, presenting comparative child poverty statistics among OECD nations.

[3] N Bala, JT Oldham, A Perry, 'Regulating Cross-Border Child Support within Federated Systems: The United States, Canada, and the European Union' (2005) *Transnational Law & Contemporary Problems* 87.

[4] Contini (n 1).

[5] Hereafter the 1956 UN Convention.

UN Convention, along with a range of international non-governmental associations and organisations exemplifying the variety of stakeholders interested in this topic.[6] In addition to the 1956 UN Convention, four additional instruments in this area were negotiated under the auspices of the Hague Conference on Private International Law in the 1950s and the 1970s, covering recognition and enforcement of foreign maintenance decisions and applicable law issues.[7]

These international instruments—the most recent drafted in 1973—attempted to address issues which, with the ever-greater mobility of persons across borders, have only continued to intensify. The United Nations has released new statistics that show that more people than ever are living abroad, with some 232 million—or 3.2 per cent of the world's population—living outside of their countries of origin.[8] This is in contrast to figures of 174 million in 2000 and 154 million in 1990.

Exemplifying a renewed international commitment to devising workable, contemporary solutions in this field, the Hague Convention of 23 November 2007 on the International Recovery of Child Support and Other Forms of Family Maintenance[9] marks a new era in international cooperation for the recovery of maintenance from abroad.

Child support and family maintenance, within the broader field of national and international family law, is of course a distinctive area of law in itself, subject to specific practical and theoretical legal complexities. However, this international legal subfield also has importance within the framework of international human rights law, and may be looked at within the context of (international) social and economic development. This chapter seeks to frame the 2007 Child Support Convention within a number of broader legal and policy perspectives. Putting the 2007 Child Support Convention into such a context will assist, it is hoped, with the promotion of the Convention, which at this time is only beginning to gather momentum as to widespread, global ratification.[10] It is hoped that the 2007 Child Support Convention, like the 1989 United Nations Convention on the Rights of the Child (the UNCRC),[11] will achieve nearly universal ratification/accession, and will surpass

[6] Eg, the International Labour Organization, the World Federation of Trade Unions and other international trade union associations, international religious organisations of the Christian and Jewish faiths, international women's and child welfare organisations, etc.

[7] These instruments include the Hague Convention of 24 October 1956 on the Law Applicable to Maintenance Obligations towards Children; the Hague Convention of 15 April 1958 Concerning the Recognition and Enforcement of Decisions Relating to Maintenance Obligations towards Children; the Hague Maintenance Convention of 2 October 1973 on the Recognition and Enforcement of Decisions Relating to Maintenance Obligations; and the Hague Convention of 2 October 1973 on the Law Applicable to Maintenance Obligations.

[8] *Population Facts No. 2013/2: The Number of International Migrants Worldwide Reaches 232 Million* (United Nations Department of Economic and Social Affairs (UN-DESA), September 2013).

[9] Hereafter the 2007 Child Support Convention.

[10] The 2007 Child Support Convention recently entered into force on 1 January 2013. At the time of writing of this chapter, the Convention had four Contracting States, and two additional signatories, the United States and the European Union (representing 27 States within the European Union where the Convention will be applicable). The 2007 Child Support Convention will come into force for the European Union on 1 August 2014 and likely for the United States within the next several years, representing extremely important economic regions and migration destinations significant for the international recovery of maintenance.

[11] The UNCRC currently has 193 States Parties (United Nations Treaty Database at www.treaties.un.org/Pages/ViewDetails.aspx?src=TREATY&mtdsg_no=IV-11&chapter=4&lang=en (accessed November 2013)).

the hitherto most widely ratified international instrument in this field, the 1956 UN Convention which has 65 Parties.[12]

II. The Innovations of the Hague 2007 Convention

The 2007 Child Support Convention and the companion 2007 Hague Protocol on applicable law[13] will replace, over time, the five international treaties which currently exist in this field.[14] The 2007 Child Support Convention should also replace a great many bilateral agreements or reciprocity arrangements,[15] while at the same time not precluding the conclusion of further bilateral or regional agreements which supplement or provide more effective measures compatible with the Convention.[16] The 2007 Child Support Convention is meant to be a single, comprehensive and unified global system for the cross-border recovery of maintenance. Indeed, it is possible that it will realise this goal, due to the number and diversity of the 70 States participating in or observing negotiations of the Convention from 2003–07, representing a great variety of the legal, political and cultural traditions of the world.[17]

The older international maintenance instruments, in addition to being numerous, potentially conflicting, and engendering unnecessary complexity, were found to have a number of structural and operational problems that had not been remedied by infrequent

[12] United Nations Treaty Database at www.treaties.un.org/Pages/ViewDetailsIII.aspx?&src=TREATY&mtdsg_no=XX~1&chapter=20&Temp=mtdsg3&lang=en (accessed November 2013). Achieving near-universal acceptance of the Convention, while realistic over the long term, is an ambitious goal given the technical nature of the instrument. Achieving such a goal may require, in particular, the availability of technical assistance for some States which lack sufficient legal and economic capacity for the implementation of the Convention. However, it should be noted that a number of developing nations have been 'early signers' of the Convention (see below (nn 48 and 49)), speaking to the Convention's universal appeal. See also Section V below, regarding other tools and supports for the Convention already or soon to be available to maximise its impact and wide application.

[13] See Arts 48 and 49 of the 2007 Child Support Convention and Art 18 of the Hague Protocol of 23 November 2007 on the Law Applicable to Maintenance Obligations.

[14] Ie the 1956 UN Convention and the four Hague Conventions (n 7).

[15] Eg, the UK's Reciprocal Enforcement of Maintenance Orders (REMO) programme (see www.gov.uk/remo-unit-helpline (accessed November 2013)), and the range of foreign reciprocating jurisdictions for the Enforcement of Family Support (Maintenance) Obligations in relation to the United States (see www.federalregister.gov/a/E8-28323 (accessed November 2013)).

[16] See Arts 51 and 52 of the 2007 Child Support Convention.

[17] Hague Conference Members adopting the final text included: Albania, Argentina, Australia, Austria, Belgium, Brazil, Bulgaria, Canada, Chile, China, Croatia, Czech Republic, Denmark, Ecuador, Egypt, Estonia, European Community, Finland, France, Germany, Greece, Hungary, Ireland, Israel, Italy, Japan, Jordan, Republic of Korea, Latvia, Lithuania, Luxembourg, Malaysia, Mexico, Monaco, Morocco, Netherlands, New Zealand, Norway, Peru, Poland, Portugal, Romania, Russian Federation, Serbia, Slovakia, Slovenia, South Africa, Spain, Sri Lanka, Sweden, Switzerland, The former Yugoslav Republic of Macedonia, Ukraine, United Kingdom of Great Britain and Northern Ireland, United States, Uruguay and Venezuela. Non-Members signing the final text included: Algeria, Burkina Faso, Colombia, Costa Rica, Dominican Republic, El Salvador, Guatemala, Haiti, Holy See, India, Indonesia, Iran, Philippines and Viet Nam. As can be seen from this list, civil and common law legal traditions were represented, as were States with Sharia law legal traditions, administrative and judicial maintenance systems, States which practice advance payments of owed support to creditors, etc.

review exercises.[18] It was considered that the 'number of cases being processed through the international machinery was very small in comparison with real needs'.[19] The existing international landscape was studied in preparation for the development of a new Convention in the field, and the best and worst features of existing regimes were highlighted and drawn out to learn from.[20]

The 2007 Child Support Convention seeks to ensure the effective international recovery of family maintenance by way of a number of inter-linking features within a modernised system. The key features of the 2007 Child Support Convention can be summarised as follows.[21] The Convention:

(1) sets out a broadly based system for the recognition and enforcement of maintenance decisions (including maintenance arrangements) made in Contracting States, including expedited procedures (Chapter V);
(2) establishes an international administrative cooperation network, where each designated national Central Authority has a wide range of specified functions to assist in the processing of Convention applications and with other operational issues (Chapters II and III);
(3) obligates free legal assistance for child support applications for children under the age of 21 (with minor exceptions) and general 'effective access to procedures' (Arts 14–17);
(4) specifies the protection of personal information (Arts 38–40);
(5) seeks to be 'technology neutral'[22] so as to take advantage of technological advances (Art 13 and preamble); and,
(6) includes a special chapter on actual enforcement of decisions, a first for a Hague Convention (Chapter VI).

In addition, a new global case management system, 'iSupport', is planned to leverage IT solutions to further support the practical and effective cross-border recovery of maintenance.[23] With iSupport, Central Authorities designated under the Convention would have the ability to communicate with each other quickly and efficiently, to manage cross-border cases, to address language barriers through technology, and to realise the swift and low-cost transfer of maintenance payments. iSupport has the potential to assist in the more efficient and standardised application of the Convention internationally, saving time and money for national authorities and effectively getting more money into the hands of creditors faster.

[18] See, eg, a description of structural, operational and other issues concerning the 1956 UN Convention (including its uncertain interaction with other international instruments in the maintenance field) in W Duncan, 'Towards a New Global Instrument on the International Recovery of Child Support and Other Forms of Family Maintenance' (Prel Doc No 3, April 2003) Permanent Bureau of the Hague Conference on Private International Law, 15–18.

[19] W Duncan, 'The New Hague Maintenance Convention and Protocol' (2008) *Yearbook of Private International Law* 313, 317.

[20] Duncan (n 18).

[21] See Duncan (n 19) for a more detailed description of the Convention's main features.

[22] P Lortie, 'The Development of Medium and Technology Neutral International Treaties in Support of Post-Convention Information Technology Systems' (2008) *Yearbook of Private International Law* 359.

[23] See P Lortie, 'Development of an International Electronic Case Management and Communication System in Support of the Future Hague Convention on the International Recovery of Child Support' (Info Doc No 1, June 2006) Permanent Bureau of the Hague Conference on Private International Law (available on the Hague Conference website, www.hcch.net, under 'Conventions' then 'Convention No 38' then 'Preliminary Documents'). See also P Lortie, ch 17 of this volume.

III. International Human Rights Law Context

On the international plane, children have been recognised as possessing economic and social rights since early in the last century. The Geneva Declaration of the Rights of the Child was drafted by the League of Nations in 1924, and the International Labour Organization has created standards for child labour since 1919.[24]

The landmark 1989 Convention on the Human Rights of Children, the UNCRC, recognises various economic and social rights of children,[25] which are most directly set out in Article 27 of the Treaty, affirming that States Parties 'recognize the right of every child to a standard of living adequate for the child's physical, mental, spiritual, moral and social development'.[26] Provisions of Article 27 are quoted in the Preamble to the 2007 Child Support Convention. Importantly, Article 27 of the UNCRC notes that parents, and others responsible for the child, bear 'primary responsibility to secure, within their abilities and financial capacities, the conditions of living necessary for the child's development'.[27] Notwithstanding this primary obligation of the parents or other guardians of children to provide for their needs, Article 27(3) additionally emphasises that States Parties, 'in accordance with national conditions and within their means', shall take measures to assist parents and others in implementing the right, and also must provide 'material assistance and support programmes', in particular with respect to nutrition, clothing and housing, in case of need.[28]

UNCRC provisions are framed more broadly by the rights enshrined in the United Nations 1966 International Covenant on Economic, Social and Cultural Rights (the 1966 Covenant), representing one of the two classical pillars of modern international human rights law, alongside the pillar of civil and political rights.[29] Under the 1966 Covenant, States have obligations of protection and assistance to the family particularly 'while it is responsible for the care and education of dependent children',[30] and must recognise the right of everyone 'to an adequate standard of living for himself and his family, including adequate clothing and housing, and to the continuous improvement of living conditions'.[31]

The 2007 Hague Child Support Convention supports and assists in tangibly realising the above-mentioned social and economic rights and, most specifically, directly implements Article 27(4) of the UNCRC that stipulates that States Parties must

> take all appropriate measures to secure the recovery of maintenance for the child from the parents or other persons having financial responsibility for the child … . In particular, where the person having financial responsibility for the child lives in a State different from that of the child, States Parties shall promote the accession to international agreements

[24] K Libal and K Neubeck, 'The Rights of the Child to an Adequate Standard of Living: Applying International Standards to the U.S. Case' in L Minkler (ed), *The State of Economic and Social Rights: A Global Overview* (Cambridge, Cambridge University Press, 2013).

[25] For a summary, see ibid 179–80.

[26] Art 27(1).

[27] Art 27(2).

[28] Thus some State obligations under Art 27(3) fall outside of the scope of the 2007 Child Support Convention, and require that supplementary policies are employed by governments in cases of family need.

[29] The 1966 Covenant is also very widely ratified, currently with 161 States Parties (United Nations Treaty Database at www.treaties.un.org/pages/ViewDetails.aspx?src=TREATY&mtdsg_no=IV-3&chapter=4&lang=en (accessed November 2013)).

[30] Art 10(1).

[31] Art 11(1).

The UNCRC thus explicitly recognises the difficulties of obtaining child support in cross-border circumstances—difficulties which by and large will be felt not only by the child, but also by the custodial parent who may be seeking support on behalf of the child—and mandates that States find international legal solutions in this respect. The 2007 Child Support Convention should be considered a fundamental contemporary tool in fulfilling this specific obligation of the UNCRC. More generally, the Convention is an exciting opportunity for the international community to build upon the rights affirmed in a number of key human rights instruments,[32] and also to support other modern United Nations Declarations and initiatives concerning the 'Right to Development', improvements in global standards of living and the eradication of poverty.[33] Scholars have noted that 'neither the Committee on the Rights of the Child nor state parties to the [UN]CRC have adequately addressed the question of children's economic and social rights and eliminating child poverty as a core obligation of states.'[34] The 2007 Child Support Convention is an important opportunity for States to demonstrate a strong commitment in this area.

IV. The Economics of Child Support and Maintenance

A. Government Perspectives

In addition to implementing their international (and/or national) human rights obligations and policy commitments, there are a number of broader economic calculations governments might make in designing and operating their national maintenance programmes, including those which address the recovery of maintenance from abroad. The collection of maintenance payments can, in some circumstances, replace governmental social security and welfare payments or, as the case may be, serve as an important supplement to the same. In aggregate, vast sums of money are implicated in owed child support and other family maintenance, reaching billions of dollars per year. For example, Australian national authorities reported working with separated parents to transfer $AUD 3.24 billion in child support for the year of 2011–12.[35] In the United States, it is reported that approximately $USD 27 billion in child support is collected and distributed annually.[36] To put these numbers in some kind of perspective, it is estimated by the World Bank that total global

[32] Most prominently the 1966 Covenant and the UNCRC, but also regional instruments such as the Additional Protocol to the American Convention on Human Rights in the Area of Economic, Social and Cultural Rights (Protocol of San Salvador), the Council of Europe European Social Charter of 1961 (rev 1966), and other instruments.

[33] Eg, the United Nations Declaration on Social Progress and Development, General Assembly, Resolution 2542 (XXIV) of 11 December 1969; the United Nations Declaration on the Right to Development, General Assembly, Resolution 41/128 of 4 December 1986; the United Nations Millennium Declaration, General Assembly, Resolution 55/2 of 18 September 2000, etc.

[34] Libal and Neubeck (n 24) 175–76.

[35] Australian Department of Human Services Annual Report, 2011–12, 135 and 152, Table 16 (available at www.humanservices.gov.au/corporate/publications-and-resources/annual-report/resources/1112/ (accessed November 2013)).

[36] As reported by the Office of Child Support Enforcement (OCSE) for the year of 2010 (see www.acf.hhs.gov/programs/css/about (accessed November 2013)).

migrant remittance flows to developing nations should reach $USD 414 billion in 2013 (see Section C below).[37]

Governments around the world have realised the importance of this policy area, and have invested in child support and family maintenance programmes in order to more fully assist parents and children in particular to establish and collect owed maintenance. Interestingly, various jurisdictions seem to evidence different 'rates of return' in terms of government monies invested in such programmes and maintenance collected: in the United States, the ratio is approximately 1:5;[38] Canada (British Columbia) reports that $CAD 10.83 is collected for every dollar invested (a ratio of approximately 1:11);[39] and, in Norway, each 1 NOK collected costs 0.035 NOK in governmental investment (a ratio of 1:29).[40] For the Australian programme, while a ratio of investment to return is not readily available, since the national Child Support Scheme started in 1988, it is reported that parents have transferred 96.9 per cent of all liabilities raised—an extremely high collection/enforcement rate.[41] However, although based on officially reported data, these figures have not been standardised among the various jurisdictions as to methodology, exact definitions of terms, unique national challenges, and other issues which would allow for a reliable comparison among domestic systems. Further study and analysis would be necessary (and could be highly worthwhile) in order to make more accurate comparisons of the relative efficiency of national maintenance systems, and the specific challenges that each State may face.

Nonetheless, from the above rough statistics, and indeed, from the descriptions of the various operators and users in the various jurisdictions, maintenance systems which are of a more 'administrative' nature (eg those which have been developed in Norway, Australia, etc), as opposed to traditional court-based systems, seem to get the most 'return on investment' of public monies. It is hoped that the 2007 Child Support Convention will invite a range of domestic reforms for the more efficient recovery of maintenance, motivated in particular by the default obligation of States Parties to provide free legal assistance, if needed, for child support applications made by creditors (including enforcement and appeal procedures):[42] this could become an expensive obligation if States do not transition to less expensive ways to process maintenance applications. Chapter VI of the Convention, concerning the enforcement of maintenance decisions, also contains provisions (in particular Article 34) which are expected to push national systems towards making more effective enforcement measures available domestically. If national reforms are indeed catalysed through the application of the 2007 Child Support Convention, this should also help with the more

[37] *Migration and Remittance Flows: Recent Trends and Outlook, 2013–2016*, Migration and Remittances Team, Development Prospects Group, World Bank, 2 October 2013 (available at www.worldbank.org (accessed November 2013)).

[38] See OCSE Annual Reports to Congress, Fiscal Year 2009 and Fiscal Year 2011, Preliminary Report (available at www.acf.hhs.gov/programs/css/resource/fy2009-annual-report and www.acf.hhs.gov/programs/css/resource/fy2011-preliminary-report (both accessed November 2013)).

[39] See the British Columbia Family Maintenance Enforcement Program Annual Report of October 2012, 24. It is reported that yearly operational costs were $CAD 17,564,060 and collection was $CAD 190,203,137 (available at www.fmep.gov.bc.ca/resources/information/ (accessed November 2013)).

[40] These figures were verbally reported at the March 2013 Heidelberg Conference plenary proceedings by Norwegian governmental officials. For more on Norway, see also Jorid Saue, Floor de Jongh Bekkali, Elisabeth Sættem and Britt Rustad, ch 11 of this volume.

[41] Australian Department of Human Services Annual Report (n 35) 151.

[42] The Convention sets out the obligation in Art 15(1), and qualifies that free legal assistance need not be provided 'if and to the extent that the procedures for that State enable the applicant to make the case without the need for such assistance' (Art 14(3)).

efficient recovery of maintenance in purely national cases in jurisdictions which have not yet invested in building effective national child support and maintenance systems.[43]

B. Perspectives of Creditors and Debtors

For creditors in particular, the 2007 Child Support Convention holds the promise of greatly decreased transaction costs in the recovery of maintenance from abroad or, more dramatically, accessible mechanisms for the recovery of maintenance in cross-border circumstances where previously there was no hope. The effective access to procedures and free legal assistance provisions of the Convention were carefully designed to ensure that as many creditors as possible, regardless of financial means, could use the new international system.[44] Likewise, the range of specifically enumerated Central Authority duties to assist with various aspects of applications available under the Convention (and including such procedures as advance provisional measures, enforcement and ongoing transfer of funds), seek to 'level the playing field' for the cross-border recovery of child support.

The protection of the rights of the maintenance debtor is also crucial, and the Convention provides for several important debtor applications for recognition and modification of a maintenance decision.[45] Central Authorities must equally help debtors, and a number of provisions related to access to justice, including effective access to procedures, are also applicable to debtors.[46] Amicable solutions are encouraged under the Convention, and Central Authorities must assist in this respect.[47]

Thus, if established and modified maintenance amounts are reasonable and sensitive to typical challenges debtors may face (per applicable law and the judgment of national competent authorities establishing or modifying the maintenance), the Convention should also have a positive effect on those owing maintenance, meanwhile helping to shift societal norms of parental accountability and engagement. Contributing to the upbringing of one's child should be a positive experience, inculcating a sense of responsibility, involvement in a child's life and satisfaction as a debtor sees the tangible results of support over time for the child (eg good health, educational and extra-curricular opportunities, etc).

C. General International Development and Poverty Reduction Perspectives

It has been interesting to observe that a number of countries currently on the Official Development Aid (ODA) list[48] are 'early signers' of the Convention.[49] Such enthusiasm

[43] The Permanent Bureau has already been informed of several plans for domestic legislative reforms in the area of maintenance inspired by the 2007 Child Support Convention. However, such domestic legislative projects, of course, also take time and resources, and require strong political leadership at the national level.

[44] A Borrás and J Degeling with the assistance of W Duncan and P Lortie, 'Explanatory Report on the Convention on the International Recovery of Child Support and Other Forms of Family Maintenance' (The Hague: Permanent Bureau of the Hague Conference on Private International Law, 2009) para 357.

[45] Art 10(2).

[46] See the Explanatory Report (n 44) paras 221 and 383.

[47] Art 6(2)(d).

[48] See the list of ODA Recipients, established by the Development Assistance Committee of the OECD (available at www.oecd.org/dac/stats/daclist (accessed November 2013)).

[49] Eg Albania, Burkina Faso, Bosnia and Herzegovina and Ukraine.

for the 2007 Child Support Convention even before it has gained significant momentum for widespread global ratification/accession,[50] in addition to underlining a commitment to the rights of children and other maintenance creditors, may also demonstrate that there is awareness that cross-border maintenance can be a type of 'international remittance', transferring funds from more mature economies to developing countries. For example, the 2007 Child Support Convention may be especially helpful with respect to parents who live or have migrated abroad for employment opportunities, but have ceased to pay (or never intended to pay) support to their child/children or other dependents.

The overall societal benefits of international migrant remittances have been well-studied in World Bank and other academic literature.[51] Like child support or family maintenance, international migrant remittances often involve small amounts of money, sent periodically on a regular basis, and directed at family or community members. International migrant remittances from abroad have been found to have the potential to be a stable and even counter-cyclical income for a receiving nation.[52] Remittances may produce a 'macroeconomic multiplier effect' in the receiving economy, and tangibly help to reduce poverty in recipient countries.[53] Such remittances are associated with increased household investments in education, entrepreneurship and health—all areas of 'high social return'.[54]

Another interesting perspective is the gendered aspect of (international) maintenance recovery as a type of remittance, if, as has been the traditional norm, it is the case that much child support is directed at female-headed single parent families. As UN Women has recently noted, 'economies rebound faster from crisis when responses focus on women's needs',[55] due to, among other things, their still-dominant child-care roles and resultant investment in areas of high social return.[56] Research has noted mothers' differential spending patterns on children, and the benefit to children which flows from patterns of many women's approaches to 'household accounting'.[57]

Furthermore, when iSupport is developed, it is planned that such a system will expedite international monetary transfers (with a scheme to reduce transfer fees), decreasing the transaction costs associated with such international currency flows. In the field of international migrant remittances, it has been noted that the high transaction costs charged by middlemen for transferring remittances can diminish the positive effects

[50] Widespread global ratifications of and accessions to the 2007 Child Support Convention are expected to gain momentum after economically and geographically significant jurisdictions become States Parties to the instrument: see (n 10).

[51] For a useful overview see D Ratha, 'Leveraging Remittances for Development' in *Policy Brief: Program on Migrants, Migration and Development* (Washington, Migration Policy Institute, June 2007). See also Ann Laquer Estin, ch 8 of this volume for a more in-depth analysis of the issue as it relates to maintenance.

[52] Ratha (n 51) 3.

[53] Ibid 3–5.

[54] Ibid 6.

[55] See UN Women press release and research materials available at www.unwomen.org/co/news/stories/2013/1/economies-rebound-faster-from-crisis (accessed November 2013).

[56] See also speech by Michelle Bachelet, then-Under-Secretary-General of the United Nations and Executive Director of UN Women, at the economics symposium 'Critical Perspectives on Financial and Economic Crises: Why Gender Matters' 21 January 2013 (available at ibid), noting that '[s]ocial protection has helped to increase resilience against economic shocks, contributing to accelerated recovery and relieving more people of poverty and deprivation'.

[57] See WiSE (Women in Scotland's Economy Research Centre) and Save the Children, Briefing Sheet: Child Poverty and Mothers' Employment Patterns—Exploring Trends (September 2012).

of these cross-border transfers.[58] Under the 2007 Child Support Convention, States are obligated to give the highest priority to the international transfer of maintenance payments.[59]

However, it is extremely important to note, of course, that the collection of child support and other forms of family maintenance is not a 'silver bullet' solution—nationally or internationally—that will single-handedly resolve child or single-parent family poverty.[60] All needs of children or single-parent families in poverty cannot be fulfilled simply by looking to private debtors, for example, if the debtors themselves are poor or impecunious, and/or lack meaningful work opportunities. Governments must also invest in child poverty reduction from public funds and have other policy strategies, as indeed is clearly recognised in Article 27(3) of the UNCRC.[61]

Child support and family maintenance, nevertheless, as acknowledged by the UNCRC, are one important piece in the puzzle, and regular child support payments have been seen to make a significant difference in bringing families above the poverty line or to contribute to closing the poverty gap,[62] speaking to the reality that a 'larger proportion of women and children live in poverty following divorce'.[63] Scholars have suggested the effective and pro-active coordination of child support and public assistance programmes as a way to meaningfully address child poverty and the impoverishment of (predominantly female) single-parent head of households.[64]

[58] See Ratha (n 51) 10, noting that '[t]he cost of sending remittances tends to be high and regressive' and that a typical migrant may send 'about $200 or less per transaction' for which transfer operators might charge flat fees representing 10 to 20% of amounts transferred. Like migrant remittances, maintenance amounts, paid periodically, can often be relatively small amounts.

[59] Art 35.

[60] Indeed, some have offered strong criticism of national approaches to child support policies which they perceive as an intentional distraction from broader efforts to address child poverty more comprehensively. See, eg, M Shaffer, 'Canada's New Child Support Guidelines: Do They Fulfill Canada's International Obligations to Children?' in I Merali and V Oosterveld (eds), *Giving Meaning to Economic, Social and Cultural Rights* (Philadelphia, University of Pennsylvania Press, 2001).

[61] See also minimum core obligations of States Parties to the UNCRC with regard to provision of 'essential foodstuffs, equal access to primary health care, basic shelter and housing, social security or social assistance coverage, family protection, and basic education', cited by Libal and Neubeck (n 24) 177.

[62] See statistics cited, eg, in M Cancian and D R Meyer, *Child Support in the United States: An Uncertain and Irregular Income Source?* (April 2005) Institute for Research on Poverty and Discussion Paper No 1298-05, 15. Recent research focusing on Colombia has found that 32 per cent of poor families that received child support were brought out of poverty, and that child support had even greater effects on extreme poverty. L Cuesta and DR Meyer, 'The Role of Child Support in the Economic Wellbeing of Custodial-Mother Families in Less Developed Countries: The Case of Colombia' (2014) *International Journal of Law, Policy and The Family*, 1–17, at 1.

[63] Shaffer (n 60) 124, quoting Federal, Provincial and Territorial Family Law Committee, Department of Justice, Canada, *Child Support: Public Discussion Paper* (Ottawa, Government of Canada, 1991) 3–4.

[64] See R Clarke, T Robinson and J Sealy-Burke, 'Gender Analysis of Child Support in the Caribbean: Legal, Socio-economic and Cultural Issues for Consideration' in M Shivdas and S Coleman (eds), *Without Prejudice: CEDAW and the Determination of Women's Rights in a Legal and Cultural Context* (London, Commonwealth Secretariat, 2010). See also the Council of Europe Parliamentary Assembly Recommendation 869 (1979) on payment by the state of advances on child maintenance.

V. Maximising the Impact of the 2007 Child Support Convention

The 2007 Child Support Convention, as a modern, comprehensive and unified system for the cross-border recovery of child support and other forms of family maintenance, holds great promise to tangibly improve the lives of children and other creditors of family maintenance around the world. The question remains, however, as to how to achieve the full potential of the instrument, and to maximise its effects.

First, as with other Hague Conventions, which also tend to be rather technical instruments within the specialised area of private international law, promotion of the Convention is of paramount importance. National policymakers must first simply know of the existence of the Convention, and also be informed of its concrete benefits and special features. Much promotion can be effected by way of the Hague Conference regional offices in Latin America and Asia, and also through partner networks of experts and practitioners in the maintenance field, such as those present at the March 2013 Heidelberg Conference.[65]

States contemplating joining the Convention must also be informed of the tools and resources to assist with its implementation, such as the Implementation Checklist[66] published by the Hague Conference, and possible technical assistance from the Permanent Bureau, as far as resources of the Hague Conference permit, or provided by other experts, such as those present at the Heidelberg Conference.[67] Much advance work has been done to assist with the effective implementation and operation of the 2007 Child Support Convention: for example, the development of standardised mandatory and recommended forms for applications under the Convention, the (electronic) Country Profile on national law and procedure, the Caseworker's Practical Handbook[68] and the iSupport project. Prospective Contracting States must be made aware of these resources, and how they can be fully employed. Also, as has been the case with other Hague Conventions, States which have completed implementation may wish to participate in a 'buddy system' to assist new or potential Contracting States.

The provision of technical assistance to States which lack capacity or resources to implement the 2007 Child Support Convention, as has been the case with the 1993 Hague Intercountry Adoption Convention,[69] might prove particularly important for some individual States to ratify or accede to the Convention.[70] However, a key challenge in the provision of technical assistance to States which request such help is the availability of

[65] See Conclusions and Recommendations Nos 1 and 2 (*Recovery of Maintenance in the European Union and Worldwide: Conclusions and Next Steps of the Heidelberg Conference from 5 to 8 March 2013*), affirming the conference's commitment to engage with the international community and to mobilise support for the effective implementation of the 2007 Child Support Convention. See www.heidelberg-conference2013.de/tl_files/downloads-papers/downloads%20ab%2031_07_2013/C+R_Heidelberg_Conference_2013_final.pdf (accessed December 2013).

[66] *Implementation Checklist 2007 Child Support Convention* (Prel Doc No 6 (rev) of May 2010), available on the Hague Conference website, www.hcch.net.

[67] See Conclusion and Recommendation No 2 (n 65).

[68] All available free of charge on the Hague Conference website, www.hcch.net.

[69] The Hague Convention of 29 May 1993 on Protection of Children and Co-operation in Respect of Intercountry Adoption.

[70] See n 12.

funds. The international community might consider establishing a trust fund or other funding mechanism for the provision of such important support to States in relation to the Hague Children's Conventions in particular.[71]

Subsequent to ratification of or accession to the 2007 Child Support Convention, the operation of the instrument must be monitored and reviewed. The Convention itself provides for Special Commission meetings to review its practical operation,[72] where officials from Contracting States can convene in order to share best practices and discuss operational challenges. The network of international child support and family maintenance professionals established by the March 2013 Heidelberg Conference and subsequent meetings should also assist greatly in building expertise, diagnosing problems and finding solutions to operational issues under the Convention.

As mentioned above, it is hoped that the 2007 Child Support Convention will serve to catalyse national reforms in the child support and maintenance area. At root, the Convention is only as good as the national systems which apply and operate the instrument, and thus progress in making national systems more effective is crucial to the overall success of the Convention. National awareness-raising and outreach to creditors[73] and debtors is also fundamental. Creditors in particular must be made aware of their rights and the mechanisms which are available to them. Debtors must be sensitised to the importance of child support and other forms of maintenance, in order that rates of voluntary payment increase, and a constructive social stigma is created around the non-payment of duly established maintenance obligations.

In short, the 2007 Child Support Convention represents a unique opportunity for the international community to give life to a number of important international human rights obligations and policy objectives concerning children and vulnerable families, in connection with a vibrant network of global maintenance experts whose actions seek to ensure that:

> both governments and the public understand the *importance of child support* and other forms of family maintenance to families around the world, and the positive impact that maintenance has upon the lives of children and their emotional, physical, spiritual and moral well-being.[74]

[71] Eg the Universal Periodic Review Voluntary Fund for Financial and Technical Assistance established by the United Nations Human Rights Council in 2007 for the purpose of strengthening compliance of individual States with international human rights obligations.

[72] Art 54.

[73] Conclusion and Recommendation No 22 (n 65), encourages implementing strategies that 'ensure that the public knows of the existence of [the 2007 Child Support Convention] so that families in need will receive assistance in recovering child support and other forms of family maintenance in cross-border circumstances.'

[74] Conclusion and Recommendation No 23 (n 65).

8

Migration, Remittances and Child Support

ANN LAQUER ESTIN

I. Introduction

Private individuals send many billions of dollars to family members living in other countries every year on a voluntary basis, most of it to developing nations, with the majority of these payments intended as family support. As the Hague Family Maintenance Convention comes into effect,[1] with its ambitious system for cross-border cooperation in the determination and enforcement of child support obligations, a careful consideration of predominant migration patterns and the voluntary international financial transfers known as remittances may be helpful in predicting where the Convention could be particularly useful. Such a comparison may also serve to motivate countries with significant remittance receipts to take the steps required to develop and improve their own child support enforcement systems so that they can ratify the Convention.

Data on global migration and remittances illustrate the patterns of movement between countries, mapping the corridors where personal financial transfers are particularly important and suggesting where cross-border child support programmes might be useful. Just as developing nations have adopted other policies designed to encourage emigrants to send remittances, these countries may look to the Hague system as a complement to the current system of voluntary global financial transfers and a possible vehicle to improve efficiency and greatly lower costs of all forms of transnational transfer of family support payments.

II. Remittances and Financial Transfers

The World Bank estimates that $440 billion was transferred across borders by individuals in 2010, with the largest share—$325 billion—sent to developing countries. The data show that remittance levels have increased significantly over the past decade, and were three times the total amount of official foreign aid in 2010. In many countries, these transfers make a significant contribution to gross domestic product (GDP), and governments may

[1] Hague Convention of 23 November 2007 on the International Recovery of Child Support and Other Forms of Family Maintenance.

work to encourage the inflow of foreign currency.[2] According to the World Bank, personal transfers proved to be more resilient than flows of foreign direct investment and private debt and equity investment during the 2008 global financial crisis. Remittance flows remained strong following the crisis, even as current migration levels declined.[3]

In compiling these statistics, the World Bank includes three types of financial transfers. 'Workers' remittances' are the portion of income that a migrant sends back to his or her country of origin in the form of funds or goods, sometimes referred to as 'personal transfers'.[4] The remittance statistics also include compensation paid to foreign employees who spent less than a year in the host country before returning home, and migrants' transfers of capital. Global financial transfers are difficult to measure, and the official statistics capture only the portion of these transfers that are sent through formal banking channels. The actual level of personal financial transfers is therefore likely to be much larger.

Anthropological studies offer an interesting counterpoint to the economic data, focusing on the financial strategies of transnational family groups. The studies suggest that decisions regarding migration are often made jointly by household members, and describe how the financial transfers that follow are embedded in a cultural and family context.[5] Typically, migrants send remittances frequently, in small amounts, through a variety of channels, including networks of traditional brokers as well as transfer services such as Western Union or MoneyGram and financial institutions such as banks and credit unions.[6] Many of these transfer systems involve high transaction costs and have only recently become subject to significant regulation.[7]

In receiving countries where transfers form a high percentage of GDP, their major purpose is to pay for immediate consumption needs of family members or related items such as children's school fees. If resources are sufficient, transfers may be saved for purposes such as building a house or starting a business in the migrant's home country. Looking at the United States and Latin America, a study prepared for the Congressional

[2] World Bank, *Migration and Remittances Factbook 2011*, 2nd edn (Washington DC, International Bank for Reconstruction and Development/World Bank, 2011). See generally D Yang, 'Migrant Remittances' (2011) *Journal of Economic Perspectives* 129, 131–32; E Rosser, 'Immigrant Remittances' (2008) *Connecticut Law Review* 1; see also A Chander, 'Homeward Bound' (2006) *New York University Law Review* 60.

[3] I Sirkeci et al, 'Introduction: Remittance Flows and Practices During the Crisis' in I Sirkeci et al (eds), *Migration and Remittances during the Global Financial Crisis and Beyond* (Washington DC, International Bank for Reconstruction and Development/ World Bank 2012) 1.

[4] See World Bank (n 2) xvi–xvii. Yang offers this definition: 'Remittances are household income received from abroad, resulting mainly from the international migration of workers. Remittances may be sent as cash or in kind, and may flow through a variety of formal or informal channels' Yang (n 2) 132.

[5] Eg M Sana and D Massey, 'Household Composition, Family Migration and Community Context: Migrant Remittances in Four Countries' (2005) *Social Science Quarterly* 509; see generally J Glick, 'Connecting Complex Processes: A Decade of Research on Immigrant Families' (2010) *Journal of Marriage and Family* 498, 507. See also eg M Binci and G Giannelli, 'Internal vs. International Migration: Impacts of Remittances on Child Well-Being in Vietnam' (2012) IZA Discussion Paper No 6523; F Magunha et al, 'Remittance Strategies of Zimbabweans in Northern England' (University of Leeds, School of Geography, 2009); I Mara et al, 'Analysis of Literature on the Effects of Remittances on Education and Health of Family Members Left Behind' (University of Fribourg, Regional Research Promotion Programme in the Western Balkans, 2012); T Nguyen and R Purnamasari, 'Impacts of International Migration and Remittances on Child Outcomes and Labor Supply in Indonesia: How Does Gender Matter?' (2011) World Bank Policy Research Working Paper 5591.

[6] Yang (n 2) 142–45. See also Rosser (n 2) 6–7, 29–32.

[7] In the United States, disclosure requirements for electronic remittance transfers were mandated by the 2010 Dodd-Frank Act and take effect in October 2013. See 15 USC § 1693o-1(a). See generally US Consumer Financial Protection Bureau, 'Report on remittance transfers' (July 2011). Other countries and the World Bank have also implemented transparency standards; see ibid 22.

Budget Office found that consumption was the primary purpose for which remitters sent funds to Mexico (70 per cent), Nicaragua (81 per cent) and the Dominican Republic (89 per cent), with the remainder of transfers intended for both consumption needs and asset accumulation.[8]

Remittance patterns are different for higher-income countries. The CBO study found that more than 80 per cent of private financial inflows to low- and middle-income countries were personal transfers, as opposed to employee compensation (17 per cent) or capital transfer (two per cent). High income countries were much more likely to have inflows of employee compensation (65 per cent) or capital transfer (16 per cent).[9] Notably, the World Bank data show that Germany and Spain are among the top ten countries in terms of remittances sent, and also among the top ten for remittances received. France also receives and sends remittances at a high level.[10]

Global financial transfers come primarily, but not exclusively, from migrant households. A survey conducted by the United States Census Bureau in 2008 questioned 50,000 households regarding international financial transfers, noting differences between the total sample and households with a foreign-born adult member. Of the total, five per cent sent money abroad to friends and relatives and one per cent received funds. Of the 'foreign-born' households, however, 27 per cent sent money abroad and four per cent received funds. The foreign-born households also sent remittances more frequently, and in larger amounts.[11] Some migrants send very large portions of their earnings, often at considerable personal sacrifice.[12]

III. Global Migration Patterns

Remittances and other personal financial transfers typically run in the opposite direction from migration. Global migration statistics illustrate the broad scope and scale of these patterns.[13] More than 215 million people—about three per cent of the world population—currently live outside the country of their birth. The United States has the largest numbers, with a total of 42.8 million immigrants, followed by Russia (12.3 million), Germany (10.8 million), Saudi Arabia (7.3 million) and Canada (7.2 million).[14] Migration patterns

[8] US Congressional Budget Office, 'Migrants' Remittances and Related Economic Flows' (February 2011) (CBO study).

[9] Ibid.

[10] Individuals in Germany sent $15.9 billion and received $11.6 billion; in Spain individuals sent $12.6 billion and received $10.2 billion, and in France individuals sent $5.2 billion and received $15.9 billion. A number of detailed case studies are presented in Sirkeci et al (eds) (n 3).

[11] E Grieco et al, 'Who in the United States Sends and Receives Remittances? An Initial Analysis of the Monetary Transfer Data from the August 2008 CPS Migration Supplement' (2010) US Census Bureau Population Division, Working Paper No 87.

[12] Yang (n 2) 133–34.

[13] These numbers are drawn from World Bank (n 2), and International Organization for Migration (IOM), *World Migration Report 2010: The Future of Migration: Building Capacities for Change* (Geneva, IOM, 2010). See also US Census Bureau, 'The Foreign-Born Population in the United States: 2010' (American Community Survey Reports, May 2012).

[14] The next five largest migration destination countries are the UK (7.0 million), Spain (6.9 million), France (6.7 million), Australia (5.5 million) and India (5.4 million).

are complex, and many countries have high rates of both emigration and immigration. Notably, India, Russia and the UK are among the top ten both as migration destination countries and origin countries.[15]

In general, the primary driver of this movement is an income differential across borders, and it is not exclusively a north-south phenomenon. The data show very high levels of migration between developing countries, with foreign born individuals forming a large majority of the population in countries such as Qatar (87 per cent), United Arab Emirates (70 per cent), and Kuwait (69 per cent). Global migration follows clear patterns, with the largest corridor linking Mexico and the United States, which has 11.6 million residents who were born in Mexico. Russia and the Ukraine form another large corridor, where migration has moved in both directions: 3.7 million people born in Russia live in the Ukraine, and 3.6 million people born in the Ukraine live in Russia. The data also show large movements from Bangladesh to India (3.3 million) and Turkey to Germany (2.7 million). Many people born in India now live in the United Arab Emirates (2.2 million), the United States (1.7 million) and Saudi Arabia (1.5 million). In addition to its immigrants from Mexico and India, the United States has particularly large population groups born in China (1.7 million) and the Philippines (1.7 million).[16]

Looking at the remittance and migration data together, the linkage is clear. Four of the top five migration destination countries—the United States, Russia, Germany and Saudi Arabia—are also among the top five sending countries for financial transfers. There is a similar correspondence between countries of emigration and receipt of financial transfers, with Mexico, India, and China all appearing among the top five on both lists.[17]

These migration data aggregate very different types of cross-border movement, including documented and undocumented, temporary and permanent relocation, and solitary migrants as well as those joining or bringing family members. With these different types of movement, there are different family issues for married and unmarried partners, parents and children, and extended family members.[18] Many of these scenarios, however, give rise to transnational family relationships that may generate international remittance flows or, if transfers are not made on a voluntary basis, may create a need for cross-border child support enforcement services.

[15] India had 5.4 million immigrants, largely from Bangladesh, and 11.4 million emigrants, for a net emigration of 6 million people. Russia had 12.3 million immigrants, and 11.1 million emigrants, for a net immigration of 1.2 million people. The UK had 7.0 million immigrants and 4.7 million emigrants, for a net immigration of 2.3 million people.

[16] Other large immigration pathways as of 2010 included Russia to Kazakhstan (2.2 million), West Bank and Gaza to Syria (1.5 million), Indonesia to Malaysia (1.4 million) and Burkina Faso to Côte d'Ivoire (1.3 million).

[17] The top ten emigration countries as of 2010 were Mexico (11.9 million), India (11.4 million), Russian Federation (11.1 million), China (8.3 million), Ukraine (6.6 million), Bangladesh (5.4 million), Pakistan (4.7 million), UK (4.7 million), Philippines (4.3 million) and Turkey (4.3 million). The top ten remittance receiving countries in 2010 were India ($55 billion) China ($51 billion), Mexico ($22.6 billion), Philippines ($21.3 billion), France ($15.9 billion), Germany ($11.6 billion), Bangladesh ($11.1 billion), Belgium ($10.4 billion), Spain ($10.2 billion) and Nigeria ($10.0 billion).

[18] The IOM identifies 'at least four categories of family migration: family reunification, family formation (or marriage migration), the migration of the entire family, and migration by sponsored family members.' IOM (n 13) 62–64. See also IOM, 'World Migration Report: 2008: Managing Labour Mobility in the Evolving Global Economy' (2008) 151–73.

IV. Public and Private Support for Families

Under the United Nations Convention on the Rights of the Child (CRC), every child has the right to a standard of living 'adequate for the child's physical, mental, spiritual, moral and social development'.[19] Parents or other adults responsible for a child have 'the primary responsibility to secure, within their abilities and financial capacities, the conditions of living necessary for the child's development', and governments must take appropriate measures to assist parents in case of need, particularly with respect to nutrition, clothing and housing.[20]

Child maintenance laws around the world reflect this duality, typically drawing financial support for children from both public and private sources. Traditional family law principles allocate primary support obligations between a child's parents, according to their respective abilities to provide for their offspring; public law and social welfare systems assure a more basic level of support for children, particularly those in poor families. Comparative assessments of child support systems reveal significant differences in the policies adopted in different countries,[21] and many families have support needs met by a combination of private and public sources. The proportion of public and private support for children around the world therefore depends on the economic circumstances of particular families, legal and public policies adopted at the national and local level, and the resources of the governments responsible for those children. The current global economic crisis has made all of these challenges more difficult, and is likely to reduce the levels of public support for children, and, accordingly, increase the need for the assistance of child support enforcement systems.[22]

Public family support and antipoverty programmes are local and national rather than international, and nations make very different choices regarding the structure and funding for these efforts.[23] The United States, for example, places greater emphasis on private support, and ties public financial support for children and families to broader policies regarding family structure, taxation, employment and poverty. Families at all income levels have access to public services for determination and enforcement of private child support obligations, with these services largely structured and funded by the national government.

[19] CRC, Art 27(1), GA Res 44/25, annex, UN GAOR, 44th Sess, Supp No 49 at 167, UN Doc A/4449 (1989). Except for the United States and Somalia, all countries of the world have ratified, acceded to, or succeeded to the CRC. The United States signed the CRC in 1995, obligating it to refrain from acts that would defeat the object and purposes of the Treaty, and it ratified two important Protocols to the CRC in 2002.

[20] CRC, Art 27(2)–(3).

[21] See M Maclean and A Warman, 'A Comparative Approach to Child Support Systems: Legal Rules and Social Policies' and J Eekelaar, 'Child Support as Distributive and Commutative Justice: The United Kingdom Experience', both in JT Oldham and M Melli (eds), *Child Support: The Next Frontier* (Ann Arbor, University of Michigan Press, 2000) 166 and 151 respectively.

[22] P Lortie, 'The 2007 Hague Child Support Convention and its Protocol on the Law Applicable to Maintenance Obligations: Challenges and Opportunities for Domestic Reforms' (2012) *International Family Law* 118, 119; P Parkinson, 'Another Inconvenient Truth: Fragile Families and the Looming Financial Crisis for the Welfare State' (2011) *Family Law Quarterly* 329, 340–43, 346–47.

[23] See generally UNICEF, *Measuring Child Poverty: New League Tables of Child Poverty in the World's Richest Countries* (Florence, UNICEF Innocenti Research Centre, Report Card 10, 2012); OECD, *Doing Better for Families* (2011), available at www.oecd.org/social/soc/doingbetterforfamilies.htm; I Garfinkel et al, 'A Re-examination of Welfare States and Inequality in Rich Nations: How In-Kind Transfers and Indirect Taxes Change the Story' (2006) *Journal of Policy Analysis and Management* 897–919.

This system is intended to reduce child poverty by assuring that private support payments are available whenever possible, and to recoup funds paid out as public assistance through the Temporary Assistance to Needy Families (TANF) programme, Medicaid, and the Supplemental Nutrition Assistance Program (SNAP).[24] The scale of the US child support enforcement programme is enormous, and households that have never qualified for public assistance comprise a large portion of the total caseload.[25] At the margins, to the extent that children have non-residential parents with employment or another source of income, the programme has helped to keep children out of poverty.[26]

At the international level, the members of the Hague Conference on Private International Law concluded the 2007 Convention on the International Recovery of Child Support and Other Forms of Family Maintenance after five years of international negotiation. In comparison with previous multilateral agreements on these issues, the new Convention imposes much more extensive public obligations, through a system of administrative cooperation between Central Authorities and the requirement that Contracting States provide free legal services for establishment and enforcement of support in international cases.[27] An important aspect of the Convention will be implementation of efficient and cost-effective systems and procedures to locate parents, determine support levels, and collect and transmit payments across borders.[28]

International law separates the public and private aspects of child support, and the new Hague system applies only to support owed by private individuals.[29] Public bodies may use the system to seek reimbursement for assistance provided in place of private maintenance.[30] The costs and benefits of this programme are asymmetrical, however, in the sense that its costs fall on governments and the benefits accrue primarily to children and families. These costs may discourage accession to the Convention, particularly for countries that do not already have an administrative infrastructure for establishing and enforcing child support.[31] To the extent that participation is likely to generate substantial

[24] Building an effective system for interstate child support enforcement was central to the project, and helped to lay the groundwork in the United States for international cooperation through bilateral agreements at the state and national level. See M Smith, 'Child Support at Home and Abroad: Road to The Hague' (2009) *Family Law Quarterly* 37, 54–58.

[25] US Office of Child Support Enforcement, *Fiscal Year 2011 Preliminary Report* (October 2012) (total of 15.8 million cases, including 8.8 million current and former public assistance cases, with total support collections of $31.2 billion).

[26] E Sorenson and C Zibman, 'Child Support Offers Some Protection Against Poverty' The Urban Institute, New Federalism: National Survey of America's Families, Series B, No B-10 (March 2000).

[27] Maintenance Convention, Arts 4–17, previous Hague Conventions, and the 1956 UN Convention on the Recovery Abroad of Maintenance (New York Convention), see generally W Duncan, 'The New Hague Child Support Convention: Goals and Outcomes of the Negotiations' (2009) *Family Law Quarterly* 1, 5–8.

[28] Eg Art 35 of the Convention. Since 2007 the Hague Conference has prepared a series of recommended forms, a Practical Handbook for Caseworkers, and a recommended Country Profile form, and plans to develop an electronic case management and communication system. See generally Lortie (n 22) 119–20.

[29] Maintenance Convention, Art 2(1) ('This Convention shall apply—a) to maintenance obligations arising from a parent-child relationship towards a person under the age of 21 years'). Note that there are significant issues regarding cross-border eligibility for public child-raising benefits in the European Union. See H Stalford, 'Old Problems, New Solutions?—EU Regulation of Cross-National Child Maintenance (2003) *Child and Family Law Quarterly* 269, 271–74.

[30] Maintenance Convention, Art 36.

[31] This was a difficult point during the negotiation of the Convention. See MH Carlson, 'United States Perspective on the New Hague Convention on the International Recovery of Child Support and Other Forms of Family Maintenance' (2009) *Family Law Quarterly* 21, 29–31; Duncan (n 27) 14.

new private revenue, roughly analogous to remittance flows, it may be worth a substantial investment of government resources to establish or improve child support enforcement systems, even in the poorest of countries, to enable ratification of the Convention.

Based on migration and remittance data, countries with large emigrant populations appear particularly likely to benefit from joining the Convention, with the prospect of a net inflow of child support funds. Additional support from non-custodial parents located in other countries should improve living standards, and may help to reduce the need for public assistance in the country where the child is habitually resident. Conversely, nations that host a large immigrant labour force may see a net outflow of child support as the system comes online. Many of these countries have already established administrative systems for establishing and enforcing support, however, and have signalled their intention to ratify. The importance of cross-border collaboration between governments to foster private family financial support gains emphasis from the CRC, which obligates States Parties to 'take all appropriate measures to secure the recovery of maintenance for the child from parents or other persons having responsibility for the child, both within the State Party and abroad.'[32] The CRC imposes a particular obligation to address circumstances in which 'the person having financial responsibility lives in a State different from that of the child' by promoting accession to international agreements—such as the new Convention—and also by making 'other appropriate arrangements' to secure payment of maintenance.[33]

V. Implementing the 2007 Convention

At the time of writing, the Convention has just come into effect amongst a small group of nations. Implementation efforts are underway in the European Union and the United States, which have signed the Convention, signalling their intention to ratify. Because the European Union and the United States receive large numbers of migrants, who make substantial financial transfers to other countries, their ratification should provide a significant incentive to other States to join as well.

Looking ahead, the data on migration and remittances suggest several distinct patterns that will be relevant. In Europe, there is a great deal of cross-border movement and a high level of economic integration.[34] Four European Union countries are among the list of sending nations with the largest annual remittances: France ($15.9 billion), Germany ($11.6 billion), Belgium ($10.4 billion) and Spain ($10.2 billion), and some portion of these funds move beyond the borders of the European Union. The inducement that EU ratification will provide to other countries in the region is suggested by the early interest expressed by Ukraine, which signed the Convention in 2010 and ratified it in 2013, and the fact that the

[32] CRC, Art 27(4).

[33] Beyond the child support system, countries might help to meet these obligations by improving the infrastructure for voluntary remittance payments, which benefit vastly more families than a system of formal support orders can reach.

[34] Ratification in the European Union follows on from implementation of internal EU Regulations on establishing and enforcing family support obligations. Council Regulation (EC) No 4/2009 of 18 December 2008 on jurisdiction, applicable law, recognition and enforcement of decisions and cooperation in matters relating to maintenance obligations, OJ 2009 L 07. See also H Stalford, *Children and the European Union* (Oxford, Hart Publishing, 2009) 122–26.

Convention came into force initially in 2013 in Norway, Albania and Bosnia-Herzegovina.[35] The substantial presence of Turkish migrants in Germany and other European countries, along with Turkey's membership of the Hague Conference and its participation in previous family law conventions, suggest that it might also find it advantageous to ratify.[36]

For the United States, which signed the Convention on the day it was concluded in 2007, support for the Convention reflects a broad national commitment to child support enforcement.[37] Many children in the United States stand to benefit from ratification of the Convention, which will improve on the patchwork of bilateral child support agreements, established at the national and state levels, which currently extend piecemeal to various European countries, numerous Canadian provinces and Mexican States, and a few other countries.[38] In addition to receiving immigrants, the United States is also a country of emigration, with at least 2.4 million people who were born in the United States now living abroad, primarily in Mexico, Canada, the UK, Germany and Australia—all countries with whom bilateral agreements have been implemented.[39] Because the United States is primarily a receiver of immigrants and a sender of remittances, however, ratification by the United States should help to make the case for joining the Convention in the many countries that send emigrants to the United States, particularly emigrants who leave without their children and other family members. This would clearly include Mexico and other countries in Latin America.

Among Hague Conference members, Australia and Canada seem likely to participate in the Convention, for the same reasons that it makes sense in Europe and the United States. Both nations are traditional countries of immigration, and have sophisticated child support systems, which include administrative cooperation in international cases. At the other end of the spectrum, China, Japan, and Russia voiced concern during the treaty negotiations about the obligations that the Convention would impose, primarily the provisions on free legal assistance and a particular procedure for simplified recognition and enforcement of maintenance decisions. These concerns were accommodated to a certain degree by the addition of what are now Articles 16 and 24, allowing a Contracting State to adopt a child-centred means test for cases involving establishment of new support orders and an alternative procedure for recognition and enforcement.[40] All three nations

[35] Regarding Albania, see (n 44).

[36] For a case study, see P Yazgan and I Sirkeci, 'Financial Crisis and Remittances from Denmark to Turkey' in Sirkeci et al (eds) (n 3) 295. Turkey has ratified or acceded to 12 Hague Conventions, including the civil procedure Conventions, the previous maintenance Conventions, and the child abduction and intercountry adoption Conventions. Turkey did not participate in the negotiations for the Maintenance Convention, however, and will need time to develop a child support enforcement infrastructure adequate to permit ratification. It will probably take at least five years before Turkey will be in a position to become a party to the Convention, see the Jean Monnet Lifelong Learning Workshop No 3 Report (2013) on Turkey available from the Centre for Private International Law, University of Aberdeen at www.abdn.ac.uk/law/research/events-150.php (accessed November 2013).

[37] See generally Carlson (n 31). Implementation in the United States will occur through federal legislation and amendments to the Uniform Interstate Family Support Act. See HR 1896, International Child Support Recovery Improvement Act, 113th Cong 1st Sess (2013).

[38] Beyond Europe and North America, the United States has bilateral agreements in effect with Australia, El Salvador and Israel. The United States has not entered into a bilateral agreement with Mexico at the national level, but many reciprocal agreements have been negotiated at the state level.

[39] World Bank (n 2). The United States makes no formal attempt to count the number of its citizens living in other countries. The US Bureau of Consular Affairs in the US State Department estimates that 7.6 million US citizens live abroad and another 65 million travel abroad annually. See www.travel.state.gov/pdf/ca_fact_sheet.pdf.

[40] Carlson (n 31) 29–31, 32–33.

are members of the Hague Conference, and have gradually embraced the other Hague Children's Conventions.[41] Like China, with its annual remittance receipts of $51 billion, the other nations at the top of the list—India ($55 billion), Mexico ($22.6 billion) and the Philippines ($21.3 billion)—are all Conference members, but will face significant challenges in implementation because they presently do not have well-established child support enforcement systems.[42] Because large numbers of individuals born in these four countries now live in the United States, and in other nations likely to ratify, there could be a significant net benefit from joining the Convention which would warrant investment in such mechanisms.

Remittances have the greatest economic impact in less-developed countries that tend to be outside the Hague network. In absolute terms, there are particularly high levels of remittances sent to Bangladesh ($11.billion) and Nigeria ($10 billion), which are not Hague Conference members and have not signed, ratified or acceded to any of the Hague conventions.[43] Of the 22 countries in which remittances represent ten per cent or more of GNP, only five are Hague Conference members: Jordan (16 per cent), Bosnia-Herzegovina (13 per cent), Serbia (13 per cent), Philippines (12 per cent) and Albania (11 per cent).[44] As noted above, Albania and Bosnia-Herzegovina have already ratified the Maintenance Convention.[45] The group includes several Caribbean and Latin American countries, which send significant numbers of emigrants to the United States and might benefit from establishing a more formal relationship for establishment and enforcement of child support as a complement to informal remittance payments.[46]

VI. Remittances and Child Support

Global migration and remittance patterns suggest the broad outlines of cross-border movement and indicate where there are likely to be significant numbers of transnational family relationships. In these corridors, personal transfers already provide a substantial

[41] China has joined the Adoption Convention, with the Abduction Convention in force for Hong Kong and Macao. Russia acceded to the Abduction Convention in 2011 and the Child Protection Convention in 2012, and signed the Adoption Convention in 2000. Japan ratified the Abduction Convention in January 2014.

[42] India and the Philippines have ratified the Adoption Convention, and Mexico has ratified both the Abduction Convention and the Adoption Convention.

[43] Although not a Hague Conference member, Burkina-Faso acceded to the child abduction and intercountry adoption Conventions during the 1990s, and was the first nation to sign the Maintenance Convention after the United States. The country has 1.0 million immigrants and 1.6 million emigrants, with most of these living in the Côte d'Ivoire. To date, it is the only low-income country that has signed the Convention.

[44] The others on this list are Tajikistan (35% of GDP), Tonga (28%), Lesotho (25%), Moldova (23%), Nepal (23%), Lebanon (22%), Samoa (22%), Honduras (19%), Guyana (17%), El Salvador (16%), Kyrgyz Republic (15%), Haiti (15%), Jamaica (14%), Bangladesh (12%), Togo (10%), Nicaragua (10%) and Guatemala (10%).

[45] Both Albania and Bosnia-Herzegovina are upper-middle income countries with large numbers of emigrants relative to national population. See R King et al, 'Gendering Migration and Remittances: Evidence from London and Northern Albania' (2006) *Population Space & Place* 409.

[46] This list includes Honduras, Guyana, El Salvador, Haiti, Jamaica, Nicaragua, and Guatemala; see (n 44). See the report on 'The Work of the Hague Conference on Private International Law and its Relevance for the Caribbean Region and Bermuda', held in Bermuda, 21–24 May 2012 in *The Judges' Newsletter* (2013) vol XIX 21–23.

amount of financial support for children, although often at a serious cost for children who remain behind when fathers and mothers are working abroad.[47]

For many reasons, child support systems will not displace voluntary remittances, not least because of the tremendous personal sacrifice and altruism that stand behind the billions of dollars sent to family members every year.[48] Children and their caretakers living in serious poverty, or in rural areas, may have difficulty finding their way to officials who can assist in obtaining free child support services abroad. Working parents who are undocumented or illegal migrants are more often employed in the underground economy, for relatively low earnings, and may be difficult to locate. To the extent that parents are regular migrants, participating in the formal economy of the place where they reside, child support establishment and enforcement becomes a more realistic possibility.

Cross-border child support will be most useful in cases of family breakdown, at the point when remittances are unlikely to continue. Divorce rates among immigrants are difficult to measure, reflecting many complex variables.[49] Rates much lower than the background rates of receiving communities would generate a large number of divorces, in light of the many millions of families concerned, and there are also reasons why rates of breakdown could be much higher for transnational and migrant families. Residential mobility has been associated with increased risks of relationship dissolution, even within a single country.[50] For transnational families, with family members living in different countries, prolonged periods of separation can take a serious toll.[51] Adults living alone at home or abroad may be drawn into new relationships, and over time migrants may stop communicating or sending money to their family at home. Families that migrate together, or form across national borders, also face unique challenges, including immigration laws that may lead to enforced separation.

Maintaining parent-child bonds across great distances is difficult, and more so after the adult relationships that nurtured those ties have ended. Norms of support and reciprocity are unlikely to operate as effectively when they are no longer reinforced by wider family and community networks. As in purely domestic situations, child support laws may help to fill the gaps that are created when parents' sense of obligation no longer produces sufficient tangible support for their children. Proceedings under the Convention are also well-adapted for cross-border family relationships that form outside the predominant migration paradigm, and outside the cultural and familial contexts that foster connections across long distances.

As more countries ratify or accede to the Maintenance Convention, opportunities may be presented to coordinate remittance and child support payments. Voluntary support transfers could conceivably be facilitated through the Central Authority system under the Convention. This could have advantages for families, particularly to the extent that transac-

[47] See V Mazzucato and D Schans, 'Transnational Families and the Well-Being of Children: Conceptual and Methodological Challenges' (2011) *Journal of Marriage and Family* 704; J Dreby, 'Children and Power in Mexican Transnational Families' (2007) *Journal of Marriage and Family* 1050.

[48] *Cf* Rosser (n 2) 10–11, 56–57.

[49] See Glick (n 5) 502–03; eg S-E Khoo and Z Zhao, 'Research Note: A Decomposition of Immigrant Divorce Rates in Australia' (2001) *Journal of Population Research* 68.

[50] See P Boyle et al, 'The Effect of Family Migration on Union Dissolution in Britain' in H Stalford et al (eds), *Gender and Migration in 21st Century Europe* (Surrey, UK, Ashgate Publishing, 2009) 11.

[51] R Frank and E Wildsmith, 'The Grass Widows of Mexico: Migration and Union Dissolution in Binational Context' (2005) *Social Forces* 919.

tion costs are subsidised or regulated. Depending on the countries and providers involved, remittance fees and foreign exchange costs may consume a significant percentage of the total transfer.[52] An alternative channel for family support payments could be helpful for transfers between less-developed countries, where transfer costs are notably higher.[53] Small remittances might be bundled and combined with child support payments before being sent to another country creating efficiencies of scale and lowering costs to individuals. To the extent that particular family corridors present specialised issues, there may be particular benefits to networking and cooperation between Central Authorities, and the nations involved might make bilateral agreements within or outside the terms of the Convention.[54]

VII. Conclusion

Statistics on migration and personal financial transfers confirm the importance of international cooperation regarding child support. The data do not reveal the family circumstances of the many millions of individuals currently living outside the countries of their birth—we do not know the numbers of children living in different countries from their parents, or the percentage of these transnational families that are still intact, in the sense that adult family members are working cooperatively to secure the best possible future for the children concerned. There are no statistics to reflect the numbers of migrants who stop sending remittances, or the dollars that might be obtained from vigorous implementation of new tools for cross-border child support enforcement. As experience in implementing the 2007 Convention is attained, and reports and data are compiled documenting case processing, a great deal of information will be gathered concerning these populations.

Child support enforcement also has the potential to bolster the impressive flow of private remittances that already run on a voluntary basis to children in many parts of the world. The existence and potential use of international enforcement measures to ensure payment of support, in and of itself, may provide an inducement for non-custodial parents to pay voluntarily and to avoid the intervention of governmental authority to enforce their parental obligations. The Permanent Bureau and member countries of the Hague Conference can benefit greatly by further study of migration and remittance patterns as they work to bring the new Convention into force, and support its adoption in countries of emigration and immigration.

[52] See US Consumer Financial Protection Bureau, *Report on Remittance Transfers* (July 2011) 12–20.

[53] See United Nations Development Programme, 'Towards Human Resilience: Sustaining MDG Progress in an Age of Economic Uncertainty' (September 2011) 135–36.

[54] Art 51 of the Convention.

9

International Maintenance Cases: Preliminary Research

HANNAH ROOTS

I. Introduction

The evolution of child support over the past four decades has seen the increasing use of data and metrics as an important driver of both policy and legislation. As child support programmes have matured, a wealth of different measures have been developed to track the effectiveness of those programmes and the impact that child support has on the lives of families and children.[1]

The development and refining of child support metrics has also enabled a focus on particular segments of the child support caseload, and with the conclusion of the 2007 Hague Convention on International Child Support and Other Forms of Family Maintenance (the 2007 Convention), international cases have become a subject of discussion within the child support community. Once the Convention comes into effect more broadly, there is expected to be substantial growth in the number of international cases, and that has led to questions about the current international maintenance caseload.

An informal survey of countries represented in the National Child Support Enforcement Association's (NCSEA) International Subcommittee in 2011 revealed that few jurisdictions[2] have systematically collected data on international child support cases, and there are differences between the data available in different countries on international cases. There have been few attempts to collect international child support caseload data with a view to finding out what commonalities or differences might exist.

[1] See eg Office of Child Support Enforcement, Administration for Children and Families, United States Department of Health and Human Services, 'FY 2011 Preliminary Report', available at www.acf.hhs.gov/programs/css/resource/fy2011-preliminary-report#fig7 (last accessed 21 December 2012).

[2] In this chapter, the term jurisdiction is used deliberately to include sub-units of a country or State. This research project collected information from individual programmes, including programmes delivered at the county, State, provincial and national level. The term country or State is used here to refer to the national entity.

Those informal conversations led to the creation of a research project to look at three very basic questions:

(1) What data about international maintenance cases are available?[3]
(2) Can that data be compared in any meaningful way to provide broader insight into international child support cases?
(3) What does the available data indicate concerning the families and cases that make up the international maintenance caseload?

In addition to the collection of 'hard data' on the international cases, it was also decided to collect qualitative information from the child support caseworkers responsible for managing international cases in the jurisdictions surveyed. The successful collection and transmission of child support depends upon these staff, and their perspective on international cases is important. The research project surveyed these caseworkers and their work to determine what does and does not work on international child support cases, and what steps could be taken to improve the management of these cases.

The overall objective was to determine what the international child support community does and does not know about international cases; and in a general sense, to find out what the cases and families look like. The collection of data and surveys in the research project resulted in preliminary conclusions, and recommendations for further research into these cases.

This chapter is divided into four sections. In the first section the methodology and a description of the data collected is presented. The second section sets out the conclusions and findings from the data. In the third section of the chapter the information and feedback received from the caseworker survey is reviewed. In the final section, the research project itself is discussed and there is a further exploration of the limitations on available data and whether the data can be compared. The final section also makes recommendations for further research.

II. Executive Summary and Highlights

The research project established that, with limitations, it is possible to collect data from different jurisdictions and to use that data to get a baseline picture of international cases. There are reliable data concerning the characteristics of families and clients receiving child support services, and, to a limited extent, the data could be compared to find similarities and differences between jurisdictions. However, the examination of more detailed data, in particular concerning payments and arrears, determined that such information was much more limited and not reliably comparable because of fundamental differences in case procedures in different programmes and the complexity of maintaining financial information.

The survey responses from caseworkers consistently showed an enthusiasm for the work, together with very similar responses in terms of the need for better technology to allow

[3] The term maintenance is used in this chapter and in our research to include both child and spousal support.

caseworkers to communicate efficiently and effectively across borders. Finally, the project provided useful experience in terms of conducting research into international cases and resulted in the development of a number of recommendations for future researchers.

A. International Caseload Highlights

(1) The size of the international caseload in the programmes responding is relatively small. With the exception of Ontario and New Zealand, these cases generally make up less than ten per cent of the overall caseload, and in most cases, amount to only one or two per cent of all cases in the caseload of the responding jurisdiction.
(2) Geographic proximity is an important factor in determining which programmes have significant numbers of cases with each other.
(3) International cases most commonly involve parents between 30 and 50 years of age, with one or two children between the ages of ten and 18.
(4) International cases are sharply divided between cases that are fully paid (no arrears) and cases where no payments have ever been made.
(5) To a large extent, the profile of an international case, on the measures looked at, resembles the profile of a domestic case.
(6) Data limitations and programme structure affected the ability of some programmes to supply comparable data.

B. Caseworker Survey Highlights

(1) Most caseworkers responding to the survey had significant experience working international cases. The median number of years of experience was seven years.
(2) Most of the caseworkers have mixed caseloads—that is, they work non-international cases as well as international cases.
(3) Communications with other programmes was the most frequently reported challenge to working these cases.
(4) The overwhelming preference of caseworkers is to communicate by email yet almost half of the respondents reported restrictions on the use of email.
(5) Obtaining clear, understandable information about what other programmes can or cannot do to assist with child support is seen as a challenge.
(6) While recognizing the challenges of working these cases, the caseworkers responding to the survey were enthusiastic and positive about their work.

C. Research Process Highlights

(1) Collecting data on international cases is possible—particularly in the area of client demographics.
(2) Whether a case is included in a programme's international caseload is a question not just of geography but also of policy. Some of the most significant differences relate to whether cases are included in the international caseload where the parents live in countries that do not have formal legal arrangements with the programme managing

the case. Research focusing on the international caseload needs to take into account that there may be cases involving a parent living in a different country that are not included in a programme's international caseload.

(3) International caseloads form a small component of the caseload in many countries, and there is rarely IT infrastructure available to produce the data required for comparative analysis.

III. Methodology

Nine child support programmes[4] were invited to participate in the research project. They included those with only a few international cases and others with many thousands of cases. In order to determine the types of variables that might affect the availability and comparability of data, large and small programmes were chosen, including those that manage cases very differently.

We developed a rudimentary data instrument and conducted an online survey of caseworkers. Participants were asked to provide feedback throughout the project and the preliminary findings were shared with them.

A. Data Collected

The participating programmes were asked to provide data for the years 2009, 2010 and 2011, in most instances. Each respondent was free to use calendar years or government fiscal years, according to the organisation of the data in their jurisdiction. Where the data concerned clients, it was requested that they be divided into two types—cases where the debtor lived in the reporting jurisdiction and the other parent and children lived abroad, and cases where the debtor lived abroad and the other parent and children lived in the reporting jurisdiction.

i. International Caseload Profile

Data were collected on the size and composition of the international caseload in each programme. The data included:

— number of international cases;
— international cases as a percentage of the overall caseload;
— identification of the countries involved;
— the average length of time the cases had been enrolled; and
— breakdown of caseload by type of family support (child support, spousal support, or support for both child and spouse).

[4] The participating jurisdictions included: Australia; New Zealand; Germany; Orange County, California; New Jersey; Los Angeles County, California; Washington State; Ontario, Canada; British Columbia, Canada. It should be noted however that caseload size and IT limitations prevented a number of responding programmes from providing all of the data requested. In addition, for some variables, data from the two counties in California were combined. Caseworkers from all nine participating jurisdictions responded to the survey.

ii. Client Profile

Data were also collected concerning the clients and families involved in international cases. This included:

— age of maintenance creditor;
— age of maintenance debtor;
— number of children involved in the case; and
— ages of the children.

iii. Maintenance Payment Information

The objective of all maintenance programmes is the transfer of payments between parents or guardians, so the collection of data concerning payments was included. This included:

— quantum of maintenance due on individual maintenance cases;
— payment profile—is the case paid in full, have there been partial payments, or is the case one where no payments have ever been received?; and
— percentage of cases receiving a payment.

iv. Enforcement Information

Enforcement practices vary considerably, depending upon the legislative authority concerning the measures available for enforcing maintenance orders. The list of available enforcement mechanisms set out in the 2007 Convention was used as a guide, and respondents were asked to indicate which of their enforcement measures were most commonly used on international cases.

v. Caseworker and Case Management Information

Caseworkers were asked to provide information on their caseloads, their experience in managing international cases, and their impressions of the challenges and rewards of managing such cases. The caseworkers were specifically asked to identify the largest barriers to managing international cases and for suggestions for improving the management of these cases.

B. Defining Key Terms

Defining the meaning of particular terms in a universal context was one of the most challenging tasks faced. The research required the collection of comparable data for analysis while avoiding the minutiae of precise legal or programmatic definitions. Not surprisingly, the conclusions contain important findings with respect to the comparability of data arising from the challenges in defining terms. Importantly, however, despite the decision to deliberately define certain elements very broadly, the research was able to reach a fair understanding of the different ways that programmes manage their cases.

The following terms were central to the data we collected:

Maintenance Case

A maintenance case included both cases where no support decision had been made (cases for establishment of support), as well as cases where a maintenance decision was being enforced or there was a case open for modification of an existing decision.

International Case

A broad definition was used. The case simply had to have a parent or parent and child living in a country other than the reporting country. As noted below, this led to some interesting differences in the extent of cases included in the research.

Maintenance Debtor/Maintenance Payer

These terms describe the person obligated to pay the maintenance, or the person against whom an application to pay maintenance is being brought.

Maintenance Creditor/Maintenance Recipient

These terms describe the person entitled to receive the family maintenance or support. This could be a parent or a child.

Debtor in Reporting Jurisdiction

These are the cases where the person required to pay maintenance, or against whom maintenance is sought, lives in the country, State, county or province that was providing the data, and the other parent and child (if applicable) live in another country.

Debtor in Another Jurisdiction

These are cases where one parent and the child (if applicable) live in the reporting jurisdiction, and the person required to pay maintenance, or against whom an application to pay is being made, lives in another country.

IV. International Caseload Findings

A. Caseload Characteristics

i. Size of International Caseload

The number of international cases in the participating programmes in 2011 ranged from 38,844 in Australia to 745 in Washington State. The total case count for all participating programmes in 2011 was 59,743 cases. As the graphs[5] below show, the caseload fluctuated over the three years in some of the reporting programmes.

[5] See n 4 above. California data included both participating county programmes.

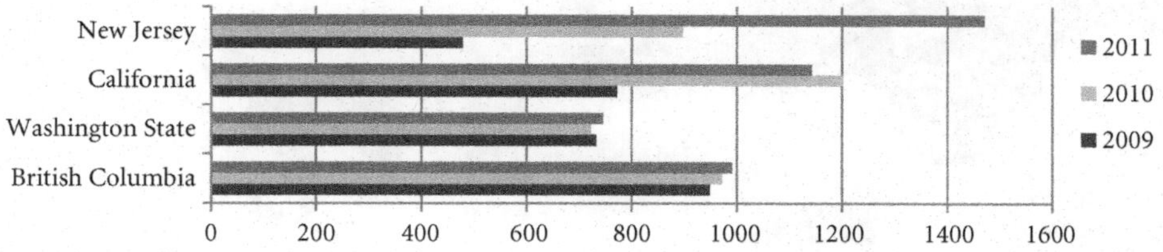

Figure 1: Total International Cases

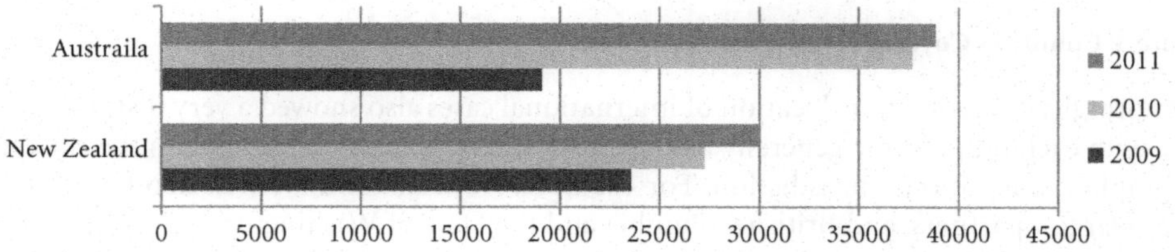

Figure 2: Total International Cases

As a percentage of the overall caseload, however, the number of international cases is very small. With two exceptions, international cases make up less than five per cent of the total maintenance caseload. The exceptions are the province of Ontario and New Zealand. New Zealand's international caseload is particularly significant in comparison to the domestic caseload and reflects the mobility of New Zealand citizens between Australia and New Zealand.

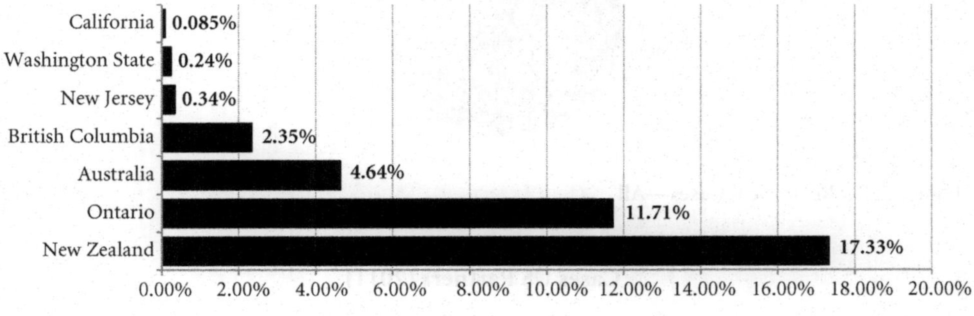

Figure 3: International Cases as a Percentage of Total

ii. Location of International Cases

Participating programmes were asked to identify the countries that were covered by their international caseload. The map below shows the global distribution of all the cases. Participants identified cases with 172 countries, which represent almost 90 per cent of nations in the world.

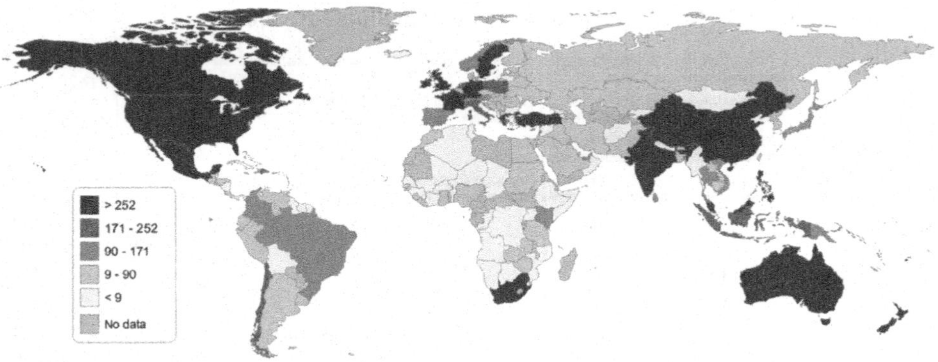

Figure 4: Countries Covered by International Cases

Interestingly, the geographic location of international cases also showed a very distinct pattern, with each programme generally having most of its international cases with the closest geographic international jurisdiction. For example, Australia and New Zealand are each other's largest partners, and British Columbia and the State of Washington are each other's largest partners. The charts below illustrate this pattern.

It appears that this pattern of proximity may relate to the importance to the parents of maintaining a connection with the children, however further research would be required to confirm this assumption.

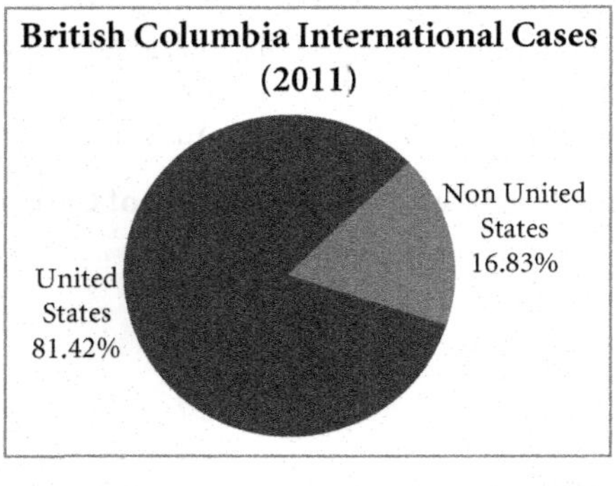

Figure 5: BC Reciprocal Cases—All

Figure 6: BC Reciprocal Cases—United States

Figure 7: Washington State International Cases

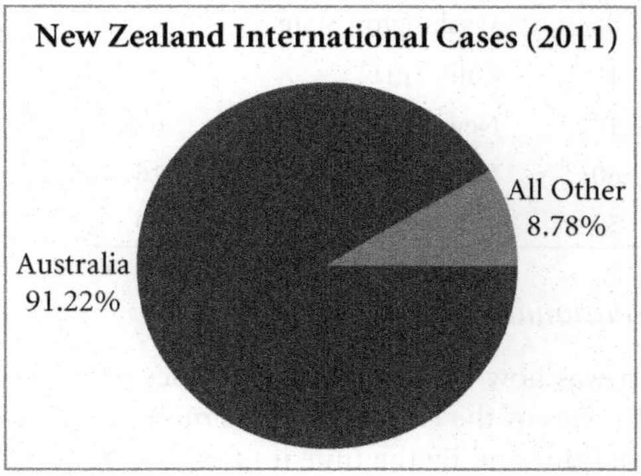

Figure 8: New Zealand International Cases

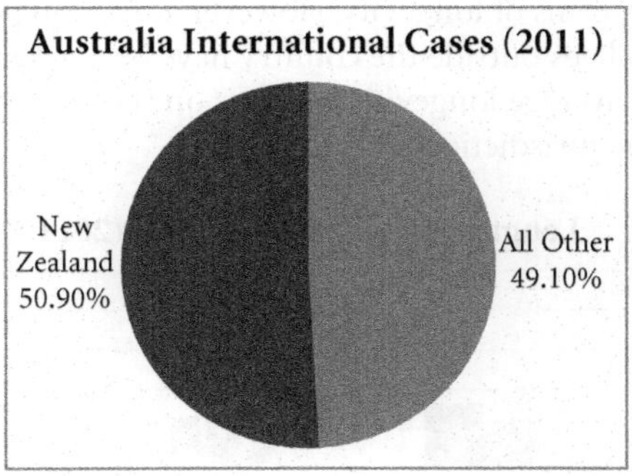

Figure 9: Australia International Cases

iii. Types of International Cases

Although the focus in the international community is often on child support, rather than on other forms of support or maintenance, and because many programmes do enforce spousal support only cases, it was important to determine the extent to which the international caseload includes spousal support only cases. The core scope of the 2007 Convention covers only applicants who have or are seeking maintenance decisions for child support or both child and spousal support, unless the two States involved have made declarations to extend their assistance to cover spousal support only decisions.

It was found that there were very few spousal support only cases in the international caseloads of those jurisdictions currently assisting with the obtaining or enforcing of spousal support only cases. In no jurisdiction were there more than 100 cases of this type. This is an interesting finding, as one of the decisions that will have to be made by jurisdictions in the lead up to the implementation of the 2007 Convention is whether to make a declaration concerning spousal support only cases.

Table 1: Number of Spousal Support Cases by Jurisdiction

Number of Spousal Support Cases (2011 Data)			
Debtor out of Jurisdiction		**Debtor in Jurisdiction**	
British Columbia	1	British Columbia	13
Washington State	0	Washington State	1
California	1	California	4
New Jersey	10	New Jersey	6
New Zealand	60	New Zealand	16
Australia	39	Australia	30

iv. Longevity of International Cases

Another area of interest was how long international cases remain open. The longevity of a case is influenced by the ages of the children, by the mobility of the parents (whether they move to another jurisdiction) and by the time it takes to collect any outstanding arrears.

The research showed found that almost three quarters of all the international cases had been open for over five years. In this respect, the international caseload is quite similar to the domestic caseload in terms of longevity. However almost 50 per cent of the cases where a debtor (paying parent) lives outside the country have been open for more than ten years, which is longer than the average longevity for cases on the domestic caseload (cases where both parents reside in the jurisdiction).

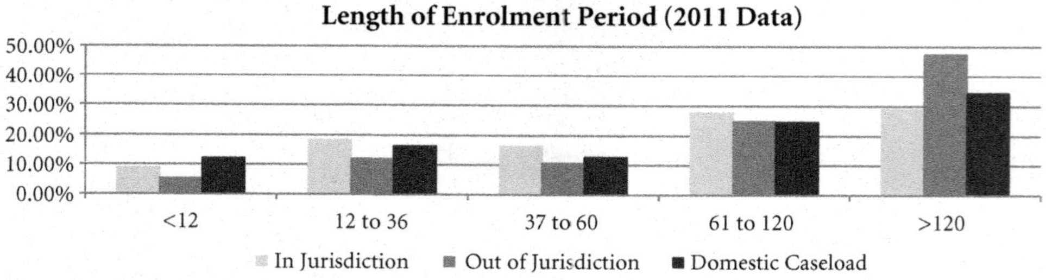

Figure 10: Length of Enrolment

v. Data Limitations

These data highlighted an interesting difference between programmes in terms of the way they treat and count cases where one parent lives in a different country. In some programmes, a case is considered an international one if one of the parents has an address in a different country. In other countries, international cases are synonymous with reciprocal cases, and the cases in that category only include those where a parent lives in a jurisdiction that has a reciprocal or legal agreement with the first country. Cases where a parent lives in another country, but there is no official reciprocal agreement with that country are not considered international cases and those cases are included in the domestic case count.

In this study, the data from British Columbia are an example of the latter approach. Only cases where a parent resides in a reciprocating jurisdiction were included by British Columbia in this research. Cases where a parent lives in a non-reciprocating jurisdiction (ie one that does not have a reciprocal arrangement with British Columbia) were not included. In contrast, Australia included all cases where one parent lives outside Australia in their data.

Similarly, the global reach of some child support programmes reflects the extent to which the programme or jurisdiction has been able to conclude reciprocal or other agreements with different countries. New Jersey, for example, has reciprocity agreements with 24 countries (including all provinces or territories in Canada), while British Columbia only has reciprocity agreements with 18 jurisdictions.

The other factor that influences the caseload size is scope of services provided by child support or maintenance programmes. Programmes that provide services across the maintenance life cycle from establishment of maintenance decisions, through enforcement and modification, necessarily have more international cases than those that provide services for the enforcement of existing maintenance decisions only. Child support programmes in the United States provide a full spectrum of services, as do those in Australia and New Zealand, while Canadian programmes offer enforcement assistance only.

vi. Australia and New Zealand—A Special Relationship

The data collected in this research study reflect the unique nature of the relationship between Australia and New Zealand in managing child support for families in those two countries. In terms of number of cases alone, the combined total of cases from the two jurisdictions made up over 90 per cent of the cases in this study. Because of the high volume of international cases[6] between these two jurisdictions, the child support programmes have well-developed practices for transmitting cases, transferring funds and managing communications.

Another factor influencing the size of the international caseload in Australia and New Zealand is the structure of their child support programmes. Both countries operate a single national child support programme. In contrast, in Canada, the United States and Germany, programmes operate at a local level, leading to significant differences in the size of the programmes within the country as well as variations between the programmes within the country.

B. Clients and Children

To determine the composition of the families on the international caseload, data concerning the ages of the maintenance paying parent (debtor) and the maintenance receiving parent (creditor) as well as the number and ages of the children were collected. Comparisons between cases where the debtor was in the reporting jurisdiction and those where the debtor was in a different country were also completed.

[6] As of May 2012, Australia administered approximately 11,580 cases (debt $NZ143.8 million) and transferred $NZ4.12 million per month to New Zealand. New Zealand administered approximately 6,457 cases (debt $NZ45.8 million) and transferred $NZ950k per month to Australia ('Jurisdictions Working Together' Presentation to 2012 NCSEA Training Conference, Denver, United States).

i. Debtor (Non-custodial Parent) Profile

The majority of debtors in international cases are between 30 and 50 years of age. There is a slight difference between cases where the debtor is in the reporting jurisdiction and those where he or she is not. Debtors in the reporting jurisdiction tend to be somewhat younger.

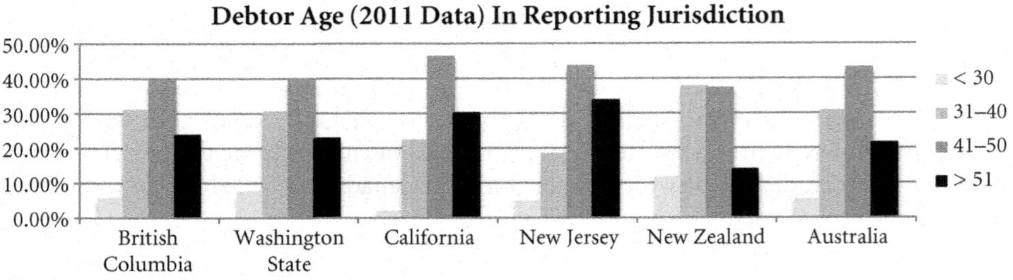

Figure 11: Debtor Age—In Reporting Jurisdiction

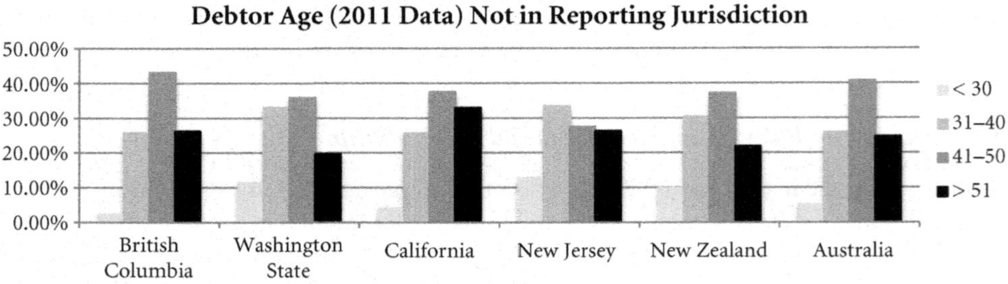

Figure 12: Debtor Age—Not In Reporting Jurisdiction

ii. Creditor (Custodial Parent) Profile

In general, creditors in these cases are younger than the debtors. Of the creditors residing in another country, 71 per cent are between 30–50 years of age. In cases where the creditor resides in the reporting jurisdiction, 68 per cent are in the 30–50 year age group. The majority are in the 41–50 year age group.

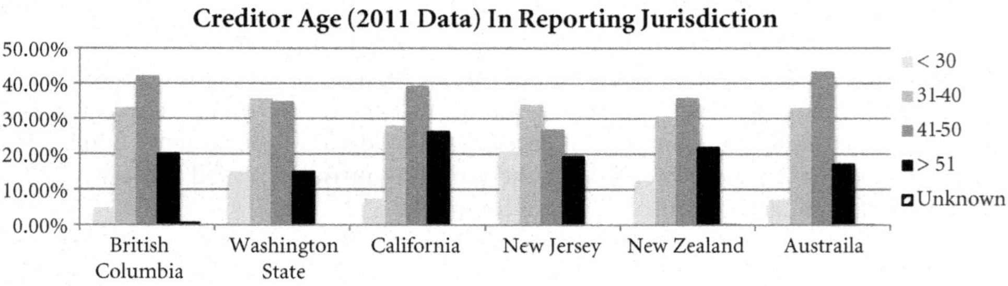

Figure 13: Creditor Age—In Reporting Jurisdiction

The data would appear to suggest that there is a greater discrepancy between the ages of creditors and debtors in cases where the creditor resides abroad. This is shown in the data below:

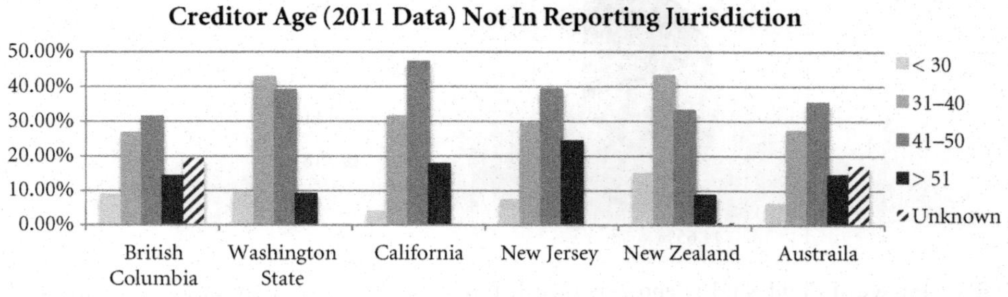

Figure 14: Creditor Age—Not In Reporting Jurisdiction

However, an examination of this data revealed that there were a large number of cases on the 'creditor—out' caseload where the age of the creditor was unknown. This is not surprising as few programmes require the age or date of birth of an out-of-country creditor in order to process a file. Often the only information collected relates to the ages of the children.

iii. Children

The families in international cases tend to be small families with an average of almost 1.6 children on cases where the child lives in another country, and just over 1.8 children where the child lives in the reporting jurisdiction.

The age distribution of these children is interesting and, with respect to the number of older children on the caseload, reflects differing policies concerning the collection of child support for children over the age of majority.[7] The age of majority also varies between jurisdictions. In all reporting programmes however, there are very few children receiving child support who are under the age of six. Most of the children who are receiving maintenance are between the ages of six and 18. In some programmes the age distribution of the children is quite different between the domestic caseload and the international caseload. This difference is explained, to some extent, by the reality that it may take a number of years between the time a child needs child support and the time that the order is finally established or enforced in an international jurisdiction.

[7] In some jurisdictions, like British Colombia, child support can continue past the age of majority for as long as the child remains dependent upon the custodial parent. In other jurisdictions (New Jersey, Ontario), the maintenance will continue until the court orders otherwise. In other jurisdictions the maintenance ends when the child reaches the age of majority.

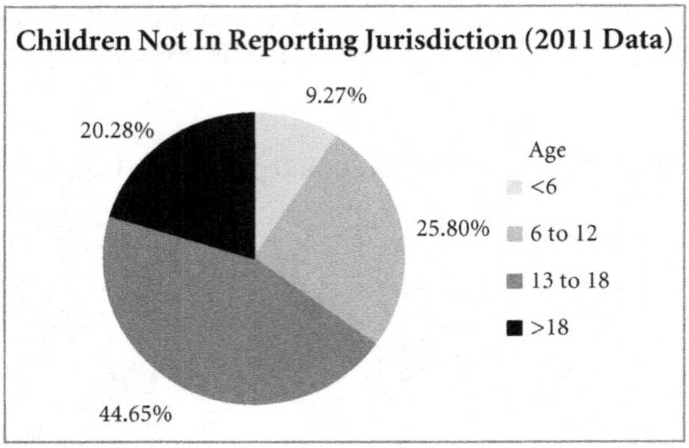

Figure 15: Age of Child Not In Reporting Jurisdiction

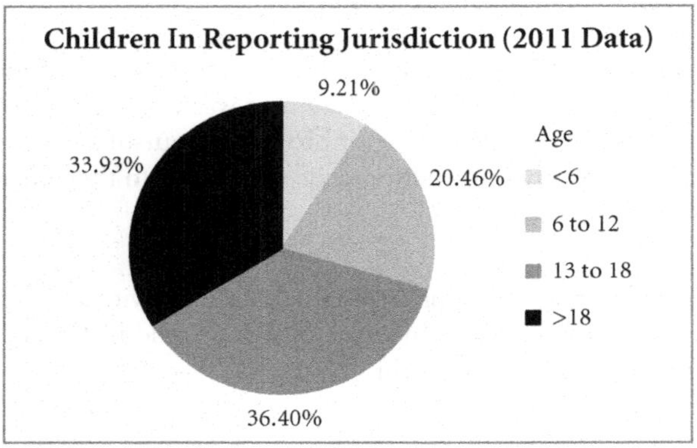

Figure 16: Age of Child In Reporting Jurisdiction

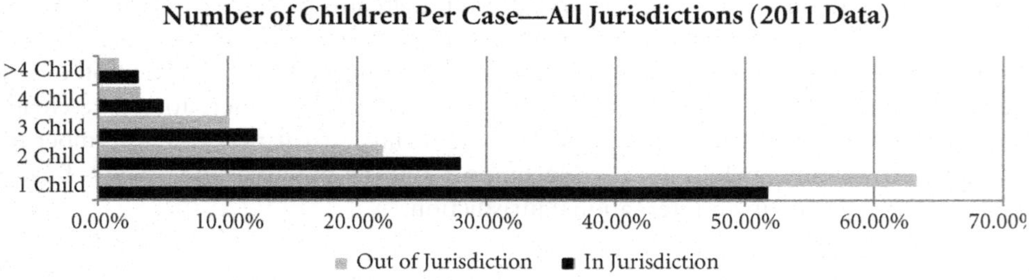

Figure 17: Number of Children Per Case

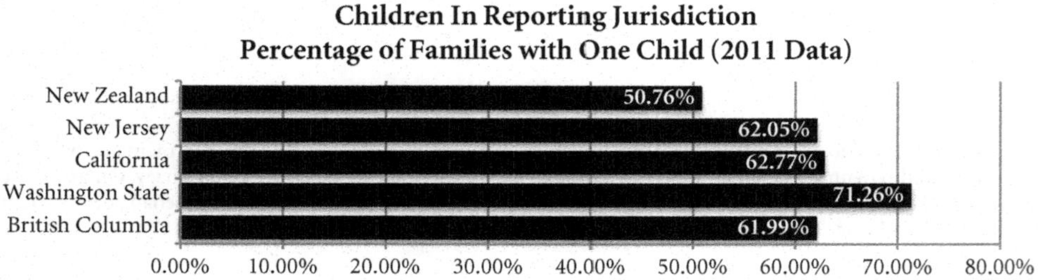

Figure 18: Percentage of Families with One Child

A slightly older age range in those programmes that included only enforcement cases was expected, in comparison to those jurisdictions that included cases where maintenance has yet to be established, as the enforcement process takes place later in the life cycle of the case. This was seen, to a limited extent, particularly with the data from British Columbia. However the larger percentage of older children also reflects British Columbia's policies concerning continued enforcement of maintenance for children over the age of majority.

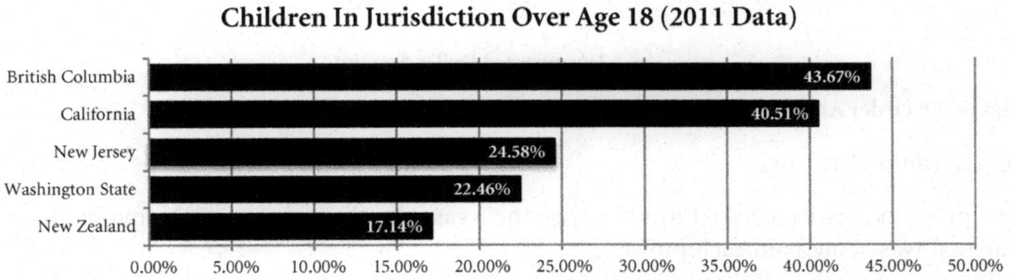

Figure 19: Children over Age 18

C. Maintenance Payment Information

One of the questions addressed by this research study was whether there was enough commonality between maintenance programmes to enable comparison of financial data. The financial aspects of maintenance can be complex, and most programmes have sophisticated information systems to track the payments due and the payments received. Obviously, in international cases, there is also the added challenge of different currencies and differences in the purchasing power of a given amount of maintenance in each country. An order for US$200 (or the equivalent amount in the local currency) may cover a greater proportion of a child's expenses in one country than another.

i. Maintenance Due

Two factors emerged from the data collected. There was a significant portion of cases reported as arrears only (cases where there is no ongoing amount for maintenance due under the order). In British Columbia and the United States over 24 per cent of their cases were classified as arrears only. Australia and New Zealand reported over 40 per cent of their cases were arrears only. This is interesting and will require further analysis as it is difficult to reconcile with the data that show that most cases involve families with children under age 19, and those children should be entitled to ongoing support. Further research into this apparent anomaly would be useful.

The distribution of due amount (the amount that the debtor is required to pay each month) was spread over the full spectrum, with no significant clustering of payment level. However, there was a small 'tail' at the end of the graph which showed a significant number of cases where the due amount was in excess of $900. As the quantum on maintenance due is generally related to the ability of the debtor to pay maintenance, this may indicate a group of debtors that have a higher income or capacity to pay. Again, further research into these findings would be useful.

A few fairly simple measures were developed to look at the payment of maintenance in these cases. Information was collected concerning payment patterns (whether cases are being paid in full, paid only partially, or not paid at all), what percentage of cases received a payment, and the average payment size of an order.

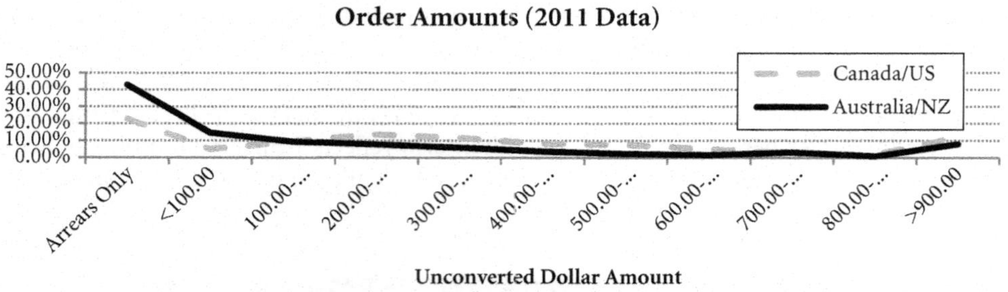

Figure 20: Order Amounts

ii. Payment Patterns

The programmes were asked to categorise their cases by the amount of the maintenance due that was being paid each month.

In cases where the debtor was in the reporting jurisdiction, the pattern of payment fell into what can be described as a 'bathtub curve'. Looking at the data from 2011, 45.24 per cent of the cases each month received ten per cent or less of the due amount. In contrast, 42.50 per cent of the cases received 90 per cent or more of the due amount. Thus, in these cases, the payers or non-custodial parents either pay close to the full amount due, or they pay very little at all.

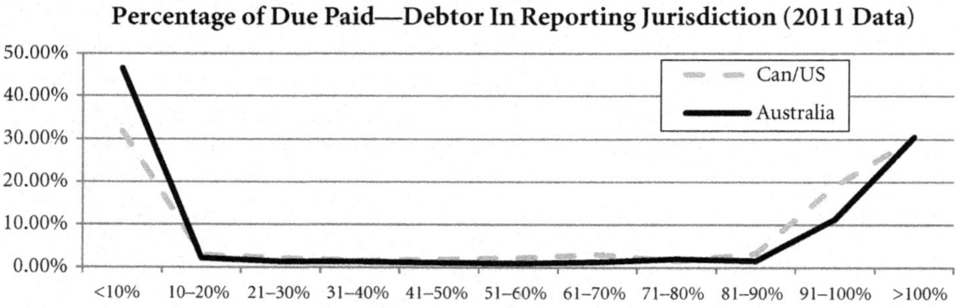

NB: NZ was unable to separate out their domestic caseload for this calculation.

Figure 21: Percentage of Due Paid—Debtor In Reporting Jurisdiction

A different pattern emerges in the cases where the debtor resides outside the country. In those cases (based on 2011 data), a much larger percentage (69.58) paid very little (ten per cent of the due amount or less), and significantly fewer cases were paid in full (22.93 per cent).

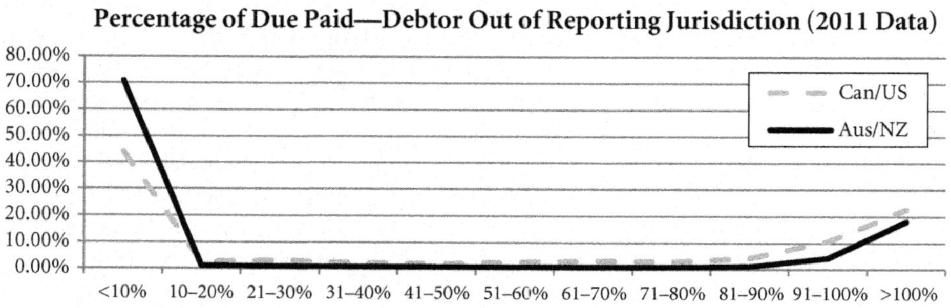

NB: NZ is included in this comparison.

Figure 22: Percentage of Due Paid—Debtor Not In Reporting Jurisdiction

The pattern of payment in the cases where the debtor is in the responding jurisdiction is quite similar to the pattern of payment in domestic cases for the same jurisdictions. This is not surprising, given the fact that most international cases are treated, for enforcement purposes, in the same way as domestic cases.

The payment pattern in cases where the payer resides out of the country most likely reflects the policy in all of the reporting jurisdictions of maintaining cases with an international element (ie cases where one parent is out of the country) in the domestic caseload for as long as the maintenance is being paid. This policy makes sense for the family, as it minimises the disruption in payments caused by the flow of payments through another country, and it avoids the extra work associated with managing international cases. It does, however, reduce the payment rates of the 'international' cases as a group. This difference is particularly evident in the data from jurisdictions such as British Columbia where the only cases included in the research are those cases where the child support agency in another country is engaged.

iii. Percentage of Cases Receiving a Payment

Data were collected on the percentage of cases receiving a payment, as the number is an interesting reflection on the 'breadth' of the child support effort. A high percentage of cases receiving a payment generally indicated that all cases are receiving attention, not just the cases that may be easier to enforce.

The data collected on this measure showed a significant amount of similarity across programmes. The percentage of cases receiving a payment where the reporting programme is responsible for the enforcement (debtor in responding jurisdiction) ranged from 62 per cent to 93 per cent; however, most programmes were clustered in the low- to mid-70 per cent range.

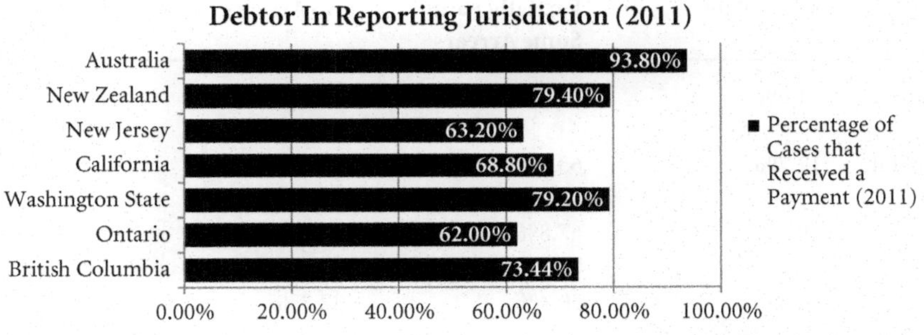

Figure 23: Percentage of Cases Receiving Payment—Debtor In Jurisdiction

The percentage of cases receiving a payment where the debtor is outside the country is generally lower, as the graph below illustrates.

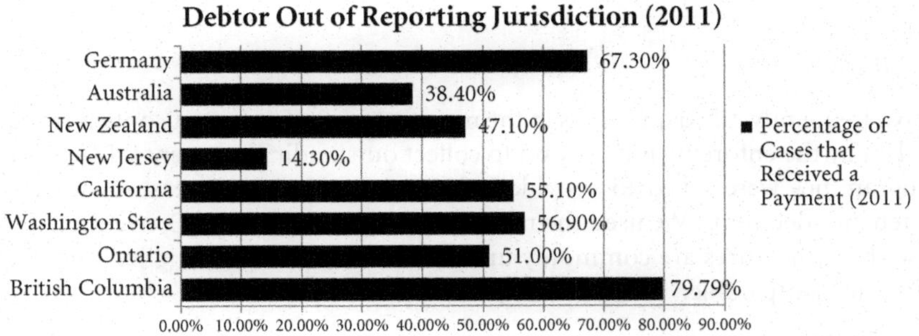

Figure 24: Percentage of Cases Receiving Payment—Debtor Not In Jurisdiction

The decision to retain cases where the maintenance is being paid, rather than transferring the enforcement of cases to another country, accounts for some of the difference between the debtor-in and debtor-out results. However, the comparability of these data is also limited by the fact that in some jurisdictions, cases where no maintenance decision had been established are included in the overall universe of international cases. For these cases, not surprisingly, no payments have ever been received, so the overall average is depressed by their inclusion.

iv. Case Arrears

The third measure collected related to outstanding arrears of maintenance. It was important to determine what proportion of international cases had arrears of maintenance, and whether there were any interesting differences in the arrears profile of cases in different jurisdictions.

In cases where the debtor lived in the reporting jurisdiction, it was found that Australia and New Zealand had very similar numbers, perhaps not surprisingly, given the nature of the reciprocal arrangements between the two countries. California, Washington State and British Columbia had similar profiles, with the majority of the cases having received some payment over the life of the case, but still having outstanding arrears.

Table 2: Payment Rates by Jurisdiction

Payment Rates—Debtor In Jurisdiction (2011 Data)			
Jurisdiction	**Never Paid**	**Partially Paid/ Some Arrears**	**No Arrears**
British Columbia	11.3%	74.2%	14.5%
Washington State	12.7%	63.6%	23.8%
California	19.9%	67.8%	12.3%
New Jersey	36.8%	30.4%	32.8%
New Zealand	2.8%	82.9%	14.4%
Australia	3.6%	82.1%	14.3%

v. Enforcement Measures

One of the most frequently asked questions in the maintenance enforcement context relates to the steps taken by the enforcing jurisdiction to collect outstanding payments. Therefore, reporting programmes were asked to provide information about the measures used to enforce maintenance decisions. We used the measures set out in the 2007 Convention as a guide, because those measures are commonly understood in the responding jurisdictions and are more easily comparable.

It is important to note that, by policy, all of the programmes participating in this research use the same tools or measures to enforce international decisions as they do to enforce domestic maintenance decisions. This is also a key requirement for enforcement of maintenance under the 2007 Convention.[8] The responses show the most commonly used enforcement measures in that jurisdiction.

The data supplied indicated, not surprisingly, that for all programmes, taking steps to locate a debtor and sources of assets and income, along with enforcement against wages, are the most frequent measures taken. Almost all programmes take steps to intercept government benefits or payments, such as income tax refunds or social security type benefits. Generally, it was not surprising to find that in terms of enforcement international cases are very similar to domestic cases.

However with respect to a number of other measures, very few respondents indicated that the measures are taken on international cases. The researchers found this to be surprising and it perhaps points to an area of further investigation or training as more countries move towards ratifying the 2007 Convention. It may well be that the listed enforcement measures are being used in some fashion in the enforcement of maintenance decisions, but the responding programme did not identify the action as such. As caseworkers begin to communicate about cases under the 2007 Convention, it is important to ensure that there is a common understanding as to what would come within a particular described measure.

The data collected were however also subject to some important limitations. With respect to a number of measures, reporting programmes indicated that their case management systems did not separate out the particular measures in any measurable way. So, for example, none of the reporting programmes were able to report on attachment of pensions or other benefits, although this measure is frequently used in most of the programmes. Similarly, many of the respondents indicated that they do not formally count voluntary payment arrangements reached with a debtor, although these may be very common.

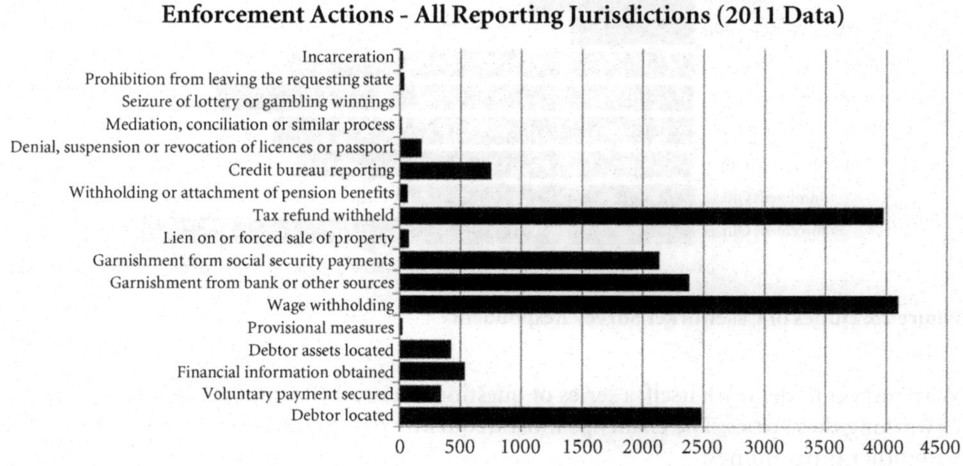

NB: Sum of all data provided.

Figure 25: Enforcement Actions by Jurisdiction

[8] See Art 33.

V. International Caseworker Survey

A. Introduction

The caseworker survey was available for completion from 19 November 2012 until 5 December 2012. One hundred and three responses to the online version of the survey were received. The Australian participants were unable to complete the survey online and submitted 13 manually completed surveys. The analysis is based on the total of 116 responses.

To put some of the answers in context, caseworkers were asked about their backgrounds and their caseloads. Most of the respondents had been working in the area of child support for between five and 12 years, with a median of seven years. Of that time most of it was spent working on international cases, although not exclusively. While approximately one-third of the caseworkers have dedicated international caseloads, the majority of respondents have caseloads where less than one quarter of their time was spent on international cases. This has interesting implications for staff training on international cases and the 2007 Convention, as the training will have to be accessible and meaningful for workers who spend only a minority of their time on international cases.

The organisation of the work involved in international child support varies significantly. The overlap in responsibility for key tasks is shown in the responses to questions about the duties carried out by respondents to the survey.

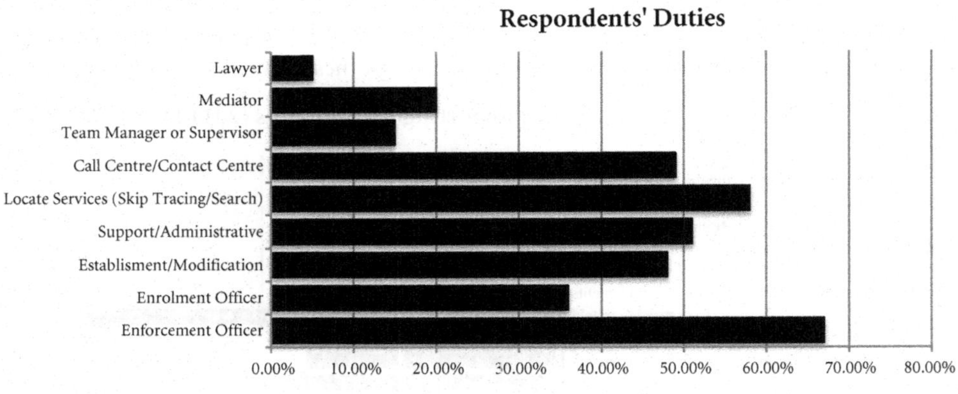

Figure 26: Duties of Caseworker Survey Respondent

With respect to the work itself, a series of questions were asked about challenges or barriers to working these cases. The challenge most frequently reported related to communications with other programmes.

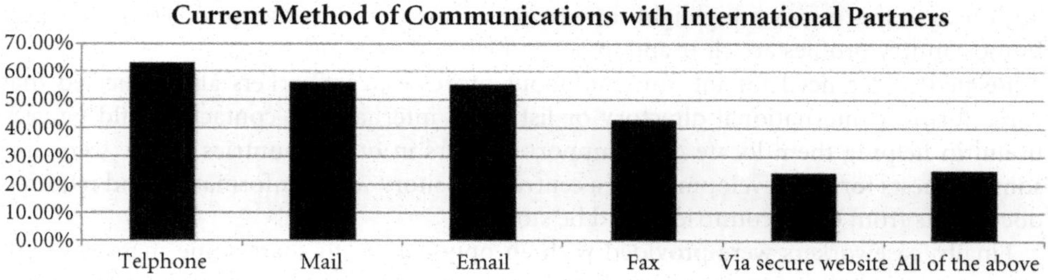

Figure 27: Current Methods of Communication with International Partners

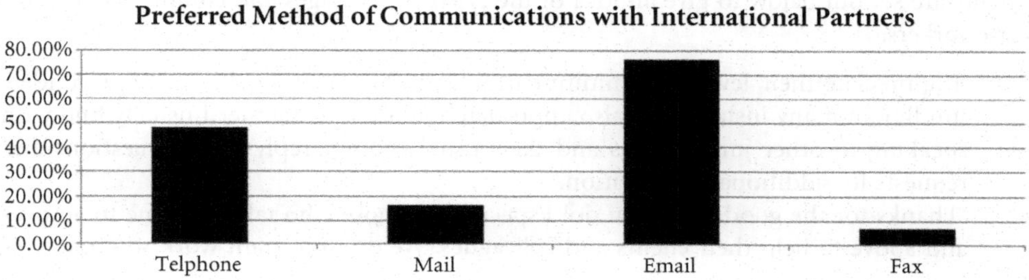

Figure 28: Preferred Methods of Communication with International Partners

Forty-eight per cent of respondents indicated that their organisation had restrictions on the use of email to communicate with other jurisdictions, and a portion of those also indicated that there were restrictions on making international phone calls. These restrictions are based on government policies concerning the protection of client personal information, applicable to all maintenance cases, and on the cost of long distance calls. Secure websites for communication are noted as an alternative option, but they are not generally regarded as being as effective or practical as email. Given that email is the overwhelming preference of caseworkers, this is an area that merits further discussion.

The focus on the use of email for communication reflected the challenges experienced by caseworkers relating to time zone differences and the length of time it takes to resolve issues by mail. Several respondents suggested that perhaps modified work hours might be one way of supporting direct communications. Almost all of the respondents felt that good communications with other countries had a direct positive impact on getting child support established and paid.

Another frequently mentioned challenge was the lack of good, clear information regarding processes for managing international cases in other countries. A number of respondents indicated that it was often very difficult to get information about what can be done in another programme or how the child support procedures work in that country. The country profiles being developed for signatories to the 2007 Convention will certainly be an important step forward in making this information available to caseworkers, and the responses to this research highlight the need to ensure that the descriptions of procedures in the country profiles are clear and understandable to caseworkers.

Related to the need for information about processes, caseworkers also indicated that some form of international directory or listing of international contacts would be very useful in helping them locate child support workers in other countries. There were also some requests for the development of a central repository where information and required documents from other countries could be stored.

Finally, caseworkers were provided with an opportunity to share some messages with caseworkers in other programmes who were also filling out the survey. Those messages have been collated and are being sent out to all the respondents. A few of those comments are set out below to give an idea of the types of messages and comments made by caseworkers.

— 'I appreciate their level of commitment given the often difficult situations (underfunding in many instances). I also appreciate the friendly manner I usually find with speaking to other jurisdictions and their usual prompt reply to my questions and requests for additional information.'
— 'Thanks for the good work you do! Especially to those who take the time to go over and above to help their clients and colleagues. We do important work so remember that.'
— 'It has always been a pleasure working with caseworkers around the world!'
— 'Your work is *so* important to the children of the world. Keep up the *excellent* work!!!'
— 'We all do a fantastic job for the children—keep up the good work.'

VI. Research Conclusions and Recommendations

As noted at the outset, one of the goals of the research project was to determine whether data on international cases could be compared and to become aware of the challenges that researchers might face in compiling data from different jurisdictions. While there were certainly areas where the data were available and could be compared, limitations were also found. This section summarises the conclusions and recommendations with respect to further research in this area.

A. Limitations on Data

i. Fundamental Differences in Structure of the Maintenance Programme

In some jurisdictions the maintenance cases in the programme are not representative of the full international maintenance caseload. This was the case, for example, with the data from the German Institute for Youth Human Services and Family Law. That programme manages 'outgoing' cases only—that is, cases where the maintenance payer or debtor lives in another jurisdiction and the maintenance recipient or creditor and children live in Germany. This limited the availability and comparability of the data.

ii. Data System/Technology Limitations

While some programmes have well-developed data systems that can extract specific data on international caseloads, in other programmes, very little data are available. As noted in the conclusions below, in many jurisdictions this simply reflects the reality that international cases only represent a small minority of cases in the maintenance programme, so they have not received the same level of IT attention as domestic cases. Thus, some jurisdictions were not able to extract significant data about their international cases because the cases could not be separated from the domestic caseload. Nonetheless, the participation of these jurisdictions in the research was very valuable as their caseworkers provided interesting insights into the casework, and through their involvement, a better understanding the challenges in the international caseload was gained.

B. Recommendations for Further Research

The research demonstrated that despite the limitations, it was still possible to gather preliminary data concerning international cases. A larger, more comprehensive research study would certainly be possible and might yield interesting information not only about the international caseload itself, but about the impact that the international collection of child support has on families and children. For example, 2011–12 data from British Columbia show that $3,649,538.95[9] was collected for international families. For a small programme, with few international families in the caseload, these recoveries are important. Globally, the amount of child support collected and transferred is significant. Further research will help to quantify the impact.

In terms of guidance for future researchers, the following recommendations are suggested:

(1) There is no uniform definition of an international case. The inclusion or exclusion of certain types of cases should be driven by the focus and purpose of the research. If the purpose is to look at all international families, the definition should be broad, including those cases that are entirely managed by one programme or jurisdiction, as that approach will give a better sense of the families that are affected by child support. Conversely, if the focus of the research is on the relationships between reciprocating jurisdictions, collaboration and improving processes, the cases to be included should be those cases where two programmes are involved and the defined processes are used.

(2) Taking the time at the outset to understand the way that international cases are managed in different jurisdictions, before the research questions are defined, will drive better outcomes. Had the researchers known more about the delivery of the child support programme in each jurisdiction prior to commencing the project, it might have been easier to collect data that would have been more comparable and useful.

(3) Understanding the delivery of the programme also assists in understanding data limitations. For example, those programmes that only manage enforcement of orders may have much more limited information concerning the income of the paying/liable parent

[9] Canadian Dollars, British Columbia Family Maintenance Enforcement Program, 2011–12 Annual Statistics.

at the time of the making of the maintenance decision, as their records do not include information concerning the basis for the maintenance decision.

(4) Size is important. The two national programmes in the study had significant numbers of cases because their programmes are delivered at the national level and not at the level corresponding to a sub-unit of the State. The input of these significantly larger programmes into the research projects is important; however, any interpretation of the data must account for the differences in volume of cases.

(5) Understanding more about cases in common and the barriers to effectively working on international cases will better prepare caseworkers to manage the changes expected as a result of the 2007 Convention. For example, knowing that many of the caseworkers are experienced, but work on both domestic and international cases, will help programmes better design training to meet caseworker needs.

(6) The level of cooperation by all countries supporting the collection of data is excellent. There is a shared interest in looking at the numbers and significant support for more research.

10

Setting Appropriate Child Support Orders and Addressing Barriers: Research and Policy Implications to Improve Payments and Compliance

MARK TAKAYESU AND STEVEN ELDRED

I. Introduction

The child support programme in the United States evolved from a welfare reimbursement, revenue-producing device for the Federal and State governments to a family-first programme designed to provide income for families. The mission of the Child Support Enforcement Programme in the United States is:

> To encourage responsible parenting, family self-sufficiency and child well-being and to recognize the essential role of both parents in supporting their children, the national child support program assures that assistance in obtaining support, including financial and medical, is available to children through locating parents, establishing paternity, establishing and modifying support obligations, and monitoring and enforcing those obligations.[1]

In Federal Fiscal Year (FFY) 2011, the United States child support programme served 15.8 million families and collected and distributed $27 billion in payments.[2] The programme served 17.3 million children. Led by the Office of Child Support Enforcement (OCSE), the United States has made consistent efforts to improve collections year by year through innovative strategies, best practices and collaboration with child support offices within other States. As a result, child support distributed collections in the United States increased 9.8 per cent or $2.4 billion from FFY 2007 to FFY 2011.

[1] US Office of Child Support Enforcement, 'National Child Support Enforcement Strategic Plan FY 2010–2014' (2013) www.acf.hhs.gov/programs/css/resource/national-child-support-strategic-plan-fy-2010-2014 (accessed January 2014).

[2] US Office of Child Support Enforcement, 'FY 2011 Preliminary Report' (2011) www.acf.hhs.gov/programs/css/resource/fy2011-preliminary-report (accessed January 2014).

In 2013, OCSE outlined a three-tier strategy approach for all States to continuously improve future child support performance.[3] These strategies represent a roadmap for States to follow and are designed to promote continuous improvement in the child support programme:

— **Focus on the fundamentals.** Make sure computer systems, new hire reporting and income withholding (e-IWO) are working well.
— **Identify the performance problem.** Identify the reason for irregular support payments, intervene early and set appropriate obligations.
— **Expand access to services.** Partner with other programmes and redirect resources to address barriers to non-payment through family-centred services.

This chapter examines tier two and tier three: understanding the reasons for irregular or non-payment of child support and addressing these reasons by expanding access to services using a family-centred services approach. In addressing both tiers, two areas of empirically based research will be explored: setting appropriate orders and barriers to child support payments. For setting appropriate orders, empirical research supports the hypothesis that practices of setting orders based on an assumed amount when actual income is not available can lead to inconsistent payments and increase arrearage debt of the non-custodial parent (NCP). In addition, the discussion explores the order amount as a proportion of the NCP's income that leads to the highest potential payment compliance and consistency. Both newly established and existing orders within the context of setting appropriate orders will be discussed as well as operational and broader policy concerns.

For the second area, empirically based research will be discussed with regards to the barriers that prevent NCPs from paying child support. These barriers include (but are not limited to) items such as low education, having a criminal history, having a history of substance abuse, having their first child at a young age, and having a high child support order amount relative to his or her monthly gross income. This research is based on a predictive modelling approach that identifies the combination of child support barriers that predicts low to high payment compliance. Using a predictive modelling approach provides insight into the relative influence setting appropriate orders have to predict future compliance for NCPs with notable barriers. For example, will setting appropriate orders for NCPs with low education or criminal history improve compliance?

Operational and broader policy implications are discussed with regards to setting orders appropriately for newly established orders and existing orders that lead to maximum payment consistency, compliance and lower arrears growth. Policy implications will also be discussed regarding the barriers that affect payments, and whether setting appropriate orders for NCPs with barriers is an effective strategy to improve long-term payment compliance. Finally, this chapter will address the effective use of family-centred services as an instrument to improve child support payments for NCPs with barriers. It is the combination of setting appropriate orders, identifying and understanding payment barriers, and effective referral to family-centred services programmes that leads to positive outcomes.

[3] V Turetsky, 'Three Tiers: A Roadmap of Strategies to Improve Program Performance' (2013) *Child Support Report* www.acf.hhs.gov/programs/css/resource/march-2013-child-support-report (accessed January 2014).

II. Setting Appropriate Orders

In the United States, appropriate child support order amounts based on the NCP's ability to make affordable child support payments, reduces arrears debt and improves payment compliance.[4]

To determine initial child support order amounts, States are required to publish child support guidelines.[5] Whether the State uses a court-based system (like California) or an administrative tribunal system, all States are required to publish set guidelines for determining the amount of support payable. The intent of the federal requirement is to promote uniformity inside each State for families setting a support obligation. Orders set as a proportion of the NCP's gross income (Ratio of Order Amount to Wage (ROTW)) vary considerably from State to State.

Ten States utilise a 'percentage-of-income' model that uses the income of the paying parent to determine the support order.[6] This method gives little or no consideration to factors such as child visitation, health-care costs or the income of the other parent. The tribunal looks at the paying parent's income and takes a set percentage (eg 17 per cent of gross income for one child, 25 per cent if there are two, etc). Thirty-eight States including California use an 'income-shares model'.[7] This model attempts to apportion support for the child as if the parents were still living together. The income of both parents is combined and a set portion of the combined income is set aside for child-rearing expense. That portion is divided between the parents according to their relative incomes. The 'paying parent' then pays the receiving parent their share of the expense. The receiving parent is expected to contribute their share through providing support in their home. California's model is the most complex in the United States,[8] incorporating variables such as parenting time shares, health costs, tax-deductible expenses, expenses of other children under the

[4] E Sorensen, L Sousa and S Schaner, 'Assessing Child Support Arrears in Nine Large States and the Nation' (2007) Urban Institute www.aspe.hhs.gov/hsp/07/assessing-CS-debt/report.pdf (accessed January 2014).

[5] 42 USC 667 (1988).

[6] Jurisdictions using the percentage-of-income model include: Alaska, Arkansas, District of Columbia, Illinois, Mississippi, Nevada, New York, North Dakota, Texas and Wyoming.

[7] Jurisdictions using the income-shares model include: Alabama, Arizona, California, Colorado, Connecticut, Florida, Georgia, Guam, Hawaii, Idaho, Indiana, Iowa, Kansas, Kentucky, Louisiana, Maine, Maryland, Massachusetts, Michigan, Minnesota, Missouri, Nebraska, New Hampshire, New Jersey, New Mexico, North Carolina, Ohio, Oklahoma, Oregon, Pennsylvania, Rhode Island, South Carolina, South Dakota, Tennessee, Utah, Vermont, Virginia, Washington, West Virginia and Wyoming.

[8] See California Family Code § 4055 et seq.

4055. (a) The statewide uniform guideline for determining child support orders is as follows: CS = K [HN—(H%)(TN)].

(b) (1) The components of the formula are as follows:

(A) CS = child support amount.

(B) K = amount of both parents' income to be allocated for child support as set forth in paragraph (3).

(C) HN = high earner's net monthly disposable income.

(D) H% = approximate percentage of time that the high earner has or will have primary physical responsibility for the children compared to the other parent. In cases in which parents have different time-sharing arrangements for different children, H% equals the average of the approximate percentages of time the high earner parent spends with each child.

(E) TN = total net monthly disposable income of both parties.

(2) To compute net disposable income, see Section 4059.

parent's responsibility, union dues, and others. A computer programme is required to perform the calculations. While administration of the programme is more difficult due to the complex formula, the requirement of a computer for the calculations means the data for this study was captured and made available for research.

When child support order amounts do not appropriately reflect the NCP's ability to pay, NCPs (especially poor NCPs) make little effort to comply with the order. In many instances, the child support order is based on 'imputed' income not related to the NCP's ability to pay. Orders based on imputed (fictional) income is based on what a NCP 'should make' and not based on actual income. In many instances, these types of cases result in default orders.

III. Process

An introduction to the establishment of orders in California is required to understand the human factors of this research. California uses a judicial-based system for its support orders. All orders, even when agreed upon by the parents, must be approved by a judicial officer in a family court. Initially, when a government support agency opens a support case, they consider available information and send the parents a 'proposed order'. Many parents come into the agency office and negotiate a mutually satisfactory agreement at that point. Some choose to go to court to convince a judicial officer that the order should be higher or lower than the proposed order. Up to one-half of the cases do not make a formal response, and the proposed order is signed by the judicial officer and becomes the order. Those cases are referred to as 'default' orders, as they had little or no participation by the paying parent. It is these orders that are the most problematic and a significant focus of this chapter.

IV. Prior Research on Setting Appropriate Orders

Previous research from the State of Washington found that arrears growth occurs when an NCP's child support order is greater than 20 per cent of an NCP's gross monthly earnings (ROTW = 20 per cent).[9] Based on the findings of this research, the State of Washington uses the 20 per cent threshold as a useful baseline in setting initial orders and is continually reducing arrears growth based on the following recommendations in their State: (1) updating the State of Washington Child Support Schedule; (2) reducing default orders;

(3) K (amount of both parents' income allocated for child support) equals one plus H% (if H% is less than or equal to 50 percent) or two minus H% (if H% is greater than 50 percent) times the following fraction:

Total Net Disposable Income Per Month	
K$0–800	0.20 + TN/16,000
$801–6,666	0.25
$6,667–10,000	0.10 + 1,000/TN
Over $10,000	0.12 + 800/TN

[9] C Formoso, 'Determining the Composition and Collectability of Child Support Arrearages, Volume 1. The Longitudinal Analysis' (2003) www.dshs.wa.gov/pdf/esa/dcs/reports/cvol1prn.pdf (accessed January 2014).

and (3) incorporating more income information such as unemployment compensation, social security benefits and labour and industry compensation into their order setting process.[10]

In addition to research demonstrating the importance of the 20 per cent threshold, other research demonstrates higher orders result in lower compliance (measured as a percentage of monthly current support paid out the month current support is due), and higher orders provide higher payments to children.[11]

It seems counterintuitive for higher orders to result in higher payments while lowering compliance and increasing arrears debt. However, these researchers commented that raising an individual father's order does not necessarily increase his payments.[12] In fact, responsible fathers actively engaging in their children's lives may have high orders leading them to make high payments. It is possible that increasing an existing order will not increase payments when it leads to lower compliance, arrears growth, and becomes a major barrier for making future child support payments. Increasing an existing order may lead to reduced payment consistency month-to-month, putting the NCP in a major disadvantage for making payments in future years.

Based on the research completed by the Research Unit from the Orange County California Department of Child Support Services (CSS), the following questions are addressed in this chapter:

— What are the effects of setting child support orders based on fictional income of the NCP?
— What is the recommended order amount (as a proportion of the NCP's income) to produce maximum payment compliance, maximum payments and reduced arrears growth?
— For existing orders, how does modifying orders appropriately affect future payments and payment compliance?
— What are the operational and broader policy concerns to improve performance?

V. What are the Effects of Setting Child Support Orders Based on the Fictional Income of the NCP?

Minimal empirical research has examined the impact of using fictional income when actual NCP income is not available for setting child support order amounts on future collectability of orders. Fictional income is widely used in child support programmes in the United States to set imputed orders when actual NCP income is not available. Some orders are based on sparse information from computer databases, common in seasonal or

[10] C Formoso and Q Liu, 'Arrears Stratification in Washington State Developing Operational Protocols in a Data Mining Environment' (2010) www.dshs.wa.gov/pdf/esa/dcs/reports/ArrearStratificationReportFinal.pdf (accessed January 2014).

[11] DR Meyer, Y Ha, and M Hu, 'Do High Child Support Orders Discourage Child Support Payments?' (2008) *Social Service Review* 93.

[12] Ibid.

part-time workers. Others are based on the average local wage for a person in their known trade (ie the parent is known to be a bricklayer). Using average local wage amounts for that trade, a monthly expected income can be derived. Government labour and taxation databases provide information on income by trade and geographic region. Often, a full-time schedule is implied, even if the NCP is not known as working full-time, or a full-time schedule is not available. In some cases, income information is not known. In those cases, most States require that the court assume that the parent is working full-time at a job that pays the government-mandated minimum wage. Such orders are used primarily in cases ending in default orders. The fallacy in this reasoning is shown in government-reported employment information. Unemployment, as of this study period, was above nine per cent nationally. For young men aged 16–24, unemployment and under-employment (people working part time, but seeking full-time work) was at record highs. About 60 per cent of men aged 16–24 were employed. Of those seeking work, unemployment ranged from 15–31 per cent by ethnicity.[13] According to the study by Guggenheim Investments, 20 per cent of jobs in the United States are part-time.[14] Reuters reports that 75 per cent of new jobs created in 2013 were part-time.[15]

Previous research found that setting inappropriate orders (high and often unaffordable orders) for NCPs with low or no reported income contributes to the majority of arrears growth in the United States. The majority of arrears owed in nine States surveyed belonged to a small number of non-custodial parents. For instance, 11 per cent of the obligors surveyed owed 54 per cent of the total arrears balance. Three quarters of these obligors, referred to as high debtors, had no reported income or income less than $10,000 per year.[16] It is possible that debtors who report little or no income may have income or assets from which to pay (underground economy, illegal activity, assets). However, experience shows that most of those reporting no income in fact have little or no income. A quarter of those with no reported income were institutionalised or disabled.[17] Although this study associates arrears growth primarily to the population of low or non-reported income, it does not investigate the impact of using fictional income on future collectability of orders.

In 2011, the Research Unit from the Orange County California CSS completed the first major guideline study examining the impact of using fictional NCP income on future child support payments. In California, if no income is available to set up a child support order, income is imputed based on a full-time monthly minimum wage amount of $1,387 per month. Basing a child support order on minimum wage income produces an order amount of $301 per month for a one child family.

CSS examined two models of the use of fictional vs. factual (actual NCP income available) income of the NCP in producing child support orders on future child support

[13] United States Bureau of Labour Statistics, US Department of Labour, 'Employment and Unemployment Among Youth—Summer 2011' (2011) press release, 24 August 2011 www.bls.gov/news.release/archives/youth_08242011.pdf (accessed January 2014).

[14] Haver Analytics, Guggenheim Investments 'Part-Time Jobs Driving Employment Growth' (2013) The Growth Mirage www.guggenheimpartners.com/perspectives/macroview/the-growth-mirage (accessed January 2014).

[15] Lucia Mutikani, '75 Per cent of Jobs Created This Year Were Part-Time Due To Weak Economy, Obamacare Concerns' (2013) The Huffington Post www.huffingtonpost.com/2013/08/21/part-time-job-creation_n_3788365.html (accessed January 2014).

[16] Sorensen, Sousa and Schaner (n 4).

[17] Ibid.

payments. CSS hypothesised how using factual income leads to setting appropriate orders, which allows the NCP to make consistent payments producing little or no arrears growth. NCPs with little or no arrears are better able to make future payments and avoid the barrier of high arrears debt (Figure 1).

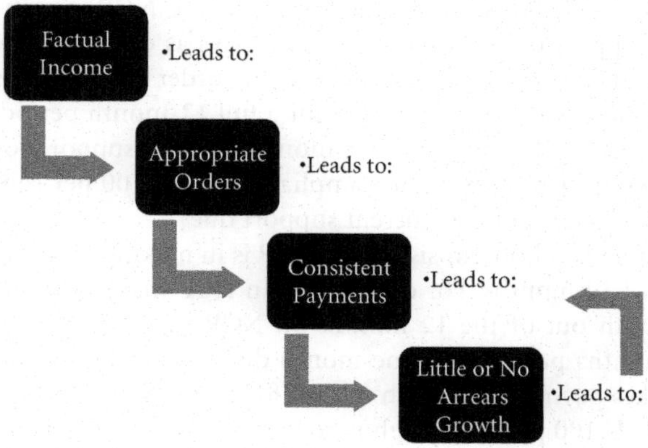

Figure 1: *Factual* Income Leads to Consistent Child Support Payments

CSS hypothesised how using fictional income leads to the setting of inappropriate orders, which results in the NCP making inconsistent payments. This results in arrears growth which deters NCPs from making future child support payments (Figure 2).

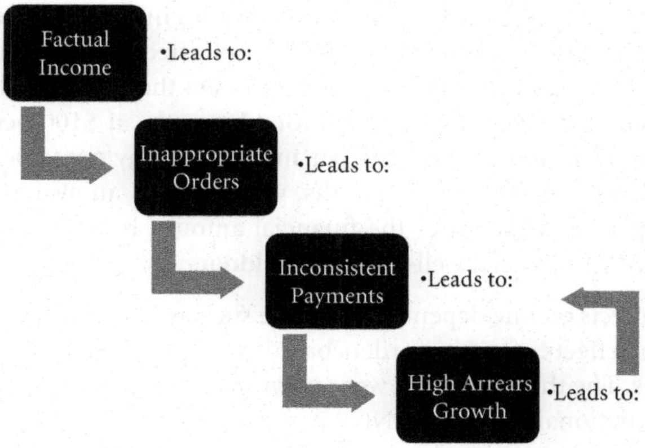

Figure 2: *Fictional* Income Leads to Inconsistent Child Support Payments

CSS examined all newly established orders in the State of California from January 2009 to December 2010, and examined future child support payments 12 months after these orders were established. Order amounts established were based on the guideline calculator (GLC) tool; however, deviation can occur depending on the circumstances of the case. The GLC tool included the NCP income data used to calculate the child support order. The entire sample analysed included 102,332 child support cases with a total of 142,730 children.

CSS evaluated the impact of fictional vs. factual income on three dependent measures:

— *Compliance* is defined as the percentage of current support collections distributed each month divided by the current support due per month for up to 12 months. This measure evaluates the financial well-being of children regarding basic living and medical needs. Generally, high percentages of compliance mean the NCP is compliant with the existing child support obligation ordered and pays as ordered. Low percentages mean the NCP is not in compliance with an existing order and pays less than ordered. Compliance for each case was determined for a full 12-month period. For example, if an NCP was ordered to pay $100 per month in child support for 12 months, and paid the full $100 each month, the compliance equals 100 per cent ($1,200 current support paid divided by $1,200 current support due).
— *Percentage of months paid* is defined by how consistent an NCP is in making monthly payments out of a maximum of 12 months. For example, if an NCP makes a single monthly payment for one month out of the 12 months an NCP was obligated to pay, then the percentage of months paid equals one month divided by 12 months, or 8.3 per cent. If an NCP makes payments for each month for 12 months, then the percentage of months paid equals 100 per cent. High percentages of payments mean the custodial parent (CP) received consistent monthly payments. Low percentages of payments mean the CP received less frequent payments. Consistency of payments is an important indicator of the ability of an NCP to comply with a child support order, and is also a measure of financial stability for the family the NCP is obligated to support.
— *Payments per child* is defined as the average monthly amount of child support paid for each child up to a maximum of 12 months. For example, if an NCP pays child support for one child for 12 months at $100 per month, then payments per child equals the total amount paid ($1,200) divided by the number of months obligated to pay (12). This represents $1,200 divided by 12 months or $100 per month. On the other hand, if an NCP is obligated to pay child support for one child for 12 months at $100 per month, but only pays six consecutive months at $100 per month, the payments per child equals $600 (total payments) divided by 12 months, which equals an average of $50 per month. Payments per child measures the financial amount received per month and is directly related to the financial well-being of children.

While prior research examined the effects on one dependent variable such as either compliance or payments, CSS examined the effects of setting orders based on fictional vs. factual income on three dependent variables. The three variables were examined simultaneously to understand the full impact of using fictional income on NCP payment behaviour.

Table 1 below summarises each of the three dependent measures in relation to the NCP's income. The number of cases profiled according to four monthly gross income levels of the NCP is presented below:

— Minimum wage	$1,387
— Low income	$0–$1,386
— Mid income	$1,388–$2,500
— High income	$2,500 +

Over 90 per cent of the minimum wage based orders are based on fictional NCP income. For the most part, all other categories are based on factual income.

Table 1: Compliance, Percentage of Months Paid, and Payments Per Child by NCP Income Category

	Number of Cases	Compliance	Percentage of Months Paid	Payments Per Child (Monthly)
Minimum Wage ($1,387)	19,983	19.9%	27.9%	$47
Low Income ($0–$1,386)	27,526	47.8%	56.0%	$68
Mid Income ($1,388–$2,500)	28,636	61.5%	74.2%	$176
High Income (>$2,500)	26,187	75.3%	85.7%	$371
Total/Average	102,332	59.1%	63.3%	$172

In Table 1, performance is higher for all performance measures as income increases from minimum wage to high income. As expected, NCPs with higher income have greater compliance, in relation to the percentage of months paid and they make higher payments per child compared to NCPs with lower income.

Several characteristics of the minimum wage group stand out in comparison with the other categories. First, this group of cases represents a large part of the sample (19.5 per cent of the total number of cases). Second, this group has the lowest performance measures in all three categories, especially compared to the low income group. The low income group is primarily composed of cases with actual income and outperforms the minimum wage group whose orders are primarily based on fictional income. Basically, using fictional income produces low compliance, low payment consistency and low payments per child.

Minimum wage orders in this study are the lowest and most difficult income group for collecting payments. The following statistics support the performance challenges of this group. In Figure 3, the study examined the percentage of cases paying zero dollars during a 12-month period comparing minimum wage cases vs. all other cases:

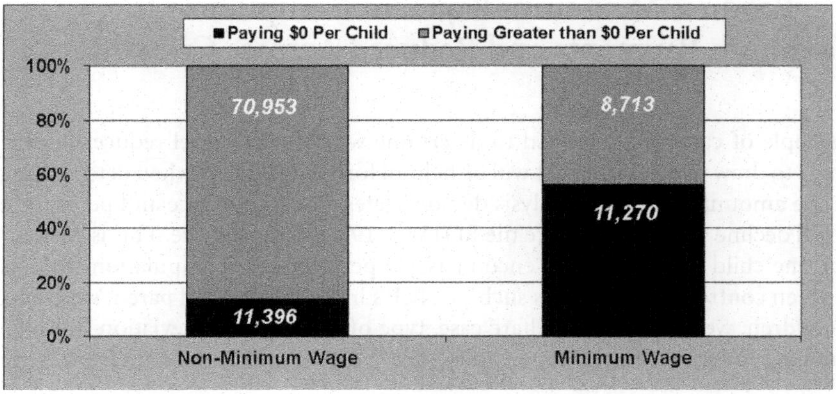

Figure 3: Percentage of Cases Paying Zero Dollars for Minimum Wage vs Non-Minimum Wage Cases

Low performance for minimum wage cases is directly associated with a high proportion of cases paying zero dollars. This fact specifically supports the hypothesis that setting orders based on imputing income at $1,387 produces cases with low probability of receiving any payment. Compared to cases based on actual income, there is a 56 per cent chance of receiving zero dollars in the next 12 months, if the order is based on fictional income. Taken a step further, there is a 70 per cent chance of receiving $1 to $50 per month, if the order is based on fictional income.

The use of orders based on fictional income impacts negatively on payments and does not lead to better compliance of orders or increases in support paid. California's data suggest in cases where there was an absence of income information, and a 'full-time minimum wage' amount was presumed, those orders were paid at a low rate and fewer dollars were collected than in other cases. Emphasis on these cases should be on identification of income sources. The hope that 'if you set it they will pay' is not supported by this study.

The use of fictional income can also be counterproductive. Most jurisdictions in the United States allow a tribunal to impute the obligor's ability to earn in a variety of instances. In some cases, the practice is justified as a sanction for uncooperative behaviour, failure to file income documents when the obligee spouse has alleged an earning capacity, or deliberate underemployment (a professional declining to become employed to avoid support obligations). Those cases were not isolated or commented on in this study. In some jurisdictions, when an obligor parent is employed part-time or at non-regular work (day labour), the tribunal or state law sets an artificial 'floor' for income. Commonly, the tribunal or policy will dictate all obligors be charged as if they were employed full-time at the local minimum wage, even if there is evidential proof that the obligor is employed at a lower rate. In such cases, this research supports the conclusion of 'imputed' income cases pay at a lower compliance rate, *and collect fewer dollars*, than when a less-than-minimum-wage income is used to calculate support. This finding was especially significant due to the high unemployment rates experienced during the study period.

VI. What is the Recommended Order Amount (as a Proportion of the NCP's Income) to Produce Maximum Payment Compliance, Maximum Payments and Reduced Arrears Growth?

The entire sample of cases was analysed to determine what ROTW level reduces performance in order to draw conclusions that will be helpful for policymakers when determining the appropriate amount to set. The analysis demonstrates that compliance and percentage of months paid decline significantly once the ROTW is 19 per cent or more. This is particularly true for one child families, which encompass 70 per cent of the population studied. This occurs when controlling for factors such as: NCP's income, custodial parent's income, number of children, welfare or non-welfare case, type of court action, deviation from the guideline amount, visitation percentage and child's age.[18] After 19 per cent ROTW, NCPs are

[18] M Takayesu and S Eldred, 'How Do Child Support Orders Affect Payments and Compliance' (2011) Orange County Department of Child Support Services www.css.ocgov.com/about/research_studies (accessed January 2014).

likely to fall out of compliance and pay irregular child support payments month-to-month. These results are consistent with prior research demonstrating arrears growth when ROTW was greater than 20 per cent.[19]

For families with two children, the threshold ranges from 19 to 29 per cent depending on the income level of the NCP. For families with three or more children, the threshold ranges from 29 to 39 per cent depending on the income level of the NCP.

Given these findings, the question becomes 'should child support policy support all orders being no more than 19 per cent ROTW for one child families to ensure orders are set appropriately?'

Setting all orders no higher than 19 per cent for one child families is a useful baseline for settings orders for child support professionals. Setting orders no higher than 19 per cent is beneficial to the CP and NCP for the following reasons:

— It increases the likelihood future monthly child support payments are compliant with the monthly order.
— It reduces the risk the NCP will fall into arrears as a result of non-compliance.
— It increases the likelihood the CP will obtain regular monthly payments on a timely basis as ordered.
— It ensures the CP is receiving the maximum amount of collections.

Maximum collections are achieved if the order is set no higher than 19 per cent ROTW because it ensures more consistent monthly payments to the CP.

VII. For Existing Orders, how does Modifying Orders Appropriately Affect Future Payments and Payment Compliance?

Thus far, the discussion has focused on the importance of setting orders appropriately using actual income to increase compliance and payments. What about existing orders? Can existing orders be modified appropriately to increase child support compliance and payments?

In the United States, modification of orders is the adjusting of the level of support owed each month. This is initiated either through a request by one of the parents, or initiated by the child support agency. For example, an NCP may request a modification to lower a child support order as a result of: losing his or her job, becoming disabled or being incarcerated. A CP may request an upward modification to provide for his or her child to pay for basic necessities as a result of increased living expenses. The child support agency may initiate a modification if notified of a change in circumstances from either party.

Orange County CSS provides child support services for approximately 79,000 cases as of October 2011. The CSS Research Unit completed two modification studies. One study

[19] Formoso (n 9).

was completed in FFY 2004,[20] and more recently for the period of May 2009 to May 2011.[21] Both studies examined the effects of modifying orders on compliance and payments for Orange County.

Three types of modifications were examined in this study: lower modifications, upward modifications and no change modifications (Figure 4).

Lower modifications are defined when the monthly current support amount is lowered from a previous existing amount. This also includes orders reserved and modified to zero dollars, as a result of the incarceration of the NCP.
Upward modifications are defined when the monthly current support amount is increased from a previous existing amount.
No change modifications are defined when the monthly current support amount remains the same from a previous existing amount.

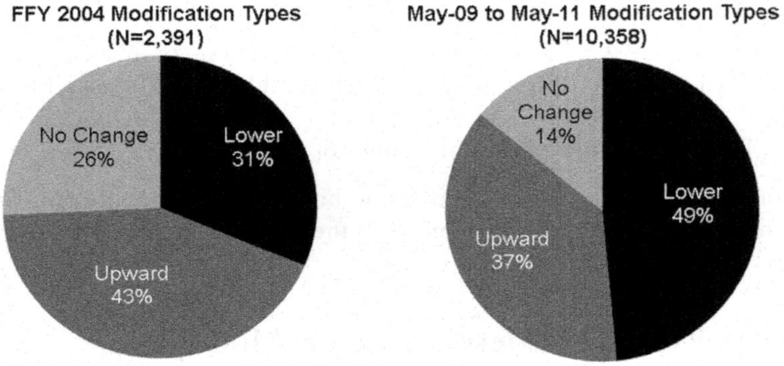

Figure 4: The Percentage of Lower, Upward, and No Change Modifications (FFY 2004 vs May 2009 to May 2011)

Compared to FFY 2004, the number of modifications nearly doubled in the later study (May 2009 to May 2011). The approximate number of modifications in a one-year period is 5,000 based on a two-year figure of 10,358. Furthermore, the proportion of lower modifications increased substantially in the later time period compared to FFY 2004. Both results reflect the economic downturn starting in 2008 which resulted in increased demand for modifications, primarily in the lower modification category.

A. The Effects of Modifying Child Support Orders on Compliance and Payments

The later study examined compliance and child support payments before modification (pre-modification) and after modification (post-modification) for 10,358 child support cases with a court order modification filing date between May 2009 and May 2011. Equal months of financial transactions were compared in pre- and post-modification time

[20] Orange County CSS, 'Impact of Judicial Modifications FFY 2004' (2005).
[21] Orange County CSS, 'Impact of Judicial Modifications FFY 2011' (2011).

periods for a maximum of 12 months. For example, if a case was modified in May 2009, up to 12 months of financial transactions were recorded 12 months after May 2009 (post) compared to 12 months before May 2009 (pre). The effects of modifications on compliance and child support payments are presented in Table 2.

Table 2: Modification Effects on Compliance and Payments by Modification Type

Lower Modifications (N=5,032)	Pre Modification	Post Modification	Variance	% Change
Current Support Due	$36,463,858	$17,831,015	–$18,632,843	–51.1%
Current Support Paid	$17,723,351	$12,253,629	–$5,469,722	–30.9%
Compliance	**48.6%**	**68.7%**	**20.1%**	**41.4%**
Upward Modifications (N=3,868)	Pre Modification	Post Modification	Variance	% Change
Current Support Due	$9,483,191	$22,669,490	$13,186,299	139.0%
Current Support Paid	$6,296,804	$14,611,525	$8,314,721	132.0%
Compliance	**66.4%**	**64.5%**	**–1.9%**	**–2.9%**
No-Change Modifications (N=1,458)	Pre Modification	Post Modification	Variance	% Change
Current Support Due	$1,893,276	$1,893,276	$0	0.0%
Current Support Paid	$1,090,336	$1,180,509	$90,173	8.3%
Compliance	**57.6%**	**62.4%**	**4.8%**	**8.3%**
Total Modifications (N=10,358)	Pre Modification	Post Modification	Variance	% Change
Current Support Due	$47,840,325	$42,393,781	–$5,446,544	–11.4%
Current Support Paid	$25,110,492	$28,045,662	$2,935,170	11.7
Compliance	**52.5%**	**66.2%**	**13.7%**	**26.0%**

For all modifications types, compliance improved by 26 per cent comparing pre- vs. post-modification time periods. Current support paid increased by 11.7 per cent and current support due dropped by 11.4 per cent. In total, modifications improved compliance significantly by reducing current support due and increasing current support paid.

Lower modifications improved compliance by the largest degree (41.4 per cent) compared to upward (–2.9 per cent) and no change (8.3 per cent) modifications. This improvement is primarily attributed to the 51.1 per cent drop in current support due. Current support paid, did not improve as a result of lower modifications.

Upward modifications did not improve compliance. However, it did improve current support paid by 132 per cent, which is primarily attributed to the 139 per cent increase in current support due.

No change modifications resulted in an 8.3 per cent improvement in compliance due to current support paid improving by 8.3 per cent. This category is of particular interest. Although a request for modification was initiated, the resulting modification ruling by the courts was a no change order and caused NCPs to increase their payments. Going through the court process and confirming that the support amount is correct may change payment behaviour, and bring a renewed awareness to paying child support.

VIII. Operational Policy Concerns (New Orders)

The study using California's guideline data found drops in compliance for new cases with an order greater than 19 per cent of an NCP's income for one child families. This information can assist caseworkers and programme managers in formulating office policy consistent with state law. A payment predictor tool was developed by the CSS Research Unit based on this study's findings: with all other case factors equal, what is the predicted payment compliance with a given NCP's gross income level and monthly child support order amount? Individual cases may have different results: low-family conflict/high participation cases are likely to pay above the predicted compliance. Obligors with less family participation or more social barriers (history of lower educational attainment, substance abuse or incarceration) are likely to pay lower than the predicted rate. Local knowledge is most useful as to the predictability of a particular case. Cases likely to pay at a low rate, either by order amount or predictive barriers, will need earlier and more thorough case support. A benefit of this research is how it assists the programme manager in identifying those cases that are most likely to pay at a low rate at the beginning of service.

IX. Operational Policy Concerns (Existing Orders)

Results of the Orange County modification study indicate that: modifications improve performance either through increasing payments through high orders (upward modifications), increasing compliance through low orders (lower modifications), or increasing payments by going through the modification process without changing the order amount.

Modifying orders based on a 19 per cent threshold has the benefit of improving compliance, while preventing arrears growth. For example, additional findings from the study indicate compliance is above 70 per cent when orders are at or below the 19 per cent threshold while orders above the 19 per cent threshold report low compliance (below 50 per cent) for a one child family. Although higher payments may result from modifying orders to higher amounts, the risk of arrears growth increases substantially. This becomes a barrier to making future consistent payments. Finally, NCPs going through the modification process increase child support payments as a result of NCPs being put through the court process.

X. Broader Policy Concerns

From a programme-wide perspective, the research in setting new orders is instructive in two main ways: the relationship between ROTW and support payment and the effects of imputing income at a higher level than obligors actually earn.

Child support compliance, in terms of rate of payment (percentage of ordered payments made) and dollars collected, are substantially determined by the ROTW of the state guideline. Policymakers are encouraged to focus on not designing high ROTW guidelines, because the results for both the paying parent and the receiving parent are not positive. 'Demand-based' systems that focus on the cost of raising a child, over the ability of the payer to pay, are counterproductive to the extent that they lead to unreasonable orders.

Finally, for setting orders where no factual income is available, it is important to set policy that emphasises the importance of taking the extra time to research factual income to set an appropriate order. Determining an order based on factual income less than the minimum wage floor is better than setting orders based on fictional income, because orders based on factual income lead to higher compliance and payments. In the following sections, empirical research focusing on barriers to child support payments will be discussed in the context of improving compliance through the use of appropriate orders. This research was conducted by the Research Unit from the Orange County California CSS using a predictive modelling approach. Policy implications and the effective use of family-centred services will be discussed as effective strategies to improve payment compliance.

XI. Barriers to Paying Child Support

The child support programme in the United States is a critical public programme and represents an important source of income for poor families, lifting a million people from poverty. Child support represents substantial income for poor and deeply poor families. For families that receive child support, previous research shows that child support represents 40 per cent of income for poor custodial families, and 63 per cent of income for families that are extremely poor. Child support income is instrumental in alleviating poverty.[22]

Knowing that child support income provides critically needed income for poor families, it is important to understand the barriers that prevent NCPs from paying child support. Previous research has noted barriers such as fatherhood at an early age, low education, incarceration and lack of health insurance are characteristic of NCPs who pay little or no child support.[23] Significant barriers were found as reasons for arrears growth and non-payment of child support.[24] These barriers include the prevalence of multiple cases, parents on public assistance, intermittent employment, mental illness, substance abuse problems and incarceration. Others have identified relationship barriers such as conflict over visitation, and NCPs concern that the CP is spending money unwisely, as obstacles to child support payments.[25]

[22] E Sorensen, 'Child Support Plays an Increasingly Important Role for Poor Custodial Families' (2010) Urban Institute www.urban.org/uploadedpdf/412272-child-support-plays-important-role.pdf (accessed January 2014).

[23] K Lippold, A Nichols and E Sorensen, 'Strengthening Families Through Stronger Fathers: Final Impact Report for the Pilot Employment Programs' (2011) Urban Institute www.urban.org/UploadedPDF/412442-Strengthening-Families-Through-Stronger-Fathers.pdf (accessed January 2014).

[24] Formoso (n 9).

[25] W Primus and K Daugirdas, 'Improving Child Well-Being by Focusing on Low-Income Noncustodial Parents in Maryland' (2000) www.abell.org/pubsitems/cd_improving_child_900.pdf (accessed January 2014).

Child support payment barriers are addressed in the context of understanding the reasons for non-payment of child support, and point to the need to examine the reasons for unemployment or inconsistent employment. Barriers that prevent consistent employment include health limitations, limited education, limited work experience and lack of English language skills. Generally, policy reforms have expressed the need to increase child support for poor NCPs with these barriers by addressing the need for income support programmes, employment services and job training programmes.

With regards to setting appropriate orders, previous research shows that NCPs who are poor pay a higher percentage of their income towards child support compared to NCPs who are not poor. For example, one quarter of the poor NCPs paying child support spent 50 per cent of their income on child support while only two per cent of non-poor fathers spent that same percentage.[26] Often the requirement to pay a high percentage leads to high arrears debt, that never gets paid, and is primarily responsible for the substantial amount of arrears owed and its growth.[27] NCPs with more barriers are expected to pay a larger portion of their income towards child support. For example, when the ratio of the NCP's monthly child support order amount to the NCP's monthly gross wages (ROTW) is at 20 per cent ROTW, the number of barriers has little effect on arrearage growth. When ROTW is higher than 40 per cent, the number of barriers increases to four or more per NCP. As indicated by the number of barriers and lowest incomes, NCPs with the most problematic lives are expected to pay an impossibly large portion of their income towards child support.[28]

The goal of the barriers study is to examine and understand the number and type of barriers that lead to low compliance and to effectively address policy implications exploring successful programmes that deal with these issues. Questions addressed in this study are:

(1) What are the barriers that lead to low compliance?
(2) What are the NCP characteristics that predict compliance?
(3) Will setting appropriate orders for NCPs with payment barriers lead towards higher compliance?
(4) What is the role of family-centred services to improve child support payments for NCPs with barriers?

XII. What are the Barriers that Lead to Low Compliance?

CSS identified barriers that lead to low compliance through a survey study that assessed NCP barriers to paying child support. This survey instrument asked the NCP questions related to his or her education level, employment and criminal history. Questions were also asked regarding his or her reasons for not making consistent child support payments.

[26] E Sorensen and H Oliver, 'Policy Reforms are Needed to Increase Child Support from Poor Fathers' (2002) www.urban.org/UploadedPDF/410477.pdf (accessed January 2014).
[27] Sorensen, Sousa and Schaner (n 4).
[28] Formoso (n 9).

These questions include dealing with the relationship of the other parent (ie the other parent decides how to spend money), perception that orders are too high, visitation and motivation factors.

CSS randomly surveyed 4,923 NCPs from a caseload of approximately 79,000 cases in Orange County as of FFY 2011. The sample population included open cases billing current support for six months or longer. Survey responses were collected by email, phone contact, or postal mail to six per cent female and 94 per cent male NCPs. Seven hundred and seventy-two NCPs responded to the survey, giving a response rate of 15.7 per cent. The completed survey responses were matched with California's state-wide Child Support Enforcement System to extract child support due and amounts paid, and other demographic information from October 2010 to September 2011.

The primary independent variables include the barriers assessed based on the questionnaire assessment. With the exception of NCP monthly income, ROTW and NCP age at first becoming a parent (which were derived from California's Child Support Enforcement (CSE) system), the values described in Table 3 represent the answers from the questionnaire. ROTW was calculated as the monthly child support order amount divided by the monthly gross wages. For example, if an NCP is obligated to pay $100 per month for one child, and has a gross monthly income of $1,387, then the ROTW is calculated as $100 divided by $1,387 or 7.2 per cent. High ROTW indicates a heavy financial burden for the NCP, and as a result may have lower compliance in payment of current support resulting in arrears growth. The list of independent variables along with their values to assess its impact on compliance are listed in Table 3.

Table 3: Independent Variables

Variable Name	Values
Income and Barriers	
Income of NCP	Income per month ranging from $0 to $90,000 per month
Education Level	College Degree, Some College, High School Diploma/GED, Did Not Complete High School
Currently Employed	Yes or No
Currently on Public Assistance	Yes or No
History of Substance Abuse	Yes or No
Criminal History	Never Convicted, Misdemeanour, Felony
Currently On Probation/Parole	Yes or No
Relationship Variables	
Other Parent Limits Visitation	Yes or No
Child Support Order is Too High	Yes or No
Support Child(ren) From Other Relationships	Yes or No
Visitation Variables	

(*Continued*)

Table 3: (*Continued*)

Visitation Days Per Month	0, 1–5, 6–10, 11–15–16–20, 21–25, 26–30
Conflict With Other Parent Limits Visitation	Yes or No
Physical Disability Limits Visitation	Yes or No
Distance Limits Visitation	Yes or No
Child Support Order	
Ratio of Order Amount To Wage	Ratio Ranging From 0–100 per cent
Demographic Variables	
NCP Age At First Becoming A Parent	Numeric Value with Range from 14 to 55 years of age
Language of NCP	English, Spanish, Vietnamese, Other
Number of Children	Numeric value ranging from 1 to 7 children

Compliance was the dependent measure defined as the percentage of current support collections distributed each month divided by the current support due per month for up to 12 months. This measure evaluates the financial well-being of children regarding basic living and medical needs. Generally, high percentage of compliance means the NCP is compliant with the existing child support obligation ordered and pays as ordered. Low percentage means the NCP is not in compliance with an existing order and pays less than ordered. Compliance for each case was determined for a full 12-month period. For example, if an NCP was ordered to pay $100 per month in child support for 12 months, and paid the full $100 each month, the compliance equals 100 per cent ($1,200 current support paid divided by $1,200 current support due).

To identify the barriers that are the most likely to cause lower compliance, CSS utilised a predictive modelling approach using a gradient boosting algorithmic model.[29] CSS used SAS® Enterprise Miner 7.1. software to develop the model. The gradient boosting approach was used to produce a predictive model based on multivariate data. The model produced a predicted compliance value for each NCP based on the combination of independent variables used to establish the model. Gradient boosting is an attractive algorithm to analyse child support data because it can be applied to classification or regression problems from a variety of response distributions (Gaussian, Bernoulli, Poisson and Laplace). Gradient boosting also models complex interactions simply and provides interpretable results.

The statistical output of the gradient boosting algorithmic model displays the relative importance of the most influential predictors. Since these measures are relative, a value of 1.0 was assigned to the most influential predictor and the others were scaled accordingly. This model was used to assess the overall influence of predictors from all of the independent variables used.

[29] J Friedman, 'Greedy Function Approximation: A Gradient Boosting Machine' (2001) *The Annals of Statistics* 1189.

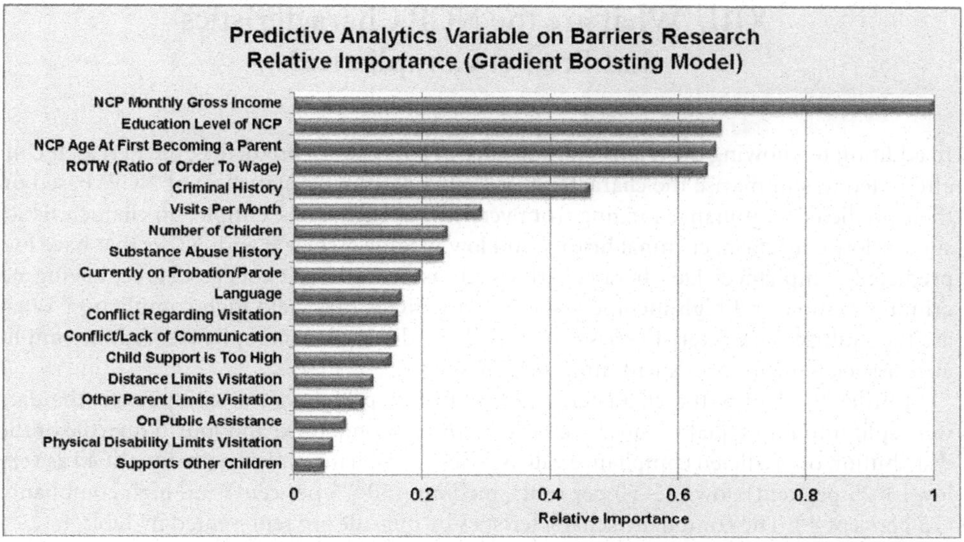

Figure 5: Model Predictors

- Based on the gradient boosting algorithmic model in predicting compliance, the most influential predictor is the NCP's monthly gross income (1.0). Relative to income, the next most influential predictor was education level of the NCP (.66) and closely followed by the NCP age at first becoming a parent (.65) and ROTW (.64). Education level of the NCP (.66), NCP age at first becoming a parent (.65) and ROTW (.64) are clustered close together. The next most influential variable is criminal history (.46) which is highly influential in comparison to visits per month (.29) and all the other variables that follow. The average squared error used to assess model fit was .085833.
- It is important to note the top ten predictors (from NCP income to language) represent primarily social economic barriers of the NCP. With the exception of being on public assistance, the other predictors can represent a perceived opinion. For example, the NCP's opinion that the 'child support order is too high' is not a good predictor to compliance. These types of predictors have less of an influence compared to social economic barriers.

Understanding the relative importance of these barriers is important in developing child support policy to address reasons for non-payment and to arrive at solutions that improve payments. For example, knowing that education is a major barrier in comparison to other barriers, do social programmes encourage education by providing incentives to new NCPs to complete high school? Knowing that ROTW is about as influential as education level, will setting appropriate orders for NCPs without a high school education help encourage NCPs to obtain an education, which can eventually lead to long-term, consistent payments?

XIII. What are the NCP Characteristics that Predict Compliance?

In addition to knowing the relative importance of compliance predictors, the Research Unit attempted to summarise the characteristics (using descriptive statistics) of NCPs based on their predicted compliance ranging from very low to high. For example, do characteristics such as low education, criminal history and low income associate with NCPs that have low predicted compliance? Do characteristics such as possessing a college degree, having no criminal history and high income associate with NCPs that yield high compliance? What are the multiple characteristics associated with predicting low compliance? Is low compliance associated with NCPs with multiple barriers?

In order to identify the characteristics that make up high vs low compliance, the data were split into four equal groups based on the first, second, third and fourth quartile of the distribution of predicted compliance values. These compliance values were identified as very low (0–25 per cent), low (25–50 per cent), medium (50–75 per cent) and high compliance (75 per cent +). The compliance characteristics by quartile are represented in Table 4.

Table 4: Predicted Compliance Characteristics

	Very Low (n=317) (0–25%)	Low (n=206) (25–50%)	Medium (n=172) (50–75%)	High (n=77) (75–100%)
Average Predicted Compliance	16.0%	34.5%	66.4%	78.2%
Average Actual Compliance	14.2%	35.0%	66.3%	82.6%
Monthly Income (Median)	$631	$1,433	$3,502	$4,619
Did Not Complete High School	35.0%	31.1%	22.7%	14.3%
Average NCP Age At First Becoming a Parent	25.4	25.9	27.7	27.8
ROTW (Ratio of Order To Wage)	45.2%	27.3%	15.1%	9.3%
Criminal History	72.6%	25.7%	34.3%	9.1%
Average Vists Per Month	4.6	3.7	6.6	2.4
Cases With 2+ Children	43.9%	25.7%	35.5%	14.3%
History of Substance Abuse	31.9%	23.8%	12.8%	5.2%
On Probation/Parole	21.8%	8.7%	2.3%	0%
Language (English is Not Primary Language)	24.9%	32.5%	27.3%	19.5%
On Public Assistance	25.9%	25.2%	9.9%	11.7%
Unemployed	64.0%	48.5%	29.7%	16.9%
Average Number of Barriers	3.3	2.5	1.9	1.5

Table 4 identifies NCP characteristics of predicted compliance ranging from very low to high. The variations in compliance in this table are strikingly clear. In examining each predicted compliance category, those with very low to low predicted compliance have significant barriers. NCPs who are predicted to have very low (n=317) to low predicted compliance (n=206) make up 68 per cent of the 772 respondents, which is a substantial percentage of the study sample.

— Characteristics of NCPs with predicted very low to low compliance are those: with lower income; who generally did not complete high school; are first time parents at a young age; have a criminal history; low visitation; two or more children; a history of substance abuse; are on probation/parole; have English as a second language; are on public assistance; are unemployed; and have a greater number of barriers.
— Characteristics of NCPs with predicted medium to high compliance include, but are not limited to, cases with higher income, higher education and less criminal history.
— Although NCPs with predicted very low to low compliance have significant barriers and low median gross income, these NCPs are expected to pay a large percentage of their gross income towards child support (ROTW of 27 per cent and above) compared to NCPs with medium to high compliance (ROTW of 15.1 per cent or less).

XIV. Will Setting Appropriate Orders for NCPs with Payment Barriers Lead to Higher Compliance?

This study demonstrates that ROTW and NCP barriers are good predictors of future compliance. However, is it possible to achieve higher compliance with an appropriate order even though the NCP has low education?

Figure 6 below reports the actual compliance level based on the NCP's education level, and whether the order was set between 0 and 19 per cent of the NCP's gross income or 19 per cent or greater. Table 5 describes the number of cases. For all education levels including NCPs not completing high school, orders between 0 and 19 per cent report higher compliance levels compared to orders of 19 per cent or greater.

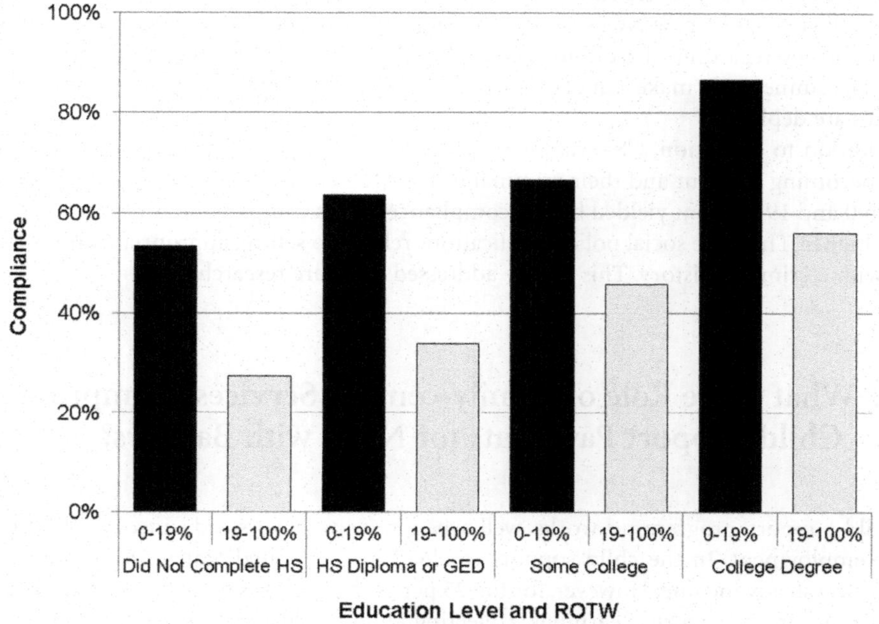

Figure 6: Compliance by Education Level and ROTW (N=714)

Table 5: Number of Cases by Education Level and ROTW

ROTW	Did Not Complete High School	High School Diploma or GED	Some College	College Degree
0–19%	90	118	88	47
19–100%	111	125	98	37

The importance of setting appropriate orders based on education level becomes important to increase the total dollars received by the family over the child's life. NCPs with less than a high school diploma or equivalency certificate earn significantly less than a person with a diploma. Based on expected compliance rates and earnings for both groups, data suggest that steering the parent into completion of a diploma or certificate could result in the family receiving up to 43 per cent more support over the child's minority. Data also show that a lower arrearage balance is built and the parent can pay off the arrears in a much shorter time.

The following is a recent example of how awareness of barriers can impact a case as applied by an Orange County commissioner. In one particular hearing, the court learned that a 20-year-old NCP had not completed high school and that the NCP was in the process of attaining a General Education Diploma. The court ordered a $50 order per month for one year. At the end of the year, the order would increase to $200 per month. The court set the $50 order to begin the following month rather than when the motion was filed to prevent the case starting in arrears. In addition, the NCP was ordered to visit a One-Stop Centre, which is a programme to assist the NCP in finding employment.

On a broad scale, reliable compliance predictors based on education levels can assist family-centred services programmes to make decisions about how much ancillary support can realistically be paid successfully. Does the social programme encourage education by providing incentives to new NCPs to complete high school? Each jurisdiction must make its own choices regarding these questions; however, with predictive research-supported data, programmes can make educated decisions about how limited social programme resources are deployed.

In addition to education, CSS examined the other top barriers including the NCP age at first becoming a parent and their criminal history. For each of these barriers, orders set between 0 and 19 per cent yielded higher compliance values compared to orders set 19 per cent or higher. There are social policy implications related to setting appropriate orders for NCPs with a criminal history. This will be addressed in future research.

XV. What is the Role of Family-centred Services to Improve Child Support Payments for NCPs with Barriers?

The child support programme works well when parents have steady income through regular employment. In the child support caseload in the United States, 75 per cent of parents have steady income. However, for the 25 per cent of parents without steady income who have no or low reported earnings, collecting child support income can be difficult.

Uncollected child support from this population constitutes 70 per cent of the unpaid child support debt.[30]

OCSE is currently undertaking a family-centred services approach to improve child support outcomes that can be effective in improving the collections for parents without steady income. Today, child support programmes are engaged in a variety of innovative strategies and projects that engage partnerships with a variety of work-oriented programmes. These strategies include outreach, referral and case management strategies that engage with fatherhood, workforce and re-entry programmes.

The child support programme is in regular contact with low-income NCPs and is uniquely positioned to link these NCPs to these services. Child support programmes also have the ability through engagement with the NCP and through data analysis to identify the underlying reasons for non-payment of child support. Child support–led programmes engaged with other work-oriented programmes have demonstrated a high level of success in improving child support collections for low-income NCPs.[31]

For example, at least 38 work-oriented programmes partnering with child support agencies are involved with at least 28 states and the District of Columbia. Court-ordered programmes, voluntary programmes and transitional job programmes are all showing success in improving child support collections. These programmes serve NCPs with low income who are mainly unemployed and have major barriers that prevent them from paying child support. The State of New York's 'Strengthening Families Through Stronger Fathers' initiative has proven to be highly successful in increasing income and child support payments for low-income NCPs with multiple employment barriers such as limited education and criminal records.

This study used predictive modelling to identify the type and number of payment barriers, and predicts compliance for these NCPs with one or a combination of these barriers. Child support programmes armed with this knowledge can provide early intervention opportunities to establish appropriate orders and refer these NCPs to overcome these barriers.

In November 2012, the Orange County CSS opened their Community Resource Centre (CRC) designed to carry out OCSE's family-centred services initiative of 2011. The CRC is a one-stop centre that includes customer interviews, family law facilitation, genetic testing, forms workshops, orientation workshops, modification workshops, and provides customers with access to community resources throughout the county. Customers using the CRC can access information regarding a variety of services such as food banks, clothing, health services, child care, employment, domestic violence, legal services, tax preparation resources, shelters, educational resources, and veterans' services. Since opening, the CRC served over 4,700 customers in its first eight months.

Future objectives of analysing child support payment barriers to predict compliance are to use predictive modelling to increase the effectiveness of the CRC and in setting appropriate orders. Knowing the number and type of payment barriers of each NCP can

[30] OCSE, 'Family-Centred Innovations Improve Child Support Outcomes' (2011) *Promoting Child Well-Being & Family Self-Sufficiency* 1 www.acf.hhs.gov/programs/css/resource/family-centered-innovations-improve-child-support-outcomes (accessed January 2014).

[31] OCSE, 'Improving Child Support Outcomes through Employment Programs' (2012) *Promoting Child Well-Being & Family Self-Sufficiency* 11 www.acf.hhs.gov/programs/css/resource/improving-child-support-outcomes-through-employment-programs (accessed January 2014).

assist staff in setting appropriate orders, increasing the probability of payment and better servicing NCPs with barriers. The Orange County Research Unit plans to evaluate the effectiveness of the CRC in improving child support collections in the future. It is anticipated that NCPs using the CRC will demonstrate higher payment compliance and payment consistency after participating in the programme.

XVI. Conclusion

Research and policy implications point to the importance of setting monthly child support orders using actual income and setting monthly orders at no higher than 19 per cent of the NCP's monthly gross income to maximise future payment compliance and payment consistency. Research demonstrates that setting appropriate orders is one of the strongest predictors to improve future payment compliance. A child support policy that adheres to these best practices can improve both payment consistency and compliance for new and existing orders.

Research has also demonstrated that where NCPs have multiple barriers, this significantly limits future payment compliance. NCPs with multiple barriers were expected to pay a much higher proportion of their monthly gross income towards child support compared to NCPs with few or no barriers. Child support policymakers, and child support professionals who are knowledgeable of NCPs' barriers on a case by case basis can use this information to set orders that are appropriate and can refer these NCPs to family-centred services. Setting appropriate orders for NCPs with barriers has been found to result in higher compliance compared to NCPs with orders set too high in proportion to their income. Referring NCPs to family-centred services has the added benefit of assisting them with the services they need to improve their long-term financial well-being and provide long-term consistent child support payments for their children.

Future research will include tracking compliance rates among parents referred to anti-barrier programmes (education, expunging criminal records, substance abuse programmes, etc). Do parents participate in these programmes? If they complete a barrier-reducing programme, does their compliance with child support orders increase as a result? Are these programmes cost-effective in terms of increasing money spent on families by increasing earning potential? Logic provides a hypothesis; long-term research and tracking will provide proof that the theory is correct.

11

Administrative Establishment and Enforcement of Child Support in Norway

JORID SAUE, FLOOR DE JONGH BEKKALI, ELISABETH SÆTTEM
AND BRITT RUSTAD

I. Introduction

Norway is a relatively small and sparsely populated country with five million inhabitants. The average birth rate is 1.88 per woman and 25 per cent of all children live with only one of their biological parents. Both parents are likely to be in employment. In Norway, 66 per cent of women between 15 and 74 years are employed, compared to 71 per cent of men.[1] In terms of the collection of child support it is positive that the employment rate is high as this increases parents' ability to provide for their children. The recovery rate of child support in Norway is relatively high at 80 per cent. There are many factors that contribute to this high success rate, and various benefits of the child support system will be discussed and analysed in this chapter. This chapter will begin by giving a brief introduction to the various bodies responsible for child support and maintenance in Norway.

There are two ministries involved in child support procedures in Norway, the Ministry of Children, Equality and Social Inclusion and the Ministry of Labour and Social Affairs. These ministries are responsible for the acts that govern child support establishment and collection, in addition to the Advance Payment of Maintenance Act, and draft regulations and changes to these acts.

The Directorate of Labour and Welfare is responsible for the establishment and collection of child support in Norway. Three subordinate agencies have different roles in handling international child support cases. In addition, there are several local offices that handle the establishment of child support in Norwegian cases.

The NAV National Office for Social Insurance Abroad is Norway's Central Authority under international child support conventions. This office is the receiving agency, and recognises foreign orders for collection in Norway. NAV National Office for Social Insurance Abroad also establishes administrative child support decisions in international cases. It is a

[1] See www.ssb.no, table 08931: Sysselsetjing og arbeidsløyse for personar 15–74. Sesongjusterte tal og trend, 3 månaders glidande gjennomsnitt, etter kjønn og alder, statistics from October 2013 (accessed January 2014).

centralised office based in Oslo, handling international social insurance and child support cases. The office has 210 employees in total, of whom 22 work in the child support unit. Good language skills are crucial for the employees. Nine of the employees come from countries other than Norway.[2] This enhances communication and good service to the parties in these cases, as well as to the cooperating States and their Central Authorities.

The Collection Agency of the Labour and Welfare Administration (the Collection Agency) is a public body which plays an important role in Norway's child support system. The Collection Agency collects child support based on national and foreign child support decisions in Norway. This office is also the requesting agency for collection abroad. The Collection Agency is a centralised unit established in 1992, located in Kirkenes next to the Russian and Finnish borders, in the north-eastern part of Norway. There are 151 employees working to collect child support and incorrectly paid social insurance benefits as well as in administration, accounting, legal services and IT.

Finally, the NAV Appeals is the administrative appellate office that handles appeals made to Norwegian child support decisions.

II. The Norwegian Child Support Model

Norway has an administrative system for the establishment and enforcement of child support. This means that the courts are not involved either in the stipulation process or the collection process. However, courts may of course be involved in high-conflict cases, if one of the parties wishes to bring the case before a judge. The administrative stipulation process is based entirely on the examination of documents, and there is no oral hearing. An administrative child support decision is enforceable in the same way as a court order. Such a decision may be brought before the courts only after all possibilities for an administrative appeal have been exhausted, but the decision continues to be enforceable until the court has reviewed the case and has made a different decision. However, it should be noted that both parties may apply immediately for a modifying administrative decision to replace the court order.

Written private agreements on child support signed by both parties are equally enforceable, but only if the agreement is enforced by the Collection Agency. This limitation does not apply to administrative decisions, where a creditor can, in theory, request the ordinary enforcement authorities to collect the money. In reality, this never happens, because the creditor would then have to pay for the services that the Collection Agency provides free of charge.

Child support establishment or modification cases are rarely brought before the courts. As a general rule, the courts do not make decisions regarding child support even if they are involved in divorce proceedings between the parties. A search in the database for judgments in Norway brings to light records of only a handful of court cases handling establishment

[2] These are Finland, Sweden, Germany, Poland, the Netherlands, Italy, Russia and Vietnam. In addition, two of the employees are fluent in French. The employees establish child support decisions written in several languages, which reduces the need for costly translation services.

of child support over the last 25 years.[3] One may safely conclude that the establishment of child support in Norway is an exclusively administrative process.

There are many benefits of using an administrative model:

- It is cost-effective.
- Cases do not take up time in the courts. Between 2004 and 2011 an average of 23,530 applications for establishment or modification of child support were handled by NAV annually. If these applications were to be handled by the courts instead, it would be necessary to employ many more judges, which would be much more costly.[4] When handling the cases in the courts, one has to find a date for a main hearing which suits both parties and their lawyers, and there is a risk that the session in court will be rescheduled and delayed. This would tend to produce a slower handling of cases.
- An administrative stipulation of child support is cheaper for parties who cannot reach a private agreement, because they do not have to be represented by a lawyer in order to ensure a fair decision.
- The parties feel closer to the public administration than to a court. The parties can call NAV and talk to a caseworker. The threshold for a party to a case to contact NAV is believed to be much lower than for a party to come forward with their views in a courtroom.
- The administrative system in general, has proved to lower the level of conflict between the parents.[5] This is especially true since the modernisation of the system in 2003, as the amount of child support payable is now calculated on the basis of the income of both parties.

The main argument against an administrative process seems to be that a court-based system is generally considered to guarantee due process for the parties to a greater extent, resulting in more correct decisions. In Norway, the amount to be paid as support follows directly from Regulations made under the Children Act. What has to be determined in order to make a decision is chiefly the income of the parties. It is not easy to see why a court hearing is more suited to clarify this matter than an administrative process. The administrative handling of cases is flexible with regards to the time and place for presenting arguments and taking steps to amend a decision. One might argue that with a system like the Norwegian system determining support, the legal protection for the parties is better taken care of through an administrative process. An administrative model for child support works in Norway because people in Norway generally have high levels of confidence in the authorities as well as the accuracy and appropriateness of administrative decisions.

[3] See www.lovdata.no (accessed January 2014).

[4] Unfortunately there are no records on the number of cases that go to court, but this happens very rarely.

[5] Act No 7 of 08 April 1981 relating to Children and Parents (The Children Act), ss 71 and 74. The Act is available in English at www.lovdata.no (accessed January 2014); the Regulation on Stipulation, s 1. See also www.ssb.no/befolkning/artikler-og-publikasjoner/naar-mor-og-far-bor-hver-for-seg (accessed January 2014).

III. Norwegian Legislation on Child Support

There are three Acts that govern child support establishment and collection in Norway: the Children Act of 08 April 1981 No 7 (the Children Act), the Advance Payment of Maintenance Act of 17 February 1989 No 2 (the Advance Payment of Maintenance Act) and the Maintenance Collection Act of 29 April 2005 No 20 (the Maintenance Collection Act).

The Children Act regulates the legal relationship between children and parents, including the establishment of child support.[6] According to this Act, parents have an obligation to bear the expenses of maintaining and educating their child.[7] A non-custodial parent is obliged to pay monthly child support.[8] The parents may agree upon the child support amount or they may apply to the National Insurance Office (NAV) for establishment of a child support decision for a minor fee.[9] The fee does not apply to international cases. Norwegian authorities have jurisdiction to establish a child support decision if the child or one of the parents lives in Norway.[10]

The Advance Payment of Maintenance Act regulates the rights to advance payments of child support.[11] A child who resides in Norway may apply for advance child support payments from the Norwegian State if the child does not live with both parents.[12] It is also a condition that the child support agreed upon or decided administratively, is collected by the Collection Agency. By applying for advance payments of child support, the custodial parent agrees to the Government's right to seek reimbursement for its expenses in child support from the non-custodial parent.

Advance payments are subject to means testing. There are three levels of advance payments, depending on the custodial parent's income.[13] If the custodial parent's annual income exceeds a certain limit, no advance payments may be made. The advance payment levels and income limits are updated annually.[14]

The Maintenance Collection Act regulates the collection of Norwegian decisions and foreign orders regarding maintenance.[15] Both parents may at any time request that the child support shall be collected by the Collection Agency.[16] The basis for collection may be a Norwegian or foreign administrative decision, private agreement or court order.[17]

[6] See www.regjeringen.no/en/doc/Laws/Acts/the-children-act.html?id=448389 (accessed December 2013) and the Children Act s 70.

[7] The Children Act, s 66.

[8] Ibid s 67.

[9] Ibid s 70, paras 1 and 2 and www.lovdata.no/for/sf/bl/bl-20011104-1250.html (accessed December 2013).

[10] The Children Act, s 83(b).

[11] See www.lovdata.no/cgi-wift/wiftldles?doc=/app/gratis/www/docroot/all/tl-19890217-002-0.html&emne=forskottering*&& (accessed December 2013).

[12] The Advance Payment of Maintenance Act, s 2. The Act is not available in English.

[13] Ibid s 5, para 1.

[14] See www.nav.no/English/English/Advance+support+payment.805368912.cms (accessed December 2013) and the Advance Payment of Maintenance Act, s 5.

[15] See www.lovdata.no/all/hl-20050429-020.html (accessed December 2013).

[16] The Maintenance Collection Act, s 5; lovdata.no/dokument/NL/lov/2005-04-29-20 (accessed December 2013). The Act is not available in English.

[17] The Maintenance Collection Act, s 2.

Child support decisions made in a State that Norway is cooperating internationally with (see section IV below) may be acknowledged and enforced in Norway, and collected in accordance with the Maintenance Collection Act if the basis for collection meets the conditions of those Conventions. In cases where a custodial parent receives advance payments of child support from the Norwegian Government, it is mandatory that maintenance payments are made through the Collection Agency so reimbursements can be made.[18]

IV. Norway's International Child Support Obligations

Norway has ratified the following international Conventions:

— The UN Convention of 1956[19]
— The Hague Conventions of 1958[20] 1973[21] and 2007[22]
— The Nordic Convention of 1962[23]
— The Lugano Convention of 2007[24]

In addition, Norway has a reciprocal agreement with the United States since June 2002.[25]

According to section 83 of the Children Act, child support may be established by the NAV National Office for Social Insurance Abroad if one of the parties or the child resides in Norway. This is a wide and simple jurisdictional rule, compared to many other States. This jurisdictional arrangement has the effect that child support may be collected in favour of children living in States other than those which are members of the international maintenance Conventions. The conditions are that the basis for collection is established in Norway (administrative establishment or private agreement between the parties) and that the non-custodial parent resides in Norway. This rule makes it possible for children in for instance Thailand, Brazil and The Philippines to receive their rightful maintenance from a parent living in Norway. This rule gives many children of Norwegian fathers opportunities that the majority of these children did not know existed.

[18] Ibid s 5, para 2.

[19] New York Convention on the Recovery of Maintenance Abroad of June 1956 (for a list of Contracting States see www.treaties.un.org/Pages/ViewDetailsIII.aspx?&src=TREATY&mtdsg_no=XX~1&chapter=20&Temp=mtdsg3&lang=en (accessed August 2013)).

[20] Convention of 15 April 1958 concerning the recognition and enforcement of decisions relating to maintenance obligations towards children (for a list of Contracting States see www.hcch.net/index_en.php?act=conventions.status&cid=38 (accessed August 2013)).

[21] Convention of 2 October 1973 on the Recognition and Enforcement of decisions relating to Maintenance obligations (for a list of Contracting States see www.hcch.net/index_en.php?act=conventions.status&cid=85 (accessed August 2013)).

[22] Convention of 23 November 2007 on the International Recovery of Child Support and other forms of Family Maintenance. Norway was the first State to ratify the Convention. (See www.hcch.net/index_en.php?act=conventions.status&cid=131 (accessed August 2013)).

[23] Convention of 23 March 1962 between Norway, Denmark, Finland, Iceland and Sweden on the enforcement of maintenance.

[24] Convention on Jurisdiction and the Recognition and Enforcement of Judgments in Civil and Commercial Matters, concluded in Lugano on 30 October 2007.

[25] Agreement between the Government of the United States of America and the Government of the Kingdom of Norway for the Enforcement of Maintenance Obligations (see www.acf.hhs.gov/sites/default/files/ocse/norway_reciprocating_agreement.pdf (accessed December 2013)).

V. Child Support Establishment in Norway

Private agreements on child support are common between Norwegian parents. These agreements save the Government time and money on establishment, modifications and appeals, and are therefore encouraged. The Children Act endorses private agreements,[26] and this is further (intentionally) encouraged through the fee for establishing and amending decisions administratively.[27] However, if parents do not agree on child support, an application may be made to NAV for establishment of the amount to be paid.

If both parents and the child(ren) live in Norway, the case is handled by a NAV office that specialises in handling child support cases. There are currently six dedicated child support offices throughout Norway. However, if one of the parents or the child lives abroad, the case is handled by NAV National Office for Social Insurance Abroad.

The Norwegian method of determining child support takes as a starting point a standardised calculation of the cost of maintaining a child based on statistics, comprising consumption and living expenses, as well as the costs of child care. The expenses used in the calculation are average expenses based on national statistics, and the amounts are updated annually.[28] Older children are more expensive to maintain than younger children. The costs are divided into four age groups; children aged 0–5, 6–11, 12–14 and 15–18. Any child care expenses need to be documented, and factual amounts are used here.

The maintenance costs are divided between the parents based on information on their income.[29] For non-respondents of the advance notice of stipulation or modification of child support, income information known by NAV and/ or the Norwegian tax authority is used. If the caseworker has no information on a party's income, imputed income is used, based on what the caseworker knows about the party's income ability. This estimated income is based on any available information regarding the party's education, work experience and former income information. If no information about the non-custodial parent can be found, income statistics are used. In that case, guidelines developed by the United Bank of Switzerland are used as a starting point.[30] However, even if the caseworker has information on a party's income, that party's earnings may be estimated if that party works less than 80 per cent of full time and does not have a reasonable ground for reduced working hours.[31]

A non-custodial parent has expenses regarding maintenance of the child during the time he or she has access to the child. For instance, to be able to have the child overnight with him or her, the non-custodial parent usually has to have a larger flat or house compared to if he or she was always living alone. The child also needs clothes and food, and expenses related to different activities will occur. When stipulating child support according to the Norwegian model, the costs related to access to the child are therefore taken into account.

[26] s 70.

[27] See www.lovdata.no/for/sf/bl/bl-20011104-1250.html (accessed December 2013).

[28] The statistics used are obtained from 'Statens institutt for forbruksforsking' (www.sifo.no) and 'Statistisk sentralbyrå' (www.ssb.no). See www.sifo.no/page/Links/Meny_engelsk_hoyre/10418/10424 for an overview of the 2011 costs (accessed December 2013).

[29] The Children Act, ss 71 and 74 and the Regulation on Stipulation, s 1.

[30] See www.ubs.com/global/en/wealth_management/wealth_management_research/prices_earnings.html (accessed December 2013).

[31] The Children Act, ss 71 and 74 and the Regulation on Stipulation, s 4.

Table 1: The Cost of Supporting a Child

Age of the child	0–5 years old	6–10 years old	11–14 years old	15 years and older
The child's consumer costs per month	3,279 kroner (approximately €404)	4,540 kroner (approximately €560)	5,256 kroner (approximately €648)	6,106 kroner (approximately €753)
The child's housing costs per month	2,232 kroner (approximately €275)	2,232 kroner (approximately €275)	2,232 kroner (approximately €275)	2,232 kroner (approximately €275)
In total	5,511 kroner (approximately €680)	6,772 kroner (approximately €836)	7,488 kroner (approximately €924)	8,338 kroner (approximately €1,029)

Note: These amounts are valid from 1 July 2013 until 1 July 2014.

Table 2: Reductions for NCPs Based on Access

Age of the child	0–5 years old	6–10 years old	11–14 years old	15 years and over
Access-level 1 (2–3,99 nights/ days per month)	198 kroner (approximately €24)	285 kroner (approximately €35)	344 kroner (approximately €42)	403 kroner (approximately €49)
Access-level 2 (4–8,99 nights/ days per month)	655 kroner (approximately €80)	943 kroner (approximately €116)	1,139 kroner (approximately €140)	1,336 kroner (approximately €164)
Access-level 3 (9–13,99 nights/ days per month)	1,773 kroner (approximately €218)	2,174 kroner (approximately €268)	2,448 kroner (approximately €301)	2,723 kroner (approximately €335)
Access-level 4 (14–15 nights/ days per month)	2,226 kroner (approximately €274)	2,729 kroner (approximately €336)	3,073 kroner (approximately €378)	3,419 kroner (approximately €421)

Note: These amounts are valid from 1 July 2013 until 1 July 2014.

The child support is reduced if the child spends a minimum of two nights per month with the non-custodial parent.[32] The reduction increases in correlation with the number of nights spent at the non-custodial parent's home.

Table 2 shows the deductions to be made in the amount payable as child support, which depends on the number of nights and days the child spends with the non-custodial parent, and takes into account that expenses increase according to the child's age. The amounts are adjusted annually.[33]

[32] The Children Act, ss 71 and 74 and the Regulation on Stipulation, s 9.

[33] www.nav.no/rettskildene/Vedlegg/Vedlegg+1+til+Hovednr.+55+Nr.+2+Beregning+av+underholdsbidrag+til+barn.+Sjabloner+og+andre+satser.104465.cms (accessed December 2013).

The reduction due to access with the child is intended both as a politically induced incentive for the non-custodial parents to spend time with their children and a compensation for the non-custodial parents who actually do so. However, in some cases the incentive backfires. Custodial parents may be negative towards access because they 'lose money' in relation to it. It is important that the access deductions find a balance between the (often opposed) interests of the parents. As the access deductions are not in any way related to the income of the custodial parent, there is a possibility that the present deduction level works too much in favour of the non-custodial parent. One might also question whether a deduction should be made when access time is as little as two days per month.

Clearly, the deductions must be considered as a part of the stipulation rules adding an element of fairness to the system, but effectively balancing all the interests involved will probably continue to present a problem. An argument put forward by custodial parents against the significant deduction for access, is that other costs related to the child(ren) are not shared between the parents according to access time. These costs may for instance be for leisure time activities, which often are paid by the custodial parent alone, even if the activity every other week falls on a weekday where the child is with the non-custodial parent. The custodial parents may therefore feel that the deduction for access to the child is unfair, as other costs are not divided in the same way. One should also take into account the practical problems that may occur, particularly when the parties are in conflict as to what has been agreed upon as access time and the extent of access in real life. However, in an evaluation of the stipulation rules presented to parliament (Stortinget) in December 2006, where the topic of access deductions was one of the main issues, the outcome of the discussion was an increase in the deductions in favour of the non-custodial parent.[34]

As the final part of the stipulation process, a payment ability assessment is made.[35] Starting with the non-custodial parent's gross income, average consumption and living expenses are subtracted, as well as average taxation and average costs for the care of other own children in the household. If the non-custodial parent shares the household with another adult, some of the consumption and living expenses are expected to be shared, and the subtracted amount is lower. If this calculation shows that the non-custodial parent does not have full payment ability, the child support amount will be reduced accordingly, or even set to zero. The amount of child support may not exceed 5/6 of the maintenance costs.[36] In addition, the total amount of child support that a non-custodial parent may be ordered to pay, may never exceed 25 per cent of his or her gross income.[37] These limits seem to have been accepted by both parties. In the evaluation of the stipulation rules presented to parliament (Stortinget) in December 2006, the limits were not discussed as being in need of amendment.[38]

International child support cases are handled differently from national cases, but there is some similarity. The rules for Norwegian cases are exhaustive. The same principles are

[34] St.meld. nr. 19 (2006–2007) Report to the Storting, White Paper, number 19 (2006–2007). See www.regjeringen.no/nb/dep/bld/dok/regpubl/stmeld/2006-2007/Stmeld-nr-19-2006-2007-.html?id=470058 (accessed December 2013).

[35] The Children Act, ss 71 and 74 and the Regulation on Stipulation, s 6.

[36] The Children Act, ss 71 and 74 and the Regulation on Stipulation, s 2.

[37] The Children Act, ss 71 and 74 and the Regulation on Stipulation, s 7.

[38] St.meld. nr. 19 (2006–2007) Report to the Storting, White Paper, number 19 (2006–2007) (n 34).

applied when stipulating child support in international cases, but they are used on a more discretionary basis. For instance, average expenses for children living abroad are set in accordance with international cost-of-living statistics. The gross income of both parties is converted into purchasing power (using Organisation for Economic Co-operation and Development (OECD) and UBS statistics).[39] Differences in taxation in the parties' countries of residence are also taken into account. Hence, the approach in international cases is more flexible, while at the same time ensuring that similar cases end up with a similar result.

When individuals make their first application for child support to the Norwegian authorities, the following information should be included:

- the address, date of birth of both parties and citizenship of the parent living abroad;
- proof of paternity;
- documentation of income;
- a decision or agreement on access to the child;
- documentation of day-care expenses;
- documentation of additional expenses for the child such as schooling and medical expenses (these may be taken into account);
- documentation of household members and other child support obligations (only necessary for non-custodial parents)

By statute, Norwegian child support decisions terminate the month the child turns 18.[40] However, payment of support may be prolonged if the child is still in secondary education.[41] Having turned 18, the child becomes a legal party to the child support case and must put forward any claim for support by him or herself. University attendance does not normally qualify for establishment of child support.[42] To ensure equal access to tertiary education for all, the Norwegian State Educational Loan Fund issues very favourable loans to all students, without demanding financial security or charging any interest until the education is completed. Since the Norwegian State Educational Loan Fund was funded in 1947, parents have no obligation to support their children through tertiary education. This is reflected in legislation and in practice.[43] However, foreign child support decisions determining child support when a child undertakes tertiary education in another country can be acknowledged and enforced in Norway through the Collection Agency. This is limited to support payments for periods before the child has reached the age of 25.

An administrative child support decision is enforceable even if it has been appealed, and the appeal has not yet been heard. Decisions made by the appellate office, NAV Appeals, are final. If the appeal is successful, and the non-custodial parent has paid too much to the custodial parent, the overpayment may be offset in future child support or, if the circumstances so warrant, be repaid.

[39] See www.stats.oecd.org/Index.aspx?QueryId=24057 (accessed December 2013).
[40] The Children Act, s 68, para 1.
[41] Ibid para 2.
[42] Ibid para 3.
[43] Ibid.

VI. Spousal Support

Maintenance for former spouses is not common in Norway. The Norwegian Ministry of Justice, in cooperation with the Marriage Act Committee, carried out two surveys on the practice of spousal support provision after separation.[44] The first survey concerned spousal support determined by the county governor of Oslo and Akershus county in 1973, and by the county governor in Hordaland county between 1 January and 30 November 1973. The other survey concerned all cases regarding spousal support determined by the county governors of Østfold, Aust-Agder, Møre and Romsdal and Troms counties from 1 January to 30 June 1985. In addition, a survey was undertaken in 1975 at Eidsivating Court of Appeal on general practice in spousal support cases.

In the survey held in 1973, of the 2,065 cases regarding separation, claims for spousal support were made in 367 of the cases, that is, in 17.8 per cent of cases. Spousal support was granted in 293 cases, that is, in 79.8 per cent of the cases where spousal support was claimed and 14.1 per cent of the total number of divorce cases. In the 1985 survey, spousal support was claimed in 93 cases (10.7 per cent) out of a total of 871 cases. Spousal support was stipulated in 31 cases, that is, 33.3 per cent of the cases where spousal support was claimed and 3.5 per cent of the total caseload regarding divorce.

The Marriage Act Committee stated in its law proposal that each of the spouses must obtain independent financial means after the marriage has ended. In the committee's view, spousal support may however be granted in exceptional cases.[45] In accordance with the Marriage Act, the mutual obligations of spouses cease to exist upon separation and divorce.[46] The same applies to a cessation of cohabitation without a separation or divorce.[47] If one of the spouses has not been employed during the marriage, he or she is expected to obtain employment if the marriage ends.

However spousal support obligations may be ordered, if the ability and opportunity of a spouse to acquire income has been reduced as a result of caring for children of the marriage, or of the distribution of common tasks during cohabitation. The other spouse may be required to pay maintenance for a limited period, not exceeding three years.[48] In other cases maintenance may only be ordered if there are special reasons for doing so.[49] Spousal support shall be assessed on the basis of the need for support of the person concerned and the economic situation of the person liable to pay support.[50]

A claim for spousal support is as a general rule handled by the courts. However, if both spouses agree, spousal support may be established administratively,[51] by NAV. The caseload is

[44] Ot. Prop. 28 (1990–1991) Law proposition to the Norwegian Parliament, number 28 (1990–1991) Chapter VII, s 2.2 (accessible at www.lovdata.no through log in version).

[45] Ot. Prop. 28 (1990–1991) Law proposition to the Norwegian Parliament, number 28 (1990–1991) Chapter VII, s 2.3 'Hver av ektefellene må etter samlivets opphør opparbeide en selvstendig økonomi. Bidrag bør likevel etter utvalgets syn kunne tilkjennes i unntakstilfeller'.

[46] Act No 47 of 04 July 1991 relating to Marriage, at Chapter 16, s 79. For the English version see www.regjeringen.no/en/doc/laws/acts/the-marriage-act.html?id=448401 (accessed December 2013).

[47] The Marriage Act, Chapter 16, s 79, para 1.

[48] Ibid para 2 and s 8, para 11.

[49] Ibid s 79, para 3.

[50] Ibid s 80.

[51] Ibid s 83.

small, with an average of 55 applications for provision or modification of spousal support per year between 2010 and 2012. As mentioned above, spouses are expected to support themselves after separation and divorce. It should be noted that the National Insurance Scheme is an important part of the picture, as adequate social security benefits are payable to persons who are disabled, etc even if the person concerned has not been in employment. The Norwegian approach is shared by the other Nordic countries, but may perhaps be foreign to other cultures.

Regardless of the national approach to spousal support, Norway has undertaken to enforce foreign decisions on spousal support even if they are not limited in time. Spousal support decisions are enforced in the same way as decisions regarding child support, in accordance with the Hague Conventions of 1973,[52] 2007[53] and the Nordic Convention.[54] A foreign decision on spousal support is usually enforced as long as it is valid in the requesting State. If the decision is no longer valid, for instance if the person to whom support is provided remarries, the debtor usually communicates this to NAV, and the support is terminated.

VII. Private Agreements on Child Support

The Ministry of Children and Families, in the consultative paper on the reform of the child support stipulation model issued in 1999, stated that one of the goals for a good child support system is that as many parents as possible reach agreements on child support, and administer payments according to the agreement, without the assistance of the State.[55] Reflecting this attitude, Norwegian law gives parents contractual freedom as regards child support.[56] Private agreements on child support and private payment of support mean that the costs to the Government of establishing, modifying and enforcing support are reduced. Also, private determination and payment of support should mean a reduced conflict level between the parents concerned, which in turn should be a benefit for the child. Private agreements are therefore encouraged.

The Children Act puts forward private agreements as the primary basis for paying support.[57] In addition, an economic incentive for the parents to arrange support privately has been introduced. A fee, currently around €115, is charged to each party when applying for administrative establishment or modification of a decision.[58] Parents on a low income (as from 1 July 2013, that means those with an annual income of less than NOK 235,101

[52] Convention of 2 October 1973 on the Recognition and Enforcement of Decisions Relating to Maintenance Obligations.

[53] Convention of 23 November 2007 on the International Recovery of Child Support and Other Forms of Family Maintenance.

[54] Convention of 23 March 1962 between Norway, Denmark, Finland, Iceland and Sweden on Enforcement of Maintenance.

[55] Consultative paper issued 28 June1999 by the Ministry of Children and Families, 'Forslag til endringer i barnebidragsregelverket, forskotteringsordningen m.v.' 98.

[56] The Children Act, s 70, para 1.

[57] s 70.

[58] Regulation made pursuant to the Children Act, s 70, para 2. See www.lovdata.no/cgi-wift/ldles?doc=/sf/sf/sf-20011104-1250.html (accessed December 2013).

(approximately €27,900)) are not required to pay the fee. The fee does not apply in international cases.

Applying for public collection on the basis of a private agreement on child support is free of charge for the parties. Information provided by the Directorate of Labour and Welfare, shows that 1,041 applications for collection of private agreements were received in 2012, submitted by one of the parents or by a child aged 18. This is compared to 13,255 applications regarding administrative establishment of child support and 8,161 applications regarding modification of child support, the same year.

As mentioned above, private agreements will not only save money for the State, but they may also have positive effects for the parents and the child. It saves the non-custodial parent from accruing debt while the case is being handled by a NAV caseworker and prevents the custodial parent from receiving no child support during this period. In addition, it is human nature to be more positive towards decisions we make ourselves. Consequently, a non-custodial parent should feel a stronger obligation to pay the support amount he or she personally has agreed on, rather than an amount determined by the authorities.

Being able to agree on the amount of support to be paid should indicate, and possibly also work towards creating, a lower conflict level between parents who have decided to cease living together. The child should benefit from this through easier and more harmonious contact with both father and mother. However, there is also a risk that the stronger party in a relationship may take advantage of the situation and bring about solutions that are unfavourable to the other party. This seems not be the case to any noticeable extent, possibly also because a disadvantageous situation may easily be remedied by seeking public assistance, in particular as regards provision and collection of support.

Using contractual freedom to determine support does not result in any greater legal insecurity for the parents compared to an administrative decision or a court order. A private agreement on child support is equally enforceable, provided that it is enforced by the Collection Agency. All enforcement measures are also available when enforcing a private agreement. Parents who have ceased to agree on the amount to be paid may at any time apply to NAV for an administrative ruling on how much child support should be paid.

Information to assist parties in reaching a private agreement on child support is provided on the Labour and Welfare Administration's website.[59] NAV has also developed a web-based child support stipulation calculator, a useful tool for the parties when entering into an agreement on child support. On feeding information on income, the age of the children and other relevant data into the calculator, the parents will see the amount of support applicable according to the Children Act.[60] Provided that the information fed into the calculator is correct, the amount provided by the web-based calculator should be the same as the amount that would be set in an administrative decision.

Private agreements are an important feature of the Norwegian child support system. From a Norwegian point of view, it would be highly preferable if States ratifying the 2007 Hague Convention refrain from making a reservation under Article 62 of the Convention towards maintenance arrangements under Article 30. Such a reservation would probably primarily be made by States where private agreements are not recognized as legally enforceable under the relevant law. It is understandable that accepting private agreements

[59] See www.nav.no/Familie/Barnebidrag/Privat+avtale (accessed December 2013).

[60] The Children Act, s 71 and the Regulation on Stipulation.

from other States for enforcement would then pose a problem, both in principle and in practice. For example, the internal legal problems could be constitutional and hence very difficult to overcome. One might also point out that the legal status of private agreements in Norway, where the agreement at any time may be replaced by an administrative decision at the request of only one of the parties, makes an agreement less suitable as a basis for enforcement than an administrative decision, which may be amended only after prescribed procedures and only if a change is warranted on the basis of the facts of the case. Based on the Norwegian experience, however, private agreements still seem to be the most effective mechanism for solving the question of child support when parents separate.

VIII. Establishment of Paternity in Norway

Paternity can be established in Norway, regardless of where the child is born, if one of the parties resides in Norway.[61] The general rule is that the man to whom the mother is married at the time of the child's birth, shall be regarded as the father of the child.[62] When paternity is not established pursuant to the pater est rule, the father may acknowledge paternity during the pregnancy or after the child is born.[63] If the child does not have a father in accordance with these provisions, the authorities shall be responsible for establishing the identity of the father.[64] Paternity is handled by local authorities administratively or established by court order. Foreign paternity decisions can be recognised in Norway.[65]

IX. Recognition and Enforcement of Foreign Maintenance Decisions in Norway

When a foreign State is a member of one of the Hague Conventions, or has a reciprocal agreement with Norway, a foreign child support order (or spousal support order) may be enforced in Norway.[66] Any foreign basis for child or spousal support must first be acknowledged for enforcement before collection in Norway can take place. NAV National Office for Social Insurance Abroad is the receiving Central Authority for requests for recognition of foreign orders for enforcement.

As of October 2013 there were 1,272 custodial parents residing in Sweden, Finland, Denmark (including the Faeroes) or Iceland, having child support collected through the Collection Agency on the basis of the Nordic Convention.[67] There were 66 custodial parents residing in the United States having child support collected through the Collection Agency

[61] The Children Act, s 81.
[62] Ibid s 3, para 1.
[63] Ibid s 4, para 1.
[64] Ibid s 5, para 1.
[65] Ibid s 85.
[66] See www.hcch.net/index_en.php?act=status.comment&csid=1067&disp=resdn (accessed January 2014).
[67] Convention of 23 March 1962 between Norway, Denmark, Finland, Iceland and Sweden on Enforcement of Maintenance.

on the basis of the agreement between Norway and the United States.[68] There were at the same time 575 custodial parents residing in other countries in the world (except Norway) having child support collected from a non-custodial parent living in Norway, through the Collection Agency. The majority of the claims in this category are received from Poland, Germany and the Baltic countries.

Nearly all foreign orders received by the Central Authority are recognised and enforced.[69] If recognition of a foreign order is refused, the reason is usually that due process cannot be proven, meaning that the non-custodial parent had not received proper notice of the proceedings and hence did not have an opportunity to be heard before the decision was made.[70] Before recognising a foreign order for enforcement, the parties are allowed to comment on the question of recognition. To be able to continue using this procedure even in cases under the 2007 Hague Convention, Norway has made a declaration in accordance with Article 63 of the Convention to apply Article 24 rather than the 'normal' procedure described in Article 23.

X. Enforcement in International Cases with Norway as the Requesting State

As of January 2013, nine per cent of the Collection Agency's caseload consisted of cases where the non-custodial parent lived abroad.[71] The Collection Agency of the Labour and Welfare Administration is the authority that requests recognition and enforcement abroad of an obligation established in Norway. As of 1 June 2011 there were 2,568 cases registered for collection under the Nordic Convention of 1962. The number of cases sent to Nordic countries, represent about 45 per cent of all the international cases.

On 1 June 2011, 566 cases were registered for collection in the United States in accordance with the 2002 reciprocal agreement between the United States and Norway. 1,146 cases were at the same time registered for collection in accordance with the Hague Conventions of 1958 and 1973. Under the Hague Conventions, Norway mainly receives child support collected from non-custodial parents in Australia, Austria, Germany, the Netherlands, Switzerland and the United Kingdom.

In many international cases, a claim for child support is unsuccessful because the non-custodial parent lives in a country which is not a party to any Convention or reciprocal agreement. However, on 1 June 2011 there were 1,996 cases registered abroad without any Convention tied to them, and up to that date in 2011 more than five million kroner were collected in those cases. In most of these cases, the non-custodial parent receives a public pension from Norway.

[68] The Government of the United States of America and the Government of the Kingdom of Norway for the Enforcement of Maintenance Obligations. See www.acf.hhs.gov/sites/default/files/ocse/norway_reciprocating_agreement.pdf (accessed January 2014).

[69] From January to April 2013 NAV National Office for Social Insurance Abroad received 137 applications for recognition and enforcement of foreign orders.

[70] From January to September 2013, nine applications for recognition and enforcement were refused.

[71] Information on how many non-custodial parents live abroad can be excerpted from the Collection Agency's caseload.

We look forward to increased cooperation with more countries as the Hague Convention of 2007 achieves more widespread ratification.[72] The 2007 Convention will probably make it easier for other States to acknowledge administratively set child support decisions. Another benefit is that the information demanded when requesting enforcement in another Contracting State will be more homogenous.

XI. Public Collection in Norway

Public collection involves no costs for the private parties, as the Government foots the bill. The total operational costs at the Collection Agency amounted in 2013 to €10.8 million, including labour costs at the Collection Agency of €9.4 million. This is, of course, an expense for the Government. However by collecting child support from the non-custodial parent; and placing the responsibility for the cost of bringing up a child on the parents, where it belongs, Norwegian society as whole saves money on public benefits which would otherwise have to be paid to the child and custodial parent. The work done by the Collection Agency is very cost-effective. For each Euro spent, nearly €33 are collected, or, to put it another way, for each Euro collected, only €0.03 are spent on operational costs.

The Collection Agency has just over 78,000 active cases. Approximately 20,000 new cases are received each year, and approximately 20,000 cases are closed each year. This means that they have a caseload of approximately 100,000 cases throughout the year. Around 72,000 of all cases are national, and around 6,000 cases are international. The publicly collected cases involve nearly 120,000 children, 80,000 non-custodial parents and 85,000 custodial parents. Thirty-two per cent of the total caseload is without arrears.

The outstanding arrears in the cases the Collection Agency is responsible for, amounted to nearly €360 million as at December 2013. In 2013, €275 million were collected by the Collection Agency. However, the same amount accrues in current cases each year, so the total amount of total arrears has remained more or less the same for many years.

Due to the Collection Agency's location in the north of Norway in Kirkenes, the caseworkers seldom meet the non-custodial or custodial parents face-to-face. Instead, the parties have access to experienced caseworkers through telephone, e-mail, letter or fax. Telephone is the primary means of communication with the parties. Many questions can be answered and problems solved through a phone call. The Collection Agency receives approximately 4,500 calls per week. The number of incoming letters, e-mails and faxes amount to approximately 1,600 per week. All incoming mail is scanned at the Collection Agency and registered electronically to the relevant case, so the caseworkers have easy access to the correspondence when handling an application or talking to a party to a case on the phone. The parties may also visit their local Labour and Welfare office for assistance. In addition, a lot of relevant information may be found on the Norwegian Labour

[72] Convention of 23 November 2007 on the International Recovery of Child Support and Other Forms of Family Maintenance.

and Welfare Administration's website, such as the statutes that form the legal basis of the Administration's services,[73] payment dates,[74] publications and forms.[75]

However, there is room for improvements in performance. The Norwegian Labour and Welfare Administration is currently going through a major IT-modernisation project (it started in 2012). The purpose of the project is to facilitate a more modern and efficient organization, and it will also provide additional means of self-service and communication. It will have effect on all public benefits administered by the Norwegian Labour and Welfare Administration, not only child support.

XII. Voluntary Payment

Nearly €110 million, approximately 40 per cent of all the child support collected, was paid voluntarily by the non-custodial parent in 2013. In these cases, collection was conducted automatically, either by automatic invoicing or usually by an electronic transfer of funds through a bank. This means that the only contact the Collection Agency has with voluntary payers would be through monthly invoice or bank statement.

When a non-custodial parent has a starting debt of child support or if debt has accrued for some other reason, the Collection Agency will enter into a dialogue with the debtor to agree on a down-payment plan in accordance with the Maintenance Collection Act.[76] The provision on a down-payment plan even allows the Collection Agency authority to enter into an agreement with the non-custodial parent entailing a monthly payment *lower* than the monthly child support, if the non-custodial parent does not have the means to support him or herself, and at the same time pay the child support due. This situation may occur for instance if the child support is set according to the non-custodial parent's income ability, but he or she chooses not to use this ability. This situation may also occur if the basis for collection is made in a foreign country, and the support amount is based on the non-custodial parent's previous income in that country, but his or her salary is lower after having moved to Norway.

As long as monthly payments are lower than the monthly support, debt will of course accrue. If the non-custodial parent's income situation (on a permanent basis) does not allow the parent to pay the support determined, he or she should apply for modification of the support amount. However, this is not always possible. If the child support is set according to the non-custodial parent's income ability, but he or she does not use his or her ability, modification will not be permitted unless the income ability has been reduced in the meantime. Another obstacle may be rules regarding jurisdiction. An application for modification must be submitted to the State that has jurisdiction, which may be a court-based jurisdiction and/or a system in which it is very costly to file a case for modification of child support.

[73] See www.nav.no/rettskildene/ (accessed January 2014).
[74] See www.nav.no/Payment+dates.352426.cms (accessed December 2013).
[75] See www.nav.no/Skjema/Skjemaer/Privatpersoner (accessed January 2014).
[76] s 10, para 2.

The purpose of reducing the monthly enforced amount is to ensure that the non-custodial parent has enough means to support him or herself, according to a modest standard of living. Documentation on income and expenses is required and is taken into account when setting the monthly amount the non-custodial parent has to pay. Payments may be deferred or made in instalments.

XIII. Enforced Collection of Child Support—Enforcement Measures

Non-voluntary payers make up about 60 per cent of the Collection Agency's total caseload. Wage-withholding and deduction from social security and pension benefits are the two main enforcement measures in use, but these methods of course only apply to employees and people receiving public benefits.[77] All jobs being offered by an employer based in Norway must be registered with a national employment registry, all income is annually reported electronically to the Norwegian Tax Authority,[78] and residents are registered in the Public Population Registry.[79] The Collection Agency has electronic access to these registers, which yield valuable information for the collection. Searches through internet and social media may enlighten the caseworker as to the source of the non-custodial parent's income, and some information might be given by the custodial parent or other third parties. The high level of employment in Norway means there are many cases where child support decisions can be enforced through wage-withholding.[80] It should also be noted that Norwegian law gives claims for child support priority over any other claim (with the exception of prepayment of taxes) when withholding from wages.[81] The limitation period for child support is ten years, which provides ample time for the enforcement.[82]

As regards enforcement measures, the Collection Agency can also collect support by withholding tax and VAT-refunds and governmental contributions such as agriculture grants.[83] The withholding of tax refunds is an important enforcement measure as the total amount collected using this method is significant. In 2013, of a total of €275 million collected, €10.6 million of this was collected by withholding tax refunds. It is also a simple, cost-effective process.

The Norwegian legislation allows for garnishment of bank accounts, real estate and shares, as well as the forced sale of real estate and personal property by the Collection

[77] The Maintenance Collection Act, s 11 and Act No 59 of 8 June 1984 relating to creditors' rights to satisfaction of claims (Satisfaction of Claims Act), s 2-7. A recent version of this section is not available in English, an old version is available at www.lovdata.no (accessed December 2013).

[78] From 2015, income will be reported to the Tax Authority each month.

[79] Act No 1 of 16 January 1970 relating to the Public Population Registry, s 1. The Act is not available in English.

[80] The unemployment rate was 3.1% as at September 2013. Unemployment has increased in the last few months due to a combination of Norwegian and international economic developments. See www.nav.no/Om+NAV/Tall+og+analyse/Arbeidsmarked/%C3%98kt+ledighet+i+august.356791.cms (accessed January 2014).

[81] Satisfaction of Claims Act, s 2-8, para 1(a), *cf* s 2-7.

[82] Act No 18 of 18 May 1979 relating to the Limitation Period for Claims, s 6. Available in English at www.lovdata.no (accessed December 2013).

[83] The Maintenance Collection Act, s 14.

Agency.[84] The Collection Agency's enforcement authority is however limited. For garnishment of real assets like vehicles, boats and other registered assets, an application for execution is sent to the ordinary enforcement authority where the non-custodial parent lives. The same applies when the Collection Agency cannot find bank accounts, shares or real estate. The Collection Agency may also use its legal authority to claim bankruptcy when a non-custodial parent does not pay child support or arrears, to force payment.[85] Bankruptcy is only claimed in a small number of cases each year. When a non-custodial parent is bankrupt or deceased, the Collection Agency will present claims against the estate and is even entrusted with taking care of the interest of the private persons to whom maintenance is owed.[86]

Where child support has not been paid, the Collection Agency may apply to the courts to impose travel restrictions on a non-custodial parent.[87] Imposing travelling restrictions on a non-custodial parent prohibits him or her from leaving the country and the non-custodial parent's passport is impounded. Normally travelling restrictions are not lifted until the child support arrears are paid in full, and security for future child support is given.[88] However, applications for travel restrictions are seldom taken to court by the Collection Agency. Freedom of movement is a human right, therefore travel restrictions are very rarely imposed as strict standards have to be met. In the years 2008, 2010 and 2011 the Collection Agency submitted one application for travel restrictions per year. In 2009, four applications were submitted to the courts. In three of the cases between 2009 and 2011, travel restrictions were not imposed as the court found the measure to be disproportionate.[89] The Collection Agency may also apply to the courts for arrest of accounts or other personal property.[90] This enforcement measure is not often used.

Furthermore, the Collection Agency may put pressure on a non paying non-custodial parent by reporting him or her to the police for non-compliance with the obligation to maintain his or her child.[91] Sentencing in these cases may result in imprisonment from between one to six months, community service and sometimes fines. The condition for a criminal charge is that the non-custodial parent has the means to pay support, but still neglects his or her responsibility, or that the non-custodial parent has income ability he or she chooses not to use. Between 2008 and 2012 an average of 49 non-custodial parents were reported to the police for non-compliance with their obligation to support their children.

Reporting non-compliant non-custodial parents to the police sends an important signal to the public; that it is a criminal offence to refrain from supporting your children when you have the ability to do so. Police reporting has both individual and general preventive effect, due to press coverage, criminal records and stigma. The Collection Agency does not contact the media in these cases, and does not comment on media inquiries related to specific cases. The reason for press coverage is that there is a general interest in Norwegian society in cases where child support is not paid.

[84] Ibid s 13. In 2012, garnishments from bank accounts were made in 72 cases.

[85] Ibid s 31, para 2.

[86] Ibid.

[87] Ibid s 15 and Act No 90 of 17 June 2005 relating to Mediation and Procedure in Civil Disputes (The Dispute Act), Chapters 32 and 33. Available in English at www.lovdata.no (accessed December 2013).

[88] The Dispute Act, s 33-11.

[89] Unfortunately, the judgments regarding travel restrictions are not publicly available.

[90] The Maintenance Collection Act, s 15 and the Dispute Act, Chapters 32 and 33.

[91] The Maintenance Collection Act, s 33, para 1.

Table 3: Non-compliance with a Child Support Order

Year	Reported to the police	Convicted	Fined	Dismissed or conditionally discharged	Acquitted	With-drawn	Not yet decided[92]
2008	80	60	3	9	1	0	7
2009	55	32	5	7	0	0	11
2010	46	19	4	1	0	0	22
2011	24	9	2	2	0	2	9
2012	39	-	-	-	-	0	39

All income-withholding measures and garnishments are registered in a national database for credit bureau reporting.[93] The main purpose of this database is protection for the debtor, in order to ensure that income-withholding orders and other garnishments do not exceed the debtor's payment ability. As a by-product, the registration in the national database may put pressure on the debtor, because being rated as an unreliable debtor may cause problems for the non-custodial parent when applying for loans, credit cards or buying mobile telephones, etc.

Income-withholding orders are accessible to all the enforcement authorities in Norway. The enforcement authority is obliged to check the database for any other income-withholding orders before deciding to impose an income-withholding order, and setting the amount to withhold under the order. This ensures that the non-custodial parent has enough means to support him or herself according to a modest standard of living. As claims for support have legal priority over all other claims, the amount to be witheld in respect of other claims has, if necessary, to be reduced to allow the support claim to be paid in full.

XIV. IT Systems

Modern IT systems are crucial for the performance and efficiency of the Collection Agency. The IT systems are built on a well-functioning regulatory framework. Forty per cent of all collection is done automatically. Wage withholding, for example, is done automatically in the majority of cases. This is possible as a result of access to electronic employment records. The Collection Agency's IT systems provide an automated check on a monthly basis of the non-custodial parent's sources of income, such as employment, pension and social security benefits.

When a child support decision is produced by NAV and registered in the system for enforcement, or if a foreign decision is acknowledged and registered for enforcement, the IT systems automatically produce an invoice. Invoices and reminders are then produced

[92] As at February 2013.

[93] Act No 2 of 07 June 1935 relating to Land and Property Registration, s 34a and Regulations made by virtue of this provision.

and sent automatically every month. Child support payments from non-custodial parents are automatically registered in the relevant child support case and forwarded electronically to the custodial parent.

The IT systems are programmed so that deadlines for different steps are set automatically in each case, for example the limitation period and when tasks must be performed or letters must be answered. This helps the caseworkers at the Collection Agency to manage the caseload well, enabling them to prioritise between tasks in order to meet deadlines. Each electronic case file provides a total overview of: child support due each month, all payments, debts, incoming and outgoing letters, memos from phone calls, and tasks to be followed up. The case files also provide information about former enforcement proceedings such as garnishment, withholding of income or tax refunds—in other words, a full history of the case.

XV. Conclusion

Norwegian results on child support collections are good, because the collection rate is very high:

— 80 per cent of children receive the full amount of child support due every month.
— An additional 15 per cent of children receive a partial payment every month.
— 40 per cent of all payments are made voluntarily, without any enforcement measures being used.

There are many possible explanations for such a high collection rate. In 2003, the model for stipulation of child support was changed from a percentage of the non-custodial parent's income, depending on how many children he or she was obliged to maintain, to the maintenance cost model where both parents' incomes are taken into consideration. In the beginning, many custodial parents criticised the model, claiming that the resulting support amounts were too low. The deductions for access time were probably the main issue of dissatisfaction.

However, since the statutory change in 2003, people have become acquainted with the maintenance cost model and the reasoning behind it. A steadily increasing number of parents choose to arrange their child support payments privately, which may be taken to imply that the majority perceive the rules on maintenance to be fair, as the private agreements are usually based on the maintenance costs following from the Children Act and accompanying Regulations. Also, the idea of dividing costs according to the income of the parents seems to be generally accepted. The web-based support calculator (see section VII above) has probably contributed to this.

One of the characteristics of the Norwegian maintenance-cost-model is that child support shall not exceed what the non-custodial parent is able to pay. This allows for setting the child support at zero if the non-custodial parents clearly would not be able to pay. Another product of this characteristic is that when the non-custodial parent becomes the mother or father of a new child, child support for previous children may be reduced. These rules are beneficial and improve collection results, because the child support stipulated does not exceed what the non-custodial parent is realistically able to pay. However, where the parent cannot pay this does not mean that the children are left with nothing. When a non-custodial parent is unable to pay, the Government assists low and middle income custodial parents in Norway with the costs of raising the child by paying advance payments of child support. Of course, in such cases the advance payments must be considered as social benefits.

Another reason for the high collection rate may be that the Norwegian legislation in general is aimed at securing the payment of child support. During the enforcement period, child support claims have priority over other claims,[94] and the limitation period is set at ten years.[95]

The high rate of employment also results in a high level of payment ability among parents. Modern IT systems within the NAV offices, which are both well integrated and cross-communicating, in addition to electronic access to updated electronic registers like the Population Registry and Inland Revenue's income registries, are also contributing factors to Norway's success. However, there are groups of people whose work and income are not found in these registries. These people choose to work in the underground economy where Norway's existing enforcement measures do not reach. This may include freelancers and self-employed persons. Non-custodial parents within these groups are the source of some grief to custodial parents and caseworkers working on these cases. The Norwegian Ministry of Labour and Social Affairs is therefore considering new enforcement measures to resolve these problem cases, such as suspension of driver's licenses and revocation of passports.

The fact that establishment and collection of child support decisions is handled within the same organisation probably contributes towards the success as well. Centralising the collection of child support at the Collection Agency instead of leaving collection to smaller local offices has improved collection results enormously. Overall, the current system in Norway is operating very well and this is clearly reflected by the high collection rate of child support in Norway.

[94] Satisfaction of Claims Act, s 2-8. Available in English at www.lovdata.no (accessed December 2013).

[95] Act No 18 of 18 May relating to the Limitation Period for Claims, s 6. Available in English at www.lovdata.no (accessed December 2013).

12

Child Support in Kazakhstan: Case for Accession to the 2007 Hague Maintenance Convention

MILANA KARAYANIDI

I. Introduction

This chapter sheds light on family law provisions related to child support in Kazakhstan, otherwise scarcely covered in publications in the English language. It analyses the basic features of child support in Kazakhstan, the procedure of enforcement of maintenance decisions and access to information and data in child support cases. It evaluates the present state of affairs on conflict of laws issues when it comes to recovery of maintenance in Kazakhstan from abroad. Finally, it builds a case for the accession to the Hague Maintenance Convention 2007 by Kazakhstan.

This chapter was first presented as a paper at the Heidelberg Conference on Recovery of Maintenance in the EU and Worldwide.[1] The methodology used to conduct this research included analysis of the relevant legislation of the Republic of Kazakhstan, international treaties, appropriate scholarly materials and available online publications related to the recovery of maintenance in Kazakhstan and abroad. The research was also based on the findings obtained upon consultation with the state authorities of Kazakhstan.

Since the legal system of Kazakhstan follows the tradition of continental (civil) law systems, judicial practice (or case law) does not represent a source of law in Kazakhstan. Courts look for guidance in law rather than in previously issued judgments. However, the Supreme Court of Kazakhstan periodically reviews decisions by lower courts and issues normative resolutions on certain issues (*postanovleniya*). These decrees by the supreme judicial body are recognised as sources of law, and they are consequently applied by judges. Review of the relevant decrees has also been part of the methodology of this research project.

[1] Heidelberg Conference 'Recovery of Maintenance in the EU and Worldwide' Germany, 5–8 March 2013.

II. Child Support in Kazakhstan

Recovery of maintenance obligations in Kazakhstan is governed by section 5 of the Family Code,[2] which came into force in January 2012.[3] The Family Code defines maintenance (or alimony) as monetary or material content, which one person is required to give to another person entitled to receive it.[4] The concept of maintenance is wider than child support alone; it includes maintenance of elderly adults by their children, alimony paid to former spouses, etc. However, this chapter will focus on child support only; and the terms 'maintenance' and 'child support' will be used interchangeably.

Around 50 per cent of all child support obligations in Kazakhstan are paid voluntarily according to child support agreements between parents. The main reasons for so many voluntary maintenance arrangements are their low cost, simplicity and effectiveness. For a reasonable fee, notary public officers throughout Kazakhstan help citizens conclude and notarise child support agreements. Upon notarisation, child support agreements constitute authentic instruments and have the effect of court enforcement orders. The requirements for the amount of maintenance are set out by law. Agreements setting the amount of maintenance lower than that prescribed by law are void.

A. Recovery of Child Support in Court

In the case of absence of an agreement between the parents, child support may be recovered in court.[5] According to the default jurisdiction rule, an action for child support should be brought to a court of general jurisdiction at the location of the defendant.[6] Also, if the claimant chooses to do so, he or she may file a maintenance suit at his or her own location, thus overriding the default jurisdiction rule.[7] A person entitled to child support (a parent on behalf of a child) may initiate court proceedings regardless of the period that has elapsed since the occurrence of the right to child support, if maintenance has not previously been paid under a child support agreement.[8] The obligation to pay maintenance, however, cannot be inherited.

Marriage is not a requirement for a successful claim for maintenance. Prior proof of paternity (official documents, such as a birth certificate with names of parents) is not a requirement either; however, if already established, it simplifies the claimant's case. If not, legal paternity can still be established in court. The claims for paternity and maintenance

[2] Code of the Republic of Kazakhstan of 26 December 2011 No 518-IV 'On Marriage and Family' (Family Code).

[3] Prior to that, the Law of the Republic of Kazakhstan of 17 December 1998 No 321 'On Marriage and Family' regulated family relationships.

[4] Family Code, Art 1(1).

[5] Ibid Art 163.

[6] Code of Civil Procedure of the Republic of Kazakhstan of 13 July 1999 No 411-I (Code of Civil Procedure), Arts 24 and 31.

[7] Ibid Art 32.

[8] Family Code, Art 164.

may be brought together.[9] The law does not differentiate between a father and a mother when it comes to responsibility to pay the child support. It is more common, however, that children remain with their mother, and the father becomes liable to pay maintenance.

Children up to 18 years old are eligible to receive child support. Also, those up to 21 years old and engaged in full-time study may be entitled to child support as well.[10] Full-time study is understood as secondary, technical and vocational, post-secondary, or higher full-time education. If parents do not voluntarily provide funds for maintenance of their children up to 18 years old (or full-time students up to 21 years old), maintenance may be secured with the help of a court.

The law sets out clear guidelines on how child support should be calculated in relation to the income of the debtor:

(a) One child—1/4 of income of the debtor;
(b) Two children—1/3 of income of the debtor;
(c) Three or more children—1/2 of earnings and (or) other income of the debtor.[11]

The amount of maintenance may be reduced or increased by courts taking into account financial or marital status of the parties and other relevant circumstances. The law does not provide an exact list of circumstances based on which courts may make such decisions. It is up to the courts to decide on a case-by-case basis. Also, there is no upper limit on the amount of maintenance, no matter how high the income of the debtor is. For debtors earning minimum wage or those with a large income, the amount of maintenance payments would still be calculated according to the guidelines above. Also, the amount of maintenance is calculated in the same way for children younger than 18 and those up to 21 who are engaged in full-time study.

The Family Code elaborates from which means of subsistence of the debtor the maintenance is secured.[12] First of all, it would be recovered from the income of the debtor. In case of insufficiency of income of the debtor, the maintenance payments would be collected from the debtor's funds in bank accounts. In case of insufficiency of these funds, an action can be brought to recover the maintenance from any other property of the debtor.

B. Financial Support from the Public Sector

The Kazakhstan Government provides limited financial support to parents for having children (birth benefits). The birth benefits are paid until a child is one year old; and they cannot substitute for child support. In certain conditions, welfare payments and benefits to raise a disabled child may be paid as well; however these appear extremely minimal in view of expenses associated with feeding and bringing up a child.

[9] Notably, if the two claims (for paternity and maintenance) are brought together, only the fee for the claim for paternity should be paid. See Decree of the Supreme Court of the Republic of Kazakhstan of 25 December 2006 'On Application by the Courts of the Republic of Kazakhstan of the Law on the Court Expenses in Civil Cases' ('О Применении судами Республики Казахстан законодательства о судебных расходах по гражданским делам'), Art 6.

[10] Family Code, Art 138(2).

[11] Ibid Art 139.

[12] Ibid Art 168.

Both working and non-working mothers are entitled to receive birth benefits after the birth of their children. They are entitled to a single fixed payment and 12 monthly child benefit payments. The single fixed payment for birth amounts to 30 monthly calculated indices (MCI)[13] for the first, second and third child, and 50 MCI for the fourth child. In 2014, these figures translate to the lump sums of 55,560 Tenge (equivalent to €221) and 92,600 Tenge (€369) correspondingly. Furthermore, monthly child benefits are paid to women who did not work prior to delivering a baby, varying from 10,186 Tenge (€40) to 15,742 Tenge (€62), until the child is one year old.

In addition, working women qualify to get additional (maternity) payments provided they paid social security payments (from their salary to the government pension fund, as required by the law since 2008).

So, if a mother has been working before the birth of her child, she makes monthly social security payments to the government pension fund. This system of women paying social security payments and subsequently receiving birth benefits has been in place in Kazakhstan since 2008. Prior to that, employers were responsible for maternity leave payment. Unfortunately, many employers sought to avoid the maternity payments by setting unreasonably short maternity leave terms or finding a way to fire women who became pregnant. The new system was introduced to protect women's rights to maternity pay. It freed employers from paying maternity fees altogether and made it the responsibility of the Government and women themselves. Thus, this system ensures that women's rights are protected and represents a positive feature in the regulation of family relationships in Kazakhstan.

So, when her child is born, a working woman receives her money back during the maternity leave from the state pension fund. She is entitled to receive:

(a) One single payment of a woman's average salary for the last 12 months multiplied by a corresponding co-efficient (ranging between 4.2 and 5.7 depending on various circumstances).
(b) Monthly payments calculated as the woman's average salary times co-efficient 0.4 minus 10% of the sum withheld by the fund for pension (but no more than 79,864 Tenge (€318).

For instance, a woman making around 125,500 Tenge (€500 Euro) per month before the child is born can get a single fixed payment of 527,100 Tenge (€2,100). There is a limit to this amount, however; even if a woman's average monthly salary equals to or exceeds ten times the minimum wage (199,660 Tenge or €795), the fixed amount would be calculated as if the average salary equals to 199,660 Tenge. In addition, the woman would receive 12 monthly payments of 45,180 Tenge (€180).

Therefore, there is a dual system of birth benefits designed for working and non-working women. For both working and non-working women, the Government guarantees a single fixed payment, and monthly payments for a year. In addition, a woman who has worked at least 12 months before the birth of the child and has paid her social security contributions to the Government as required by the law, would receive a single lump sum and 12 monthly

[13] The monthly calculated index (MCI) is a flexible amount determined yearly taking into account inflation and other factors. This rate is widely used in civil, administrative and criminal law to calculate fines, taxes, minimal starter capital for legal entities, government subsidies, etc. At the moment, the MCI for year 2014 constitutes 1,852 Tenge, according to the Law on Republican Budget for 2014–16, Art 10(4).

payments as well. The amounts of these, however, differ depending on the average monthly salary of the woman.

Thus, the governmental system of birth benefits provides advantages to women giving birth to children in Kazakhstan. However, it cannot substitute for maintenance since the birth benefits only support a mother during the first year of her child's life.

C. Procedure for Enforcement of Maintenance Decisions

Recognition and enforcement of court orders on maintenance is in the hands of judicial and administrative authorities and private organisations (employers of debtors). It should be noted that a court enforcement order on maintenance and a notarised maintenance agreement have the same legal effect. Therefore, enforcement of a maintenance agreement is carried out in the same way as that of a court enforcement order.

First, a court issues an order on maintenance obligations with the monthly amount of maintenance specified therein. The enforcement order is given to an officer of the court (bailiff). Recently, in addition to state bailiffs, the institution of private bailiffs has been introduced. Kazakhstan is currently learning from the practice of other European countries about how private bailiffs operate. For instance, in January 2013, private officers of the court from Kazakhstan and the European Union exchanged knowledge and ideas on best practice during seminars in the Kazakhstan cities of Ust-Kamenogorsk and Shymkent.[14]

After the officer of the court receives a court enforcement order, he or she submits it to the employer of the debtor. The employer of the debtor must withhold the required amount from the debtor's income and pay it to the person entitled to receive maintenance. The officer of the court oversees the promptness and accuracy of the maintenance payments.[15] If the employer does not cooperate, he is subject to administrative liability (eg in case of non-enforcement of the court order or failure to provide information on the status of the debtor's employment, the amount of his income, the maintenance payments, etc).[16]

The debtor him or herself must also report any changes of address or of place of work to the officer of the court. Non-compliance by the debtor with the court order or failure to inform the officer of the court of these changes may lead to administrative liability. In particular, the debtor may be charged with a fine up to 10 MCI (18,520 Tenge or around €73) or detained in prison for up to ten days.[17]

D. Access to Procedure

The Kazakhstan Government facilitates some access to information on procuring child support. The Ministry of Justice provides a freely accessible Family Code on its website and

[14] Delegation of the European Union in Kazakhstan, 'The European and Kazakhstani private bailiffs to exchange their best practices' (2013) Press-centre of the Delegation, 25 January 2013 www.eeas.europa.eu/delegations/kazakhstan/press_corner/all_news/news/2013/25.01.2013_en.htm (accessed November 2013).

[15] Law of the Republic of Kazakhstan of 2 April 2010 No 261-IV 'On Enforcement Procedure and the Status of Officers of the Court', Art 102.

[16] Code of the Republic of Kazakhstan of 30 January 2001 No 155-II 'On Administrative Violations' (Code on Administrative Violations), Art 526.

[17] Code on Administrative Violations, Art 524.

provides answers to interested parties relating to family law.[18] There is also a phone line facilitated by the Ministry of Justice, allowing anyone in Kazakhstan to benefit from a free consultation on the interpretation of the legislation. There are other non-official sources of information on getting maintenance as well.[19]

In addition, information on recovery of maintenance can be obtained from an attorney. By law, all attorneys are required to provide free legal assistance to citizens on questions related to maintenance.[20] This legal assistance must be provided immediately following the request of a potential claimant to the lawyer. If it is impossible to provide legal aid immediately, an applicant must be notified of the office hours or convenient time, which cannot exceed three working days from the date of first application. Duration of legal consultation in such cases should not exceed one hour. If necessary, this period may be extended. A person can get free legal assistance on the same question only once. The lawyer can be reimbursed for his services by the Government later, upon provision of an application and a report on services rendered. The Government sets the rate and the procedure for remuneration for such service.

In addition to the limited free legal assistance, potential claimants can always hire an attorney to handle their cases for maintenance. It is up to the attorney and the potential client to determine the amount of payment for such services.

The civil procedure in Kazakhstan does not foresee appointment of a lawyer to plaintiffs and defendants automatically. In fact, one may choose to hire a lawyer or to represent oneself in court in civil proceedings. Not consulting a lawyer can be a disadvantage in court, because lawyers are well informed about the law and its latest developments, and they are very familiar with the court procedure. Clearly, this is of great benefit to the person fighting for maintenance in court.

In situations of financial hardship, citizens may be exempt from paying the lawyer's fees for representation in court. This may be determined by the head of the establishment where the lawyer works (the Bar Association or a law firm) or by an individual attorney if he or she is operating without registration of a legal entity. In such a case, the lawyer either does not get paid, or gets paid by the firm for whom he or she works.

E. Access to Information on Assets

The State does not provide access to information on income and assets of debtors for the purpose of child support or maintenance. An employer cannot provide any person with information about their employee without the consent of the employee.[21] Also, the content of primary documents and registers of accounting (including those containing the information on pay) constitutes a commercial secret.[22] Moreover, any information on income of taxpayers is confidential.[23]

[18] See, generally, www.adilet.gov.kz (accessed April 2014).

[19] For instance, www.zakon.kz (accessed January 2014).

[20] Law of the Republic of Kazakhstan of 5 December 1997, No 195-I 'On Advocacy', Art 6(1)(3).

[21] Labour Code of the Republic of Kazakhstan of 15 May 2007 No 251, Art 67.

[22] Law of the Republic of Kazakhstan of 28 February 2007 No 234-III 'On Accounting and Financial Accountability', Art 12.

[23] Code of the Republic of Kazakhstan of 10 December 2008 No 99-IV 'On Taxes and Other Obligatory Payments to the Budget' (Tax Code), Art 557.

Therefore, there is no way to obtain information on the debtor's income from the state authorities or the employer of the debtor, and the only way to get such information is through an officer of the court (bailiff). The officer of the court has the right to obtain information on, for example, the income and assets of the debtor from the state authorities and other organisations in Kazakhstan.

III. Recovery of Maintenance from Abroad

Having reviewed the basic features of law and procedure of recovery of maintenance in Kazakhstan, it is time to analyse recovery of maintenance across the border. This section will consider the provisions of private international law in the sphere of child support and maintenance, in particular:

(a) What are the applicable law rules regarding child support or maintenance?
(b) What are the international jurisdiction rules in matters relating to child support?
(c) What are the rules on recognition and enforcement of foreign judgments, of authentic instruments and of maintenance agreements?

A. Applicable Law

The domestic law of Kazakhstan asserts that in relations with a foreign element, rights and liabilities of parents and their children are determined in accordance with the law of the country where they have lived together.[24] In the absence of such a common place of residence, the law of the State of which the child is the citizen applies. At the request of the claimant in child support proceedings, the law of the State where the child habitually or permanently resides shall apply. The law of Kazakhstan shall apply to Kazakhstani citizens living abroad.

Parties with no common place of residence may sign an agreement on child support, and choose the law of a certain (third) State to apply to their relations, such as repayment of maintenance obligations. Thus, the principle of party autonomy in family relationships is observed and enforced in Kazakhstan. Theoretically, parties may choose a body of law that has no factual connection with the parties, or that provides little or no child support. However, the likelihood of this happening appears low. At the stage of enforcement, a court would most likely support the choice of parties regarding the law of the country where the child resides. Had the parties chosen the law prescribing no or little child support, such an agreement would be declared void in court by action of an interested party, if it violates the rights of the person eligible to receive maintenance in the amount foreseen by the law of the forum.[25]

In addition, the matters of relationships of parents and children living in different countries may be regulated by international treaties. Provisions of international law prevail

[24] Family Code, Art 277.
[25] Ibid Art 160.

over the rules of national law of Kazakhstan, and the Family Code in particular. In case of conflict between the international law provisions and the national law, the rules of international law apply.[26] So, the party autonomy to choose a certain body of law to apply to a maintenance agreement (otherwise permitted in Kazakhstan) may be limited in cases where parties are from Kazakhstan and from another State-signatory to an international instrument that does not recognise such party autonomy in family matters. In such cases, the choice may be limited by the international instrument.

At the present moment, the international treaties relating to recovery of maintenance in force in Kazakhstan include the New York Convention on the Recovery Abroad of Maintenance 1956[27] and the Minsk Convention on Legal and Judicial Assistance.[28]

Kazakhstan acceded to the New York Convention on the Recovery Abroad of Maintenance in 2000.[29] In accordance with the New York Convention, each Contracting State designates a body, which acts as a Transmitting and Receiving Agency. A claimant from one Contracting State may make application to the Transmitting Agency in his or her State regarding maintenance obligations. The Transmitting Agency then transmits the request to the Receiving Agency in the State of the respondent. Kazakhstan's Transmitting and Receiving Agency is the Committee on Judicial Administration to the Supreme Court of the Republic of Kazakhstan. At this time, no cases have been discovered demonstrating examples of the New York Convention work in practice involving parties from Kazakhstan. So, the effectiveness of the New York Convention is hard to determine.

At the regional level, the Minsk Convention applies in relation to cooperation between the judicial and administrative organs of the Member States of the Commonwealth of Independent States (CIS—some of the former Soviet Union republics).[30] Inter alia, the Treaty concerns family relations. It established that:

> rights and obligations of parents and children, including those on maintenance, shall be determined in accordance with the law of the Contracting State, where the parties have common residence; in absence of such common place of residence of parents and children, their rights and liabilities shall be determined in accordance with the law of the Contracting State where the children reside.
>
> In accordance with the plaintiff's request in maintenance cases, the law of the Contracting State where the child predominantly resides shall apply.[31]

[26] Ibid Art 4(2). Also, see the Constitution of the Republic of Kazakhstan adopted on 30 August 1995.

[27] The Convention can be found at the United Nations Treaty Collection at www.treaties.un.org/UNTC/ (accessed November 2013). Currently, the Convention has 65 parties to it, including 64 United Nations Member States and the Holy See.

[28] Minsk Convention on Legal Assistance in Civil, Family and Criminal Matters 1993, subsequently re-signed with some amendments in 2002 in Kishinev, Belarus.

[29] Law of the Republic of Kazakhstan of 30 December 1999 No 33-II 'On Accession of the Republic of Kazakhstan to the Convention "On Recovery of Maintenance"'.

[30] The parties to the Convention are Armenia, Azerbaijan, Belarus, Georgia, Kazakhstan, Kyrgyzstan, Moldova, the Russian Federation, Tajikistan, Turkmenistan, Uzbekistan and Ukraine. The Convention entered into force in 1994, and was subsequently reviewed and a new Convention, known as the Kishinev Convention, was adopted in 2002 with minor changes. The Kishinev Convention is in force for Armenia, Azerbaijan, Belarus, Kazakhstan, Kyrgyzstan and Tajikistan. Russia, Ukraine, Georgia and Moldova have signed the Convention but have not ratified it, so it has not yet come into force for them.

[31] Minsk Convention, Art 32(1); Kishinev Convention, Art 35(1).

So, the Minsk Convention excludes party autonomy and connects a maintenance dispute to the law of the country of residence of the children. The Convention does not solve the issue when a child may be resident in more than one country. It may be assumed that in such cases, the law of the Contracting State, where the child mainly and predominantly resides, shall apply. The criteria for determining the child's closest connection to a State may be derived from the court's domestic law.

Therefore, provisions of these international treaties and the local laws lay out the conflict of laws rules for international maintenance disputes. These provisions, including the New York Convention, are incomplete; they differ and lack uniformity. This chapter will go on to discuss possible accession to the Hague Maintenance Convention 2007, as a possible way to improve this situation.

B. Jurisdiction

As mentioned above, the general jurisdiction rule in Kazakhstan establishes that civil actions should be filed at the location of the defendant.[32] Special (alternative) jurisdiction overrides the general jurisdiction rule in matters of maintenance, and provides a choice to the claimant either to file at the location of the defendant, or at the location of the claimant.[33] If the location of the defendant is unknown, the court has to initiate an official investigation with the state authorities (Ministry of Internal Affairs and the agency for fighting economic and corruption crimes) searching for the defendant.[34]

In proceedings with a foreign element, Article 416(3) of the Code of Civil Procedure empowers the relevant Kazakhstan courts to consider cases related to child support. That means that courts in Kazakhstan have the potential authority to hear and decide international maintenance cases.

At the regional level, the Minsk Convention provides that actions against parties located in a State-signatory to the Convention, shall be brought to the courts of that State notwithstanding the citizenship of the party.[35] Thus, the Convention adheres to the general jurisdiction rule—filing at the location of the defendant. However, the general rule can be overridden by the provision related to the family relations: 'in cases involving relationships between parents and children, the court of the Contracting State shall have the jurisdiction, the law of which is applicable'.[36] The applicable law of the Convention is the law of the Contracting State where the children reside. Therefore, the Convention empowers the court of the Contracting State, at the territory of which a child resides, with jurisdiction in maintenance cases. It establishes a straightforward uniform mechanism of determining which law shall apply, and which courts shall have jurisdiction in maintenance cases. The solution of establishing the applicable law first (the law of the State where the child resides), and then determining the competent judicial authorities (the courts of that State) may appear unusual to States other than parties to the Minsk Convention. Applicable law

32 Code of Civil Procedure, Art 31.
33 Ibid Art 32.
34 Ibid Art 135.
35 Minsk Convention, Art 20.
36 Ibid Art 32(3); Kishinev Convention, Art 35(3).

does not normally define jurisdiction. On the territory of the post-Soviet bloc, however, this approach is embedded into the system and seems to work effectively.

Notably, the Minsk (Kishinev) Convention applies strictly in international disputes involving parties from States in which the Convention has entered into force.[37] The effect of the Minsk Convention is as follows: when a child resides in Kazakhstan, the Kazakhstan law shall apply, and the Kazakhstan courts shall have jurisdiction. The Minsk (Kishinev) Convention is not automatically activated just because a child is resident in Kazakhstan, however; when a child is resident in Kazakhstan, but the parents live elsewhere and not in the countries parties to the Minsk Convention, the Convention does not apply.

In some cases involving parties from Kazakhstan and non-CIS countries, bilateral agreements may prescribe jurisdiction rules in maintenance cases or in civil cases in general. There are a few such bilateral agreements. For instance, there is an Agreement between the Republic of Kazakhstan and the United Arab Emirates (UAE) on legal (judicial) cooperation in civil and commercial matters.[38] The Agreement does not specify special rules regarding maintenance cases or any family matters in particular. It adheres to the general rule of jurisdiction in all civil matters, empowering with jurisdiction the courts of the State where the defendant is domiciled (or resident). Under Kazakhstan law, the domicile of an individual is understood as a place where he is permanently or predominantly resident. Additionally, the courts of the Contracting State may have jurisdiction, if the liabilities of the defendant are due to be performed in that State, or the damage was inflicted in that State, or he or she voluntarily submitted to the jurisdiction of that State, etc.[39]

C. Enforcement

Recovery of maintenance in Kazakhstan presents certain challenges and can depend on many factors, such as cooperation and responsibility of the parents, success of a maintenance claim, effectiveness of a bailiff enforcing the court enforcement order, cooperation and promptness of the employer of the debtor, etc. When crossing the border of Kazakhstan, recovery of maintenance becomes even more complex.

Foreign judgments shall be generally enforced in Kazakhstan if prescribed by the law or an international agreement according to the principle of reciprocity.[40] Conditions for recognition and enforcement of judgments are provided by an applicable international treaty or by the law of Kazakhstan.

When it comes to enforcement of court judgments and orders, a lot depends on the existence of an international agreement on legal and judicial cooperation between Kazakhstan and another State. When an enforcement mechanism is prescribed by such an agreement, maintenance orders are easier to enforce both in Kazakhstan and in the corresponding state. There may be different requirements, such as the necessity for a document to be authorised or provide a document with an Apostille. Also, foreign instruments may

[37] In regard to Kazakhstan, the Minsk Convention applies when an international dispute involves parties from Kazakhstan and Georgia, or Moldova, or the Russian Federation, or Turkmenistan, or Uzbekistan or Ukraine. The Kishinev Convention (essentially, the Minsk Convention with some changes) applies when the parties are from Kazakhstan and Armenia, or Azerbaijan, or Belarus, or Kyrgyzstan or Tajikistan.

[38] Signed in Abu Dhabi, 16 March 2009, entered into force on 22 September 2012.

[39] The Agreement between the Republic of Kazakhstan and the United Arab Emirates, Art 19.

[40] Code of Civil Procedure, Art 425.

be enforced straight away if an international treaty provides for such enforcement and recognition. There are only a few States with which Kazakhstan has bilateral agreements on judicial cooperation providing the legal background for enforcement of judgments and court orders from these States.[41]

If there is no international treaty between Kazakhstan and the country in question, enforcement proceedings of foreign enforcement documents in Kazakhstan will be executed in accordance with the civil procedure laws of Kazakhstan.[42] As for enforcing Kazakhstan court orders in other countries, sometimes, unfortunately, a child support agreement fully corresponding to the requirements of the law in Kazakhstan may not be recognised and enforced by foreign judicial bodies, if there is no international treaty in place, or the document is not appropriately authorised.

Therefore, in summary, international recovery of maintenance depends on which countries the parties are from:

(a) On the domestic level in Kazakhstan, recovery of maintenance is least problematic.
(b) At the regional level of neighbouring CIS countries which have acceded to the Minsk (or Kishinev) Convention, the situation is less straightforward.
(c) In cases involving Kazakhstan and other non-CIS countries, recovery of maintenance becomes more problematic, and sometimes, even impossible.

So, the further one goes from Kazakhstan, the more difficult it is to recover child support for parents with children remaining in Kazakhstan.

IV. Case for Accession to the Hague Maintenance Convention 2007

Regulation of recovery of child support across the border of Kazakhstan requires major improvement. One of the logical solutions would be for Kazakhstan to accede to the existing network of countries who have signed the Hague Maintenance Convention 2007.

A question may be raised: why accede to the new international instrument, if the New York Convention on Recovery of Maintenance is already in place? The answer is that the New York Convention is not a convention on enforcement. It does not provide an effective mechanism for enforcing foreign judgments and authentic instruments on maintenance. Also, the difficulties in applying the New York Convention 'are to a much greater extent due to differences in the standard of living between the countries, … frequently incompatible religious or philosophical convictions and … systematic bad faith of maintenance debtors'.[43]

[41] These States include Iran, Lithuania, Mongolia, North Korea, Pakistan, South Korea, Turkey, and the UAE. See S Akimbekova, 'Recognition and Enforcement of Foreign Judgments in the Republic of Kazakhstan' (2013) *Jurist* 4, 71–73, available at www.zakon.kz/4562001-priznanie-i-privedenie-v-ispolnenie.html (accessed November 2013).

[42] In particular, the Code of Civil Procedure and the the Law on the Enforcement Procedure and the Status of Officers of the Court (n 6 and 17).

[43] M Pelichet, 'Note on the operation of the Hague Conventions relating to maintenance obligations and of the New York Convention on the Recovery Abroad of Maintenance' (1995) Prel Doc 1, September 1995. Also see the Hague Conference on Private International Law, 'General Conclusions of the Special Commission

Kazakhstan already benefits from three other Hague Conventions (the Apostille Convention 1961, the Hague Convention on Protection of Children and Co-operation in respect to Inter-country Adoption 1993, and the Hague Convention on the Civil Aspects of International Child Abduction 1980). The Conventions work effectively and bring a lot of advantages to parties from Kazakhstan. To decide whether accession to the Hague Maintenance Convention 2007 would be beneficial for Kazakhstan, its main points need to be compared to the corresponding national legal provisions in Kazakhstan.

A. Marital Status of Parents

The Hague Maintenance Convention shall apply, and the maintenance may be recovered regardless of the marital status of the parents (Article 2(4)). This is in accordance with the national law of Kazakhstan, where a child being legitimate is not a requirement for a successful claim of maintenance. This point is very important. If Kazakhstan accedes to the Hague Maintenance Convention, it might benefit more Kazakhstani children with unmarried parents, one of whom resides abroad. While in some countries such children may be regarded as illegitimate and not entitled to child support, thanks to the Hague Convention, single parents from Kazakhstan will be able to recover maintenance without being married.

B. Grounds for Refusal of Enforcement

The Hague Maintenance Convention foresees situations when enforcement of a foreign court decision may be refused. Article 22 establishes that a foreign decision may be refused recognition and enforcement if it is manifestly incompatible with the public policy of the State addressed; if it was obtained by fraud; if the same parties have pending proceedings with the same purpose which were initiated first; if the decision is incompatible with a decision of another court between the same parties with the same purpose; in a case where the respondent does not appear for the proceedings and certain other conditions are met; and if the decision was made breaching the restrictions on bringing the proceedings (Article 18).

These provisions do not contradict the national legal provisions on recognition and enforcement of foreign judgments in Kazakhstan. As discussed earlier, the current Kazakhstani law foresees enforcement of foreign judgments or court orders only if directly prescribed by an international agreement, by a national law, or, in the absence of such, according to the principle of reciprocity. So, if an order originates from a country, with which Kazakhstan does not currently have an intergovernmental agreement on judicial cooperation in civil matters, the Kazakhstani judge would follow the principle of reciprocity and decide whether enforcement of Kazakhstani court judgments is reflected in the law and (or) court practice of the corresponding State. In the absence of such reciprocity, the judge may consider refusing enforcement of such a foreign judgment.

of November 1995 on the Operation of the Hague Conventions Relating to Maintenance Obligations and the New York Convention of 20 June 1956 on the Recovery Abroad of Maintenance' www.hcch.net/index_en.php?act=conventions.publications&dtid=35&cid=131 (accessed November 2013).

Also, a court may refuse enforcement if provided by an interested party with proof of the following:

(a) The case was considered by an incompetent (foreign) court;
(b) The proceedings were held in the absence of the interested party with no proper notification;
(c) The three-year limitation period had expired;
(d) There was an earlier court decision in force between the same parties on the same subject matter and on the same grounds.[44]

Additionally, the concept of public policy or 'ordre public' may lead to non-enforcement of foreign judgments made contrary to public policy in Kazakhstan, as expressed in the Kazakhstani legislation.[45] So the local legal grounds for non-enforcement are in line with those listed in the Hague Maintenance Convention 2007. Moreover, the grounds for refusal of enforcement foreseen in the Hague Maintenance Convention 2007 are broader and include additional cases (such as pending proceedings between the same parties with the same purpose, or court decisions obtained by fraud). Acceding to the Convention would integrate these additional provisions into the national legislation. This would complement and enrich the current law and protect Kazakhstani citizens against foreign decisions obtained in bad faith.

C. Age of Children

The Hague Convention applies to maintenance obligations arising from a parent-child relationship towards a person under the age of 21 years (Article 2(1)(a)). This is compatible with the provisions of the national law in Kazakhstan, considering that children up to 18 years are entitled to receive child support, and, if they are under 21 years old and engaged in full-time study they can still benefit from maintenance.

D. Maintenance Arrangements

Under the Hague Maintenance Convention, a maintenance arrangement made in a Contracting State shall be entitled to recognition and enforcement as a court decision, provided that it is enforceable as a decision in the State of origin (Article 30). This provision is consistent with the national law in Kazakhstan, which regards notarised maintenance arrangements as equal to court enforcement orders, officially drawn up by courts in maintenance cases. If Kazakhstan accedes to the Hague Maintenance Convention, authentic Kazakhstani agreements on child support will be easily recognised and enforced—in States Party to the Convention.

[44] Supreme Court of the Republic of Kazakhstan, Regulatory Decision of 11 July 2003 'On Court Decision' ('О судебном решении'), para 30.

[45] Civil Code of the Republic of Kazakhstan of 27 December 1994, Art 1090; Code of Civil Procedure, Art 425.

E. No Fee for the Applicant

Article 8(2) of the Convention provides that 'Central Authorities may not impose any charge on an applicant for the provision of their services under the Convention save for exceptional costs arising from a request for a specific measure under Article 7'. Considering the financial situation of the general population in Kazakhstan, it is a very positive provision that the applicant will not have to pay extra fees trying to recover maintenance from abroad. The minimum wage in Kazakhstan only amounts to €79 a month.[46] For some families, even the nominal charge for services for international recovery of child support may constitute half their monthly income. Thus, the fact that the Central Authority bears its own costs and does not request any fees from applicants, save for certain exceptional circumstances, represents a significant advantage when taking into consideration accession to the Hague Convention.

F. Protection of Data

A very important aspect of the Hague Maintenance Convention which makes the Convention attractive for ratification by Kazakhstan is protection of personal data. In particular, the Convention guarantees that personal data gathered or transmitted under the Convention shall be used only for the purposes for which they were gathered or transmitted (Article 38). Moreover, the transmittal form and the acknowledgement form (Annexes to the Convention), which are to be submitted together with an application for maintenance by the Central authority, contain confidentiality and personal data protection notices. Strict protection of personal data constitutes one of the main advantages of the Hague Convention for Kazakhstani parties.

G. Transfer of Funds

Article 35 encourages Contracting States to promote the use of the most cost-effective and efficient methods available to transfer maintenance payments. No problem should arise in this regard in Kazakhstan, since the financial system in Kazakhstan is developed and sophisticated enough for any types of international bank transactions, money transfers, or any other type of payments.

H. Types of Enforcement Measures

The Hague Maintenance Convention requires that the Contracting States shall make available in their domestic law effective measures to enforce decisions under the Convention. Such measures may include: wage withholding, garnishment from bank accounts and other sources, deductions from social security payments, lien on or forced sale of property,

[46] The minimum monthly wage in Kazakhstan is currently 19,966 Tenge or €79. This amount is calculated annually by the Government taking into account various economic circumstances and figures; it gradually increases every year. See Law on Republican Budget for 2014–16, Art 10(1).

tax refund withholding, withholding or attachment of pension benefits, credit bureau reporting, denial, suspension or revocation of various licences (eg, driving licences) and the use of mediation, conciliation or similar processes to bring about voluntary compliance (Article 34).

Some of these measures are not exactly ideal for Kazakhstani parties, such as deductions from social security payments (undesirable and complicated), tax refund withholding (tax refunds are non-existent in Kazakhstan), or credit bureau reporting (also non-existent in Kazakhstan). Kazakhstan is not required to have such measures as these are merely part of an illustrative list in the Convention. Kazakhstan does have effective enforcement measures including: seizure of a debtor's property, preventing the debtor from taking certain actions (such as leaving Kazakhstan), prohibiting access to or limiting the debtor in the use of his property (including money), seizing title documents, and prohibiting third parties from transferring property (including money) to the debtor.

I. Designation of Central Authorities

If Kazakhstan joins the Hague Maintenance Convention, a network of Central Authorities should be established instead of designating a single Central Authority in the country's capital city. In particular, the presence of a Central Authority at least in the cities of Almaty, Astana and Atyrau is desirable for the convenience of the local people.

Also, when taking recovery of maintenance to the international level, one must keep in mind that the main languages used in the courts of Kazakhstan are Kazakh and Russian. A Central Authority to be designated in Kazakhstan according to the Hague Maintenance Convention should employ qualified individuals with adequate knowledge of foreign languages (at least English and French).

Based on this analysis and in connection with the Heidelberg Conference on Recovery of Maintenance in the EU and Worldwide, an enquiry was made by the author to the Ministry of Justice of the Republic of Kazakhstan regarding the possibility of ratification of the Hague Maintenance Convention and Protocol.

The Committee on Implementation of Resolutions of the Ministry of Justice of the Republic of Kazakhstan, having considered the enquiry, informed the author as follows.[47] A proposal has been initiated by the Ministry of Justice of the Republic of Kazakhstan to join the Convention, which was supported by the Ministry of International Affairs of the Republic of Kazakhstan. Development of the draft law on ratification of this Convention has begun.

The Convention has been found to correspond to the requirements for international treaties pursuant to national law.[48] Also, the Convention does not contain any provisions that would contradict the Constitution of the Republic of Kazakhstan, the Family Code and the laws of the Republic of Kazakhstan. Thus, the Ministry of Justice concluded that no changes need to be made to the legislation of the Republic of Kazakhstan.

[47] Committee on Implementation of Resolutions of Ministry of Justice of the Republic of Kazakhstan, Letter of 27 February 2013 No 15-03-10/1414 to M Karayanidi, on file with the author.

[48] Law of the Republic of Kazakhstan of 30 May 2005 No 54 'On International Treaties of the Republic of Kazakhstan'.

V. Conclusion

This chapter has discussed recovery of maintenance in Kazakhstan and analysed the considerations for accession to the Hague Maintenance Convention by Kazakhstan. The analysis has led to several conclusions.

Review of the current situation in Kazakhstan has shown that a sound domestic system for recovering child support is in place. Consideration of the latest developments in civil procedure on enforcing maintenance decisions suggest that certain positive improvements have been taking place. Among others, there is the introduction of private bailiffs and the existence of thorough protection of personal data and information on assets in Kazakhstan, etc.

However, the research has highlighted that matters are rather more unsatisfactory when it comes to the recovery of maintenance from abroad. The existing rules on the recovery of maintenance in relations with a foreign element are diverse and incomplete. The New York Convention on Recovery of Maintenance from Abroad does not provide for enforcement of maintenance judgments and foreign instruments; the mechanism of recovery of maintenance through transmitting and receiving authorities seems outdated and needs improvement. The Minsk Convention regulating conflict of laws issues shows a promising basis for legal and judicial cooperation among the independent States of the former Soviet Union. However, the Convention lacks an effective mechanism of enforcement and is limited in its territorial application.

The most relevant provisions of the Hague Maintenance Convention from the point of view of a lawyer in Kazakhstan were tested for compatibility with the national legislation in Kazakhstan. No major contradictions have been found. Indeed, most of the provisions have been found consistent with the existing rules of Kazakhstan law on child support and beneficial to Kazakhstani parties. Similarities between Kazakhstani regulation of maintenance and the Hague Maintenance Convention treatment of the fundamental issues (such as marriage, age of children, authentic maintenance arrangements and data protection) support the argument for the accession to the Convention by Kazakhstan. Moreover, the most advantageous feature of the Hague Maintenance Convention for Kazakhstan would be effective international enforcement of maintenance decisions and authorised instruments. Kazakhstan residents would have access to Central Authorities and legal aid at no cost to themselves in order to establish child support decisions in another Contracting State, usually where the debtor lives, or to enforce abroad a child support decision or maintenance agreement that they have already obtained in Kazakhstan. Overall, the research has shown that, in the interests of more effective recovery of maintenance from abroad, Kazakhstan should accede to the Hague Maintenance Convention.

13

Maintenance Obligations in the Brazilian Legal System

INEZ LOPES

I. Introduction

Family law issues are no longer limited to national borders, and international legal cooperation is an important principle to assure cross-borders rights. The objective of this chapter is to explain Brazilian law on maintenance obligations.

This chapter is divided into eleven parts. It provides an overview of family law according to the Brazilian Federal Constitution and presents the concept of maintenance obligations and maintenance as a basic human right in domestic law. It examines the legal nature of maintenance obligations, and how maintenance obligations in the Brazilian legal system involve the analysis of concepts such as: marriage, civil union, same-sex marriage, child support, child support in a paternity investigation, unborn child support, grandparents, elderly parents, and family collateral line. In addition, it analyses extrajudicial maintenance agreements and legal proceedings. It also studies maintenance obligations in private international law from the Brazilian perspective. Finally, this text presents Brazil's policy on the implementation of the 2007 Hague Convention and its Protocol on the Law Applicable to Maintenance Obligations and assesses new challenges for recognition and enforcement of foreign maintenance decisions.

II. An Overview of Family Law according to the Brazilian Federal Constitution

The family is a natural social organisation, and States and societies are committed to protecting this institution. Following the principles of human dignity and human rights, people have the right to marry or to cohabit. Spouses and cohabitees have equal rights and common responsibilities during and potentially after the relationship. As stated by Article 226, paragraph 3 of the Brazilian Constitution, civil unions or cohabitees is recognised as a family institution and the law has to facilitate its conversion into marriage when required.[1]

[1] Art 226, para 3 reads:
Para efeito da proteção do Estado, é reconhecida a união estável entre o homem e a mulher como entidade familiar, devendo a lei facilitar sua conversão em casamento.

In addition, Law No 9.278 of 10 May 2009 came into force in order to regulate 'civil unions' or cohabitees. It establishes rights and duties for such partnerships related to child support responsibilities, common property, support obligations and the right to bring legal actions before family courts instead of civil courts. For instance, in the case of dissolution of marriage or a civil union, parents have the obligation to protect their children and to sustain their basic needs.[2] In relation to liabilities at the constitutional level, spouses and cohabitees have the same rights and common responsibilities in protecting their children.

According to the Brazilian Federal Constitution, the family is considered to be the cornerstone of society and is given special protection by the State. The family concept is broad as the family entity includes parents and their descendants.[3] Furthermore, the Federal Constitution establishes that family, society and the Brazilian State have the common responsibility of assuring fundamental basic rights and preventing violations, discrimination, negligence, oppression, cruelty and exploitation of these rights.[4]

All children are protected at the constitutional level regardless of the status of their parents. As stated by Article 227, all children, irrespective of whether they were born inside or outside wedlock, or adopted, have the same rights under the law.[5] The Constitution prohibits any sort of discrimination on the basis of children's legitimacy, or whether they are adopted.

Before the 1988 Brazilian Constitution, such discrimination used to exist. This discrimination applied to children born outside of marriage or adopted children.[6] The law distinguished between legitimate and illegitimate children, or adopted children, and their rights were unequal. For instance, in the case of rights of succession, the illegitimate child was entitled to only half the inheritance that a legitimate child could receive, under Article 2 of Law No 883 of 21 October 1949 (repealed by Law No 12.004 of 29 July 2009).[7]

Therefore, the 1988 Constitution was a defining point in the affiliation system. Consequently, all laws which contain reference to children's legitimacy were repealed by the constitutional order; even those adjectives which contain negative connotations such as bastard, spurious or adulterine, were banned.

The Federal Constitution recognises the principles of solidarity and reciprocity among family members, as stated in Articles 229 and 230:

> Article 229. It is the duty of parents to assist, raise and educate their under-age children and it is the duty of children of age to help and assist their parents in old-age, need or sickness.
>
> Article 230. It is the duty of the family, society and the State, to assist the elderly, ensuring their participation in the community, defending their dignity and well-being and guaranteeing their right to life.

[2] Brasil, Superior Tribunal de Justiça, *Civil—Alimentos—Revisão,* Recurso Especial No 450164—SP (2002/0077943-8), Terceira Turma Relator Ministro Ari Pargendler, Recorrente Rafael B Birmann, 15 March 2004.

[3] Art 226, para 4 reads:

Art 226. A família, base da sociedade, tem especial proteção do Estado.

§ 4º - Entende-se, também, como entidade familiar a comunidade formada por qualquer dos pais e seus descendentes.

[4] In accordance with the provisions laid down in Art 227- of Brazilian Federal Constitution.

[5] Art 227, para 6 states that:

Children, born or not during a marriage relation, or adopted, shall have the same rights and qualifications, prohibited any discriminatory designations related to affiliation.

[6] Under Art 1605 of 1916 Civil Law Code (Law No 3071).

[7] Law No 883/1949 provided that children born outside of wedlock could be recognised only after the separation of a couple. Law No 6.515/77 modified Art 1 of Law No 883/1949 so that children born outside the marriage could be recognised at any time (including during the marriage).

Consequently, while parents have a duty to protect their children until they reach the age of majority, which is set at 18 years old, children must assist their elderly parents indefinitely. This might include the possibility of being responsible for the maintenance obligation.

Assistance between family members involves more than providing food in order to survive. There is particular emphasis on protecting people in a family institution in a broad sense. Stakeholders have to contribute to assuring a child and an adolescent's rights which have absolute priority under Article 227. In practice, this assistance contributes to the creditor's rights to life, health, food, education, leisure, professional training, culture, dignity, respect, freedom, and family and community life.

III. Concept of Maintenance Obligation

In the Brazilian legal system, there has been some debate among jurists as to the meaning of the word 'maintenance'.[8] Maintenance is not limited to the necessities for survival but includes other things that are essential for living in accordance with the social context of a particular person according to doctrine and case law.[9] Usually, the right to maintenance is recognised by law,[10] and maintenance will be fixed by agreement or by a judge.

Additionally, maintenance is defined as 'a legal obligation which aims to guarantee the fundamental needs of persons unable to meet those needs themselves'.[11] The first Brazilian Civil Code (1916) had not defined the concept of maintenance and because of the absence of a definition it was interpreted as a support duty, involving not only physical well-being (sustaining the body) but also intellectual and moral aspects (cultivation and education of the spirit and of the rational human being).[12]

Due to the lack of a clear definition in the 1916 Civil Code, the concept of maintenance was defined by doctrine,[13] which has been taken into account by judges. For instance, Clóvis Bevilaqua, the Code's author, when analysing the previous civil code, said that maintenance meant financial support, housing, clothing, support during treatment of disease, and school education and instruction.[14] In this sense, there are two approaches to the meaning of the word maintenance discussed by doctrine. The *minimum standard of maintenance approach* concerns basic needs that are essential for surviving, such as food, housing and medication. In contrast, the *reasonable maintenance approach* goes beyond the

[8] These debates used to point out differences between maintenance in 'common' and legal meaning, since the time of Portugal's Acts ('Ordenações') in the nineteenth century up to Law No 5.478/1968. Jurists such as Pontes de Miranda, Clóvis Bevilaqua, Yussef Said Cahali, Orlando Gomes and Antônio Joaquim Ribas were among those who promoted discussions on these issues.

[9] See SG Porto, *Doutrina e Prática dos Alimentos,* 4th edn (São Paulo, Revista dos Tribunais, 2011) 17–20.

[10] Civil Code, Law No 10.406/2002, Arts 1.694–1.170 and Law No 5.478/1968, provisions for maintenance recovery proceedings.

[11] O Gomes, *Direito de Família,* 7th edn (Rio de Janeiro, Forense, 1988) 455.

[12] E Almeida, *Direito de Família* (Jacintho Ribeiro dos Santos, 1925) 314, in YS Cahali, *Dos Alimentos*, 8th edn (Revista dos Tribunais, 2013) 16.

[13] See (n 8).

[14] C Bevilaqua, *Código Civill dos Estados Unidos do Brasil. Edição histórica* (Rio de Janeiro, Ed Rio, 1975) 863.

minimum standard and includes education, entertainment, medical and dental care and financial status.[15]

According to the Brazilian Civil Code, Law No 10.406, of 10 January 2002, maintenance obligations apply to parents and children and include both *necessarium vitae* and *necessarium personae*. This can be extended to other family members, such as grandparents, brother and sisters.[16] However, this duty cannot undermine the obligation on a capable adult to provide for him or herself, nor take away from the maintenance debtor what is needed for his or her basic needs as stated in Articles 1695 and 1696:[17]

> Article 1695. Support is owed when the claimant does not have sufficient property, and cannot provide through his work, for his own maintenance and the person from whom support is claimed can pay it without forfeiting what is necessary for his own sustenance.
>
> Article 1696. The right to support is reciprocal between parents and children, and extends to all the ascendants; the obligation falls to those nearest in degree, in order.

Beyond the reciprocal commitments between family members, Brazil also has social rules in terms of the law of maintenance obligations in order to achieve a fair maintenance amount, over and above the duty to support.[18] It takes into account multiple aspects of social rules that are necessary for a person's development including the components of maintenance obligations essential to the right to live with dignity in accordance with individual and social human rights.

IV. Right to Maintenance: Basic Human Rights

The right to maintenance for children is based upon reciprocal obligations between parents and children, and the obligation may be extended to ascendants and descendants and in certain situations may reach a collateral relative, in accordance with the Civil Code:

> Article 1697. In the absence of ascendants, descendants have the duty (of maintenance), in the order of intestate succession, and in the absence of all of them, to full or half siblings.

In relation to a collateral relative's right to maintenance, there is a limitation of responsibility from the second degree of the collateral line. Even though the Article cited above distinguishes between full and half siblings, the interpretation is that any half-brothers and half-sisters can claim maintenance among themselves. If a father has died and the mother and grandparents have no way to support a child, there will be a maintenance obligation to brothers and sisters without undermining their own support.[19] The courts also recognise the legitimacy of claiming child support from half siblings, because they are related by

[15] Brasil, Superior Tribunal de Justiça, Agravo em Recurso Especial No 276979-MG (2013/0006385-0) Decisão monocrática Relator Ministro Ricardo Villas Bôas Cueva, Agravante E P DOS S, Judgment 19 June 2013.

[16] See items 4 and 6 of this Article.

[17] L Rose, *The Brazilian Civil Code in English* (Rio de Janeiro, Renovar, 2008) 367.

[18] Cahali (n 12) 16.

[19] Brasil, Tribunal de Justiça do Rio Grande do Sul, 8a. Câmara Cível, Relator Claudir Faccenda, 18 October 2007 RT 868-359; Tribunal de Justiça de São Paulo, 8a. Câmara Cível, 25 August 1999 JTJ 229-28.

blood.[20] The main purpose is to provide brothers and sisters with basic maintenance like food and housing in order to meet the minimum standard of living.[21]

However, even though the maintenance obligation is founded on the principle of reciprocity, it depends on the debtor's financial conditions, and it does not apply fully to family law as stated by the Civil Code.[22] The principle is not normally applicable to a minor child. However, if a minor child inherits a fortune, he or she might be required to pay maintenance to their relatives, depending on the degree of affinity based upon the possibility to pass maintenance obligations to heirs under Article 1700 of the Civil Code.[23]

It is very important to emphasise that the fundamental principles of maintenance rights and responsibilities, are for the dignity of human beings and family solidarity. Both principles are constitutionally based.[24] The law protects vulnerable people in family law matters, ensuring the needs of all people (from children to the elderly) are met. The Superior Court of Justice will not accept the judgment of a lower court that discharges a father's child support based only on the fact that the child has reached 18 years old; it maintains the obligation until the final decision of the special appeal.[25]

In addition, maintenance obligations are decided by a judge based upon two criteria: to meet someone's need (a person who makes the request) and the ability of the debtor to pay (a person from whom maintenance is requested and who is legally responsible for the obligation). The Superior Court of Justice clarifies that the potential family members are responsible for the reciprocal maintenance obligation, such as parents, spouses and cohabitees. Nevertheless, to determine the amount payable it will be necessary to take account of the creditor's needs and the financial resources of the debtor (the ability to pay maintenance).[26]

According to the Brazilian legal system, it is possible to issue a maintenance arrest warrant which may be used only in the case of non-fulfilment of the duty by the debtor in order to ensure the creditor's basic human rights are met among family relatives. However *habeas corpus* has been used to question the issuing of an arrest warrant for non-fulfilment of duties of support, because this has not been considered an appropriate legal proceeding in order to examine evidence with the aim of ascertaining the wealth and earning ability of the debtor, the needs of the creditor, or any overvalue of maintenance.[27]

[20] Brasil, Tribunal de Justiça de São Paulo, 3a. Câmara Cível, 15 March 1979, RT 546-103.

[21] Cahali (n 12) 478.

[22] Art 1.695 reads 'são devidos os alimentos quando quem os pretende não tem bens suficientes, nem pode prover, pelo seu trabalho, à própria mantença, e aquele, de quem se reclamam, pode fornecê-los, sem desfalque do necessário ao seu sustento'.

[23] Art 1.700 reads: 'a obrigação de prestar alimentos transmite-se aos herdeiros do devedor, na forma do Art 1.694'.

[24] Art 1, III and Art 229.

[25] Brasil, Superior Tribunal de Justiça, Agravo Regimental na Medida Cautelar No 12032/DF (2006/0208375-3) Terceira Turma Relatora Ministra Nancy Andrighi, Agravante VSN de A, 6 February 2007.

[26] Brasil, Superior Tribunal de Justiça, *Direito Civil e Processual Civil—Família—Alimentos—Provisionais*, Recurso Especial No 1170224-SE (2009/0240135-1) Terceira Turma Relatora Ministra Nancy Andrighi, Recorrente OLF e outros, Brasília, 23 November 2010.

[27] Brasil, Superior Tribunal de Justiça, *Execução de Alimentos*, Recurso Ordinário em Habeas Corpus No 33720-SP (2012/0183284-1) Quarta Turma Relatora Ministra Maria Isabel Gallotti, Recorrente N K M, 5 March 2013. For other case examples, see RHC 31922/PA; RHC 28821/RS; RHC 30729/TO.

V. Legal Nature and some Characteristics of Maintenance Obligations

The legal nature of maintenance is considered both a personal and patrimonial right, as it is based on human and economic solidarity between family members and also establishes mutual assistance as an ethical obligation.[28] This solidarity can be extended to the debtor's descendants because Article 1700 of the Civil Code states that the maintenance obligation is transmitted to debtors' heirs.

Maintenance obligations are divided into categories, known in the Brazilian system as: natural or necessary, and civil or appropriate.[29] Necessary or natural maintenance comprises basic needs, in accordance with Article 1694, paragraph 2 and Article 1704 of the Civil Code. Civil or appropriate maintenance refers to other needs a person might have in order to keep the same social conditions, like education and entertainment, as stated in Article 1694 of the Civil Code, or upholding the same standard of living that the person had before needing maintenance support.

A maintenance obligation in Brazil is a personal and non-waivable right because its primary goal is to protect life, subsistence and physical integrity under Article 1707 of the Civil Code. Notwithstanding this, there is an understanding by the Council of Federal Justice that spouses can waive their rights on divorce in accordance with Statement No 263. The Statement declares that Article 1707 of the Civil Code does not prevent the waiver in a divorce or a separation of cohabitees from being effective. Nevertheless, spouses or cohabitees can only exercise their rights to maintenance as a non-waivable prerogative during the existence of their relationship.

Additionally once a maintenance obligation is fixed by the court, whether provisional or definitive, it cannot be refunded. The Superior Court of Justice has held that even if the debtor has paid more than the amount due in child support, the debtor has no right to claim compensation.[30]

Cahali affirms that maintenance is not based on solidarity but on joint obligations, and is therefore divisible.[31] In this sense, the Superior Court of Justice has decided that the main responsibility to pay child support belongs to parents, but the subsidiary obligation should be divided between paternal and maternal grandparents according to their resources, taking into account two characteristics: divisibility and the possibility of division.[32]

[28] CR Gonçalves, *Direito Civil Brasileiro—Direito de Família*, vol 6, 9th. edn (São Paulo, Saraiva, 2012) 499–500.

[29] AMG Louzada, *Alimentos—Doutrina e Jurisprudência*, (Belo Horizonte, Del Rey, 2008).

[30] Brasil, Superior Tribunal de Justiça, *Direito Civil—Alimentos*, Recurso Especial No 1318844–PR (2011/0179694-9) Terceira Turma Relator Ministro Sidnei Beneti, Recorrente CT e outros, 7 March 2013.

[31] Cahali (n 12) 138.

[32] Brasil, Superior Tribunal de Justiça Civil, *Alimentos—Responsabilidade dos Avós*, Recurso Especial No 658139-RS (2004/0063876-0) Quarta Turma Relator Ministro Fernando Gonçalves, Recorrente IGS e outro, 11 October 2005.

VI. Maintenance Obligations in the Brazilian Legal System

A. Maintenance and Marriage

When analysing the duty of support in wedlock, the Superior Court of Justice has decided that maintenance between spouses is reciprocal and based upon need and ability to pay after the end of marriage. The role of women has changed in society and they generally have a more independent economic life nowadays. For this reason, if a woman works and can sustain herself through her own means, she will have no right to claim maintenance from her ex-spouse unless she proves her need. The maintenance obligation between ex-spouses is based upon assistance and cannot be *ad aeternum*; however it might be necessary for a certain time, considering the situation and the facts.[33]

Hence, when spouses get divorced, both can be responsible for temporary maintenance. For women who were not working for the duration of the marriage, there is a right to maintenance and this right will exist until she returns to work. Once she gets a job and can sustain herself, her ex-husband will cease to have the maintenance obligation.[34] Nonetheless, this right to support may last indefinitely in exceptional circumstances, such as a spouse's permanent incapacity to work or the practical impossibility of entering the labour market.[35]

Article 1708 of the Civil Code of 2002 says that the marriage, the civil union, or cohabitation of the creditor with another person, ends the duty of support by the debtor. In a claim before a local court to discharge a former husband of the duty to support his former wife due to the latter's new relationship, the judges of Sao Paulo Court of Justice upheld the complaint; and concluded that there can be an obligation to pay household expenses. This decision was partially modified on appeal. The judgment given by the Superior Court of Justice revised the decision and discharged the debtor's duty to pay the cost of tax, water, electricity and the telephone in the property, which was occupied by his children and his ex-wife, who was already living with a new partner.[36]

The understanding of the Superior Court of Justice in regard to the legal obligation to pay maintenance between former spouses is based on assistance and not on compensation.[37] The main idea is that there is no economic dependence between them during the time of the marriage. However, maintenance compensation may be applicable as an extraordinary regime of separation of property, especially when a wife is dedicated

[33] Brasil, Superior Tribunal de Justiça, *Direito Civil Família—Revisional de Alimentos,* Recurso Especial No 933355-SP (2007/0055175-0), Terceira Turma Relatora Ministra Nancy Andrighi, Recorrente MRO, 25 March 2008.

[34] Ibid.

[35] Brasil, Superior Tribunal de Justiça, *Civil—Processual Civil—Alimentos—Exoneração,* Recurso Especial No 1205408-RJ (2010/0145953-6) Terceira Turma Relatora Ministra Nancy Andrighi, Recorrente SAC, 21 June 2011.

[36] Brasil, Superior Tribunal de Justiça, *Civil e Processual Civil—Alimentos—Exoneração,* Recurso Especial No 1087164-SP (2008/0195848-4) Terceira Turma Relatora Ministra Nancy Andrighi Recorrente NLP, 2 October 2011.

[37] Case law examples include Brasil, Superior Tribunal de Justiça, Recurso Especial No 933355-SP; Recurso Especial No 1205408; Recurso Especial No 886537-MG; Recurso Especial No 1087164-SP; Recurso Especial No 1143762-SP; Recurso Especial No 1025769-MG; Recurso Ordinário em Habeas Corpus No 21514-GO; Habeas Corpus No 187202-RJ.

exclusively to the family, with no job or income. The Superior Court of Justice has not given a judgment on this matter.

B. Maintenance in Civil Unions and Same-Sex Marriage

Civil unions are recognised on the constitutional level, according to Article 226, paragraph 3, which acknowledges a relationship between a man and woman as a family. The provision determines that law shall facilitate the union's conversion into marriage, when required. In 1994, Law No 8971 was created to regulate the rights to maintenance and to succession in civil unions. Some years later, the Civil Code of 2002 established a civil union as a family entity which has the same rights as marriage. However, there is a proviso that this will not apply where the parties to the civil union are prohibited from marrying according to the provisions laid down in Articles 1521 and 1723, paragraph 1.

In a judgment given by the Supreme Federal Court, it was decided that the union between persons of the same sex deserves to be treated according to the same rules and requirements. A family formed by a same sex union, called 'união homoafetiva', cannot suffer any discrimination, and shall have the same rights, privileges, obligations and benefits that may be available to partners of different sex civil unions.[38] These benefits include social security, the ability to adopt a child and maintenance obligations. Recently, in light of the declaration of unconstitutionality of different treatment given to civil unions between same sex persons by the Supreme Federal Court, the National Council of Justice has published Resolution 175/2013, which prohibits competent authorities from refusing to authorise or register a civil marriage, or convert a civil union into a marriage where the parties are of the same sex.

Following the human rights principles of equality and dignity, the Superior Court of Justice has decided that a same-sex civil union is to be considered as one of several modalities of family entity. Furthermore, the Brazilian constitutional principles of equality, human dignity and non-discrimination, for instance, are the cornerstones to apply the same legal effects that apply to heterosexual couples. In case of separation, both persons have the same rights to share the assets acquired during the relationship. Although some properties are registered solely in the name of one of the partners, there is no need to prove the existence of common efforts because it is based on the assumption that they were obtained during the common life.

C. Child Support

According to the Superior Court of Justice, both father and mother have a joint obligation and each one assumes an independent status in relation to maintenance obligations.[39]

[38] Brasil, Supremo Tribunal Federal, *Benefício de Pensão por morte união homoafetiva*, Agravo Regimental no Recurso Extraordinário No 687432-MG Primeira Turma Relator Ministro Luiz Fux, Agravante Caixa de Previdência dos Funcionários do Banco Do Brasil—Previ, 18 September 2012.

[39] Brasil, Superior Tribunal de Justiça, *Processual Civil e Direito Civil—Ação de Alimentos*, Recurso Especial No 964866-SP (2007/0148321-5) Quarta Turma Relator Ministro João Otávio de Noronha, Recorrente JRR, 1 March 2011.

Thus, both parents have the main duty to support, which may be extended to ascendants and descendants.

The duration of child support is until the child is 18 years old, the age of majority, in accordance with Article 5 of the Civil Code. However, Brazilian courts have extended this right up until undergraduate education.[40] According to the Superior Court of Justice's judgment, the maintenance obligation does not cease automatically at the age of majority, further maintenance payments after that are possible based upon kinship relations. In addition, there is case law that considers that there is a rebuttable presumption (*praesumptio iuris tantum)* that children over 18 should continue receiving maintenance when they are attending university as undergraduates or undertaking technical training. Therefore, parents' maintenance obligations are limited to the conclusion of undergraduate courses or technical training, and the Superior Court of Justice has upheld a ruling discharging a father from the obligation to pay child support to his daughter while she completed a master course.[41]

In relation to international legal cooperation, there is a constitutional requirement that letters rogatory are legal instruments of communication between national and foreign courts and they will not be automatically granted. It will depend on a proceeding known as *exequatur* that will be decided by the Superior Court of Justice.[42] Thus, any necessity for notification, finding out the whereabouts of a person, taking evidence, and other courts' demands coming from abroad, must be communicated to the debtor in Brazil by letters rogatory.[43] There is also a constitutional requirement that foreign judgments can only be recognised by the Superior Court of Justice and then enforced before federal courts. If a child or adolescent is an applicant in a lawsuit, federal prosecutors must protect their rights.

In relation to the basis of jurisdiction, Article 88 of the Brazilian Code of Civil Procedure sets out grounds of concurrent jurisdiction for local decisions with international links, as follows:

> Article 88—The Brazilian judicial authority is competent when:
>
> I—The defendant, whatever his nationality, is domiciled in Brazil;
>
> II—The obligation must be performed in Brazil;
>
> III—The case is based on an incident that took place or arises from an action taken in Brazil.

Nevertheless, Article 89 of the Brazilian Code of Civil Procedure sets out a requirement for exclusive jurisdiction at the international level when cases are related to immovable property located in Brazil or in succession cases when property is situated in Brazil.

[40] Brasil, Superior Tribunal de Justiça, *Processual Civil—Civil—Ação de Alimentos*, Recurso Especial No 1218510-SP (2010/0184661-7) Terceira Turma Relatora Ministra Nancy Andrighi, Recorrente CEM, 27 September 2011.

[41] Brasil, Superior Tribunal de Justiça, *Direito de Família e Processual Civil—Recurso Especial—Omissão e Contradição—Inexistência—Alimentos*, Recurso Especial No 1312706-AL (2012/0046782-0) Quarta Turma Relator Ministro Luis Felipe Salomão, Recorrente JCJ, 21 February 2013.

[42] A letter rogatory is an instrument of international legal cooperation which contains a formal request from a court to a foreign court or vice versa for the purpose of service of process and taking evidence. The Superior Court of Justice is the competent body to concede the *exequatur* to the letters rogatory in order to produce effects and to be fulfilled, according to Art 105, I, i, of the Brazilian Constitution.

[43] Brasil, Superior Tribunal de Justiça, Carta Rogatória No 6947-CH (2012/0135694-8) Decisão monocrática Relator Ministro Felix Fischer, Interessado CZ, 14 December 2012; Carta Rogatória No 6588-CH (2012/0039614-4) Decisão monocrática Relator Ministro Ari Pargendler, Interessado FCT, 9 May 2012.

In relation to territorial jurisdiction, according to Article 100, II, of the Brazilian Civil Procedural Code, the competent court for disputes of maintenance obligations is that of the domicile or residence of the child, spouse, or any person who has the right to claim maintenance. This rule is also applicable in the case of revision of the maintenance obligation and represents the second stage after the jurisdiction of Brazilian courts has been decided.[44]

i. Child Support in Paternity Investigations

The recognition of paternity is a non-waivable right. A mother has no right to dismiss a paternity investigation claimed before the court if there has been a DNA test, with confirmation of paternity. The interest of the child and the determination of the truth are important.[45]

It is also possible for the child, who may be represented or assisted by his or her mother, to bring an action for a paternity investigation together with an action for child support. In this case, the obligation of the debtor will be due from the date of the judicial notice.[46]

According to Brazilian law, the Public Prosecutor's Office (*Ministério Público* in Portuguese) is also permitted to bring an action on behalf of the child in order to seek paternity. The National Judicial Magistrate of the National Council of Justice (CNJ) has launched a programme, known as 'Pai Presente',[47] that directs judges and prosecutors to ask public schools to inform them of children who do not have a registered father and start proceedings in order to discover the father. The aim is to achieve the recognition of fatherhood of all children who attend public schools in Brazil and who do not have a declared father on their birth certificate. It must be noted that while it is not yet a formal legal action, this proceeding, which is administrative in nature, may develop into one, if the result is inconclusive. Brazilian law allows the Public Prosecutor's Office to start legal proceedings in order to determine the child's father, if this information is not on the child's birth certificate. This action may result in maintenance as well.

ii. Unborn Child Support

An unborn child has *locus standi* to bring an action for maintenance or for a paternity investigation with support, represented by his or her mother. Law No 11.804, 5 November 2008, gives pregnant women the right to maintenance. The purpose is to assure the dignity of birth.[48] It should be noted that it is only the father and no other members of the family who can be the defendant in a claim for unborn child support.

[44] There is a new code of civil procedure project being discussed in Congress, currently at an advanced stage, which has a new express rule for maintenance in Art 22, I, which states that the Brazilian judicial authority is competent to proceed and judge actions related to maintenance when the creditor is domiciled or resident in Brazil.

[45] Brasil, Superior Tribunal de Justiça, *Civil e processual—Ação de Investigação de Paternidade,* Recurso Especial No 472608-AL (2002/0136005-7) Quarta Turma Relator Ministro Aldir Passarinho Júnior, Recorrente Natália dos Reis Vieira—menor impúbere, 18 March 2003.

[46] Precedents Nos 1 and 277/STJ.

[47] The 'Pai presente' programme (or 'Acting father' programme) was launched by Resolution No 16 of National Judicial Magistrate, of National Council of Justice, in 17 February 2012. See www.cnj.jus.br/programas-de-a-a-z/infancia-e-juventude/pai-presente (accessed October 2013).

[48] Gonçalves (n 28) 575.

The maintenance payable includes an amount sufficient to cover the additional expenses of the term of pregnancy from conception to delivery, including any special dietary requirements, medical appointments, hospital admissions, childbirth, medicines, and other necessary preventive and therapeutic prescriptions.[49] However, the unborn child support does not mean that the paternity has already been recognised. The Justice Court of Rio Grande of Sul held that the award may be set to contribute to the maintenance of the mother. If there is evidence of paternity, it is reasonable to fix child support in favour of the unborn child until it is possible to perform the DNA test.[50]

Once the child is born, there will be an automatic conversion from unborn child support to child support, in terms of Article 6, Law No 11804/2008.[51] However, in the case of a negative DNA result, the mother will be responsible for committing an unlawful act.[52]

D. Grandparents' Maintenance

Although the main responsibility to pay child support lies with parents, grandparents may also be responsible in some circumstances. This is based on the principle that ascendants and descendants may be responsible for maintenance in accordance with the Civil Code. The grandparents will only have the obligation to make the payment, full or partial, in cases where parents cannot pay maintenance, based upon subsidiary and complementary principles.[53]

E. Elderly Parents' Maintenance

In general, the maintenance duty between parents and children is reciprocal, and one of the characteristics is that there is a joint obligation between them. However, parents' primary responsibility is to support their children.

According to the Superior Court of Justice, maintenance is due by kinship governed by the Civil Code, in accordance with Article 1698. These are joint obligations, because every debtor has an autonomous duty in relation to the maintenance creditor, subject to balancing the ability to pay with the corresponding need of the maintenance creditor.[54]

Nevertheless, Law No 10741/2003, known as the Elderly Statute, has attributed a solidarity obligation to provide maintenance when the creditors are elderly, which differs from that provided in the Civil Code. The Superior Court of Justice has decided that by virtue

[49] According to the provisions set out in Art 2 of Law No 11804/2008.

[50] Brasil, Tribunal de Justiça do Rio Grande do Sul, Agravo de Instrumento No 70045908373 Sétima Câmara Cível Relator Sérgio Fernando de Vasconcellos Chaves, 31 October 2011.

[51] Brasil, Tribunal de Justiça do Distrito Federal, *Processo Civil—Civil—Ação De Alimentos Gravídicos,* Processo No 20090710241625APC, Terceira Turma Cível, Relator João Mariosa, Apelante M.J.S, 15 March 2010.

[52] According to the provisions set out in Art 186 of the Civil Code.

[53] Brasil, Superior Tribunal de Justiça, *Civil e Processual—Ação de alimentos dirigida contra os avós paternos,* Recurso Especial No 576152-ES (2003/0142789-0) Quarta Turma Relator Ministro Aldir Passarinho Junior, Recorrente JGOS—menor impúbere, 8 June 2010; *Civil—Processual civil—Obrigação alimentar avoenga,* Recurso Especial No 1211314-SP (2010/0163709-4) Terceira Turma Relatora Ministra Nancy Andrighi, Recorrente JOAB e outro, 15 September 2011.

[54] Brasil, Superior Tribunal de Justiça, Direito *Civil e Processual Civil—Ação de alimentos proposta pelos pais idosos em face de um dos filhos,* Recurso Especial No 775565-SP (2005/0138767-9) Terceira Turma Relatora Ministra Nancy Andrighi, Recorrente Roberto Wagner de Souza, 13 June 2006.

of the special nature of this law, it prevails over the specific provisions of the Civil Code. Therefore the maintenance obligation is due to elderly people based upon kinship and on a solidarity obligation. The statute also guarantees the elderly the right to choose one of the debtors in compliance with Article12.[55]

For instance, an elderly person has claimed provisional support from his siblings in a *post mortem* paternity investigation before a court. Once the paternity was confirmed by DNA examination, the judge upheld the claim and fixed the amount of the provision. The bases for his claim were that he was old, in a miserable situation and his three adult sons were unemployed with no ability to pay any support. The Superior Court of Justice decided that considering the paternity confirmed by examination, half-brothers have the duty to support an elderly sibling under the solidarity obligation established by Article 11 of the Elderly Statute.[56]

F. Maintenance in Family Collateral Line

The Brazilian Civil Code establishes that members of the family have reciprocal duties of mutual assistance, but this duty is limited to the second degree of the collateral line.[57] Therefore, the primary obligation to pay maintenance belongs to the closest relatives. Only when these relatives are absent or when they are financially unable to provide support are other members of the family required to fulfil this duty. This could be: ascendants, grandparents, and descendants (up to brothers and sisters) based upon the subsidiary principle.[58]

The maintenance obligation is based upon the law, which provides an exhaustive list of non-declarative criteria of those who are responsible for support.[59] The understanding of the Superior Court of Justice is that this limits liability up to the second degree of collateral relatives. The law does not include uncles and nephews.

VII. Maintenance Legal Proceedings

A. Extrajudicial Maintenance Agreement

Although the majority of cases in Brazil concerning maintenance obligations are decided by courts, an extrajudicial agreement between parents or a child's legal representatives may

[55] Ibid.

[56] Brasil, Superior Tribunal de Justiça, *Processo Civil e Direito Civil Família—Alimentos provisionais,* Recurso Especial No 1170224-SE (2009/0240135-1) Terceira Turma Relatora Ministra Nancy Andrighi, Recorrente OLF, 23 November 2010.

[57] Arts 1697 and 1698.

[58] Brasil, Superior Tribunal de Justiça, *Processo Civil e Direito Civil—Família—Alimentos Provisionais,* Recurso Especial No 1170224-SE (2009/0240135-1) Terceira Turma Relatora Ministra Nancy Andrighi, Recorrente OLF e outros, 23 November 2010.

[59] Brasil, Superior Tribunal de Justiça, *Prisão Civil—Prestação de alimentos—Tios e Sobrinhos,* Habeas Corpus No 12079–BA (2000/0009738-1) Quarta Turma Relator Ministro Salvio de Figueiredo Teixeira, Impetrante Fernando Santana, 12 September 2000.

establish the conditions for support. However, in order for the agreement to be valid and effective, it is mandatory that the public prosecutor or the public attorney be involved in the agreement. The participation of at least one of these officials is compulsory; otherwise the agreement might be dismissed by courts.[60] '[I]ntervention of the public prosecutor member is required to ensure that children['s] interests are preserved' otherwise the agreement may be declared void.[61] Consequently, if a debtor does not fulfil his or her obligations, the agreement can be enforced before a court as an extrajudicial title pursuant to Article 585, II of the Civil Procedure Code.[62]

When the agreement is made abroad, it has to be recognised before the Superior Court of Justice in order to be enforceable. The maintenance case lies under the scope of concurrent jurisdiction when there is the possibility of suing either in Brazil or in a foreign jurisdiction. Article 90 of the Civil Procedure Law does not recognise international *lis pendens*. So elements of time and factual circumstances will be considered in judgments when there are conflicts of jurisdiction. This means that Brazilian courts are competent to open a judicial proceeding on maintenance obligations and shall refuse any argument concerning the existence of an equivalent legal proceeding which has already been filed in another country on the grounds of not recognising international *lis pendens*. Only after the recognition by the Superior Court of Justice will the foreign decision have *res judicata* effects. According to Rechsteiner, competence concentration into a single jurisdictional body favours uniform jurisprudence and a *securité de droit*.[63]

Under the Brazilian system, a foreign decision needs to be brought as a new action before the Superior Court of Justice, which will not review the merits. The decision is made by the President of the court and it is quite quick. However, if the defendant does not agree, and replies to the action, the case is remanded to the Superior Court of Justice plenary and it becomes a contested case of recognition. It is essential to highlight that one of the most important procedural requirements for recognition is that the defendant is given adequate notice and an opportunity to be heard in court. If this does not happen, the Superior Court of Justice will deny recognition of the foreign decision.

In the case of contested recognition of a foreign judgment, the Superior Court of Justice has held that an extrajudicial agreement on child custody recognised by a German administrative body, when in accordance with the foreign law, has the same effect as a judgment,[64] so it can have extraterritorial effect in Brazilian territory as a precedent of the Supreme Federal Court.[65] The court says that there is concurrent jurisdiction between Brazilian and foreign jurisdictions to decide custody and child support when a child is currently living in Brazil with his mother, while his father lives in another country. But the Superior Court

[60] Brasil, Superior Tribunal de Justiça, *Civil e Processual—Ação de alimentos—Acordo extrajudicial,* Recurso Especial No 896310-RS (2006/0210357-3) Quarta Turma Relator Ministro Aldir Passarinho Júnior, Recorrente ENS e outro, 5 February 2009.

[61] Ibid.

[62] Brasil, Superior Tribunal de Justiça, *Processual Civil—Execução de Alimentos,* Recurso Especial No 858270-MS (2006/0120463-6) Terceira Turma Relator Ministro Paulo de Tarso Sanseverino, Recorrente WGZJ e outro, 22 March 2011.

[63] BW Rechsteiner, *Direito Internacional Privado—Teoria e Prática*, 11th edn (São Paulo, Saraiva, 2010) 298.

[64] Brasil, Superior Tribunal de Justiça, *Pedido de homologação de provimento administrativo que assentou acordo de guarda compartilhada na Alemanha,* Sentença Estrangeira Contestada No 5635-DF (2010/0140983-2) Corte Especial Relatora Ministra Laurita Vaz, Recorrente GMB, 18 April 2012.

[65] Brasil, Supremo Tribunal Federal, *Sentença Estrangeira Contestada* (SEC 5526-NO). Relatora Ministra Ellen Gracie Data do julgamento Tribunal Pleno Requerente: Kare Vorland, 22 April 2004.

of Justice has dismissed the requirement of recognition of foreign judgments made by the father for the following reasons:

a) Decisions regarding the custody and child support do not undergo the effects of res judicata, when the facts have been modified after the agreement celebrated in 2001;
b) The Brazilian courts have granted temporary custody of the child to the mother, and provisional maintenance for the father taking into account that the last domicile of child and the couple in a civil union ended in 2009 was in Brazil (article 7 of Introductory Law to the Rules of the Brazilian Law);
c) In this context, the foreign agreement that has the same subject is recognised, but when modified and reconsidered by a domestic court, albeit temporarily, this implies the coexistence of two contradictory titles in blatant affront to the sovereignty of national jurisdiction.[66]

It should be noted that Article 4, paragraph 3 of Resolution No 9 of the Superior Court of Justice allows for the possibility of provisional measures while recognition of foreign decisions is pending.

B. Maintenance Recovery Proceedings

Law No 5478 of 25 July 1968 is a special law on maintenance and establishes a special procedure for maintenance recovery that applies to children and other family members. This procedure is quicker than normal proceedings. Along with the application the applicant should provide the birth certificate or some other form of evidence that establishes the duty to provide maintenance, such as the marriage certificate or the proof of a civil union. If this documentation is not provided the plaintiff has to bring an action in a regular proceeding.

A child may bring an action before the court, represented or assisted by the custodian. The Superior Court of Justice held that although a claim in the name of the mother is not technically adequate, child support necessitates that this complaint be heard.[67]

Furthermore, the Public Prosecutor's Office is permitted to bring an action before a court to recover maintenance on behalf of a child or adolescent under Article 201, III of Law No 8.069/90 (Statute of Children and Adolescents).[68] The public defender's offices also play an important role in ensuring that legal aid is provided when needed by a child, adolescent or any other vulnerable person in order to recover maintenance.

The Brazilian judicial system is organised into federal and state branches. Proceedings for the recovery of maintenance are held before state courts. The competent court is the court where children or maintenance applicants are domiciled or resident according to Article 100, II, of the Civil Procedural Court.

The Brazilian procedure for litigation can be divided into five stages. There are pleadings by claimant and defendant, then a conclusive opening order, followed by the evidentiary

[66] Ibid.

[67] Brasil, Superior Tribunal de Justiça, *Direito de família—Ação de reconhecimento e dissolução de união estável*, Recurso Especial No 1046130- MG, (2008/0075284-3) Terceira Turma Relatora Ministra Nancy Andrighi, Recorrente GGDAC, 6 October 2009.

[68] The Superior Court of Justice accepted the request of the Public Prosecutor of Minas Gerais and recognised its capacity to bring an action to recover maintenance on behalf of a child. Brasil, Superior Tribunal de Justiça, *Processual Civil Ação de Alimentos,* Recurso Especial No 1113590-MG (2009/0026873-9) Terceira Turma Relatora Ministra Nancy Andrighi, Recorrente A DOS S, 24 August 2010.

stage, and then the decision-making stage. The final stage is the appeal for those who opt to challenge the decision. Provisional measures for maintenance obligations can be established by judges until a final decision is given.[69] The amount payable may be either a fixed amount or a percentage of the debtor's net salary in accordance with their earnings.

When the application is upheld by the court, the provisional maintenance amount will be replaced with the definitive one. In order to determine the date on which the debtor should start making the payment obligation of definitive maintenance, there are two references fixed by jurisprudence: one that will be due from the defendant's receiving notice and the other from the trial. According to the Superior Court of Justice, it will be retroactive up to the notice of motion pursuant to Article 13 when the amount granted is higher than the provisional amount fixed before the judgment.[70] However, when the amount fixed by a final decision is below the provisional one, the obligation starts from the date of the judgment because of the non-refundable principle.[71]

In regard to enforcement, there is a special provision in the Civil Procedure Code.[72] Courts have often made use of their ability to withhold the debtor's income.[73] The judge can issue an order to arrest a debtor under Article 733, paragraph 1 of the Civil Procedure Code. A maintenance arrest warrant is considered appropriate when the debtor did not fulfil his obligation to pay maintenance for a period of three consecutive months before the application in court, as well as other unfulfilled obligations of paying maintenance during the litigation, in accordance with Precedent No 309/STJ.[74] An arrest warrant is only

[69] In accordance with Arts 2 and 4 of Law No 5478/1968.

[70] Brasil, Superior Tribunal de Justiça, *Família—Alimentos*, Agravo Regimental No Agravo de Instrumento No 982233-PR, (2007/0269815-8) Quarta Turma Relator Ministro Aldir Passarinho Junior, Agravante CDVL, 17 June 2008.

[71] Brasil, Superior Tribunal de Justiça, *Execução—Alimentos—Prisão do alimentante,* Agravo Regimental no Recurso Especial No 1175407-RS (2010/0004261-8) Terceira Turma Relator Ministro Massami Uyeda, Recorrente MLSK, 28 August 2012.

[72] Arts 732–735 of the Civil Procedure Code read:

> Art. 732. A execução de sentença, que condena ao pagamento de prestação alimentícia, far-se-á conforme o disposto no Capítulo IV deste Título.
>
> Parágrafo único. Recaindo a penhora em dinheiro, o oferecimento de embargos não obsta a que o exequente levante mensalmente a importância da prestação.
>
> Art. 733. Na execução de sentença ou de decisão, que fixa os alimentos provisionais, o juiz mandará citar o devedor para, em 3 (três) dias, efetuar o pagamento, provar que o fez ou justificar a impossibilidade de efetuá-lo.
>
> § 1° Se o devedor não pagar, nem se escusar, o juiz decretar-lhe-á a prisão pelo prazo de 1 (um) a 3 (três) meses.
>
> § 2° O cumprimento da pena não exime o devedor do pagamento das prestações vencidas e vincendas.
>
> § 3° Paga a prestação alimentícia, o juiz suspenderá o cumprimento da ordem de prisão.
>
> Art 734. Quando o devedor for funcionário público, militar, diretor ou gerente de empresa, bem como empregado sujeito à legislação do trabalho, o juiz mandará descontar em folha de pagamento a importância da prestação alimentícia.
>
> Parágrafo único. A comunicação será feita à autoridade, à empresa ou ao empregador por ofício, de que constarão os nomes do credor, do devedor, a importância da prestação e o tempo de sua duração.
>
> Art 735. Se o devedor não pagar os alimentos provisionais a que foi condenado, pode o credor promover a execução da sentença, observando-se o procedimento estabelecido no Capítulo IV deste Título.

[73] In accordance with the provisions set out in Art 734.

[74] Brasil, Superior Tribunal de Justiça, *Alimentos—Inadimplência de débito alimentar—Prisão civil,* Recurso em Habeas Corpus No 37055-GO (2013/0108826-8) Terceira Turma Relator Ministro João Otávio de Noronha, Recorrente KJAO, 4 June 2013.

possible for a failure to pay maintenance, and does not include debts related to courts' or attorneys' fees.

Even though the right to maintenance of the creditor is considered to be without limit of time[75] by doctrine and case law, there is a procedural limitation pursuant to Article 206, paragraph 2 of the Civil Code, which prescribes two-year instalments for the debtor. Cancellation of the obligation is subject to a judicial decision, with the right to appeal (Precedent No 358/STJ).

VIII. Maintenance Obligations in Private International Law

The family does not recognise political borders.[76] Since people have begun to move more freely across borders, the number of requests for international legal cooperation relating to maintenance obligations has increased. According to the Department of Assets Recovery and International Legal Cooperation (DRCI) of the Ministry of Justice, 45 per cent of international legal cooperation cases in civil matters are for maintenance obligations.[77]

In the Brazilian legal system, maintenance obligations in cross-border litigation are governed by national and international law, national conflict rules, and are based upon reciprocity and international legal cooperation principles. In regard to family law in the context of private international relations, family rights are governed by the law of the person's domicile.[78] Maintenance obligations are ruled by domestic law when the creditor and debtor both live in Brazil, regardless of their nationality. When the creditor and debtor have their residence in different countries the conflict of jurisdiction is governed by Article 88, sections I and II, of the Civil Procedure Code (Law No 5869, 11 January 1973). This provision establishes two rules of international jurisdiction: the *lex domicilie* (the plaintiff's domicile) or *lex fori* (the place where the obligation has to be fulfilled). In this context, Vicente Greco Filho affirms that the latter rule is more favourable to the creditor as it establishes national competence where the obligation is fulfilled.[79]

The Superior Court of Justice has decided that in accordance with the international procedural system, jurisdiction is not exercised exclusively but concurrently with the foreign jurisdiction in the matters of maintenance recovery.[80] In addition, the judgment states that the action brought before the foreign court is not subject to *lis pendens*, nor does it prevent

[75] This means that there is no statute of limitations for maintenance actions.

[76] E Jayme, 'O Direito Internacional Privado e a Família no umbral do século XXI—Conferência do Rio de Janeiro, 15 de março de 2002, PUC-Rio' in CL Marques and N Araújo (eds) *O Novo Direito Internacional estudos em homenagem a Erik Jayme* (Rio de Janeiro, Renovar, 2005) 27.

[77] DRCI, Ministry of Justice www.portal.mj.gov.br/main.asp?View={64D38BA9-C9D4-49D9-9B30-63ACD42B2476}&BrowserType=IE&LangID=pt-br&params=itemID%3D{4F479356-2E84-4ECB-9E12-C515E6605F17}%3B&UIPartUID={2868BA3C-1C72-4347-BE11-A26F70F4CB26} (accessed May 2013).

[78] In accordance with Art 7 of the Introductory Law to the Rules of Brazilian Law (Decreto-Lei No 4657, 4 September 1942).

[79] V Greco Filho, 'Alimentos em Direito Internacional Privado e sua Ação Extraterritorial' *Justitia*, vol 100 (São Paulo, 1977) 95108.

[80] This means that Brazilian and foreign courts are both competent to bring an action and make decisions on maintenance recovery, as confirmed by the Superior Court of Justice in case SEC 5635-DF.

the Brazilian courts from accepting the same claim or case and vice versa in terms of Article 90 of the Civil Procedure Code.[81]

The Bustamante Code was adopted by the VI Pan-American Conference in Havana, in 1928 (Decree No 5647, 8 January 1929) with the aim of establishing common rules on private international law. This Treaty has been considered a source of principles of private international law extending beyond the 15 Latin American State parties.[82] According to Article 68, the provisions referring to maintenance obligations between relatives are considered international public policy, which prohibit renunciation and ceding of these rights.[83]

In the United Nations system, the Convention on the Recovery Abroad of Maintenance, New York, 20 June 1956 (Law Decree No 10, 13 November 1958) was a great step toward assuring maintenance obligations rights, facilitating international procedural civil law to improve difficulties in recovering maintenance abroad. The General Attorney's Office of the Republic is the Central Authority for this international Treaty and its role goes beyond transmitting and receiving intermediate administrative information. Both the Supreme Federal Court and Superior Court of Justice have acknowledged that the General Attorney's Office of the Republic can represent the interests of the maintenance claimant by proposing the recognition and enforcement of a foreign decision before the national court based on the New York Convention.[84] The Superior Court of Justice understands that there is no necessity of diplomatic or consular legalisation of foreign documents when they are transmitted between official Central Authorities.[85]

It is worth noting that the Convention establishes two types of Central Authority—one that sends requests for cooperation (the sending or transmitting authority) and another that receives such requests in a given country (the receiving authority).[86] These Authorities act as intermediary institutions under the Convention. In Brazil, the Attorney General is designated to perform both functions, as specified by Article 26 of Law No 5478/1968 (Law of Maintenance) and Decree No 56.826 of 2 September 1965. Therefore, the New York Convention was the first instrument to ensure an open channel of cooperation in the area of the recovery of maintenance from abroad.

According to this Treaty and Law No 5478/1968, concerning conflicts of competence, when the creditor lives abroad and the debtor lives in Brazil, the competent court to

[81] Brasil, Superior Tribunal de Justiça, *Divórcio—Partilha de bens estrangeiros—Alimentos e guarda de filhos*, Sentença Estrangeira Contestada No 4127-US (2011/0125464-9) Corte Especial Relatores Ministros Nancy Andrighi e Teori Albino Zavascki Recorrente JGF, 29 August 2012.

[82] A Schulz, AM Tuñon and RV Meza, *The American Instruments on Private International Law: A Paper on their Relation to a Future Hague Convention on Exclusive Choice of Court Agreements*, Preliminary Document No 31 of June 2005. Available at www.hcch.net/upload/wop/jdgm_pd31e.pdf (accessed January 2014).

[83] Although the Bustamante Code is still in force, there are only a few cases citing this Treaty before the Brazilian Supreme and Superior courts and none of them are related to family law. However, it remains largely a source for doctrinal articles and research.

[84] Brasil, Superior Tribunal de Justiça, *Processual Civil Divórcio por mútuo consentimento—Alimentos*, Sentença Estrangeira Contestada No 2772-FR (2007/0276626-9), Corte Especial Relator Ministro Castro Meira, Recorrente LT, 5 November 2008; Supremo Tribunal Federal, Sentença Estrangeira No 8359-PT (2012/0097720-0) Decisão Monocrática Relator Ministro Felix Fischer, Requerente Procuradoria-Geral da República, Interessado IRM, 19 September 2012.

[85] Brasil, Superior Tribunal de Justiça, Sentença Estrangeira No 4703-NL (2009/0124980-3) Decisão Monocrática Relator Ministro Cesar Asfor Rocha, Requerente Ministério Público Federal, Interessado DPA, 23 August 2010.

[86] New York Convention, Art 2.

recover maintenance is a federal one in Brazil, if the request is made through the Central Authority.[87] However, when the debtor lives abroad and the creditor is in Brazil, the Superior Court of Justice affirms that a state court is competent to decide on maintenance recovery.[88]

Meanwhile, when the debtor lives in Brazil and seeks to revise and reduce the amount of maintenance payable to a creditor who lives abroad, the Superior Court of Justice has upheld that the competent court is the state court in the place where the debtor is domiciled, since it is the debtor who brings an action with the aim of reducing the amount of maintenance. The court has decided that the New York Convention is not applicable because it applies only to claims of maintenance recovery and not to an action for revising and reducing the amount of the obligation.[89] When Brazil ratifies the Hague Convention 2007, the debtor will only be able to seek modification in the State where the creditor is habitually resident as prescribed by Article 18 of the Convention.[90]

The Department of Assets Recovery and International Legal Cooperation (DRCI) of the National Secretariat of Justice of the Ministry of Justice is another Central Authority responsible for applications that do not fall under the New York Convention. There is still the possibility of requesting international legal cooperation through diplomatic means, based upon the reciprocity principle, which is processed by the Ministry of External Relations.

In addition to the bilateral agreements signed by Brazil and other States, relating to maintenance obligations or family matters, there is the Inter-American Convention on Maintenance Obligations concluded in Montevideo, Uruguay on 15 July 1989 from the IV Inter-American Conference on Private International Law. It was enacted in Brazil by Decree No 2428 of 17 December 1997, approved by Legislative Act 1, of 28 February 1996. The Convention covers applicable law, jurisdiction and international cooperation procedures. It applies when the maintenance creditor has their domicile or habitual residence in a State party and the debtor has their domicile or habitual residence, assets, or income in another State.[91]

Nadia de Araújo believes that this Treaty adopted a modern method of private international law, using the principles and designation of an alternative connection rule. The Convention leaves it to the competent authority to choose the applicable law that is more favourable to the creditor, whether that be the law of the domicile or residence of the creditor or the law of the domicile or residence of the debtor.[92] The Brazilian Central Authority for the Inter-American Convention on Maintenance Obligations is the DRCI. However,

[87] In accordance with the provisions of Art 26.

[88] Brasil, Superior Tribunal de Justiça, *Ação de Alimentos, Devedor residente no exterior e credor no Brasil,* Conflito de Compêtencia No 20175-SP (1997/0054515-6) Segunda Seção, Relator Ministro Carlos Alberto Menezes Direito, Autora Valéria Cristina Aguayo Antunes, 14 October 1998.

[89] Brasil, Superior Tribunal de Justiça, *Conflito negativo de competência—Ação revisional de alimentos—Alimentando residente no exterior, Convenção de Nova Iorque,* Conflito de Competência No 103390-SP (2009/0032608-2) Segunda Seção, Relator Ministro Fernando Gonçalves, Autor ND, 23 September 2009.

[90] See (n 44).

[91] Art 1.

[92] N Araújo, *Direito Internacional Privado: teoria e prática brasileira,* 5th edn (Rio de Janeiro, Renovar, 2011) 538.

despite the advantages of this Convention, it has not been used as much as the New York Convention.[93]

In regard to international procedural cooperation, the Treaty states that foreign judgments have extraterritorial effectiveness among State parties when a foreign judgment fulfils the requirements listed in Article 11 of the Convention. Further, the decision has to be enforced before the competent domestic court. However, it is important to highlight that a foreign decision has to be recognised by the Superior Court of Justice, in accordance with Article 105, I (a) of the Brazilian Constitution, before it can be enforced by a federal court.

IX. Brazilian Policy on the Implementation of the 2007 Hague Convention

In 2004, the Ministry of Justice created the Department of Assets Recovery and International Legal Cooperation (DRCI), a Central Authority, whose competency was established by Declaration No 6061of 15 March 2007, Annex I:

I—to articulate, integrate and propose actions of the Government in aspects related to combating money laundering, transnational organized crime, asset recovery and international legal cooperation;

II—to promote the articulation of the organs of the executive, legislature and judiciary, including the Federal and State prosecutors, with regard to combating money laundering and transnational organized crime;

III—to negotiate and coordinate the implementation of international legal cooperation;

IV— to perform the function of central authority for the processing of requests for international legal cooperation;

V— to coordinate the activities of the Brazilian Government in international forums on preventing and to combat money laundering and transnational organized crime, asset recovery and international legal cooperation;

VI—to instruct, advise and coordinate the implementation of international legal cooperation active and passive, including letters rogatory; and

VII—to promote the dissemination of information on asset recovery and international legal cooperation, preventing and combating money laundering and transnational organized crime in the country

This department is responsible for international legal cooperation in civil and criminal matters, and it is a Central Authority for bilateral and multilateral treaties related to family issues in private international law, except for the 1956 New York Convention on the Recovery Abroad of Maintenance and the 1980 Hague Convention on Civil Aspects of International Child Abduction.

[93] Ibid 540.

A. Study Group on the 2007 Hague Convention and Protocol

DRCI has been fully involved in both the international instruments (Convention of 23 November 2007 on the International Recovery of Child Support and Other Forms of Family Maintenance and the Protocol on the Law Applicable to Maintenance Obligations) contributing to the development of the transnational recovery of child support.

The National Secretariat of Justice (SNJ) of the Ministry of Justice established the Study Group on Child Support, by Portaria No 16, of 15 June 2009. According to Article 3, the main objective of the study group was to publish a report containing proposals on any possible reservations necessary in the case of Brazil's ratification of both instruments.

The study group worked together with scholars in order to support the Secretariat in future work with other agencies of the Executive on the Convention and its Protocol. The creation of this group was a consequence of the involvement of the DRCI with the 2007 Hague Maintenance Convention and its Protocol.

Since the DRCI was created in 2004, it has participated fully in the work of the Hague Conference on the maintenance project regarding the content of the final text of the Convention and its Protocol. During the negotiation period, Brazil made considerable efforts to ensure a broad scope of application of the Convention. This included proposals to include applications for child support for those under 21 years old and the provision of legal aid for these applicants under the Hague Convention of 2007.

The study group published its final report in 2010, which analysed the two regulatory instruments, and suggested a basis for future work among the executive bodies.

B. Working Group on the 2007 Hague Convention and Protocol

Continuing the policies for matters related to the international recovery of child support and family maintenance, two executive bodies (the Ministry of Justice and the Ministry of External Relations) decided to create a working group. The Portaria Interministerial No 500, of 21 March of 2012, established a permanent working group on the Hague Convention and Protocol.[94] This working group comprises the following representatives of administrative bodies: (i) SNJ; (ii) Office of Legislative Affairs (SAL) of the Ministry Justice; (iii) Legal Counsel (CONJUR) of the Ministry of Justice; (iv) Secretariat General for Brazilian Communities Exterior (SGEB), the Ministry of External Relations; and (v) Legal Counsel (CONJUR) of the Ministry of External Relations. At its first meeting, the working group decided to invite other representatives and academics to represent civil society.

The main objectives of the working group included the preparation of an essential document[95] for signature and ratification of the Convention and the Protocol. The working group must also translate the final text of both instruments into Portuguese, and write a report containing further proposals. In addition, it may come up with a list of possible reservations to the Convention, which would be made in the process of signature and

[94] Art 1.

[95] This document will be an important instrument, sending a message to National Congress supporting the signature and the ratification of both international legal instruments, suggesting possible reservations (which may include jurisdiction matters) and also presenting implementing provisions for the correct functioning of this new system of international legal cooperation.

ratification by Brazil, and produce other documents deemed relevant for the functioning of the working group.

Hence, the creation of this new working group highlights Brazil's willingness to work proactively towards an international system of cooperation on maintenance issues. The Brazilian authorities recognise the need to improve international legal cooperation in this area, and acknowledge that this requires a well-structured legal framework if further progress is to be made.

At present, this working group has discussed both instruments, analysed the report of the study group, and translated both instruments into Portuguese. It has also prepared a final report explaining the importance of these international treaties. National Congress has to approve the treaties for them to be ratified by the president in accordance with Article 49, I and 84, VIII, of the Federal Constitution.

X. New Challenges for Recognition and Enforcement of Foreign Decisions in Maintenance Obligations

International legal administrative cooperation between States has been one of the greatest advances in facilitating the exercise of rights beyond national borders. The States' commitment to guaranteeing people access to justice in other jurisdictions through international treaties is important in overcoming poor cooperation based only on reciprocity through diplomatic means.

The development of Central Authorities as administrative and legal bodies is a milestone in private international law. They have contributed both to facilitating communication as contact points for claimants, and to improving transnational legal and administrative services. Likewise, the role of Central Authorities is no longer limited to receiving and transmitting documents. The positive experiences with the New York Convention of 1956 on the Recovery Abroad of Maintenance extended the functions of Central Authorities and performed a 'safeguard' function.[96] The Central Authority must assist children in obtaining their maintenance, which includes applying for recognition and enforcement of a foreign decision rendered in another country before the Superior Court of Justice.

Conversely, although the effectiveness of cross-border demands has been advanced by international legal cooperation, letters rogatory for judicial communications (notification, intimation), or taking evidence, many people still cannot afford the costs of applying for recognition and enforcement of foreign judgments abroad. Brazilians from abroad can qualify for legal assistance with the Public Defender that will take care of the recognition process before the Superior Court of Justice. Foreigners living in Brazil also enjoy legal aid in Brazil. The problem is for Brazilians or even foreigners living in Brazil to apply for measures in foreign countries that do not provide free legal assistance in civil matters. In this sense, there is a special need to rethink the concept of legal aid or legal assistance, which includes public attorneys or defenders. Otherwise, borders will provide barriers for those

[96] SG Cano, 'Evolución de las Técnicas de Cooperación Internacional entre Autoridades en el Derecho Internacional Privado' in *Boletin Mexicano de Derecho Comparado* (Mexico, Universidad Nacional Autónoma de México, 2005) 104.

who want to escape maintenance obligations based upon no international access to justice or no legal aid provided by the required State.

Both Hague instruments are important in strengthening international legal cooperation among States and assuring circulation of cross-border decisions in maintenance matters. Central Authorities no longer only receive and transmit documents, but in fact cooperate among themselves to provide efficient public services. If a request for international legal cooperation cannot be enforced in the requested country, the Central Authority should send the document back, explaining not only the reason but also what is necessary in order for the decision to be enforceable.

Country profiles help explain systems and should prevent Central Authorities sending requests that would be dismissed because of an offence against public policy or that cannot be granted under the law. This will hopefully create a multicultural dialogue among countries.

Additionally, the greatest challenge for the international recovery of maintenance is ensuring the provision of legal aid because there are different concepts and systems concerning this topic. In child support cases creditors are, in principle, entitled to free legal aid under the Convention and only when their action fails as a result of their bad faith may the State seek to recover its costs in providing legal aid.[97] States should also consider signing the Hague Convention 25 October 1980 on International Access to Justice.

Another important issue that requires further discussion is the transfer of funds, especially for small amounts, between Member States for maintenance payments and the time spent by the creditor to receive money. Even though Article 6 of the 2007 Hague Convention establishes, for Central Authorities, the function of facilitating collection and transfer of payment, it will depend much more on countries' policies on guaranteeing prompt international public legal service. Good future developments would be cross-border strategies and mechanisms for reducing costs of transferring small amounts of maintenance, creating fee waivers for very low values, and direct discount of the value from the pay slip to the beneficiary's bank account. The use of new technologies through electronic means is vital to the successful functioning of the system on the international recovery of maintenance.

XI. Conclusion

In a globalised society, family issues are no longer limited to national borders, and transnational litigation related to maintenance obligations is on the rise. Although local decisions may have transnational effects, the effectiveness of foreign judgments depends on international legal and administrative cooperation as important principles in enforcing cross-borders rights.

States' sovereignty and their right to self-determination to establish their legal systems and jurisdiction must assist with international cooperation as the key to creating common values among diverse people involved in private international relations. However,

[97] See Arts 15 and 43(2) of the Convention and P Beaumont, 'International Family Law in Europe—The Maintenance Project, the Hague Conference and the EC—A Triumph of Reverse Subsidiarity in Europe' (2009) *Rabels Zeitschrift für ausländisches und internationales Privatrecht* 509, 530–32.

the effectiveness of these rights in cross-border family conflicts depends on their access to justice wherever they are or whenever they have to do so.

Although Brazil has been engaged in several international law treaties concerning private international matters on global and regional levels mainly related to maintenance obligations (the New York Convention and the Inter-American Convention), the ratification of both Hague instruments, the Convention and Protocol, is important to enhancing cooperation in cross-border litigation. In addition, these instruments contribute to strengthening private international law in family matters based upon human rights principles such as the dignity of human beings and family solidarity. State boundaries should not be allowed to undermine this right.

14

Argentina's Regulation of Maintenance Obligations: Implementation of the 2007 Hague Convention

NIEVE RUBAJA

I. Introduction

In order to establish the framework of this chapter and to appreciate the main essence of the right to maintenance in Argentina, it is important to consider some background information. First, the human rights treaties to which Argentina has become a Party have a special legal force according to Argentina's National Constitution, especially since its last reform in 1994. Among these treaties,[1] the Convention on the Rights of the Child creates special provisions regarding the welfare of children and their adequate development, emphasising the right to maintenance in Article 27. In addition, this right has been considered as a consequence of the right to survival and, thus, of the right to life.

Furthermore, according to the premise that the fundamental human rights should be contemplated progressively, the Argentinean State has implemented public policies or programmes to ensure this right.[2] Also, the domestic legislation has been adapted to fit the standards established in the human rights treaties[3] and judicial decisions have been taken by the Supreme Court and other provincial courts in this sense.[4]

[1] Some of them refer to the guarantee of the adequate standard of living, including maintenance: the Universal Declaration of Human Rights, Art 25.1, the American Declaration of the Rights and Duties of Man, Art 11, and the International Convention on Economic, Social and Cultural Rights, Art 11.

[2] Eg Universal Child Allowance for the Social Protection of the Children, Decree 1602/2009, and Universal Allowance for Pregnancy, Decree 1602/2009.

[3] Eg Law 26.061/2005 for the Integral Protection of the Rights of Children and Adolescents provides priority allocation to public policies and programmes in favour of the realisation of the right to maintenance. Neither this law nor the Bill for the reform of the Civil and Commercial Code submitted to Congress for consideration, which will be referred to later, have taken advantage of those opportunities to go further and provide the subsidiary obligation of the State to provide maintenance.

[4] Eg *Rodríguez, Karina Verónica v Estado Nacional* [2006] Corte Suprema de Justicia de la Nación R. 1148.XLI; *Quiñone, Alberto Juan v Provincia de Buenos Aires* [2006] Corte Suprema de Justicia de la Nación; *ML* [2003] Corte Suprema de la Provincia de Buenos Aires; *Defensor de menores v Provincia de Entre Ríos* [2002] Tribunal Superior de Justicia de Entre Ríos. In this last case the provincial government has been forced to grant a family without economic resources access to a public programme to guarantee the fulfilment of their rights and the novelty was that a supermarket was obliged to provide the children and their parents with some products, allowing the enterprise to compensate its debts with the tax authority.

Therefore, the right to access to maintenance, especially regarding children, should be considered as a fundamental right.

Finally, this perspective implies a special and prior protection for fulfilling this fundamental right based on Argentina's international obligations in this sphere. This understanding has an impact on the treatment and interpretation of the right to access to maintenance, from both a legislative and judicial point of view.

II. Substantive Law

In Argentina the substantive law of maintenance is regulated in the Civil Code. There have been several changes, the last of which was in 2009 by means of Law No 26579.

According to this regulation, this obligation arises from ascendants, descendants, affinities, siblings, half siblings, spouses and parent-child relationships.[5] Probably, this wide range of possibilities is a consequence of cultural values, especially because Argentina's population is mainly of immigrant descent. During the First and Second World Wars European families settled in Argentina. The urgency and the economic possibilities meant that family members came separately: first, the men (including fathers, cousins and uncles) used to work and save some money so that women and children could then travel. Therefore, the concept of family in Argentina is broader than merely that of a nuclear family.

Regarding child support obligations it is important to consider that nowadays, after Law 26579, the age of majority is 18, but the maintenance obligation lasts until 21; unless the child over 18, or his or her parents, prove that he or she is able to meet these needs. The obligation covers maintenance, education and recreation, clothing, housing, assistance and expenditure by reason of disease. It could be enforced in cash or in kind. This right to assistance seeks to cover the child's needs in whole for his or her entire development, apart from those which are essential for his or her survival. These needs do not have to be proved; only the parentage has to be stated by means of a birth certificate.

Since there are no charts or guidelines to calculate the amount of the support obligation, the child's lifestyle prior to divorce is taken into account or, in other cases, the child's needs—as they are defined in this context—have to be covered while considering the debtor's income and his or her own needs. If the debtor is unable to provide the child with the maintenance obligation, the public sector does not provide financial support in its place.

The Bill for the unification of the Civil and Commercial Code submitted to Congress[6] features some innovations in this field, compared to the current legislation. These include:

(i) domestic partnerships: included for the first time in Argentina's system; the parties have to assist each other and contribute to household expenses;

[5] According to the Civil Code, a donee is also obliged to pay maintenance in favour of the donor (Art 1873).

[6] The Bill for the reform, update and unification of the civil and commercial law was proposed by the Executive branch by means of Decree 191/2011. A commission, composed of Ricardo Lorenzetti, Elena Highton de Nolasco—both Ministers of the National Supreme Court—and Aída Kemelmajer de Carlucci—former Minister of Mendoza Supreme Court, was given responsibility for its development. After the Executive branch introduced some changes to the project presented by the commission, the Bill was submitted to Congress on 7 July 2012. A Special Commission composed of members from the Chambers of Senators and Deputies has been designated for the draft analysis. The Senator's Chamber voted in favour of the Bill on 28 November 2013; in 2014 the Deputy's Chamber will vote. The Bill has 2,671 articles; it includes a Title for Private International Law and a section on maintenance.

(ii) divorce: only if the creditor is affected by a serious illness, prior to the divorce, which does not allow him to support himself; if the creditor cannot afford his or her own expenses or the creditor is not able to provide for himself—taking into account their age, the possibilities of access to employment of the creditor and who kept the family house—only for a specific period of time; or if they agree on maintenance.[7]

(iii) the obligation towards the spouse or domestic partner's children; pregnant women; unrecognised children; children from the age of majority until 25 years of age, if their studies or professional development do not allow them to satisfy their own needs.[8]

The maintenance obligation for children covers the same aspects and it goes further, including the necessary expenses for developing a profession or occupation.

III. Procedural Law

In Argentina, competence to make a decision in these cases and to recognise and enforce a maintenance decision lies with the judicial authorities. The Civil Code determines that the procedure adopted must be the fastest one. However, as a consequence of the federal system, the procedural law depends on each province's regulation,[9] which implies differences in the treatment that they offer in some aspects, for example: mediation as a mandatory stage prior to trial, terms, evidence and urgent measures, among others.

In order to deal with this process several institutions offer free legal assistance including: universities, bar associations, national and local governments, etc.

Regarding access to information on the debtor's assets or income, state government offices, banks and official registers, among others, facilitate this. Some information can be requested by lawyers and other information only upon request by a court, according to the procedural regulation in each case. Certain tax information is excluded based on the protection of official secrecy.

Registers of defaulting debtors, which depend on the provincial governments, can be found in some provinces. The orders for the debtors to be registered lie with judicial authorities. This limits the debtor's actions only in the public scope in the territory of the province involved. Some possible consequences can be: being prevented from opening bank accounts; obtaining credit cards; obtaining all permits, licences, and authorisations for commerce; being a public officer.

[7] It is important to state that the Bill includes significant modifications on divorce rules. The principal changes are: no requirement for grounds for divorce or an agreement between the spouses; provisions regarding economic compensations; compulsory agreements between the spouses on the consequence of the divorce (*Convenio Regulador*); and provisions regarding use of the family residence.

[8] The Bill also includes the possibility for children who live without their parents, either abroad or in a distant place in the country, to be authorised by a judge or a diplomatic representation to go into debt in order to satisfy their own needs or urgent requirements. Teenagers do not need such authorisation, only the acceptance of the adult in charge, according to the applicable law.

[9] Argentina has a representative, republican, and federalist form of government, consisting of the union of 23 provinces and the Autonomous City of Buenos Aires (since the constitutional reform of 1994). These retain all those powers which were not delegated to the national government, according to Arts 121 and 126 of the National Constitution. Thus, the Legislative branch is in charge of passing general laws (civil, commercial, penal codes, employment legislation and other areas of competence of the federal government) for all the country, while the procedural legislation and provincial issues are within the competence of the provincial governments.

The Bill includes some provisions on procedural matters, such as the retroactive effects of the judicial decisions to the time of the first formal extrajudicial request for maintenance; ensuring the enforcement of decisions by appropriate measures judicially ordered; higher interest rate for maintenance debts; possibility of ensuring future payments with preventive measures; joint and several liability of the person responsible for retaining part of the debtor's salary or income, in case he does not do so.

IV. Private International Law

Argentina's system provides different sources of solutions to family maintenance problems in cases that present foreign elements or contacts with more than one State. On the one hand, there are international conventions to which the State is a party; on the other hand, there is the Civil Code that applies in those cases in which the conventions do not. Furthermore, the Bill before parliament includes a section referring to family maintenance in private international law.

However, there is scarce practical application of these sources, as will be explained below.

A. International Sources

The international conventions, with special legal force in accordance with Argentina's constitutional system, are: Montevideo Civil International Law Treaties of 1889 and 1940, the United Nations Convention on the Recovery Abroad of Maintenance, adopted in New York on 20 June 1956 (the New York Convention), the Inter-American Convention on Support Obligations, adopted in Montevideo on 15 July 1989 (the Inter-American Convention). In addition, as regards preventive measures, the Inter-American Convention on Execution of Preventive Measures, adopted in Montevideo on 8 May 1979 and the Protocol of Preventive Measures, adopted in Ouro Preto, Brazil, on 16 December 1994, are in force.[10]

[10] In the inter-American field there is also the Bustamante Code, Cuba, 1928, which is still in force between Bolivia, Brazil, Costa Rica, Cuba, Chile, Ecuador, El Salvador, Haiti, Guatemala, Honduras, Nicaragua, Panama, Peru, Dominican Republic and Venezuela. Even though dispositions in this subject matter are scarce, they paved the way for the consideration of the maintenance obligations as an autonomous issue as well as revealing a tendency towards creditor benefit as a priority. They establish that the main connecting factor to regulate this obligation is the creditor's personal law and that public policy should be considered as a mandatory rule to prevent the application of an unfavourable law to the creditor (Arts 67–68).

It is also important to mention that in the Mercosur scope the new Protocol of 2012 on International Jurisdiction, Applicable Law and International Cooperation in Matrimony and Domestic Partnerships issues was signed in December 2012. Although it is not yet in force, it includes domestic partnerships, which are not included in all the Member States or associates. Even though this document does not provide special rules for maintenance obligations, such obligations could be considered to be included in the personal effects of domestic partnerships or divorce matters. Provisions on children are also not covered.

i. Montevideo Civil International Treaties

The Montevideo Civil International Law Treaties (the 1889s is in force between Argentina, Bolivia, Colombia, Paraguay, Peru and Uruguay; the 1940s is in force, between Argentina, Paraguay and Uruguay) do not have specific rules on this subject, particularly considering the autonomy that the maintenance obligation has nowadays; they only offer tangential solutions.[11]

ii. The New York Convention[12]

In practice, this Convention is the one mainly relied upon because it is the instrument that gives answers to most of the maintenance cases in Argentina. This Convention has been highly efficient in its application, especially in the area of providing legal assistance to creditors. However, some difficulties that mar its effectiveness have been identified, the more significant of these being unavoidable expenses, such as the documents' translation and legalisation, and international transfer fees. At the moment most transfers of funds take place:

(a) through bank transfers: these have compulsory costs and are less than expeditious because of the time required between the deposit and the withdrawal of the payment;
(b) through money transfer companies: even though these have higher costs, they are faster;
(c) through debit cards issued by a bank in the debtors' residence banks; creditors are able to withdraw the payment in other States.

Nevertheless, at the moment these options are affected by the restrictions that the Argentine Government has imposed on the withdrawal of foreign currency either in Argentina or abroad.[13]

Some ways of overcoming these difficulties in the practical application of the Convention have been considered. For example, if the transfers are made by official banks, no expense should be incurred. Thus, the representative of the absent creditors has been advised to ask judges to order international transactions without any costs, invoking the gratuitousness that inspired the Convention. In addition, possible agreements with the professional associations representing official translators have been contemplated as a

[11] All the Member States in the Montevideo's Treaties are parties to the Inter-American Convention. Taking this into account, it is important to consider that the Inter-American Convention seeks in its text to limit neither the provisions of existing or future bilateral or multilateral conventions on this subject entered into by the States Parties, nor the more favourable practices that those States may observe in this area (Art 30). Thus, the coordination between these instruments should be resolved according to the benefit of the creditor in each case.

Some of the Member States in the Montevideo's Treaties are also parties to the New York Convention (Argentina, Bolivia, Colombia and Uruguay).

[12] The New York Convention is currently in force in 65 countries (12 of which are Latin American).

In Argentina, around 500 cases a year are processed by the Central Authority (the Ministry of Justice acts both as the transmitting and receiving agency): 60% are incoming cases and 40% outgoing. The former came principally from Chile (60%) and Mexico (almost 20%); the rest from Spain, Switzerland, France, Brazil, Colombia, Australia and Belgium. The latter go mainly to Chile (65%) and Spain (20%); the rest to Mexico, Italy, Switzerland, Germany, Colombia, France, Netherlands, Israel, Austria and Brazil.

[13] According to the Central Bank Communication A 5530 of 26 July 2012, the transfer of money for maintenance obligations from US $300 to US $1,500 should be only by a debit from a bank account and those over US $1,500 need the pre-authorisation of the Central Bank.

way of reducing or avoiding altogether this kind of expenditure in regard to maintenance obligations.[14]

Although the New York Convention applies to the majority of maintenance cases that arise in Argentina, there are no judicial decisions on the application of this Convention. This could be because solutions are mainly of an administrative nature. When solutions come from the courts, as a consequence of the power of attorney (according to Article 3.3) and the application of the law of the debtor's State (Article 6.3), these cases are solved as domestic ones.

iii. The Inter-American Convention

Lastly, the Inter-American Convention brings together important criteria for international jurisdiction and applicable law among the States parties.[15] Both creditors and judges may take advantage of this regulation—the former, by choosing the judicial authority who will hear the claim and, therefore, the applicable law that might offer the best solution for their own interests; the latter, by implementing and interpreting the Convention rules, for defining their competence, the applicable law or for analysing the indirect jurisdiction issues. Thus, the more States that become parties to this Convention, the wider the standardisation of criteria.

This Convention has introduced a new possibility into Argentina's legal system: as regards the creditor, support claims may be heard by the judicial or administrative authorities of the State to which 'the debtor is connected by personal links such as possessing property, receiving income or obtaining financial benefits' (*Foro del Patrimonio,* Article 8(c)).[16] This option should be considered as an alternative among other connections that the text offers: domicile or habitual residence of the creditor; domicile or habitual residence of the debtor. Additionally, there is a possibility for the judicial or administrative authority of another State to have jurisdiction if the defendant appears before it absent a jurisdictional challenge, allowing choice of court agreements.[17]

[14] Moreover, some consulates (eg, the Italian consulate) offer the possibilities of free translation services, in cases involving child support obligations only.

[15] The scope of this Convention includes child support obligations owed because of the child's minority and spousal support obligations arising from the matrimonial relationship between spouses or former spouses (Art 1). Furthermore, a State may declare that the Convention will be applied to support obligations in favour of other creditors (Art 3), eg Colombia extended the scope to descendants, ancestors, adopted children, adoptive parents, siblings, an individual who made a substantial donation (if that donation has not been rescinded or revoked) and to a constant partner in a common-law marital union. See www.oas.org/juridico/english/sigs/b-54.html (accessed January 2014).

[16] The possibilities mentioned in this Article should not be considered to be exhaustive (they could also include property, usufruct, salaries and employment benefits, bank deposits, among others); these should be considered on a case-by-case basis by the court.

Nevertheless, the term 'personal links' was discussed in some depth during the Conference, choosing that proposed by the United States delegation. It means that the link should be relevant in order to avoid the possibility of assuming an exorbitant jurisdiction, see the *Proceedings of the Fourth Inter-American Specialized Conference on Private International Law*, II, 165.

In conclusion, the main problem that has been identified regarding this forum is the possible absence of connection between the court and the case. This has prompted criticism of the doctrine. See generally DP Fernandez Arroyo, 'Compétence exclusive et compétence exorbitante dans les relations privées internationales' (2006) 323 *Hague Academy Collected Courses* 157.

[17] In terms of the setting the jurisdiction, a distinction is made between actions to increase or reduce the amount of support, in order to protect the creditor. Thus, actions for increments may be heard by any of the authorities mentioned in Art 8; actions to discontinue or reduce support shall be heard by the authorities of the State that set the amount of support (Art 9).

The essence of this fundamental human right, that the Convention seeks to ensure and become effective, makes this new possibility reasonable and justified. Nevertheless, the debtor's right of defence should be always guaranteed, as well as fundamental principles of public policy of the States involved in any given case. Concretely, the intervention of the public order should be reduced in accordance with the nature of the right sought to be protected.[18]

Furthermore, this new alternative will probably simplify the enforcement of the support order because of the location of the property in the same State as the judge who will hear the support claim. Perhaps, in some cases, that may be the only way of fulfilling this right; especially given the disadvantages of filing the claim in one State and enforcing the judgment where the debtor's assets are located: higher costs, waste of resources and time, order's recognition needs, among others. Undoubtedly, these extremes could pose a risk to the debtor's assets, for instance by allowing their reduction or the debtor's insolvency.

Presenting the support claim to the authorities of the State where the debtor has his patrimony could also pose some disadvantages, particularly when this place is geographically away from the parties' habitual residence, carrying possible difficulties in the appreciation of their personal circumstances. However, in some cases, this alternative could make the difference between enforcing this essential right or not.

Ultimately, at the time of filing the case the creditor should weigh up the advantages and disadvantages of each option offered by the Convention. Then he or she will be able to choose the option best suited to his or her interests; in other words, the one which offers the best solution to his or her particular problem. In conclusion, the more options the creditor has, the more chances he or she has to enforce his or her rights.

Regarding the applicable law the Convention offers a flexible methodology with several alternative connections, whose choice depends on the competent authority. The criteria should be based on the 'most favourable to the creditor' between: the law of the State of domicile or habitual residence of the creditor or the debtor (according to Article 6).[19]

However, this Convention is not as effective in promoting international cooperation on the recognition and enforcement of decisions. It fails to include regulations to reduce and facilitate such cooperation with the same efficiency as the Hague Convention of 2007 or the EU Regulation of 2008, offering only a basic system for cooperation (Articles 11–18).[20] Mercosur may be able to deal with this challenge in Latin America.

The Inter-American Convention presents the same problems as the New York Convention regarding the costs demanded by transfers of funds. Inter-institutional agreements with banks—public or private—and money transfer companies could be a solution to this issue. Consequently, the payment of commissions would be avoided and the transfers would

[18] Notice that Art 22 requires that, in order for this exception to apply, the solution should be 'manifestly contrary to its fundamental principles of public policy'.

[19] The domicile's connection has been criticised especially in the case of children because this place will depend on their parents' location. Nevertheless, there are more possibilities to choose the law which may be more favourable to the creditor. Furthermore, beside these four options the court should also give effect to the *lex fori* if it is more favourable to the creditor: according to Art 21 'the provisions of this Convention may not be construed in such a way as to restrict the rights of the support creditor under the law of the forum'. See especially R Santos Belandro, *Convención Interamericana sobre obligaciones alimentarias. Reglas de conflicto materialmente orientadas hacia la protección de las personas* (Uruguay, Fundación de Cultura Universitaria, 1999) 135.

[20] Traditional requirements for the *exequatur* are minimised. See eg LE Rapallini, 'Cobro de alimentos en el extranjero: perspectivas de la Convención Interamericana sobre obligaciones alimentarias' in *Seminario de Derecho Internacional. Cooperación jurídica en materia de derecho de familia y niñez* (2011) OEA/Sec General DDI7doc 13/11.

be carried out expeditiously. Mercosur could also be a suitable scope to deal with these agreements.

Additionally, the scarce practical application of this Convention has been explained by the lack of dissemination of this instrument and the Central Authorities' functions among lawyers, judges and advisors.[21] In addition, the fact that five of the State parties have not designated Central Authorities affects the proper development and efficiency of this treaty.[22] Petitions within the scope of the Convention are probably handled by other instruments (eg, Inter-American Conventions on Proof and Information on Foreign Law; Extraterritorial Validity of Foreign Judgments and Arbitral Awards; Taking of Evidence Abroad; Execution of Preventive Measures; the Hague Conventions of 1954, 1965, 1970; the Protocols of Las Leñas 1992 and Ouro Preto1994—Mercosur—and other bilateral instruments).

B. National Law

Argentina's Civil Code treats international support claims differently depending on whether these arise in matrimonial cases or cases involving parentage and other family issues. For the former, both from the perspectives of applicable law and competent jurisdiction, the regulation reflects clearly the intention of the legislator to favour the spouse with a credit. Therefore, Article 228 proposes several possibilities regarding the competent authority, leaving the decision to the creditor, between: the judge of the matrimonial domicile, the domicile of the debtor, the residence of the creditor, the location of the enforcement of the obligation or, if there is an agreement, the place where this has been settled as long as it matches the residence of the debtor. However, if the demand is connected to the legal separation, divorce or marriage annulment process, the same judge will also have jurisdiction in this matter. This flexibility is helpful given the nature of the right to be protected and to the position of the creditor in these kinds of proceedings.

In reference to the applicable law in this field, Article 162, through a conflict of laws rule, determines that the right to the support and the admissibility, opportunity and scope of the agreement, if any, will be governed by the law of the matrimonial domicile. This last concept is defined in the first part of this Article as the last place where they effectively lived together.

However, the quantum of the support obligation may be determined by the law of the debtor's domicile, if it is more favourable to the creditor, according to the last part of this Article. This shows that in the first instance, the Article chooses a connection with a specific temporal scope to guarantee the principles of due process and predictability; nevertheless, it extends the possibilities for determining the amount. Evidently, this solution is intended for the creditor's benefit.

Provisional measures depend on the law of the place of the proceedings.

[21] Judicial precedents are hard to find because of this. See, however, the case cited at (n 30).

[22] Those States are: Belize, Costa Rica, Guatemala, Panama and Paraguay www.oas.org/dil/esp/tratados_autoridades_centrales_Convencion_Interamericana_sobre_Obligaciones_Alimentarias.htm (accessed January 2014).

In the case of maintenance obligations arising from a parental or family relationship, Argentina's system does not contain any specific regulations on private international law. Therefore, solutions should be found by the analogical application of either international sources or rules relating to spousal maintenance.

Notwithstanding the fact that this is probably where the majority of the cases with foreign elements in family conflicts arise, there is also very little case law in the application of this source.[23]

Argentina's draft Civil and Commercial Code includes a Title on private international law issues, in which a Chapter provides rules related to family maintenance conflicts.

Two provisions underpin all the cases. On the one hand, Article 2629 provides solutions to jurisdictional problems in three different paragraphs. Firstly, it indicates that the support claims could be filed, by the creditor's choice, with the courts of either the creditor's or the debtor's domicile or habitual residence. Remarkably, it also includes the option, taken from the Inter-American Convention, to bring a claim where the debtor's assets are located, as long as this option is reasonable in the circumstances.[24]

Secondly, conflicts between spouses or domestic partners may be heard by the courts of the place where they effectively last lived together, the domicile or habitual residence of the debtor, or by the authority which dealt with the dissolution of that union.

Lastly, if an agreement has been settled, the creditor has the alternative to file a claim with the court where the obligation is to be enforced, or where the agreement was concluded, as long as it matches the simple residence of the debtor.

On the other hand, Article 2630 provides answers to applicable law issues in these cases. The court must choose between the laws of the domicile of the creditor or the debtor, whichever is more favourable to the creditor's interests.

Together with this, agreements on support matters would be governed by the law of the domicile or the habitual residence of either party at the time of their conclusion, by their own choice. Otherwise, the applicable law should be the one which regulates maintenance issues.[25]

To conclude, matrimonial support obligations will be governed by the law of the parties' last domicile, where they last effectively lived together, or by the law of the State applicable to the dissolution or annulment of the marriage.

[23] Eg *BM and CI v MyCA* [1985] Cámara Nacional de Apelaciones en lo Civil, Sala A. This was a case in which mother and daughter, who lived in Argentina, filed a demand for maintenance against their father and husband, who lived in Spain. The determination of the international jurisdiction was reasoned by the analogical application of the Montevideo Treaties, based on the urgency of the measure, with the result that the Argentinean jurisdiction was accepted; *NSR y O v ORM* [1998] Cámara Nacional de Apelaciones en lo Civil, Sala J held that the enforcement of a decision in the United States was not possible because of the absence of international instruments applicable for that purpose.

[24] This last requirement assures the proximity between the forum and the case.

[25] This scope for party autonomy should be considered as an important alternative which can provide effective, economical and quick solutions to these problems. Nevertheless, this possibility is limited to the choice of some connecting factors and to a certain time in accordance with the subject matter.

V. Advantages of Implementing the 2007 Hague Convention[26]

The 2007 Hague Convention offers several advantages to Argentina. First, it will be applied to cases in which the other country involved is also a party to the Convention. That is to say that the more States which ratify the Convention the greater its impact will be on Argentina. Furthermore, in Argentina's current legislation, this Convention will also be useful as a source for application by analogy in some cases.

Some of the main improvements include the following.

A. Standardisation of Criteria

The text offers important commitments to the uniform interpretation and application of its provisions among the State parties.[27] These benefits will cover interpretation issues (eg, the definitions in Article 3), the scope of intervention of the Central Authorities (eg, Articles 5–6), details regarding applications (eg, Chapter III), the procedural aspects, terms and use of forms, among others.

Additionally this benefit will impact on the standardisation of Argentina's procedural regulations in the different provinces for international cases, basically, because of the diversified treatment that the federal system provides.

Evidently, all these pros will positively affect maintenance cases and will allow the procedures to become faster and without extra costs. Lastly, fundamental human rights can be met.

The more States that ratify the Convention, the greater the impact will be for reaching a wider level of standardisation of criteria. In addition, the Review Special Commissions at The Hague will help to enhance its uniform interpretation as time goes on.

B. Cooperation

Lack of effective regulation in regard to cooperation aspects, both in international and national Argentine sources, hinder the possibilities of finding proper and fair solutions in maintenance cases.[28]

[26] Since the applicable scope of the Convention in Art 2 a) includes maintenance obligations arising from a parent-child relationship towards a person under the age of 21, it is important to state that according to Argentine law, which considers that the childhood begins with the conception, it would include unborn children.

This Convention ensures coordination with the other conventions that are in force. In Argentina, on the one hand, the Convention will replace the New York Convention between the Contracting States if both of them are Parties to the Hague Convention, insofar as its scope of application as between such States coincides with the scope of application of this Convention (Art 49). On the other hand, the Convention will not affect any international instrument concluded before to which Contracting States are Parties and which contains provisions on matters governed by this Convention (Art 51). Therefore, the Montevideo International Law Treaties will be replaced by this Convention; and the Inter-American Convention will be applied as long as its solutions are as effective as those of the Hague Convention, according to the spirit and purpose of the Convention (Art 52 of the Hague Convention refers to the 'Most effective rule').

[27] This is a goal expressly mentioned in Art 53 as well as the monitoring of the practical operation of the Convention in Art 54.

[28] Although Argentina's Central Authority has been highly efficient in some of the functions it is required to undertake by the New York Convention, its development has been limited to the possibilities outlined in the text

Furthermore, the fact that the conventions in force are not well known to judges and lawyers, negatively affects these kinds of proceedings.[29]

The only case in which a court has applied the Inter-American Convention illustrates the problem of lack of cooperation.[30] The Central Authorities (Argentina and Peru) could have fostered the fastest and most expeditious solution for two girls; however, only the competent authorities heard it and the negative answer came more than two years later.[31] A Peruvian couple got divorced and presented the Peruvian courts with an agreement on the maintenance obligations for their daughters. Later, the mother asked the courts for an increase in the amount agreed upon. Later, the mother and the two girls moved to San Nicolás, Buenos Aires, where she filed a claim for the opening of a bank account in which the debtor had to deposit the money for the maintenance obligation and to which the money deposited in Peru could be transferred. Three different judicial authorities, including the Supreme Court of Buenos Aires' province, understood that the competent authority in the case was the Peruvian judge: because the demand was about the enforcement of the agreement and not a new action or the modification of the maintenance amount (these last two options would have allowed Argentine jurisdiction based on Articles 8 and 9 of the Inter-American Convention). The petition was rejected. Notwithstanding the fact that this outcome is probably the reasonable one according to the interpretation of the Convention text, neither of the authorities informed the creditor or the Central Authorities about these circumstances, and the opportunity for cooperation was lost.[32]

Evidently, a failure of cooperation implies the obstruction of justice in this case. Had the Central Authorities cooperated with each other, the girls' fundamental human right to maintenance would have been met.

Taking into account that the mechanism sought by the 2007 Convention is based on an efficient system of administrative cooperation, it should provide solutions at different stages of proceedings, both prior to the case being heard and in cases before the courts themselves (eg, mediation, appeals or enforcement actions).[33]

and also depends on its application by other Member States. Argentina's Central Authority receives and analyses petitions; advises on the scope of the Convention in accordance with the requirements of the local regulations of the debtor's State; offers help in obtaining documents or social reports on the creditor's circumstances for presenting them in the debtor's State; searches for information on the debtor's location in foreign consulates in Argentina; asks that the transfer of money abroad takes place without costs; recommends the provision of free legal assistance abroad; among others.

[29] This arises, among other reasons, from the lack of specific courts for private international law cases in Argentina. In addition there are some provinces in which the courts are competent to hear actions on civil, commercial, administrative, employment and mining issues, and they attend to international cases very rarely.

[30] *CCA v FEDB* [2012] Corte Suprema Provincia de Buenos Aires C 114775.

[31] It is important to note that Peru is not a State party to the New York Convention.

[32] Eric Jayme understands postmodern private international law as being characterised by the collaboration of judges in different countries. This kind of collaboration is institutionalised, especially in the shape of the Central Authorities. E Jayme, 'Identité culturelle et intégration: le droit privé postmoderne' (1995) 251 *Hague Academy Collected Courses* 257.

[33] Central Authorities' functions are described in Art 6. They are now considered to be much wider than those provided by any other convention of administrative cooperation (such as the Conventions of 1980 on International Child Abduction and of 1993 on Protection of Children and Inter-country Adoption) since they were specially drafted to deal with the weaknesses of the existing cooperation systems. I Goicoechea, 'El nuevo Convenio de La Haya de 2007 y su posible impacto en América Latina' in N Lloveras and M Herrera (eds), *El derecho de familia en Latinoamérica* (Buenos Aires, Nuevo Enfoque Jurídico, 2009).

The Central Authorities carry out several important functions.[34] The extension of the role of the Central Authorities can be seen in the definition in Article 3(c) of the obligation to provide legal assistance, which states that it encompasses 'all' that is necessary for the person to assert her or his rights effectively.[35] Also, assistance to be provided in establishing parentage, when necessary for the recovery of maintenance (Article 6(2)(h)), should be considered as an important innovation in Argentina.

Lastly, it is important to state that the ratification of this Convention will imply the assumption by Argentina of international obligations in regard to Central Authority development.

C. Recognition and Enforcement of Decisions

Given that international sources in Argentina are not particularly effective in this field, and the disadvantages of Argentina's federal system, which results in different procedural approaches being taken from province to province, the ratification of the Convention will bring a practical and indispensable tool for ensuring the fundamental human right to maintenance.

Its implementation will counterbalance the flaws of Argentina's system and it will be a major innovation and improvement in this area. That is to say, it will be an effective tool in this field as well as offering a standardised treatment of maintenance issues all over the country, especially in dealing with issues of interpretation.[36]

In this regard it is also important to mention that, notwithstanding the lack of direct jurisdictional rules,[37] the several options that Article 20 offers for the bases for recognition and enforcement of decisions will be a significant advance in Argentina's regulation, which takes mainly the bilateral criteria for determining the indirect jurisdiction.[38] Although the Convention offers the possibility of making reservations in accordance with Article 62, it creates more options than the national law.[39] For example, Article 20.1(b) allows recognition and enforcement in another Contracting State if 'the respondent has submitted to the jurisdiction either expressly or by defending on the merits of the case without objecting to the jurisdiction at the first available opportunity'.

In addition, provisions on procedure will also result in important improvements. The Convention offers two different alternatives for the recognition and enforcement of decisions in Articles 23 and 24. The former seeks a faster and shorter procedure and is

[34] Especially in Chapters II and III.

[35] Goicoechea (n 33).

[36] Seen in Art 19 which contains a broad definition of the terms 'decision' and 'administrative authority'; particularly taking into account the fact that treatment of this issue in Argentina is limited to the courts and that only judicial decisions may be enforced (even private agreements need the approval of the courts).

[37] Art 18.1 only states limits on proceedings to modify a decision or to make a new decision when a decision is made in a Contracting State where the creditor is habitually resident, with some exceptions (Art 18.2).

[38] The analysis of the jurisdiction of the authority who took the decision to recognise should be carried out according to the Argentinean rules (Procedural National Code, Art 517.1—the majority of the provincial codes follow these criteria).

[39] Some of the possibilities offered by the Convention in this Article are included in some of Argentina's international sources: eg the Inter-American Convention on Support Obligations, Art 8; the Bilateral Convention with Italy on Judicial Assistance and Recognition and Enforcement of Decisions in Civil Aspects, Art 22(a), (e), (i) and (f).

consistent with Argentina's constitutional principles. Undoubtedly, this alternative will bring more benefits, added to the limited possibilities of refusing the recognition and enforcement of decisions, being limited only to *ex officio* review on the ground of public policy.[40]

The pros will be mainly found in the agility and efficiency of the mechanisms proposed since a huge failure of Argentina's system is the inordinately slow progress of cases through the courts.

D. Assistance in Establishing Parentage

The assistance provided in Article 6.2(h) for establishing parentage where necessary for the recovery of maintenance, will bring a great benefit in this field. Notwithstanding the fact that nowadays courts allow a provisional obligation of maintenance pending an action on parentage, it is necessary to file a different procedure from the maintenance one. No assistance is provided for the filiation process at the moment unlike the Convention.[41] Therefore, this obligation in the Convention will also have a favourable impact on the creditor's position.

E. Effective Measures to Enforce Decisions

According to Argentina's federal system, each province regulates the measures to enforce decisions. Some possible actions could be wage withholding, freezing the debtor's assets, economic and penal sanctions[42] and registers of defaulting debtors, among others.

As there is no standardisation of criteria and a wide range of possibilities for enforcing the decisions, effective measures depend mainly on the creativity of the judges. For example, in a case in which a debtor had been asked several times to meet his obligation, the judge realised that the debtor was used to travelling abroad. Therefore, in that particular case the most effective measure for enforcing the maintenance obligation was to forbid the debtor from leaving the country, even though such a measure was not one offered by the current legislation in that province.[43]

[40] Nevertheless, Argentina could choose the alternative of declaring, in accordance with Art 63, that it will apply the procedure for recognition and enforcement set out in Art 24.

[41] Despite the free legal assistance that is offered in Argentina after a party has proved his or her inability to meet the costs of the process him or herself, even for DNA tests, the assistance that is provided under the Convention could be faster and broader. Providing assistance 'could mean obtaining relevant documents in relation to the establishment of parentage by presumption, acting on a request to contact the putative father to obtain a voluntary acknowledgement of paternity, initiating judicial proceedings for the establishment of parentage, or assisting with arrangements for a voluntary DNA test of the presumed parent'. A Borrás and J Degeling, with the assistance of W Duncan and P Lortie, 'Explanatory Report: Convention of 23 November 2007 on the International Recovery of Child Support and other Forms of Family Maintenance', Hague Conference on Private International Law www.hcch.net/upload/expl38e.pdf (accessed December 2013) 43.

[42] Penal sanctions are applied only when the debtor who avoids the enforcement of the maintenance obligation does not provide the fundamental resources for survival, Law No 13944/1950. The sanction may take the form of a fine or imprisonment. However, imprisonment could exacerbate the debtor's economic situation, as well as the creditor's. Therefore, the wisdom of applying these sanctions would have to be analysed in every case.

[43] *PAJ v RGA* [2010] Tribunal de Familia No 5 Rosario, Provincia de Santa Fe. In this case the judge took into account the fact that the debtor had been properly notified about the petition.

The ratification of the Convention will be both a challenge and an improvement in this regard. On the one hand, Argentina will have to improve its domestic regulation according to Article 34 by making available effective measures to enforce decisions under the Convention; on the other hand, it will work towards the creditor's best interests and it will allow the State to respond to the international obligations assumed.[44]

F. Transfer of Funds

Given the difficulties that Argentina faces regarding the transfer of funds (see earlier in the chapter) the implementation of the Convention will bring several advantages in this area; especially because of the commitment involved in Article 35.[45] This will result in a substantial benefit to the creditor and will be a real improvement to an area that seriously hinders the efficiency of other Conventions in maintenance actions.

G. Other Relevant Aspects: Free Legal Assistance for Child Support Applications, Legalisation, and Translation of Documents

Other benefits of the implementation of the Convention are related with unavoidable costs as well as faster results, which are particularly important in these types of cases. Throughout our discussion of the Convention, it is clear that the concern about costs is ever-present, for example in the guarantee in Article 15 that free legal assistance in child support cases will be offered.[46] The Convention provisions will bolster Argentina's current reality towards costs.

In addition, provisions regarding the simplification of bureaucracy and the reduction of costs will have a positive impact in Argentina (eg, Articles 12.9, 28, 37, 41 and 45.3). Experience shows that some creditors simply cannot afford to pay certain expenses and, sometimes, these results in proceedings being delayed for several months or even abandoned altogether. These kinds of barriers are totally contrary to the letter and the spirit of Conventions.

VI. Challenges Posed by the Implementation of the 2007 Hague Convention

The ratification and implementation of this Convention will bring several advantages; nevertheless it is very important to create the proper scenario for its success and to face

[44] For the observance of this compromise Art 34.2 provides some examples of enforcing measures.

[45] Art 35: 'Transfer of funds (1) Contracting States are encouraged to promote, including by means of international agreements, the use of the most cost-effective and efficient methods available to transfer funds payable as maintenance. (2) A Contracting State, under whose law the transfer of funds is restricted, shall accord the highest priority to the transfer of funds payable under this Convention.'

[46] Arts 8, 14, 16 and 17 also deal with free legal assistance.

Argentina's international responsibility for the obligations that will be assumed in this Convention as well as those which arise from human right treaties.

Some of the challenges are discussed here.

A. Difficulties Arising from Argentina's Federal System

The implementation of the Convention will have the effect of unifying several domestic procedural elements that are included in its scope. Nevertheless, because of Argentina's federal system, it would be necessary to review any procedural aspects of the system that could obstruct the proper application of the Convention; perhaps, passing a national law of procedure would be a possible solution.

Determining the Central Authority could also pose a challenge. Currently, the Transmitting and Receiving Agency for the New York Convention is the Ministry of Justice. Given the size of the country, it is complemented in its work by the provincial ministries or those supporting the judiciary. The Central Authority assigned in the Inter-American context is the Ministry of Foreign Affairs. Either could be designated for this function.

B. Need for Training

Argentina is a large country with many judges. In some areas they have to hear cases in several fields of law (eg civil, family, commercial, administrative, employment and mining). Sometimes, they do not encounter an international family case very often and therefore they are not aware of the current tools at hand. Therefore, training is a major need, specifically in the practical application of the Convention. Liaison judges, as provided for in the 1980 Hague Convention, would be useful for understanding the Convention's provisions, especially the interpretation issues, amongst others.[47]

C. Need for Resources

In order to implement the Convention's objectives successfully, a wide range of available resources are crucial, such as economic, human, infrastructure and technological resources, among others.

Not only will this be reflected in the application of the Convention itself, but also in the advantages of the technological development in the 'iSupport' software.[48]

[47] The provision of information sought in Art 57 will also be an indispensable tool for the proper and efficient application of the Convention.

[48] Among other benefits, it has been noted that: 'The system would help significantly to improve communications between Central Authorities and alleviate translation problems and costs as it could operate in different languages. Such a system could assist the daily operations of the Central Authorities established under the Convention and help to improve standards of case management. The system could also generate the required statistics as part of the means of monitoring the operation of the Convention'. See especially Borrás and Degeling (n 41) 16. See also P Lortie, 'The Development of Medium and Technology Neutral International Treaties in Support of Post-Convention Information Technology Systems—The 2007 Convention and Protocol' (2008–09) XIV *The Judges' Newsletter* 14 and see Philippe Lortie, ch 17 of this volume.

In addition these resources will be useful for reviewing the practical operation of the Convention, both in Argentina and between the States parties.[49]

D. Need for Dissemination of Information

It is not only some judges who are unaware of these tools, neither are a great number of the parties that participate in these kinds of proceedings, such as lawyers, advisers, public officers, etc.

It is essential to offer proper public information on the existence and content of the Convention so that it becomes a practical and handy tool for all citizens.

VII. Conclusions

Argentina's system provides different sources—international and domestic—that offer solutions to family maintenance problems in cases with foreign elements or contacts with more than one State. In addition, a Bill has been submitted to Argentina's Congress for consideration. The proposed legislation includes several innovations in the field of maintenance with the specialisation and the guarantees needed to fulfil this fundamental human right.

One of the distinctive features of Argentina's regulation is the potential to file international support claims where the assets of the debtor are located. Currently, this option is included as a direct jurisdictional rule that unifies the criteria in the Inter-American context; it will probably also be part of the Civil and Commercial Code in the near future. Furthermore, as this option may apply to a broad spectrum of cases, it could bring the solution in a given case.

What is more, this possibility could be considered as going beyond those available in the European Union Regulation; even taking into account the several alternatives that it presents, since *Foro del Patrimonio* is not overtly mentioned and, perhaps, it is not even included in the terms of Article 7 as a *forum neccesitatis*.[50] This option is not included within the scope of the Hague Convention, not even in regard to the regulation of the indirect jurisdiction for the enforcement of decisions or agreements on maintenance. However, such a direct rule of jurisdiction is not prohibited by the Hague Convention as it does not regulate the jurisdictions that can be relied upon by the maintenance creditor.

As a conclusion, the more options the creditor has to file his or her support claim, the more chances there are to fulfil this fundamental human right and all the others that depend on it. Time and practice will tell us just how efficient *Foro del Patrimonio* is.

Nevertheless, in Argentina's legal system difficulties exist especially regarding the enforcement of maintenance obligations. Not only are there failings in the legislation in

[49] An ambitious programme for the Administrative Co-operation Working Group has helped in this regard. See especially W Duncan, 'The New Hague Child Support Convention: Goals and Outcomes of the Negotiations' (2009) *Family Law Quarterly* 18.

[50] On this possibility, see J Carrascosa González, 'Alimentos', in A Calvo Caravaca and J Carrascosa González (eds), *Derecho Internacional Privado* volume II (Granada, Comares, 2012) ch XXII, 449.

this regard—both international and national—but there are also practical problems related to costs that are impossible to avoid and that frustrate the efficiency of solutions.

Against this background, it can be seen that there are several advantages of ratifying and implementing the 2007 Hague Convention. Furthermore, it would be used as an analogical source in cases that are outside its scope as a way of counterbalancing the absence of regulation in Argentina.

Notwithstanding the pros of implementation, certain challenges must be overcome in order to achieve the Convention's goals and to take on the international responsibility that Argentina would assume with its ratification as well as those that arise from the international human rights treaties.

In the meantime, the contribution of the international community, as the Heidelberg Conference proposed, is fundamental for observing, studying, analysing, and for inspiring more agile, effective and simple solutions that allow the enforcement of the maintenance right.

15

Recovery of Child Support in Nigeria

OLANIKE ADELAKUN-ODEWALE

I. Introduction

The concept of child maintenance stipulates an ongoing, periodic payment made by a parent, usually separated or divorced, or a guardian, for the financial benefit of a child of a marriage or other relationship. Although child maintenance is not statutorily defined in Nigeria, it has been decided by the courts that custody of a child connotes not only the control of a child, but carries with it the concomitant implication of the preservation and adequate care of the child's well-being—physical, mental and moral; this responsibility includes his or her needs in terms of food, shelter, clothing and the like.[1]

There are three different types of marriage that a man and a woman can contract in Nigeria which are statutory marriage, customary marriage and Islamic marriage.[2] As Nigeria is a multi tribal society, the customs of its people are as varied as the number of ethnic societies. In other words, there is no single customary law for Nigerians. The various ethnic communities have their different customs as they relate to marriage. This chapter explores the topic of marriage generally in relation to the major accepted customs, as recognized by the superior courts of Nigeria.

Marriage under Nigerian customary law is largely polygamous. A polygamous marriage is a voluntary union for life of one man with one or several wives.[3] There is no limit to the number of wives a man can marry under customary law. Islamic law marriage possesses most of the features of customary law marriage with the limitation that a man may not take more than four wives if he cannot justly look after them.[4]

There seems to be a societal belief that all child maintenance matters in Nigeria will be decided in favour of the mother. While it is true that under most customary law systems in Nigeria, the father is duty bound to pay child maintenance, this is not uniform or universal and does not apply to any statutory marriage under the Matrimonial Causes Act.[5]

[1] *Alabi v Alabi* (2008) All FWLR (pt 418) 245, 296.

[2] Marriage is strictly a union of one man to one woman or more, depending on the nature of marriage. Same-sex marriage is prohibited and criminalised in Nigeria by the Same Gender Marriage (Prohibition) Bill of 2011 which was further affirmed by a voice vote of the National Assembly in May 2013.

[3] EI Nwogugu, *Family Law in Nigeria* (Ibadan, Heinemann, 2001) lxxxi.

[4] Quran 4:3.

[5] 1970 Cap M6, Laws of the Federation of Nigeria 2004.

Under the Islamic law that is applicable in the Northern region of Nigeria, custody of a child, whether male or female, is usually granted to the mother[6] but the father is under an obligation to maintain the children of the marriage according to the doctrines of Islamic law. Furthermore, where the children are in the custody of someone else, such as a relative, the father is still under an obligation to maintain the children. In the case of an orphaned child, the burden shifts to the grandparents. Where the grandparents are dead or unable to provide maintenance to the child, the obligation devolves on the collateral relations of the child. However the obligation is restricted to the collaterals within the prohibited degrees of relationship by priority of being entitled to inherit from the child, had the child been dead.[7]

Under the customary law, a father has exclusive custody of the children of the marriage[8] and this custodial right extends to the father's family.[9] This is due to the fact that Nigerian societies are patrilineal in nature. However, it is the practice of customary courts in Lagos State of Nigeria to award the custody of children over seven years old to the father irrespective of whether he is capable of taking care of the child or not and this has been justified on the ground that the father paid a dowry on the mother and therefore owns the mother.[10] A woman may have custody of children of tender age at the time of the divorce but this is only a temporary position and between this time and the time of return to the father, the father is under a duty to maintain the children.[11] This position has been enforced by the courts in a number of cases including but not limited to *Mesike v Mesike*,[12] *Eborah v Eborah*,[13] *Adejoke v Adejoke*.[14]

II. Maintenance Obligations in Nigeria

The obligation to claim child maintenance in Nigeria depends largely on whether the claim is based on a statutory application or customary law.[15] Maintenance obligations under the Matrimonial Causes Act 1970 (MCA) must conform to the provisions of the Matrimonial Causes Act and Rules[16] and the Child's Rights Act 2003 to uphold the best interests of the child.[17]

The maintenance obligation under Nigerian statutes depends largely on the parent with custody of the child and other factors which shall be discussed in the course of this chapter but, broadly speaking, a maintenance obligation in Nigeria has its history in alimony

[6] *Alabi v Alabi* (2008) All FWLR (pt 418) 245, 298.

[7] S Arfat, 'Islamic Perspective of the Children's Rights: An Overview' (2013) 2 *Asian Journal of Social Sciences & Humanities* 304.

[8] MC Onokah, *Family Law* (Ibadan, Spectrum Books, 2003) 178.

[9] *Abiakam v Anyanwu* (1975) 5 ECSLR 305.

[10] B Owasanoye, 'The Regulation of Child Custody and Access in Nigeria' (2005–06) 39 *Family Law Quarterly* 421.

[11] Onokah (n 8) 180.

[12] Suit No 82/67 of 2 February 1968.

[13] Suit No 10/68 of 5 March 1968.

[14] *Lagos Weekend Newspaper* of 10 May 1989.

[15] Nigerian law is complex and dual in nature due to multiple ethnicity and cultural diversity and as a result, both the statutory and customary laws on child maintenance are recognised, provided the custom in question is not repugnant to natural justice, equity and good conscience and not inconsistent with any law in force.

[16] Matrimonial Causes Act (MCA) 1970 Cap 220 Laws of the Federation of Nigeria 2004.

[17] Child's Rights Act 2003 Cap C50 Laws of the Federation of Nigeria 2004.

pendent lite and the rule concerning the calculation of maintenance on the basis of one fifth of the joint income of the spouses. In this light section 70 of the MCA provides as follows:

(1) Subject to this section, the court may, in proceedings with respect to the maintenance of a party to a marriage, or of children of the marriage, other than proceedings for an order for maintenance pending the disposal of proceedings, make such order as it thinks proper, having regard to the means, earning capacity and conduct of the parties to the marriage and all other relevant circumstances.
(2) Subject to this section and to rules of court, the court may, in proceedings for an order for the maintenance of a party to a marriage, or of children of the marriage, pending the disposal of proceedings, make such order as it thinks proper, having regard to the means, earnings capacity and conduct of the parties to the marriage and all other relevant circumstances.
(3) The court may make an order for the maintenance of a party notwithstanding that a decree is or has been made against that party in the proceedings to which the proceedings with respect to maintenance are related.
(4) The power of the court to make an order with respect to the maintenance of children of the marriage shall not be exercised for the benefit of a child who has attained the age of twenty-one years unless the court is of the opinion that there are special circumstances that justify the making of such an order for the benefit of that child.

It is clear from the above provisions, especially from subsections 1 and 2 that an order for maintenance can be made during a matrimonial cause proceeding or in the absence of a pending proceeding but subject to the same yardstick.[18]

Islamic law, applicable in Northern Nigeria, does not view maintenance of a wife and children as recommended but mandatory. Where the father reneges on this obligation, the law will compel compliance to fulfil the obligation. The husband subject to Islamic law is under a legal mandate to maintain his wife no matter how wealthy the wife may be and to maintain his children who have not attained the age of maturity. For female children the father's maintenance obligation continues towards them for as long as they are unmarried and remain under parental care.[19]

Although Islamic law is applicable as a form of customary law in the Northern region of Nigeria, some of the populace of the region are not subject to Islamic law. This section of the populace either applies its own ethnic law or the statutory law on child maintenance and this is determined by the nature of the marriage conducted by the parties in question.

Maintenance obligations under customary laws of Nigeria differ depending on the customary law to which the parties are subject. The prevalent customary laws of Western Nigeria on maintenance obligations vary but generally, custodial rights are exclusive to the father and even when custody is awarded to the mother, this is in cases of very young children and the custodial right reverts to the father when the child grows older.[20] In rare

[18] *Olu-Ibukun v Olu-Ibukun* (1974) All NLR 463, 469.

[19] Arfat (n 7).

[20] *Mesike v Mesike* Suit No 82/67 of 2 February 1968; *Eborah v Eborah* Suit No 10/68 of 5 March 1968; *Adejoke v Adejoke* Lagos Weekend Newspaper of 10 May 1989.

cases however, the mother may contest the custody rights based on the best interests of the child.[21] This seldom happens though due to societal influence and prevailing customs.

Under the customary laws of Eastern Nigeria, women have no custody rights except for children who are still being breastfed. Immediately after weaning such children, custody reverts to the father.[22] This is based on the premise that upon payment of the bride price, a wife becomes the property of the husband. However, upon divorce, the wife's father or guardian has the customary obligation to refund the bride price[23] while the husband retains custody of the children and is therefore responsible for the maintenance of the children.

On child maintenance claims, the mother is under no obligation at all to maintain or contribute towards the upbringing of the child. However, where the bride price has not been paid, such a child is deemed to be the child of the wife's father who would be responsible for maintaining the child, with the biological father being under no legal obligation to maintain the child.[24] In fact, the biological father has no paternal right over the child until he pays the bride price in full. It is noteworthy at this point that in the light of section 42 of the Nigerian Constitution, a custom that is discriminatory cannot stand the test of time. Thus in *Edet v Essien*,[25] the court held that a custom that is contrary to natural justice, equity and good conscience is invalid and thus the test of a custom not being repugnant to natural justice, equity and good conscience or violating any law in force is relevant in child maintenance issues.[26]

Thus the issue of custody, and therefore maintenance, will be determined in the light of the validity of the customary law marriage as happened in Agani v Atule[27] where the court concentrated on whether the claimant of the children contracted a valid customary law marriage with their mother and custody was awarded to the mother in accordance with customary law when the putative father was unable to prove the existence of a valid marriage.[28]

III. Applicable Laws on Child Maintenance

The legal regulation of child custody in Nigeria is complex in several ways due to the fact that, as noted earlier, Nigeria has a tripartite system of laws and the appropriate court authorised to resolve a particular custody dispute, as well as the substantive norms to be applied, depend on which form of marriage the parents celebrated—statutory, customary, or Islamic.[29]

Where the marriage conducted is a statutory marriage, the various Federal and State laws of Nigeria relating to matrimonial causes will be applicable to determine custody and

[21] *Olayemi v Adeyemi* (unreported) Suit No JD/22A/60 where the wife appealed to Jos High Court which reversed the Customary Court decision based on the welfare principle.

[22] *Eborah v Eborah* (n 20) Unreported, Suit No 10/68 of 5 March 1968.

[23] Nwogugu (n 3) 220.

[24] *Ogbu v Esien* (unreported) Suit No MD/152A/1980.

[25] (1932) 11 NLR.

[26] *Mojekwu v Ejikeme* (2000) 5 NWLR 402.

[27] Suit No MD/102A/1975 of 3 April 1977.

[28] A similar decision was reached in lyorzua Bito v Tarbere Shigba, (Unreported) Suit No MD/123A/1977 of 8 July 1979.

[29] Owasanoye (n 10) 405–27.

maintenance orders. However, in determining this, there will be the need to prove that there is a valid statutory marriage in existence and that the supposed marriage is not void or voidable at the instance of any of the parties thereto.[30] Where the supposed statutory marriage is defective, the relevant laws would not be applicable and the marriage would be deemed to be a customary law marriage.[31]

On 20 November 1989, the United Nations General Assembly adopted the UN Convention on the Rights of the Child (CRC), whilst the African Union Assembly of Heads of States and Governments adopted the African Union Charter on the Rights and Welfare of the Child (AUCRCW) in July 1990. Nigeria signed both instruments and ratified them in 1991 and 2001 respectively. In 2003, Nigeria gave internal effect to the UN Convention on the Rights of the Child by the Child's Rights Act,[32] and this has been given effect to in 26 States in Nigeria. Some States in Northern Nigeria[33] refused to pass the Child's Rights Law mainly because of the provision on marriageable age which contradicts the prevailing custom that permits child marriage. The effect is that the States that have refused to give effect to the Child's Rights Act by enacting a state version of the law cannot be bound by the provisions of the Child's Rights Act. This is simply because the issue of child justice administration falls under the concurrent list of the Constitution[34] over which the National Assembly lacks the power to make binding laws for the States of the federation as a result of which the Child's Rights Act is only applicable in the Federal Capital Territory of Nigeria.

Under section 70 of the MCA, a court can make an order for maintenance for a party to the marriage or of children of the marriage suggesting that a maintenance order could potentially be made in favour of the male spouse and a mother could be ordered to pay maintenance for children. It could be considered quite progressive that Nigerian matrimonial law has removed a common law distinction that reinforced women's lower status. However, the customary law influence on the judges has made judges reluctant to grant maintenance orders against the female spouse and also, very few Nigerian men may be willing to bring maintenance actions against their wives in favour of the children.

Furthermore, Part IV of the MCA generally provides for the making of orders for maintenance, custody and settlements in favour of a husband, wife, children or adopted children of a marriage. In respect of maintenance, the MCA, by virtue of section 70(1), makes provision for the maintenance of a spouse or child of a marriage. The Infants Law of 1958 which is applicable to all States carved out of the former Western region of Nigeria is to the effect that custody issues should be resolved in the best interests of the child.[35]

In situations where the parties conducted both a statutory and customary law marriage, the statutory marriage prevails over the customary law marriage such that statutory laws will apply to determine custody and maintenance issues.[36]

[30] This is essential due to the negligence of some parties in ensuring that the valid requirements of a statutory marriage under Nigerian law are met; such as being celebrated by a licensed authority, giving the required notice, etc.

[31] *Obiekwe v Obiekwe* [1963] 7 ENLR 196, 199.

[32] Cap C50, Laws of the Federation of Nigeria, 2004; K Agary: 'Rights of a Child' *Punch Newspaper* of 13 May 2012.

[33] Specifically Adamawa, Bauchi, Borno, Enugu, Gombe, Kaduna, Kano, Katsina, Kebbi, Sokoto, Yobe and Zamfara States of Nigeria.

[34] Part II of 2nd Schedule to s 4(2) of 1999 Constitution.

[35] s 25 of the Infants Law of Oyo State.

[36] *Ali v Ali* [1966] 2 WLR 620.

As legislation establishing customary courts and area courts[37] has emerged so too have rules regulating custody and maintenance orders. These statutes empower the courts to administer the customary law prevailing in the area of jurisdiction of the courts so far as it is not repugnant to natural justice, equity and good conscience or incompatible with any written law in force in the State. They have also introduced the welfare principle by providing that in any matter relating to the guardianship of children, the interest of those children shall be the first and paramount consideration'.[38]

Thus it was held in *Joseph Ala v Akegh Achigbe*[39] that the statutes cover custody of children born under customary law marriages and appear also to cover custody of illegitimate children.

So it can be said that the applicable laws and rules in Nigeria include the Child's Rights Act, Matrimonial Causes Act and Rules, the various Infant Laws of the States, the various rules of courts and prevailing customary laws.

IV. Requirements to Claim Child Maintenance in Nigeria

In the case of a statutory marriage, application for maintenance of a child will normally arise alongside a proceeding for a matrimonial cause which, inter alia, includes divorce and judicial separation.[40] The Court of Appeal held in the case of *Ugbah v Ugbah*[41] that the reliefs of maintenance of a wife as well as education and welfare of the children of the marriage are not independent but must be ancillary to the main relief for the dissolution of marriage, nullity, judicial separation or restitution of conjugal rights[42] or jactitation of marriage.[43] Thus, an action for child maintenance cannot be brought prior to a matrimonial cause action.[44]

The MCA provides that both the mother and the father have equal responsibility to maintain the children of their marriage. Where however a parent or both parents fail to maintain the children, such children cannot enforce their right to maintenance in the absence of a proceeding for a matrimonial cause.[45] Where a parent omits to provide the necessities of life for his or her child under the age of 14 years thus resulting in danger to the child's life and health, proceedings may be brought by the relevant authorities to punish and deprive the parent of his or her custodial rights.[46]

[37] Such as Area Courts Edict 1967, Laws of Kwara State; Area Courts Edict 1968, Laws of Benue State; Customary Courts Edict 1978, Laws of Anambra State; Customary Courts Edict, 1981, Laws of Imo State.

[38] EN Uzodike 'Custody of Children in Nigeria—Statutory, Judicial and Customary Aspects' (1990) 39 *International and Comparative Law Quarterly* 419–33.

[39] Suit No MD/98A/972 of 1 June 1973.

[40] Part IV of the MCA deals with making of orders for maintenance, custody and settlements.

[41] [2009] 3 NWLR (pt 1127) 108; *Adekoya v Adekoya* (1999) 3 NWLR 607.

[42] MCA, ss 47–51.

[43] MCA, s 52.

[44] This is further made clear by the wording of s 70 of the MCA: 'maintenance pending the disposal of proceedings'.

[45] MCA, s 70.

[46] Children and Young Persons Law Cap C10 Laws of Lagos State of Nigeria 2004, s 27; *Head of Federal Military Government v Warri Juvenile Court, Ex parte Saka* (1981) 3 LRN 208.

Section 14(2) of the Child's Rights Act has however extended the child's right by providing that the child's right to maintenance by his or her parent or guardian can be enforced by the child in the family court whether or not there is a proceeding for a matrimonial cause. In effect, if a child is of the view that the parents are not fulfilling their obligation to take care of him or her, the child can initiate an action in the family court for maintenance from the parents. It can be safely assumed that, since all child maintenance cases must be in the best interests of the child, a child of a customary or Islamic law marriage can benefit from the provisions of the Child's Rights Act.

However, in practice this may be difficult because Nigerian society would frown on any child who takes a legal action against his or her parents in a court of law. The traditional beliefs tilt towards viewing such a child as an enemy of the parent and the societal belief that parties to a court matter cannot be friends thereafter. This approach by society hinders the development of this aspect of the law, thus there is a need to further educate the public on the objective of the Child's Rights Act and the need to take care of children.

Under the various customary laws of Nigeria, paternity of a child is the most important requirement to pay child support. Customary law admits as legitimate children born in lawful wedlock and also extends legitimacy to children born outside wedlock but whose paternity their father or putative father has acknowledged. Also, Islamic law in certain circumstances admits as legitimate, children born out of wedlock.[47] Once a claimant can show that the spouse against whom the claim is sought has always been responsible for the maintenance of the child in question before the divorce or separation or pending suit, the claimant is entitled to claim child support. It is immaterial that the child was born out of wedlock insofar as the father has expressly or impliedly acknowledged paternity.

Although the practice was to exclude a child born out of wedlock—as happened in *Onwudijoh v Onwudinjoh*[48] where it was held that a child born out of wedlock has no right of inheritance—this practice was abolished by section 42(2) of the 1999 Constitution (as amended) which is to the effect that 'no citizen of Nigeria shall be subjected to any disability or deprivation merely by reason of the circumstances of his birth'.[49] This position affirmed that already taken by the Nigerian court in *Ukeje v Ukeje*.[50]

A. Age Limit for Maintenance

Age is an important consideration in the determination of the welfare of a child.[51] Under section 277 of the Child's Rights Act a child is a person under the age of 18 years and by virtue of the same Act,[52] orders relating to maintenance of a child shall cease to have effect when the child attains the age of 18 except where otherwise directed.[53]

[47] PO Itua, 'Legitimacy, Legitimation and Succession in Nigeria: An Appraisal of Section 42(2) of the Constitution of the Federal Republic of Nigeria 1999 as amended on the Rights of Inheritance' (2012) 4 *Journal of Law and Conflict Resolution* 31–44.

[48] (1957) 2 ENLR 6.

[49] Art 18(3) of the African Union (AU) Charter on the Rights and Welfare of the Child 2001 also provides that no child shall be deprived of maintenance by reason of the parents' marital status.

[50] (2001) 27 WRN 142.

[51] *Anyaso v Anyaso* [1998] 9 NWLR (pt 564) 150, 184.

[52] First Schedule, ss 55(14), 3(1)(b).

[53] Ibid.

However, by virtue of section 70(4) of the MCA, the power of the court to make an order with respect to maintenance of children of a marriage shall not be exercised for the benefit of a child who has attained the age of 21 years. However, the court can still exercise discretion to a child of the marriage who is over 21 years old where the court is of the opinion that there are special circumstances that justify the making of such an order for the benefit of that child.[54] In *Ajai-Ajagbe v Ajai-Ajagbe*,[55] the court refused to extend maintenance to the youngest child of a marriage who was 27 years old. In deciding whether or not to extend maintenance to a child above the age of 18, there is a need to consider the best interest of the child in every individual case such as if the child has a disability or special need.

In the Northern region of Nigeria where Islamic law operates, child maintenance continues till the child attains the age of puberty.[56] Puberty in this instance differs from puberty for the purpose of marriage. For female children, child maintenance continues for as long as they are unmarried and remain under parental care, even after attaining puberty[57] and for male children, until they are financially capable of maintaining a family. There is no specific age to determine majority under Islamic law in Nigeria but in practice the age ranges from nine for girls to 18 for boys, although for girls the age of menstruation is generally accepted. Where there is doubt as to the age of majority, a statement by the child in question that he or she has reached puberty is adequate.

Under the various customary laws of Nigeria, there is no uniform marriageable age and this does cause conflict in Nigerian laws. Generally, it is accepted that marriageable age is the age of maturity. However, marriageable age in the Eastern region of Nigeria has been fixed by statute and thus by virtue of section 3(1) of the Age of Marriage Law, Eastern Nigeria, marriageable age has been fixed at 16 for both genders.[58] The law regarding marriageable age in Western Nigeria is not laid down in any legislation. Puberty and financial capacity are the determining factors.

Under the various customary laws, there is no stipulated age limit to benefit from child maintenance but in the light of the marriageable age, it can be safely argued that the age limit to benefit from child maintenance is the marriageable age as applicable under the relevant customary law.

V. Assessment of Child Maintenance

Section 70(1) of the MCA is to the effect that 'the court may, in proceedings with respect to the maintenance of a party to a marriage, or of children of the marriage, other than for proceedings for an order of maintenance pending the disposal of proceedings, make orders as it thinks proper, having regard to the *means, earning capacity and conduct* of the parties to the marriage and all other relevant circumstances.'(Emphasis added.)

[54] MCA, s 70(4).
[55] (1978) 10–12 CCHCJ 182.
[56] Quran 4:6 in accordance with Islamic law.
[57] Arfat (n 7) 304.
[58] *Emeakuana v Umeojiako* (1979) ENLR 151.

In as much as the court has discretion[59] in granting a maintenance order, there are nevertheless clear principles for the assessment of maintenance and it is clear that the means, earning capacity and conduct of the parties are the important factors that Nigerian courts rely on. The principles are clearly stated in section 4 of the first Schedule to section 55(14) of the Child's Rights Act in conjunction with section 70 of the MCA to the effect that the court shall, in making a maintenance order, consider all the circumstances of the case including the income, earning capacity,[60] property, conduct of the parties to the marriage and other financial resources of the party to which the maintenance order applies as well as his financial needs, obligations and responsibilities and all other relevant circumstances.

Also, the financial needs of the child, the income, earning capacity, property, physical or mental disability of the child and the manner in which the child is being or is expected to be brought up must all be considered in calculating child maintenance. In *Eziashi v Eziashi*,[61] Akhigbe J stated that the fact that one spouse is in a much better financial position than the other to bring up the child may be decisive.

The principles guiding assessment of awards were enumerated in *Menakaya v Menakaya*[62] as follows:

(a) The income, earning capacity, property and other financial resources which each of the parties has or is likely to have in the foreseeable future;
(b) The financial needs, obligations, and responsibilities which each of the parties has or is likely to have in the foreseeable future;
(c) The standard of living enjoyed by the family before the breakdown of the marriage;
(d) The age of each party to the marriage and the duration of the marriage;
(e) Any physical or mental disability of either of the parties to the marriage;
(f) The contributions made by each of the parties to the welfare of the family including any contribution made by looking after the house and caring for the family; and
(g) In the case of proceedings for divorce or nullity of marriage, the value of either party to any benefit like a pension, which by reason of the dissolution or annulment of the marriage that party will lose the chance of acquiring.

The court went further to state that where there are children of the marriage, the court must, in the assessment of maintenance and education of the children, lean in favour of their welfare.[63] In sum, the paramount interest of the child should be of utmost relevance in assessing maintenance.[64]

The court will not consider the question of custody or make an order for custody if the parties seeking such custody have not set out their plans and arrangements for the upbringing of the children of the marriage. This shows that a strong emphasis is put on the ability of a party to provide for the material well-being of the children.[65]

This would make assessment of maintenance easy where the claimant provides adequate information backed with evidence as to the earnings of the respondent. However, where the

[59] *Anyaso v Anyaso* [1998] 9 NWLR (pt 564) 150, 176.
[60] MCA, s 70(1); *Olu-Ibukun v Olu-Ibukun* (1974) ECSLR 706, 711.
[61] Suit No B/255/80 (unreported) High Court Benin.
[62] [1996] 9 NWLR (pt 472) 256, 301.
[63] *Menakaya v Menakaya* at 301; see also *Buwanhot v Buwanhot* [2009] 16 NWLR (pt 1166) 22; *Tabansi v Tabansi* [2009] 12 NWLR (pt 1155) 415.
[64] *Anyaso v Anyaso* [1998] 9 NWLR (pt 564) 150.
[65] Uzodike (n 38).

court is unable to make an assessment due to lack of adequate information or for any other reason, the claimant shall make an application to the court to obtain a certificate of means of the respondent. The court shall, upon this application, enquire into the resources of the parties to the marriage to which the application relates and to the capability of each of the parties to earn income, and issue a certificate of means with respect to those resources and capabilities.[66]

The procedure is usually to force the defendant to disclose his or her assets under oath, with the consequence of an action for perjury if he or she fails to do so truthfully. Also, the evidence relied on in the matrimonial proceedings will be taken into consideration in determining the income and assets of the defendant. This system is inadequate in assisting the courts in assessing the respondent's income in order to make a maintenance order. In as much as the law safeguards the petitioner's interests by making the respondent declare his or her assets on oath with the likely exposure to an action against him or her for perjury,[67] in practice, parties still lie under oath. It appears that this is an area which the Government must look into urgently and provide other measures to ensure adequate declaration of assets such as shifting the burden of proof of assets on to the respondent in an action for child maintenance.

Also, the court is under an obligation to consider the current market forces as dictated by the price index so that the current buying power of the Nigerian naira is taken into consideration in making an award.[68]

The court also has the power to vary the order in due course on application of either of the parties.[69] There is a conflict of views in the Nigerian courts on the fraction of the joint income of the parties to be used as a rule to measure maintenance.[70] It has been agreed however that the conduct of the parties will influence the quantum of maintenance to be awarded.[71]

Under the customary law of Western Nigeria, the guide to calculating child maintenance is very similar to the provision under the Act. The amount which the father had always been committed to before the divorce or separation would be a starting point in assessing the amount of maintenance.[72]

It is unknown to the Nigerian customary laws for a man to claim maintenance against his wife. Rather the divorced wife has the right to claim maintenance for herself and her children. In *Ejimbe v Ejimbe*,[73] a husband who sought monthly maintenance for himself and for each of his five children against his wife had the application dismissed. Rather the court made an order against him for the maintenance of the children.

Under the customary law of Eastern Nigeria, child custody lies with the father and the mother is under no obligation to pay child support to the father. The father has the sole responsibility of maintaining the child and where he is not capable, the obligation shifts to the child's paternal grandfather.[74] If the child is being breastfed, as a result of which

[66] Matrimonial Causes Rules, Order XIV Rule 18; *Obe v Obe* Suit No WD/94/86.

[67] Criminal Code Act Cap C38 Laws of the Federation of Nigeria 2004, ss 117 and 118.

[68] *Anyaso v Anyaso* [1998] 9 NWLR (pt 564) 150, 183.

[69] s 73(1)(j)(iv).

[70] *Adeyemi v Adeyemi* (1972) 2 UILR 494; *Negbenebor v Negbenebor* (1971) 1 ANLR 210; *Okala v Okala* (1973) ECSNLR 67.

[71] *Ajai-Ajagbe v Ajai-Ajagbe* (1979) HCLLR 183, 191; *Okala v Okala* (n 70).

[72] *Sulaimon v Sulaimon* Suit No CCM/187/2011 of 11 August 2011.

[73] Suit No WD/59/85 of 3 March 1989.

[74] *Eborah v Eborah* (n 20).

custody lies with the mother, the father is duty bound to provide for the sustenance of the mother and child in the sum of whatever he can afford until the child is weaned.

Under Islamic law which is prevalent in Northern Nigeria, maintenance of children includes accommodation, food, drink, clothing and education, and everything that the child needs, and the calculation of the payment is to be based on what is reasonable, considering the husband's financial situation.[75] This is based on the Quranic provision that 'Let the rich man spend according to his means; and the man whose resources are restricted, let him spend according to what Allah has given him. Allah puts no burden on any person beyond what He has given him. Allah will grant after hardship, ease.'[76]

If the parties cannot decide on the amount payable as child maintenance, then the Sharia court judge or the Sheik[77] responsible for the marriage is to decide the amount after considering the means of the father. In calculating child maintenance based on this requirement, the status of the husband and the standard of living that the child had been used to would be taken into consideration.[78]

VI. Means of Securing a Debtor's Subsistence

The courts have wide powers in this respect under sections 73, 92, 93, and 105 of the MCA.

Statutorily, where a party has defaulted in paying maintenance as ordered by the court, an application may be made ex parte to the High Court for an attachment of earnings order.[79] The affidavit in support of the application shall state the particulars of the maintenance order, the amount of the arrears due to the applicant under the maintenance order, particulars of any proceedings taken by the applicant to enforce the maintenance order, particulars of the employer of the defendant to the application and particulars of the defendant and of his work.[80]

Where the earnings order is made, the applicant shall deposit a copy of the order with the Registrar of the court and the Registrar shall see to it that a sealed copy of the order is served on every person on whom a sealed copy is required by law.[81]

Also, by virtue of section 4 of the third Schedule to section 92 of the MCA, where a person has been in default of payment of maintenance to the tune of four payments in the case of a weekly payment or two payments in any other case, or where it can be shown that the defendant has wilfully and persistently refused to pay maintenance, the court may give an order to the person who appears to be the defendant's employer in respect of his earnings or part of his earnings to take out of the earnings the payment as prescribed by the court.[82]

[75] Fatwa No 20473 available at www.islamqa.info/en/ref/20473 (accessed October 2013).
[76] Quran 65:7.
[77] Meaning an Islamic scholar.
[78] Conclusion reached based on several interviews with some Islamic scholars of Northern Nigeria.
[79] MCA, s 92.
[80] Matrimonial Causes Rule, Order XVII Rule 8.
[81] Rule 10.
[82] *Bairbre Oloyede v Hector Oloyede* (1971) 2 UILR 13.

Where this kind of order is made, the order shall stipulate the amount so attached and that the payment should be made to a named officer of the court. The payment is deemed to be made by the defendant in discharge of the maintenance payment in respect of the amount so paid by the employer.[83]

Failure to comply with an attachment order is an offence punishable on conviction with a fine of not more than 200 naira.[84] The defence available to such defendant is that he took reasonable steps to comply with the order.[85] It is clear that this area of Nigerian law is inadequate and vague. With the present Nigerian economy, it is making a mockery of the justice system to impose a fine of 200 naira for non-compliance with an important statutory provision.

Also, the law gives no insight into what 'reasonable steps' may be. A defendant could easily take advantage of this provision of the law and claim, based on any excuse, that he took reasonable steps to comply with the law. Thus the duty to determine what qualifies as reasonable steps to comply with the order is left to the discretion of the courts.

Under Western Nigerian customary law, the appropriate mode to enforce a debtor's subsistence is for the customary courts to order that the prescribed fee be paid into court on a specified date of each month. Where the party ordered to pay defaults, the applicant would go back to the customary court that gave the maintenance order to inform it of the default. The judge would invite both parties to see him or her and try to mediate and appeal to the father's conscience to continue payment.[86] If the father continues to default, the appropriate practical order is to remand the father for a few days to ensure compliance.

Where this also fails, there does not appear to be any judicial machinery in place for the enforcement of child maintenance at the customary court level. The only available remedy is for the claimant to express her grievances to the husband's parents or the husband's extended family who may be forced to take up the responsibility to maintain the child.

In the Northern region of Nigeria where Islamic law operates, the practice is to approach the Shariah court that gave the maintenance order and file an enforcement application. This application will be heard and the party in default will be instructed to pay the arrears and where circumstances allow, the order as to maintenance may be varied especially if the defaulting party is out of a job.

VII. Public Support in Child Maintenance

In Nigeria, an assessment of orphans and vulnerable children conducted with UNICEF support in 2004 showed that there were about 7 million orphans and this number keeps rising by the day.[87]

In this regard, section 50 of the Child's Rights Act provides that a child development officer, a police officer or any other person authorised by the Minister may bring a child before the court if 'he has reasonable grounds for believing that the child is an orphan or

[83] MCA, ss 6–8, 3rd Schedule, s 92.

[84] Equivalent to US $1.2; MCA, s 32(1), 3rd Schedule, s 92.

[85] MCA, s 32(2), 3rd Schedule, s 92.

[86] *Sulaimon v Sulaimon* Suit No CCM/187/2011 of 11 August 2011.

[87] EN Uzodike, 'New Legislative Approach towards Child Protection and other Family Law Developments in Nigeria', Salt Lake conference seminar paper www.law2.byu.edu/isfl/saltlakeconference/papers/isflpdfs/Uzodike.pdf (accessed October 2013).

is deserted by his relatives'. The court may then commit the child to the care of any person whether a relative or not, who is willing to undertake the care of the child.

Furthermore, section 178 of the Child's Rights Act also makes provision for the accommodation and maintenance of the State Government for children looked after by it such that the State is under an obligation to identify children in need of maintenance and to offer maintenance, even where the children live with their families. However, this situation is a far cry from what happens in reality, though some States are working towards achieving this objective by adopting the Child's Rights Act[88] and enacting the State version of the law subject to changes deemed necessary.

As in the Convention on the Rights of the Child, the Nigerian Government also has responsibilities and as such in the Lagos State Child Rights Law,[89] the State Government has a duty to protect and provide necessary goods for children in need in the State and also to help their families to take good care of them. That duty means that the State Government must: provide a policy framework that will ensure the rights of the child; reduce infant and maternal mortality rates; provide medical and health care; provide adequate nutrition and safe drinking water, hygienic and sanitised environments; combat diseases and malnutrition; support and mobilise, through local and community resources, the development of primary health care for children; and provide accommodation, maintenance and/or financial support, advice and other services to children and their families.[90]

Furthermore, Nigeria, through the Ministry of Women's Affairs, developed a National Plan of Action (NPA) for Orphans and Vulnerable Children (OVC) through the UNICEF assisted process that began in 2004 and was officially launched in 2007.[91]

There are several non-governmental agencies and orphanages with the sole purpose of providing care and education for vulnerable children. However, the orphanages that exist are not government funded and they are insufficient to cope with the situation. They rely largely on funding from international and domestic donations. The public sector, especially religious groups, make donations to these vulnerable children from time to time but the number of people willing to make such donations is few compared to the number of vulnerable children.

In the Northern part of Nigeria, the concept of Shariah law operates such that responsibility for and compassion towards the child is a matter of religious importance as well as social concern. Whether the parents are alive or deceased, present or absent, known or unknown, the child is to be provided with the best possible care. Where there are executors or relatives close enough to be held responsible for the child's welfare, they shall be directed to discharge this duty. But if there is no next of kin, care for the child becomes a joint responsibility of the Muslim community, designated officials and commoners alike.[92]

88 Such as the South Western States.

89 Child's Rights Law 2007.

90 Agary (n 32).

91 R Bray, 'A Literature Review of Child Carers in Angola, Nigeria, Uganda and Zimbabwe' (2009) Save the Children UK Research Report www.crin.org/docs/SCUK_lit_review.pdf (accessed January 2014).

92 Arfat (n 7) 302.

VIII. Access to Procedure by the State

The Legal Aid Council (LAC) of Nigeria was established under the Legal Aid Act No 56 of 1976.[93] The Council focuses on the provision of relief for victims of arbitrary arrest, unlawful detention and prosecution, and minimising the abuses of human rights. The organisation also provides mediation centres for minor civil disputes such as civil claims arising from criminal activities against persons who qualify for Legal Aid under the Act; mediation on disputes on various issues such as landlord/tenant, master/servant, employer/employee, husband/wife, inheritance and family matters, etc.

The categories of services provided by the Council are representation at the police station and in courts, advice and assistance (written or in conference) including writing letters, negotiating, mediation and providing a wide range of services which include legal counselling, financial/welfare assistance to a target group namely, women and children either standing trial or in custody, payment of convicts' fines and integration into society, and provision of mobile legal aid clinics.

The service is free for Nigerian citizens where the individual's income does not exceed the minimum wage, or those with higher incomes who cannot afford to pay private legal practitioners. The service is limited due to a shortage of state funding and skilled personnel.[94]

It is noteworthy that most Nigerian citizens are unaware of the Legal Aid Scheme as a result of which access to justice becomes very limited if not impossible for the indigent population. For those who are aware of the existence of the Legal Aid Council, the average Nigerian mentality is that anything that has to do with the court is trouble. Many Nigerians, whether educated or not, believe that bringing a matter before the courts results in bad publicity and that they will not get justice. This is due, largely, to the slow dispensation of justice. It is however hoped that with the creation of family courts in most state High Courts, matrimonial matters will be attended to promptly due to the sensitive nature of these types of disputes.

Currently, the Legal Aid Council has initiated a project to make the public aware of their existence and the availability of their services to the citizens of Nigeria. So far, the project has been helpful in making Nigerians aware of their rights and how they can seek legal redress.

Also, complementing the work of the Legal Aid Council are the federal Ministry of Women's Affairs and Social Development and the state Ministries of Women's Affairs and Social Development which are essentially social service oriented, with functions and responsibilities of policy formulation, articulation and implementation of programmes and activities geared towards the promotion of the interests and welfare of women, children, the elderly, people with disabilities and the vulnerable generally.[95]

The broad mandate of the Ministry is to advise the Government on gender and children issues; issues affecting persons with disabilities and the aged; initiate policy guidelines and lead the process of gender equality and mainstreaming at both the national and international levels.[96]

[93] Cap L9 Laws of the Federation of Nigeria 2004.

[94] Ibid.

[95] Ministry of Women's Affairs, Nassarawa State Official website www.nasarawastatenigeria.com/?p=349 (accessed February 2014).

[96] Nigerian Federal Ministry of Women's Affairs and Social Development.

The Child Development Department was set up under one of the programmes of the Department of the federal Ministry of Women's Affairs and Social Development established by Decree 42 in 1992, under the then National Commission for Women (NCW). The Commission was later upgraded to the federal Ministry of Women's Affairs and Social Development in 1994.[97]

This Ministry mediates in collecting child maintenance on behalf of the spouse with custody from the spouse who is under the obligation to pay maintenance. However, in cases where there is no means of support or where the party mandated to pay child support cannot be traced, it falls on the Ministry to pay child support to the spouse with custody of the child as part of their development programmes. However the number of cases being dealt with is greater than the funding available to the Ministry.

There are also several NGOs that focus on child's welfare and rights[98] that provide assistance to work for parents who have been denied maintenance or maintenance enforcement due to lack of knowledge on their rights or limited funds. These NGOs sometimes initiate maintenance proceedings on behalf of the aggrieved party.

The media have also been of great help in this respect mainly by airing live programmes where aggrieved parties can complain of default or lack of maintenance by a spouse. The procedure is for anyone with a grievance in child maintenance matters to approach the programme makers before the show and explain what has happened and the fact that they lack the capacity to maintain the child on his or her own.

The aggrieved party is then put on air and given the opportunity to relate his or her story after which a public appeal would be made to the defaulting spouse and the account details of the aggrieved party would be aired with the appeal to the general public to pay whatever they can to assist the party directly into his or her account.

It is noteworthy that women gain the sympathy of the public more than men basically because the African culture sees it as the male obligation for the father to maintain his children.

IX. Participation in International Conventions

Nigeria, as a member of the African Union, ratified the African Union (AU) Charter on the Rights and Welfare of the Child (AUCRWC) on 23 July 2001. The AUCRWR expressly provides that no child shall be deprived of maintenance by reference to the parents' marital status.[99] Thus, it appears that the African Court on Human and People's Rights may have constructive jurisdiction on child maintenance issues where the national courts have failed to mete out justice in this respect. This can be achieved by bringing an individual complaint before the African Committee of Experts on the Rights and Welfare of the Child for violation of the child's right to maintenance as protected by the AUCRWC.[100]

[97] www.womenaffairs.gov.ng/departments/child_development.htm (accessed February 2014).

[98] Such as Child Adolescent and Family Survival Organization (CAFSO), Child Rescue and Survival Project (CREASUP), Child Right Action Coalition (CRAC), Save the Child, Hope for Children, etc.

[99] Art 18(3).

[100] The Committee has its mandate under Arts 32–46 ACRWC.

Nigeria has ratified the United Nations Convention on the Rights of the Child which provides that parents or guardians shall have the primary responsibility for the upbringing and development of the child, which includes the right to adequate maintenance by the parents.[101]

These international instruments have been given domestic effect in Nigeria by the Child's Rights Act 2003. However, before an individual can institute an action to enforce a right at a regional or international court such as the African Court, such an individual must have exhausted the judicial process of his or her country and must still be dissatisfied by the decision. It goes without saying that before a child can enforce his or her maintenance right in a regional court; he must have gone through the judicial process in Nigeria up to the Supreme Court which is the apex court.

The problem then is the capacity of a child to sue in a court of law. In as much as the Child's Rights Act[102] ensured adequate representation of a child in court, a child cannot, as of right, commence an action in a court in Nigeria, except through a next friend.[103]

X. Recognition and Enforcement of Child Maintenance in Nigeria

Relying on child support related statutes in Nigeria, the courts have the competence to recognise and enforce child maintenance decisions.[104] However where a matter of child maintenance is brought before an administrative body such as the ministry of Women's Affairs of any State of the federation, the administrative body is duty bound to mediate and advise the parties to seek recourse to the courts if mediation fails.

For instance, section 73(1)(h) of the MCA empowers the court to make a permanent order, an order pending the disposal of a proceeding, or an order for a fixed term or for a life or joint lives or until further order. The section further empowers the court to vary the terms of an order made upon the satisfaction of certain criteria.[105] The courts also have the competence to determine the mode and manner of payment of maintenance in the best interests of the child.

Furthermore, jurisdiction to determine the enforcement of maintenance orders by registration or by attachment of earnings or by other means lies in the courts.[106] Also, matters of assessment of maintenance, default in payment of amount assessed, determination of claims for maintenance and other related issues are the responsibility of the court.[107] The following provisions of the MCA are useful for child maintenance enforcement:

> 88 (1) Subject to rules of court, a court having jurisdiction under this Act may enforce by attachment or other process an order made by it under this Act for payment of maintenance or costs or in respect of the custody of, or access, to children.

[101] UN CRC, Art 8.

[102] s 155 guarantees right to a counsel and to free legal aid in hearing and determining any matter concerning a child in court.

[103] Who is expected to be a person in *loco parentis*.

[104] MCA, s 88(1).

[105] Ibid s 73(1)(j)(iv).

[106] Ibid s 88(1).

[107] Ibid ss 70–74, 96, 105.

...

89.(2) A decree registered in a court under this section may, subject to rules of court, be enforced as if it had been made by the court in which it is registered.

90.(1) Where a decree made under this Act orders the payment of money to a person, any moneys payable under the decree may be recovered as a judgment debt in a court of competent jurisdiction.

...

91.(1) Where pursuant to this Act, a court has made an order for payment of maintenance, the order may be registered in accordance with rules of court in a court of summary jurisdiction of a state of the federation, and an order so registered may, subject to rules of court, be enforced in the same manner as if it were an order for maintenance of a deserted wife made by the court of summary jurisdiction.

In the Western region of Nigeria, competence to recognise and enforce a child maintenance decision lies with both judicial and administrative bodies. The customary courts have the powers to recognise and enforce a child maintenance decision.[108]

Likewise, where a child maintenance decision has been made, local administrative bodies such as the community leaders can step in to enforce the maintenance decisions. This is done mainly by calling the parties and appealing to the party in default to obey the decision laid down by the courts. Where this fails, the only recourse is to seek redress in the court of law for enforcement.

It is worthy of note that, by way of customary practice, the media contribute to effective child maintenance recognition and enforcement by airing several programmes[109] in the local dialect where aggrieved parties can appear and share their story. The mediators invite the parties involved and hear both parties out after which they allow the audience to contribute by calling in to the programme. In most cases, the children of the marriage are brought on the programme. The mediators thereafter make an order relating to child maintenance and they monitor compliance. Where a party defaults, the defaulting party is invited on to the programme and scolded on air.

This method has been very effective because the fear of embarrassment has led to a compliance level of over 70 per cent. No responsible father would want his name mentioned as defaulting in fulfilling his obligation to his children. This could cost him his reputation, as a result of which most people comply.

In the Eastern region of Nigeria, where a child who has not been weaned is in the custody of the mother, the elders of the community have the responsibility of enforcing a maintenance decision until the father gains custody of the child. Elders of the community in this respect mean the family head or the village head.

[108] *Dawodu v Dawodu* (Unreported) CCHCJ/5/74.

[109] Such as 'Agborodun', 'So da bee', etc meaning 'mediator' and 'is it good' respectively.

XI. Recognition and Enforcement of Foreign Judgments

In order for an order of a foreign court to be recognised, one of five conditions prescribed by section 81 of the MCA must be satisfied. These conditions are:

(a) at the time the divorce proceeding was initiated, the petitioner was domiciled in the country in which the divorce was obtained;
(b) the petitioner was a deserted wife who was domiciled in the foreign country, either immediately before her marriage or immediately before her desertion;
(c) the wife had been a resident of the foreign country for three years immediately preceding the initiation of divorce proceedings;
(d) the divorce was recognised as valid by the law of the parties' domicile at the date of divorce; or
(e) the divorce would be recognised as valid under the rules of private international law.

The recognition and enforcement of a foreign judgment on maintenance further depends on the reciprocal arrangement between Nigeria and the nation seeking enforcement. A reciprocal arrangement is governed by international Conventions,[110] and this implies that foreign maintenance orders in favour of individuals in reciprocating countries can likewise be registered and enforced by Nigerian courts against Nigerian residents. The precise nature of reciprocity available between Nigeria and another jurisdiction depends on the Convention or agreement to which the other country is a signatory. Presently, there are no treaties on recovery of child maintenance to which Nigeria is a party.

Under the Maintenance Orders Act 1921,[111] a maintenance order made by any court in England or Ireland may be registered and enforced in Nigeria. Once the order is registered in a Nigerian court, it has the force and effect of an order originally obtained in the court that registered it. If the original order was issued by a superior court, it will be registered in a High Court but in other cases, the registration will be made at the Magistrates court.[112]

The Act has been extended by proclamation under section 11 to The Gambia, Ghana, Sierra Leone, New South Wales, St. Vincent, Grenada, British Guyana, Victoria, Commonwealth of Australia, Northern Rhodesia, Western Australia, Union of South Africa,[113] New Zealand, including the Cook Islands and The Island of Jersey.[114] Also, Nigeria has a pending Reciprocal Enforcement Maintenance Order with Wisconsin.[115]

The Nigerian courts have powers to confirm the authenticity of a maintenance order made in a foreign country and where such a provisional order has been confirmed, it may be varied or rescinded in like manner as if it was originally made by a magistrate, and where on an application for rescission or variation, the magistrate is satisfied that it is necessary to remit the case to the court which made the order for the purpose of taking

[110] Reciprocal Enforcement of Maintenance Orders www.nidirect.gov.uk/reciprocal-enforcement-of-maintenance-orders (accessed January 2014).

[111] Laws of the Federation of Nigeria Cap M1, 2004.

[112] Maintenance Orders Act (MOA) 1921, s 3.

[113] Now Republic of South Africa–Reciprocal Enforcement of Maintenance Orders Act 1963 (Act 80 of 1963) www.justice.gov.za/ilr/intmnt.html (accessed January 2014).

[114] Schedule to the MOA. For further analysis of the Commonwealth scheme for recognition and enforcement of maintenance orders see Richard Frimpong Oppong, ch 4 and James Ding, ch 6 of this volume.

[115] www.acf.hhs.gov/programs/cse/po/DCL/2004/dcl-04-21.htm (accessed January 2014).

any further evidence, the magistrate may so remit the case and adjourn the proceedings for the purpose.[116]

In enforcing a foreign order, a court of a magistrate in which an order has been registered or confirmed shall take all such steps for enforcing the order as may be prescribed. Every such order shall be enforceable in like manner as if the order were for the payment of a civil debt recoverable summarily and a warrant of distress or commitment issued by a magistrate for the purpose of enforcing any order so registered or confirmed may be executed in any part of Nigeria in the same manner as if the warrant had been originally issued or subsequently endorsed by a court having jurisdiction in the place where the warrant is executed.[117]

Under section 11 of the Act, the reciprocal recognition and enforcement shall extend to any Commonwealth country or British colony which has reciprocal provisions for the enforcement of maintenance orders made by courts in Nigeria.

XII. Conclusion

The Nigerian MCA 1970 which codifies the laws on divorce, annulment, judicial separation, custody, maintenance and settlement of disputes was fashioned out of English law and has since then not been modified to meet the changing demands of society. The Child's Rights Act 2003 was enacted to complement the provisions of the MCA, nonetheless the statutes do not address all that is essential to truly protect and uphold the best interests of the child. Though the statutes recognise the need to consider the best interests of the child in child support cases, they are not detailed enough to meet the changing demands of Nigerian and global societies.

As much as the effort of the Nigerian Government is commendable in giving effect to the ratified UNCRC via the Child's Rights Act, the fact that family matters fall within the concurrent list of the Nigerian legislature has undermined the effectiveness of the Act throughout the country, thus there is a need to adopt and enact specific legislation on recovery of domestic and international child support.

XIII. Recommendation

Presently, Nigeria is not a party to the Hague Convention on the Civil Aspects of International Child Abduction 1980, the Hague Convention on the International Recovery of Child Support and Other Forms of Family Maintenance 2007, or to any other international Convention with specific rules on custody or maintenance orders. The Hague Convention on the International Recovery of Child Support and Other Forms of Family Maintenance 2007 is a very important convention on the recovery of child maintenance.

[116] MOA, s 6.
[117] MOA, s 7.

The Convention is open to all sovereign States as well as Regional Economic Integration Organisations.[118]

Though there are several regional treaties to which Nigeria is a signatory that deal partly with the issue of maintenance,[119] there is no specific international or regional treaty that deals with the issue of child support recovery and maintenance that Nigeria has ratified and given effect to. This makes it crucial to ratify the Hague Convention and give effect to it in Nigeria by creating a specific law that deals with the recovery of child maintenance issues.

Furthermore, there is the need to make the public, especially women, aware of their rights after a divorce, in order to reduce the customary influence on the rights of the child to parental support. In this light the laws on children should be simplified and made available to children, who are the stakeholders, at every level of education. Also leaflets in both the official and local languages should be made freely available nationwide on the issue of child support.

Finally, the various Ministries of Women's Affairs and Social Development in the States of the federation should be encouraged to open zonal offices in all the local government areas in the country, where they can have direct access to the stakeholders at the grass roots level and provide legal aid, awareness campaigns and support to women and children who are unable to afford the legal fees for litigation for the purpose of recovering child support wherever such a dispute arises. This further stresses the need to ratify the Hague Convention which allows for free legal assistance for child support applications for a child under 21 years old.[120]

[118] The Hague Convention on the International Recovery of Child Support and Other Forms of Family Maintenance www.hcch.net/index_en.php?act=conventions.text&cid=131 (accessed January 2014).

[119] Such as the African Charter on the Rights and Welfare of the Child 1990.

[120] Art 15.

16

The Interface between Maintenance and Cross-border Surrogacy

KATARINA TRIMMINGS*

I. Introduction: Surrogacy and its Global Market

A surrogate mother can be defined as a woman who carries a child pursuant to an arrangement made before she became pregnant, and made with the sole intention of the resulting child being handed over to another person or other persons and the surrogate mother relinquishing all rights to the child.[1] There are two types of surrogacy: traditional surrogacy and gestational surrogacy. In traditional surrogacy, the surrogate mother becomes pregnant with the sperm of the intended father (usually by insemination, and seldom through sexual intercourse) or is inseminated with a donor sperm. As a result, the surrogate mother is genetically related to the child. In gestational surrogacy, an embryo is created by in-vitro fertilisation using the egg of the intended mother (or a donor egg) and the sperm of the intended father (or a donor sperm). As a result, in gestational surrogacy, the surrogate mother has no genetic relationship with the child.

Despite controversies over ethical aspects of surrogate motherhood, surrogacy has become an increasingly popular method of reproductive technology. It is no exaggeration to say that the modern world has already witnessed the development of an extensive international surrogacy market.[2] This market, although initially largely unnoticed, has recently attracted a great deal of interest by the media. In spite of its expanding nature, cross-border surrogacy remains completely unregulated at the global level, leaving parties to cross-border surrogacy arrangements at a serious risk of exploitation and resulting in complex legal problems in individual cases of cross-border surrogacy arrangements.

* The author wishes to express her thanks to an anonymous reviewer for their thorough review of the chapter and valuable comments and suggestions which significantly contributed to improving the quality of the chapter.

[1] For an in-depth analysis of the problem of cross-border surrogacy see K Trimmings and P Beaumont, 'General Report on Surrogacy' in K Trimmings and P Beaumont (eds), *International Surrogacy Arrangements: Legal Regulation at the International Level* (Oxford, Hart Publishing, 2013).

[2] The term 'market' is used here to indicate that the vast majority of cross-border surrogacy arrangements are entered into on a commerical basis; ie the surrogate mother receives compensation for her reasonable pregnancy-related expenses plus additional remuneration for her 'services'. Nevertheless, it must be acknowledged that there are also cross-border surrogacy cases where no remuneration or even compensation is involved. These cases usually take place with the help of a family member or a close friend of the intended parents.

The first part of this contribution outlines the different ways in which countries have responded to the legal challenges posed by surrogacy arrangements. This analysis sets the scene and provides the necessary background for the examination of the interface between cross-border surrogacy and maintenance which is attempted in the second part of the chapter. This chapter is in principle an analytical and conceptual piece of work which explores how the relevant issues could be dealt with under the new maintenance regime: the Hague Convention on the International Recovery of Child Support and Other Forms of Family Maintenance[3] (the 'Hague Maintenance Convention' or 'Convention') and the Protocol on the Law Applicable to Maintenance Obligations[4] (the 'Protocol'). Undeniably, a lot will depend on specific domestic substantive rules on legal parenthood/maintenance, which this chapter, however, does not aim to cover. All case scenarios used in the chapter are purely hypothetical.

II. Preliminary Issues: Applicability of the Convention and of the Protocol to Cases Involving Surrogacy

Prior to the substantive analysis, it is considered essential that the preliminary question of the applicability of the new maintenance instruments to cases involving surrogacy be addressed. The problem of surrogacy in the context of maintenance was not considered during the negotiations of the new maintenance instruments, and, as a result, there is no reference to surrogacy in either the Convention or the Protocol. Nevertheless, the core scope of the Convention includes 'maintenance obligations arising from a parent-child relationship towards a person under the age of 21 years'[5] so the key question is whether there is a parent-child relationship between the creditor and the child. This will be subject to a preliminary question on parentage which is not governed by the Convention.[6] However, Central Authorities are required to provide assistance in establishing parentage where necessary for the recovery of maintenance,[7]and establishment of parentage is part of 'free legal assistance' under Article 15 of the Convention.[8] Assistance on the problem of parentage can be sought under Article 6(2)(h) in relation to an application under Article 10(1)(c) or as a request for a specific measure under Article 7.[9] Article 7(1) expressly covers requests for specific measures under Article 6(2)(h) which includes requests for the establishment of

[3] Hague Convention on the International Recovery of Child Support and Other Forms of Family Maintenance, 23 November 2007 (Hague Maintenance Convention).

[4] Protocol on the Law Applicable to Maintenance Obligations, 23 November 2007 (Protocol).

[5] Hague Maintenance Convention, Art 2(1)(a).

[6] More generally on the problem of preliminary questions (alternative terminology 'incidental questions') see eg P Beaumont and P McEleavy, *Anton's Private International Law*, 3rd edn (Edinburgh, W Green, 2011) paras 4.71–4.79; S Goessl, 'Preliminary Questions in EU Private International Law' (2012) *Journal of Private International Law* 63–76; and T Schmidt, 'The Incidental Question in Private International Law' (1992) 233 *Hague Academy Collected Courses* 315–33.

[7] A Borrás and J Degeling, 'Explanatory Report on the Convention on the International Recovery of Child Support and Other Forms of Family Maintenance' (Explanatory Report on the Convention), November 2009, para 385, available at www.hcch.net/upload/expl38e.pdf (accessed January 2014).

[8] Hague Maintenance Convention, Art 6(2)(*h*).

[9] Explanatory Report on the Convention (n 7) para 172.

parentage.[10] Article 10 sets out specific categories of applications available to a creditor in a requesting State. Among these categories is an application for 'establishment of a decision in a requested State where there is no existing decision, including where necessary the establishment of parentage'.[11] The establishment of parentage under the Convention can only be requested in conjunction with a request to establish a maintenance decision; that is, where a decision on the establishment of maintenance cannot be reached for lack of a proof of parentage. Indeed, 'a separate application for the establishment of parentage is not available under the Convention.'[12] The actual procedure for the establishment of parentage in relation to Articles 6(2)(h) and 10(1)(c) will be subject to the domestic law of the requested Contracting State.[13]

Nevertheless, an application under Article 10(1)(c) is subject to paragraph 3 of the same Article which states that 'applications in paragraphs 1 *c)* to *f)* and 2 *b)* and *c)* shall be subject to the jurisdictional rules applicable in the requested State.'[14] Consequently, jurisdictional rules of the forum may restrict the situations in which an application for establishment, including establishment of parentage, might be made.[15] Nevertheless, such a limitation seems highly unlikely as it is normal for many countries to allow applications for establishment in the debtor's jurisdiction.[16] Indeed, it is the general ground of jurisdiction in most States—*actor sequitur forum rei*. There are obvious reasons of speed and efficiency behind this jurisdictional ground as it is not necessary to comply with international requirements for the service of documents on the respondent or employ procedures for the recognition and enforcement of foreign judgments.[17]

Another important rule in relation to the preliminary question of parentage can be found in Chapter V of the Convention which deals with the problem of recognition and

[10] See ibid para 193. Art 7(1) imposes on the requested Central Authority an obligation to 'take such measures as are appropriate if satisfied that they are necessary to assist a potential applicant in making an application under Article 10 or in determining whether such an application should be initiated.'

[11] Hague Maintenance Convention, Art 10(1)(c). The requested Central Authority will be obliged to take 'all appropriate measures' to 'provide assistance in establishing parentage'. Explanatory Report on the Convention (n 7) para 172. See also para 244 stating that: 'If parentage must be determined before the maintenance decision can be established, that is authorised by sub-paragraph *c)*.'

[12] Ibid para 247. The Explanatory Report also sheds light on the reasons behind this approach. It explains that Art 10(1)(c) represents a compromise between those delegates who advocated a separate application for the establishment of parentage and those who advocated a total exclusion of parentage issues from the scope of the Convention. Various reasons were presented by the latter delegates in support of their approach, including that 'establishing parentage for the restricted purposes of maintenance was against public policy in their jurisdictions, or that the *erga omnes* effect of a decision on parentage prevailed in their jurisdiction, meaning that if parentage is established, it is established for all purposes, not just maintenance.' Ibid.

[13] Contracting States are expected to indicate in their respective country profiles how the establishment of parentage will be carried out. Explanatory Report on the Convention (n 7) para 252. A copy of the Country Profile form can be found on the Hague Conference website at www.hcch.net/upload/wop/maint2011pd03e.pdf (accessed January 2014) (see 44 of the form 'Establishment of Parentage'). However, no country profiles have been uploaded yet. See www.hcch.net/index_en.php?act=conventions.publications&dtid=42&cid=131 (accessed January 2014). For a summary of the different approaches to the issue of parentage in relation to maintenance see P Lortie, 'Parentage and International Child Support: Responses to the 2002 Questionnaire and an Analysis of the Issues' Prel Doc No 4, April 2003, available at www.hcch.net/upload/wop/maint_pd04e.pdf (accessed January 2014) ('Parentage and International Child Support').

[14] Para 3 also directs that the proceedings be governed by the forum's procedural and substantive rules: 'Save as otherwise provided in this Convention, the applications in paragraphs 1 and 2 shall be determined under the law of the requested State'. See also Explanatory Report on the Convention (n 7) para 245.

[15] Ibid para 245.

[16] Ibid para 246.

[17] Ibid.

enforcement. Specifically, Article 19(2) states that 'if a decision does not relate solely to a maintenance obligation, the effect of this Chapter [Chapter V] is limited to the parts of the decision which concern maintenance obligations.' Consequently, if a decision on maintenance also includes a decision on the establishment of parentage, the maintenance obligation can be recognised and enforced independently from the question of parentage. The decision on the establishment of parentage does not necessarily have to be recognised and enforced under the Convention.[18]

The scope of the Protocol in Article 1(1) is even broader than the scope of the Convention referring to a 'family relationship, parentage … including a maintenance obligation in respect of a child regardless of the marital status of the parents.' Article 1(2) goes further and gives the Protocol application to decisions on maintenance obligations even if the underlying relationship referred to in Article 1(1) does not exist.

The law applicable to parentage is not governed by the Protocol.[19] Given the Protocol's silence, the Explanatory Report to the Protocol recommends that States apply the law designated to govern the maintenance obligation also to the preliminary issue of the existence of parentage.[20] The Report, however, acknowledges that this solution is not binding on the Contracting States and that they may instead resolve the preliminary issue by applying the law designated by the forum's conflicts rules.[21]

It is acknowleged that given the lack of reference to surrogacy in the Convention or the Protocol, doubts might arise over the applicability of the instruments to cases involving surrogacy. Undoubtedly, given the role of domestic law in relation to the establishment of parentage as a preliminary question to maintenance, some potential maintenance relationships will not be given effect in some systems. Similarly, maintenance obligations established in one system might be refused recognition in other systems on the grounds of public policy; although, as of yet, there is no evidence as to how these issues will be approached by courts in different jurisdictions. Nevertheless, it is believed that as far as the private international law issues of indirect jurisdiction, applicable law and recognition and enforcement are concerned, and based on the wording of the instruments as analysed above, the Convention and the Protocol are both applicable to maintenance cases involving surrogacy.

III. Domestic Approaches to Surrogacy

Domestic legal responses to surrogacy differ widely between jurisdictions. Generally speaking, some countries decided to regulate surrogacy, some to prohibit it and some to ignore it. Jurisdictions that chose to regulate surrogacy further differ on, for example, whether surrogate

[18] Ibid para 438. See also 'Parentage and International Child Support' (n 13) paras 34–38.

[19] See A Bonomi, 'Explanatory Report on the Protocol of 23 November 2007 on the Law Applicable to Maintenance Obligations' (Explanatory Report on the Protocol), October 2009, para 24, available at www.hcch.net/upload/expl39e.pdf (accessed January 2014).

[20] Ibid. This recommendation is based on the interpretation that had been suggested for the 1956 and 1973 Maintenance Obligations Conventions 'whereby the law designated to govern the maintenance obligation can also apply to the preliminary issue of the existence of a family relationship within the meaning of Article 1(1)'. Bonomi (ibid) refers to the Explanatory Report on the Maintenance Obligations Conventions (Enforcement-Applicable Law) of 1973, drawn up by M Verwilghen, paras 125 et seq.

[21] Explanatory Report on the Protocol (n 19).

mothers should be allowed to receive payments beyond reasonable pregnancy-related expenses (known as 'commercial surrogacy') or whether surrogacy agreements should be legally enforceable.

In a more specific way, according to their domestic approaches to surrogacy, countries can be grouped into three categories: 'anti-surrogacy' jurisdictions, jurisdictions with a relatively neutral approach to surrogacy, and 'surrogacy-friendly' jurisdictions. The term 'anti-surrogacy jurisdictions' refers to countries where surrogacy in both its forms—altruistic and commercial—is outlawed. This group includes for example Germany, France, China and certain US States.

Countries with a relatively neutral approach to surrogacy comprise two alternative approaches. First, the term refers to countries where surrogacy is regulated whilst only altruistic surrogacy is permitted. Two distinct regulatory approaches can be identified among these countries: statutes which require court/special committee pre-approval of the surrogacy arrangement (eg Greece, South Africa, Israel and the US State of Virginia), and statutes which do not require such pre-approval (eg the UK and Australia—New South Wales, Queensland, South Australia and the Australian Capital Territory). Second, the category of countries with a relatively neutral approach to surrogacy covers jurisdictions where both forms of surrogacy (ie altruistic or commercial) remain unregulated (eg Belgium, Ireland, Japan and some US States).

Typically, in both, the 'anti-surrogacy' jurisdictions and jurisdictions with a relatively neutral approach to surrogacy, legal motherhood in surrogacy cases follows the general rule for the establishment of legal motherhood, that is, the 'birth' or 'gestational' rule. According to this approach, a woman who gives birth to a child is viewed as the legal mother of the child, even if she is biologically unrelated to the child. In relation to altruistic surrogacy, the situation is slightly different in some of the countries that require formal pre-approval of the surrogacy arrangement. In these jurisdictions the official pre-approval of the surrogacy arrangement will result in an automatic acquisition of legal parenthood by the intended parents from the moment of the birth of the child.[22]

The final category of countries is the 'surrogacy-friendly' jurisdictions. The term refers to countries where commercial surrogacy is legal and is performed on a relatively large scale. In relation to legal motherhood, these countries depart from the traditional birth rule in surrogacy cases, including commercial surrogacy arrangements. Instead, alternative approaches that can be referred to as the intent test and the genetics test are applied. According to the intent test, the intent of the parties as expressed in the surrogacy agreement controls the determination of the legal motherhood (or more generally, legal parenthood). When applying the genetics test, the child's legal mother is determined on the basis of genetics.

IV. Cross-Border Surrogacy

The variety of domestic responses to surrogacy has led to widespread *forum shopping* where infertile couples seeking to have a child through surrogacy travel from one country

[22] Examples of such jurisdictions are Greece, South Africa and the US State of Virginia. For more details see Trimmings and Beaumont (n 1) 458–60.

to another, purposely choosing 'surrogacy-friendly' jurisdictions as their destinations. Indeed, 'surrogacy-friendly' countries have become 'hubs' of the international commercial surrogacy market, attracting intended parents from both 'anti-surrogacy' jurisdictions and jurisdictions with a relatively neutral approach to surrogacy.

As already mentioned, there is a complete void in the international regulation of surrogacy arrangements. In the absence of a global legislative response, highly complex legal problems arise from these arrangements. Among these problems, the most prevalent are the question of legal parenthood and the nationality of the child. In addition to these difficulties, other legal hurdles can easily be envisaged. Undoubtedly, a cross-border maintenance dispute is one of them. Although available case-law indicates that there has not yet been cross-border litigation over maintenance in the context of surrogacy, theoretically, there are three broadly defined situations which can result in such a claim. First, situations where the surrogate mother decides to keep the child and seeks child maintenance from the intended father and/or the intended mother; second, situations where the intended father and/or the intended mother make a claim for child maintenance against the surrogate mother; and third, situations where, following a breakdown of the intended parents' relationship, one of the intended parents seeks child support from the other intended parent or from the surrogate mother. Admittedly, there is a wide variety of potential sub-scenarios within these three categories, depending on, in particular, the type of surrogacy arrangement (ie traditional or gestational surrogacy) and the genetic make-up of the child. Nevertheless, it must be pointed out that, given the dynamics of the international surrogacy market, some of the cases that can be foreseen are more realistic than others.

A. Three Hypothetical Case Scenarios

The following part of the chapter examines three hypothetical cases of cross-border maintenance claims in surrogacy cases.

Scenario 1: The Surrogate Mother Decides to Keep the Child and Seeks Child Maintenance from the Intended Father

In a domestic context, this scenario arose for the first time in the UK in 2011 in a surrogacy case of *CW v NT & Anor.*[23] The case involved a traditional, altruistic surrogacy arrangement. The intended parents, Mr and Mrs W, entered into an informal agreement with a single woman, Miss N, after meeting her through a surrogacy website. The surrogate mother was inseminated with the intended father's sperm and the parties agreed that the surrogate mother would be paid £10,000 in expenses. However, during the pregnancy, the surrogate mother decided to keep the baby and refused to continue with the agreement. Under English law, the surrogate mother and the intended father were considered to be the child's legal parents. The intended father applied for a residence order, but his application was refused by the High Court and a residence order was made in favour of the surrogate

[23] [2011] EWHC 33 (Fam) (21 January 2011).

mother. Following this decision, the intended father was ordered by the Child Support Agency to pay £568 in child support every month.[24]

For the purposes of this analysis, let us assume that the case occurred in a cross-border setting: Intended parents, habitually resident in Country X, entered into a traditional altruistic surrogacy arrangement with a surrogate habitually resident in Country Y. The intended parents come from an anti-surrogacy jurisdiction, whilst Country Y is a jurisdiction with a relatively neutral approach to surrogacy where surrogacy is regulated and only altruistic arrangements are permitted, and no formal pre-approval of the surrogacy arrangement is required[25] (comparable to the UK).[26] Although altruistic surrogacy is lawful in Country Y, surrogacy agreements are not enforceable. The legal mother of a child born to a surrogate in Country Y is always the birth mother (whether or not she is also the genetic mother). As the surrogate mother is single, the intended father, being the genetic parent, is viewed in Country Y as the legal father of the child. Although Country X is an anti-surrogacy jurisdiction, general rules on legal parenthood (in particular the rule that the woman who gave birth to a child is viewed as the child's legal mother) are identical with the rules applicable in Country Y.

Halfway through the pregnancy the surrogate mother changes her mind and decides to keep the baby. The surrogate mother is granted custody of the child in Country Y and decides to seek maintenance from the intended father who is habitually resident in Country X. Assuming that both countries are Contracting States to the Hague Maintenance Convention and to the Protocol, the surrogate mother can pursue two alternative avenues:

(a) she may seek establishment of a maintenance order in Country X (Article 10(1)(c) of the Hague Maintenance Convention in combination with Article 4(3) of the Protocol).

or

(b) she may seek recognition and enforcement in Country X of a maintenance order made in Country Y (Chapter V of the Hague Maintenance Convention).

a. Establishment of a Maintenance Order in Country X

At the outset of the analysis it ought to be pointed out that the jurisdictional rules of the forum (ie Country X) may restrict the possibility of making an application for establishment of maintenance.[27] Nevertheless, such a limitation is unlikely.[28] Therefore, assuming that the forum allows an application for establishment, the maintenance obligation will be governed, in accordance with Article 4(3) of the Protocol, by the law of Country X as the law of the forum. However, if no maintenance obligation exists under this law (ie in the words of the Protocol, the surrogate mother is unable, by virtue of this law, to obtain maintenance from the intended father), the law of the habitual residence of the surrogate

[24] A Ahmad, 'Surrogate Mother who Kept Baby Wins Claim for Support', *Bionews* 18 April 2011, available at www.bionews.org.uk/page_93040.asp (accessed January 2014).

[25] See section III above.

[26] For a detailed analysis of the UK approach to surrogacy see M Wells Greco, 'National Report on Surrogacy: United Kingdom' in Trimmings and Beaumont (n 1) 367–86.

[27] Hague Maintenance Convention, Art 10(3). See relevant discussion in section II above.

[28] Hague Maintenance Convention, Art 10(3). See also Explanatory Report on the Convention (n 1) para 246.

mother, ie Country Y will apply.[29] Nevertheless, if this is the case, it will be open to Country X to exclude the applicable law where its effects are manifestly contrary to the public policy of the forum.[30]

b. Recognition and Enforcement in Country X of a Maintenance Order Made in Country Y

Alternatively, the surrogate mother can apply for a maintenance order in Country Y. In this case, the maintenance obligation will be governed, in accordance with Article 3(1) of the Protocol, by the law of Country Y as the law of the State of the habitual residence of the creditor. Assuming that such a maintenance obligation exists under the law of Country Y, the surrogate mother will then seek, in accordance with Article 20 of the Hague Maintenance Convention, the recognition and enforcement in Country X of the maintenance order made in Country Y. The recognition and enforcement may, however, be refused on the grounds of public policy—that is, if it is manifestly incompatible with the public policy of the requested State (Country X).[31] Additionally, Article 20(2) allows for a reservation but this is coupled with a duty to establish in Article 20(4) and (5).

It is thought that this is a relatively simple case where the public policy defence is not likely to succeed in either of the alternative avenues (establishment or recognition). The surrogate mother and the intended father are both the genetic and the legal parents of the child. Most, if not all, legal systems acknowledge the genetic father's maintenance obligation towards his child.[32] The fact that the child was conceived in the context of a traditional surrogacy arrangement is irrelevant, especially if the arrangement was altruistic. It is suggested that the situation would remain the same even if the arrangement involved gestational surrogacy, that is, a donor or the intended mother's ovum was used instead of the surrogate mother's ovum. The 'birth rule', which is applicable as the general rule for the establishment of legal motherhood in both Country X and Country Y[33] is clear: the woman who gives birth to a child is the child's legal mother. Consequently, even if the surrogate mother was not genetically related to the child, it is believed that she would still be entitled to seek establishment of maintenance or recognition of a maintenance order without the public policy defence being likely to succeed.[34]

Scenario 2: The Intended Father and/or the Intended Mother Make a Claim for Child Maintenance Against the Surrogate Mother

A different conclusion on the applicability of public policy might, however, be reached if one of the countries involved is a 'surrogacy-friendly' jurisdiction. Nevertheless, the facts

[29] Protocol, Art 4(3). If the surrogate mother has no right to maintenance for her child from the biological intended father under the law of the forum or her habitual residence she can seek maintenance under the law of the common nationality of herself and the intended father if they have one (Art 4(4))—but on these facts it is highly unlikely that they will have a common nationality.

[30] Protocol, Art 13.

[31] Hague Maintenance Convention, Art 22(a). Although Art 22 contains six alternative reasons for refusing recognition and enforcement of a decision on maintenance, only the public policy ground is dealt with in the analysis below given the relevance of this ground in the context of surrogacy arrangements.

[32] This consideration excludes sperm donors.

[33] See section III above.

[34] The Explanatory Report to the Convention makes it clear that '[t]he public policy exception should in any case have only a very limited application'. See Explanatory Report on the Convention (n 7) para 245.

of the case will first need to be adjusted. The reason is that in 'surrogacy-friendly' countries surrogacy arrangements (including commercial surrogacy) are in principle enforceable and therefore the scenario of a surrogate mother keeping the child and claiming maintenance from the intended father is not entirely realistic. (She would have to abscond with the child and obtain habitual residence in a 'surrogacy non-friendly' jurisdiction first). So let us assume that intended parents habitually resident in Country A, which is an anti-surrogacy jurisdiction, enter into a commercial surrogacy arrangement with a single surrogate mother habitually resident in Country B which is a 'surrogacy-friendly' jurisdiction. An embryo is created using the genetic material of the intended parents. The surrogate mother is therefore genetically unrelated to the child (ie it is a gestational surrogacy case). After the baby is born, the surrogate mother hands it over to the intended parents. Country B, being a 'surrogacy-friendly' jurisdiction considers the intended parents to be the legal parents of the child. Back home in Country A, however, only the intended father will be regarded as the legal father of the child.[35] Although the intended mother is also genetically related to the child, the law of Country A will not view her as the legal mother.[36] Country A, as an anti-surrogacy jurisdiction, will apply the birth rule to the establishment of legal motherhood and will therefore consider the surrogate as the child's legal mother (despite the lack of a genetic link). Against this background, the intended father decides to seek child maintenance from the surrogate mother. Assuming that both countries are Contracting States to the Hague Maintenance Convention and the Protocol, two avenues will be open to the intended father: (1) to seek establishment of a maintenance order in Country B (Article 10(1)(c) of the Hague Maintenance Convention in combination with Article 4(3) of the Protocol); or (2) to seek recognition and enforcement in Country B of a maintenance

[35] Although this is a general expectation, admittedly, there are nuances in the approach to legal parenthood in different anti-surrogacy jurisdictions. In particualr, the genetic link between the child and the intended father might not always be sufficient per se for the establishment of legal parentage. See eg two recent decisions of the French Supreme Court, both dated 13 September 2013, as reported and analysed by C Bidaud-Garon and H Fulchiron, 'Dans les limbes du droit, À propos de la situation des enfants nés à l'étranger avec l'assistance d'une mère porteuse' (2013) *Dalloz* 2349–57; C Petit, 'Statut juridique des enfants nés d'une gestation pour autrui réalisée à l'étranger' (2013) *Dalloz* 2377–82; and M Fabre-Magnan, 'Le refus de transcription : la Cour de cassation gardienne du Droit' (2013) *Dalloz* 2384–88.

[36] There are, nevertheless, rare exceptions to this general rule in some anti-surrogacy jurisdictions. See eg a decision of the Court of Appeal of Bari, Italy, dated 13 February 2009 as reported in (2009) *Rivista di diritto internazionale privato e processuale* 699. For comments on this case see C Campiglio, 'Lo stato di figlio nato da contratto internazionale di maternità' (2009) *Rivista di diritto internazionale privato e processuale* 599; and R Baratta, 'La reconnaissance internationale des situations juridiques personnelles et familiales' (2011) 348 *Hague Academy Collected Courses* 396–98. It might be noted that a comparable observation can be made in relation to countries with a relatively neutral approach to surrogacy where the general expectation of the indended mother not being viewed as the legal mother of the child applies in the same way as in anti-surrogacy jurisdictions (for more details, including a comment on the exceptions to this general rule see section III above). See eg decisions of the Austrian Constitutional Court (Verfassungsgerichtshof) No B 13/11-10 of 14 December 2011 and No B 99/12 UA of 11 October 2012 where both intended parents were recognised as the legal parents of children born through surrogacy abroad. For analysis of these decisions see B Lurger, 'Das österreichische IPR bei Leihmutterschaft im Ausland-das Kindeswohl zwischen Anerkennung, europäischen Grundrechten und inländischem Leimutterschaftsverbot' (2013) *IPrax* 282–89; and European Parliament, 'A Comparative Study on the Regime of Surrogacv in EU Member States' ('Comparative Study on the Regime of Surrogacy') 2013, 101–04, available at www.eurogender.eige.europa.eu/sites/default/files/EST93673.pdf (accessed January 2014). See also a decision of the High Court of Ireland in the case of *M.R & Anor v An tArd Chlaraitheoir & Ors* [2013] IEHC 91 where the Court found that the intended mother was also the legal mother of twins born through a surrogacy arrangement entered into between the intended parents and the intended mother's sister. The intended parents were also the genetic parents of the children and there was no dispute between them and the surrogate as to the question of legal parentage. For a short comment on this case see 'Comparative Study on the Regime of Surrogacy' 71.

order made in Country A (Chapter V of the Hague Maintenance Convention). It is expected that, given the underlying differences in approaches towards legal motherhood in surrogacy cases and towards the enforceability of surrogacy arrangements between Country A and Country B, the intended father is in both cases bound to stumble on public policy. Indeed, it is likely that Country B would consider it manifestly contrary to public policy to order a surrogate mother who is not the legal mother in the eyes of its law to support a child who is looked after by the intended parents whom the forum views as the legal parents of the child. It must be pointed out that it is not envisaged to be a common scenario that an intended father would seek maintenance from the surrogate mother. In most cases, the principal motivation for the surrogate mother to enter into a surrogacy arrangement is the financial incentive. Consequently, given her financial position, it is unlikely that the intended father would sue her for maintenance.

Scenario 3: Following a Breakdown of the Intended Parents' Relationship, One of the Intended Parents Seeks Child Support from the Other Intended Parent

A more realistic scenario of a maintenance claim arises where the intended parents split in the course of or after the surrogacy process and one of them claims child support from the other. For the purposes of this analysis, let's assume that, in an initially purely domestic commercial surrogacy arrangement, an embryo is created using a donor sperm and a donor egg. All parties are habitually resident in one 'surrogacy-friendly' jurisdiction, Country C. Country C is a common law jurisdiction comparable to the US State of California.[37] In Country C, commercial surrogacy operates on the basis of judicial precedent. Several decades ago, the Supreme Court of Country C developed the 'intent-based' approach to the establishment of legal parenthood in surrogacy cases, and judicially confirmed the enforceability of surrogacy arrangements.[38] In practice, the intent of the parties is often formalised through a 'pre-birth parentage order' which declares the intended parents as the legal parents before the child is born.[39] Once the 'pre-birth parentage order' has become final, it is enforceable against all parties who participated in the proceedings. This implies

[37] For analysis of the US approach to surrogacy, including California, see S Snyder, 'National Report on Surrogacy: United States of America' in Trimmings and Beaumont (n 1) 387–96. See also Trimmings and Beaumont (n 1) 449–51.

[38] As early as in 1993, the California Supreme Court, in the case of *Johnson v Calvert* developed the 'intent-based' approach to the establishment of legal parenthood in surrogacy cases, and endorsed the enforceability of surrogacy arrangements. *Johnson v Calvert* 5 Cal 4th 84, 19 Cal Rptr 2d 494, 851 P2d 776 (cert denied 510 US 874, 114 S Ct 206, 126 L Ed 2d 163) (Cal 1993). For analysis of the case, see eg D Morgan, 'A Surrogacy Issue: Who is the Other Mother?' (1994) *International Journal of Law and the Family* 386; A Vorzimer, 'The Egg Donor and Surrogacy Controversy: Legal Issues Surrounding Representation of Parties to an Egg Donor and Surrogacy Contract' (1999–2000) *Whittier Law Review* 415, 415–17; L Behm, 'Legal, Moral and International Perspectives on Surrogate Motherhood: The Call for a Uniform Regulatory Scheme in the United States' (1999) *DePaul Journal of Health Care Law* 557, 572–77; K Rothenberg, 'Gestational Surrogacy and the Health Care Provider: Put Part of the "IVF Genie" Back Into the Bottle' (1990) *Law, Medicine & Health Care* 345, 345–46.

For a detailed analysis of legal parentage and surrogacy see K Trimmings and P Beaumont, 'Parentage and Surrogacy' in J Scherpe (ed), *Research Handbook on European Family Law* (Cheltenham, Edward Elgar Publishing, 2014, forthcoming).

[39] For a comment on the concept and applicability of the 'pre-birth parentage order' in the US see S Snyder and M Byrn, 'The Use of Prebirth Parentage Orders on Surrogacy Proceedings' (2005–06) *Family Law Quarterly* 633, 634. The authors, however, explain that pre-birth parentage orders are not appropriate in all surrogacy scenarios. In the light of the decision in *Moschetta*, a successful outcome is likely to depend on the genetic make-up

that, in the eyes of the law of Country C the intended parents will be considered as the legal parents of the child, although neither of them is genetically related to the child. The surrogate mother will be viewed only as the 'carrier' with no legal obligations once the child has been handed over to the intended parents. Following the birth of the child, the intended parents split. The intended mother then removes the child to her native country (Country D), which is an 'anti-surrogacy' jurisdiction, where she becomes habitually resident. The intended father remains in Country C and refuses to take any responsibility for the child. The intended mother therefore seeks child maintenance from the intended father. She relies on Article 10(1)(c) of the Hague Maintenance Convention and seeks the establishment of maintenance in Country C. It is submitted that, using this avenue, she should be able to succeed. Although neither she nor the intended father is regarded as the legal parent in Country D, they are both regarded as the legal parents in Country C, in accordance with the 'pre-birth' order. Country C as a common law jurisdiction will not ratify the Protocol and Country C will apply its own law as the law of the forum to the maintenance obligation.[40] (Nevertheless, in practical terms, the applicable law is the same as it would be under Article 4(3) of the Protocol if the Protocol applied.) It is possible that, as the intended father is not the genetic father of the child, he will attempt to dispute the existence of his legal parenthood so the issue of parentage will arise as a preliminary question in the course of the maintenance proceedings.[41] This question will again be governed by the law of Country C as the law of the forum. As the intended father is viewed as the legal father in Country C, it is believed that he is more than likely to be ordered to pay child maintenance by the court of Country C, and this is irrespective of the fact that there is no genetic link between him and the child.

Alternatively, the intended mother might decide to seek a maintenance order in Country D and then get this order recognised and enforced in Country C. It is thought that this avenue is, however, not likely to achieve the desired outcome for the following reasons. The intended mother's application for establishment of maintenance before a court of Country D will be governed, in accordance with Article 3(1) of the Protocol, by the law of Country D as the law of the State of the habitual residence of the creditor. It can again be expected that the intended father will challenge the existence of his legal parenthood in the course of the maintenance proceedings so the issue of parentage will again arise as a preliminary question. The law applicable to parentage is not governed by the Protocol;[42] however, the Explanatory Report to the Protocol recommends that States apply the law designated to govern the maintenance obligation also to the preliminary issue of the existence of a parentage.[43] Assuming that the law of Country D applies to the main issue of maintenance and that Country D follows the recommendation of the Explanatory Report to apply to the preliminary issue of parentage the same law as applicable to the main question, the

of the child. Ibid. (For an extracted version of the article, see S Snyder and M Bryn, 'The Use of Prebirth Parentage Orders in Surrogacy Proceedings' (2006) *GPSolo (ABA General Practice, Solo & Small Firm Division)* 14).

[40] Explanatory Report on the Protocol (n 19).

[41] Ibid para 24.

[42] Ibid. See relevant comment in section II above.

[43] Explanatory Report on the Protocol (n 19). This recommendation is based on the interpretation that had been suggested for the 1956 and 1973 Maintenance Obligations Conventions 'whereby the law designated to govern the maintenance obligation can also apply to the preliminary issue of the existence of a family relationship within the meaning of Article 1(1)'. Bonomi refers to the Explanatory Report on the Maintenance Obligations Conventions (Enforcement-Applicable Law) of 1973, drawn up by M Verwilghen, paras 125 et seq.

establishment of parentage will be governed by the law of Country D. As no parentage exists between the presumed debtor and the child under the law of Country D, it is suggested that no maintenance obligation exists either.[44]

V. Conclusion

The aim of this contribution was to explore in a very preliminary way some of the legal problems that might arise in the area of maintenance in cases involving cross-border surrogacy. As the chapter has demonstrated, the interface between cross-border surrogacy and maintenance is likely to produce extremely complex scenarios. Although these scenarios have not yet been tested before national courts; given the expanding nature of cross-border surrogacy, it is only a matter of time before courts are confronted with such issues.

Given the primarily analytical nature of this chapter, the conclusions arrived at in the above three case scenarios should be viewed as principally theoretical. Undoubtedly, further research is needed in this area. A work that combined a substantive comparative law approach with private international law would be particularly desirable. This method would allow for a detailed examination of the nuances in the approach to the concepts of legal parenthood and maintenance in different jurisdictions, and the practical effect of these nuances on cases arising in the cross-border context.

[44] Nevertheless, this conclusion should not be regarded as definite as variations in the approach might occur. See eg decisions of the French Supreme Court in two cross-border surrogacy cases, both dated 6 April 2011: Cour de Cassation, Chambre Civile 1, 6 April 2011, 09-66.486, Publié au bulletin, and Cour de cassation, civile, Chambre civile 1, 6 April 2011, 10-19.053, Publié au bulletin. In these judgments, the Court expressed the view that the refusal to transcribe foreign birth certificates stating the intended parents as the legal parents did not deprive the children of their legal link with either their father or their mother as had been established abroad. Although the exact meaning of the decisions is not entirely clear, the statement does cast doubt on the general validity of the above conclusion. For analyses of these decisions see eg D Berthiau and L Brunet, 'L'ordre public au préjudice de l'enfant' (2001) *Dalloz* 1522–29; and P Hammje, 'Maternité pour autrui, possession d'état et état civil' (2011) *Revue Critique De Droit International Privé* 722.

Part Three

International and European Union Matters

17

Developing an Electronic Case Management and Communication System for the 2007 Hague Child Support Convention and 2009 EU Maintenance Regulation

The iSupport Project

PHILIPPE LORTIE

I. Background

A. History

On 23 November 2007, after more than four years of negotiations, more than 70 States,[1] as well as the then European Community, successfully concluded the Hague Convention on the International Recovery of Child Support and Other Forms of Family Maintenance (the 2007 Convention),[2] as well as its Protocol on the Law Applicable to Maintenance Obligations (the 2007 Protocol).[3] Both instruments employ rules of private international law to build bridges at the international level between the different domestic legal systems for the recovery

[1] The following Members of the Hague Conference have signed the Final Act: Albania, Argentina, Australia, Austria, Belgium, Brazil, Bulgaria, Canada, Chile, China, Croatia, Czech Republic, Denmark, Ecuador, Egypt, Estonia, European Community, Finland, France, Germany, Greece, Hungary, Ireland, Israel, Italy, Japan, Republic of Korea, Latvia, Lithuania, Luxembourg, Mexico, Monaco, Morocco, Netherlands, New Zealand, Norway, Peru, Poland, Portugal, Romania, Russian Federation, Serbia, Slovakia, Slovenia, South Africa, Spain, Sri Lanka, Sweden, Switzerland, Ukraine, United Kingdom of Great Britain and Northern Ireland, United States of America, Uruguay and Venezuela. The following Observers (non-Member States) have also signed the Final Act: Algeria, Burkina Faso, Colombia, Costa Rica, Dominican Republic, Guatemala, Haiti, India, Indonesia, Iran, Philippines and Viet Nam. The following intergovernmental organisations attended: Commonwealth Secretariat and Mercosur. The following non-governmental organisations attended: International Society of Family Law (ISFL), International Association of Women Judges (IAWJ), International Bar Association (IBA), Defence for Children International (DCI), National Child Support Enforcement Association (NCSEA), International Social Services (ISS) and the International Union of Latin Notaries (UINL).

[2] The text of the 2007 Convention can be found on the Hague Conference website at www.hcch.net under 'Conventions' then 'No 38' (accessed April 2014).

[3] The text of the 2007 Protocol can be found on the Hague Conference website, under 'Conventions' then 'No 39' (accessed April 2014).

of maintenance. A year later, the European Union concluded the Council Regulation (EC) No 4/2009 of 18 December 2008 on Jurisdiction, Applicable Law, Recognition and Enforcement of Decisions and Co-operation in Matters relating to Maintenance Obligations (the 2009 Regulation)[4] which provides for a similar cooperation system as the 2007 Convention.

B. Statistics

The 2007 Convention and the 2009 Regulation are designed to offer children and other family members a simpler, swifter and more cost-effective international system of recovery of maintenance. Hundreds of thousands of children and other family members worldwide could benefit from these instruments. They will also contribute to the reduction of welfare/social security dependency. Statistics show that in countries such as Australia, Canada, New Zealand and the United States, there is on average one international child support case per 1,000 inhabitants. In addition, based on a rough extrapolation of statistics from the 1980 Hague Child Abduction Convention[5] and the previously mentioned statistics, it appears that there are between 500 and 1,000 international child support cases per international child abduction case in these four countries. Therefore, based on the 2003 Statistical Report on the 1980 Child Abduction Convention,[6] there could be between 240,000 and 480,000 child support cases between Australia, Canada, New Zealand, the UK and the United States. Based on these statistics, there could be between 110,000 and 220,000 cases between these States and the Members of the European Union (excluding the UK). Furthermore, there could be between 200,000 and 400,000 cases between the 28 Members of the European Union. Finally, altogether, these 32 States could have between themselves between 550,000 and 1,100,000 child support cases. However, at this time the 2007 Convention is not in force for any of these States.[7] On the other hand, the 2009 Regulation is applicable between all European Member States (with the exception of Denmark only insofar as it modifies the Brussels I Regulation) but the Regulation only covers decisions rendered after 18 June 2011.

C. General Description of the Project

The 2007 Convention and the 2009 Regulation are built on a solid system of administrative cooperation according to which the Central Authorities transmit to each other applications for establishment, recognition and enforcement, and modification of maintenance decisions. Access to child support procedures set up by the Convention and Regulation is virtually free of charge.[8] The Convention and the Regulation are flexible instruments which include thorough systems of recognition and enforcement adapted to all national systems of recovery of maintenance, whether these systems are court based or administrative

[4] [2009] OJ L7/1. The text of the 2009 Regulation can be found on the European Judicial Atlas in Civil Matters website at www.ec.europa.eu/justice_home/judicialatlascivil/html/index_en.htm, under 'Family Law' (accessed January 2014).

[5] The text of the 1980 Convention can be found on the Hague Conference website at www.hcch.net under 'Conventions' then 'No 28' (accessed April 2014).

[6] See the Hague Conference website at www.hcch.net, under 'Conventions', 'No 28' then 'Practical information documents' (accessed April 2014).

[7] The 2007 Convention will come into force for the European Union on 1 August 2014 since the European Union approved the Convention on 9 April 2014.

[8] See Arts 8 and 14–17 of the 2007 Convention, and Arts 44–47 and Recitals 32 and 36–37 of the 2009 Regulation.

based.[9] They offer modern solutions regarding enforcement and allow public bodies to benefit from these systems.

The Permanent Bureau (the Secretariat) of the Hague Conference on Private International Law is now seeking the support and assistance of interested Members and of its Member Organisation,[10] as part of its Supplementary Budget process, to facilitate the further development of an electronic case management and Internet-based communication system (the 'iSupport' system) in support of this new international treaty framework.[11] The collaboration of service providers (information technology vendors and banks) with an interest in the development and implementation of such systems, and possibly their operation and maintenance, is also called upon.

As the 2007 Convention, 2009 Regulation and 2007 Protocol build bridges at the international level between the different domestic legal systems for the recovery of child support and other forms of family maintenance, the iSupport system will provide an electronic bridge between interested States to communicate, process data and transfer payments under these international instruments. This cooperation could be made possible by the electronic migration of the required Convention, Regulation and Protocol data from the domestic case management systems, where they exist, to the international system and vice versa. The iSupport system will also provide the beginning of an electronic solution to those States and organisations that have not yet embraced e-government practices in this area. It may also inspire them to develop domestic systems in the future.[12] It is the intention of the Permanent Bureau to facilitate the development of the iSupport system in an inclusive manner, with all interested States and organisations, as it did for the development of the 2007 Convention and 2007 Protocol, in accordance with its general working methods.

II. The Objective—The Use of Information Technology for the International Recovery of Child Support and Other Forms of Family Maintenance

A. The Call for the Use of Information Technology Solutions

The international recovery of maintenance calls for the application of information technology solutions for many reasons:

— the very large number of cases involved, which is steadily increasing;
— maintenance cases often have a long life-span (in some countries child support can last until the age of 25 years);

[9] See Art 19(1) and (3) of the 2007 Convention and Art 2(2) and Recitals 12, 37 and 43 of the 2009 Regulation.

[10] The European Union.

[11] At the time of writing, the Permanent Bureau of the Hague Conference on Private International Law learned that the European Commission had awarded the iSupport project a co-financing Action Grant of about €720,000 for the development of Phase I of iSupport in response to a collective co-financing effort of about €180,000 from 12 partners (ie, Austria, Finland, France, Germany, Latvia, Netherlands, Norway, Romania, Switzerland, the Council of Bars and Law Societies of Europe (CCBE), the Institute of Legal Information Theory and Techniques (ITTIG) of the Italian National Research Council and the *Union Internationale des Huissiers de Justice* (UIHJ)).

[12] As domestic norms such as the Uniform Interstate Family Support Act (United States) and the Interjurisdictional Support Orders Act (Canadian provinces and territories) track the same data, a similar system, with small adjustments, could be used for the recovery of maintenance obligations within the United States or Canada.

- maintenance cases are subject to a high number of transactions, such as regular modifications (ie variations of the needs of the creditor and of the resources of the debtor) or recurrent electronic transfers of funds for example;
- a high number of transactions are repetitive and can be standardised;
- communications take place regardless of time zones;
- a vast amount of information about the state of the law in the different countries has to be available in real time;
- means of communications have to overcome language barriers.

It is in response to this environment that the Preamble of the 2007 Convention states that 'the States signatory to the … Convention … [seek] to take advantage of advances in technologies and to create a flexible system which can continue to evolve as needs change and further advances in technology create new opportunities'. Furthermore, Article 12(7) of the 2007 Convention provides that Central Authorities, charged with the operation of the cooperation system established under the Convention, shall employ the most rapid and efficient means of communication at their disposal. In that respect the Convention will require the use of website databases to provide real time information about its operation,[13] will invite the use of electronic fund transfers[14] and will be geared towards the use of cross-border electronic case management and communication systems.[15]

B. Development of Legal Texts that Accommodate the Use of Information Technology Solutions

In order to accommodate effectively the use of information technology at the global level, it was necessary to develop a text that would be medium and technology-neutral, that is, a text that could be used either in a paper environment, an electronic environment or a combination of the two. This neutrality would also allow the text to pass the test of time as technologies will evolve. There are several reasons upon which this decision rests.

First, at present very few judicial or administrative authorities around the world deliver or accept electronic data. Where the information and documents could be transmitted electronically between Central Authorities, some of the information and documents in the State of origin may only exist in paper form and can only be filed in such form with the competent authority in the requested State. In this respect, Article 13 of the 2007 Convention provides that '[a]ny application made through Central Authorities of the Contracting States in accordance with this Chapter, and any document or information appended thereto or provided by a Central Authority, may not be challenged by the respondent by reason only of the medium or means of communication employed between the Central Authorities concerned'.

Secondly, the objective was to develop a text that could stand alone from functional equivalents found in domestic law, or the lack thereof, and the different technologies available within the different States. Worldwide, less than 55 States have enacted legislation that provides functional equivalents for concepts such as 'signature', 'writing', 'original', 'sworn'

[13] Art 57.
[14] Art 35.
[15] Art 13.

and 'certified'. States that have done so have either implemented the 1996 UNCITRAL Model Law on Electronic Commerce[16] as such or have drawn upon it. Where this has been the case, even fewer States have extended the application of their legislation beyond the context of commercial activities such as the area of family law and more specifically the field of child support and other forms of family maintenance. Furthermore, in the light of this lack of functional equivalents in domestic laws of a number of States it was clear that, where possible, other drafting techniques would have to be relied upon to find solutions.

The text of the 2007 Convention is autonomous from the solutions found in domestic law regarding information technology. The Convention uses neutral terms in relation to medium and technologies so that it can be used in either a paper or electronic environment or a combination of the two. Therefore, the Convention avoids terms such as 'signature' (when what is actually required is a simple identification of the user), 'writing', 'original', 'sworn' and 'certified' as much as possible.[17] In this respect, it should be noted that some of the solutions adopted for this purpose have been drawn from the area of uncontested claims. It is important to remember that in the area of child support the establishment of paternity or the amount of maintenance are the most contested issues, not the documentary evidence per se. Furthermore, the text as drafted provides for the protection of personal data,[18] confidentiality[19] and non-disclosure of information,[20] without endangering the principles of due process. As a result, the 2007 Convention and the 2009 Regulation could be operational in an electronic environment such as the one provided by iSupport.

C. The Use of Mandatory and Recommended Forms to Standardise Communications and Alleviate Language Barriers

Since the beginning of the work on the international recovery of child support and other forms of family maintenance, the value of mandatory and recommended forms to be used primarily between Central Authorities for the transmission and receipt of applications has been emphasised again and again.[21] They facilitate the presentation of information and provide the opportunity to summarise and list documents for specific applications while reducing documentary requirements to a minimum. While they may not act as substitutes for certain required documents, they may reduce the need for full translations. Familiarity with mandatory and recommended forms, even when translated into different languages, facilitates the handling of applications. The forms developed for the 2007 Convention and 2009 Regulation make use of 'tick-boxes' and avoid 'open-text' answers as often as possible,

[16] Consult www.uncitral.org/uncitral/en/uncitral_texts/electronic_commerce/1996Model.html to obtain the text of the Model Law (accessed January 2014).

[17] For a more detailed analysis of these issues see P Lortie, 'The Development of Medium and Technology Neutral International Treaties in Support of Post-Convention Information Technology Systems—The Example of the 2007 Hague Convention and Protocol' (2008) *Yearbook of Private International Law* 359, and P Lortie and P Gingras, 'Développement et mise en œuvre pratique d'un traité international tirant profit des technologies de l'information : l'exemple des nouvelles conventions de La Haye sur le recouvrement des aliments' in *Compte-rendu de Lég@l TI 2008—Droit et technologies de l'information* (Cowansville, Québec, Éditions Yvon Blais) 71–90.

[18] Art 38 of the 2007 Convention and Art 62(1)–(3) of the 2009 Regulation.

[19] Art 39 of the 2007 Convention and Art 62(4) of the 2009 Regulation.

[20] Art 40 of the 2007 Convention.

[21] Mandatory and recommended forms are widely used under other Hague Conventions.

with the latter required for names of parties and competent authorities and their contact details, dates of birth, maintenance amounts, etc. Thus, making these forms available in different languages will allow countries to overcome language barriers; it will be possible to complete a form in English and to read it in Spanish, with the exception of 'open-text' answers which in most cases would not need to be translated as explained above.[22] The mandatory and recommended forms will encourage consistent practices, regular operation and uniform interpretation of the Convention and Regulation. They will assist with the swift transmission of documents and information. Finally, the use of these forms will be an essential component of a common multilingual international electronic case management and communication system under the 2007 Convention.

III. The Desired Outcome—The Development of a Common Multilingual International Electronic Case Management and Communication System

A. General Description of iSupport

The Permanent Bureau of the Hague Conference began examining the possibility of developing a common multilingual international electronic case management[23] and Internet-based communication system[24] for the 2007 Convention—the iSupport system—during the last three years of negotiations of the Convention. The system would contribute to the effective implementation of the 2007 Convention and 2009 Regulation and lead to greater consistency in practice in the different States since it would follow the language of these instruments. The system would also help significantly to improve communications between Central Authorities[25] and could alleviate translation problems as it could operate in different languages.[26] Such a system could contribute to the daily operations of the Central Authorities set up under both the Convention and the Regulation and help considerably to improve standards of case management by promoting paperless processing. The system could also generate the required statistics[27] as part of the means of monitoring operation of both the Convention and Regulation. In addition to the management and monitoring of cases, the system could provide instructions to banks with regard to

[22] 'Open-text' answers would be completed using alphabetical characters agreed upon by the users.

[23] Under the system envisaged, all the information pertaining/belonging to a Central Authority would be stored on servers within that Central Authority. Information/data would not have to be stored with third parties.

[24] This would be a secured system guaranteeing integrity, irrevocability, identification/authentification, access control and confidentiality of the information communicated. For further information regarding these concepts, see the Report drawn up by Philippe Lortie, First Secretary, 'Transfer of Funds and the Use of Information Technology in relation to the International Recovery of Child Support and other Forms of Family Maintenance', Prel Doc No 9 of May 2004, for the attention of the Special Commission of June 2004, and annex to Prel Doc No 9. Both documents are available on the HCCH website at www.hcch.net, under 'Conventions', 'No 38' then 'Preliminary Documents'.

[25] Art 5 of the 2007 Convention and Art 50 of the 2009 Regulation.

[26] Arts 44 and 45 of the 2007 Convention and Arts 20, 28, 40, 59 and 66 of the 2009 Regulation.

[27] Art 54(2) of the 2007 Convention and Art 74 of the 2009 Regulation.

electronic transfers of funds[28] and could send and receive secured online communications and applications[29] under the 2007 Convention and 2009 Regulation. Finally, the system would generate significant savings.

B. Functional Requirements

The development of the iSupport system will be based mainly on already adopted functional requirements, such as those provided by the texts of the 2007 Convention, 2009 Regulation and 2007 Protocol, the mandatory and recommended forms,[30] Country Profile[31] and the Practical Handbook for Caseworkers on the operation of the 2007 Convention.[32] Experience from States equipped with electronic case management systems[33] as well as the experience of the Hague Conference with the iChild case management system[34] will provide other useful examples of functional requirements. In accordance with industry practice, a cost-effective development of functional requirements that would meet the needs of all States would be one developed with the assistance of 20 per cent of the States that would represent about 80 per cent of the case load.[35]

Phase I should at a minimum include the development of the case management and Internet-based communication systems. Phase II would be aimed at the development of an electronic fund transfer module. Phase III could deal with statistical reporting and performance measurements. Phase IV could focus on linking the electronic version of the Country Profile with the electronic case management system in order to automatically generate functional requirements specific to States.

C. Technical Requirements

It will be important to know the technical requirements of all interested States in order to develop a single common system that can be deployed, interconnected and/or integrated on any globally accepted industry standard of platform or environment without the need to make costly modifications. Technical requirements will range from the types of systems on which iSupport will have to be deployed to the security protocols that will have to be followed.

[28] Arts 11(1)(f) and 35 of the 2007 Convention and Art 51(2)(f) of the 2009 Regulation.

[29] Art 12(7) of the 2007 Convention and Art 58(7) of the 2009 Regulation.

[30] The recommended forms can be found on the Hague Conference website at www.hcch.net under 'Work in Progress' then 'Maintenance Obligations' (accessed April 2014).

[31] The electronic Country Profile can be found on the Hague Conference website, ibid, under 'Conventions' then 'No 38' and 'Country Profiles' (accessed April 2014).

[32] The Practical Handbook for Caseworkers can be found on the Hague Conference website, *ibid.*, under 'Conventions' then 'No 38' and 'HCCH Publications' (accessed April 2014).

[33] Eg Australia, Canada, Finland, Netherlands, New Zealand, Norway, Sweden and the United States.

[34] The iChild case management system under the Hague Convention of 25 October 1980 on the Civil Aspects of International Child Abduction has been developed in cooperation with WorldReach Canada and the Government of Canada. It is available free of charge to all States Parties to that Convention. It is implemented in more than seven Central Authorities worldwide.

[35] This would include the States listed above in n 28 with the addition of other key States from the European Union.

D. Main Features of the iSupport System

iSupport should include at a minimum the following features:

- secured access web-based application running on locally hosted servers with little interactions with PC-based applications for low-cost deployment;
- individual databases for each participating State hosted locally, if preferred, in order to ensure appropriate protection of personal data and confidential information;
- possible migration/integration of relevant data between locally implemented web-based systems and iSupport in order to avoid work duplication;
- standardised case-based record keeping system respecting filing and archiving requirements of participating States;
- self-contained server-to-server secured Internet-based communication system for transmission between participating States and, where applicable, territorial units, of electronic messages, notes to file and multilingual requests and applications under the Convention;
- case management system to initiate, process, follow-up and provide status reports on outgoing and incoming applications under the Convention assisted by a task management and alert system in line with Convention requirements;
- cross-border electronic transfer of funds which will include the transmission of disbursement information for monitoring purposes;
- statistical and performance measurement reporting systems to assist strategic planning at both domestic and international levels;
- single desktop platform with access to all relevant Hague Conference information such as Central Authority contact details, Country Profiles, Convention and Protocol Status Charts, Practical Handbook, User Manual and Implementation Guide;
- multitasking provided by minimising several cases at once;
- software available in English, French and Spanish and any other language participating States are willing to finance.

E. Development Process to be All Inclusive and Coordinated by the Secretariat of the Hague Conference

The Secretariat of the Hague Conference, which holds the institutional memory regarding the development of the 2007 Convention and 2007 Protocol and has a coordinating role in ensuring the proper implementation and application of these instruments, will facilitate the development of iSupport with the assistance of working groups of States experts[36] and an advisory group of industry professionals, and through decisions made by interested States. The Secretariat will coordinate the input of States interested in the development of the system at each stage of the development process, from the establishment of the

[36] Different Working Groups of States experts could be established to deal with issues such as: (1) functional requirements for case management; (2) functional requirements for Internet-based communications; (3) functional requirements for electronic transfer of funds; (4) technical requirements for system deployment; (5) technical requirements for Internet based communications; (6) public procurement; (7) contractual matters; (8) financial issues; (9) pilot project and deployment; and (10) Caseworker User Manual.

functional and technical requirements of the system to its deployment. iSupport will be developed in close cooperation with interested Members of the Organisation.

VI. Conclusion—Financial Issues

From 2014 until 2016, and beyond, the Hague Conference will need, in addition to its Regular Budget, assistance in kind or by way of financial contributions in order to facilitate the development of Phases I and II of the iSupport system.[37]

The costs for the deployment of a pilot project (including hardware, implementation (cross-mapping/integration of international and domestic databases where necessary), translation of software into languages other than English, French and Spanish, and customised features) would be borne by interested States. Maintenance and upgrade costs related to operation could be recovered by user fees or interest on the payment transfers, or a combination of the two, if interested States so wished. The Permanent Bureau hopes that either these funds generated from the operation of iSupport and/or additional funding will help secure sufficient resources for the Permanent Bureau to monitor and review iSupport. It is hoped that development aid funding will allow underdeveloped States and States in transition to implement iSupport.

iSupport will open the door to an array of possibilities to improve the international recovery of child support and other forms of family maintenance. A bright future lies ahead. However, as for any pioneering work, there will also be challenges ahead which should make the work even more interesting.

[37] At the time of writing, the Permanent Bureau of the Hague Conference on Private International Law learned that the European Commission had awarded the iSupport project an Action Grant of about €720,000 for the development of Phase I of iSupport. See, above n 11.

18

Child Maintenance and Authentic Instruments—A German Perspective

ANA-SABINE BOEHM, NATALIE FAETAN AND ISABELLE JÄGER-MAILLET

I. Introduction

In Germany, authentic instruments play an important role in child maintenance law. The reasons for this may well have to do with the fact that they represent a simple and cost-effective enforcement order that is based on mutual agreement.[1] The use of authentic instruments relieves the burden on the courts. Voluntary authentication on the part of the debtor generally has a positive influence on the debtor's acceptance of his maintenance obligations and without entailing any enforceability limitations with respect to maintenance claims in comparison with court judgments.

This chapter explains how an authentic maintenance obligation instrument is established in Germany and which guarantees of the parties are preserved by the authentic form. Second, the enforceability of German authentic instruments abroad and the available legal remedies, particularly with respect to the international context, will be discussed.

II. Establishing an Authentic Instrument

The drawing up of authentic instruments is subject to strict requirements in Germany. They are intended to guarantee that all parties accept the authenticated obligations knowledgeably and with an awareness of the legal consequences of their actions. In particular,

[1] Enforceable authentic instruments in the area of child maintenance have mainly been used in Germany since the enforcement law was reformed in 2002, expanding the scope of application of § 794 para 1 no 5 of the German Code of Civil Procedure (Zivilprozessordnung (ZPO)) with the goal of relieving the courts. In this regard, see P Gottwald, *Münchner Kommentar Zivilprozessordnung* (Munich, CH Beck, 2012) Art 57 Council Regulation (EC) No 44/2001 of 22 December 2000 on jurisdiction and the recognition and enforcement of judgments in civil and commercial matters (Brussels I Regulation) margin no 1 with further refs; J Fleischhauer, 'Vollstreckbare Notarurkunden im europäischen Rechtsverkehr- neue notarielle Zuständigkeiten nach der Brüssel I Verordnung' (2002) *Mitteilungen des Bayerischen Notarvereins* 15. See, on similar developments in France, JJ Bourdillat, 'Le titre exécutoire notarié: le consensus exécutoire' (1994) *Revue Huissiers* 679.

parties who are 'weaker' with respect to economic, language or cultural factors need to receive equal protection. Moreover, the instruments' enforceability is subject to strict requirements that guarantee the debtor a high level of protection from improper claims.

A. Formal Requirements

The term 'authentic instrument' is defined in German procedural law[2] as an 'instrument that has been prepared in the prescribed form by a public authority within the confines of their competence or by a publically appointed person within the confines of his appointed business circles'. The word 'instrument' is used here to mean the embodiment of declarations of intent.

The requirements according to which a written declaration of intent becomes an authentic instrument are mainly governed by the German Authentication Act enacted 28 August 1969 (Beurkundungsgesetz (BeurkG)).

i. Competence to Authenticate

Only certain public authorities are entitled to establish instruments in an authenticated form.

As a rule, notaries in Germany have a general competence to authenticate.[3] Furthermore, § 1 BeurkG allows the State by law to endow other persons with the competence to authenticate, where appropriate with substantive limitations.

In child maintenance law, authentic instruments drawn up by youth welfare offices play a significant role. The competence of authentication officials in youth welfare offices to authenticate maintenance obligation declarations is based on the German Social Code, Eighth Book—Child and Youth Welfare (Sozialgesetzbuch (SGB VIII))[4] and implies the right to authenticate 'self-commitments to fulfil maintenance claims of descendants or their legal successors, provided that the descendant has not turned 21 at the time of authentication'.[5] The youth welfare offices are part of the municipal administration. Their competence to authenticate in legal maintenance matters is substantiated in that the State's mandate to support children and families includes assistance in the recovery of maintenance by simplifying the process of establishing maintenance orders.

In cases with a cross-border context, the authorisation of consular officers representing Germany abroad is of practical relevance[6] as well, provided that the party with maintenance obligations (the debtor) does not have any other extrajudicial possibility of establishing an enforceable maintenance order in the State where he or she resides.

[2] § 415 para 1 ZPO.

[3] § 1 para 1 BeurkG.

[4] § 59 para 1 no 3 of the German Social Code, Eighth Book—Child and Youth Welfare (SGB VIII).

[5] For more on this, see B Knittel, *Beurkundungen im Kindschaftsrecht* (Cologne, Bundesanzeiger Verlag, 2013) margin no 364, 365.

[6] §§ 2, 10 German Consular Act (KonsularG). However, the consular agent only provides authentication to the extent necessary. It does not therefore compete with German notaries. The authentications of the consular agent are supplementary services that would not otherwise be possible.

Family courts are also authorised to publicly authenticate a settlement concerning maintenance obligations concluded before the court (§ 127a of the German Civil Code); however, this will not be examined in any greater detail here.

ii. Authentication Procedure

In German civil procedural law, authentic instruments enjoy a high degree of evidentiary value. They establish full proof of the authenticity of the authentic instrument issued by the public authority or the authentication officials.[7] This trustworthiness is guaranteed by adhering to a strictly formalised procedure that is regulated in the German Authentication Act.[8]

Characteristic of authenticating declarations of intent as per the German Authentication Act is first and foremost the duty of neutrality of the authentication official.[9] To avoid conflicts of interest, it is prohibited for the authentication officials or their close relatives to have any kind of personal interest in the establishment of the authentic instrument.

The authentication official has the duty to establish personal assurance of the identity of the persons submitting declarations.[10] This is generally done by examining identification documents. As an important part of the proceedings, the entire record of the declarations must be read to the parties in the presence of the authentication official and then approved and personally signed by them and the authentication official (§ 13 paragraph 1 BeurkG). For authentications with a cross-border element, the authentication official must make sure before the authentication procedure that the parties have mastered the German language to a sufficient degree. If this is not the case, this must be expressly declared in the record, and the record must be translated to the person concerned instead of being read aloud. The translation may be performed by the authentication official him or herself or by an interpreter (§ 16 BeurkG).

With respect to the contents of the instrument, the authentication official is subject to a number of legally standardised duties to inspect and instruct.[11] These are to ensure that the parties do not make any declarations whose contents or scope they have not completely understood. In particular, the authentication official is to probe the intent of the parties, clarify the facts, instruct the parties concerning the scope of the matter and express their declarations clearly and unequivocally in the record.[12] In the process, the official must take care to ensure that errors and ambiguities are avoided, and also that inexperienced and inexpert parties are not disadvantaged. If foreign law is applicable or if there are any ambiguities, the authentication official is to point this out to the parties and make note of this in the document. The authentication official is not obligated to provide instruction on the contents of foreign law.

The efficiency of these prescriptions is guaranteed by the particular training of the authentication officials. In most German States, notaries are certified legal practitioners, comparable to judges and lawyers. The authentication officials in youth welfare offices are civil servants or employees and have extensive specialist knowledge in the field of

[7] § 415 para 1 ZPO.

[8] The German Authentication Act (BeurkG) applies either directly, by virtue of reference (eg § 10 para 3 KonsularG) or as per § 1 para 2 BeurkG.

[9] §§ 6, 7 BeurkG.

[10] § 10 Abs 2 BeurkG.

[11] §§ 17–21 BeurkG.

[12] § 17 para 1 BeurkG.

maintenance law. They are therefore not limited to recording declarations, but also consult with the parties prior to the authentication with respect to the legal impact of their declaration. If there are any doubts, for example, concerning the legal capacity to contract of the person making the declaration or his or her true intent, the authentication official may refuse the authentication or make a note in the authentic instrument accordingly.

Finally, the German Authentication Act regulates how authentic instruments are treated once they have been successfully established.[13] This is largely comparable to the treatment of court judgments. As a rule, the personally signed original of the authentic instrument remains with the authenticating authority.[14] In legal relations, the original document is represented by duplicates of the record. Only the depositary of the original document may issue duplicates. This ensures that the duplicates are identical to the original document. However, a duplicate does not necessarily have to be a facsimile of the original document. This is why duplicates do not always have the parties' signatures. The signatures are then substituted by the comment 'signed'. In legal relations, this regularly leads to the objection that the debtor was not personally involved in the issuance of the instrument. In such a case, the authenticating authority can be requested to issue a certified photocopy of the original document.[15]

Taken as a whole, the German Authentication Act grants the parties similar guarantees as with court proceedings, both with regard to protecting the interests of the party accepting obligations as well as with the evidentiary value of the authentic documents. Due to the authentication official's duties to inspect and instruct, the individual making the declaration is notified of potential problematic issues by professionally competent persons so that he or she can seek the advice of the authentication official or of a lawyer beforehand. The duty to read the report guarantees that the individual making the declaration is aware of the exact contents and legal consequences of his or her declaration. This is the reason for the high trustworthiness that German authentic instruments enjoy.

iii. Costs

In Germany, notarial authentications involving the obligation to fulfil child maintenance claims are free of charge.[16] The authentication activities of youth welfare offices are generally provided free of charge as well.[17] This regulation avoids time-consuming and costly court proceedings and promotes consensual solutions.

While youth welfare offices are not allowed to levy either fees or charges for expenses, notaries are permitted to invoice for expenses incurred. This may result in additional costs, especially if the translation requirement applies.

[13] §§ 44 et seq. BeurkG.

[14] Original consular documents constitute an exception and can be kept in the deposit of the District Court of Berlin Schöneberg upon request (§ 10 para 3 no 5 of the German Consular Act).

[15] § 51 para 3 BeurkG.

[16] § 62 para 1 BeurkG, part 2, 2nd preliminary remark, para 3 GNotKG-KV (German Court and Notary Charges Act—Schedule of Values).

[17] As per § 64 para 1 SGB X; only Brandenburg has made use of the right to charge fees in § 97c SGB VIII.

B. Conditions of Enforceability

i. Submission to Immediate Enforcement

Unlike in France, for example,[18] German authentic instruments are not automatically enforceable. Instead, the party who is obligated to an enforceable action (payment of maintenance) must submit his entire assets to immediate enforcement of the claim by expressly stating so in the authentic instrument.[19] The submission clause needs to be authenticated in the same way as the other declarations in the maintenance obligations instrument and is therefore also subject to the instruction duties described above for the protection of the debtor.

ii. Granting Enforcement and Legal Succession in Title Clauses

In order to enforce the terms of an authentic instrument, an executable copy of the authentic instrument must be issued by the office detaining the original document of the instrument.[20] This is usually the same office that authenticated the declaration. An exception to this is executable copies of consular instruments, which may only be issued by the District Court of Schöneberg if the original document is deposited there.[21]An executable copy of an authentic instrument is characterised by an enforcement clause,[22] and it is generally only issued once to prevent claims from being asserted against the debtor under different enforcement orders. The enforcement clause confirms that the enforcement arising from the authentic instrument may be instigated[23] if the enforcement order is also served on the debtor and if a two-week period has elapsed from service of the order (see below).

With respect to legal succession in title, the new creditor can apply for a fully or partially executable copy with a legal succession clause referring to him or her. This case is particularly relevant in maintenance matters if anyone entitled to maintenance (referred to here as 'creditor' or 'maintenance creditor') receives social security benefits from different public authorities[24] and thus the maintenance claims pass on to the public body by virtue of a *cessio legis* (transfer by operation of law). In order to receive an executable copy of the maintenance order, the legal succession in title has to be known to the competent authority or has to be proven by the successor by public records of documents or documents that have been publicly certified.[25] The decision to grant a legal succession clause (or to refuse this) may be appealed.[26]

One of the general responsibilities of the office authorised to issue an executable copy is the issuance of enforceability certificates in terms of international legal instruments such as

[18] Fleischhauer (n 1) 15.

[19] § 794 para 1 no 5 ZPO (and s 60 SGB VIII for instruments of youth welfare offices).

[20] § 724 ZPO.

[21] See (n 14).

[22] For similar proceedings in France, though without an enforcement clause being necessary, see C Lefort 'Actes notariés revêtus de la formule exécutoire' in Guinchard and Moussa (eds), *Droit et pratique des voies d'exécution* (Paris, Dalloz, 2009) margin no 124.12.

[23] Knittel (n 5) margin no 499 et seq.

[24] N Hartig and I Jäger-Maillet 'Durchsetzung übergegangener Ansprüche im Ausland' in C Schmidt (ed), *Internationale Unterhaltsrealisierung* (Baden-Baden, Nomos, 2011) s 11 margin no 1.

[25] § 727 ZPO.

[26] § 732 ZPO and § 54 BeurkG.

the Lugano Convention[27] or the Brussels I Regulation[28] or of extracts of decisions in terms of the EC Maintenance Regulation.[29]

iii. Serving the Enforcement Order

Another condition for enforcing authentic instruments is serving[30] them on the debtor.[31] It is the responsibility of the maintenance creditor to arrange service of the authentic instrument. If the maintenance debtor lives in Germany, this service is subject to German service provisions.[32] For evidence purposes, an enforcement officer is generally commissioned to carry out the service, since he or she can subsequently issue a certificate with respect to the service contents, time and type. In case of service abroad, international service provisions[33] are applicable.

§ 60 paragraph 2 SGB VIII allows for a simplified procedure of service for authentic instruments issued by youth welfare offices. Pursuant to this, they can also be personally served by the authentication official by physical delivery (often immediately following the authentication process) on the basis of § 173 ZPO.[34] In this case, the day of the physical delivery is to be noted on the original document. Physical delivery is the usual mode of service.

iv. Waiting Period under § 798 ZPO

As per § 60 paragraph 1 SGB VIII in connection with § 798 ZPO, the enforcement arising from a youth welfare instrument with submission to immediate enforcement begins at the earliest two weeks after it has been served on the debtor. However, it must be noted that an enforcement act is effective, albeit contestable, even if it is undertaken without observing the waiting period.[35] The enforcement becomes effective once the period has elapsed. The purpose of the waiting period is to prevent the debtor from being surprised by enforcement. However, enforcement should not be delayed unnecessarily either.

C. Instrument Contents

The parties in a maintenance relationship are free to choose the place of authentication. However, they are bound by the requirements of the applicable conflict of laws and the

[27] Convention on Jurisdiction and the Recognition and Enforcement of Judgments in Civil and Commercial Matters concluded 16 September 1988 in Lugano (Lugano Convention).

[28] Council Regulation (EC) No 44/2001 concluded 22 December 2000 on the Jurisdiction and the Recognition and Enforcement of Judgments in Civil and Commercial Matters (Brussels I Regulation).

[29] Annex I to IV of Council Regulation (EC) No 4/2009 concluded 18 December 2008 on Jurisdiction, Applicable Law, Recognition and Enforcement of Decisions and Cooperation in Matters Relating to Maintenance Obligations (EC Maintenance Regulation).

[30] §§ 750, 798 ZPO.

[31] Unlike in Germany, French notarial instruments can be enforced without the need for service (2nd civ, 22 March 2001, no 02-11.353). The rationale for this is that the instrument reflects the express will of the parties and thus no opportunity to lodge a complaint is necessary.

[32] § 166 et seq. ZPO.

[33] Regulation (EC) No 1393/2007 of the European Parliament and of the Council of 13 November 2007 on the Service in the Member States of Judicial and Extrajudicial Documents in Civil or Commercial Matters (Service of Documents), and Repealing Council Regulation (EC) No 1348/2000; Hague Convention on the Service Abroad of Judicial and Extrajudicial Documents in Civil or Commercial Matters concluded 15 November 1965 (Art 17) et al.

[34] Knittel (n 5) margin no 541.

[35] K Stöber in R Zöller (ed), *Zivilprozessordnung Kommentar* (Cologne, Dr Otto Schmidt, 2012) § 798 margin no 3.

substantive law of the particular place of authentication. From the German perspective, the question of which substantive law is applicable to the facts of a maintenance matter relating to the laws of a foreign State depends directly on the EC Maintenance Regulation and the international Conventions.[36]

As with Article 4 of the Hague Convention on the Law Applicable to Maintenance Obligations 1973[37] and Article 18 Einführungsgesetz zum Bürgerlichen Gesetzbuch[38] before it, Article 3 of the Hague Maintenance Protocol 2007[39] regards the law of the creditor's state of habitual residence as the main connecting factor, expressly providing that changes in the habitual residence are to be respected. This general rule is based on the idea that the law of the State of habitual residence is the law most closely related to the actual living circumstances of the creditor.[40]

Now for the first time, Article 15 of the EC Maintenance Regulation in connection with Articles 7 and 8 of the Hague Maintenance Protocol 2007 provides for the designation of the applicable substantive law. Article 7 of the Hague Protocol 2007 permits the designation of the applicable law for a particular proceeding in a given State while Article 8 allows the designation by the maintenance parties of the applicable law without any connection with particular proceedings. These options are intended to increase party autonomy.

The designation of applicable law option is limited in various ways for the protection of certain persons, such as underage children. First, it requires a particular form as per Article 7(2) of the Hague Protocol 2007, which is a minimum requirement that can be extended by national law.[41] The designation of applicable law is limited with respect to persons in that it excludes children under the age of 18.[42] Article 8(4) contains a special regulation for renouncing the right to maintenance. Because of the consequences for the creditor of renouncing the right to maintenance, this issue is excluded from the scope of the law designated by the parties. The admissibility of renouncing the right to maintenance is determined according to the law of the habitual residence of the creditor at the time the designation of law is made.[43] These limitations serve first and foremost to protect the weaker party in the maintenance relationship. Article 8(1) limits the range of options available to the parties

[36] Now the Hague Protocol on the Law Applicable to Maintenance Obligations concluded 23 November 2007 (hereafter Hague Protocol 2007) available at www.hcch.net/index_en.php?act=conventions.text&cid=133 (accessed December 2013).

[37] Hague Convention on the Law Applicable to Maintenance Obligations concluded 2 October 1973 (hereafter Hague Maintenance Convention 1973) available at www.hcch.net/index_en.php?act=conventions.text&cid=86 (accessed December 2013).

[38] Introductory Act to the German Civil Code (EGBGB).

[39] Hague Convention on the International Recovery of Child Support and Other Forms of Family Maintenance concluded 23 November 2007.

[40] HJ Dose '§ 9 Auslandsberührung' in P Wendl and Dose (eds), *Unterhaltsrecht in der familienrichterlichen Praxis* (Munich, CH Beck, 2011) 1428 margin no 13.

[41] See A Bonomi, 'Explanatory Reporton the Hague Protocol 2007', para 119, available at www.hcch.net/upload/expl39.pdf (accessed December 2013).

[42] Art 8(3). The Bonomi Report, ibid para 146, says this is such a clear provision that it requires no further comments. See, for more detail, M Andrae '§ 9 Auslandsberührung' in T Rauscher (ed), *Europäisches Zivilprozess- und Kollisionsrecht* (Munich, Sellier, 2010), Verordnung (EG) Nr.4/2009 des Rates vom 18. Dezember 2008 über die Zuständigkeit, das anwendbare Recht, die Anerkennung und Vollstreckung von Entscheidungen und die Zusammenarbeit in Unterhaltssachen, Art 8 margin no 17.

[43] Waiving future claims for child maintenance, even partially, is not admissible under German law (§§ 1614 para 1, 134 German Civil Code (BGB)). However, a certain amount of discretion is permitted. The limit is set by case law at about 1/5. For this reason, the current settlement agreements in child maintenance law in *common law jurisdictions* may be problematic within the German legal system. In German law, they are only acceptable as indemnification agreements between the parents, since the child is generally a contracting party and legally represented by the caring parent with custody.

in terms of choosing the applicable law so that there is a real connection between the law designated and the maintenance relationship at the relevant time.

The chosen law determines the admissibility, conclusion and substantive effectiveness as well as the content of a maintenance agreement, its variation and annulment. In this context, the parties to the agreement will be able to establish the amount of the maintenance claim, currency issues and the basis for calculating the maintenance as well as indexation.

From the German perspective, in accordance with Article 11 EGBGB, the form of the agreement depends either on the chosen law or the law of the place where the agreement was concluded. Where the chosen law changes, this alone will not cause the agreement to be reassessed. However, the new maintenance law will determine whether and under what conditions the agreement can be modified or annulled.[44]

If German law is the applicable law, German substantive law does not stipulate a specific form for agreements that involve child maintenance. Drawing up authentic instruments in this area therefore does not result from a statutory form requirement, but rather from the need to create enforceable maintenance titles. Thus the potential contents of the authentic instruments are solely limited by the substantive limitations of contractual freedom (eg inadmissibility of renouncing the right to future claims for child maintenance as per § 1614 BGB). The contents of the authentic instrument may involve arrears as well as current maintenance. The maintenance obligation may be expressed as a unilateral declaration of the maintenance debtor, as a contract between the maintenance debtor and the maintenance creditor, or as a contract in favour of third parties between the parents of the child entitled to maintenance. In practice, purely unilateral declarations tend to be rare, since generally the authenticated unilateral declarations of the debtor are either based on an agreement between the parties or have been made the subject matter of an agreement when the creditor receives the authentic instrument without objecting to the contents.[45] For example, this is the case if the authentic instrument is handed to the creditor and the creditor does not object to the authenticated maintenance payments.[46]

III. Implementing German Authentic Instruments Abroad

The multilateral, cross-border significance of authentic instruments as enforcement orders first began with the Brussels Convention 1968.[47] Article 50 of the Convention states that authentic instruments formally drawn up or registered and enforceable in one Contracting

[44] See Andrae (n 42) Art 11 margin no 9.

[45] This possibility appears to have been confirmed by the German Federal Supreme Court in its decision dated 2 December 2009, in which it gave its opinion on the requirements for varying a unilateral declaration: BGH, (2010) *Zeitschrift für das gesamte Familienrecht* 195.

[46] This is especially valid for variation instruments of youth welfare offices as well. Even these declarations are usually either attributable to a previous settlement of the parties or are to be viewed as an offer to conclude a new agreement in terms of § 145 BGB: see Knittel (n 5) margin no 259.

[47] Brussels Convention on Jurisdiction and the Enforcement of Judgments in Civil and Commercial Matters concluded 27 September 1968 (Brussels Convention 1968).

State shall be declared enforceable in another Contracting State on application and after the exequatur procedure established for court judgments has been carried out.

Prior to this, civil law claims specified in an authentic instrument could be enforced abroad on a bilateral basis. The Jenard Report on the Brussels Convention 1968 cites the bilateral agreements between the six original Contracting States. Germany, for example, had made bilateral agreements with Belgium[48] and the Netherlands.[49] The Convention with the Netherlands even dealt explicitly with maintenance orders issued by a youth welfare office.[50]

Soon afterwards, the Hague Recognition and Enforcement Maintenance Convention 1973 left the equal treatment of authentic instruments with court judgments with respect to their enforcement in other Contracting States up to the choice of the Contracting States. Pursuant to Article 25, any Contracting State may declare at any time on the basis of reciprocity that it will extend the provisions of the Convention to authentic instruments.

The declaration option was mainly directed at notarial deeds, but otherwise not much practical importance was ascribed to this kind of enforcement order.[51] Since then, only four States have actually made use of this option: Germany, the Netherlands, Sweden and Ukraine.[52]

The Lugano Convention followed for the EFTA States.[53] It was designed to operate in parallel with the Brussels Convention 1968, and for this reason authentic instruments fall within the scope of both of these Conventions (even though the representatives of the EFTA States did not see any practical necessity for including authentic instruments within the scope of an enforcement convention and regarded such enforcement orders as an Austrian peculiarity).[54]

Once the Brussels I Regulation took effect on 1 March 2002, the authentic instrument became an integral part of European enforcement law.[55] Even States that do not use authentic instruments for maintenance in their legal practice are required to declare the enforceability of instruments from Member States. Accordingly, they are clear enforcement orders in terms of the European Enforcement Order Regulation[56] and the EC Maintenance Regulation, which followed later.

[48] The Convention between the Federal Republic of Germany and the Kingdom of Belgium signed on 30 June 1958 on the Mutual Recognition and Enforcement of Judgments, Arbitration Awards and Authentic Instruments in Civil and Commercial Matters.

[49] The Convention signed on 30 August 1962 between the Federal Republic of Germany and the Kingdom of the Netherlands on the Mutual Recognition and Enforcement of Judgments and Other Enforceable Instruments in Civil and Commercial Matters.

[50] Art 16 para1 lit b of the German/Dutch Convention.

[51] See the Verwilghen report on the Hague Recognition and Enforcement Maintenance Convention 1973, para 104, available at www.hcch.net/upload/expl23-24.pdf (accessed December 2013).

[52] See the full status table available at www.hcch.net/index_en.php?act=conventions.statusprint&cid=85 (accessed December 2013).

[53] Convention on Jurisdiction and the Recognition and Enforcement of Judgments in Civil and Commercial Matters concluded 16 September 1988.

[54] Compare p 80 of the Jenard and Möller report on the Convention On Jurisdiction And The Enforcement Of Judgments In Civil And Commercial Matters concluded on 16 September 1988 in Lugano [1990] OJ C 189/57.

[55] Art 76 of the Brussels I Regulation.

[56] Regulation (EC) No 805/2004 of the European Parliament and the Council of 21 April 2004 regarding the Introduction of a European Enforcement Order for Uncontested Claims (European Enforcement Order Regulation).

Beyond the European Union, an authentic instrument may internationally become a basis for enforcement abroad as a 'maintenance arrangement'[57] under the Hague Convention 2007.[58]

A. Recognition and Declaration of Enforceability

i. Definition of an Authentic Instrument in Terms of International Enforcement Instruments

Neither the Brussels I Regulation nor the Conventions state what is to be understood by an authentic instrument. A definition of the term is first found in the EC European Enforcement Order for Uncontested Claims Regulation, in Article 4(3):

> a) a document which has been formally drawn up or registered as an authentic instrument, and the authenticity of which:
>
> i) relates to the signature and the content of the instrument; and
>
> ii) has been established by a public authority or other authority empowered for that purpose by the Member State in which it originates;
>
> or
>
> b) an arrangement relating to maintenance obligations concluded with administrative authorities or authenticated by them.

Another comparable definition followed in the EC Maintenance Regulation.[59]

While these definitions still leave it up to the national law of the Member States to state precisely what is to be understood by an authentic instrument, there are three important criteria that must be adhered to so that an instrument falls within the scope of the Regulation. Authentication must be carried out by an agency authorised to do this in the Member State; the trustworthiness of both the content of the instrument as well as the signature underneath must be guaranteed; and pursuant to Article 25 the instrument must be enforceable in the State of origin. The definition is based on the criteria that the European Court of Justice laid down in 1997[60] for proceedings in accordance with the Brussels Convention 1968. The European Court of Justice case law[61] is applicable for the Lugano Convention[62] and for the Brussels Convention 1968.

[57] The Convention provides for the recognition and enforcement of 'maintenance arrangements' (Art 30) which include agreements concerning maintenance drawn up in the form of an authentic instrument or otherwise authenticated by or concluded or registered or filed with a competent authority (Art 3(e)). The text of the Convention is available at www.hcch.net/index_en.php?act=conventions.text&cid=131 (accessed December 2013).

[58] However the extent of this right depends on the extent to which Contracting States reserve the right not to recognise and enforce a maintenance arrangement (Art 30(8)). Ukraine has utilised this reservation, see www.hcch.net/index_en.php?act=conventions.statusprint&cid=131 (accessed December 2013).

[59] Art 2(1)(3) EC Maintenance Regulation.

[60] Case C-260/97 *Unibank A/S v Christensen* [1999] ECR I -3715, paras 15–20.

[61] Ibid.

[62] See Art 1 protocol no 2 on the uniform interpretation of the Lugano Convention.

Furthermore, maintenance agreements or obligations concluded before administrative authorities are included in the definition of an authentic instrument according to several international enforcement instruments.[63]

ii. Recognition and Declaration of Enforceability in the System of the EC Maintenance Regulation

a. Extent of the Recognition Obligation

According to the legal system of their State of origin, enforceable authentic instruments do not develop any *res judicata* or other procedural effect that qualify for recognition in the sense of an extension of effect. To date, recognising authentic instruments which include maintenance obligations has not been regulated in European procedural law.[64] With regard to maintenance obligations, for the first time[65] Article 48 of the EC Maintenance Regulation regulates the cross-border recognition of enforceable authentic instruments of an EU Member State in another Member State according to Chapter IV of the Regulation. The Regulation does not contain a definition of recognition.

However, Article 48 of the EC Maintenance Regulation does not provide a substantive recognition of the legal situation[66] since, according to the legal systems of the Member States, there is no effect comparable to legal force that pertains to the authentic instruments with respect to the effects of the legal act attested by the instrument. According to the legal systems of the Member States, only facts are regularly included in the evidentiary value of an instrument, not substantive legal results.[67] The lack of a corresponding effect

[63] Art 57(2) of the Brussels I Regulation; Art 2(1)(3) of the EC Maintenance Regulation; Art 57(2) of the Lugano Convention 2007; Art 3(e) of the Hague Convention 2007.

[64] In Art 57 of the Lugano Convention and Art 57 of the Brussels I Regulation, it is clear that the recognition of authentic instruments as a requirement to be admitted for enforcement is not regulated. The provision is restricted to the declaration of enforceability for instruments established and enforceable in the first state. Art 30 of the Hague Maintenance Convention 2007 cannot be legally compared, even though the term recognition is used for maintenance arrangements. Here, recognition is to be understood in the context of the term 'enforcement'. It is to be regarded as a synonym for the declaration of enforceability, or the registration, of maintenance arrangements.

[65] *Cf* the corresponding regulation of Art 46 of Regulation (EC) No 2201/2003 of 27 November 2003 concerning Jurisdiction and Recognition and Enforcement of Judgments in Matrimonial Matters of Parental Responsibility or Chapter V of Regulation (EC) No 650/2012 of the European Parliament and of the Council concluded 4 July 2012 on Jurisdiction, Applicable law, Recognition and Enforcement of Decisions and Acceptance and Enforcement of Authentic Instruments in Matters of Succession and on the Creation of a European Certificate of Succession.

[66] For a restrictive interpretation, see H-P Mansel, K Thorn and R Wagner, 'Europäisches Kollisionsrecht 2010: Verstärkte Zusammenarbeit als Motor der Vereinheitlichung' (2011) *Praxis des Internationalen Privat- und Verfahrensrechts* 5; R Geimer et al, *Internationales Zivilprozessrecht*, (Cologne, Verlag Dr Otto Schmidt, 2009) margin no 2865a et seq are also critical, unlike the European Commission, which regarded designing a substantive recognition of legal authentic instruments for civil status and succession as viable; see H-P Mansel et al for more details, *ibid*, p 2 et seq. and R Wagner, 'Inhaltliche Anerkennung von Personenstandsurkunden—ein Patentrezept? Überlegungen aus internationalprivatrechtlicher Sicht' (2011) *Zeitschrift für das gesamte Familienrecht* 609.

[67] Andrae (n 42) Art 48 margin no 6, W Hau 'Annex 2 of 110 FamFG' in H Prütting and T Helms (eds), FamFG Kommentar (Cologne, Verlag Dr Otto Schmidt, 2013) Annex 2 of § 110 FamFG margin no 158, correctly rejecting the view that the substantive legal result is to be assumed, though this is possibly the opinion of K Hilbig 'Art 48 Margin no 6' in Geimer and Schütze (eds), *Internationaler Rechtsverkehr in Zivil- und Handelssachen* (Munich, CH Beck, 2013) Art 48 margin no 6; see also T Rauscher on the same subject in T Rauscher, *Europäisches Zivilprozess- und Kollisionsrecht* (Munich, Sellier, 2010) Art 46 Regulation (EC) No 2201/2003 margin no 1; S Dornblüth, *Die europäische Regelung der Anerkennung und Vollstreckbarerklärung von Ehe- und Kindschaftsentscheidungen*, (Tübingen, Mohr-Siebeck, 2003) 63; K Paraschas in Geimer and Schütze,

in the first State would cause the extension of an effect related to a substantive legal status to fail in the second State.[68] Recognition is therefore not permitted as blanket recognition of a legal status, not even in principle, but only within a certain context,[69] namely in the context of enforcement.[70] A consequence of adopting the formal evidentiary effects is that only the factual process actually authenticated by the authentication official is to be taken into consideration—for example, the making of the declarations of intent while the declaring parties are all present along with the wording of the declarations recorded in the instruments.[71] The equivalence of authentic instruments to judicial decisions regulated by Article 48 of the EC Maintenance Regulation is thus confirmed.

b. Recognition and Declaration of Enforceability Procedure

According to Chapter IV of the EC Maintenance Regulation, recognition and enforcement means that, for the procedure that is to be adhered to in the sense of the two-corridor system, the distinction needs to be made as to whether the Member State of origin is bound by the Hague Maintenance Protocol 2007 (Article 17 et seq) or not (Article 23 et seq).[72]

According to Article 48(1) of the EC Maintenance Regulation, the common requirement for equating authentic instruments with judicial decisions is their enforceability in the Member State of origin. The term enforceability is not defined in more detail by the EC Maintenance Regulation. Since the issuance of an executable copy or another kind of copy by the Member State of origin is not envisaged, it must be presumed that an *enforcement declaration* is not necessary for establishing 'enforceability' in the sense of Article 48(1). In order to ensure that the instrument is subject to the Regulation and has enforceable contents, the Member State of enforcement should stipulate in its own national law

Internationaler Rechtsverkehr in Zivil- und Handelssachen, Art 46 of Regulation (EC) No 4/2009 margin no 4, 10. This view is otherwise refuted by Art 59 of Regulation (EC) No 650/2012; for a thorough discussion on this, see M Buschbaum, 'Rechtslagenanerkennung aufgrund öffentlicher Urkunden?' in *Festschrift Martiny* 42 with other references.

[68] Concerning the question of a recognition principle for conflict of laws, *cf* also the parallel discussions with respect to the legislative recommendation for the mutual recognition of civil status instruments, see H-P Mansel et al (n 66) 3 et seq, or with respect to the Succession Regulation, M Buschbaum and C Kohler, 'Die "Anerkennung" öffentlicher Urkunden' (2010) *Praxis des Internationalen Privat- und Verfahrensrechts* 313 et seq.

[69] *Cf* also in this respect the comments by D Henrich, 'Anerkennung statt IPR: eine Grundsatzfrage' (2005) *Praxis des Internationalen Privat- und Verfahrensrechts* 422.

[70] According to M Buschbaum 'Europäisches Nachlasszeugnis und Annahme öffentlicher Urkunden-neue Mechanismen zur grenzüberschreitenden Nachlassabwicklung und ihr Verhältnis zum materiellen Sachenrecht' in R Geimer and J Hager (eds), *Die europäische Erbrechtsverordnung im Überblick* (Baden-Baden, Nomos, 2013) 41, at fn 6 it speaks against an isolated adoption of the formal evidentiary effects in the context of Art 48 of the EC Maintenance Regulation that such an adoption is initially regulated in Art 59 Regulation (EC) No 650/2012 and thereby in the form of an independent provision on the acceptance of authentic instruments dissociated from enforcement. In contrast, in Art 48 of the EC Maintenance Regulation, the term recognition is used in the context of enforcement, and thus as an enforcement requirement; Hau (n 67) Annex 3 as per § 110 FamFG margin no 158 as well as § 108 FamFG margin no 6, that pursuant to Art 48 of the EC Maintenance Regulation, states that the formal evidentiary effects are to be adopted, but not the substantive legal result.

[71] According to most legal systems of Member States, substantive aspects are not the subject matter of the formal evidentiary value of the authentic instrument, *cf* § 415 ZPO for the German legal status. If, according to the legal system of another Member State, the evidentiary value of an instrument also refers to the accuracy of content and the effectiveness of the substantive legal status, a partial recognition should be considered.

[72] See also the transitional provision of Art 75(2), whereby instruments from states bound to the Hague Maintenance Protocol 2007 that were issued before 18 June 2011 and fall within the temporal scope of the Brussels I Regulation, are likewise to be considered as enforceable in accordance with Chapter IV section 2.

that a confirmation of at least these aspects must be granted before the instrument can be used for enforcement. In German law, it is therefore necessary to provide an enforcement clause.[73] Article 17(1) of the EC Maintenance Regulation is accordingly applicable for authentic instruments and settlements if the Member State of origin is bound by the Hague Maintenance Protocol 2007. This is true of all EU Member States except for the UK and Denmark. Recognition occurs *ipso jure* and without the possibility of objection. Article 48(1) in connection with Article 17(1) of the EC Maintenance Regulation divests the courts of the other Member States of the competence to decide in this regard. Even violating public policy does not constitute grounds to refuse recognition.

If the Member State of origin is not bound by the Hague Maintenance Protocol 2007, then the judicial settlements and authentic instruments likewise need to be recognised *ipso jure*. A *révision au fond* is excluded according to Article 42. A judicial decision concerning recognition can be made per Article 23(2) and (3). A procedure to determine recognition as well as an incidental recognition is possible. According to Article 48, which refers to the provisions with respect to recognition in Chapter IV, the grounds for refusing recognition in Article 24 apply. The grounds for excluding judicial settlements and authentic instruments are not separately regulated (which is somewhat different to the provisions of Articles 57 and 58 of the Lugano Convention and the Brussels I Regulation) and are geared towards decisions. As in the Lugano Convention and the Brussels I Regulation, the public policy proviso would have been sufficient in and of itself. While the incompatibility between authentic instruments or between authentic instruments and decisions could possibly constitute grounds for exclusion pursuant to Article 24(c), the wording/formulation of Article 24(d) does not apply to authentic instruments. With respect to the public policy obstacle to recognition of authentic maintenance obligation instruments, it should be pointed out that it is hardly possible for authentication procedure to violate procedural public policy.[74] It would seem more likely that the enforcement may contradict the second State's substantive public policy in exceptional cases. A public policy violation may come into question if the maintenance obligation is not commensurate with the economic circumstances of the debtor and seriously overburdens him financially. Depending on the procedural configuration in the individual codes of procedure, the debtor will not be able to receive adequate legal protection by means of a modification application and a judicial decision.

[73] *Cf* accordingly also §§ 8 et seq, § 55 para 3 Gesetz zur Ausführung zwischenstaatlicher Verträge und zur Durchführung von Verordnungen und Abkommen der Europäischen Gemeinschaft auf dem Gebiet der Anerkennung und Vollstreckung in Zivil- und Handelssachen (German Act for the Implementation of International Treaties and for the Implementation of European Community Regulations in the Area of Recognition and Enforcement in Civil and Commercial Matters, (AVAG)). The legal clarity and thus rapid enforcement of maintenance would be improved if the Member States provided information on the type of authentic instruments admissible in national legal systems and the national requirements on proving enforceability in the European Judicial Atlas or the Justice Portal.

[74] For this reason, it is not possible to draw on the lack of international authentication jurisdiction from the perspective of the enforcement state, *cf* Andrae (n 42) Art 57 margin no 8. From the practical experience of DIJuF (German Institute for Youth Human Services and Family Law) with the cross-border enforcement of child maintenance, it should also be pointed out that, in enforcement proceedings, maintenance debtors regularly invoke alleged deficiencies of the authentic instrument of obligation. When a duplicate without the liable parent's signature is available, objections to forged signatures or, in connection with status authentications and language-related difficulties, lack of awareness of having expressed a legally relevant declaration of intent with respect to the maintenance obligation, are raised.

iii. Recognition and Declaration of Enforceability under the Hague Maintenance Convention 2007

Authentic instruments involving maintenance arrangements are admissible in accordance with the complex regulation for recognition and declaration of enforceability of Article 30 in connection with Article 3(e) of the Hague Maintenance Convention 2007.

a. Concept of Maintenance Arrangement in the Hague Maintenance Convention 2007

As per Article 3(e) of the Hague Maintenance Convention 2007, a maintenance arrangement refers to a written agreement relating to maintenance payments that has either been formally drawn up as an authentic instrument or registered by a competent authority (sub-paragraph i) or has been certified or registered by a competent authority or has been authenticated by or concluded, registered or filed with a competent authority (sub-paragraph ii) and may be the subject of review and modification by a competent authority.

What is questionable, according to this definition, is the extent to which unilateral obligation declarations that are publicly authenticated also fall within the material scope of application of the Hague Maintenance Convention 2007 as a maintenance arrangement.

According to the wording of Article 3(e), a maintenance arrangement refers to an agreement that comes about under the conditions standardised in (i) and (ii). A substantive meaning in the sense of a contractual arrangement between two opponents is not expressed by the wording. According to the Explanatory Report on the Hague Maintenance Convention 2007 by Borrás and Degeling, the Contracting States engaged in extensive discussions about whether authentic instruments and private agreements should fall within the material scope of the Convention.[75] Here, the term 'maintenance arrangement' is used to include both authentic instruments and private agreements between the parties. The subject matter of the discussions was not only the various types of legal declarations that are able to be enforced, but rather—independently of the type of legal act—the *legally enforceable form* of the authentic instrument as such.[76] From the sense and purpose of the Convention it is clear that alternative amicable arrangements for concluding a maintenance dispute are encouraged (*cf* Article 6(2)(d) of the Hague Maintenance Convention 2007). The wording may lead to the assumption that unilateral obligation declarations are not covered by the material scope of the Convention. The Explanatory Report itself is not unambiguous with respect to the exclusion of unilateral declarations. Their exclusion—provided they are linked to a prior or subsequent agreement with the creditor—would,

[75] A Borrás and J Degeling, 'Explanatory Report on the Convention on the International Recovery of Child Support and Other Forms of Family Maintenance', November 2009, para 72 available at www.hcch.net/upload/expl38.pdf (accessed December 2013). The Report emphasises in para 552 the 'great advantages' of including maintenance arrangements in the scope of the Convention of promoting amicable solutions and the use of ADR.

[76] According to the Explanatory Report, ibid 26, no 74, the unilateral obligations declarations seem to be covered by sub-para (ii) of Art 3(e): 'In Germany and Austria maintenance arrangements are often concluded with the child welfare authority (Jugendamt).' From the authors' perspective the maintenance arrangements are only authenticated by German youth welfare offices. As they regularly contain unilateral maintenance declarations of the maintenance debtor, they are, however, based on a prior written or oral agreement with the maintenance creditor or become an agreement at a later point of time when the authentic instrument is received by the maintenance creditor (*cf* 6). Therefore, sub-para (i) should be applicable to German authentic instruments on maintenance obligations drawn up by a notary public or a youth welfare office.

however, contradict the sense and purpose of the Convention. A restrictive interpretation of Articles 3(e) and 30 of the Hague Maintenance Convention 2007 would not sit well with a variety of legal developments to enhance the significance of authentic instruments in cross-border legal relations.[77] Thus, unilateral maintenance declarations in the form of an authentic instrument should be part of Articles 3(e) and 30 of the Hague Maintenance Convention 2007 at least where there is a mutual consent between the parties and the unilateral declaration reflects that mutual consent in written and enforceable form. Alternatively, since such unilateral declarations are comparable to agreements pursuant to Articles 3(e) and 30 and not covered by the Convention's scope, the rules of those Articles of the Convention should be applied by way of analogy to them.

b. Procedural Provisions

Article 30 of the Hague Maintenance Convention 2007 determines the entire procedural treatment of maintenance arrangements with respect to recognition and the declaration of enforceability as well as the cooperation of the authorities. It contains some independent provisions and also refers to other provisions.

Article 30(2) extends the applicability of the system of cooperation between the Central Authorities—pursuant to Article 10—to maintenance arrangements. Article 30(3) contains a procedural regulation with respect to the documents that need to be provided for the recognition and declaration of enforceability proceedings, whereby, in addition to the complete wording of the maintenance agreement, a certificate confirming the enforceability of the agreement in the State of origin is to be provided as well. According to this, it is imperative that the arrangement in the particular case meets the requirement of enforceability as a judicial decision in the State of origin.[78]

Article 30(4) deals with the grounds for refusal with respect to an application for recognition and enforcement of a maintenance arrangement: public policy, fraud or falsification and an incompatible decision rendered between the same parties and having the same purpose. The grounds for refusal are all discretionary under the Convention but at least the public policy ground can be invoked at first instance.[79]

Article 30(5) then expressly regulates the analogous application of the procedural regulations of Chapter V (namely mutatis mutandis), except for the regulations in Articles 20, 22, 23(7), 25(1) and (3), which are not meant to apply. Differences in the procedure are regulated further with respect to the procedural options of Articles 23 and 24.

Article 30(6) contains the requirements for suspending the recognition and declaration of enforceability proceedings, and Article 30(7) and (8) standardise exceptions for the recognition and declaration of enforceability for maintenance arrangements. Article 30(7) permits Contracting States to accept applications for recognition and enforcement concerning maintenance arrangements only when they are brought through Central Authorities.[80] Article 30(8) entitles a Contracting State to reserve the right not to recognise

[77] Especially in the European Union.

[78] Explanatory Report (n 75) para 558.

[79] See Art 30(4) and (5). By contrast, Art 24 of the Maintenance Regulation and Art 57 of the Lugano Convention and of the Brussels I Regulation only allow the grounds for refusal to come into play in the appeal proceedings.

[80] Norway has made this declaration, see www.hcch.net/index_en.php?act=conventions.statusprint&cid=131 (accessed December 2013).

and enforce a maintenance arrangement. Thus, there is no unlimited regulation for enforcing authentic instruments on a global scale. However, this would be essential in the interest of equivalent treatment of authentic instruments and the functionally comparable 'judgments by consent' of the common law legal systems. These involve judicial decisions that are able to be reached by expedited proceedings due to the debtor agreeing to pay the debt. In maintenance disputes, this means is resorted to particularly often in amicable arrangements for the purpose of establishing an enforceable order in favour of the creditor. Since, pro forma, judgments by consent involve judicial decisions, they are readily enforceable in the Contracting States, whereas the enforceability of the authentic instruments depends on whether the Contracting States have avoided making the reservation under Article 30(8). Therefore, it would be preferable if States do not make the reservation.[81]

B. Enforcement

Enforcement can be readily executed in Germany from an enforceable German instrument.

In cross-border cases, the enforcement takes place based on an instrument that has been officially declared enforceable, a directly enforceable instrument or a *European enforcement order*.

Enforcement is carried out in accordance with the law of the enforcement State (Article 41 of the EC Maintenance Regulation and Article 32 of the Hague Maintenance Convention 2007). No international or European legal basis exists for harmonised regulation of enforcement law. However, certain minimum standards are created internationally, namely promptness, non-discrimination and effectiveness (see Articles 32 to 34 of the Hague Maintenance Convention 2007) and in the EU, equivalence (Article 41(1) of the EC Maintenance Regulation) and effectiveness (general principle of EU law). There are no special features as a result of the nature of the authentic instrument. As a rule, the same enforcement instruments are available as for enforcing other enforcement orders. The legal remedies permitted in the context of enforcement are admissible for enforcement of authentic instruments.

IV. Modification Options and Legal Remedies

Authenticated statutory maintenance obligations can change, with respect to grounds or amount, or cease. This therefore raises the question as to which modification and defence options are available to the maintenance debtor in an international context.

A. Amicable Modification of German Authentic Instruments

German authentic instruments may be amicably rendered ineffective, limited and/or replaced by a new instrument. In cross-border cases, it is important to pay attention to any changes of applicable law.

[81] Regrettably the Ukraine has made this reservation, see www.hcch.net/index_en.php?act=conventions.statusprint&cid=131 (accessed December 2013). *Cf* Fleischhauer (n 1) 22.

If the parties are in agreement that the statutory maintenance obligation has decreased or no longer applies, then the authenticated maintenance obligation may be wholly or partially cancelled by means of an informal agreement. It is important to bear in mind this does not void the enforceability of the existing authentic instrument. As a rule, an improper claim against the debtor will be prevented by the creditor wholly or partially renouncing the right to the enforcement of the authentic instrument. If the creditor were nevertheless to initiate the enforcement, the debtor would be able to successfully defend him or herself against these measures.[82]

If the parties are in agreement that the statutory maintenance obligation has increased and that an enforceable maintenance order should be drawn up for the new amount owed, the new maintenance obligation must be authenticated. In order to avoid misunderstandings, the previous instrument will be referred to in the new instrument and a comment made with respect to the fact that, and to what extent, the effects of the previous instrument have been amicably annulled. Insofar as all claims (especially arrears) arising from the previous instrument have been satisfied, the creditor generally hands over the executable copy of the previous instrument to the debtor to ensure that no claims can be made against the latter concerning the old maintenance order.

B. Judicial Modification and Defence Options

If the parties cannot agree, it is necessary to initiate court proceedings. As to which proceedings are admissible, this will depend on the goals of the applicant. For example, the substantive contents of the instrument or its enforceability may be called into question. Moreover, the enforcement measures initiated may be objected to.

The question of delimiting the potential proceedings is not uncontroversial even in purely German cases. In cases with an international scope, this is even harder to answer, since the various systems exhibit profound differences that result in proceedings with the same objective as to content being characterised differently in international proceedings. This can give rise to doubts as to the international jurisdiction of the courts appealed to and the compatibility of national proceedings with international enforcement instruments.

i. Legal Situation in Germany

a. Modification of Authentic Instruments

In relation to the *substantive requirements* of the variation of authentic instruments, it is necessary to distinguish between unilateral declarations and contractual obligations.

According to German procedural law,[83] it is possible to modify an authentic instrument based on an *agreement* if the circumstances present at the time of authentication (in particular the financial situation of the parties, the needs of the maintenance creditor, new maintenance obligations of the debtor, legal situation) have changed so much in the

[82] See below section IV.B.i.b.

[83] § 239 German Act on the Procedure in Family Matters and in Matters of Non-contentious Jurisdiction (FamFG).

meantime that the maintenance amount owed has changed in accordance with the civil law rules.[84]

What first needs to be done is inspect whether the parties have stipulated modification options in the authentic instrument and whether certain requirements or even the exclusion of modification have been arranged. If there are no evident indications of such an agreement, a breach or disruption relating to the basis of the agreement may justify the modification.[85] German law[86] defines the basis of an agreement (*Geschäftsgrundlage*) as the objective and subjective circumstances[87] on which the agreement has been established. What is relevant to maintenance, however, are generally the objective circumstances that formed the basis of the maintenance calculation at the time the authentic instrument was drawn up. With respect to subsequent modification options, it is reasonable in this respect to expressly list these circumstances in the authentic instrument. If this was not done, they can also be derived from interpretation of the instrument or from the correspondence between the parties prior to the agreement.

Concerning *unilateral declarations*, the above-mentioned principles of frustration of contract cannot be used due to lack of a contractual basis. According to case law from the German Federal Court of Justice, the relevant legal and factual circumstances need to have changed so much subsequently that the payment of the maintenance in the ordered amount cannot reasonably be expected from the debtor.[88] However, the Federal Court of Justice[89] does not postulate the event of exceeding a certain materiality limit.[90]

The Federal Court of Justice[91] makes an exception with respect to authentic instruments that have been drawn up either without previously conferring with the maintenance creditor or within the context of a dispute against the will of the latter; in such cases, it permits an application to determine maintenance (*Unterhaltsfestsetzungsverfahren*) with respect to the entire amount claimed despite the existence of a (partial) enforceable order in the form of a unilateral commitment.[92] The background to this is that the maintenance creditor has a right to the establishment of an enforceable order relating to the full statutory maintenance amount and that he or she cannot be expected to have to deal with two different orders (a unilateral commitment concerning a partial amount and a court decision concerning the amount in dispute).[93]

[84] Eg see R Bömelburg in H Prütting and T Helms (eds), *FamFG Kommentar* (Cologne, Dr Otto Schmidt, 2013) § 239 margin no 18 or M Klein in Schulte-Bunert and Weinreich (eds), *FamFG-Kommentar* (Cologne, Luchterhand, 2011) § 239 margin no 1.

[85] § 313 BGB.

[86] § 313 para 1 BGB.

[87] C Grüneberg in O Palandt (ed), *Bürgerliches Gesetzbuch* (Munich, CH Beck, 2013) § 313 margin no 3, 4.

[88] BGH (2007) *Zeitschrift für das gesamte Familienrecht* 715 margin no 11; D Schmitz 'Verfahrensrecht' in P Wendl and HJ Dose (eds), *Das Unterhaltsrecht in der familienrichterlichen Praxis* (Munich, CH Beck, 2011) § 10 margin no 279.

[89] BGH (2011) *Zeitschrift für das gesamte Familienrecht* 1041, BT-Drucks 16/6308, 258.

[90] The modification of court decisions assumes that a so-called materiality limit will be exceeded by approximately 10%, pursuant to § 238 FamFG.

[91] Decision dated 2 December 2009, (2010) *Zeitschrift für das gesamte Familienrecht* 195.

[92] For more on this debate in German literature, see Schmitz (n 88) § 10 margin no 275, R Bork, F Jacoby and D Schwab, *FamFG Kommentar* (Bielefeld, Ernst und Werner Gieseking Verlag, 2013) § 239 margin no 11; HU Graba, 'Zur Abänderung der Jugendamtsurkunde' (2005) *Zeitschrift für das gesamte Familienrecht* 678, 679.

[93] Knittel (n 5) margin no 371.

Modification proceedings do not allow the case to be reviewed completely, but only for the ongoing maintenance obligation to be adjusted to the changed situation.[94] Thus, maintenance orders cannot be modified with respect to maintenance in arrears, pursuant to § 239 FamFG.

With regard to the timing of the modification, unlike court decisions which accrue legal force, a retroactive modification of an instrument is generally possible in terms of procedure.[95] Only substantive grounds can conflict with a retroactive modification. In particular, a retroactive increase in the maintenance amount can only be asserted once a notice of default has been issued, that is, a request to provide information or a request to pay.[96]

Other limitations, such as grounds of protection of trust, may not be asserted. In particular, the German legislator assumes that the creditor is sufficiently protected by German enrichment law.[97] Accordingly, a creditor who has received too much will, as a rule, not have to pay back the wrongly paid maintenance if he or she is not in a financial position to do so, and acted in good faith when spending the maintenance amounts received.[98]

b. Cancelling Enforceability of the Authentic Instrument (Action Raising an Objection to the Claim being Enforced)

An action raising an objection to the claim being enforced (*Vollstreckungsabwehrantrag*)[99] may be employed to have the enforcement arising from the authentic instrument declared inadmissible after enforcement measures have been initiated, thus eliminating its enforceability.[100] This application is generally used to assert pleas by way of avoidance or estoppels, such as fulfilment, subsequently effective maintenance or enforcement waivers, the conclusion of a cancellation agreement or compensation, or refutation of a declaration due to an absence of intent as per § 119 et seq BGB. With particular regard to authentic instruments, it must be borne in mind that the preclusion clause of § 767 paragraph 2 ZPO does not apply, which means that pleas arising before the instrument is drawn up can also be asserted (§ 797 paragraph 4 ZPO).

c. Defence Against Specific Enforcement Measures (Debtor Protection Rules)

The German Code of Procedure provides for debtor protection rules in the form of limits of exemption from seizure of earned income[101] or seizure prohibitions for certain earnings[102] or objects.[103] The latter only limit the enforceability of the maintenance order with

[94] Schmitz (n 88) § 10 margin no 267; BGH (1995) *Zeitschrift für das gesamte Familienrecht* 665.

[95] BGH (1984) *Zeitschrift für das gesamte Familienrecht* 888.

[96] § 1613 para 1 BGB.

[97] § 818 para 3 BGB.

[98] F Klinkhammer, *Der Unterhaltsprozess* (Cologne, Luchterhand, 2009) ch 5 margin no 388; I Rasch 'Verfahren in Unterhaltsstreitsachen' in U Ehinger, G Griesche and I Rasch (eds), *Handbuch Unterhaltsrecht* (Cologne, Dr Otto Schmidt, 2010) XIV margin no 870.

[99] As per § 767 ZPO.

[100] H Putzo '§ 767 ZPO' in H Thomas and H Putzo (eds), *Zivilprozessordnung Kommentar* (Munich, CH Beck, 2011) § 767 margin no 12; R Lackmann '§ 767 ZPO' in HJ Musilak (ed), *Kommentar zur Zivilprozessordnung* (Munich, CH Beck, 2008) § 767 margin no 2.

[101] § 850c ZPO.

[102] § 850a and b ZPO.

[103] § 811 ZPO.

respect to time, object or quantity, without calling the enforceability or the existence of the maintenance order into question.

ii. Delimitation Issues in Cross-Border Legal Relations

It is undisputed in Germany and internationally that maintenance obligations, which typically involve recurring payments, do not necessarily persist indefinitely. The question whether, for instance, modification proceedings or enforcement defence measures are to be initiated in certain factual circumstances is contentious in German intra-State law.[104] Such delimitation issues particularly affect authentic instruments, since their existence is not protected by legal force.[105] The issues are aggravated in cross-border legal relations due to the profound systemic differences[106] and the additional recognition obligations that need to be taken into consideration.

If an authentic instrument is drawn up in one State and enforced in another State, this may call into question for the debtor whether he should proceed against the enforcement measures, against the existence, or against the enforceability, of the authentic instrument. This may well raise the question of where the admissible proceedings are to be initiated (international jurisdiction) and to what extent the competence of the enforcement court appealed to as determined by national law is compatible with the provisions (recognition obligations) of the international enforcement instruments. Neither the EC Maintenance Regulation nor the Hague Maintenance Convention 2007 contains clear delimitation rules with respect to whether one kind of proceeding enforcement (Article 41 of the EC Maintenance Regulation and Article 34 of the Hague Maintenance Convention 2007) or another modification proceeding (Articles 8 and 21(2) of the EC Maintenance Regulation and Article 18 of the Hague Maintenance Convention 2007) is legally justified. It can also be gathered from the Regulation that, as per Article 41 of the EC Maintenance Regulation, the enforcement measures are subject to the autonomous enforcement law of the enforcing state, while the procedural requirements of establishment of support orders are subject to the law of the State that is competent as per Article 3 et seq of the EC Maintenance Regulation. Just how the legal remedies that exist in the EU Member States are able to be assigned to one procedure or another is yet unclear. While a definition of the enforcement procedure is completely lacking, an attempt at a definition of the modification decision[107] can be found in Articles 21(2) and 24(2) of the EC Maintenance Regulation.[108] However, this is too imprecise to solve problems involving conflict of laws between different legal systems and/or legal remedies.

In order to avoid conflicts of jurisdiction and undesirable forum-shopping as well as to guarantee the efficiency of the international enforcement instruments, a harmonised

[104] In certain constellations, the German Federal Court of Justice actually permits both kinds of proceedings (eg for forfeiture: BGH (1990) *Zeitschrift für das gesamte Familienrecht* 1095).

[105] § 767 para 2 ZPO, § 238 para 2 FamFG.

[106] C Strasser, 'Abänderung und Vollstreckung von Unterhaltstiteln aus dem EU-Ausland in Deutschland' (2007) *Familie, Partnerschaft, Recht* 451.

[107] 'A decision which has the effect of modifying an earlier decision on maintenance on the basis of changed circumstances'.

[108] Art 8 of the EC Maintenance Regulation also expressly refers to modification proceedings but it does not contain any practical definition.

regulation of the international jurisdiction with respect to the possible legal remedies depending on the goal of the proceedings and a precise definition of the legal means falling under Article 41 EC Maintenance Regulation appears to be desirable. Until then, the existing national legal remedies against authentic instruments are to be qualified and applied in conformity with European law depending on their legal nature.[109]

The following practical examples in the scope of application of the EC Maintenance Regulation serve to illustrate the problems described.

(1) In German law, the modification proceedings are systematically assigned to the procedure of establishing support orders.[110] Another international procedural qualification should be ruled out, since, in accordance with § 239 FamFG, the proceedings are used to call into question the existence of the claim determined in the authentic instrument and, as a rule, pursue the establishment of a substitute order (see above).[111] Furthermore Article 8 of the EC Maintenance Regulation is to be interpreted as a limitation of the provisions of Article 3 et seq. If the creditor is the applicant, he may choose to file the proceedings either at his or her habitual residence,[112] or at the habitual residence of the debtor,[113] or if maintenance is an ancillary matter at the court with jurisdiction to deal with status issues or parental responsibility.[114] If the debtor is the applicant, only the courts at the habitual residence of the defendant are competent, pursuant to Articles 3(a) and 8 of the Regulation, if the original decision was given in that State.[115]

The debtor protection rules, for example within the meaning of § 850 ZPO (see above) are obviously to be assigned to the enforcement proceedings, since they limit neither the existence nor the enforceability of the authentic instruments, but only temporarily the recoverability of the authenticated child maintenance claim for the protection of the debtor. Therefore, these provisions are subject to German intra-State law when enforcement measures are being executed in Germany.

What is considerably more difficult is the international procedural qualification of the action raising an objection to the claim being enforced pursuant to § 767 ZPO. The precise legal nature of these proceedings is already disputed in German law.[116] The prevailing opinion in the literature presumes a procedural action requesting a modification of a legal relationship (*prozessuale Gestaltungsklage*),[117] since the exclusive matter in dispute is the cancellation of the enforceability of the maintenance order.[118] Moreover, the decision

[109] Case C-464/01 *Gruber v Bay* [2005] ECR I-439 on the Brussels Convention 1968.

[110] § 231 FamFG.

[111] In Germany, a modification application is a claim for benefits (*Leistungsantrag*) and, at the same time, an application for a change of status (*Gestaltungsantrag*), whereby it is verified whether the continuously changing economic circumstances or other circumstances have developed in a way other than expected since the maintenance order was made (BGH (1984) *Zeitschrift für das gesamte Familienrecht* 470, and (2005) 479).

[112] Art 3(b) of the EC Maintenance Regulation.

[113] Ibid Art 3(a).

[114] Ibid Art 3(c) and (d).

[115] But see the exceptions to this rule in ibid Art 8(2). For cross-border issues, German intra-State law (§ 28 AUG, German Implementation Law) stipulates a special jurisdiction of the central family courts at the *seat* of the Higher Regional Court (*Oberlandesgericht*), in derogation from § 231 FamFG. In particular, this serves to focus competencies in the area of international law.

[116] A Halfmeier, 'Die Vollstreckungsgegenklage im Recht der internationalen Zuständigkeit' (2007) *Praxis des internationalen Privat- und Verfahrensrechts* 381 et seq.

[117] C Seiler '§ 767 ZPO' in H Thomas and H Putzo (eds), *Zivilprozessordnung Kommentar* (Munich, CH Beck, 2011) § 767 margin no 1; BGH (2005) *Zeitschrift für das gesamte Familienrecht* 1832.

[118] Halfmeier (n 116) 381; Seiler (n 117) § 767 margin no 3.

allegedly does not produce an effect until it is submitted to the executing authority and does not accrue legal force.[119] In summary, the opposing view says that in an action raising an objection to the claim being enforced, the matter in dispute is not limited to the enforceability of the existing maintenance order, but also refers to the original claim established in the order.[120] These opinions appear to better harmonise the goal of European enforcement instruments than the currently prevailing opinion in case law and the literature.

While § 767 ZPO is systematically located in the enforcement part of ZPO and is directed against the enforceability of the instrument, the admissible objections, on the other hand, which concern the existence of the enforceable claim, and the exclusive intra-State jurisdiction of the family court at the habitual residence of the maintenance creditor,[121] speak for assigning the enforcement defence proceedings to the procedure for establishing the support order and not to the enforcement procedure. With respect to European Union law, another characterisation would hardly be compatible with the recognition obligations[122] resulting from the EC Maintenance Regulation and the concentration of the competence to decide on the merits in the State of origin, since an enforcement characterisation would ultimately enable an inadmissible review as to the substance of the maintenance order through the back-door. A review of the authentic instrument in the Member State performing recognition or enforcement (to its full extent, anyway) is, however, not stipulated by the EC Maintenance Regulation (see above). Therefore, the recognition obligation states that objections to the enforceability of the maintenance obligation instruments or to substantive and content-related grounds for invalidity are to be submitted exclusively to the courts of the Member State of origin.[123] The international jurisdiction of the German enforcement defence court is therefore determined by Article 3 et seq of the EC Maintenance Regulation.[124] In this respect, it is doubtful whether objections to the claim established in a foreign enforcement order can be asserted as per §§ 66 AUG, 767 ZPO (instead of the proceedings in accordance with repealed § 44 AUG).[125] In order not to challenge the individual act of enforcement, but rather the enforceability of the maintenance order itself, the view taken here is that, pursuant to Article 3(a) of the EC Maintenance Regulation, the application should be filed at the courts of the habitual residence of the maintenance creditor in the State of origin.[126]

(2) There is a similar problem with respect to France. The enforcement law there stipulates that objections such as fulfilment, set-off or limitation be asserted at the enforcement court appealed to concerning the specific enforcement measure (*opposition*).[127] The Cour de Cassation even partly allows the enforcement judge to inspect the substantive validity of authentic instruments.[128] With respect to the issue of limitation, the EC Maintenance

[119] Halfmeier (n 116) 382.

[120] Ibid.

[121] For authentic instruments, jurisdiction for the court being appealed to with respect to an action raising an objection to the claim being enforced arises from § 797 para 5 ZPO, in derogation from § 767 para 1. In maintenance matters, § 797 para 5 ZPO is in turn supplanted by § 232 FamFG.

[122] For the scope of the recognition obligation, see section III.2.

[123] Indirectly in this way as well: recital 13.

[124] Halfmeier (n 116) 388.

[125] Bundesrat DS 311/12 dated 25 May 2012.

[126] See also in this respect: recital 13 of EC Maintenance Regulation.

[127] Lefort (n 22) margin no 153.11 et seq.

[128] Civ 2ème, 18 June 2009, no 08-10.843, D-2009, 1768, com. Avena-Robarnet.

Regulation contains a clarifying provision in Article 21(2), according to which the most favourable prescription term for the maintenance creditor shall be valid for any ambiguities that arise concerning the applicable statute of limitations so that the question of admissible proceedings and international jurisdiction that has been very relevant for practitioners hitherto has lost practical significance, since the French enforcement court may well have to apply the more favourable foreign law.

With respect to the other objections, it is possible for conflicts of jurisdiction to arise in regard to German authentic instruments establishing maintenance obligations or even for irreconcilable decisions to ensue, since the debtor can theoretically go with the same plea both to the French enforcement court as well as to the German court at the habitual residence of the maintenance creditor in the context of actions raising an objection to the claim being enforced within § 767 ZPO. To resolve this conflict, the above statements on the interpretation of the German action raising an objection to the claim being enforced in compliance with European Union law would accordingly apply with the corollary that the existence of authentic instruments or substantive objections to the established maintenance claim may only be asserted in the State of origin of the authentic instrument or, if there is a change of residence, where the creditor is habitually resident.

(3) In England and Wales, the competence of the enforcement courts (especially the magistrates' courts) is even wider in scope than those in France or Germany. As a rule, they are authorised according to local enforcement law to inspect applications of the debtor, which correspond to a German modification application with respect to content (conclusive modification of the established support amount for the future) and go even further in legal effects (irrevocable remission of accrued arrears,[129] granting of redemption by instalments) if the maintenance debtor at the time the enforcement proceedings were executed is not able to comply with his or her maintenance obligation. Due to issues that had arisen in the past, certain provisions of the Magistrates' Court Act 1982[130] were declared inapplicable in the course of implementing the EC Maintenance Regulation, insofar as maintenance orders have been registered for enforcement within Chapter IV of the EC Maintenance Regulation. However, this did not eliminate the fundamental systemic differences. First of all, the new provisions only applied insofar as a maintenance order was recognised and registered on the basis of Chapter IV of the EC Maintenance Regulation. The problem therefore persists with respect to maintenance orders subject to the Brussels Convention 1968 (concerning authentic instruments drawn up before 1 March 2002) or the Brussels I Regulation (authentic instruments registered before 18 June 2011); however, the latter contains recognition obligations similar to those of the EC Maintenance Regulation. Moreover, the competence of the enforcement courts to order the fulfilment by instalment and the deferral of the maintenance amounts[131]—where evident—is not excluded. Depending on how the decision of the English enforcement court is expressed, such an order of deferral or payment by instalment can have the same effect as a seizure limit and thus merely limit the enforceability of the German authentic instrument temporarily. However, if the decision has a conclusive effect, the due-date conditions of the established maintenance claim will be modified. This constitutes a conclusive modification of the German authentic

[129] Magistrates' Courts Act 1982, s 95; *Bernstein v O'Neill* 1989 (unreported)—on file with the author.
[130] Magistrates' Court Act 1982, ss 60(a), 95(b).
[131] Magistrates' Courts Act 1982, s 75.

instrument, which is obviously no longer compatible with the recognition obligations arising from the EC Maintenance Regulation (see above). To ensure the *effet utile* of the EC Maintenance Regulation, an assignment of these English enforcement provisions, as in the case of the German enforcement defence proceedings or the French *opposition*, to the proceedings of establishing maintenance orders seems inevitable. In a German/English case, therefore, a modification application of the maintenance debtor residing in England would need to be initiated in the State of residence of the maintenance creditor (here in Germany), even though the modification proceedings would be assigned to the enforcement proceedings according to English national law. A consequential problem of this 'intervention' in the system of English enforcement law could be, however, that there is a risk that insufficient debtor protection will be granted, insofar as the English enforcement law does not provide for any other protective mechanisms in terms of seizure limits. Article 21 of the EC Maintenance Regulation stipulates that the enforcement can be suspended if the enforceability is suspended in the State of origin. In the time period between initiating enforcement defence or modification proceedings in the State of origin and the decision, the enforcement State may be obligated to enforce the maintenance order. The debtor can avoid this by initiating provisional measures against the maintenance order in the State of origin, insofar as the interim measures are accordingly processed quickly. Since this is not always the case in practice, the English courts will find themselves faced with the difficult task of interpreting their competence (especially concerning complete or partial deferral of the fulfilment obligations) in compliance with European Union law so that the content of the EC Maintenance Regulation does not become ineffective, leaving the debtor with no protection. The difficulty of this task clearly shows the need for the adoption of additional harmonising regulations concerning the defence against enforcement measures arising from maintenance orders. This particularly applies to enforcement stemming from authentic instruments, since practice shows that, when it comes to enforcement, foreign courts (especially in the Member States that are unfamiliar with authentic instruments) have even less compunction about getting involved with the substantive objections of the maintenance debtors, since its *res judicata* effect cannot be used as a counter-argument.

V. Outlook

Authentic instruments have played a significant role in previous legislative acts of the EU in the context of enforcement. A new development in the area of authentic instruments can currently be observed in the Regulation proposed by the EU Commission for promoting the free movement of citizens and businesses by simplifying the acceptance of certain authentic instruments within the European Union.[132]

Based on the EU Commission's Green Paper, 'Less bureaucracy for EU citizens: promoting free movement of authentic instruments and recognition of the effects of civil status records', dated 14 December 2010,[133] the Commission presented a proposal for a Regulation

[132] COM (2013) 228 final.

[133] COM (2010) 747 final, also printed in BR-Drucks 831/10. Also H-P Mansel, D Coester-Waltjen, D Henrich and J Kohler, 'Stellungnahme im Auftrag des Deutschen Rats für Internationales Privatrecht zum

on 24 April 2013 concerning the promotion of free movement of citizens and businesses by simplifying the acceptance[134] of certain authentic instruments within the European Union.[135] According to this, the proof of their authenticity by legalisation or apostille that was previously regularly required for certain authentic instruments from other Member States is to be dispensed with.[136] Only in cases of doubt may a public authority of a Member State request further proof. Regarded as authentic instruments in terms of this proposal are instruments that have been drawn up by authorities of the Member States and have evidentiary value with respect to birth, death, name, marriage, registered partnership, parenthood, adoption, residence, EU citizenship, nationality, real estate, legal status and representation of a company or other undertaking, intellectual property rights as well as the absence of a criminal record. Civil status records,[137] in particular, are included in the scope of application of the proposal. Besides the abolition of legalisation, the proposal includes the preparation of multilingual forms in all official languages for civil status records that are intended to make translation unnecessary in the future.

Pursuant to Articles 1 and 2, the proposal exclusively refers to the free circulation of authentic instruments, though not to the recognition of the legal effects of civil status records. Another instrument is to be developed in future for the latter.[138]

It will be interesting to see how far the legal developments progress. Currently, the legislative competence of the EU is still in doubt, since the Commission is basing its proposal on Article 21(2) of the Treaty on the Functioning of the European Union (TFEU) (Measures for Free Movement) and Article 114(1) TFEU (Measures for Strengthening the Single Market), even though it involves a measure of judicial cooperation in accordance with Article 81(2) TFEU.[139]

With respect to the likely effects of the draft on legal maintenance practice, it is evident from the outset that to date the circulation of decisions and instruments from other

Grünbuch der Europäischen Kommission—Weniger Verwaltungsaufwand für EU-Bürger: 'Den freien Verkehr von öffentlicher Urkunden und die Anerkennung der Rechtswirkungen von Personenstandsurkunden erleichtern.' COM (2010) 747 final (2011) *Praxis des internationalen Privat- und Verfahrensrechts* 335; H-P Mansel, 'Kritisches zur "Urkundsinhaltsanerkennung"' (2011) *Praxis des internationalen Privat- und Verfahrensrechts* 341; M Buschbaum, 'Anerkennung von Rechtslagen aufgrund von Personenstandsurkunden' (2011) *Zeitschrift für das Standesamtwesen* 106; R Wagner, 'Anerkennung von Personenstandsurkunden—was heißt das?' (2011) *Deutsche Notarzeitschrift* 176.

[134] The definition of the 'acceptance' of authentic instruments, henceforth shaped by Art 59 of the EU Succession Regulation (eg *cf* Art 2(1) COM (2013) 228) is incorrect in connection with the discontinuation of legalisation and, moreover, prone to cause interpretation problems. To be correct the future legislative act should speak of the 'use' of authentic instruments.

[135] COM (2013) 228 final.

[136] To date, these instruments have been subject to the free consideration of evidence, § 438 para 1 ZPO. The authenticity was generally proven by legalisation pursuant to § 438 para 2 ZPO. Domestic authentic instruments have hitherto already incorporated the presumption of authenticity, § 437 para 1 ZPO.

[137] According to the Commission's Green Paper, this definition includes 'records executed by an authority in order to record the life events of each citizen, such as birth, filiation, adoption, marriage, recognition of paternity, death and also a surname change following marriage, divorce, a registered partnership, recognition, change of sex or adoption'. COM (2010) 747 final, 11.

[138] Compare the statements under section IV on Outlook in this contribution.

[139] S Leible 'Artikel 81' in R Streinz (ed), EUV/AEUV (Munich, CH Beck, 2012) Art 81 AEUV, margin no 54. The designation of the legal basis could be politically motivated as well, in order to expand the scope of application of the Regulation to the Member States that are not participating in the measures of judicial cooperation (Denmark) or have reserved the right to opt-in with respect to such measures: Ireland and the UK; N Dethloff and L Hauschild, 'Familienrecht im Rahmen der justiziellen Zusammenarbeit in Zivilsachen—Das besondere Gesetzgebungsverfahren gem. Art 81 III AEUV' (2010) *Familie, Partnerschaft, Recht* 489, 490.

Member States is already enjoying a certain facilitation via the EC Maintenance Regulation. However, since civil status records are not enforceable—meaning that no 'recognition' as per Article 48(1) of the EC Maintenance Regulation takes place, and the civil status merely represents a preliminary question,[140] so that the release from legalisation as per Article 65 of the EC Maintenance Regulation does not take effect—this facilitation does not apply in the area of civil status records.

According to the Commission's proposal, the authentic instruments of Member States, the authenticity of which—as with German authentic instruments (and civil status records) as well—will be assumed (§ 437 paragraph 1 ZPO), would be able to be regularly resorted to directly in future, without a formalised proof of authenticity in the form of legalisation or an apostille being required beforehand.[141]

However, the substantive inspection by competent authorities[142] of a legal status confirmed in a civil status record (eg relative status) will not be changed by this.

[140] Preliminary questions are conditions of legal relations or legal positions (aside from any required facts) that the conflict of laws or the relevant maintenance regulations imply for the legal consequence to occur or the claim to come about, *cf* HJ Sonnenberger, *Münchner Kommentar BGB* (Munich, CH Beck, 2010) Introduction, margin no 533. As a rule, preliminary questions are to be connected independently, *cf* G Uecker 'Internationales Familienrecht' in H Scholz, N Kleffmann and S Motzer (eds), *Praxishandbuch Familienrecht* (Munich, CH Beck, 2013) part P 'Internationales und interlokales Familienrecht', margin no 13. Therefore, the effectiveness of the contracted marriage is a preliminary question for spousal (separation) maintenance, the evaluation of which may be governed by a different applicable law than that applicable to the maintenance claim itself.

[141] *Cf* hitherto for foreign authentic instruments, § 438 ZPO.

[142] On the substantive right of inspection of the registrar for marriages contracted abroad, see the BGH, decision dated 4 October 1990, XII ZB 200/87 (1991) *Zeitschrift für das gesamte Familienrecht* 300 et seq.

19

Innovations of the 2007 Hague Maintenance Protocol

MIRELA ŽUPAN

I. The Hague Protocol—Introductory Notes

The Protocol of 23 November 2007 on the Law Applicable to Maintenance Obligations (Hague Protocol)[1] is a landmark achievement in both international and European Union private international law. Innovations introduced by the Hague Protocol can be observed on several levels from different standpoints. One such innovation relates to its negotiation and adoption and its impact on the legal framework in maintenance matters. Others relate to its substance, more precisely the choice of law and the connecting factors employed.

This chapter addresses both levels of novel approaches inherent in the Hague Protocol. The first part deals with techniques of legal standardisation in private international law, the interrelations and interdependence of unification within the European Union and the Hague Conference on Private International Law (HCCH). The second part of the chapter analyses the choice of law rules applied in the Hague Protocol, comparing them to the previous Hague Conventions, and discussing the costs and benefits of the newly adopted solutions.

II. Combining International and European Union Instruments—A Novelty in Legal Standardisation

Over the past decade there has been an increasing international convergence in the unification of maintenance issues on both the European Union and global level. There has also been a development in the relationship between the HCCH and the EU, that is, the interrelation of the major forum for private international law unification (HCCH) and the forum that only recently plays an important role in the unification of private international law (the EU). After the Amsterdam Treaty, the EU was endowed with new legislative

[1] Protocol of 23 November 2007 on the Law Applicable to Maintenance Obligations, available at www.hcch.net/index (accessed 30 June 2013).

competence in private international law,[2] consequently the role of the EU and its Member States in the negotiation and conclusion of international Conventions in the area of private international law has been significantly altered as well.[3] A great deal has been written on this subject, debating whether the HCCH and the EU are becoming competitors or collaborators; must one party lose the battle, or is there a mutual win-win scenario?[4] In the context of this chapter, this becomes even more interesting because the maintenance project is the only parallel action undertaken by each of these institutions so far.[5] The answer to the aforementioned questions was first displayed in the pattern of the maintenance projects themselves.

A. Unification of Applicable Law Rules in Both Maintenance Projects

It is well known that applicable law in maintenance matters has been subject to the universal unification efforts of the HCCH for a long period of time.[6] Yet, due to a limited number of signatory States[7] the effects of these unification attempts were insignificant. Therefore, the issue of applicable law remained one of the most controversial parts of contemporary maintenance projects: both the HCCH and the EU wanted to launch a comprehensive Convention/Regulation, dealing with all aspects of private international law.[8] Yet, the outcome was a true innvation in legal standardisation, as will be explained. First and foremost, it should be recalled that unification in this field has always been very limited. The reason is that States can generally be categorised into one of two major groups in the area of private international law of maintenance: States which favour conflict of laws rules that may lead to the application of a foreign law and States that require the application of the law of the forum.[9] The former wanted to use the opportunity of global negotiations

[2] NA Baarsma, *The Europeanisation of International Family Law* (The Hague, TMC Asser Press, 2011) 75–93; T Helms, 'Neues europäisches Familienkollisionrecht' in AL Verbeke et al (eds), *Confronting the Frontiers of Family and Succession Law. Liber Amicorum Walter Pintens* (Antwerp, Intersentia, 2012) 681–701.

[3] P Beaumont and P McEleavy, *Anton's Private International Law* (Edinburgh, W Green & Son, 2011) 894–95.

[4] A Malatesta et al (eds), *The External Dimension of EC Private International Law in Family and Succession Matters* (Milan, CEDAM, 2008).

[5] In 1999 the Special Commision of the Hague Conference decided to start work on the new Hague Maintenance Convention, whilst in 2004 the EU launched a Green Paper on Maintenance Obligations, COM (2004) 254 final initiating work on the Maintenance Regulation. See W Duncan, 'The New Hague Child Support Convention: Goals and Outcomes of the Negotiations' (2010) *Family Law Quaterly 1*; UP Gruber, 'Die neue EG-Unterhaltsverordnung' (2010) *Praxis des Internationalen Privat- und Verfahrensrechts* 128–38; K Siehr, 'The EU Maintenance Regulation and the Hague Maintenance Protocol of 2007. Recognition of Foreign Judgments and the Public Policy Defence' in Permanent Bureau (ed), *A Commitment to Private International Law. Essays in honour of Hans van Loon* (Cambridge, Intersentia, 2013) 529.

[6] Hague Convention of 24 October 1956 on the Law Applicable to Maintenance Obligations towards Children; Hague Convention of 2 October 1973 on the Law Applicable to Maintenance Obligations.

[7] The 1956 Convention has 13 whereas the 1973 Convention has 15 Contracting States.

[8] D Looschelders and S Boos, 'Das grenzüberschreitende Unterhaltsrecht in der internationalen und europäischen Entwicklung' (2006) *Zeitschrift für das gesamte Familienrecht* 374.

[9] Although at first glance these systems seem completely diverse, they both try to ensure that the outcome is in the child's best interest. However, they differ in method. One seeks to provide procedural economy and the other to achieve the best outcome in each case. The Special Commision on the International Recovery of Child Support and Other Forms of Family Maintenance (7–18 June 2004), Working Document No 13 E, 2; for a detailed discussion see D Martiny, 'Maintenance Obligations in the Conflict of Laws' (2004) *Hague Academy Collected Courses* 131–289; D Martiny, 'Is Unification of Family Law Feasible or Even Desirable' in AS Harkamp et al (eds), *Towards a European Civil Code* (Nijmegen, Kluwer, 2011) 429–59.

on cross-border maintenance obligations to modernise the outdated provisions of the earlier HCCH Maintenance Conventions, whereas the latter States were never parties to those Conventions in the first place.[10] It is noteworthy that European States form the majority of Contracting States to the HCCH Maintenance Conventions, and that they were mostly interested in a new modernised regime. Yet, not only did the HCCH intend to modernise the Conventions, it also wanted to attract more signatories. The HCCH therefore analysed the necessity of developing a modernised instrument on applicable law.[11] A nominated working group on applicable law drafted a comprehensive questionnaire and held numerous meetings,[12] only to report finally that a compromise between these two polarised groups could not be achieved.[13] As one of the focal issues of the HCCH was to conclude a comprehensive Convention comprising all aspects of private international law, it became evident that this could not be achieved in one piece of legislation. The possibility of drafting optional provisions on applicable law remained a possibility, the content and subsequently the status of which was negotiated in the years that followed.[14] Finally, the Special Commission on Maintenance Obligations decided these provisions needed to be in a formally separate Protocol. This could be accessed by States acceding to a new Hague Maintenance Convention, while States not interested in unifying the choice of law rules could still join the renewed system of recognition and enforcement.[15]

The most controversial aspect of the EU Commission Proposal for the Maintenance Regulation[16] related to the introduction of applicable law provisions to replace the national rules of the Member States. Why was the issue of applicable law of such importance within the EU maintenance system? The cornerstone of the EU jurisdictional regime is predictability of the forum. Since it retains jurisdictional rules that lead to a multitude of fora (and a singularity of jurisdiction is not an option that could be employed to ensure predictability), it becomes clear that unification of applicable law helps to ensure predictability.[17] As the UK could not accept the inclusion of such provisions, it originally did not opt in to the proposed Regulation within the first three months after it was proposed by the Commission. To enable the participation of as many Member States as possible, Chapter III on applicable law was then modified in the Council in order to establish a two-track system. Subsequently the UK opted in to the Council Regulation (EC) No 4/2009 of 18 December 2008 on Jurisdiction, Applicable Law, Recognition and Enforcement of Decisions, and

[10] Report on the first meeting of the Special Commission on the international recovery of child support and other forms of family maintenance, Prel Doc No 5/2003, 30–32.

[11] M Pelichet, 'Note on the operation of the Hague Conventions relating to Maintenance Obligations and of the New York Convention on the Recovery Abroad of Maintenance', Prel Doc No 1/1995, 17–57; Note on the desirability of revising the Hague Conventions on Maintenance Obligations and including in a new instrument rules on judicial and administrative cooperation, Prel Doc No 2/1999, 16–41.

[12] Questionnaire relating to the Law Applicable to Maintenance Obligations, Prel Doc No 12/2004.

[13] Proposal by the Working Group on the Law Applicable to Maintenance Obligations, Prel Doc No 14/2005.

[14] Form of the Rules on Applicable Law and Possible Final Clauses, Prel Doc No 20/2006; Working Draft on Applicable Law, Prel Doc No 24/2006; Report of the Working Group on Applicable Law, Prel Doc No 27/2007.

[15] Working Draft on Applicable Law—Draft Additional Provisions, Prel Doc No 28/2007.

[16] Proposal for a Council Regulation on jurisdiction, applicable law, recognition and enforcement of decisions and cooperation in matters relating to maintenance obligations, COM (2005) 649. For criticism see M Hellner, 'The Maintenance Regulation: A Critical Assessment of the Commission's Proposal' in K Boele-Woelki et al (eds), *European Challenges in Contemporary Family Law* (Antwerp, Intersentia, 2008) 343ff.

[17] G Calster, 'To Unity and Beyond? The Boundaries of European Private International Law and the European Ius Commune' in AL Verbeke et al (eds), *Confronting the Frontiers of Family and Succession Law. Liber Amicorum Walter Pintens* (Antwerp, Intersentia, 2012) 1459–85.

Cooperation in Matters Relating to Maintenance Obligations[18] (Maintenance Regulation) after it was adopted.[19]

In the end, to please both sides, the HCCH adopted an optional Hague Protocol to the Convention of 23 November 2007 on the International Recovery of Child Support and Other Forms of Family Maintenance (Hague 2007 Maintenance Convention), while the EU omitted its own applicable law provisions, and instead referred to the Hague Protocol. A solution previously suggested by scholars prevailed:[20] the Hague Protocol rules were 'mirrored' in the EU Regulation. This approach led to some novel points in legal standardisation, both in the Hague Conference on Private International Law and in the EU. In the long history of the Hague Conference, this was the first time it had drafted an instrument called a 'Protocol'. Protocol is commonly used as a term for an 'instrument that amends, supplements or clarifies a multilateral treaty … normally open to participation by the parties to the parent agreement'.[21] Despite the definition, the 2007 Protocol is not dependent on the Hague 2007 Maintenance Convention, as prescribed in Article 23(3). The term merely suggests that there is a 'common origin and functional connection' between these two texts.[22] The main advantage of a Protocol lies in the fact that although it is interconnected to parent agreements, it provides greater detail on particular points.

B. Novelty in Legal Standardisation at a European Union and a Universal Level

On several points, the Hague Protocol is a textbook example of the external competence of the EU, and a novelty in its legal standardisation. Several issues need to be discussed in relation to the EU accession to this international Convention. In order to understand the legal background of such an outcome, it is necessary to review the doctrine on the status of international agreements in EU law.[23] The *ERTA* doctrine established by the Court of Justice of the European Union (CJEU) was clearly employed to justify the exclusive competence of the EU in the area of private international law. The Union's external competence is exclusive to the extent that an international Convention affects internal EU rules or alters their scope. In situations of EU exclusive external competence, the role of Member States and the EU as actors in negotiating and concluding international agreements has been altered. Therefore, only the EU, but not the Member States, can accede to international agreements falling into exclusive EU competence.[24] Keeping in mind the expansion of the EU instruments adopted in the framework of the European Area of Freedom, Security and Justice after the Treaty of Amsterdam; the *ERTA* doctrine contributed to a gradual, but in the end

[18] [2009] OJ L 7/1.

[19] LA Buckley, 'European Family Law: The Beginning of the End for Proper Provision?' (2012) *Irish Journal Of Family Law* 31.

[20] Hellner (n 16) 352.

[21] United Nations, *Treaty Handbook* (New York, Treaty Section of the Office of Legal Affairs, 2006) 62.

[22] A Bonomi, 'The Hague Protocol of 23 November 2007 on the Law Applicable to Maintenance Obligations' (2008) *Yearbook of Private International Law* 337.

[23] S Barriati, *Cases and Materials on EU Private International Law* (Oxford, Hart Publishing, 2011) 31–41.

[24] A de MS Pedro and J-S Bergé, 'The Place of International Agreements and European Law in the European Code of Private International Law' in M Fallon et al (eds), *Quelle architecture pour un code européen de droit international privé* (Brussels, Peter Lang, 2011) 388.

significant, broadening of the areas belonging to the Union's exclusive competence.[25] It is a fact that the EU gained internal competence that was transferred to external competence, also generated by the accession of the EU to the HCCH.[26] From the EU perspective, the accession to the Hague Conference was a necessary step in enabling the EU to exercise its external competence in the field of international cooperation in civil matters. Due to a high level of international cooperation in the framework of the HCCH, and a substantial number of Conventions and areas covered by HCCH activities, the full membership of the EU to the HCCH (3 April 2007) is a landmark development in the entire modern history of private international law.[27] The EU can accede to the Conventions to the extent that the matters governed by the Conventions fall within its competence.[28]

Another important question is 'what are the implications of such external competence for maintenance issues?' The Hague 2007 Maintenance Convention and the Hague Protocol are strong examples of international instruments that the EU has decided to conclude alone. Even in these situations that undoubtedly fall within the scope of EU exclusive external competence, fragmentation among its Member States may still persist. Due to the special position of the UK, Ireland and Denmark in respect to Title V of the Treaty on the Functioning of the European Union (TFEU),[29] it may be the case that these Member States are not bound by an EU Decision concerning accession to a particular Convention—regardless of the EU exclusive external competence. The Hague Protocol is in this sense a textbook example. For the purposes of the Decision of 2009 on the accession to the Hague Protocol, the EU does not include Denmark and the UK.[30] In the end, even though Article 3 reveals that the EU exercises competence over all the matters governed by the Protocol and that its Member States are bound by the Protocol by virtue of its conclusion by the EU, in practice that is not the case for Denmark and the UK.

C. Costs and Benefits of Merging the HCCH and the EU Maintenance Choice of Law Rules

What follows here is an attempt to assess the costs and benefits of this merger on the international and European Union levels regarding maintenance issues.

It is thought that an international Convention may, under certain circumstances, render the establishment of an EU regime unnecessary. This is particularly true for international

[25] See Art 3(2) TFEU; A Rosas, 'The Status in EU Law of International Agreements Concluded by EU Member States' (2011) *Fordham International Law Journal* 1306.

[26] A Schulz, 'The Accession of the European Community to the Hague Conference on Private International Law' (2007) *International Comparative Law Quarterly* 947.

[27] The EU has become a member of the Hague Conference as a Regional Economic Integration Organisation; S Szabó, 'Brief Summary of the Evolution of the EU Regulation on Private International Law' (2011) *Iustum Aequum Salutare* 144. See the 2007 revision of the Statute of the Hague Conference.

[28] JJ Kuipers, 'The European Union and the Hague Conference on Private International Law—Forced Marriage or Fortunate Partnership' in H Waele and JJ Kuipers (eds), *The European Union's Emerging International Identity: Views from the Global Arena* (Leiden, Brill, 2011) 159.

[29] Protocol (No 21) on the position of the United Kingdom and Ireland in respect of the area of Freedom, Security and Justice; Protocol (No 22) on the position of Denmark; Consolidated versions of the Treaty on the European Union and the Treaty on the Functioning of the European Union—Protocols—Annexes—Declarations annexed to the Final Act of the Intergovernmental Conference which adopted the Treaty of Lisbon—Tables of equivalences [2008] OJ C 115/1.

[30] Pedro and Bergé (n 24) 388.

agreements with universal application (its provisions are applicable with respect to all situations concerning the relevant subject matter).[31] Under such circumstances it may be appropriate for the EU legislator to include a provision referring to the relevant international treaty. Yet, EU legislation that incorporates an international Convention containing a set of conflict of laws rules by reference is rather rare. The ratio lies in the fact that it is considered unusual that international Conventions adopted by the EU would then make the relevant EU legislation redundant.[32] The first time that the EU used such a direct reference to an international treaty was regarding maintenance matters. Nowadays the most prominent example of such incorporation is to be found in Article 15 of the Maintenance Regulation which refers to the applicable law rules in the Hague Protocol being applied in the Member States bound by that instrument. The situation is even more unusual as the Hague Protocol has only recently entered into force, but it was already applied in the EU as of 18 June 2011 on a provisional basis pursuant to Article 4(2) of the Council Decision on the conclusion of the Hague Protocol.[33] At the time the EU ratified the Hague Protocol it still required a second ratification, since the EU is considered as one party for the purposes of ratification of the Protocol. The peculiarity lies in the fact that a Hague Protocol was applied at the regional level before it entered into force on the international level.[34]

Such a novel development on the unification scene can be beneficial for other reasons as well. It may be in line with the European Council's Stockholm Programme which 'highlights the importance of starting work on consolidation of the instruments adopted so far in the area of judicial cooperation in civil matters'.[35] International agreements and the special position of the EU in their conclusion and negotiation can offer an appropriate framework to standardise both levels (intra-European and towards third States), particularly from the perspective of eventual codification of EU private international law. It would be in line with the imperative towards 'consistency of Union legislation'.[36] It has already been argued that the EU has employed an internationalist approach to harmonisation of law here. With this approach, the EU has clearly admitted that this matter could be more adequately addressed at a global level, rather than merely at a regional level. Since the EU has built its *acquis* on the merits of the work of the HCCH,[37] it has proven that it has taken reverse subsidiarity seriously.[38]

[31] K Kreuzer, 'Gemeinschaftskollisionsrecht und universales Kollisionsrecht (Selbstisolation, Koordination oder Integration?)' in D Baetge et al (eds), *Die richtige Ordnung Festschrift für Jan Kropholler zum 70. Geburtstag* (Tübingen, Mohr Siebeck, 2008) 147–48.

[32] D Sehnálek and J Turoňová, 'Nařízení o výživném a postavení mezinárodních smluv v Evropské unii' (Council Regulation on Maintenance Obligations and the Position of International Treaties in the EU law) (2010) 3 *Právník* 233.

[33] Council Decision of 30 November 2009 on the conclusion by the European Community of the Hague Protocol of 23 November 2007 on the Law Applicable to Maintenance Obligations [2009] OJ L331/17.

[34] P Mankowski, 'Hängepartie dank Kodifikationspolitik—Oder die neuen Leiden des Internationalen Unterhaltsrechts' (2010) *Zeitschrift für das gesamte Familienrecht* 1487.

[35] Stockholm Programme [2010] OJ C 115/1.

[36] The Action Plan implementing the Stockholm Programme was communicated on 20 April 2010, see Communication from the Commission to the European Parliament, the Council, the European Economic and Social Committee and the Committee of the Regions, 'Delivering an Area of Freedom, Security and Justice for Europe's Citizens', COM (2010) 171 final. The Action Plan mentions further actions, eg 'continue to support the Hague Conference on Private International Law'.

[37] P Bremner, 'The EU Maintenance Regulation: A Qualified Success for European Family Law' (2010) *King's Student Law Review* 23.

[38] P Beaumont, 'International Family Law in Europe—The Maintenance Project, the Hague Conference and the EC: A Triumph of Reverse Subsidiarity' (2009) *Rabels Zeitschrift für ausländisches und internationales Privatrecht* 509.

This novel approach to legal standardisation provides examples of some drawbacks and risks as well. Having in mind the special position of some Member States in Title V TFEU, and consequently facing the fact that not all Member States are bound by the Council Decision,[39] the result leads to fragmentation within the EU.

The essential aim of the EU Maintenance Regulation is to simplify recognition and enforcement of maintenance claims.[40] This aim is achieved by abolishing *exequatur* for decisions given in a Member State bound by the Hague Protocol. Such a legal framework erases the border that would impede the free circulation of judgments: a maintenance order of one Member State goes directly to an enforcement judge of another Member State. On the other hand, the enforcement of a maintenance decision of a Member State not bound by the Hague Protocol is subject to a declaration of enforceability in other Member States.[41] In its initial Proposal the Commission stressed the intrinsic link between abolition of *exequatur* and the applicable law harmonisation:

> Thus, the conflict-of-laws rules accompany and facilitate the elimination of 'intermediate measures' at the stage of recognition: the decision is less problematic to accept if it is given in accordance with a law designated according to harmonised rules.[42]

The United Kingdom has opted into the Maintenance Regulation but not to the Hague Protocol. From the UK standpoint, the application of foreign law other than the *lex fori* was unacceptable.[43] The UK has used its *opt in* as a negotiating tactic in order to advance its own interests. On the other hand, not opting in initially enabled the UK to respect its international obligations towards the Hague Conference.[44] The consequence is that the abolition of *exequatur* depends on the issue of applicable law. Moreover, we face a two-track regime in the treatment of foreign maintenance orders. It has been pointed out that the special position of the UK and its subsequent influence of *acquis* content is unwelcome and unjust.[45] If one reviews this objectively, the outcome is actually rather unjust for the UK: with almost no objection it allows the enforcement of each Member States' judgments while UK judgments are subject to additional controls in other Member States when submitted for enforcement.

To this end, one possible weakness of the approach to replace EU legislation by an international Convention lies in the possibility that the relevant Hague Protocol would not achieve significant international acceptance. In such situations, the solution would not be convenient in the end.

[39] According to Art 3 of the 2009 Decision on the conclusion by the European Community of the Hague Protocol of 23 November 2007 on the Law Applicable to Maintenance Obligations ([2009] OJ L 331/17), the declaration that the Member States of the EC would be bound by the Protocol by virtue of its conclusion by the EC included a statement that, for the purpose of such declaration, the term 'European Community' does not include Denmark and the UK.

[40] G Smith, 'The EU Commission's Draft Regulation on Maintenance Obligations' (2006) *International Family Law* 72.

[41] At present, only the UK and Denmark have not acceded to the Protocol, which has been ratified by the EU, see Council Decision of 30 November 2009 on the conclusion by the European Community of the Hague Protocol of 23 November 2007 on the Law Applicable to Maintenance Obligations [2009] OJ L 331/17.

[42] Proposal for a Council Regulation on jurisdiction, applicable law, recognition and enforcement of decisions and cooperation in matters relating to maintenance obligations, COM (2005) 649.

[43] M Pfeiffer, 'Choice of Law in International Family and Succession Law' (2012) *The Lawyer Quarterly* 298.

[44] Bremner (n 37) 9–12.

[45] Bremner (n 37) 10.

III. Basic Scheme of Applicable Law Rules in the Hague Protocol

If we now change the focus to the content of the Hague Protocol, the first interesting point is its scope of application. The Protocol differs from customary 'protocols' concerning the scope of application, because, even though enacted parallel to the Hague 2007 Convention, the Protocol itself has a broader scope than the Convention.[46]

A close look at the basic scheme of applicable law rules in the Hague Protocol indicates further novelties. Most of them are a welcome innovation. If the new Protocol is compared to the Hague 1973 Convention, at first glance it may appear that the primary connecting factor, the creditor's habitual residence, is retained. The very familiar cascade system is also apparent. However the situation is much more complex and many innovations are introduced, even to these principal rules.

A. (Old) Cascade of Connecting Factors (Renewed)

Generally speaking, on some issues the Hague Protocol retained certain principles of its predecessors, whereas in certain areas it went one step further. The vertical approach of the earlier Hague Conventions is reflected through the primacy of the connection of the creditor's habitual residence and the cascade reference system, whereas the greatest novelty is undoubtedly the introduction of party autonomy into the system of conflict of laws rules. A closer analysis shows that even in the first instance, the solutions of the predecessors have been retained in general terms; however the structure of the rules as well as the order of connecting factors have been reversed.

The basic applicable law rule in Article 3 refers to the application of the law of the creditor's habitual residence, and it applies unless the Hague Protocol provides otherwise.[47] The Hague Protocol immediately deals with *conflits mobiles*, as in the case of a change of the creditor's habitual residence, the law of the State of the new habitual residence is applicable as from the moment when the change occurs.

By further applicable law rules the Hague Protocol follows the principle of favouring creditors by introducing subsidiary connections conducive to the realisation of the right to maintenance. In a legal and technical sense, this is called the 'cascade' system based on subsidiary connections.[48] The cascade system works in a way that a subsidiary connection is applied only if the previous connection deprives the creditor of his or her right to maintenance.[49] The intention of the entire 'cascade' system is to increase the creditor's

[46] Bonomi (n 22) 338.

[47] UP Gruber, 'Das Haager Protokoll zum internationalen Unterhaltsrecht' in B Bernreuther et al (eds), *Festschrift für Ulrich Spellenberg* (Munich, Sellier, 2010) 183–84; Bonomi (n 22) 341; F Ferrand, 'The Council Regulation (EC) No 4/2009 of 18 December 2008 on Jurisdiction, Applicable Law, Recognition and Enforcement of Decisions and Cooperation in Matters Relating to Maintenance Obligations' in B Campuzano Díaz et al (eds), *Latest Developments in EU Private International Law* (Cambridge, Intersentia, 2011) 97.

[48] AE Von Overbeck, 'Private International Family Law in Europe' in AG Chloros (ed), *Reform of Family Law in Europe* (Deventer, Kluwer, 1978) 289.

[49] A Bucher, *L'enfant en droit international privé* (Geneva, Helbing & Lichtenhahn etc, 2003) 214.

chances of success. Compared to the debtor the creditor is in a weaker economic position,[50] hence we can argue that the principle of maximum efficiency is reflected by this rule.[51] However, to what extent certain laws favour creditors is questionable.[52] It also means that if a present connection provides any, even wretchedly inadequate maintenance, it applies irrespective of the fact that maintenance is more favourable to the creditor by the law of the subsidiary connection with respect to the amount, the charging system and any other criteria.[53] In this sense, a contradiction arises in relation to the hypothesis that the social circumstances of the creditor have priority. This is because it does not leave any possibility of a real *in favorem* approach to the creditor—if the creditor argued that some other law is more favourable to his or her claim then the authority must reject such objections. The cascade system was introduced into the applicable law system of maintenance by the Hague 1973 Convention, and is retained in the Hague Protocol with certain changes. The cascade system of the Hague Protocol is implemented through several rules. If a creditor is not entitled to maintenance by the law of his or her habitual residence, the *lex fori* applies. Even in the earlier Hague Conventions the *lex fori* was used as a subsidiary connection, but in relation to Article 6 of the Hague 1973 Convention, the Protocol has switched the subsidiary connections: common nationality has been relocated to the second position due to the application of the *lex fori*. This order of connections stems from the fact that the common nationality connection is of minor importance when determining maintenance obligations. The application of the *lex fori* facilitates the work of the authority seised, which may immediately apply its own law without being required to investigate the substance of the law of the parties' common nationality, resulting in a quick procedure and lower costs.[54] If the creditor is unable to obtain maintenance under the law of his or her habitual residence or the *lex fori* then the law of the common nationality of the parties is to be applied.

There is another parallel track of the Hague Protocol cascade system. Namely, pursuant to the provisions of the elective international jurisdiction rules, the maintenance creditor may decide to initiate proceedings in the State of the debtor's habitual residence. In that case, the aforementioned instruction of Article 3 and Article 4(2) does not apply. Instead, the substantive law of the court seised, which is also the law of the debtor's habitual residence, should be applied. In this case the jurisdictional criterion simultaneously determines the application of substantive norms. It is met by the cumulative achievement of two conditions: the assumption is that the creditor knowingly instituted a proceeding in the

[50] M Verwilghen, *Explanatory Report on the 1973 Hague Maintenance Conventions* (Hague, Acts and Documents of the Twelfth Session, 1975) para 144; P De Cesari, 'Alimenti' in M Sesta (ed), *Codice della famiglia. Le fonti del diritto italiano* (Milan, Giuffrë, 2007) 3880; G Badiali, 'Le obbligazioni alimentari nel nuovo doritto internazionale privato italiano' in F Salerno (ed), *Convenzioni internazionali e legge di riforma del diritto internazionale privato* (Padua, Cedam, 1997) 101; R Wagner, 'Ein neues unterhaltsrechtliches Übereinkommen aus Den Haag' (2005) *Zeitschrift für das gesamte Familienrecht* 418.

[51] F Majoros, *Les conventions internationales en matière de droit privé. Abrégé théorique et traité pratique (Paris, Pedone,* 1976) 281.

[52] Martiny (n 9) 182; Y Lequette, 'Le droit international privé de la famille á l'épreuve des conventions internationales' (1994) *Hague Academy Collected Courses* 101.

[53] M Pertegás Sender, 'La responsabilité parentale, l'enlèvement d'enfants et les obligations alimentaires' in P Wautelet (ed), *Actualités du contentieux familial international* (Bruxelles, Larcier, Commission Université-Palais, 2005) 216.

[54] Report of the Working Group on applicable law, HCCH, Prel doc No 22/ June 2006, 5; Gruber (n 47) 186; Bonomi (n 22) 342; Ferrand (n 47) 98; Bremner (n 37) 19.

State of the debtor, so that he also opted for the application of its substantive law.[55] Hence, one has to assume that the creditor knows that in this case the assumed application of the law of the *forum* is more favourable to him or her, both in terms of the amount of maintenance, and the fact that the procedure will be faster and more cost-effective. However, if under that law the creditor cannot obtain maintenance from the debtor, the law of the creditor's habitual residence applies. Finally, if the creditor cannot obtain maintenance from the debtor under the law of the forum or the law of his or her own habitual residence, the law of the State of their common nationality applies, if there is any.

The aforementioned provisions imply that, unlike the Hague 1973 Convention, the Hague Protocol provides for a dual cascade system of subsidiary reference. When it comes to maintenance obligations between spouses, ex-spouses or parties to a marriage which has been annulled, the primary rule of Article 3 shall not apply if the following two conditions established by Article 5 are met: (1) one of the parties disagrees; (2) the law of another State has a closer connection with the marriage. Furthermore, to some extent the Protocol standardises an open and clear framework connecting factor of the closest connection:if any last common habitual residence of the spouses exists, the decision maker should pay particular attention to whether the law of the last common habitual residence should be considered as having a closer connection with the marriage than the law of the creditor's habitual residence.

The final novelty lies in the possibility for a debtor to contest a claim on the grounds that there is no such obligation under either the law of the State of the debtor's habitual residence or under the law of the State of the parties' common nationality, if there is one.[56] Such a special defence rule is prescribed for maintenance obligations other than those arising from a parent-child relationship towards a child, and those referred to in Article 5.[57]

B. Party Autonomy in Maintenance Matters

Until very recently, party autonomy was only marginally represented both in national and cross-border maintenance obligations.[58] Nevertheless, it is interesting that from the first drafts, both the Hague 2007 Convention and the Maintenance Regulation, in terms of party autonomy, foresaw limited *optio iuris* as the primary applicable law.[59]

Traditionally, the provisions relating to family law had an obligatory character, and parties were not allowed to dispose of their rights and obligations, even in international situations. In this context, party autonomy has traditionally not been associated with family law relationships and until recently maintenance has not been mentioned in relation to the

[55] A Bonomi, 'Explanatory Report to the Protocol of 23 November 2007 on the Law Applicable to Maintenance Obligations' (The Hague, Permanent Bureau, 2009) 19–20.

[56] F Bartl, *Die neuen Rechtsinstrumente zum IPR des Unterhalts auf internationaler und europäischer Ebene* (Tübingen, Mohr Siebeck, 2012) 41.

[57] Art 6 of the Hague Protocol.

[58] F Rigaux amd M Fallon, *Droit international privé* (Brussels, Larcier, 2005) 192, fn 12.

[59] E Jayme and CF Nordmeier, 'Neue Wege im Internationalen Unterhalsrecht: Parteiautonomie und Privatisierung des ordre public' (2010) *Praxis des Internationalen Privat- und Verfahrensrechts* 377; J Hirsch, 'Das neue Haager Unterhaltsübereinkommen und das Haager Protokoll über das auf Unterhaltspflichten anzuwendende Recht' in D Coester-Waltjen et al (eds), *Europäisches Unterhaltsrecht* (Göttingen, Universitätsverlag Göttingen, 2010) 34.

choice of applicable law.[60] In terms of maintenance obligations, there is a significant trend in substantive legal systems towards encouraging family law subjects to think about their needs and to organise their family relationships amicably. This move towards flexibility also influences the position of party autonomy in private international law. Since the interests of the State interfere here (maintenance as part of the social policy particularly) as well as the interests of third parties, there has been also a growing number of opponents to the concept of party autonomy.[61] The academic community is recording an increasing number of supporters of a limited party autonomy in the area of private international family law in general and therefore also in the context of maintenance.[62] Although provisions of the 1973 Hague Convention did not allow the parties to choose the applicable law, jurisprudence drifted away from the Convention a long time ago.[63] Moreover, although criticised by doctrine,[64] the judgment of the Dutch Hoge Raad[65] surely had a great impact on inserting this criterion into the newly adopted instruments on maintenance.

Limited party autonomy is an important novelty in the newly adopted system of international maintenance.[66] In the Hague Protocol, party autonomy is set out in two directions, with separate assumptions and form. In the first case, Article 7 provides that the parties can choose the *lex fori* for the purpose of a particular proceeding that has been or will be instituted in a certain State. The effect of this choice is limited to that particular proceeding so that if it was not initiated, or if it was suspended, the choice would subsequently lose its legal effect. Even if subsequently a proceeding to amend the decision on maintenance was initiated before the forum, the choice of law pursuant to Article 7 in relation to an earlier proceeding is not binding, and the applicable law is determined on the basis of objective connections. The intention of this rule is to enable the parties to gain information regarding the substantive regime and its favourability to their application, while taking into account the elements of cost effectiveness and simplicity, to choose the initial law as the applicable law.[67] If they do not know which authority will be in charge of the proceeding, the intention is lost, so the choice *pro futuro* has no effect.[68]

[60] AE von Overbeck, 'L'irrésistible extension de l'autoinomie en droit international prive' in *Nouveaux itinéraires en droit, Hommage à François Rigaux* (Bruxelles, Bruylant, 1993) 619.

[61] A Bucher, 'La famille en droit international privé' (2000) *Hague Academy Collected Courses* 76.

[62] Wagner (n 50) 417–18; see also special issue 'International Family Law and Party Autonomy' (2012) *Nederland Internationaal Privaatrecht*.

[63] See *W.P.P. v W.* Obergericht Zürich, 15 April 1975, BIZR 75 (1975) No 13, 23 (1977) *Annuaire suisse de droit international* 326–33; at the same time other Contracting States appplied the Hague 1973 Convention, see OLG Karlsruhe, 24 August 1989 (1990) *Zeitschrift für das gesamte Familienrecht* 313–14.

[64] K Boele-Woelki, 'Artikel 8 Haager Unterhaltsübereinkommen steht einer Rechtswahl nicht entgegen' (1998) *Praxis des Internationalen Privat- und Verfahrensrechts* 492.

[65] Hoge Raad, 21 February 1997, NIP, 1997 No 70; for commentary see M Sumampouw, 'Article 8 Hague Maintenance Convention 1973 Set Aside in Favour of Party Autonomy: One Step Too Far Supreme Court' (1998) *Netherlands Internaitonal Law Review* 115–28; AE von Overbeck, 'Obligations "alimentaires" entre époux après divorce: autonomie ou rattachement objectif?' in A Rieg (ed) *Le rôle de la volonté dans les actes juridiques. Etudes à la mémoire du professeur Alfred Rieg* (Brussels, Bruylant, 2000) 839–54.

[66] Jayme and Nordmeier (n 59) 377; Hirsch (n 59) 34; D Martiny, 'Objectives and Values of (Private) International Law in Family Law' in J Meeusen et al (eds), *International Family Law for the European Union* (Antwerp, Intersentia, 2007) 90.

[67] M Andrae, 'Haager Protokoll von 23 November 2007 über das auf Unterhaltspflichten anzuwendente Recht' in T Rauscher (ed), *Europäisches Zivilprozess- und Kollisionsrecht: Kommentar: Brüssel IIa-VO, EG-UnterhaltsVO* (Munich, Sellier, 2010) 924; Gruber (n 47) 189; M Pertegás, 'Beyond Nationality and Habitual Residence: Other Connecting Factors in European Private International Law in Family Matters' in J Meeusen et al (eds), *International Family Law for the European Union* (Antwerp, Intersentia, 2007) 338.

[68] Hirsch (n 59) 35; Bonomi (n 55) 16, fnn 62–67; Gruber (n 47) 189–90; Andrae (n 67) 929; Ferrand (n 47) 99.

Another form of limited party autonomy is provided for by Article 8 of the 2007 Hague Protocol, which is substantially similar to the actual *lex autonomiae* that used to be typical only in contract law. The scope of application is however limited due to the protection of the weaker party. It does not apply to maintenance obligations in respect of a person under the age of 18.[69] On the contrary, Article 7 allows the choice of the forum even when it affects children or incapacitated persons. In Article 8, it is the 'right' to designate the applicable law, which is not limited to a particular proceeding that is already instituted or will be initiated. The effects of that choice persist until the time the parties agree otherwise. Legal certainty is achieved by choosing the applicable law because the parties know in advance which law is applicable irrespective of the forum before which the proceeding is conducted. Some of the difficulties arising from the application of objective connections that are of variable character, for example, *conflicts mobiles*, are avoided in this way.[70]

There are multiple restrictions of the *lex autonomiae* provided for by Article 8 of the Hague Protocol. Through the first paragraph, the provision limits the choice to just a few laws, so that this rule can be considered a statement of the *lex connexitatis* principle, because the options offered are used in order to avoid the choice of law that is in no way related to the subject.[71] The following laws may be designated:

> a) the law of any State of which either party is a national at the time of the designation; b) the law of the State of the habitual residence of either party at the time of designation; c) the law designated by the parties as applicable, or the law in fact applied, to their property regime; d) the law designated by the parties as applicable, or the law in fact applied, to their divorce or legal separation.

The first two options were barely questioned. In regard to the law of the party's nationality, if one of the parties had dual or multiple nationalities, the rule should be interpreted as it may be the law of any nationality a person has.[72] On the contrary, in the negotiations of the Hague Protocol, the other options were subject to much discussion, and their implications are still being discussed. Article 8 allows parties to designate the same applicable law in divorce/matrimonial property matters, and in maintenance. But connecting the choice of the law of maintenance with the law applicable to divorce/matrimonial property should be prohibited, because it would mean that the choice of the law applicable to maintenance was done blindly and not a conscious decision of the parties involved. Options in Article 8(1)(c) and (d) refer to the law designated by the parties as applicable to their matrimonial property regime and to their divorce and legal separation or the law that was actually applied to those issues. This solution is disadvantageous, because it has unnecessarily created a very complex system and a wide choice of applicable laws; the options provided for under points c) and d) depend on the national conflict of laws rule applicable to the respective issues, thereby undermining the uniqueness of a unified instrument. If the parties take advantage of this option and associate the choice of the law applicable to maintenance with the law applicable to matrimonial property regimes or divorce, the parties have in fact made a valid choice of law in relation to maintenance. However this is dependent on

[69] G Rühl, 'Choice of Law by the Parties in European Private International Law' in J Basedow et al (eds), *Max Planck Encyclopedia of European Private Law* (Oxford, Oxford University Press, 2012).

[70] Bonomi (n 22) 353.

[71] Ibid 354; Andrae (n 67) 933; Gruber (n 47) 190–91; Ferrand (n 47) 100.

[72] Bonomi (n 55) 31, fn 131.

the validity of the choice of law in relation to these other issues. In other words, as the law applicable to property or divorce itself is not governed by the Hague Protocol, it depends on the provisions of private international law in force in the State of the forum. If the conflict of laws rules of the forum do not provide a *lex autonomiae*, such an invalidity of that choice also entails invalidity of the law chosen to govern maintenance as well.[73] This concern is most apparent where the choice of law applicable to maintenance is combined with the choice of the law applicable to divorce, because only a few national private international law rules allow choice of law for divorce. The result is that a choice valid in one State is often invalid by the rules of another forum. This argument has partly lost its merits since Regulation 1259/2010 on the law applicable to divorce has been enacted.[74]

In relation to Article 8(1)(c) of the Protocol which connects the law applicable to maintenance with the law designated for the matrimonial property regime, the scope of party autonomy in the latter should be considered. It is significant that the Hague 1978 Convention on the Law Applicable to Matrimonial Property Regimes allows a choice of law in a range unknown to the Hague Protocol (eg the law of domicile, the law of the location of real property (Articles 3(4) and 6(4) of the Convention)), and therefore Article 8(1)(c) may significantly expand the range of maintenance laws the parties may choose from. If in relation to the property regime the choice is not valid under the rules of the forum, it shall be deemed null and void, and this invalidity extends to the choice in relation to maintenance.

Furthermore, the Hague Protocol enables the choice of the law that was *actually applied* to matrimonial property matters. In this case reference is made to the situation where a competent court of the forum has already designated the law applicable to a property regime. Furthermore, if in accordance with its conflict of laws rules the court applied the rules of the forum related to property matters, then the choice of that law by the parties remains within the framework of Article 8, and it is not a choice made under Article 7 which would be valid only in that proceeding. Moreover, if the property is finally decided upon in a single proceeding, and subsequently the maintenance proceeding is conducted separately, the parties may take advantage of this option and also choose the law that was actually applied to the property matters. This option is not limited to the period that the property issue related proceeding is being conducted. The result is that there is a wider range of laws that can be chosen and, at the same time, there is one legal order applicable to all issues. The Hague Protocol of 2007 provides for an analogous rule in terms of determining the application of the law chosen for divorce, and the law that is actually applied to the divorce. Here all of the aforementioned applies mutatis mutandis in relation to binding the choice for the matrimonial property regime.

The advantage of this solution is that only one law is applicable to every claim posted in one proceeding. Answers to all of the questions are then searched for in the same legal system, which is beneficial as it is a systematic set of legal rules that work best 'as a package'. This is important because the status related issues of divorce, matrimonial property and maintenance are interconnected in most national systems—in some systems, the property consequences of the marriage must be determined for a divorce to be allowed, especially for

[73] Ibid 33; Gruber (n 47) 191.

[74] Council Regulation (EC) No 1259/2010 of 20 December 2010 implementing enhanced cooperation in the area of the law applicable to divorce and legal separation [2010] OJ L 343/10. Art 5 of the Regulation allows parties to choose the applicable law.

consensual divorce. Moreover, in some systems, delineation of property and maintenance issues is unclear or impossible, so this solution represents a bonus.[75]

Restrictions on the choice of the applicable law under the Hague Protocol are further evident through Article 8(4) and (5). The designated law does not affect all aspects of maintenance obligations. The question of whether the creditor can renounce his or her right to maintenance shall be determined by the law of the State of the habitual residence of the creditor at the time of the designation. Furthermore, Article 8(5) introduces substantive control which gives the authority the possibility to set aside the chosen law, if it finds that the application of the law chosen by the parties leads to manifestly unfair or unreasonable consequences for any of the parties.[76] The underlying purpose of the treaty makers in these two rules is to protect ignorant or uninformed parties of an agreement on the designation of law that is harmful to them.[77] The difference is that paragraph 4 protects only the creditor by imposing the rule of a number of national legislators, concerning the impossibility of renouncing the rights to maintenance to the level of a compulsory international regulation. In paragraph 5, the protection extends to both creditors and debtors. This rule serves the function of an escape clause, which takes into account substantive justice. The 'functionally closest connection' here is clearly expressed as the rule that indicates concern over substantive impacts of the applicable law, that is, disregarding Savigny's 'blindness' in relation to a concrete result.[78] At the same time, the authority seised replaces the law chosen by the objectively applicable law.[79]

In both types of the *lex autonomiae*, the Hague Protocol also provides for additional assumptions regarding the form of the agreement on the choice of applicable law: it must be made and signed by both parties, in writing, or the information contained therein recorded in any medium which is readily accessible, so as to be usable for subsequent reference (Article 7(2) and Article 8(2)). These are the minimum formal requirements with respect to the agreement that may be supplemented by more stringent requirements of the Contracting States. The 'social control' of maintenance agreements ensures that the parties' consent with respect to the agreement is freely given: in that respect a Contracting State may prescribe an additional requirement of obligatory recourse to legal advice before signing the agreement.[80]

In the examples above, the Hague Protocol introduces restrictions on the admissibility of the choice of applicable law, but it does not answer the question pertaining to which law governs the existence and validity of an agreement on the choice of applicable law. These questions should be judged according to the law chosen by the parties.[81]

Protectionist family policies of many countries are manifested by frequent expressions of concerns that the interests of the weaker side will be jeopardised by the application of

[75] Gruber (n 47) 191. See also Csongar István Nagy, ch 23 and Maarja Torga, ch 24 of this volume, highlighting the problems caused by applying different laws to spousal maintenance and to their matrimonial property regime.

[76] Andrae (n 67) 938; Gruber (n 47) 192.

[77] Ferrand (n 47) 100.

[78] TM de Boer, 'Facultative Choice of Law, The Procedural Status of Choice of Law Rules and Foreign Law' 257 (1996) *Hague Academy Collected Courses* 279.

[79] Bonomi (n 55) 23.

[80] Andrae (n 67) 936; Ferrand (n 47) 100.

[81] It is applied in Art 10 of the Hague 1978 Convention; Art 3 (5) and Art 10 of the Rome I Regulation (Reg No 593/2008). Bonomi (n 55) 35, fn 151.

party autonomy.[82] Therefore, the innovative solution was to introduce two types of party autonomy, one of which is linked to the initiation of proceedings in a State, for the choice of whose law the parties can then decide. The connection of party autonomy with the choice of the *lex fori* is significant, and the link between the law of the forum and party autonomy can be interpreted as an emphasis on the choice of the appropriate court of justice. A quick resolution of the dispute and the correct application of the law are crucial for resolving an international family dispute.[83] However, forcing this connection can also be seen as a compromise, and therefore 'scoring points' with those countries that find it difficult to abandon the *lex fori* approach. Another aspect of party autonomy includes the choice of applicable law before a dispute arises, the option that resembles the scenario of contractual relationships. Although this is not a manifestation of complete autonomy, such a radical rule in the field of international family law stresses the importance of legal certainty and predictability of applicable law. It also reflects the increasingly liberal attitude of national legislators toward dispositive provisions in the field of maintenance agreements.[84]

If we consider party autonomy as a connecting factor in maintenance cases, the choice is always limited. The restriction occurs in the form of a choice between a certain number of connections pointing to the fact that the legal relationship is also objectively connected with a specific law, which corresponds to the fundamental ratio of the closest connection in private international law. 'Limited party autonomy' can therefore be understood as a special type of junction between a subjective and an objective connection. By a rather subjective act of choice the parties affect the choice of applicable law, because the possibility of choosing is reduced to just those legal systems with which the relationship is connected anyway! So what is respected here is the basic principle of the conflict of laws reference to a law of closest connection. The closest connection is established by a subjective act of choice which enhances the already existing close connection. If an open framework connection of the closest link is said to be the judge in the role of the legislator, then limited party autonomy is said to be the parties in the role of the legislator.[85] Another common feature of party autonomy for a wider range of family relationships lies in strict formal assumptions which aim to protect a weaker contracting party, increase legal certainty and ensure informed consent as to the choice of law.

There are a number of advantages, as well as a few dangerous disadvantages of this connecting factor. The greatest danger of party autonomy lies in the possibility that the home country does not recognise such a choice, which results in 'limping' legal relationships and undesirable legal uncertainty. In contrast, many advantages can be listed. The fundamental advantage of party autonomy in relation to other connections is legal certainty made by the disposition of the parties themselves in their relationship. Autonomy provides the necessary flexibility and justice in a particular case. Party autonomy is increasingly being viewed from the perspective of economic opportunism in dealing with international cases, which

[82] Compare the responses of France and Austria to the Green Paper (www.ec.europa.eu/justice_home) to the Proposal by the Working Group on the Law Applicable to Maintenance Obligations, Prel Doc No 14 March 2005, paras 36–40 (accessed 30 June 2013).

[83] Pertegás (n 67) 338.

[84] Ibid 339.

[85] M Župan, *Pravo najbliže veze u hrvatskom i europskom me unarodnom privatnom ugovornom pravu* (Rijeka, Pravni fakultet, 2006) 256.

is not negligible.[86] The last remark relates to the legislative technique that employs limited party autonomy to interact among fragmented private international law instruments. This enables parties to choose the law applicable to other interconnected aspects of their claim (divorce, parental rights, etc) ensuring consistency between laws relating to various parts of a claim. This approach indicates that coordination has already played an important role in the overall legislative process, beyond the EU borders.[87]

IV. Concluding Remarks

The first part of this chapter dealt with the regulatory framework of two maintenance projects: one conducted by the Hague Conference and the other by the European Union. The legal prerequisites for the merging of an international instrument (the Hague Protocol) into EU law have been described in depth. Subsequently, the analysis of costs and benefits of such a novel approach to legal standardisation was presented. It is clear that a degree of fragmentation still exists amongst EU Member States regarding the choice of law in maintenance matters in addition to the abolition of *exequatur* as a cornerstone of judicial cooperation in civil matters, which has been subjected to the applicable law regime. Despite these drawbacks, the main benefit of this 'mirrored' approach to the choice of law rules is in avoiding the multiplicity of legal sources. Regarding the interplay between the EU and the HCCH displayed on maintenance matters, the outcome is a true relief. Instead of being competitors, the HCCH and the EU established themselves as complementary partners.

A closer analysis of the rules on applicable law contained in the Hague Protocol reveals many innovations in comparison to the previous regime of the Hague 1973 Convention. Even though Article 3 stands at the beginning of the Hague Protocol reference system and points towards the application of the law of the State where the creditor is habitually resident; this provision is subordinated to (a) the connecting factors of Article 7 and Article 8—if (adult) parties choose the applicable law; and (b) Article 4(3)—if the creditor has seised the competent authority of the State where the debtor has his or her habitual residence, then the law of the forum shall apply. Moreover, the application of the law determined in accordance with Article 3 can be subject to objections by one of the parties in cases of maintenance obligations between spouses and ex-spouses (see Article 5).

The importance of Article 3 is revealed by its conjunction with the jurisdictional criteria (both direct and indirect). As the habitual residence of maintenance creditors is regarded as the most favourable forum for maintenance dispute resolution, and this connecting factor is applied as the default choice of law rule, we essentially reach the point of applying the *lex fori*. By considering the interconnection between jurisdictional rules and choice of law rules, it appears that the philosophy that lies behind them differs. The applicable law rules serve the Savigny principle of the closest connection of a relationship and a legal system, whereas the jurisdictional rules aim at ensuring a fair and efficient judicial procedure (easy access to evidence, etc). However, connecting the merits of a dispute with the forum State

[86] MJ Whincop and M Keyes, *Policy and Pragmatism in the Conflict of Laws* (Aldershot, Ashgate, 2001) 38–42.

[87] A Bonomi, 'The Interaction Among the Future EU Instruments on Matrimonial Property, Registered Partnerships and Successions' (2011) *Yearbook of Private International Law* 231.

may play a decisive role in determining international jurisdiction. It is more likely that fair and efficient procedures are guaranteed through this connection and it is easier to understand the social background of a case.[88] For these reasons the philosophy of the Hague Protocol has its merits.

The well-known 'cascade' system has been retained for many of its benefits, however in comparison to the Hague 1973 Convention it has been renewed. We can identify two important innovations: (a) the hierarchy of connecting factors has been modified. The two connecting factors: *lex fori* and the common nationality are being used in accordance with their function in the course of contemporary life; and (b) the Hague Protocol introduces a two-track cascade system. The second track represents a true innovation as, subject to certain conditions, the law of the forum is the principal connecting factor. The two conditions that have to be met are the following: first of all the national authority seised is located in the debtor's State of habitual residence, secondly the proceedings must be instituted by the creditor. In this case, a principle was introduced by which a jurisdictional criterion simultaneously determines the application of substantive norms. The assumption is that the creditor knowingly instituted a proceeding in the State of the debtor, so that they also opted for the application of substantive law. It must be noted that the second track is allowed only for certain categories of maintenance obligations namely those relating to children towards their parents, creditors under 21, and parents towards their children.

Yet another innovation relates to the closest connection principle introduced. When it comes to maintenance obligations between spouses, ex-spouses or parties to a marriage which has been annulled, the primary rule of Article 3 shall not apply if the following two conditions are met: one of the parties disagrees, and the law of another State has a closer connection with the marriage. Furthermore, to some extent the Hague Protocol standardises the closest connection principle. If any last common habitual residence of the spouses exists, then the law of that State should be considered as a candidate for being the law closest to the marriage. Still, this is not a presumption, but just an indication.[89]

Finally, the most commonly highlighted innovation of the Hague Protocol is the introduction of party autonomy. From the first Protocol draft, limited party autonomy was foreseen. By using autonomy of will at the time of increased mobility of parties, one can be sure that their rights and obligations will not be subject to different legal regimes each time there is a change in circumstances underlying objective connections.[90] Limitation of party autonomy commonly refers to the choice of those laws, which are fairly closely related to the subject matter, or to the parties themselves.

It is crucial that the function of party autonomy, as well as the entire system of the conflict of laws found in the Hague Protocol considered here, is the reconciliation and compromise of those legal systems that favour the application of the law of the forum for family disputes, as opposed to those that apply the conflict of laws method. A *lex fori* approach for the applicable law is widely practised in both of these systems. It serves to promote legal certainty, efficiency and simplicity. The impact of the application of *lex fori* is generally achieved in conjunction with the rules of international jurisdiction. Therefore, there is a 'functional synchronisation' between the international maintenance instruments.

[88] M Bogdan, *Private International Law as Component of the Law of the Forum* (Hague Academy of International Law, AIL-POCKET, 2012) 100.

[89] Bonomi (n 22) 349.

[90] Hellner (n 16) 354.

Ultimately, it should be recognised that, due to the diversity of conflict of laws solutions within national systems, the introduction of autonomy of will is the only possible compromise available. Therefore, Professor Jayme underlines that the rationale of human rights and promotion of self-determination of the individual are merely a cover for a solution that promotes the integration of legal systems.[91] It is this autonomy, as a guiding principle of the conflict of laws, which has the potential to eradicate some of the difficulties arising from the fragmented private international family law, both on a European Union and a universal level.[92]

[91] E Jayme, 'Party Autonomy in International Family and Succession Law: New Tendencies' (2009) *Yearbook of Private International Law* 3.

[92] Baarsma (n 2) 131.

Part Four

European Union Perspective

20

Setting the Scene—The EU Maintenance Regulation

BURKHARD HESS AND STEFANIE SPANCKEN

I. Introduction

On 18 June 2011, the date of entry into force of the European Union (EU) Maintenance Regulation,[1] the EU legal framework in cross-border maintenance matters changed significantly. With the Maintenance Regulation, the EU legislator was responding to developments in European society and family life. In recent decades the EU has witnessed increased migration[2] leading to a growing number of international families. Apart from this demographic trend in population, the divorce rate[3] and the number of births outside marriage have both increased,[4] reflecting the development from the 'traditional family', that is, parenthood following marriage, to new types of family life. From a practitioner's perspective maintenance cases with cross-border elements are difficult to resolve. This is based on great differences in the EU Member States' substantive maintenance law[5] as well as on the co-existence of different legal sources in maintenance matters and ineffective recovery systems. However, maintenance is an important topic since it goes beyond a mere monetary claim: it guarantees the creditor's welfare and has a direct impact on public funds which often advance payments.

The Maintenance Regulation comprises all aspects of private international law; it contains provisions on jurisdiction, recognition and enforcement, legal aid and administrative cooperation. When analysing the Maintenance Regulation one has to bear in mind its

[1] Council Regulation (EC) No 4/2009 of 18 December 2008 on jurisdiction, applicable law, recognition and enforcement of decisions and cooperation in matters relating to maintenance obligations [2009] OJ L7/1.

[2] On 1 January 2012, 20.7 million (4.1%) of the EU population were nationals of a non-Member State. In addition, there were 13.6 million persons living in an EU Member State with citizenship of another EU Member State, Eurostat, 'Migration and migrant population statistics', available at www.epp.eurostat.ec.europa.eu/statistics_explained/index.php/Migration_and_migrant_population_statistics (accessed January 2014). During 2011 there were an estimated 1.7 million immigrants to the EU from third States and 1.3 million people previously residing in an EU Member State migrated to another Member State, Eurostat, ibid.

[3] Eurostat, 'European social statistics' (Luxembourg, Publications Office of the European Union, 2013) 34.

[4] Eurostat, 'Marriage and divorce statistics', available at www.epp.eurostat.ec.europa.eu/statistics_explained/index.php/Marriage_and_divorce_statistics (accessed January 2014).

[5] For an overview of maintenance law in the EU Member States, see R Fucik, 'Unterhaltsansprüche in der Europäischen Union' (2007) *Interdisziplinäre Zeitschrift für Familienrecht* 97.

interdependence with the 2007 Hague Child Support Convention[6] and the 2007 Hague Protocol on Applicable Law.[7]

II. From the Tampere Council to the EU Maintenance Regulation

The creation of a Regulation aiming at simplifying the cross-border recovery of maintenance has been on the Commission's agenda since 1999, when the Tampere European Council agreed a plan to try in the coming years to simplify and accelerate cross-border litigation on maintenance claims. For this purpose the European Council recommended abolishing the *exequatur* procedure among the Member States.[8] The European Commission recognised the importance of the cross-border recovery of maintenance claims in the EU Judicial Area and stressed that effective recovery is essential for the welfare of EU citizens as well as for decreasing the burden on public finances. In 2004, the European Commission adopted a Green Paper,[9] followed by an ambitious and far-reaching legislative Proposal in 2005.[10] The Commission's Proposal had a very broad substantive scope covering not only all aspects of private international law, but also partially harmonising enforcement measures.[11] Since Member States rejected those influences on their national sovereignty, the rules creating a kind of 'European enforcement system' were eliminated in subsequent negotiations and are not contained in the final text of the Regulation.

As family law matters do not fall within the co-decision procedure, the Maintenance Regulation was adopted by the Council of the EU by unanimity.

III. Main Achievements of the EU Maintenance Regulation

The Maintenance Regulation implements the principle of mutual recognition of judgments as set out in the Programme of 30 November 2000[12] as it (partially) abolishes

[6] Convention of 23 November 2007 on the International Recovery of Child Support and Other Forms of Family Maintenance.

[7] Hague Protocol of 23 November 2007 on the Law Applicable to Maintenance Obligations.

[8] Tampere European Council 15 and 16 October 1999, Presidency Conclusions No 34, available at www.europarl.europa.eu/summits/tam_en.htm (accessed January 2014). An earlier attempt to adopt an EU instrument was unsuccessful; the Rome Convention of 6 November 1990 between the Member States of the European Communities on the Simplification of Procedures for the Recovery of Maintenance Payments has never entered into force.

[9] Green Paper on Maintenance Obligations, COM (2004) 254 final.

[10] Proposal for a Council Regulation on jurisdiction, applicable law, recognition and enforcement of decisions and cooperation in matters relating to maintenance obligations, COM (2005) 649 final.

[11] For a detailed analysis of the Proposal, see M Hellner, 'The Maintenance Regulation: A Critical Assessment of the Commission's Proposal' in K Boele-Woelki et al (eds), *European Challenges in Contemporary Family Law* (Antwerp, Intersentia, 2008) 343 and H Dörner, 'Der Vorschlag für eine europäische Verordnung zum Internationalen Unterhalts- und Unterhaltsverfahrensrecht' in H Menkhaus and F Sato (eds), *Japanischer Brückenbauer zum deutschen Rechtskreis, Festschrift für Koresuke Yamauchi zum 60. Geburtstag* (Berlin, Duncker & Humblot, 2006) 81.

[12] Programme of measures for the implementation of the principle of mutual recognition of 30 November 2000, [2001] OJ C12/1.

exequatur proceedings and provides for a free circulation of maintenance decisions within the EU Area of Freedom, Security and Justice. Prior to its entry into force, maintenance obligations fell within the scope of the Brussels I Regulation[13] and the Regulation creating a European Enforcement Order.[14] The latter has already abolished *exequatur* for maintenance decisions, but its scope is limited to uncontested claims.

One of the main achievements of the Maintenance Regulation consists in the abolition of *exequatur* for all maintenance decisions issued in a Member State bound by the Hague Protocol. A maintenance decision will be recognised and enforced in another Member State without additional measures being required and without the possibility of opposing its recognition. Another main achievement consists in providing free legal aid to all maintenance creditors under the age of 21.[15] The guarantee of effective access to justice is underlined by the establishment of a cooperative network of Central Authorities which support creditors and debtors in processing their applications and facilitates the cross-border dialogue between the Member States.[16]

The main issues relating to the Regulation are outlined briefly below.

A. Broad Scope of Application

The Maintenance Regulation has a very broad scope of application and covers 'maintenance obligations arising from a family relationship, parentage, marriage or affinity'.[17] However, due to the European legislator's reluctance to define terms used in the Regulation, uncertainties with regard to the scope of application, in particular concerning the definition of the term 'family relationship', may arise. Moreover, drawing the demarcation line between maintenance obligations and related areas such as matrimonial property law[18] and succession law[19] will be challenging for courts applying the Regulation.

B. Jurisdiction

In terms of jurisdiction, the Maintenance Regulation follows a creditor-friendly approach by providing for several grounds of jurisdiction of equal rank in Article 3 between which the creditor can choose.[20] Compared to the Brussels I Regulation jurisdictional regime, the Maintenance Regulation has a broader scope based on its universal application. The Regulation applies regardless of whether the defendant has his or her habitual residence in a Member State or not.[21] By employing the concept of 'habitual residence' as the main

[13] Council Regulation (EC) No 44/2001 of 22 December 2000 on jurisdiction and the recognition and enforcement of judgments in civil and commercial matters [2001] OJ L12/1.

[14] Council Regulation (EC) No 805/2004 of the European Parliament and of the Council of 21 April 2004 creating a European Enforcement Order for uncontested claims [2004] OJ L143/15.

[15] Art 46(1) of the Maintenance Regulation.

[16] Ibid Arts 49–63.

[17] Ibid Art 1(1).

[18] On this issue see Csongar István Nagy, ch 23 and Maarja Toorga, ch 24 of this volume.

[19] On this issue see Jayne Holliday, ch 25 of this volume.

[20] For a detailed analysis of the jurisdictional rules, see W Hau, 'Das Zuständigkeitssystem der Europäischen Unterhaltsverordnung—Überlegungen aus der Perspektive des deutschen Rechts' in D Coester-Waltjen et al (eds), *Europäisches Unterhaltsrecht* (Göttingen, Göttinger Universitätsverlag, 2010) 57.

[21] Recital (15) of the Maintenance Regulation.

connecting factor, the Maintenance Regulation follows recent developments in private international law. Moreover, it allows parties to agree on the competent court and therefore enhances party autonomy in maintenance cases.[22] In order to ensure effective access to justice, the Maintenance Regulation provides for subsidiary jurisdiction and a *forum necessitatis* rule.[23] It should be noted that the jurisdictional system in the Maintenance Regulation is exhaustive; it does not leave room for national rules being applied.

C. Applicable Law: Referral to the Hague Protocol

Prior to the entry into force of the Maintenance Regulation, two Hague Conventions laid down applicable law rules on maintenance matters.[24] Both Conventions had only limited practical effect.[25] For the sake of legal certainty and foreseeability the European Commission decided to include such rules in the Maintenance Regulation. However, unlike the initial Proposal[26] the Regulation does not contain applicable law rules, but Article 15 refers to the applicable law rules of the 2007 Hague Protocol.[27] For reasons of simplification the EU legislator opted for a referral solution instead of creating two parallel applicable law regimes. The EU declared that it would provisionally apply the Hague Protocol as of 18 June 2011.[28] Subsequent to the ratification of Serbia the Hague Protocol has entered into force on 1 August 2013.[29] The most striking innovation in the ambit of maintenance obligations is the possibility to designate the applicable law.[30]

D. Recognition and Enforcement: Two-track System

In the area of recognition and enforcement the Maintenance Regulation establishes two separate tracks depending on whether the maintenance decision originates in a Member State that is bound by the Hague Protocol or not. For those Member States which are

[22] Ibid Art 4. It should be noted that the agreement has to fulfil certain requirements in order to be valid. On the topic of choice of court agreements, see Matthias Abendroth, ch 26 of this volume.

[23] Arts 6 and 7 of the Maintenance Regulation.

[24] Hague Convention of 24 October 1956 on the law applicable to maintenance obligations towards children and Hague Convention of 2 October 1973 on the law applicable to maintenance obligations.

[25] The 1956 Convention has 14 and the 1973 Convention has 15 Contracting States.

[26] Arts 12–21 of the Proposal for a Council Regulation on jurisdiction, applicable law, recognition and enforcement of decisions and cooperation in matters relating to maintenance obligations, COM (2005) 649 final.

[27] For a detailed analysis of the Hague Protocol, see A Bonomi, 'The Hague Protocol of 23 November 2007 on the Law Applicable to Maintenance Obligations' (2008) *Yearbook of Private International Law* 333; N Conti and V Bißmaier, 'Das neue Haager Unterhaltsprotokoll von 2007' (2011) *Der Familien-Rechts-Berater international* 62; J Hirsch, 'Das neue Haager Unterhaltsübereinkommen und das Haager Protokoll über das auf Unterhaltspflichten anzuwendende Recht' in D Coester-Waltjen et al (eds), *Europäisches Unterhaltsrecht* (Göttingen, Universitätsverlag Göttingen, 2010) 17.

[28] Art 4(2) of Council Decision of 30 November 2009 on the conclusion by the European Community of the Hague Protocol of 23 November 2007 on the Law Applicable to Maintenance Obligations [2009] OJ L331/17.

[29] The current status of ratifications is available at www.hcch.net/index_en.php?act=conventions.status&cid=133 (accessed January 2014).

[30] Art 8 of the 2007 Hague Protocol. For further details on the Hague Protocol rules see Mirela Župan, ch 19 of this volume. Her contribution is in the previous Part of the book because of its relevance internationally as well as to the EU.

bound by the Hague Protocol[31] provisions on abolition of *exequatur* apply[32] whereas for Danish and UK decisions intermediate procedures are still required. Building on the well-known Brussels I provisions on recognition and the declaration of enforceability, the Maintenance Regulation introduces new time limits for this second track.

E. Administrative Cooperation

Chapter VII of the Maintenance Regulation contains extensive provisions on administrative cooperation, which are essentially based on the provisions of the 2007 Hague Child Support Convention.[33] Both instruments reflect the important role that Central Authorities play in the cross-border recovery of maintenance by providing for a long list of duties to be performed which cover the whole application process.[34]

IV. Conclusion

The Maintenance Regulation is an important legal instrument, which reduces obstacles in the cross-border recovery of maintenance and helps creditors to effectively pursue their claims. Its objectives are manifold: simplifying the citizen's life by eliminating all obstacles which prevent the recovery of maintenance within the EU, guaranteeing legal certainty and predictability, reducing formalities and costs for the maintenance creditor and ensuring the effective access to justice.

Whether the ambitious objectives of the EU legislator have been realised in the Maintenance Regulation will be outlined and analysed in the course of this part of the book. As the conclusions of the Heidelberg Conference have shown[35] there are still some deficiencies which need to be overcome. Most importantly, knowledge of the new instruments has to be promoted among legal practitioners and Central Authorities to ensure that the Regulation has full effect.

We would like to take this opportunity to warmly thank all contributors for sharing their ideas on this important topic.

[31] All Member States except for Denmark and the UK.

[32] Arts 17–22 of the EU Maintenance Regulation. For a critical analysis on the provisions on recognition and enforcement, see Ilaria Viarengo, ch 27 of this volume.

[33] P Beaumont, 'International Family Law in Europe—The Maintenance Project, the Hague Conference and the EC: A Triumph of Reverse Subsidiarity' (2009) *Rabels Zeitschrift für ausländisches und internationales Privatrecht* 509, 525.

[34] For an analysis of the role and functions of Central Authorities in the Maintenance Regulation see Burkhard Hess and Stefanie Spancken, ch 22 of this volume. For an analysis of a statistical survey completed by the Central Authorities of the early operation of the Regulation see Lara Walker and Paul Beaumont, ch 21 of this volume.

[35] Conclusions & Recommendations available at www.heidelberg-conference2013.de/tl_files/downloads-papers/downloads%20ab%2031_07_2013/C+R_Heidelberg_Conference_2013_final.pdf (accessed January 2014).

21

Empirical Study on the Early Operation of the EU Maintenance Regulation

LARA WALKER AND PAUL BEAUMONT

I. Introduction

This chapter is based on the results of an empirical study that was carried out on the first year of operation of the EU Maintenance Regulation.[1] The data were collected as part of the work for a project on maintenance that was funded by the EU. In order to collect the data a questionnaire was sent to each of the Central Authorities operating under the Regulation.[2] The period covered by the questionnaire was 1 October 2011 to 30 September 2012. However, many of the questionnaires were returned late so in some cases the information may include applications sent outside these dates.[3] This is the first data collected on the cross-border recovery of maintenance within the European Union.[4]

The questionnaire covered incoming and outgoing maintenance applications. The objective was to discover how many applications there had been and whether new provisions, such as legal aid and the inclusion of requests for specific measures are working well under

[1] Council Regulation (EC) 4/2009 of 18 December 2008 on jurisdiction, applicable law, recognition and enforcement of decisions and cooperation in matters relating to maintenance obligations [2009] OJ L7/1 (Maintenance Regulation). The international equivalent of this instrument is the Hague Convention of 23 November 2007 on the International Recovery of Child Support and Other Forms of Family Maintenance (2007 Convention).

[2] The questionnaire is available at www.heidelberg-conference2013.de/research-aberdeen.html (accessed January 2014).

[3] Eg the information provided by the Central Authority for England and Wales only covers the period from January 2012 to 30 September 2012.

[4] When the European Commission carried out its impact assessment on the need for a new instrument on maintenance it had no data on the number of applications in this area and instead based the arguments on ancillary information that could give some indication on the scale of the problem, such as migration data and intra-community marriage and divorce statistics. Green Paper on Maintenance Obligations, COM (2004) 254 Final. Therefore, even just the raw data on the total number of applications circulated (section III below) have been very useful and important for international organisations, national governments and practitioners working in this area.

the Regulation. The questionnaires were completed to a different level by each Central Authority and therefore there are more data on some States than others. The Central Authorities that completed the questionnaire are: Belgium, Czech Republic, Estonia, France, Finland, Greece, Hungary, Ireland, Italy, Latvia, Lithuania, Malta, Poland, Portugal, Romania, Slovenia, Sweden, England and Wales and Northern Ireland. Some Central Authorities provided us with some overall data. These are: Austria, Cyprus, Germany, Gibraltar, Luxembourg, Netherlands, Slovakia, Spain and Scotland. No information at all was collected from Bulgaria, and Gibraltar reported that there had been no applications in the relevant period.

The main problem that Central Authorities faced when filling out the questionnaire was the data available to them on their databases. Where databases do exist they all seem to be different.[5] The feedback also highlighted that the databases were not always reliable. The information gained was analysed and is presented in this chapter in order to provide some insight into how the Regulation is working in practice, the number of applications that are circulating under it, and initial findings on how long it is taking to process applications under the new system. The information was entered into the SPSS system in a number of different databases in order to analyse the data. The authors take account of the difficulties highlighted above and are aware that the data may not always be accurate. However, the data provided will be presented and, given the high volume of applications, the authors are confident that there is enough information to give an overview of the operation of the Regulation.

II. Designation and Structure of Central Authorities

Each State must designate a Central Authority to discharge the duties which are imposed on it by the Maintenance Regulation.[6] However, States can designate any body as the Central Authority, and therefore the structure and organisation is different in each State. Some Central Authorities are constituted of trained lawyers and other professionals and some are made up entirely of civil servants. Some Authorities deal specifically with maintenance and other Authorities, usually smaller ones, such as Luxembourg and Scotland, deal with other issues such as child abduction. Examples of different types of bodies that act as Central Authorities are: social insurance agencies, like in Sweden—Försäkringskassan; an independent enforcing organ, like in the Netherlands—Landelijk Bureau Inning Onderhoudsbijdragen (LBIO); and a ministerial department, like in Germany—Bundesamt für Justiz.

[5] Spain reported that as of 1 February 2013 they still did not have an electronic database. Electronic databases will be discussed in section X below.

[6] Art 49 of the Regulation and Art 4 of the 2007 Convention.

States can also assign specially designated ministerial departments like in England and Wales and the Czech Republic. However, even here the construction of these two Central Authorities is significantly different. There are five practitioners working at the Reciprocal Enforcement of Maintenance Order Unit (REMO) (the Central Authority for England and Wales) and they are solely responsible for maintenance applications. None of these practitioners are legally trained and where they have a legal problem they should report to the Ministry of Justice, the ministerial department responsible for 'justice' matters. However, the body designated in the Czech Republic (Office for International Legal Protection of Children) is made up of 26 people: 15 lawyers, three psychologists and eight administrative staff. This Authority also deals with child abduction and child protection, but it is clear that the office is extremely well staffed (particularly given the size of the State). There are also States like Finland which have two bodies that deal with different functions. There is the Ministry of Justice and the public body Kansaneläkelaitos (the Social Insurance Institution of Finland). This only begins to tell the story of the different structure and organisation of Central Authorities in each Member State and highlights the different backgrounds and experiences of the practitioners.[7] This indicates another reason why it was difficult to collect the data, because every Central Authority has different powers, resources and allocation of duties.

III. Overall Data

In the Regulation's first year of operation there have been over 4,162 applications. The Central Authority for England and Wales had the highest number of incoming applications (862)[8] and Malta and Gibraltar had the least, zero. Several States such as: Belgium, Czech Republic, Estonia, Finland and Greece had around 130 applications. The first graph below shows the distribution of all incoming cases between the Member States. The second graph is designed to display information on the population of the Member States that participated in the study.[9]

[7] Information gained whilst carrying out the empirical study and at the Heidelberg Conference March 2013. See also I Curry-Sumner, 'Administrative Co-operation and Free Legal Aid in International Child Maintenance Recovery: What is the Added Value of the Regulation?' (2010) 3 *Nederlands Internationaal Privaatrecht* 611, section 3.2.

[8] However, it should be noted that the figures for England and Wales only account for nine months (January–September 2012) rather than 12 so the figure is actually higher. Having said that the months missing are from the early stages of the Regulation and Ireland reported that they received no applications in the first six months. This highlights that the uptake of the Regulation was slow. At the Heidelberg Conference it was suggested that the figures were lower than expected, which could suggest a lack of knowledge and awareness of the new system. However, it is difficult to reach concrete conclusions on this as this is the first set of data collected on the recovery of maintenance within the EU.

[9] The figures were taken from the CIA World Factbook at www.cia.gov/library/publications/the-world-factbook/wfbExt/region_eur.html (accessed June 2013).

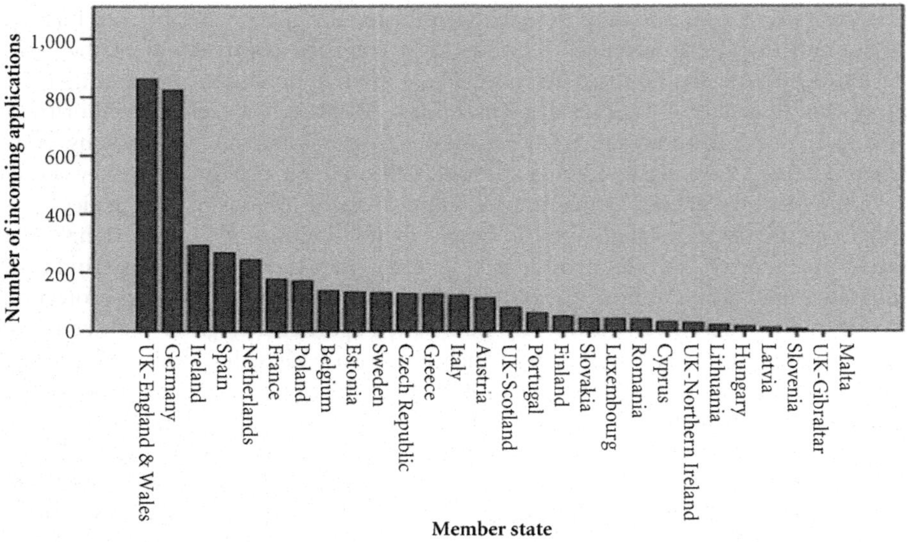

Figure 1: Total Number of Incoming Applications Per Member State

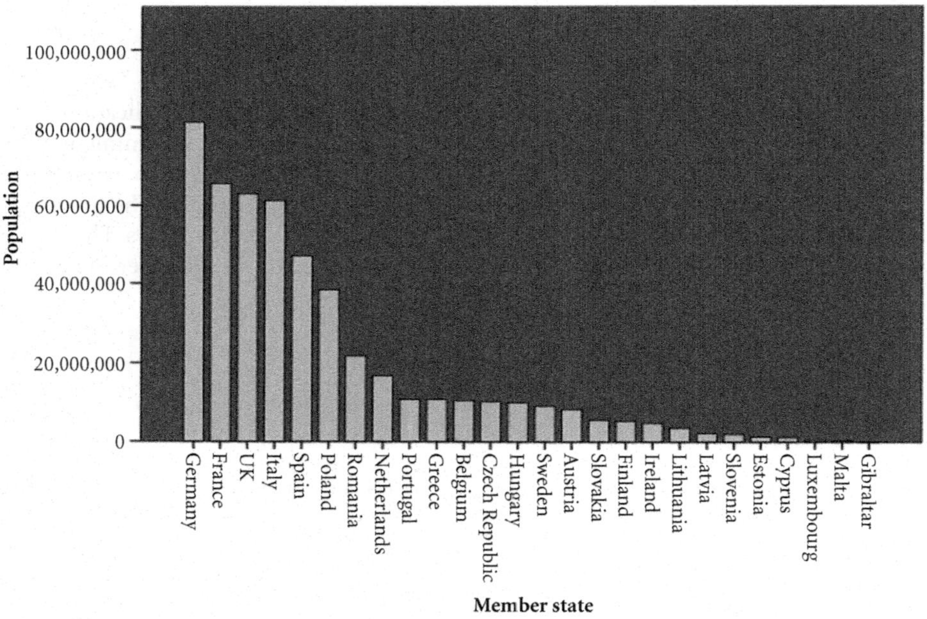

Figure 2: Population Per Member State

Germany, France and the UK have the highest populations but Germany and the UK have by far the highest number of incoming applications. The distribution of population and number of applications between the Member States is not necessarily related. The diagram below shows the relationship between number of incoming applications and population of the Member State, with a best fit line, to determine whether there is any correlation between the two.

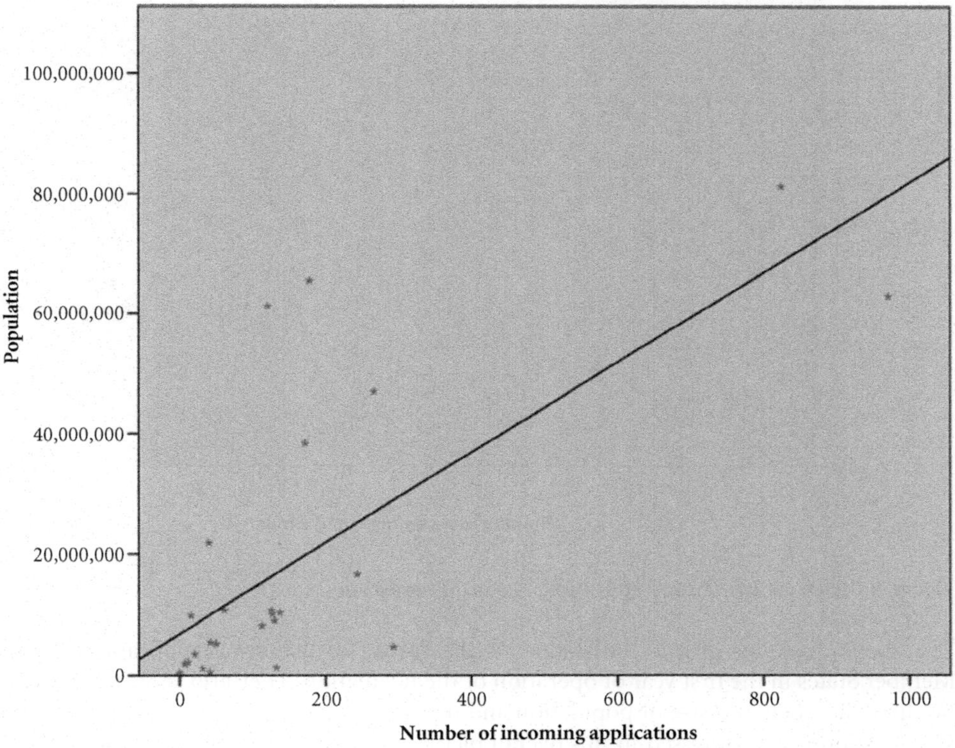

Figure 3: Population and Number of Incoming Applications

In the diagram, each Member State is represented by a star. France, Italy and Ireland do not fit with the general pattern. France has the second highest population, but only received 178 applications. Italy has the fourth highest population but only received 121 applications, whereas Ireland received 293 applications but has a lower population than the majority of Member States. Germany has the highest population but less incoming applications than the UK (as a whole) by around 150 cases. In terms of percentage, 14.8 per cent of the total EU population lives in the UK, but the UK received 21.9 per cent of the total incoming applications. The best fit line indicates that there is not necessarily a direct correlation between the number of incoming cases and the size of the population. The following graph indicates the pattern clearly.

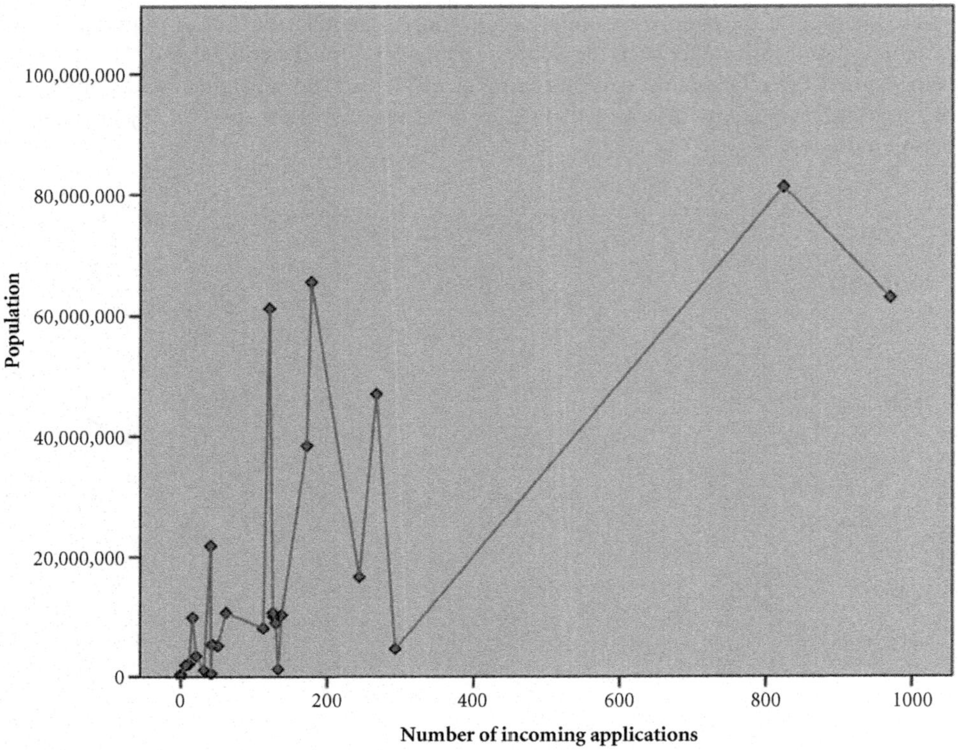

Figure 4: Pattern of Incoming Applications Against Population

The above diagrams give an indication of the spread of incoming applications across Member States in the first year of operation of the Regulation. They also show that there is no direct link between size of population and number of applications received. The other key question to be addressed in this overall picture is which State sent these applications. The majority of applications received (according to the information provided) were sent by Poland (indicated in diagonal stripes). Member States which received the vast majority of total applications from Poland are: England and Wales, Germany, Italy, the Netherlands, Greece, Sweden and Ireland. In respect of other Member States most applications received by Finland came from Estonia and vice versa. An overall picture can be seen in the graph below which displays information on applications received by Member States which is split into the sending State by pattern.[10]

[10] A table of this information is available at Annex I. Unfortunately there are no data on which States sent applications to Austria, France or Spain.

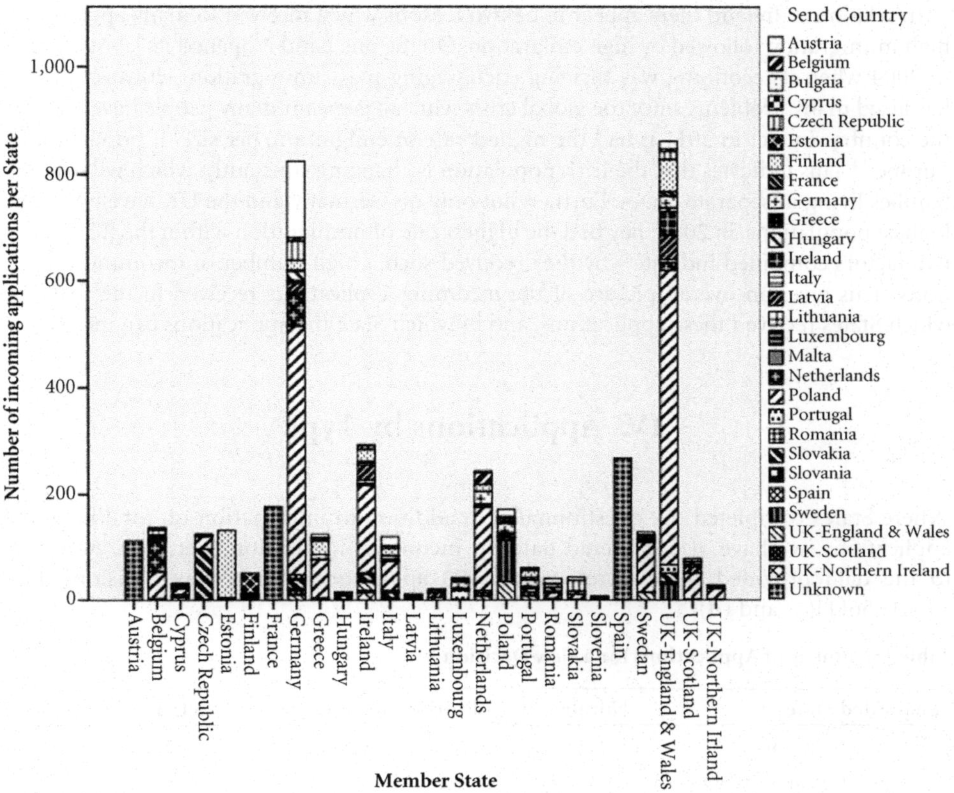

Figure 5: Applications Received, Divided by Sending State

It is unsurprising that Finland and Estonia have applications between each other because they are geographically very close and also the language is similar. In relation to Polish citizens they originally wanted to move away in order to find better work prospects. When Poland first joined the EU in 2004, the only three States that opened their labour markets to polish citizens were the UK, Ireland and Sweden.[11] This was before the economic crisis, so both the UK and Ireland had thriving economies at this time. Prior to this Germany had been a popular State for Poles to emigrate to, but since the labour market did not open until much later, Poles began to move to the UK and Ireland instead.[12] Then when the Netherlands opened its borders in 2007, this also became a popular destination country. However, as a result of the global crisis it was reported in 2008 that around half of the EU citizens who had moved to the UK since 2004 had returned to their State of origin.[13] These trends in migration begin to explain why there are so many applications from Poland, particularly to Germany, the UK, Ireland, Sweden and the Netherlands. Italy opened its labour market to Poles in 2006, indicating why they also have a number of applications from Poland. It is unclear why Greece received a number of applications from Poland.

[11] www.migrationinformation.org/Profiles/display.cfm?ID=800 (accessed June 2013).

[12] Ibid.

[13] Ibid.

In relation to Ireland there appear to be two reasons why it received so many applications: high immigration followed by high emigration. On the one hand it opened its labour market in 2004 when its economy was thriving encouraging mass immigration. However, Ireland has faced many problems since the global crisis which has meant many people have since left the country. In fact in 2011 it had the highest rate of emigration, per size of population, in Europe.[14] This indicates that the Irish population is changing constantly, which will result in families living in separate States. Further, not only do Germany and the UK have two of the highest populations, in 2011 they had the highest rate of immigration within the EU.[15] These two factors combined indicate why they received such a high number of incoming applications. This gives an overall picture of the incoming applications received in the first year, which States received these applications, and in which State the applications originated.

IV. Applications by Type

Where States completed the questionnaire, in addition to information on total incoming applications, we have also gathered data on incoming applications per type. According to the data provided there were at least 193 applications for a new decision under Article 56(1)(c) and (d).

Table 1: Number of Applications for a New Decision

Requested State	Number of applications received under Article 56(1)(c) and (d)
Belgium	2
Czech Republic	2
Estonia	1
Finland	7
Greece	1
Hungary	2
Ireland	29
Italy	2
Latvia	3
Lithuania	4
Poland	56
Portugal	7
Romania	2
Sweden	11
UK-England & Wales	63
UK-Northern Ireland	1
Total	**193**

[14] www.epp.eurostat.ec.europa.eu/statistics_explained/index.php/Migration_and_migrant_population_statistics (accessed June 2013).

[15] Ibid.

There were a lot less applications for modification of a decision. There were at least seven applications for modification by creditors and only three made by debtors.

Table 2: Number of Applications for Modification of a Decision by Creditors

Requested State	Number of applications received under Article 56(1)(e) and (f)
Belgium	1
Finland	2
Ireland	1
Lithuania	1
UK-England & Wales	2
Total	**7**

Table 3: Number of Applications for Modification by a Debtor

Requested State	Number of applications received under Article 56(2)
Hungary	1
Ireland	1
UK-England & Wales	1
Total	**3**

The majority of applications, 1,649, were made under Article 56(1)(a) for recognition or recognition and declaration of enforceability of a decision.

Table 4: Number of Applications for Recognition or Recognition and Declaration of Enforceability

Requested State	Number of applications received under Article 56(1)(a)
Belgium	116
Czech Republic	115
Estonia	29
Finland	38
Greece	54
Hungary	21
Ireland	186
Italy	113
Latvia	5
Lithuania	8
Portugal	1
Romania	17
Slovenia	4
Sweden	123
UK-England & Wales	794
UK-Northern Ireland	25
Total	**1,649**

Finally there were at least 186 applications made under Article 56(1)(b) for enforcement of a decision.

Table 5: Number of Applications for Enforcement

Requested State	Number of applications received under Article 56(1)(b)
Belgium	17
Czech Republic	10
Estonia	31
Finland	3
Greece	2
Ireland	64
Italy	6
Latvia	6
Lithuania	7
Portugal	28
Romania	2
Slovenia	3
UK-England & Wales	5
UK-Northern Ireland	2
Total	**186**

V. Legal Aid

Under the Regulation free legal aid should be provided in all child support applications.[16] This is a new development which was heavily influenced by the 2007 Convention.[17] Consequently, the questionnaire sought to recover data in this area to identify whether the new requirement was working. Unfortunately, the questions on legal aid were not answered well and not many Central Authorities provided data in this area. Therefore, it is impossible to reach any concrete conclusions. In particular, States that received a high number of incoming applications such as England and Wales, Germany, Spain, France, the Netherlands and Poland did not provide data on legal aid. Consequently data on legal aid were only provided in around a quarter of all applications.

[16] Art 46.

[17] For a description and analysis of the provisions see P Beaumont, 'International Family Law in Europe—The Maintenance Project, the Hague Conference and the EC: A Triumph of Reverse Subsidiarity' (2009) 73 *Rabels Zeitschrift* 509, I Curry-Sumner, 'Administrative Co-operation and Free Legal Aid in International Child Maintenance Recovery: What is the Added Value of the Regulation?' (2010) 3 *Nederlands Internationaal Privaatrecht* 611, section 4 and P Beaumont and L Walker, 'Administrative and Judicial Cooperation in the Hague 2007 Maintenance Convention' in J Forner Delaygua, C González Beilfuss, R Viñas Farré (eds), *Entre Bruselas y la Haya. Estudios sobre la unificación internacional y regional del Derecho internacional privado Liber Amicorum Alegría Borrás* (Marcial Pons, Madrid, 2013) 185, 186–92.

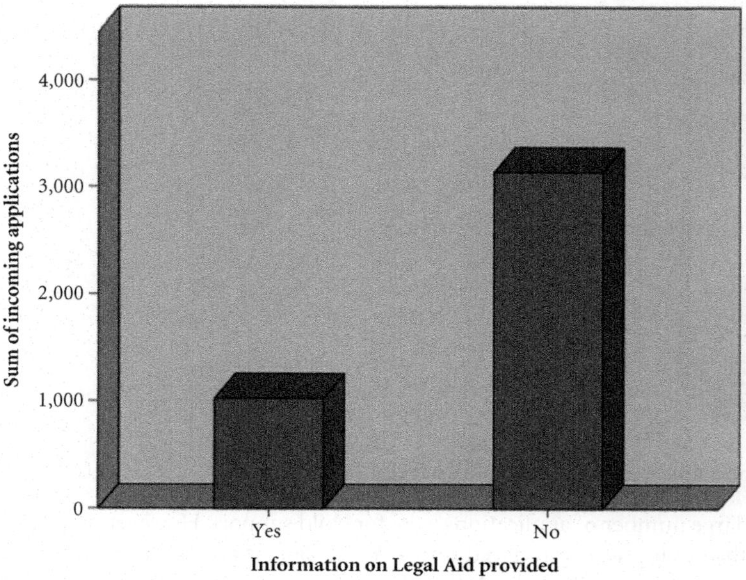

Figure 6: Number of Applications where Data were Provided on Legal Aid

Where data on legal aid were given, it would appear that legal aid was provided in the majority of child support cases and no applications were declared manifestly unfounded, under Article 46(2). However, this could only be determined in relation to applications falling under question 1. In respect of applications under question 3 the outcome is not necessarily clear. This is an area where the questionnaire would need to be changed if a future study is carried out because more data are needed in order to determine how the provisions are being applied. One thing that can be established from the data collected in this area is how many applications there were for child support and how many applications for other forms of family maintenance.

Table 6: Child Support and Other Forms of Maintenance by Receiving State

Requested State	Type		Total
	Child support	Other form	
Belgium	129	7	136
Czech Republic	126	1	127
Estonia	57	4	61
Finland	50	0	50
Greece	56	1	57
Hungary	20	3	23
Ireland	30	250	280
Italy	109	12	121
Latvia	16	0	16
Slovenia	8	0	8
Total	**601**	**278**	**879**

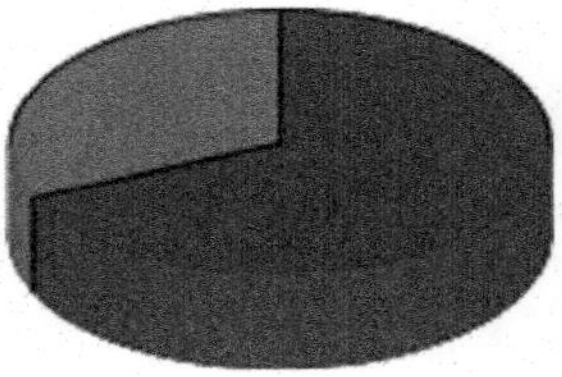

Figure 7: Child Support and Other Forms of Maintenance

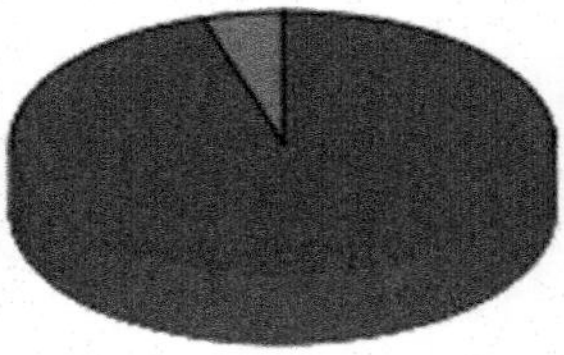

Figure 8: Child Support and Other Forms of Maintenance

This indicates that a large number of applications were for child support. However, according to Ireland, none of the applications it received under Article 56(1)(a) (186 applications) or Article 56(1)(b) (64 applications) fell under Article 46. This is quite confusing as the majority of all other applications were for child support so this does not appear to be correct. This could be skewing the statistics, so it is better not to include Ireland when analysing the data.

Table 7: Child Support and Other Forms of Maintenance by Receiving State

Requested State	Type		Total
	Child support	Other form	
Belgium	129	7	136
Czech Republic	126	1	127
Estonia	57	4	61
Finland	50	0	50
Greece	56	1	57
Hungary	20	3	23
Italy	109	12	121
Latvia	16	0	16
Slovenia	8	0	8
Total	**571**	**28**	**599**

When Ireland is not included it is clear that nearly all applications made under the Regulation to these particular States were for child support (95 per cent). Although, as the Greek Central Authority pointed out, this is not necessarily decisive because in the case of applications which involve more than one applicant, not all the applicants will be entitled to free legal aid. The application may include an award for spousal support or include a child who is over the age of 21.[18] Therefore, when data are collected in the future it will be important to amend the questionnaire to determine how many applications there are for: child support for persons under 21, child support for older children, and other forms

[18] Email correspondence, Marina Dolia, 30 December 2012 and 21 June 2013.

of maintenance. This will be important not only to determine if legal aid is being provided but also for the overall statistics. However, it should be borne in mind that applications purely for spousal support will not necessarily go through Central Authorities and therefore it will not be possible to collect full statistics in this area solely by collecting data from Central Authorities. It is clear that the data collected in relation to legal aid are incomplete. Therefore, it is impossible to reach any clear conclusions and it is hoped that more extensive and coherent data will be collected in this area when future research is carried out.

VI. Requests for Specific Measures

In addition to the ability to make full applications, the new instruments introduce the possibility to make requests for specific measures.[19] This allows Central Authorities to make a specific request rather than wasting time and resources on a full application when an answer to a particular question is unclear. This could be for example to locate the debtor if it is unclear to the applicant where he or she actually lives, so rather than make a full application it is better to check that he or she lives in that State first. A request can also be made to determine if the debtor has sufficient funds to pay a maintenance obligation. This is important, because where the debtor's means are very limited the cost of the international transfer could be higher than the obligation and in such cases it would be pointless to proceed with an application. Requests can be made to:

(a) help locate the debtor or the creditor;[20]
(b) help obtain relevant information concerning the income and, if necessary, other financial circumstances of the debtor or creditor including the location of assets;
(c) facilitate the obtaining of documentary or other evidence;
(d) provide assistance in establishing parentage where necessary;
(e) initiate or facilitate the institution of proceedings to obtain any necessary provisional measures which are territorial in nature and the purpose of which is to secure the outcome of a pending maintenance application;
(f) facilitate the service of documents.

All the requests available relate to one of the specific functions that Central Authorities are expected to carry out.[21] There were at least 1,463 requests made in the first year of operation of the Regulation.[22]

A. Types of Requests Made

The vast majority of requests were made in order to locate one of the parties, presumably the debtor (see the chart below). Unfortunately, not all Central Authorities provided

[19] See Art 53 of the Regulation and Art 7 of the 2007 Convention.

[20] It should be noted that under the Regulation this request is non-discretionary. The requested Central Authority must always carry out this request, under Art 53(2). Under the 2007 Convention, the requested Central Authority only needs to proceed with the request where they are 'satisfied that they are necessary to assist an applicant in making an application under Article 10 or in determining whether such an application should be initiated' (Art 7(1)).

[21] See Arts 51 and 53 of the Regulation.

[22] This number is the total number of incoming requests received by the Central Authorities who filled in the relevant part of the questionnaire.

information on what the request was for. If these requests are excluded (as in the chart below) requests to locate a party account for 88 per cent of all requests. If the unknown requests are included these account for 20 per cent, so requests to locate a party account for 70 per cent of all requests.

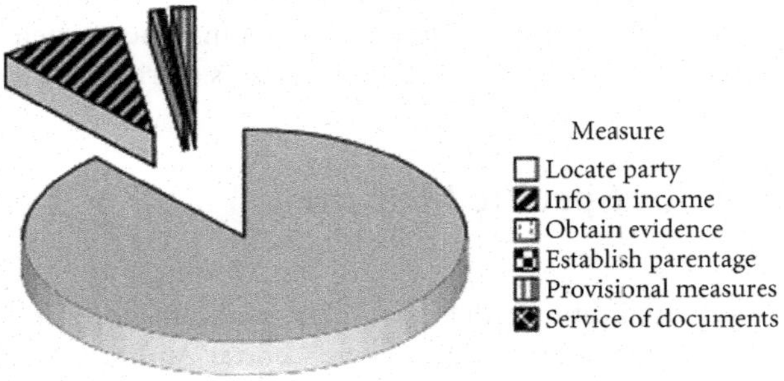

Figure 9: Requests for Specific Measures

The data collected suggests that many creditors do not know where their ex spouse, ex partner or the father of their child is living and a much smaller, but not insignificant, number of applicants want to receive information on the income or assets of a party (9 per cent). All other types of requests are very infrequent. In terms of requests received by specific States, the spread was more or less even (see the graph below).[23]

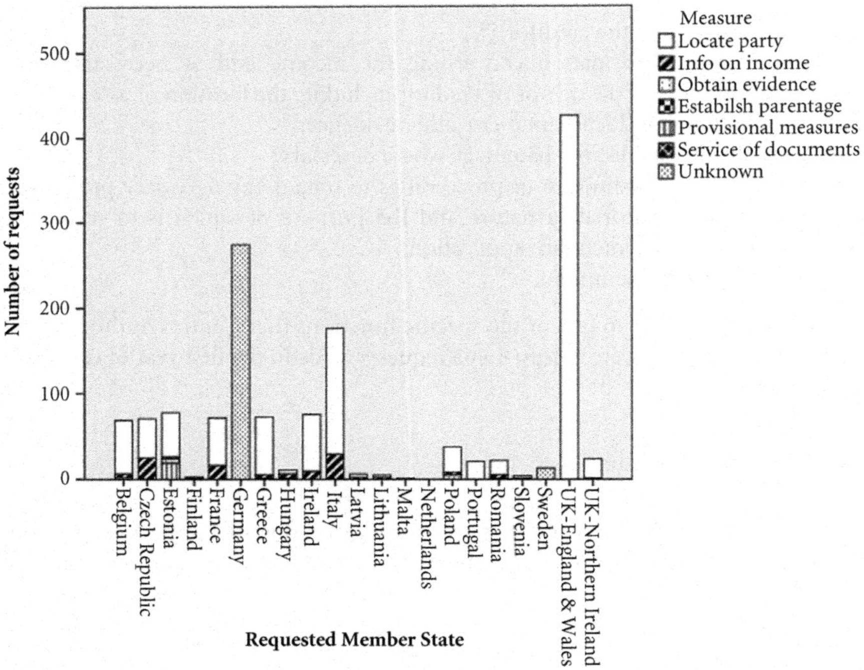

Figure 10: Requests Received by Member State

[23] A breakdown of the information in this graph can be found in Annex II.

It is unfortunate that we do not know what the requests sent to Germany were for, since they received the second highest number of requests (274). All requests sent to England and Wales and Northern Ireland (as well as the majority of requests received by the Republic of Ireland) are to locate a party. Maybe this is because the creditor is aware that the debtor is residing somewhere in the British Isles but they are not sure where. Most other States received requests for both the location of a party or for information on the income or assets of a party. The most interesting is Estonia who also received a number of requests for provisional measures (24 per cent). The other interesting point is that there were only three requests for establishment of parentage, Belgium received two and Romania one, suggesting that establishment of parentage is not in reality a problem in the majority of cross-border maintenance cases.[24] The majority of the requests received by these States were sent by Poland, 749. Of these requests 531 (70 per cent) were to find the location of a party, 28 (4 per cent) were to gain information on the income or the assets of the party and one request was made to obtain evidence.[25]

B. Requests that Resulted in a Full Application

In order to determine how well this new system is working the questionnaire sought to gain information on the number of requests that turned into a full application. The hope was that these requests are meaningful, so that in the majority of cases the debtor is actually found and therefore a full application can be made rather than Central Authorities just going on fishing expeditions and sending out the same request to a number of States. Unfortunately it was very difficult at this stage to gather data on the number of requests that had turned into a full application. At the time the questionnaires were returned it was reported that only 55 (around 4 per cent) of all requests received had turned into a full application. In the majority of cases, 942 (around 65 per cent), the Central Authority reported that they did not know the outcome. (The graph below indicates which requests turned into full applications per State).[26]

[24] There was a lengthy discussion on this during the negotiations of the Convention when deciding whether legal aid should be provided for establishing paternity (see Proceedings of the XXIst Session, November 2007, PV no 15).

[25] In respect of the other 189 requests (20%) it was not reported what the request was for.

[26] A breakdown of this information can be found in Annex IV on the Centre for PIL website.

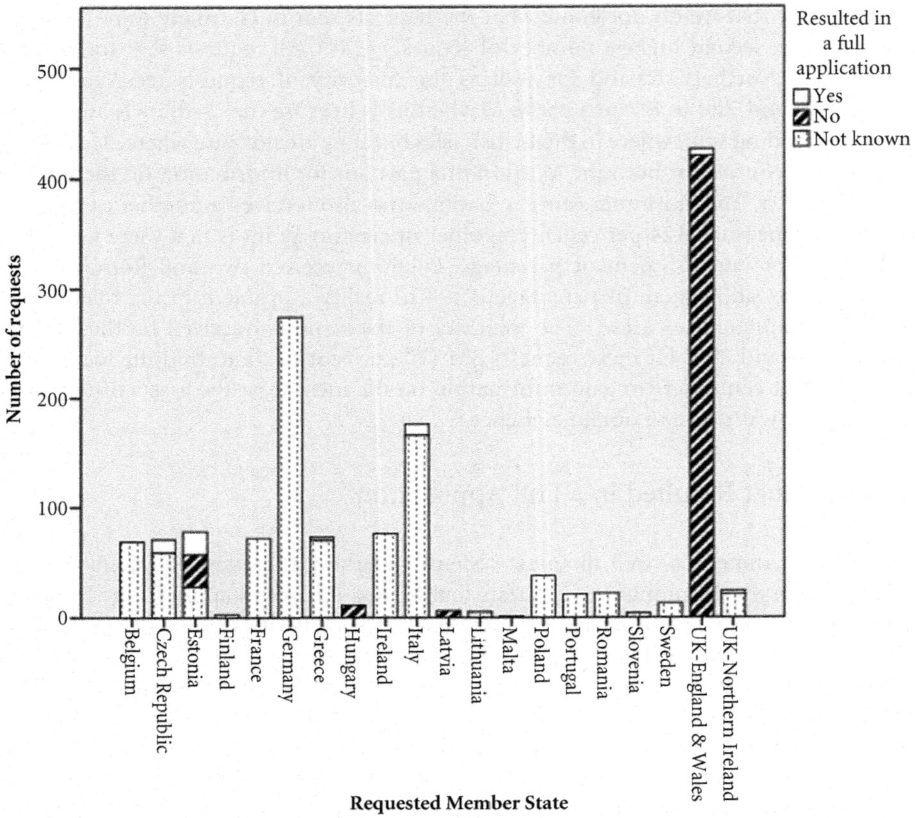

Figure 11: Requests that Resulted in a Full Application

This is definitely an area where further research should be carried out. The main problem here could be that the study was carried out too early to determine the outcome.[27] However, some States have managed to indicate the outcome in at least some of the cases and the Central Authority for England and Wales in every case. Given that the majority of requests have been sent in order to locate the debtors there are two potential problems that could arise in this area. The first conclusion is that Central Authorities are going on fishing expeditions and sending requests to more than one State because they have no idea where the debtor actually is. The second conclusion is that the outcome of these requests is delayed because Central Authorities are finding it very difficult to locate debtors and fulfil their function in Article 51(2)(b).[28] As such it is imperative that further research is carried out at a later date to discover what is happening here. In relation to the latter, it is very important that Central Authorities are provided with sufficient powers and resources (such as electronic access to the relevant registers) to enable them to be able to locate

[27] This was indicated by both the Swedish and Belgium Central Authorities in their responses (email correspondence 30 November 2012 and 27 November 2012).

[28] In relation to locating debtors generally, the Finnish Central Authority reported that three incoming applications for recognition and enforceability under Art 56(1)(a) had been refused because the debtor was not found.

the necessary parties as quickly and easily as possible. In the case of the former, Central Authorities should not be wasting their time and resources, or those of the requested Central Authorities, sending pointless requests. They should at least try to gain some indication of where the debtor might be before proceeding with requests.

C. Option to Recover Costs

Unlike the rest of the Regulation, where Central Authorities must cover their own costs, they are allowed to recover the costs in relation to a request for a specific measure.[29] However, they are only supposed to recover 'exceptional costs'.[30] It is also stated that costs related to 'locating the debtor shall not be regarded as exceptional'.[31] A Central Authority is only allowed to recover 'exceptional costs' where they have prior consent from the applicant.[32] Given that the majority of requests were related to locating the debtor, one would expect that Central Authorities rarely recovered their costs under Article 54(2). The majority of Central Authorities did not answer this part of the questionnaire, but the table below indicates the practice by the Authorities that did.

Table 8: Recovery of Costs

Recovery of Costs under Article 54(2)					
Requested State		**Costs recovered?**			**Total**
		Yes	**No**	**Not known**	
Estonia	Number of requests	0	75	3	78
	As a percentage	0.0%	96.2%	3.8%	
Finland	Number of requests	0	3	0	3
	As a percentage	0.0%	100.0%	0.0%	
Hungary	Number of requests	2	9	0	11
	As a percentage	18.2%	81.8%	0.0%	
Ireland	Number of requests	0	76	0	76
	As a percentage	0.0%	100.0%	0.0%	
Italy	Number of requests	176	0	0	176
	As a percentage	100.0%	0.0%	0.0%	
Latvia	Number of requests	0	6	0	6
	As a percentage	0.0%	100.0%	0.0%	
Sweden	Number of requests	13	0	0	13
	As a percentage	100.0%	0.0%	0.0%	
UK-England & Wales	Number of requests	0	426	0	426
	As a percentage	0.0%	100.0%	0.0%	
Total		**191**	**595**	**3**	**789**

[29] See Art 54.
[30] Art 54(2).
[31] Ibid.
[32] Art 54(3).

This indicates that the majority of these Authorities: Estonia, Finland, Ireland, Latvia and England and Wales did not recover their costs at all. Hungary recovered their costs in two out of 11 requests. Only five of the requests received by Hungary were for the location of a party,[33] so the recovery of costs in two requests could in this case be justified as exceptional costs. Both Sweden and Italy recovered their costs in every request. A possible explanation for this could be that these States misunderstood the question or inserted the numbers in the wrong column by accident. However, if it is presumed that the questionnaire was filled in correctly then this could suggest that the Italian and probably the Swedish Central Authorities are misinterpreting this provision in the Regulation.

In relation to Sweden it is not clear what the requests were for so this may have been justified. However, given the high number of requests for the location of a party, generally, it seems highly unlikely that none of the requests received by Sweden were for this. Further it seems unlikely that the Central Authority would incur 'exceptional costs' in relation to every request. Italy cannot be justified in recovering costs in all 176 requests. They could not legitimately argue that they incurred 'exceptional costs' in so many requests. In addition 147 of these requests were for the location of a party.[34] Although requests can be made to locate either party and Central Authorities are only barred from recovering costs in relation to locating debtors, it is expected that the majority of requests will be made in order to locate debtors, rather than the other way around. Therefore, provided the questionnaire was completed correctly, it has to be concluded that the Italian Central Authority is in violation of Article 54 of the Regulation for recovering their costs in respect of every request.

VII. Meeting the Time Requirements

When carrying out their work under the Regulation, Central Authorities are expected to meet certain time requirements. Along with the general obligation to 'process a case as quickly as a proper consideration of the issues will allow',[35] Central Authorities have to meet the specific time requirements in Article 58(3), (4) and (9). First, Central Authorities are meant to acknowledge receipt of the application, inform the requesting State what steps have been taken or will be taken to deal with the application, and they may also request additional information from the requesting State.[36] They should do this within 30 days of receiving the application. During this time they should also provide the requesting Authority with 'the name and contact details of the person or unit responsible for responding to inquiries regarding the progress of the application.'[37] Secondly, they must inform the requesting Central Authority of the status of the application within 60 days of acknowledging receipt.[38]

[33] See Annex III on the Centre for PIL website.

[34] See Annex III on the Centre for PIL website.

[35] Art 58(6).

[36] Art 58(3).

[37] Art 58(3). It is noted that under the Convention the Central Authority has six weeks to do this (Art 12(3)).

[38] Art 58(4). The equivalent provision in the Convention requires that this is done in three months (Art 12(4)). This is probably more sensible as it is unlikely much progress will have been made between the two time periods given in the Regulation.

At the outset, these requirements appear fair. In the first case the requested Central Authority has a month to decide how it should proceed with the application and inform the requesting Central Authority of this. It then has up to two months to provide the requesting Central Authority with an update on the progress. However, the second time requirement may be too close to the first, and little progress may have been made in 60 days. It would appear that meeting these requirements is proving harder than expected in practice.[39] This might be because of the high volume of applications, compared to a lack of personnel, although it is expected that applications will in fact increase as time goes on.[40] It might also be because the current databases are inefficient and therefore Central Authorities are finding it difficult to keep track of applications and what stage they are at. Finally, Central Authorities might be prevented from meeting the requirements due to national laws of procedure.

A. The 30-day Requirement

According to the Central Authorities that completed the relevant part of the application the 30-day requirement in Article 58(3) was met in around 76 per cent of applications.[41] However, the overall figure is not a true representation of the practice across the States (as highlighted in the table below). It should also be noted that this figure could even be slightly optimistic as Central Authorities were responding in relation to their own practice.[42]

Table 9: Meeting the 30-day Requirement

Requested State and Art 58(3) (30-day requirement)				
Requested State		**Art 58(3) met**		**Total**
		Yes	**No**	
Belgium	Number of applications	38	100	138
	As a percentage	27.5%	72.5%	
Czech Republic	Number of applications	122	5	127
	As a percentage	96.1%	3.9%	
Estonia	Number of applications	80	53	133
	As a percentage	60.2%	39.8%	

(*Continued*)

[39] It is unclear why the two instruments differ in this particular area. It would be preferable if the time limits were the same as it is not sensible to require the same Authorities to complete the same tasks within a different time scale under the two instruments.

[40] See section III above.

[41] This is based on data provided in respect of incoming applications to that Central Authority. So the data are reliant on the Central Authority being honest in relation to how often they met the requirements.

[42] Where data were provided on outgoing cases the requesting Central Authorities indicated that requested Central Authorities only managed to meet the 30-day requirement in around 54% of cases. However, because only some Central Authorities provided these data, they do not necessarily correspond with the data on incoming cases. Eg data in respect of Bulgaria, France, Austria, Luxembourg, Spain and Scotland are also included (but this only covers applications received by those States that were sent by the States who completed the questionnaire and not all the applications they received). Because not all States answered the full questionnaire the data on incoming cases are more reliable as we get to see the full picture in the State that answered the relevant questions.

Table 9: (*Continued*)

Requested State and Art 58(3) (30-day requirement)				
Requested State		**Art 58(3) met**		**Total**
		Yes	**No**	
Finland	Number of applications	51	0	51
	As a percentage	100.0%	0.0%	
Greece	Number of applications	125	1	126
	As a percentage	99.2%	0.8%	
Hungary	Number of applications	14	2	16
	As a percentage	87.5%	12.5%	
Italy	Number of applications	120	1	121
	As a percentage	99.2%	0.8%	
Latvia	Number of applications	11	0	11
	As a percentage	100.0%	0.0%	
Portugal	Number of applications	60	2	62
	As a percentage	96.8%	3.2%	
Slovenia	Number of applications	1	6	7
	As a percentage	14.3%	85.7%	
Sweden	Number of applications	127	3	130
	As a percentage	97.7%	2.3%	
UK-England & Wales	Number of applications	611	251	862
	As a percentage	70.9%	29.1%	
UK-Northern Ireland	Number of applications	26	2	28
	As a percentage	92.9%	7.1%	
Total	Applications	**1,386**	**426**	**1,812**
	Percentage	**76.5%**	**23.5%**	

According to the data provided there is quite a disparity between the Central Authorities in this respect. Both Finland and Latvia met the requirement in all cases. Latvia had a very small number of incoming cases, only 11, and initially they had two people working at the Central Authority but there have been three since March 2012.[43] Finland had more cases, but 51 is still relatively low. There are two practitioners working on maintenance applications at the Finnish Central Authority. The majority of Central Authorities reported that they meet the time requirement in around 90 per cent of applications. This seems viable and these Central Authorities should be considered to be functioning effectively. England and Wales and Estonia should seek to meet the requirement more often in order to function more efficiently. However, it is recognised that incoming applications to these States

[43] Email correspondence with Linda Strazdina, 3 December 2012. It should also be noted that these practitioners only work on maintenance, they are not in charge of other instruments such as Brussels IIa.

are high. England and Wales received 862 applications in a nine-month period.[44] It has been suggested that they have to deal with around 180 new applications a month, the majority of which are incoming, and there are five practitioners working at that Central Authority.[45] Estonia had 133 incoming applications, but there is only one practitioner working there at present.[46] This Central Authority could be more efficient if the current practitioner had some assistance.

The major causes for concern are the Slovenian and Belgian Central Authorities. The Slovenian Central Authority only had seven incoming applications, and they only managed to meet the requirement in one of these applications. There is no further information on the structure of this Central Authority, or the national law, but this is clearly not good enough. The Belgian Central Authority only met the requirement in around 27 per cent of applications but they had many more incoming applications, 138. The poor performance by the Belgian Central Authority in meeting the time requirements, appears to be related to national laws of procedure rather than the efficient or inefficient practice of the Central Authority. This is because, when completing the questionnaire, they only included applications 'for which a royal decree was effectively sent within the allotted time'.[47] It would be very difficult to meet the requirement if a royal decree had to be sent in each case. This could mean that the Belgian practice breaches the EU principle of effectiveness, because this national administrative practice makes this provision of the Regulation 'excessively difficult' to meet.[48] States should refrain from imposing cumbersome national laws of procedure where possible, in order to ensure that the process under the Regulation operates as efficiently and expeditiously as possible.

B. The 60-day Requirement

The feedback in respect of the 60-day requirement in Article 58(4) was even worse. The requirement was only met in 29 per cent of applications.[49] Again the figures were very different in each State that completed this part of the questionnaire. However, poor performance under Article 58(3) does not necessarily indicate poor performance under Article 58(4) and vice versa (see table below). Finland and Latvia maintained their 100 per cent record. Estonia met the requirement in the vast majority of cases, and the worst performers were: Portugal,[50] Italy, England and Wales and Belgium.

[44] See Annex I.

[45] Informal discussion with one of the practitioners at 'A year on—Taking stock of the EU Maintenance Regulation' event hosted by Dawson Cornwell in June 2012.

[46] Email correspondence and informal discussion at the Heidelberg Conference 2013.

[47] Email correspondence, 27 November 2012.

[48] See C-147/01, *Weber's Wine World Handels-GmbH and Others* v *Abgabenberufungskommission Wien* [2003] ECR I-11365, 11418.

[49] In this case, there was not much difference between the data provided by requested Central Authorities and requesting Central Authorities. Where information was given on outgoing cases requesting Central Authorities reported that the requirement was met by the requested Central Authority in around 27% of applications.

[50] There are five practitioners working at the Portuguese Central Authority, email correspondence 6 November 2012.

Table 10: Meeting the 60-day Requirement

Requested State and Art 58(4) (60-day requirement)				
Requested State		**Art 58(4)**		**Total**
		Yes	**No**	
Belgium	Number of applications	13	125	138
	As a percentage	9.4%	90.6%	
Czech Republic	Number of applications	124	3	127
	As a percentage	97.6%	2.4%	
Estonia	Number of applications	126	7	133
	As a percentage	94.7%	5.3%	
Finland	Number of applications	51	0	51
	As a percentage	100.0%	0.0%	
Greece	Number of applications	53	73	126
	As a percentage	42.1%	57.9%	
Hungary	Number of applications	9	7	16
	As a percentage	56.2%	43.8%	
Italy	Number of applications	0	121	121
	As a percentage	0.0%	100.0%	
Latvia	Number of applications	11	0	11
	As a percentage	100.0%	0.0%	
Portugal	Number of applications	0	62	62
	As a percentage	0.0%	100.0%	
Slovenia	Number of applications	3	4	7
	As a percentage	42.9%	57.1%	
Sweden	Number of applications	80	50	130
	As a percentage	61.5%	38.5%	
UK-England & Wales	Number of applications	45	817	862
	As a percentage	5.2%	94.8%	
UK-Northern	Number of applications	12	16	28
Ireland	As a percentage	42.9%	57.1%	
Total	Applications	**527**	**1,285**	**1,812**
	Percentage	**29.1%**	**70.9%**	

Although 'no sanctions are imposed on the requested Central Authority for failure to deliver speedy and timely responses to applications'[51] within the text of the Regulation, this should not stop the Commission from bringing an action against a State for failure

[51] Curry-Sumner (n 17) 611, section 3.5.2.

to meet these targets because they are a 'requirement' under the Regulation. Therefore, States must ensure that the requirements are met, in order to comply with the principle of 'effectiveness'.[52] It is clear from the feedback that the majority of Central Authorities are not functioning efficiently when it comes to fulfilling the requirements in Article 58(3) and (4). These tasks are fairly minimal, all that is required in reality is receipt of the application, some contact details and an update of the application. If Central Authorities are not achieving these menial tasks it is questionable how effectively they are carrying out their specific functions since these functions will generally be much more difficult to carry out. Although some difficulties have been identified, the overall picture is incomplete. State bodies should ensure that Central Authorities are suitably staffed and that personnel are given the appropriate equipment to carry out their tasks and keep track of applications.

VIII. Recognition and Enforcement: Problems with Interpretation?

Although there are two procedures under the Regulation, the quantitative research suggests that the distinction between the two procedures is not necessarily clear and at this stage the majority of applications are still going through an enforceability process (probably because of the transitional provisions in Article 75). Articles 17 to 19 clearly abolish the *exequatur* process, but how this fits with the various available applications in Article 56 of the Regulation is unclear. This is partly because there is a disconnection between the procedures for recognition and enforcement in Articles 17 to 24 and the available applications in Article 56. The text is very far away from the available applications and there is no indication in Article 56 of which applications should apply to which procedures. Further, the available applications in Article 56 are based on the applications in Article 10 of the Maintenance Convention. This is slightly concerning given that the procedures for enforceability or strict enforcement are very different under the two instruments.[53]

A. Available Applications

Article 56(1)(a) of the Regulation covers applications for recognition and for a declaration of enforceability and therefore should be used in relation to outgoing applications from the UK and Denmark and, on a transitional basis, to outgoing applications from other EU Member States in relation to decisions not yet subject to the abolition of *exequatur* (see Article 75). Article 56(1)(b) covers applications for enforcement and therefore should be used for all post-transitional outgoing applications from Protocol States and for applications from non-Protocol States seeking actual enforcement of a decision that has already

[52] The principle of effectiveness is underpinned by Art 4(3) TEU, the overarching proposition is that States must take measures to ensure their obligations under the Treaties, or any secondary legislation, are fulfilled. For an analysis of the principle see P Craig and G de Búrca, *EU Law Text, Cases and Materials*, 5th edn (Oxford, Oxford University Press, 2011) 223–37.

[53] For a brief explanation see L Walker, 'From Brussels I and the Maintenance Convention to the Maintenance Regulation: Is the Resulting Maintenance Regulation Consistent with the Other EU PIL Instruments?' (2013) 6 *Nederlands Internationaal Privaatrecht* 167, section 2.2.

been declared enforceable in the requested State. Article 56(1)(a) allows a creditor to make an application for 'recognition or recognition and declaration of enforceability of a decision'. The equivalent provision in the Convention covers 'recognition or recognition and enforcement of a decision'.[54] The difference in the text in both instruments clarifies the position as regards enforceability. The fact that the term 'and enforcement' was not included in the Regulation makes it clear that Article 56(1)(a) should only apply to enforceability. However, procedures for enforcement where no enforceability is required are not so clear. Article 56(1)(b) allows a creditor to make an application for 'enforcement of a decision given or recognised in the requested Member State', the equivalent provision in the Convention covers the 'enforcement of a decision made or recognised in the requested State'.[55] The distinction here is not so clear, because the replacement of the word 'made' with 'given' makes no difference. One would usually seek to enforce a decision originally given in the 'requesting' State, not the 'requested' State. Therefore, one might be misled into believing that there is a type of application missing. Fundamentally the type of application that should apply to the majority of applications circulated under the Regulation, to which the procedures in Articles 17 to 21 apply. This would be for 'the enforcement of a decision given in the requesting State'. Technically, the language of Article 56(1)(b) does cover all judgments from Hague Protocol States in the EU because those decisions are 'automatically' recognised in the other EU Member States under the Regulation without the need for any procedure. Thus the application for enforcement of such a decision is for enforcement of a decision that has been automatically already 'recognised' in the requested State. However, the problem is that the same reasoning applies to decisions from a non-Protocol State because they are automatically recognisable in other EU Member States without any special procedure (Article 23(1)) and therefore one could be misled by the wording of Article 56(1)(b) into believing that because the UK or Danish decision is automatically recognised in other EU Member States, an application can be made for enforcement under Article 56(1)(b) without having sought a declaration of enforceability first. Therefore, from a statistical point of view and from the point of view of clarity for the user it would be better to divide up the different types of decisions falling within Article 56(1)(b) in a future revision of the EU Maintenance Regulation. This was suggested in the Conclusions of the Heidelberg Conference:

> Consideration should be given to amending Article 56(1)(b) and Annex VI of Council Regulation 4/2009 to reduce the current risk of confusion by separating applications for actual enforcement of decisions given in the requested Member State (which apply to all Member States) from: a) applications for actual enforcement of decisions given in other Member States bound by the Hague Protocol 2007 which are automatically recognised in the requested State without a declaration of enforceability; and, b) applications for actual enforcement of decisions given in other Member States not bound by the Hague Protocol which have already been the subject of a declaration of enforceability in the requested State.[56]

[54] Art 10(1)(a) of the Convention.
[55] Art 10(1)(b) of the Convention.
[56] See conclusion 5(e) of the Heidelberg Conference. This section was included based on the findings of the empirical study carried out for the Heidelberg project. However, there were debates between the partners whilst constructing the conclusions as to whether such an amendment would really be necessary. It was concluded that for the sake of clarity it would be preferable if there was a change in the text.

Therefore, it is unsurprising that the figures provided in this area are slightly confusing given the lack of clarity in the Regulation. There is some assistance in the recitals, but again the terminology used is not entirely clear because it is not consistent, therefore interpretation can be ambiguous. The terminology in Recital 26 on recognition and declaration of enforceability is clear enough and matches the wording in the second part of Article 56(1)(a). 'For decisions on maintenance obligations given in a Member State not bound by the 2007 Hague Protocol, there should be provision in this Regulation for a procedure for recognition and declaration of enforceability.' However, Article 56(1)(a) also allows a creditor to make an application purely for 'recognition' and although this is not mentioned in Recital 26 it is provided for in Article 23(2) of the Regulation. The link between the available applications in Article 56(1)(a) and (b) and the systems established in the two tracks and the transitional provisions is slightly confusing and it may not necessarily be clear to practitioners which procedure they should use, especially when some have had no specific training on the Regulation or general legal training.

B. Practice

The practice under the first year of the Regulation suggests that the procedures in this area are not clear. It would appear that Central Authorities are generally always making an application under Article 56(1)(a). The information provided suggests that there have been at least 1,649 applications under Article 56(1)(a) and only 186 applications for enforcement under Article 56(1)(b).[57] The abolition of *exequatur* for all judgments coming from EU Hague Protocol States means that one would expect the figures to be reversed. In fact there were only 179 outgoing cases from the UK, and one might have thought that these should be the only cases under Article 56(1)(a).[58] From discussions with practitioners working at Central Authorities a misconception is that it is believed that all applications involving the UK still need to go through the *exequatur* process, when it is only outgoing applications, not incoming. However, at this stage of the operation of the Regulation the transitional provisions are very important. Therefore in accordance with Article 75(1) of the Regulation if a maintenance decision in a Protocol State arises from proceedings that were instituted there before 18 June 2011 then the decision still needs to go through the enforceability stage under the Regulation as the original decision was not made according to the rules of the Protocol. Given that our survey related to the period just after the entry into force of the Regulation it is not unreasonable to infer that a large majority of maintenance decisions in Protocol countries arose from proceedings that were instituted before 18 June 2011. Hopefully in future surveys this transitional problem will have a negligible impact on the results.

[57] A factor that contributes towards the disparity in the figures is that applications that were commenced before June 2011 still need to go through the old system. This is because the application of the law designated under the Hague Protocol is a condition for the abolition of *exequatur*. Therefore, because the Protocol did not apply previously the system under Arts 17–19 of the Maintenance Regulation cannot be used for these cases. However, it is considered that this alone cannot account for such high numbers of applications under the old system (see the discussion on old and new States below). The lack of clarity on which type of application to use could also be a factor.

[58] Except for cases from Denmark, but these applications were not included in the study.

In relation to applications for enforceability and enforcement, around 90 per cent of applications were for enforceability and only 10 per cent were for enforcement, so only one in ten applications of this type were for enforcement.

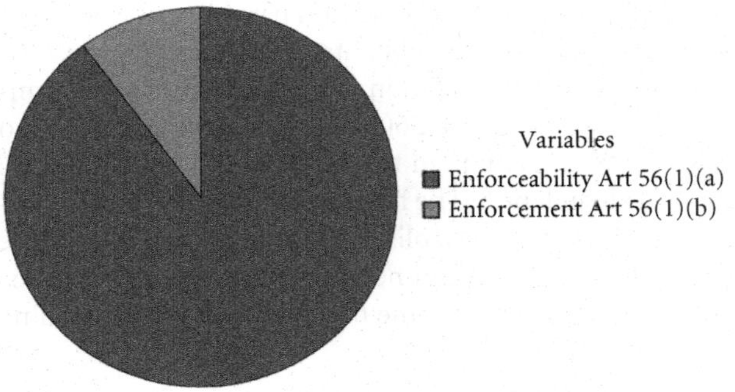

Figure 12: Applications under Art 56(1)(a) and (b)

However, when this matter is investigated further it can be seen that this ratio of 1 in 10 is not true across all the Member States. The graph below compares incoming applications for enforcement with incoming applications for enforceability in each State that completed the relevant part of the questionnaire.

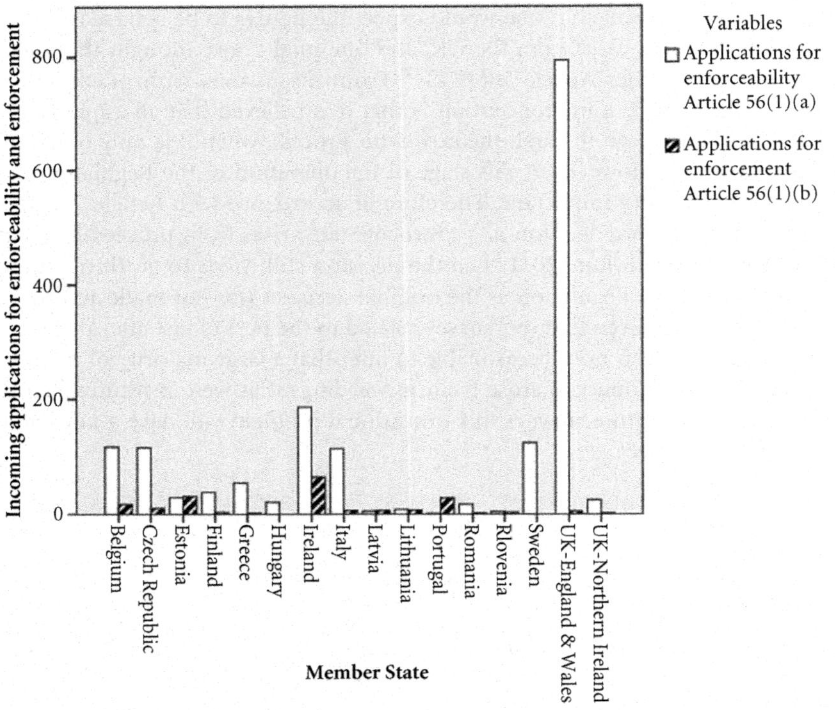

Figure 13: Incoming Applications for Enforceability and Enforcement by Member State

As can be seen from the graph England and Wales have a vast number of incoming applications for enforceability (99.4 per cent) and very few applications for enforcement. As they have by far the most applications, this is possibly skewing the results.[59] The high number of incoming applications for enforceability could also support the assertion that some of those working at Central Authorities believe, wrongly, that all applications involving the UK must go through the *exequatur* stage.[60] In contrast to the high number of applications for enforceability received by England and Wales, the majority of applications received by Portugal were for enforcement. Estonia received slightly more applications for enforcement than enforceability, and Latvia, Lithuania and Slovenia received similar amounts of each type of application. Numbers and percentages are displayed in the table below.

Table 11: Applications for Enforceability and Enforcement

		56(1)(a)	56(1)(b)	Total
		Enforceability	**Enforcement**	
Estonia	Number of applications	29	31	60
	As a percentage	48.3%	51.7%	
Latvia	Number of applications	5	6	11
	As a percentage	45.5%	54.5%	
Lithuania	Number of applications	8	7	15
	As a percentage	53.3%	46.7%	
Portugal	Number of applications	1	28	29
	As a percentage	3.4%	96.6%	
Slovenia	Number of applications	4	3	7
	As a percentage	57.1%	42.9%	

Although the overall figures are affected by the transitional application of the old rules in Brussels I, this alone probably does not account for such high numbers of applications for enforceability.

A further consideration could be whether there are any patterns in the States sending the applications. This could give some indication as to whether some Central Authorities seem to understand the procedure more than others. For example, are applications for enforceability commonly sent by certain States and applications for enforcement sent by a different pool of States? The two graphs below indicate incoming applications split into patterns by sending State. The first graph deals with enforceability and the second graph enforcement.

[59] The data from England and Wales are skewing the results slightly. If data from England and Wales are excluded then just over 80% of applications are for enforceability and around 20% for enforcement, so around 1 in 5. The figure is still much higher than one would expect given the abolition of the *exequatur* process.

[60] The Scottish Central Authority reported that incoming applications were being sent on the wrong forms.

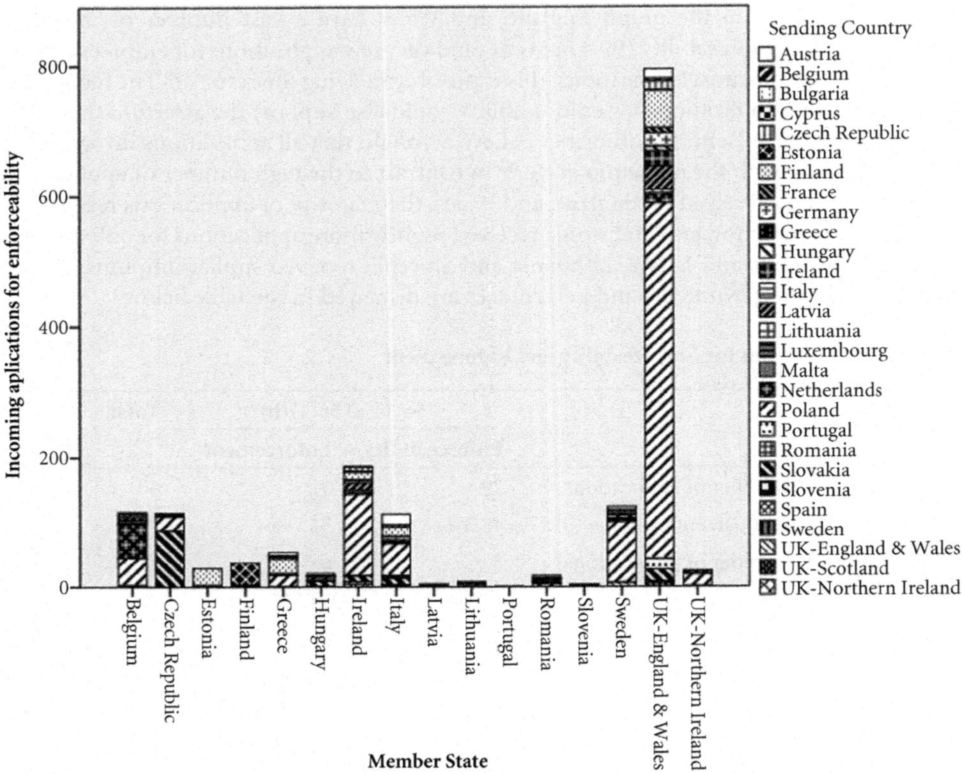

Figure 14: Incoming Applications for Enforceability Split by Sending State

In the graph above, a vast number of the applications were sent by Poland, indicated in diagonal stripes. The Czech Republic received a number of applications from Slovakia, and Belgium received a few from the Netherlands.

In the graph on enforcement, for the first time Poland is not the State that sent the most applications.[61] Notably, Sweden has received no applications for enforcement, and the vast majority of applications it received for enforceability were sent by Poland. We see a larger spread of Member States than in previous graphs, notably Finland, the Netherlands and Latvia. This could suggest that these Central Authorities are more aware of the new process than the Polish authority,[62] but it is not decisive. Although Finland is sending more applications for enforcement than other States it still sent more applications for enforceability than enforcement (around 70 per cent of applications under Article 56(1)).[63]

[61] See figure 4 above, where the majority of applications came from Poland (see also Annexes I and II).

[62] According to these States shown in the graph, 980 of the applications they received under Art 56(1)(a) and (b) were sent by Poland. 926 of these (94.5%) were for enforceability and 54 were for enforcement.

[63] This means three in ten of the applications sent by Finland were for enforcement, which is higher than the overall figure of one in ten.

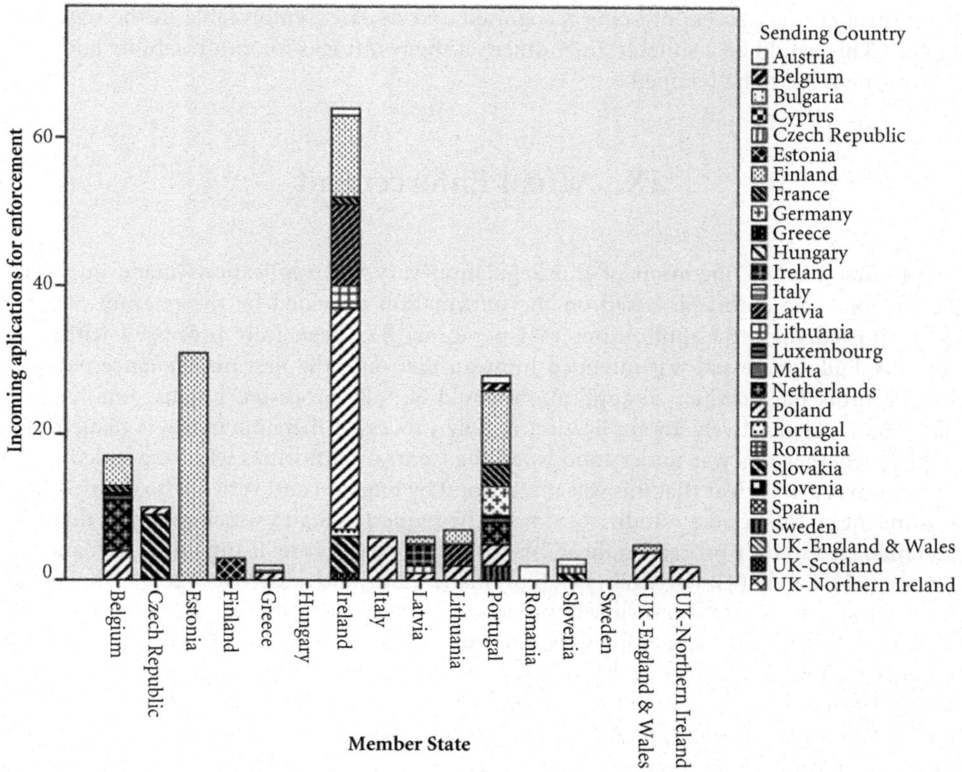

Figure 15: Incoming Applications for Enforcement Split by Sending State

Although there is an explanation for the disparity in the figures, the new system is slightly confusing and therefore Central Authorities could use more guidance. There is a lack of clarity in this area and in the absence of an explanatory report it would have been preferable if Article 56 specifically stated which of the available applications should apply to the different procedures for recognition and enforcement. It would be very useful if the European Commission developed a Practice Guide for Central Authorities. This guide should specify clearly how the procedures for recognition and enforcement fit with the applications in Article 56. It would also be useful to increase the various applications in Article 56, when the Regulation is revised, so that there is an application that relates specifically to enforcement of a maintenance decision given in the requesting State.[64] It might be helpful for statistical purposes to divide up such applications into two groups: (a) where the decision was given in another EU Member State that is bound by the Hague Protocol and therefore the decision has been automatically recognised and is automatically enforceable in the requested State; and (b) where the decision was given in another EU Member State that is not bound by the Hague Protocol (Denmark or the UK) but has previously

[64] See conclusions and next steps of the Heidelberg Conference, para 5(e).

been through the process of being recognised and declared enforceable in the requested State.[65] This would be a suitable amendment if the two tracks for enforceability and strict enforcement are to be retained.

IX. Actual Enforcement

In the first year of operation of the Regulation very few applications made under the Regulation were enforced. Based on the information provided by the relevant States it was reported that 183 applications (4.4 per cent) had been fully processed within six months. Fully processed was intended to mean that once the first maintenance payment had been discharged then an application would be fully processed because enforcement had begun. Alternatively an application is fully processed if maintenance is denied. It is unclear whether this was understood by all the Central Authorities who responded to the questionnaire. It is clear that this was understood by England and Wales, who queried what was meant by this term a number of times. The requested States which reported that they had managed to fully process applications within six months are: Estonia (81), Finland (2), Greece (51), Latvia (4), Portugal (17), Slovenia (2), England and Wales (26).[66] The overall feedback suggests that it is possible to process applications relatively quickly under the new system, but this is not happening very often so far. It is hoped that the process will speed up once Central Authorities and States become used to the new system.

In relation to cases that were fully processed in nine months not much development was made. After nine months 226 (5.4 per cent) of applications had been fully processed, only an increase of 1 per cent despite States having an extra three months to complete the applications.[67] One of the reasons for this could be because not many applications had actually been pending for nine months at the time the questionnaires were returned.[68] Therefore it would be very useful to complete this study at a later date to determine how long it takes to process applications. Such a study could also ask how many applications were processed in a year and determine the amount of applications that it took over a year to process. When the Regulation is functioning effectively and applications are being processed efficiently, then the majority of applications should be processed in under a year. This is especially true for child support applications because once parentage is established the requirement to pay child support is indisputable, although the amount payable may vary.

[65] One of the strengths of the Convention compared to the Regulation is that the Convention requires (Art 32(3)) that in the case of an application made through Central Authorities for a declaration of enforceability, actual 'enforcement shall proceed without the need for further action by the applicant'. If the declaration of enforceability is retained for any States when the Regulation is reviewed this automatic progress to actual enforcement for cases brought through Central Authorities should be introduced into the Regulation.

[66] A full table containing all the results provided and percentages can be found in Annex V on the Centre for PIL website. Unfortunately it is believed that the data provided by Estonia and Greece, might include data on requests for specific measures and not just full applications.

[67] Estonia processed one more case, Portugal three more and England and Wales 39 more (see table two in Annex V on the Centre for PIL website for full results).

[68] Eg the Irish Central Authority reported that they received no applications for the first six months therefore it would be very unlikely that they had had any applications pending for nine months given the time period of the questionnaire.

In addition to information on how long it takes to process an application the questionnaire also sought to find out how much money had been recovered from requested States in respect of maintenance obligations. Not many Central Authorities answered this part of the questionnaire. The information provided under question 5 is listed below. This includes basic information on the amount of money recovered from the requested State as well as additional information where this was provided.

- Hungary recovered €409 from Germany
- Latvia recovered 5480.18 LVL from Germany
- Latvia also recovers 360 LVL per month from Germany
- Latvia recovers 85 LVL per month from England and Wales
- Northern Ireland recovers €45 per week from Ireland (paid directly to applicant)
- Czech Republic recovered 345,705 CZK from Germany (8.6 per cent of total amount)
- Czech Republic recovered 80,879 CZK from Ireland (12.5 per cent of total amount)
- Czech Republic recovered 12.606 CZK from Netherlands (21 per cent of total amount)
- Czech Republic recovered 42,423 CZK from Slovakia (1.9 per cent of total amount)
- Czech Republic recovered 20,000 CZK from Spain (2.3 per cent of total amount)
- Czech Republic recovered 92,625 CZK from Sweden (18.7 per cent of total amount)
- Czech Republic recovered 21,571 CZK from England and Wales (0.9 per cent of total amount)
- Portugal recovered €50,000 from the Netherlands
- Sweden recovered 3,484 SEK from Germany (55.2 per cent of total amount)
- Sweden recovered 19,994 SEK from Poland (7.8 per cent of total amount)

Belgium reported that it cannot produce such data since the Belgian Central Authority does not centralise any payments.[69] Overall the limited data collected on enforcement show that the new system is viable. However, it suggests that there is still a long way to go and it will take time before the Regulation is operating efficiently in each of the Member States.

X. Information Technology (IT) Solutions

The importance of effective IT solutions cannot be emphasised enough, especially given the expected high case loads under the new instruments. Information gained during the empirical research indicates some problems with the IT systems currently in place. It also highlighted that it would be preferable if all States used the same system to create coherence and common standards.[70] At present, each database holds different types of information, which was indicated by the fact that each Member State could answer different parts of the

[69] Email correspondence 27 November 2012.

[70] Data were also stored in different ways. So some databases store information on number of applications and others number of applicants (in particular Sweden). So in Sweden if you had two applications, one involving one person and one involving three people, on their database it would be counted as four, but only counted as two applications on other databases.

questionnaire. In this respect, the Spanish Central Authority reported in January 2013 that it still was not using an electronic database, despite the fact that the Regulation had been in force for a year and a half.[71]

Even where databases did exist some errors were apparent. For example, in the answer to the questionnaire a Central Authority would say that legal aid had been provided but there were no cases registered in the first column (number of applications) so it was unclear how legal aid could have been provided when there were no applications for that State. In one case one of these queries was followed up. It had been indicated in question 5 that money had been recovered from Austria in respect of a maintenance obligation (2,070 SEK). However in question 4(b) no outgoing cases had been registered to Austria. The Central Authority was contacted in order to see where the problem lay. Three possible conclusions were considered.

(1) Question 4 was wrong and the number of applications had been missed off by accident;
(2) when the payment was made the database automatically deleted the file because the obligation had been discharged (this would not have been ideal and it would have been better if the file had just changed colour or moved to a different folder to indicate that it was no longer active); or
(3) Question 5 was wrong and there had been no applications sent to Austria.

The response received indicated the third option. There were in fact no applications sent to Austria so no money had been received. The Central Authority concluded that their 'system is definitely in need of a major checkup'.[72] Errors which suggest maintenance payments have been paid when they have not are a major cause for concern, even more so if they relate to a real application and the obligation has not actually been discharged. Therefore it would be preferable if all Central Authorities used one system that was designed specifically with the instruments in mind. Such a database would be able to store appropriate data and it could also be centrally managed so that any problems could be identified quickly and easily rectified in each State.[73]

The Hague Conference on Private International Law is working very hard to set up a system called iSupport which is designed to help with the effective application of the Convention. However, the system would also work for the Regulation. At the moment

[71] Email correspondence 29 January 2013. The delegates at this Authority individually counted the applications in order to provide information on the total number of incoming cases. However, other delegates reported that even where they did have databases they did not store the information in the correct way so still every application had to be counted individually in order to answer some or all of the questionnaire (such as: Finland, Estonia, England and Wales and Ireland). It would be much easier if databases could generate statistics or highlight when the time period was up in respect of each application, to assist Central Authorities in monitoring applications, the progress they are making as a Central Authority and to help them to adequately and efficiently fulfil their duties.

[72] Email correspondence with the Swedish Central Authority, 5 December 2012.

[73] The partners of the Heidelberg project, in conclusion no 3 of the Conclusions and Recommendations from the Conference, suggest that a 'coherent set of statistics, performance indicators, and analytic reports on the use of the Regulation in all Member States is essential to evaluate the implementation of the Regulation and to support improvements in its use. The use of a common IT system (see C and R 17 below) for keeping statistical data on the operation of Council Regulation 4/2009 (and the Hague Convention 2007) would be a great step forward in improving the enforcement of maintenance and the accountability of Central Authorities. A common IT system with the capability of analytical reporting could periodically assess future opportunities for programme improvement.'

there are insufficient funds to fully set up the programme, and even when it is activated States will be free to decide whether to use this programme. However, it is considered that if the objectives of the instruments are to be achieved Central Authorities need the efficiency gains that would come if their State was using the iSupport programme or another uniformly agreed database. Key features of the iSupport system are that it can store all the necessary information in respect of each application, it can generate statistics and it can translate the necessary forms.[74]

This programme was developed because it was considered that the international recovery of maintenance requires

> the application of information technology for many reasons: the very large number of cases involved which is still increasing; maintenance cases often have a long life span (in some countries child support can last until the age of 25); maintenance cases are subject to a high number of transactions such as for example regular modifications (i.e. variations of the needs of the creditor and of the resources of the debtor) or regular transfer of funds; a high number of repetitive transactions take place which can be standardised; communications take place regardless of time zones; a vast amount of information has to be available in real time; and means of communications have to address language barriers.[75]

It is believed that the main need for an effective system is primarily in relation to child support cases, because Central Authorities need to assist with the ongoing enforcement of obligations. Child support cases last for many years (both instruments cover obligations until the child is 21) and they may need to be modified. Therefore an effective technical system and database will make it simpler, as changes to the payments can be updated and it will enable Central Authorities to easily keep track of the payments and whether they are being discharged or not. This should make it easier for Central Authorities to efficiently ensure that the correct payments are being made on time. Any suitable system should be able to do this, however there are some benefits for all Hague Contracting States and EU Member States making use of the iSupport system. Not only would it assist with the effective and efficient implementation of the instruments, but it would 'lead to greater consistency in practice in different States as it would follow the language of the Convention. The system would also help to significantly improve communications between Central Authorities'.[76] This would need to be a key feature of any technical system as effective administrative cooperation will be imperative if the instruments are going to operate efficiently.

The iSupport programme has already been designed and contains several key features.[77] In respect of actual enforcement the design has a case specific function. This function includes 'a "Transfer of Funds" module that will assist the enforcement and monitoring of

[74] So an authority in the UK can fill in the form in English and send it to Spain. When the form is opened in Spain it will be in Spanish. This is very clever and will help lower costs under the systems. Information gained at the Heidelberg Conference 2013.

[75] P Lortie, 'The Development of Medium and Technology Neutral International Treaties in Support of Post-Convention Information Technology Systems: The Example of the 2007 Hague Convention and Protocol' (2008) 10 *Yearbook of Private International Law* 359, 359–60.

[76] Ibid 364. See also Philippe Lortie, ch 17 of this volume.

[77] See information document no 1 of June 2006, 'Development of an international electronic case management and communication system in support of the future Hague Convention on the international recovery of child support and other forms of family maintenance', available at www.hcch.net/upload/maint_info1e2006.pdf (accessed June 2013).

electronic transfer of funds.'[78] It would be great for this to be available to those working at Central Authorities in order to fulfill their duties in relation to enforcement. It is also useful to have an effective electronic system so that funds get transferred as quickly as possible and to be able to store all the information on one database. Therefore, a programme that has been designed by the Hague Conference specifically for the Convention would fulfill this need well and it would be great if it could be up and running soon and if all Contracting States were to take advantage of it. It would also be excellent if the EU made use of the iSupport system not only for external Convention cases but also for internal cases under the Regulation.[79] It is very encouraging to note that since the Heidelberg Conference the EU has agreed to generously fund further development of the iSupport system in recognition of its huge potential utility for improving the effectiveness of the Convention and the Regulation.

XI. Conclusion

The empirical data gleaned from our questionnaire survey give a good first indication of the number of applications and requests for specific measures circulating under the Regulation. They show clearly which States received the most applications, England and Wales and Germany, and which State sent the most applications, Poland.

However, the data gathered in more specific areas are incomplete. There are a variety of reasons for this: Central Authorities having difficulties filling in the questionnaire because of the information available to them, the Regulation not being in force long enough for progress to be made in particular areas by the date of the survey, the transitional period whereby all maintenance decisions relating to proceedings instituted before 18 June 2011 still require an *exequatur* process, and the fact that there are some areas where the questionnaire could have been designed better. The gathering of the first set of statistics has been a learning curve for all those involved and any data collected in the future should provide a clearer picture on how the Regulation works in practice since the majority of these problems can be resolved.

Despite this the data collected do still give some indication of how the Regulation is being implemented. They suggest that there have been many requests relating to the location of debtors. At this point not many of these requests have resulted in full applications, so it is difficult to tell whether this means there were a number of spurious requests sent. There is also an indication that there may be a misunderstanding of when Central Authorities are allowed to recover their costs. Further, the study implies that some Central Authorities are finding it very difficult to meet the time requirements in Article 58. This is likely to be the result of a variety of factors such as: insufficient staffing, ineffective databases and overburdensome national laws of procedure. States should appropriately staff Central Authorities and remove procedural obstacles where possible.

[78] Ibid para 17.

[79] Once the system is ready, it should be simple to make any minor changes necessary so that the system could also work for the Regulation (Heidelberg Conference 2013).

It is imperative that appropriate training seminars and programmes are provided and that a guide to good practice for the Regulation is produced. These elements should assist Central Authorities to carry out their tasks under the Regulation in the future. This is because practitioners will understand the Regulation better and be clearer on what is expected of them. Practitioners would also be assisted if they had efficient databases that could help them monitor applications, and their progress, in order to assist them with fulfilling the time requirements and facilitating the ongoing enforcement of maintenance obligations.

Although the current data give some indication of how the Regulation is operating, further research is required when the Regulation has been in force longer. Future data collection should be followed up by interviews with practitioners in order to check any disparities in the information provided. These data should provide more definitive answers in areas such as: how many requests for specific measures are turning into full applications, how long it is taking for applications to be enforced and how many applications for child support there are, compared to applications for other forms of maintenance. It is also hoped that more information will be provided on legal aid. The data collected this time in this area were minimal and incomplete, so no conclusions could be drawn. More comprehensive data collected at a later date would supplement the initial findings and appropriate conclusions could be reached in the areas where the current data do not provide definitive answers. This in turn would lay the foundation for a review of the EU Maintenance Regulation to allow for evidence-based reform. One tentative conclusion we can reach in relation to that reform is the advantage of increasing the number of applications referred to in Article 56 to make the work of Central Authorities easier, to ensure the correct procedures under the Regulation are followed and to facilitate the collection of more accurate data.

Annex I

Sending Member State (according to information provided by the requested State on incoming applications)															
		AT	BE	CY	CZ	EE	FI	FR	DE	GR	HU	IE	IT	LV	LT
Requested Member State	Austria (AT)		0	0	0	0	0	0	0	0	0	0	0	0	0
	Belgium (BE)	2		0	3	0	8	4	3	0	1	1	0	1	0
	Cyprus (CY)	1	0		0	1	4	0	0	4	0	0	0	1	0
	Czech Republic (CZ)	2	0	0		0	0	0	0	0	0	1	0	1	0
	Estonia (EE)	0	0	0	0		128	0	1	0	0	0	0	3	0
	Finland (FI)	0	0	0	0	40		0	0	0	0	0	0	2	0
	France (FR)	0	0	0	0	0	0		0	0	0	0	0	0	0
	Germany (DE)	144	6	0	36	0	18	3		0	17	5	0	17	3
	Greece (GR)	6	2	2	3	0	26	0	9		0	0	1	0	0
	Hungary (HU)	2	0	0	1	0	0	0	0	0		1	0	0	0
	Ireland (IE)	2	0	0	6	2	22	2	4	0	0		0	28	6
	Italy (IT)	17	0	0	5	0	14	1	5	0	3	0		0	2
	Latvia (LV)	0	0	0	0	0	3	0	0	0	0	5	0		1
	Lithuania (LT)	0	0	0	0	0	4	0	0	0	0	4	0	8	
	Luxembourg (LU)	0	3	0	0	1	1	3	12	0	0	0	0	0	1
	Malta (MT)	0	0	0	0	0	0	0	0	0	0	0	0	0	0
	Netherlands (NL)	4	22	0	0	0	12	1	23	0	3	0	1	1	1
	Poland (PL)	13	3	0	2	0	4	4	17	0	0	5	0	0	0
	Portugal (PT)	2	4	0	0	0	14	4	13	0	0	0	0	0	0
	Romania (RO)	9	1	0	1	0	1	0	6	0	6	2	0	1	0
	Slovakia (SK)	6	0	0	20	0	0	0	0	5	1	0	0	0	0
	Slovenia (SI)	1	0	0	1	0	0	0	0	0	0	0	0	0	0
	Spain (ES)	0	0	0	0	0	0	0	0	0	0	0	0	0	0
	Sweden (SW)	5	0	0	3	0	0	0	1	0	4	1	0	2	1
	England & Wales (GBEW)	5	5	0	14	1	59	9	22	1	6	45	0	45	6
	Scotland (GBS)	0	0	0	1	1	5	1	0	0	4	5	0	11	0
	Northern Ireland (GBNI)	0	0	0	0	0	1	0	0	0	0	5	0	0	0
Total		231	46	2	96	46	324	32	116	10	45	80	2	121	21

LU	MT	NL	PL	PT	RO	SK	SI	ES	SW	GBEW	GBS	GBNI	Unknown	Total
0	0	0	0	0	0	0	0	0	0	0	0	0	113	**113**
2	0	60	50	2	0	1	0	0	0	0	0	0	0	**138**
0	0	0	11	0	0	4	0	0	1	5	0	0	0	**32**
0	0	2	23	0	0	96	0	0	1	1	0	0	0	**127**
0	0	0	1	0	0	0	0	0	0	0	0	0	0	**133**
0	0	1	1	0	0	1	0	0	5	1	0	0	0	**51**
0	0	0	0	0	0	0	0	0	0	0	0	0	178	**178**
0	1	60	466	7	3	16	2	1	10	9	0	0	0	**824**
0	0	1	72	0	2	2	0	0	0	0	0	0	0	**126**
0	0	0	2	0	2	7	0	1	0	0	0	0	0	**16**
0	0	4	165	3	0	13	0	0	2	16	1	14	0	**293**
0	0	1	55	2	3	9	3	0	0	1	0	0	0	**121**
0	0	0	1	0	0	0	0	0	0	1	0	0	0	**11**
0	0	0	5	0	0	0	0	0	0	0	0	0	0	**21**
	0	2	1	17	0	0	0	0	0	1	0	0	0	**42**
0		0	0	0	0	0	0	0	0	0	0	0	0	**0**
0	0		158	4	0	0	0	1	6	7	0	0	0	**244**
0	0	4		0	1	4	0	0	80	35	0	0	0	**172**
1	0	3	6		0	0	0	0	8	7	0	0	0	**62**
0	0	1	10	0		1	0	0	0	2	0	0	0	**41**
0	0	0	9	0	0		0	1	1	0	0	0	0	**43**
0	0	1	2	0	0	1		0	1	0	0	0	0	**7**
0	0	0	0	0	0	0	0		0	0	0	0	267	**267**
0	0	3	94	0	2	0	0	0		14	0	0	0	**130**
0	0	15	551	16	0	18	0	4	30				0	**862**
0	0	1	49	0	0	0	0	0	2				0	**80**
0	0	1	20	0	0	1	0	0	0				0	**28**
3	1	160	1752	51	13	174	5	7	147	100	4	14	558	**4,102**

Annex II

Sending Member State (according to information provided by the requested State on incoming requests for specific measures)														
		AT	BE	CY	CZ	EE	FI	FR	DE	GR	HU	IE	IT	LV
Requested Member State	Belgium (BE)	0		0	0	0	3	0	9	0	2	0	0	1
	Czech Republic (CZ)	0	0	0		0	0	0	0	0	0	0	0	0
	Estonia (EE)	0	0	0	0		75	0	1	0	0	0	0	2
	Finland (FI)	0	0	0	2	0		0	0	0	0	1	0	0
	France (FR)	0	0	0	0	0	0		0	0	0	0	0	0
	Germany (DE)	25	1	0	10	1	7	0		0	5	2	2	7
	Greece (GR)	1	2	0	0	0	3	0	7		0	0	0	0
	Hungary (HU)	6	0	0	0	0	0	0	0	0		0	0	0
	Ireland (IE)	0	2	0	0	0	0	0	5	0	1		0	2
	Italy (IT)	9	1	0	3	1	5	0	11	0	3	0		0
	Latvia (LV)	0	0	0	0	0	1	0	3	0	0	0	0	
	Lithuania (LT)	0	0	0	0	0	0	0	0	0	0	0	0	1
	Malta (MT)	0	0	0	0	0	0	0	0	0	0	0	0	0
	Poland (PL)	0	0	0	2	0	1	1	5	0	0	0	0	0
	Portugal (PT)	1	2	0	0	0	3	0	9	0	0	0	0	0
	Romania (RO)	3	1	0	0	0	0	0	8	0	0	0	0	0
	Slovenia (SI)	0	0	0	0	0	0	0	0	0	0	0	0	0
	Sweden (SW)	1	0	0	2	0	0	0	0	1	0	0	0	1
	England & Wales (GBEW)	2	3	0	6	0	10	1	26	0	7	5	0	4
	Northern Ireland (GBNI)	0	0	0	0	0	0	0	0	0	0	1	0	1
Total		48	12	0	23	4	108	2	84	1	20	9	2	19

LT	LU	MT	NL	PL	PT	RO	SK	SI	ES	SW	GBEW	GBS	GBNI	Unknown	**Total**
0	0	0	3	39	0	1	1	0	0	10	0	0	0	0	**69**
0	0	0	1	11	0	0	59	0	0	0	0	0	0	0	**71**
0	0	0	0	0	0	0	0	0	0	0	0	0	0	0	**78**
0	0	0	0	0	0	0	0	0	0	0	0	0	0	0	**3**
0	0	0	0	0	0	0	0	0	0	0	0	0	0	72	**72**
0	0	0	6	183	1	3	4	0	0	16	1	0	0	0	**274**
0	0	0	0	57	0	2	1	0	0	0	0	0	0	0	**73**
0	0	0	2	0	0	0	3	0	0	0	0	0	0	0	**11**
0	0	0	0	55	0	0	2	0	1	1	2	0	5	0	**76**
0	0	0	0	130	0	4	6	0	0	3	0	0	0	0	**176**
0	0	0	0	2	0	0	0	0	0	0	0	0	0	0	**6**
	0	0	0	4	0	0	0	0	0	0	0	0	0	0	**5**
0	0		0	0	0	0	0	0	0	0	1	0	0	0	**1**
0	0	0	0		0	2	0	0	0	25	2	0	0	0	**36**
0	0	0	0	3		0	0	0	0	2	1	0	0	0	**21**
0	0	0	0	5	0		2	0	0	0	1	0	0	0	**22**
0	0	0	0	1	0	0	2		0	1	0	0	0	0	**4**
0	0	0	0	6	0	0	0	0	1		1	0	0	0	**13**
0	0	0	7	234	2	1	31	0	0	87				0	**426**
0	0	0	0	19	0	0	1	0	0	2				0	**24**
0	0	0	19	749	3	13	112	0	2	147	9	0	5	72	**1,463**

Annex III

Requested State		Requests received under Art 53						Total
		locate party	info on income	obtain evidence	establish parentage	provisional measures	unknown	
Belgium	Number of requests	63	4	0	2	0	0	69
	As a percentage	91.3%	5.8%	0.0%	2.9%	0.0%	0.0%	
Czech Republic	Number of requests	46	25	0	0	0	0	71
	As a percentage	64.8%	35.2%	0.0%	0.0%	0.0%	0.0%	
Estonia	Number of requests	52	2	5	0	19	0	78
	As a percentage	66.7%	2.6%	6.4%	0.0%	24.4%	0.0%	
Finland	Number of requests	2	1	0	0	0	0	3
	As a percentage	66.7%	33.3%	0.0%	0.0%	0.0%	0.0%	
France	Number of requests	56	16	0	0	0	0	72
	As a percentage	77.8%	22.2%	0.0%	0.0%	0.0%	0.0%	
Germany	Number of requests	0	0	0	0	0	274	274
	As a percentage	0.0%	0.0%	0.0%	0.0%	0.0%	100.0%	
Greece	Number of requests	68	4	1	0	0	0	73
	As a percentage	93.2%	5.5%	1.4%	0.0%	0.0%	0.0%	
Hungary	Number of requests	5	5	0	0	0	1	11
	As a percentage	45.5%	45.5%	0.0%	0.0%	0.0%	9.1%	
Ireland	Number of requests	67	9	0	0	0	0	76
	As a percentage	88.2%	11.8%	0.0%	0.0%	0.0%	0.0%	
Italy	Number of requests	147	29	0	0	0	0	176
	As a percentage	83.5%	16.5%	0.0%	0.0%	0.0%	0.0%	

Requested State		Requests received under Art 53						Total
		locate party	info on income	obtain evidence	establish parentage	provisional measures	unknown	
Latvia	Number of requests	4	2	0	0	0	0	6
	As a percentage	66.7%	33.3%	0.0%	0.0%	0.0%	0.0%	
Lithuania	Number of requests	3	2	0	0	0	0	5
	As a percentage	60.0%	40.0%	0.0%	0.0%	0.0%	0.0%	
Malta	Number of requests	0	0	0	0	0	1	1
	As a percentage	0.0%	0.0%	0.0%	0.0%	0.0%	100.0%	
Poland	Number of requests	30	3	0	0	0	5	38
	As a percentage	78.9%	7.9%	0.0%	0.0%	0.0%	13.2%	
Portugal	Number of requests	21	0	0	0	0	0	21
	As a percentage	100.0%	0.0%	0.0%	0.0%	0.0%	0.0%	
Romania	Number of requests	17	4	0	1	0	0	22
	As a percentage	77.3%	18.2%	0.0%	4.5%	0.0%	0.0%	
Slovenia	Number of request	3	1	0	0	0	0	4
	As a percentage	75.0%	25.0%	0.0%	0.0%	0.0%	0.0%	
Sweden	Number of requests	0	0	0	0	0	13	13
	As a percentage	0.0%	0.0%	0.0%	0.0%	0.0%	100.0%	
UK-England & Wales	Number of requests	426	0	0	0	0	0	426
	As a percentage	100.0%	0.0%	0.0%	0.0%	0.0%	0.0%	
UK-Northern Ireland	Number of requests	23	1	0	0	0	0	24
	As a percentage	95.8%	4.2%	0.0%	0.0%	0.0%	0.0%	
Total	Requests	**1033**	**108**	**6**	**3**	**19**	**294**	**1,463**
	Percentage	70.6%	7.4%	0.4%	0.2%	1.3%	20.1%	

Annex IV

Requests that resulted in a full application					
Requested State		Resulted in full application?			Total
		yes	no	not known	
Belgium	Number of requests	0	0	69	69
	As a percentage	0.0%	0.0%	100.0%	
Czech Republic	Number of requests	12	0	59	71
	As a percentage	16.9%	0.0%	83.1%	
Estonia	Number of requests	21	29	28	78
	As a percentage	26.9%	37.2%	35.9%	
Finland	Number of requests	0	0	3	3
	As a percentage	0.0%	0.0%	100.0%	
France	Number of requests	0	0	72	72
	As a percentage	0.0%	0.0%	100.0%	
Germany	Number of requests	0	0	274	274
	As a percentage	0.0%	0.0%	100.0%	
Greece	Number of requests	3	0	70	73
	As a percentage	4.1%	0.0%	95.9%	
Hungary	Number of requests	0	11	0	11
	As a percentage	0.0%	100.0%	0.0%	
Ireland	Number of requests	0	0	76	76
	As a percentage	0.0%	0.0%	100.0%	
Italy	Number of requests	10	0	166	176
	As a percentage	5.7%	0.0%	94.3%	
Latvia	Number of requests	0	6	0	6
	As a percentage	0.0%	100.0%	0.0%	
Lithuania	Number of requests	0	0	5	5
	As a percentage	0.0%	0.0%	100.0%	
Malta	Number of requests	0	0	1	1
	As a percentage	0.0%	0.0%	100.0%	
Poland	Number of requests	0	0	38	38
	As a percentage	0.0%	0.0%	100.0%	
Portugal	Number of requests	0	0	21	21
	As a percentage	0.0%	0.0%	100.0%	
Romania	Number of requests	0	0	22	22
	As a percentage	0.0%	0.0%	100.0%	

Requests that resulted in a full application					
Requested State		Resulted in full application?			Total
		yes	no	not known	
Slovenia	Number of requests	0	0	4	4
	As a percentage	0.0%	0.0%	100.0%	
Sweden	Number of requests	0	0	13	13
	As a percentage	0.0%	0.0%	100.0%	
UK-England & Wales	Number of requests	6	420	0	426
	As a percentage	1.4%	98.6%	0.0%	
UK-Northern Ireland	Number of requests	3	0	21	24
	As a percentage	12.5%	0.0%	87.5%	
Total	Total requests	**55**	**466**	**942**	**1,463**
	Percentage	3.8%	31.9%	64.4%	

Annex V

Table 1: Fully Processed Within Six Months

Requested State		6 months				Total
		fully processed	pending	not applicable	unclear	
Austria	Number of applications	0	0	0	113	113
	As a percentage	0.0%	0.0%	0.0%	100.0%	
Belgium	Number of applications	0	138	0	0	138
	As a percentage	0.0%	100.0%	0.0%	0.0%	
Cyprus	Number of applications	0	0	0	32	32
	As a percentage	0.0%	0.0%	0.0%	100.0%	
Czech Republic	Number of Applications	0	127	0	0	127
	As a percentage	0.0%	100.0%	0.0%	0.0%	
Estonia	Number of applications	81	48	4	0	133
	As a percentage	60.9%	36.1%	3.0%	0.0%	
Finland	Number of applications	2	49	0	0	51
	As a percentage	3.9%	96.1%	0.0%	0.0%	
France	Number of applications	0	0	0	178	178
	As a percentage	0.0%	0.0%	0.0%	100.0%	
Germany	Number of applications	0	0	0	824	824
	As a percentage	0.0%	0.0%	0.0%	100.0%	
Greece	Number of applications	51	75	0	0	126
	As a percentage	40.5%	59.5%	0.0%	0.0%	
Hungary	Number of applications	0	15	1	0	16
	As a percentage	0.0%	93.8%	6.2%	0.0%	
Ireland	Number of applications	0	0	0	293	293
	As a percentage	0.0%	0.0%	0.0%	100.0%	
Italy	Number of applications	0	115	6	0	121
	As a percentage	0.0%	95.0%	5.0%	0.0%	
Latvia	Number of applications	4	7	0	0	11
	As a percentage	36.4%	63.6%	0.0%	0.0%	
Lithuania	Number of applications	0	0	0	21	21
	As a percentage	0.0%	0.0%	0.0%	100.0%	
Luxembourg	Number of applications	0	0	0	42	42
	As a percentage	0.0%	0.0%	0.0%	100.0%	
Netherlands	Number of applications	0	0	0	244	244
	As a percentage	0.0%	0.0%	0.0%	100.0%	

Requested State		6 months				Total
		fully processed	pending	not applicable	unclear	
Poland	Number of applications	0	0	0	172	172
	As a percentage	0.0%	0.0%	0.0%	100.0%	
Portugal	Number of applications	17	45	0	0	62
	As a percentage	27.4%	72.6%	0.0%	0.0%	
Romania	Number of applications	0	0	0	41	41
	As a percentage	0.0%	0.0%	0.0%	100.0%	
Slovakia	Number of applications	0	0	0	43	43
	As a percentage	0.0%	0.0%	0.0%	100.0%	
Slovenia	Number of applications	2	5	0	0	7
	As a percentage	28.6%	71.4%	0.0%	0.0%	
Spain	Number of applications	0	0	0	267	267
	As a percentage	0.0%	0.0%	0.0%	100.0%	
Sweden	Number of applications	0	130	0	0	130
	As a percentage	0.0%	100.0%	0.0%	0.0%	
UK-England&Wales	Number of applications	26	613	223	0	862
	As a percentage	3.0%	71.1%	25.9%	0.0%	
UK-Scotland	Number of applications	0	0	0	80	80
	As a percentage	0.0%	0.0%	0.0%	100.0%	
UK-Northern Ireland	Number of applications	0	28	0	0	28
	As a percentage	0.0%	100.0%	0.0%	0.0%	
Total	Applications	**183**	**1395**	**234**	**2,350**	**4,162**
	Percentage	4.4%	33.5%	5.6%	56.5%	

Table 2: Fully Processed Within Nine Months

Requested State		9 months				Total
		fully processed	pending	not applicable	unclear	
Austria	Number of applications	0	0	0	113	113
	As a percentage	0.0%	0.0%	0.0%	100.0%	
Belgium	Number of applications	0	138	0	0	138
	As a percentage	0.0%	100.0%	0.0%	0.0%	
Cyprus	Number of applications	0	0	0	32	32
	As a percentage	0.0%	0.0%	0.0%	100.0%	
Czech Republic	Number of applications	0	127	0	0	127
	As a percentage	0.0%	100.0%	0.0%	0.0%	
Estonia	Number of applications	82	47	4	0	133
	As a percentage	61.7%	35.3%	3.0%	0.0%	
Finland	Number of applications	2	49	0	0	51
	As a percentage	3.9%	96.1%	0.0%	0.0%	
France	Number of applications	0	0	0	178	178
	As a percentage	0.0%	0.0%	0.0%	100.0%	
Germany	Number of applications	0	0	0	824	824
	As a percentage	0.0%	0.0%	0.0%	100.0%	
Greece	Number of applications	51	75	0	0	126
	As a percentage	40.5%	59.5%	0.0%	0.0%	
Hungary	Number of applications	0	15	1	0	16
	As a percentage	0.0%	93.8%	6.2%	0.0%	
Ireland	Number of applications	0	0	0	293	293
	As a percentage	0.0%	0.0%	0.0%	100.0%	
Italy	Number of applications	0	115	6	0	121
	As a percentage	0.0%	95.0%	5.0%	0.0%	
Latvia	Number of applications	4	7	0	0	11
	As a percentage	36.4%	63.6%	0.0%	0.0%	
Lithuania	Number of applications	0	0	0	21	21
	As a percentage	0.0%	0.0%	0.0%	100.0%	
Luxembourg	Number of applications	0	0	0	42	42
	As a percentage	0.0%	0.0%	0.0%	100.0%	
Netherlands	Number of applications	0	0	0	244	244
	As a percentage	0.0%	0.0%	0.0%	100.0%	
Poland	Number of applications	0	0	0	172	172
	As a percentage	0.0%	0.0%	0.0%	100.0%	

Requested State		9 months				Total
		fully processed	pending	not applicable	unclear	
Portugal	Number of applications	20	42	0	0	62
	As a percentage	32.3%	67.7%	0.0%	0.0%	
Romania	Number of applications	0	0	0	41	41
	As a percentage	0.0%	0.0%	0.0%	100.0%	
Slovakia	Number of applications	0	0	0	43	43
	As a percentage	0.0%	0.0%	0.0%	100.0%	
Slovenia	Number of applications	2	5	0	0	7
	As a percentage	28.6%	71.4%	0.0%	0.0%	
Spain	Number of applications	0	0	0	267	267
	As a percentage	0.0%	0.0%	0.0%	100.0%	
Sweden	Number of applications	0	130	0	0	130
	As a percentage	0.0%	100.0%	0.0%	0.0%	
UK-England & Wales	Number of applications	65	574	223	0	862
	As a percentage	7.5%	66.6%	25.9%	0.0%	
UK-Scotland	Number of applications	0	0	0	80	80
	As a percentage	0.0%	0.0%	0.0%	100.0%	
UK-Northern Ireland	Number of applications	0	28	0	0	28
	As a percentage	0.0%	100.0%	0.0%	0.0%	
Total	Applications	**226**	**1,352**	**234**	**2,350**	**4,162**
	Percentage	5.4%	32.5%	5.6%	56.5%	

22

The Effective Operation of the EU Maintenance Regulation in the Member States

BURKHARD HESS AND STEFANIE SPANCKEN

I. Introduction

A European Union legal instrument can only be effective where it is given full effect by the Member States. This chapter focuses on two issues, which are crucial for the effective operation of the Maintenance Regulation[1] in the Member States. Based on the results of a questionnaire distributed among the Central Authorities, the chapter begins with an analysis of implementation of the Regulation in the Member States (section II). It specifically explores whether and to what extent Member States enacted implementing legislation in order to ensure the appropriate application of the Maintenance Regulation. The chapter also addresses the cooperative framework of the Regulation in comparison to other legal instruments in cross-border family matters (section III). In this regard, obstacles experienced by the Central Authorities in the first year of application will be identified in order to critically assess the provisions of Articles 49 to 63 of the Maintenance Regulation.

The questionnaire covered issues on the implementation of specific aspects of the Regulation in the national legal system as well as questions on the Regulation's cooperative framework. In total, 23 Central Authorities[2] responded. This is the first information collected on the implementation of the Regulation in the Member States and on the functioning of the Regulation's cross-border cooperation mechanisms. The main problem Central Authorities faced when completing the questionnaire was the small number of maintenance cases dealt with under the Regulation. However, the answers have already revealed considerable room for improvement in ensuring the effective application of the Regulation.

[1] Council Regulation (EC) 4/2009 of 18 December 2008 on jurisdiction, applicable law, recognition and enforcement of decisions and cooperation in matters relating to maintenance obligations [2009] OJ L7/1 (Maintenance Regulation).

[2] Those Central Authorities are Austria, Cyprus, Czech Republic, Denmark, Estonia, Finland, Germany, Greece, Hungary, Ireland, Italy, Latvia, Lithuania, Luxembourg, Malta, Netherlands, Poland, Portugal, Romania, Slovenia, Slovakia, Sweden as well as England and Wales. Additionally, the questionnaire was completed by the Croatian Ministry of Social Politics and Youth, which started to operate as the Central Authority under the Maintenance Regulation after Croatia's accession to the EU on 1 July 2013.

II. The Implementation of the Maintenance Regulation in the Member States

A. Introduction

In European Union civil procedure law, tensions arise at the interfaces between directly applicable EU instruments and national procedural law.[3] EU Regulations are often drafted in a very general and conceptual way aiming at coordinating the heterogeneous national procedural laws. In order to ensure a uniform application of EU law and enhance legal certainty in the European Judicial Area, direct implementing measures are becoming increasingly important.[4]

In the context of maintenance, implementation is an issue not only of EU law, but also of international law. In order to ensure the effective operation of the 2007 Hague Child Support Convention[5] and the Additional Protocol,[6] supplementary implementing measures of State Parties are also needed. The United States have already drafted implementing legislation entitled the International Child Support Recovery Improvement Act of 2013[7] on the basis of the International Child Support Recovery Improvement Act of 2012. The latter was never passed by the Senate. Equally the German[8] and English[9] legislators have recently enacted implementing legislation. For the purposes of implementation, the Permanent Bureau of the Hague Conference has drawn up a Draft Implementation Checklist.[10] State Parties are also encouraged to use the Country Profile form to provide information to other States.[11]

[3] F Eichel, 'Europarechtliche Fallstricke im Vollstreckbarerklärungsverfahren nach dem AVAG und dem neuen Auslandsunterhaltsgesetz (AUG)' (2011) *Zeitschrift für Gemeinschaftsprivatrecht* 193.

[4] B Hess, *Europäisches Zivilprozessrecht* (Heidelberg, CF Müller, 2010) § 4 para 18.

[5] Convention of 23 November 2007 on the International Recovery of Child Support and Other Forms of Family Maintenance, available at www.hcch.net/upload/conventions/txt38en.pdf (accessed October 2013). It entered into force on 1 January 2013, subsequent to its ratification by Norway and Albania. On 1 February 2013 Bosnia and Herzegovina became the third State Party and on 1 November 2013 Ukraine became the fourth State Party to the Convention. For an overview of the Hague Maintenance Convention see E Long, 'The New Hague Maintenance Convention' (2008) *International and Comparative Law Quarterly* 984.

[6] Protocol of 23 November 2007 on the Law Applicable to Maintenance Obligations, available at www.hcch.net/upload/conventions/txt39en.pdf (accessed October 2013). It entered into force on 1 August 2013, subsequent to the ratification by the European Union and Serbia. For an overview of the Protocol see A Bonomi, 'The Hague Protocol of 23 November 2007 on the Law Applicable to Maintenance Obligations' (2008) *Yearbook of Private International Law* 333.

[7] It is available at www.gpo.gov/fdsys/pkg/BILLS-113hr1896rfs/pdf/BILLS-113hr1896rfs.pdf (accessed September 2013). The recent draft act was passed by the House of Representatives on 19 June 2013. For the US view, see M Carlson, 'United States Perspective on the New Hague Convention on the International Recovery of Child Support and Other Forms of Family Maintenance' (2009) *Family Law Quarterly* 21.

[8] Act on the Implementation of the 2007 Hague Convention [2013] BGBl I, 273; see further K Hilbig-Lugani, 'Die Änderungen im AUG und AVAG durch das Durchführungsgesetz zum Haager Unterhaltsübereinkommen 2007' (2013) *Der Familien-Rechts-Berater international* 74.

[9] The International Recovery of Maintenance (Hague Convention 2007 etc.) Regulations 2012, SI 2012/2814. For Scotland, see the International Recovery of Maintenance (Hague Convention 2007) (Scotland) Regulations 2012, SSI 2012/301. For Northern Ireland, see the International Recovery of Maintenance (Hague Convention 2007 etc.) Regulations (Northern Ireland) 2012, SSI 2012/413.

[10] Draft Implementation Checklist—2007 Child Support Convention, Prel Doc No 6, September 2009, www.hcch.net/upload/wop/maint_pd06e2009.pdf (accessed October 2013).

[11] Prel Doc No 3 final, September 2012, www.hcch.net/upload/wop/maint2011pd03e.pdf (accessed October 2013).

The implementation of an international convention by specific domestic legislation seems to be common in the process of ratifying an international treaty.[12] The ambit of implementation depends on the content of the respective international treaty: self-executing treaties usually do not require any implementation whereas non self-executing treaties have to be transposed into the domestic legal orders to have full effect. International conventions often consist of self-executing and non-self-executing provisions, and State Parties must respectively adopt implementing measures. When adopting these measures, States have a wide margin of discretion. Under international law, they must adopt effective and transparent measures, but there is usually no review of national laws. Accordingly, the Draft Implementation Checklist of the 2007 Child Support Convention[13] drawn up by the Permanent Bureau of the Hague Conference is not mandatory, but can assist States in the implementation process on a voluntarily basis. However, the implementation of international conventions generally entails very different outcomes.[14]

Although from a technical perspective implementation seems to be very similar in EU law and in international law, there are considerable differences concerning the regulatory framework: EU law formally requires Member States to enact implementing legislation whenever it is 'necessary' to do so, but it also limits their legislative margin of discretion. Further, it provides for specific standards (the principles of effectiveness and equivalence), which are directly applicable to implementing legislation. Finally, the European Commission has the power to supervise the implementation of EU law by Member States.[15]

B. Concept of Implementation

As a legal term, implementation is expressly used in Article 291 of the Treaty of the Functioning of the European Union (TFEU). According to this provision, Member States shall adopt all measures of national law necessary to implement legally binding Union acts. However, this article does not provide for any definition, nor does it clarify the concept of implementation. Originating from the Latin verb *implere* implementing can be used as a generic term to describe the procedure, which gives full effect to the operative content of EU instruments at national level in compliance with the objectives of the particular instrument.[16] This rather broad definition comprises implementation on a normative level as well as the execution of EU law by national administrations and courts. In the context of this chapter, the term is only used as implementation on a normative level.

[12] Germany has a long tradition of enacting comprehensive legislation implementing international conventions on private international law, especially in the context of the recognition and enforcement of foreign judgments in civil law matters (eg Anerkennungs- und Vollstreckungsausführungsgesetz (AVAG) [2009] BGBl I, 3830) and in international family law (eg Adoptionsübereinkommens-Ausführungsgesetz (AdÜbAG) [2001] BGBl I p 2950 or International Family Law Procedure Act [2005] BGBl I, 162). The 1980 Hague Abduction Convention has been implemented by many countries, see A Dyer, 'The Hague Convention on the Civil Aspects of International Child Abduction—Towards Global Cooperation' (1993) *The International Journal of Children's Rights* 273, 274.

[13] Draft Implementation Checklist—2007 Child Support Convention, available at www.hcch.net/upload/wop/maint_pd06e2009.pdf (accessed December 2013).

[14] On the implementation of the 1980 Hague Abduction Convention, see Dyer (n 12) 274.

[15] In particular, the EU Commission is able to launch infringement proceedings according to Art 258 TFEU.

[16] See also S Hölscheidt, 'Probleme bei der Durchsetzung des Unionsrechts in den Mitgliedstaaten'(2009) *Die Öffentliche Verwaltung* 341; W Schroeder, 'Nationale Maßnahmen zur Durchführung von EG-Recht und das Gebot der einheitlichen Wirkung' (2004) *Archiv des öffentlichen Rechts* 3, 9.

i. Why do Regulations Require to be Implemented?

The classical ambit of implementation on a normative level concerns the transposition of directives, since directives are binding only regarding the results to be achieved, but give Member States the choice of form and methods for implementing legislation.[17] In principle, only after their incorporation into national law do directives have binding legal effect.[18] In contrast, the legal framework and the legal effects of EU Regulations are different. The starting point is the definition of a Regulation in Article 288(2) TFEU, according to which a Regulation 'shall have general application [and] … shall be binding in its entirety and directly applicable in all Member States'.[19] Due to its immediate effect, a Regulation in principle does not require any transposition into national law.[20] From its entry into force it is directly applicable in the EU Member States. Therefore, any implementation seems to be superfluous and inadmissible.[21] Yet, due to their conceptual character, EU Regulations might entail the enactment of national implementing provisions ensuring and facilitating their effective application.[22] Moreover, national provisions inconsistent with the prevalent Regulation are to be removed or adapted.[23]

These objectives are reflected in the explanatory memorandum of the Member States' acts in the context of the Maintenance Regulation. Not surprisingly, the legislative purposes of implementing legislation are manifold: apart from the objective of facilitating the application of the EU instrument in the domestic framework,[24] Member States have adopted implementing acts in order to remove inconsistencies between the Regulation and domestic law.[25] Sometimes national provisions are adapted to ensure that they comply with the Regulation. Moreover, national implementing provisions help to facilitate parties and courts in finding the respective legislation in European Union law.[26]

[17] M Nettesheim, in E Grabitz, M Hilf and M Nettesheim (eds), *Das Recht der Europäischen Union* (Munich, CH Beck, 2013) Art 288 TFEU para 112; M Herdegen, *Europarecht*, 15th edn (Munich, CH Beck, 2013) § 8 para 37.

[18] M Ruffert, in C Callies and M Ruffert (eds), *EUV/AEUV Das Verfassungsrecht der Europäischen Union mit Europäischer Grundrechtecharta*, 4th edn (Munich, CH Beck, 2011) Art 288 AEUV para 23. However, the CJEU has exceptionally recognised vertical direct effects of directives in the absence of implementing measures, namely in case the time limit for implementation has passed and the provision is unconditional and sufficiently precise, see Case 41/74 *Van Duyn v Home Office* [1974] ECR 1337; Case 148/78 *Pubblico Ministero v Ratti* [1979] ECR 1629 and Case 8/81 *Becker v Finanzamt Münster-Innenstadt* [1982] ECR 53.

[19] This formulation is also used in the Maintenance Regulation.

[20] Case C-34/73 *Fratelli Variola S.p.A. v Amministrazione italiana delle Finanze* [1973] ECR 981, para 10; Case C-94/77 *Fratelli Zerbone Snc v Amministrazione delle finanze dello Stato* [1978] ECR 99, paras 22–27.

[21] W Schroeder, *Grundkurs Europarecht*, 2nd edn (Munich, CH Beck, 2011) § 6 para 35; K Riesenhuber, in J Basedow, K Hopt, R Zimmermann (eds), *Handwörterbuch des Europäischen Privatrechts II* (Tübingen, Mohr Siebeck, 2009) 1648.

[22] Hölscheidt (n 16) 343.

[23] Schroeder (n 21) § 6 para 36.

[24] Stated inter alia by Germany, Ireland, Malta, the Netherlands and Sweden.

[25] Mentioned by Estonia and Sweden.

[26] In this regard, the general German practice to incorporate provisions implementing EU Regulations in civil procedural matters in the 11th book of the Code of Civil Procedure seems to be laudable. However, in implementing the Maintenance Regulation, the German legislator has adopted a different approach and enacted a self-standing implementing act.

ii. Risks

The enactment of implementing provisions may also complicate the application of EU law as it entails the co-existence of different legal sources and therefore enhances legal uncertainty. Moreover, there is a risk that implementing legislation surpasses the stage of mere implementation and infringes mandatory requirements of EU law due to conflicting provisions. In case the national legislator enacts identical or partly overlapping provisions, these provisions may conceal directly applicable provisions of EU law, which leads to a lack of transparency. The role attributed to the national legislator is often not clearly determined by the EU instrument.[27]

Especially in the context of cross-border recovery of maintenance, the intrinsic link between the Hague instruments and the Regulation causes additional problems. It is not surprising that three Member States[28] have drafted overall implementing legislation for both the Maintenance Regulation and the Hague Child Support Convention. The Dutch and Romanian acts additionally serve to implement the 2007 Hague Protocol. After the implementation of the EU legislation, the binding effect of the Hague instruments does not fundamentally differ from the direct effect of EU Regulations. Consequently, it seems to be appropriate to implement both instruments in a uniform way.

iii. Legal Basis for Implementing Measures

EU primary law provides a general legal basis for implementing legislation.[29]

Article 4(3) of the Treaty on European Union (TEU) stipulates that 'The Member States shall take any appropriate measure … to ensure fulfilment of the obligations arising out of the Treaties or resulting from the acts of the institutions of the Union. The Member States shall facilitate the achievement of the Union's tasks and refrain from any measure which could jeopardise the attainment of the Union's objectives.'

From the obligation to effectively apply EU law, one can deduce the obligation to implement an EU Regulation if the domestic order of the respective Member State is not sufficiently prepared to receive the European instrument.[30] Article 4(3) TEU on one hand imposes a duty to adopt implementing measures where necessary and, on the other hand, a duty to abstain from any measures potentially jeopardising the attainment of the objectives of the Treaty. Therefore, it limits the Member States' legislative autonomy.[31] However, it does not govern the modalities or procedures of implementation in the national systems, which leads to a broad autonomy of the Member States.

[27] On the Brussels I and Brussels IIa Regulations, see Eichel (n 3).

[28] Those Member States are Germany, the Netherlands and Romania. In Germany the provisions implementing the 2007 Hague Child Support Convention have been incorporated into the Foreign Maintenance Act by virtue of the Act on the implementation of the Hague Child Support Convention [2013] BGBl I, 273. The changes to the Foreign Maintenance Act are illustrated by Hilbig-Lugani (n 8) 74.

[29] Apart from this general legal basis there are other specific legal bases such as Art 291 TFEU. It has to be noted that Art 291 TFEU is not applicable to EU Regulations, see M Kotzur, in R Geiger, D Khan and M Kotzur (eds), *EUV/AEUV Vertrag über die Europäische Union und Vertrag über die Arbeitsweise der Europäischen Union*, 5th edn (Munich, CH Beck, 2010) Art 291 AEUV para 2.

[30] R Streinz, in R Streinz (ed), *EUV/AEUV Vertrag über die Europäische Union und Vertrag über die Arbeitsweise der Europäischen Union*, 2nd edn (Munich, CH Beck, 2012) Art 4 EUV para 32.

[31] Case C-443/03 *Götz Leffler v Berlin Chemie AG* [2005] ECR I-9611, para 50, *cf* also Riesenhuber (n 21) 1648.

Unlike directives, the obligation of the Member States to implement Regulations cannot be directly deduced from their legal status, but from the existing margins for manoeuvre.[32] The Court of Justice of the European Union (CJEU) held that room for manoeuvre exists insofar as EU law does not regulate the subject matter exhaustively.[33] Therefore, the extent to which domestic implementing rules are needed depends primarily upon the Regulation's content and regulatory density.[34] Secondly, frictions between the national law and the Regulation may entail implementing rules.[35] Those frictions may either be of an organisational and institutional nature, meaning that they may arise as the result of the absence of an institutional framework necessary to ensure the effective practical application of the Regulation, or they may be of a procedural nature in the sense that procedural rules need to be adapted due to new procedures established by the EU instrument.

In practice, the leeway available to the national legislator is limited as national provisions directly implementing Union law are subject to the intense scrutiny of the CJEU.[36] This strict examination is justified by the importance attached by the European legislator to the direct application of the Regulation and its uniform and consistent implementation throughout the EU Member States.

C. Restrictions of Implementation Powers

The autonomy given to Member States for implementation is not limitless. Powers conferred upon the national legislator are restricted by pertinent principles of EU law. According to the CJEU case law, limitations arise particularly from the principles of equivalence and effectiveness. A further restriction can be deduced from the principle of uniformity, which implies that Union law must be uniformly applied in the Member States.

The principle of equivalence implies that national implementing rules must not be less favourable than those governing rights originating in domestic law.[37] In comparison to the implementation of directives, the principle of equivalence does not seem to be of paramount significance, since any party may invoke the rights conferred by the Regulation without referring to national implementing laws. Particularly in the context of European procedural law, the principle of equivalence prohibits Member States from introducing additional (and sometimes sophisticated) remedies against enforceable titles coming from other Member States.[38]

[32] R Streinz, in R Streinz (ed), *EUV/AEUV Vertrag über die Europäische Union und Vertrag über die Arbeitsweise der Europäischen Union*, 2nd edn (Munich, CH Beck, 2012), Art 4 EUV para 32.

[33] Cases 205 to 215/82 *Deutsche Milchkontor v Germany* [1983] ECR 2633, para 17.

[34] Hess (n 4) § 4 para 21.

[35] Case 168/85 *Commission v Italy* [1986] ECR 2945, para 13; Case C-160/99 *Commission v France* [2000] ECR I-6137, para 23.

[36] Hess (n 4) § 4 para 18 and § 11 para 13.

[37] Case C-443/03 *Götz Leffler v Berlin Chemie AG* [2005] ECR I-9611, para 50.

[38] It appears that the German legislature infringed the principle of equivalence by introducing a specific head of jurisdiction for the so-called 'Vollstreckungsgegenklage' against foreign judgments (s 12 AVAG) which does not exist in general procedural law, *cf* B Hess, 'Die Zulässigkeit materiellrechtlicher Einwendungen im Vollstreckbarerklärungsverfahren nach Art. 43 ff. EuGVO' (2008) *Praxis des internationalen Privat- und Verfahrensrechts* 25.

The principle of effectiveness imposes on EU Member States the obligation of not unnecessarily hindering the operation of EU law.[39] Thus, the principle of effectiveness imposes a duty to abstain from any measures which might potentially jeopardise the attainment of the objectives of the Regulation.[40] Accordingly, the principle obliges Member States to remove national legislation inconsistent with the Regulation in order to ensure legal certainty and predictability.[41] In our view, the principle of effectiveness also imposes on the Member States the duty of indicating in the specific context of their national systems references to the pertinent EU Regulations in order to provide for sufficient guidance to parties and courts in the application of EU law.[42]

In the light of the principles of equivalence and effectiveness it is questionable whether Member States enacting more detailed or more restricted provisions than prescribed by the Regulation are not infringing those principles. One example is the German Implementing Act (AUG), since its section 33 provides for additional grounds for suspension of enforcement. It could be questioned whether section 33 AUG is compatible with the Maintenance Regulation,[43] as the latter calls for the acceleration of enforcing maintenance decisions. However, Article 21 of the Maintenance Regulation expressly leaves room for additional grounds of refusal or suspension of enforcement under domestic law. Nevertheless such a provision illustrates the lack of transparency due to the difficult interplay between the Regulation and domestic law.

Section 44 AUG in its original version allowed substantive objections (eg fulfilment, exemption) against the action to be enforced at the appeal stage. This provision was contrary to the Regulation's operative content and is to be considered as infringing the principle of effectiveness.[44] Following a recent CJEU decision on the Brussels I Regulation[45] the German legislator removed section 44.[46]

D. Prohibition on Reproducing the Provisions of the Regulation

Due to the primacy of a Regulation, it is unnecessary and generally inadmissible to repeat any provision of directly applicable EU law at national level.[47] Such a practice might undermine the awareness of national parties and courts of the legal nature of the provision and

[39] Case C-231/96 *Edis v Ministero delle Finanze* [1998] ECR I-4951, para 34; Case C-215/04 *Konstantinos Adeneler and Others v Ellinikos Organismos Galaktos (ELOG)* [2006] ECR I-6057, para 95; Schroeder (n 16) 23; Case C-443/03 (n 37) para 50.

[40] Case C-443/03 (n 37) para 50, *cf* also Riesenhuber (n 21) 1648; W Frenz, *Handbuch Europarecht*, 5th edn (Berlin, Heidelberg, Springer Verlag, 2010) para 865.

[41] *Cf* A von Bogdandy and S Schill, in E Grabitz, M Hilf and M Nettesheim (eds), *EUV/AEUV* (Munich, CH Beck, 2013) Art 4 EUV para 74; Riesenhuber (n 21).

[42] Hess (n 4) § 11 para 13. An example of insufficient implementation of EU procedural law relates to the Small Claims Regulation. As most EU Member States did not enact any implementing legislation, the mere existence of this specific procedure is unknown to many courts and litigants, Hess (n 4) § 4 para 18 and § 10 para 87.

[43] K Hilbig, in R Geimer and R Schütze (eds), *Internationaler Rechtsverkehr in Zivil- und Handelssachen* (Munich, CH Beck, 2011) Art 21 EuUntVO para 83.

[44] B Hess, 'Die Verordnung Nr. 4/2009/EG zum Unterhaltsrecht (EU-Unterhaltsverordnung)' in C Schmidt (ed), *Internationale Unterhaltsrealisierung: Rechtsgrundlagen und praktische Anwendung* (Baden-Baden, Nomos, 2011) para 22; Eichel (n 3) 194.

[45] Case C-139/10 *Prism Investments BV v Jaap Anne van der Meer* [2011] ECR I-9511.

[46] Act on the Implementation of the Hague Child Support Convention [2013] BGBl I, 273.

[47] Case C-39/72 *Commission of the European Communities v Italian Republic* [1973] ECR 101, para 16.

the date of its entry into force[48] as well as of the exclusive competence of the CJEU for its interpretation (Article 267 TFEU). Only in exceptional circumstances, especially for the sake of coherence and in order to make EU provisions comprehensible, may singular provisions of applicable EU law be reflected in national law.[49] Nevertheless, reproducing or paraphrasing the wording of the Regulation is a dangerous and—therefore, prohibited—technique, as even a slight deviation from the original wording may lead to misinterpretation and conceal the Union nature of a provision.[50] Co-existing provisions at EU and national level have to be critically assessed in the light of legal certainty. Implementing rules have to be drafted in such a way that individuals are able to know the full extent of their rights under Union law and to rely on them before domestic courts.

The Finnish and German Implementing Acts include some provisions replicating the directly applicable provisions of the Maintenance Regulation on legal aid.[51] Section 22(1) and (2) AUG repeats the provision of Article 46 of the Maintenance Regulation with different wording[52] and section 23 replicates in essence the provision of Article 47(2) of the Maintenance Regulation, but makes use of slightly different wording. Further examples can be found in the Irish[53] and Maltese[54] implementing acts.

E. Prohibition on Completing Lacunae in the Regulation

National legislators have to abstain from supplementing potential lacunae of the Regulation by introducing additional procedures. A much discussed example of an additional procedure relates to Article 58 of the Maintenance Regulation. According to its second paragraph the Central Authority of the requesting Member State must transmit an application for maintenance to the Central Authority of the requested Member State when satisfied that the application complies with the requirements of the Maintenance Regulation. The German implementing act stipulates, however, that an application for assistance in maintenance matters is subject to prior examination. A judge of the local court examines whether

[48] Ibid para 17.

[49] Case C-272/83 *Commission of the European Communities v Italian Republic* [1985] ECR 1057, para 27.

[50] As a result, national courts might not refer preliminary questions to the CJEU on the correct interpretation and application of EU law.

[51] ss 22, 23 AUG 2011 (Germany). The Finnish implementing act reproduces the content of Art 46(1) of the Maintenance Regulation, but specifies the relevant point in time, ie the child has to be under the age of 21 at the time the application becomes pending, see section 4 of the Act on the Central Authority in Finland in Certain International Matters Relating to Maintenance.

[52] s 22 AUG 2011 provides 'Granting of legal aid can be refused only where the application is vexatious or manifestly unfounded' whereas Art 46(2) of the Regulation provides that free legal aid may only be refused if it is considered 'that ... the application or any appeal or review is manifestly unfounded'.

[53] Reg 9(3) SI 274/2011 stipulates 'Where the application is for the enforcement of a decision, the Master of the High Court shall declare the decision enforceable immediately on completion of the formalities provided for in Article 28, without any review under Article 24 and shall make an enforcement order in relation to the decision'.

[54] Art 7(2) of the International Maintenance Obligations Order (Malta) stipulates 'An appeal against the declaration of enforceability shall be lodged within thirty days of service of such declaration. Provided that if the party against whom enforcement is sought has his habitual residence in a Member State other than that in which the declaration of enforceability was given, the time for appealing shall be forty-five days and shall run from the date of service of the decision'.

the application is vexatious or manifestly unfounded under section 9(1) AUG 2011.[55] Yet, the Maintenance Regulation does not provide for a general ban of vexatious or manifestly unfounded applications.[56] Against this backdrop, the additional examination proceedings seem to be problematic for the following reasons. There is no corresponding provision in the Maintenance Regulation allowing such examination by a court. Further, the examination causes delays in most cases where the application is not vexatious or manifestly unfounded. Therefore the additional examination does not meet the Regulation's objectives. Moreover, its vague wording is a potential source of misinterpretation. It is not up to the national legislator to provide for an additional safeguard against the potential misuse of applications.

The foregoing considerations demonstrate that the implementation of an EU Regulation clearly differs from the general concept of implementing an international treaty. However, as shall be demonstrated with regard to the Maintenance Regulation, the differences between implementing an international and a European instrument have not yet been entirely recognised by legal doctrine or by the practice of EU Member States.

F. Matters in the Maintenance Regulation Requiring Implementation

The dense framework of European standards does not entail uniform implementation throughout the Union. As will be outlined below the Maintenance Regulation appears as a typical example for the divergent implementation of European law by the Member States. Sixteen Member States (Bulgaria,[57] Denmark,[58] Estonia,[59] Finland,[60] France,[61] Germany,[62]

[55] The wording of this provision is borrowed from s 114 ZPO (German Code of Civil Procedure), which governs the general conditions for granting legal aid.

[56] Art 58(8) provides that the Central Authority may refuse to process an application only if it is manifest that the requirements of this Regulation are not fulfilled.

[57] Act of 7 December 2010 amending the Code of Civil Procedure.

[58] Ministerial Order implementing the Maintenance Regulation ('Bekendtgørelse om gennemførelse af underholdspligtforordningen') BEK No 69 of 29 January 2009; Ministerial Order on the use of the Maintenance Regulation ('Bekendtgørelse om anvendelse af underholdspligtforordningen') BEK No 649 of 15 June 2011; Ministerial Order on the use of Maintenance Regulation ('Bekendtgørelse om anvendelse af underholdspligtforordningen') BEK No 1064 of 30 August 2013, which entered into force on 6 September 2013.

[59] Ülalpidamiskohustuste määruse rakendamise määrus (Regulation No 30 on implementing the Maintenance Regulation of 9 June 2011) RT I, 14 June 2011, 6.

[60] Act on the Central Authority in Finland in Certain International Matters Relating to Maintenance ('Laki Suomen keskusviranomaisesta eräissä elatusapua koskevissa kansainvälisissä asioissa') of 10 December 2010/1076 and Act on Application of the Council Regulation on Maintenance Obligations ('Laki elatusvelvoitteita koskevan neuvoston asetuksen soveltamisesta') of 10 December 2010/1077.

[61] 'Décret No 2011-1043 du 1er septembre 2011 relatif aux mesures conservatoires prises après l'ouverture d'une succession et à la procédure en la forme des référés' [2011] JORF No 0203, 14884.

[62] 'Gesetz zur Durchführung der Verordnung (EG) No 4/2009 und zur Neuordnung bestehender Aus- und Durchführungsbestimmungen auf dem Gebiet des internationalen Unterhaltsverfahrensrechts' whose Article 1 contains the reformed Auslandsunterhaltsgesetz of 23 May 2011 (Foreign Maintenance Act) [2011] BGBl I, 898; see K Niethammer-Jürgens, 'Gesetz zur Durchführung der VO (EG) No 4/2009 und zur Neuordnung bestehender Aus- und Durchführungsbestimmungen auf dem Gebiet des internationalen Unterhaltsverfahrensrechts' (2011) *Der Familien-Rechts-Berater international* 60.

Hungary,[63] Ireland,[64] Latvia,[65] Lithuania,[66] Luxembourg,[67] Malta,[68] the Netherlands,[69] Romania,[70] Sweden[71] and the UK)[72] have adopted implementing legislation to assist the effective operation of the Maintenance Regulation.[73]

The following map shows the state of play regarding implementing legislation in the Member States:

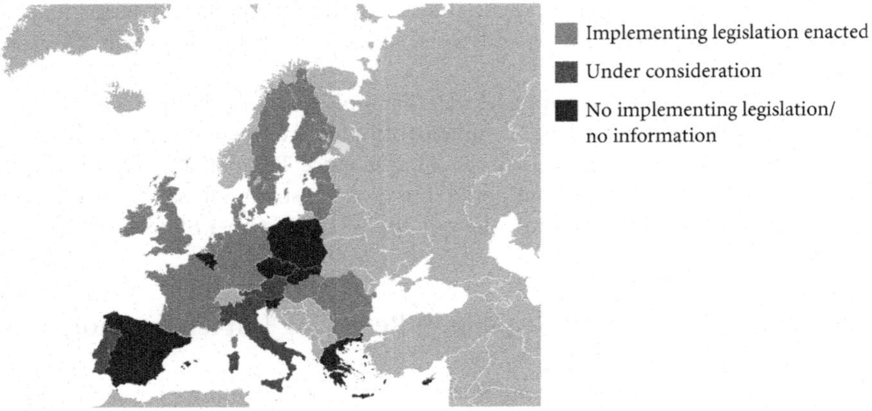

[63] 'Törveny a határon átnyúló tartási ügyekben a központi hatósági feladatok ellátásáról' [2011] *Magyar Közlöny* (Hungarian *Official Journal*) No 69, 14998.

[64] SI 274/2011 'European Communities (Maintenance) Regulations 2011' [2011] *Iris Oifigiúil* 819 and SI 612/2011 'European Communities (Maintenance) (Amendment) Regulations 2011' [2011] *Iris Oifigiúil* 1666.

[65] Regulations of the Cabinet of Ministers No 571 of 19 July 2011 [2011] *LatvijasVéstnesis* (*Latvian Herald*) No 117, 4515.

[66] Law on supplementing Law to Chapter 9 and supplementing the Annex to Law of Implementation of European Union and International Legal Acts Regulating Civil Procedure No. XI-2081 which entered into force on 30 June 2012 [2012] *Valstybés Žinios* (*Official Gazette*) No 76-3928.

[67] 'Loi du 3 août 2011 portant mise en application du règlement (CE) No 4/2009 du 18 décembre 2008 relatif à la compétence, la loi applicable, la reconnaissance et l'exécution des décisions et la coopération en matière d'obligations alimentaires, modifiant le Nouveau Code de Procédure Civile' [2011] *Mémorial A* (*Legal Gazette*) No 175, 2973.

[68] 'International Maintenance Obligations Order' [2011] *Government Gazette* No 18828.

[69] 'Uitvoeringswet internationale inning levensonderhoud' [2011] *Stb.* No 460.

[70] 'Law No 36/2012 on certain measures required to implement certain regulations and decisions of the Council of the European Union as well as private international law instruments in the field of maintenance obligations' [2012] *Monitorul Oficial al României* (*Official Journal of Romania*) No 183.

[71] Regulation (2011:603) containing additional provisions for the EU Maintenance Regulation ('Lag med kompletterande bestämmelser till EU:s underhållsförordning') and Regulation (2011:704) containing additional provisions for the EU Maintenance Regulation ('Förordning (2011:704) med kompletterande bestämmelser till EU:s underhållsförordning').

[72] The principal statutory instrument is SI 2011/1484 'The Civil Jurisdiction and Judgments (Maintenance) Regulations 2011' (*CJJMR* 2011).

[73] A compilation of the national implementing acts is available at www.heidelberg-conference2013.de/legal-bases.html (accessed December 2013).

The implementing provisions were either adopted by the parliament[74] or by members of the executive (Estonia, Ireland,[75] Latvia, Malta,[76] England and Wales).[77] The number of implementing provisions varies across the Member States and indicates the different regulatory density in the Member States' implementing acts.[78]

In three Member States[79] no implementing measures have been adopted, but the governments are examining the need for developing implementing rules. Eight Member States[80] did not adopt or plan to adopt implementing acts referring to the direct applicability of the Regulation. Following the entry into force of the Maintenance Regulation several Member States (eg Bulgaria,[81] Estonia, Latvia and Luxembourg) changed or amended their Code of Civil Procedure or their Private International Law Acts. The EU Commission has also enacted measures implementing the Maintenance Regulation.[82]

When it comes to the implementation of an EU Regulation, Member States must first scrutinize the (remaining) room for setting an implementing framework to the mandatory instrument. This can only be done by assessing which provisions of the Regulation require supplementary provisions.

i. Minimalist Implementation

As a first step, a minimum set of rules shall be identified which mandatorily require implementation. The starting point is Article 71 of the Maintenance Regulation, which provides for a list of implementing measures to be communicated from the Member States to the European Commission. Accordingly, Article 71 of the Maintenance Regulation contains a compilation of necessary implementation measures. The provision refers to three different implementing measures. First, Member States must designate and communicate the competent authority/court; secondly, they have to indicate the competent authority/court to hear the remedies against the declaration of enforceability (Article 32 of the Maintenance Regulation) as well as the applicable procedures (Article 33 of the Maintenance Regulation). Thirdly, Member States must indicate the permitted languages for the translations of enforceable titles and for communication between Central Authorities.

Article 71 of the Maintenance Regulation has been applied differently, according to the different practices of the Member States. Two Member States, Estonia[83] and Malta,[84]

[74] Finland, Germany, Hungary, Luxembourg, the Netherlands and Romania.

[75] SI 274/2011 and SI 612/2011 were adopted by the Minister for Justice and Equality in exercise of his powers conferred by s 3 of the European Communities Act 1972. Statutory instruments constitute a subordinate form of law. According to the definition provided by s 1 of the Statutory Instruments Act 1947, statutory instrument means 'an order, regulation, rule scheme or bye-law made in exercise of a power conferred by statute'.

[76] The International Maintenance Obligations Order was adopted by the Prime Minister in exercise of his powers conferred by Art 4(2) of the European Union Act 2011.

[77] Regulations adopted by the Secretary of State for Justice in exercise of the powers conferred by s 2(2) of the European Communities Act 1972.

[78] Eg the Dutch implementing act contains 12 articles whereas the German act comprises 77 provisions.

[79] Austria, Italy and Portugal.

[80] Belgium, Cyprus, the Czech Republic, Greece, Poland, Slovenia, Slovakia and Spain.

[81] A new Chapter 58a has been introduced into the Code of Civil Procedure, which implements certain provisions of the Maintenance Regulation.

[82] Commission Implementing Regulation (EU) No 1142/2011 of 10 November 2011 establishing Annexes X and XI to Council Regulation (EC) No 4/2009 on jurisdiction, applicable law, recognition and enforcement of decisions and cooperation in matters relating to maintenance obligations [2011] OJ L293/24.

[83] Regulation No 30 on implementing the Maintenance Regulation of 9 June 2011.

[84] International Maintenance Obligations Order, SL 460.25.

adopted a minimalist approach by limiting their legislative activities to the mere fulfilment of the notification requirements of Article 71 of the Maintenance Regulation.[85] From the perspective of effectiveness, this approach seems to be problematic, because the implementing legislation is by itself very hard to understand. It remains to be seen whether the courts and the parties will be able to recognise the Regulation as the pertinent legal instrument.

Against the backdrop of general European procedural law, the list contained in Article 71 of the Maintenance Regulation does not appear to be unusual. Several EU Regulations[86] require Member States to designate the courts or judicial authorities exercising jurisdiction under the Regulation. In the Maintenance Regulation this obligation relates to Articles 19(1),[87] 21,[88] 27(1),[89] and 32(2).[90] Furthermore, the Member States must designate procedural rules applicable to the appropriate review procedure[91] and relating to the enforcement procedure for the purposes of Article 21.[92]

As Chapter VII of the Regulation sets up a system of administrative cooperation, Member States have to establish an organisational framework encompassing the designation of their Central Authorities and/or public bodies including a description of their functions.[93] Practical importance can also be attributed to the indication of languages accepted with regard to the inter-state communication (Article 59 of the Maintenance Regulation) or concerning the translation of documents.[94]

ii. Implementation by Reference to National Systems

Some provisions of the Maintenance Regulation refer to the different legal systems of the Member States (in specific areas of law) and permit a kind of variable implementation. An

[85] The Estonian implementing Regulation enumerates the required information with the exception of the information requested in Art 71(e) of the Regulation, since Estonia has not designated public bodies in accordance with Art 51(3). The Maltese implementing act is also limited to the requested information except for Art 71(1)(b) and (e), since the Maltese national law does not provide for a redress procedure nor for public bodies for the purpose of Art 51(3).

[86] Art 39(1) of the Brussels I Regulation in connection with Annex II, Art 43(2) of the Brussels I Regulation in connection with Annex III. Further see Arts 21(3), 29(1), 33(2) in connection with Art 68 of the Brussels IIa Regulation.

[87] Member States have to communicate the courts having jurisdiction in accordance with Art 71(1)(c).

[88] Competent authorities have to be communicated to the Commission, Art 71(1)(f).

[89] D-C Bittmann, 'Europäische Unterhaltsverordnung', in M Gebauer and T Wiedmann (eds), *Zivilrecht unter europäischem Einfluss*, 2nd edn (Stuttgart, Munich et al, Boorberg, 2010) ch 36, para 145; Hilbig (n 43) Art 27 EuUntVO para 1; W Hau, in H Prütting and T Helms (eds), *FamFG-Kommentar*, 2nd edn (Cologne, Otto Schmidt, 2011) Annex 3 to § 110 para 132. Pursuant to Art 71(1)(a) Member States have to communicate the courts or authorities with competence to deal with applications for a declaration of enforceability.

[90] The competent courts or authorities have to be communicated to the Commission, Art 71(1) (a).

[91] Bittmann (n 89) para 99; Hilbig (n 43) Art 19 EuUntVO, para 4, M Andrae and M Schimrick, in T Rauscher (ed), *Europäisches Zivilprozess- und Kollisionsrecht-EuZPR/EuIPR* (Munich, Sellier, 2010) Art 19 EG-UntVO, para 14. According to Art 71(1)(c) Member States are obliged to communicate the review procedure and the names and contact details of the courts having jurisdiction. The communications of the Member States are published on the European Judicial Atlas in Civil Matters available at: www.ec.europa.eu/justice_home/judicialatlascivil/html/index_en.htm (accessed December 2013).

[92] Bittmann (n 89) ch 36, para 123. Pursuant to Art 71(1)(f) Member States have to communicate information on the names and contact details of the authorities with competence in matters of enforcement for the purposes of Art 21 which are published on the European Judicial Atlas in Civil Matters.

[93] Pursuant to Arts 49(3), 71(1)(d) Member States are requested to communicate the designated Central Authority/ies including their contact details. The designated public bodies have to be communicated to the Commission in accordance with Art 71(1)(e) of the Regulation.

[94] Arts 20(1)(d), 28(1)(c) and 40(3) of the Maintenance Regulation. The languages accepted have to be communicated, Art 71(1)(g).

example is Article 61 of the Maintenance Regulation, which sets out the Central Authority's tasks of locating the debtor, obtaining the relevant information about the debtor's income[95] and ensuring that the Central Authority has access to the information. In this context, the Regulation refers to the organisational infrastructure of the Member States. Member States may designate public authorities or administrations holding the information concerned and decide on the arrangements for accessing information.[96] This reference technique illustrates the importance of a Regulation as an instrument of coordination.

As far as the implementation of Article 61 of the Maintenance Regulation is concerned there are divergent solutions. In some Member States there was no need to designate authorities since the existing framework already enabled the Central Authority to directly access the relevant registries.[97] The Luxembourgian Central Authority has direct electronic access to certain registers held by public bodies.[98] The data accessible is determined by a separate Regulation, which especially excludes any transfer of data on the health of the person concerned.[99] Latvia and Romania adopted a broad approach by imposing a general duty on all public bodies to give the necessary information to the Central Authority.[100] Other Member States, however, designated specific public authorities authorised to provide the Central Authority with the information needed.[101] The latter approach seems to be appropriate as it provides for transparent responsibilities (and for a corresponding protection of data) in the processing of maintenance cases.

iii. Additional Implementation in EU Member States

The third type of national implementation transgresses the framework of the Maintenance Regulation by providing for additional provisions, which shall facilitate the application of the Regulation by national authorities. The starting point of these rules seems to be laudable. The efficient application of the Regulation in the context of the framework of national law may require adjustments at the domestic level. However, enacting additional implementing provisions for an EU Regulation might be a risky task.

As an example, section 28 of the German implementing act, establishes concentration of jurisdiction for the purpose of Article 3(a) and (b) of the Maintenance Regulation.[102] If

[95] Art 51(2)(b) and (c) of the Maintenance Regulation.

[96] Recital 33.

[97] Eg in Estonia and Sweden.

[98] Art 3 of the Act of 3August 2011.

[99] 'Règlement grand-ducal du 3 août 2011 portant exécution des articles 2 et 3 de la loi du 3 août 2011 portant mise en application du règlement (CE) No 4/2009 du 18 décembre 2008 relatif à la compétence, la loi applicable, la reconnaissance et l'exécution des décisions et la coopération en matière d'obligations alimentaires, modifiant le Nouveau Code de procédure civile' [2011] *Mémorial A* (*Legal Gazette*) No 175, 2974.

[100] Eg s 2 of the Latvian implementing act stipulates that all State and municipal authorities, courts and judicial authorities are obliged to assist the Central Authority with the information needed. s 19(1) of the Irish act requires any holder of a public body financed by means of moneys provided by the Oireachtas to provide the requested information. The Romanian implementing act provides for a non-exhaustive list of authorities to be approached by the Central Authority, Art 12(2) of Law No 36/2012.

[101] Eg s 3 of the Act on the Central Authority in Certain International Matters Relating to Maintenance (Finland); ss 16(2), 17(1) AUG 2011 differing according to whether the obtaining of information is necessary for the establishment or modification of a decision or for the recognition, declaration of enforceability and enforcement of the decision (Germany); Art $31^5(5)$ of Act No XI-2081 (Lithuania); Art 23 of the LBIO Act (the Netherlands); Art 12(2) Law No 36/2012 (Romania); Reg 4 Sch 2(1) CJJMR 2011 (England and Wales).

[102] Reg 3 of the Irish implementing act confers jurisdiction for the purposes of Art 3(a) and (b) upon the circuit court or district court. Jurisdiction may be exercised by the judge of the circuit or of the district court circuit in which the creditor or debtor, as the case may be, is habitually resident.

one of the parties is habitually resident abroad, competence lies with the local court with jurisdiction over the seat of the Higher Regional Court in whose district the domestic party is habitually resident.[103] In principle, there is no need to enact supplementary provisions on jurisdiction due to the regulatory density of the Regulation. Articles 3ff contain extensive provisions on jurisdiction including jurisdiction *ratione loci*.

This provision has been criticised for several reasons. First, its compatibility with the Regulation is questionable since Article 3 of the Maintenance Regulation exhaustively regulates jurisdiction issues and includes venue.[104] The German legislator, however, does not characterise the provision as governing venue, but as an organisational measure.[105] Secondly, it leads to the result that maintenance creditors habitually resident in Germany are deprived of the privilege of bringing proceedings before the proximate court of their habitual residence.[106] Especially in large Federal States this situation disadvantages maintenance creditors. Therefore, it has been suggested that elective jurisdiction be introduced where the maintenance creditor is habitually resident in Germany.[107] Providing for a concentration of jurisdiction for the purposes of Article 3 of the Maintenance Regulation seems to be reasonable in terms of concentrating knowledge and experience, but would be more convincing if documents could be handed in at the courts electronically.[108]

G. Conclusion: Best Practices

The outline of some of the Regulation's provisions has revealed that, although being a self-executing instrument, it contains several non-exhaustive provisions, which entail the creation of legal infrastructure by the Member States in order to effectively apply the Regulation. The mere fact that the European legislator has adopted a Regulation, which is immediately applicable and takes precedence over domestic law of the EU Member States, does not exclude the need for implementing legislation. The comparative evaluation of the implementing legislation of the Member States has also revealed significant variations.

[103] A similar concentration of jurisdiction has been introduced by the German legislator when implementing the European Order for Payment, s 1086 ZPO (German Code of Civil Procedure).

[104] T Rauscher, 'Urteilsanmerkung zu OLG Frankfurt: Zuständigkeitskonzentration bei Unterhaltsverfahren nach der EG-UntVO' (2012) *Familienrecht und Familienverfahrensrecht* 216.

[105] BT-Drucks. 17/4887, 42; *cf* also M Heger, 'Gerichtliche Zuständigkeiten nach der EuUntVO für die Geltendmachung von Kindes-, Trennungs- und Nacheheunterhalt' (2013) *Familie Partnerschaft Recht* 1, 4.

[106] M Kasenbacher, 'Zuständigkeitsfragen für Unterhaltsverfahren mit Auslandsbezug' (2012) *NJW-Spezial*, 516, 517; see also Decision OLG Frankfurt am Main - 1 UFH 43/11 (2012) *Zeitschrift für das gesamte Familienrecht* 1508, annotated by T Rauscher (n 104) 216 and C Schmidt, 'Anmerkung zu OLG Frankfurt aM 11.01.2012, 1 UFH 43/11, Zuständigkeitskonzentration bei Unterhaltsverfahren mit EU-Auslandsberührung' (2012) *Das Jugendamt* 43. On the contrary, Art 5(2) of the Brussels I Regulation provides the creditor with a *forum actoris* based on the assumption that he or she is the weaker party.

[107] Schmidt (n 106) 42, 44.

[108] This possibility is provided for by s 1087ff of the Code of Civil Procedure implementing the European Order for Payment Procedure.

However, it seems possible to cautiously present the following guidelines, which could be used as best practices:

(1) European Regulations do not leave much room for manoeuvre for the national legislators to adopt comprehensive implementing legislation. Accordingly, a cautious approach of the national lawmakers seems to be advisable.
(2) Implementing legislation is mainly needed in the areas where a European instrument explicitly requires corresponding legislation at the domestic level. In these areas Member States should place priority on implementing strategies to ensure the effective and uniform application of the Regulation throughout the European Union.
(3) Implementing legislation should avoid friction between the existing national procedural law and EU law.
(4) According to the CJEU case law, implementing provisions shall not repeat any provisions of a Regulation that are directly applicable in order to avoid inconsistent interpretation and a lack of transparency. In addition, Member States are not empowered to close perceived lacunae of the European instruments.
(5) In the implementing context, Member States need the support of the EU Commission. Accordingly, the Commission should—comparable to the Hague Conference—develop implementing guidelines or checklists which help Member States to adopt implementing measures in accordance with the requirements of the Regulation.
(6) It could be useful for Member States to provide guidance on how to apply the Regulation and the implementing acts in practice.
(7) Regarding access to the relevant data, Member States could follow the model of Luxembourg and establish a direct electronic access to certain registers holding personal data including a safeguard mechanism.
(8) Member States should be given the possibility of entering and updating the information requested under Article 71 of the Maintenance Regulation online. This would increase the effectiveness of the communication duties under the Maintenance Regulation.

III. Cross-border Cooperation in Maintenance Cases

A. Introduction

Cross-border cooperation has a longstanding tradition in international family law and especially in the area of maintenance. Its importance has been emphasised by William Duncan who stated that it is 'an essential, and perhaps the most important, element in the new instrument on the international recovery of maintenance'.[109] The reasons for its significance are manifold. The system of cross-border cooperation responds to the needs and particularities of the parties. In cross-border maintenance cases, creditors are confronted with practical and legal obstacles when seeking to enforce their claims in a

[109] W Duncan, 'Towards a New Global Instrument on the International Recovery of Child Support and Other Forms of Family Maintenance Report 2003' para 15, available at www.hcch.net/upload/wop/maint_pd03e.pdf (accessed January 2014).

foreign country. The maintenance creditor is often regarded as the weaker party who depends on regular payments. Swift and flexible adaptations without any bureaucratic obstacles are needed due to socio-economic changes in the creditor's life.[110] In cases involving children, the guarantees enshrined in the United Nations Convention on the Rights of the Child of 1989—especially those of Articles 3 and 27—must also be taken into account.

B. Concepts of Cross-border Cooperation in Family Law Matters

i. The Different Stages of Administrative Cooperation

In the past cooperation was mainly performed through diplomatic or consular channels.[111] This form of cooperation is characterised by a high level of formalisation[112] and appears as an act of foreign policy.[113] Due to the existing administrative hierarchies and the large number of officials involved, this communication channel has proved to be inefficient and slow.[114] Moreover, the application of the *lex fori* leads to a plurality of procedural laws involved, which might cause delays in proceedings.[115] From the parties' perspective this type of cooperation was disadvantageous, because the decision whether to cooperate was left to the discretion of the acting executive body without being of a mandatory nature. Correspondingly, parties were not entitled to claim the performance of cooperative measures.[116]

The second level of integration constitutes the system of transmitting and receiving agencies under the 1956 New York Convention.[117] It is the first international instrument providing for a global framework of administrative cooperation in matters relating to maintenance obligations towards children and other family dependents without governing any aspects of private international or international procedural law.[118] It is rather limited to a mere technical and organisational approach.[119] Each Contracting State has to designate

[110] P Schlosser, 'Jurisdiction and International Judicial and Administrative Co-operation' (2000) *Hague Academy Collected Courses* 13, 284.

[111] A Borrás, 'La cooperación internacional de autoridades: En particular, el caso del cobro de alimentos en el extranjero' (2008) *Anuario Español de Derecho Internacional Privado* 129, 130; G Droz, 'Évolution du rôle des autorités administratives dans les conventions de droit international privé au cours du premier siècle de la Conférence de La Haye' in *Études offertes à Pierre Bellet* (Paris, Litec, 1991) 130; H Linke and W Hau, *Internationales Zivilverfahrensrecht* (Köln, Schmidt, 2011) § 3 para 102.

[112] D McClean, *International Co-operation in Civil and Criminal Matters* (Oxford, Oxford University Press, 2002) 16.

[113] B Hess, 'Nouvelles techniques de la coopération judiciaire transfrontière en Europe' (2003) *Revue critique de droit international privé* 215, 219. For the French perspective see S Corneloup and V Corneloup, 'Le contentieux de la coopération des autorités centrales dans le cadre des conventions de La Haye. Compétence administrative ou judiciaire?' (2000) *Revue critique de droit international privé* 641.

[114] McClean (n 112) 16.

[115] Hess (n 113) 215, 219.

[116] B Hess, 'Neue Formen der Rechtshilfe in Zivilsachen im Europäischen Justizraum' in R Krause, W Veelken and K Vieweg (eds), *Gedächtnisschrift für Wolfgang Blomeyer* (Berlin, Duncker & Humblot, 2004) 617, 620.

[117] New York Convention of 20 June 1956 on the Recovery Abroad of Maintenance [1957] United Nations Treaty Series, vol 268, 3. The Convention has been ratified by 24 EU Member States.

[118] I Curry-Sumner 'International Recovery of Child Support: Are Central Authorities the Way Forward?' in B Verschraegen (ed), *Family Finances* (Vienna, Jan Sramek, 2009) 175, 176; Schlosser (n 110) 287.

[119] Curry-Sumner (n 118) 178.

one or more bodies acting as Transmitting and Receiving Agencies.[120] The duties to be performed by the Agencies are described in general clauses without any system sanctioning their non-performance.[121] In the practice of the Convention it appeared that some Agencies did not fulfil their obligations properly, which has caused operational problems in the recovery of maintenance.[122] A further obstacle relates to the non-harmonised and non-standardised procedures applicable, which require national implementing legislation. The Contracting States have adopted heterogenous national legislation for the purposes of the Convention.[123] In the light of legal certainty and predictability this might prove disadvantageous. Moreover, the 1956 Convention pursues a creditor-based approach insofar as the assistance of the agencies was only beneficial for the maintenance creditor.[124]

The system established under the 1956 New York Convention has suffered from numerous legal and practical problems and has therefore proved ineffective. Under the Convention the role of the Agencies differed according to the respective Contracting State. In some states the Agency mainly served the purpose of a letterbox.[125]

ii. The Concept of Central Authorities and their Functions

The system of cooperation through Central Authorities developed first in the 1960s in the framework of the Hague Conference on Private International Law.[126] It is characterised by concentrating responsibilities with one interlocutor in each state[127] and appears as a form of 'institutionalised co-operation'. However, due to profound differences in the internal organisation of the States the structure and capacity to act as Central Authorities are not defined in the international instruments, but left to the internal law of the States.

In the area of family law matters the first international convention establishing the concept of Central Authorities comprehensively was the 1980 Hague Abduction Convention.[128] Its cooperative framework shows the following characteristics. First, Central Authorities are the main vehicle to pursue the Convention's principal objective, that is, in all cases where one of the exceptions to return does not apply, to swiftly restore the status quo

[120] Art 2(1) and (2).

[121] See Arts 3(4) and 6(1).

[122] I Curry-Sumner 'Administrative Co-Operation and Free Legal Aid in International Child Maintenance Recovery. What is the Added Value of the European Maintenance Regulation?' (2010) *Nederland Internationaal Privaatrecht* 611, 612; Hague Conference, 'Towards a new global instrument on the international recovery of child support and other forms of family maintenance' (2003) Prel Doct No 3, 13, 15.

[123] Curry-Sumner (n 118) 178.

[124] M Kurucz, 'The 2007 Hague Maintenance Convention: Response to Practical Demands' (2012) *International Family Law* 103.

[125] Curry-Sumner (n 118) 185.

[126] A Borrás, 'La cooperación internacional de autoridades: En particular, el caso del cobro de alimentos en el extranjero' (2008) *Anuario Español de Derecho Internacional Privado* 129, 131; M del Carmen Seoane de Chiodi, 'New Trends in Networks and Co-Operation Among Central Authorities: Mediation as an Alternative Means for the Solution of Controversies and the Role of the Central Authority in its Application in International Return and Access Procedures' (2012) *International Family Law* 65.

[127] Federal States can designate more than one Central Authority, Art 6(2) of the Hague Child Abduction Convention 1980, Art 6(2) of the Adoption Convention 1993, Art 29(2) of the Child Protection Convention 1996, Art 4(2) of the Hague Child Support Convention 2007 and Art 49(2) of the Maintenance Regulation.

[128] Convention of 25 October 1980 on the Civil Aspects of International Child Abduction, www.hcch.net/upload/conventions/txt28en.pdf (accessed October 2013). All EU Member States have become Contracting States. For a detailed analysis of the concept and functions of Central Authorities in the framework of the Abduction Convention, see L Silberman, 'Co-operative Efforts in Private International Law on Behalf of Children: The Hague Children's Conventions' (2006) *Hague Academy Collected Courses* 261, 317.

ante.[129] Secondly, the Convention provides for direct bilateral cooperation by means of exchange of information. It therefore simplifies procedures. Thirdly, the Central Authority helps to protect the vulnerable party. Article 7 of the Abduction Convention lists a broad range of duties to be performed by Central Authorities. Article 7(1) illustrates the overall duty of cooperation whereas Article 7(2) specifies the principal tasks to be carried out by the Central Authorities.[130] The functions listed in Article 7(2) follow the different stages of involvement in a case of the removal or retention of a child.[131] The duties imposed on the Central Authorities can also be performed with the assistance of other intermediaries. The system of cross-border cooperation via Central Authorities has an optional character (Article 29 of the Abduction Convention).[132] It served as the basis for the subsequent conventions in family law matters such as the 1993 Convention on Protection of Children and Co-operation in Respect of Intercountry Adoption[133] and the 1996 Convention on Jurisdiction, Applicable Law, Recognition, Enforcement and Co-operation in Respect of Parental Responsibility and Measures for the Protection of Children.[134] The 1993 Adoption Convention is characterised by a division of responsibilities between the Central Authorities, which are jointly responsible for taking the adoption decision.[135] This co-decision making process constitutes a new dimension of administrative cooperation. In contrast to its predecessor conventions private accredited bodies may perform certain functions.[136]

The 1996 Child Protection Convention contains modernised forms of cooperation and introduces a novelty in cross-border cooperation by permitting the transfer of jurisdiction to another Contracting State better placed to assess the best interests of the child (a limited *forum non conveniens* rule in Article 8). The application of this rule implies prior interaction between the authorities of both states involved in the case. Moreover, the 1996 Convention institutes a procedure for mandatory consultation prior to a decision on the placement of a child or on the provision of care.[137]

[129] E Pérez-Vera, *Explanatory Report on the 1980 Hague Child Abduction Convention* (The Hague, HccH, 1982) para 35, Silberman (n 128) 276.

[130] E Pérez-Vera (n 129) para 88. The list in Art 7(2) is non-exhaustive.

[131] Ibid para 90.

[132] Droz (n 111) 139; Silberman (n 128) 319.

[133] Text of the Convention available at www.hcch.net/upload/conventions/txt33en.pdf (accessed September 2013). For a detailed analysis of the Convention see eg Silberman (n 128) 430ff.

[134] Text of the Convention available at www.hcch.net/upload/conventions/txt34en.pdf (accessed September 2013). To date, not all of the EU Member States have ratified the Convention. The EU itself has no powers to ratify it, since the Convention is lacking a so-called REIO clause. For an overview of the Convention see P Nygh, 'The New Hague Child Protection Convention' (1997) *International Journal of Law, Policy and the Family* 344.

[135] Art 17. See also H van Loon, 'International Co-operation and Protection of Children with regard to Intercountry Adoption' (1993) *Hague Academy Collected Courses* 191, 336; H van Loon, 'Hague Convention of 29 May 1993 on Protection of Children and Cooperation in Respect of Intercountry Adoption' (1995) *The International Journal of Children's Rights* 463, 465; Schlosser (n 110) 326.

[136] Arts 9 and 22(1) of the Adoption Convention. See further van Loon (n 135) 466; N Meyer-Fabre, 'La Convention de La Haye du 29 mai 1993 sur la protection des enfants et la coopération en matière d'adoption internationale' (1994) *Revue critique de droit internatonal privé* 259, 276.

[137] Art 33(2); P Lagarde, *Explanatory Report on the 1996 Hague Child Protection Convention* (The Hague, 1998) 593; Schlosser (n 110) 309.

a. Designated Authorities under the Maintenance Regulation

In accordance with Article 49(1) of the Maintenance Regulation each Member State has to designate a Central Authority, which shall discharge the duties imposed by the Regulation and shall act as a focal point for international cooperation at the administrative level.[138] The term 'Central Authority' is not defined by the Regulation in order to accomodate the differences in domestic law.

Concerning the designated authorities a great variety can be detected. The majority of Member States designated the Ministry of Justice or a subordinated institution. A few Member States (Slovenia, Denmark and Lithuania) designated the Ministry for Labour, Social Affairs and Family Matters or an institution subordinated to these ministries. However, some Member States designated other bodies or agencies than the Ministries: for example in Luxembourg the General Public Prosecutor's Office and in Sweden the Social Insurance Agency carry out the functions of the Central Authority. Moreover, some Member States (the Netherlands and Latvia) designated an independent public maintenance enforcing body (the Office for International Legal Protection of Children in the Czech Republic) or a specific Minister or Ministers (the Lord Chancellor in England and Wales and the Scottish Ministers in Scotland).[139]

Most of the Central Authorities designated by the Member States were already designated under other Union legislation (eg the Brussels IIa Regulation)[140] or international conventions in family matters (eg the Hague Child Abduction Convention, the Hague Convention on Inter-country Adoption or the Hague Convention on Protection of Children). As an exception from this general rule, Latvia designated the Maintenance Guarantee Fund for the purposes of the Maintenance Regulation whereas the Ministry of Justice has been the Central Authority within the framework of other international conventions in family matters. With the exception of Italy all of the designated Central Authorities have longstanding experience in dealings with maintenance cases.

b. Central Authority Functions under the Maintenance Regulation

Under the Maintenance Regulation, Central Authorities have to perform a wide range of functions covering the whole application procedure.[141] The provisions of Articles 49 to 58 of the Maintenance Regulation essentially follow Articles 4 to 12 of the 2007 Hague Child Support Convention[142] and are divided into general (Article 50 of the Maintenance Regulation) and specific functions (Article 51 of the Maintenance Regulation).

[138] By virtue of Art 49(3) of the Maintenance Regulation Member States have to communicate the designated authorities including their contact details to the European Commission. This obligation is repeated by Art 71(1)(d). The information has to be updated regularly in order to facilitate cross-border cooperation.

[139] See the Civil Jurisdiction and Judgments (Maintenance) Regulations 2011, SI 2011/1484, Sch 1, para 2. The functions in England and Wales are in practice exercised by the Reciprocal Enforcement of Maintenance Unit (REMO), which is an associated office of the Ministry of Justice, G Smith, 'The Recognition and Enforcement of Maintenance Orders under the EU Maintenance Regulation: An Overview' (2012) *Family Law* 39, 41.

[140] Council Regulation (EC) 2201/2003 of 27 November 2003 concerning jurisdiction and the recognition and enforcement of judgments in matrimonial matters and the matters of parental responsibility [2003] OJ L338/1 (Brussels IIa Regulation).

[141] Recital 31. See also L Walker, 'From Brussels I and the Maintenance Convention to the Maintenance Regulation' (2013) *Nederland Internationaal Privaatrecht* 167, 168.

[142] P Beaumont, 'International Family Law in Europe–The Maintenance Project, the Hague Conference and the EC: A Triumph of Reverse Subsidiarity' (2009) *Rabels Zeitschrift für ausländisches und internationale Privatrecht* 509, 516. For a detailed comparison of the provisions on cooperation see Curry-Sumner (n 122) 611ff.

In some matters, in particular regarding access to and transmission and use of information, the European instrument goes further than the Hague instrument.[143] Moreover, regular meetings in the framework of the European Judicial Network (Article 60 of the Maintenance Regulation) are intended to strengthen cooperation between the Central Authorities.

Apart from an investigative role, the Central Authority under the Maintenance Regulation provides support and may act on behalf of the maintenance creditor in (court) proceedings. It constitutes a positive development that applications through Central Authorities are also beneficial to the debtor.[144]

iii. Direct Communications

A third type of cooperation consists of direct contacts between officials and their counterparts in another state. Provisions on direct judicial communication have been introduced in several legal instruments in family law matters.[145] The advantages of this innovative cooperation are manifold. Using direct communication channels in individual cases saves time and money for the parties. In the framework of the Brussels IIa Regulation, every Member State must designate a liaison judge who shall promote and facilitate direct contact between the competent judges.[146] Solving legal issues on a direct bilateral basis could help to increase parties' acceptance and enhance mutual trust in the Member States' legal systems.[147] However, language barriers have given rise to severe problems and might lead to misunderstandings.

Given the advantages of direct communications between the officials involved it is regrettable that the Maintenance Regulation is lacking a provision allowing direct communications between courts of different Member States.[148]

iv. Conclusion

The foregoing overview has revealed that the cooperative framework in the international instruments in family law matters shows common features. The role of the Central Authority has been modified and reinforced over the past decades.[149] On the one hand the duties to be performed by Central Authorities have increased. At the same time the extensive responsibilities are described with greater precision.[150] On the other hand the organisational structure of the Central Authorities in the Member States seems to have improved. The vast majority of Member States have designated experienced institutions under the Maintenance Regulation. The increasing number of responsibilities underlines the significance of Central Authorities as 'major players' in the cross-border recovery of

[143] Beaumont (n 142).

[144] Art 56(2) of the Maintenance Regulation.

[145] Eg Council Regulation (EC) 2201/2003 of 27 November 2003 concerning jurisdiction and the recognition and enforcement of judgments in matrimonial matters and the matters of parental responsibility [2003] OJ L338/1 (Brussels IIa Regulation).

[146] E Carl and M Menne, 'Verbindungsrichter und direkte richterliche Kommunikation im Familienrecht' (2009) *Neue Juristische Wochenschrift* 3537, 3538.

[147] Ibid 3537, 3542.

[148] P Reuß, in R Geimer and R Schütze (eds), *Internationaler Rechtsverkehr in Zivil- und Handelssachen* (Munich, CH Beck, 2011) Art 1 para 13.

[149] See also Borrás (n 126) 134ff; del Carmen Seoane de Chiodi (n 126) 65ff.

[150] Art 51 of the Maintenance Regulation, Art 6 of the Hague Child Support Convention.

maintenance and responds to the internationalisation of families and changes in society.[151] However, as has been examined, the Authorities designated under the Maintenance Regulation vary across the European Union. Consequently, each Authority is embedded in a different legal environment, which complicates uniform application.[152] Regarding the working methods of Central Authorities a wider use of information technologies can be detected, which accelerates case handling.[153]

All in all, aspects of sovereignty have decreased for the benefit of administrative cooperation taking into account the parties' interests. The Maintenance Regulation is another example of a certain shift from traditional pure private international law techniques to instruments extensively governing administrative procedures.[154]

C. Functions Performed by the Central Authorities

The effectiveness of the Regulation depends on the Central Authorities' operating effectiveness. Especially in maintenance cases, which involve long-term relationships, Central Authorities fulfil fundamental functions for reaching effective and swift solutions. If, for example, a Central Authority only consists of little more than a post office box, it cannot handle maintenance cases effectively. In this respect it seems to be fruitful to analyse the different strategies and procedures of Central Authorities when performing their functions as described in the Regulation (Articles 50 to 53 of the Maintenance Regulation).

i. Locating the Debtor or Creditor

One of the main challenges in the cross-border recovery of maintenance consists of locating the debtor. It involves a disproportionate effort for the maintenance creditor to obtain information on the debtor's whereabouts.

Concerning the procedure to locate the debtor or the creditor some differences between the Member States can be detected. In some Member States (inter alia in Austria, the Czech Republic, Luxembourg and Sweden) the Central Authority has direct (electronic) access to pertinent registers such as the population register or the social security register. In other

[151] W Duncan, 'Future Developments in International Family Law with Special Emphasis on Cross-border Child Protection' in K Boele-Woelki et al (eds), *Convergence and Divergence in Private International Law: Liber Amicorum Kurt Siehr* (Zürich et al, Schulthess, 2010) 221, 224.

[152] *Cf* Curry-Sumner (n 118) 192.

[153] Art 12(7) of the 2007 Child Support Convention obliges Central Authorities to employ the most rapid and efficient means of communication at their disposal. In the context of information technology, it is also worth mentioning the INCADAT and INCASTAT databases operating under the Abduction Convention. Those databases contain a compilation of national case law. Regarding maintenance cases, the iSupport system will introduce an electronic case management system. For an overview of the iSupport system see: C Parra Rodríguez, 'De la cooperación administrativa a la era de los formularios' (2008) *Anuario Español de Derecho Internacional Privado* 217, 221. For the current status of the development of iSupport see Hague Conference Update (2013) *International Family Law* 85 and Philippe Lortie, ch 17 of this volume. For the use of IT in maintenance matters see P Lortie, 'The Development of Medium and Technology Neutral International Treaties in Support of Post-Convention: Information Technology Systems—The Example of the 2007 Hague Convention and Protocol' (2008) *Yearbook of Private International Law* 359.

[154] Borrás (n 126) 150 characterises this development as 'fenómeno de la administrativización del Derecho Internacional Privado'; H van Loon, 'The Increasing Significance of International Co-operation for the Unification of Private International Law', in T de Boer (ed), *Forty Years On: The Evolution of Postwar Private International Law* (Deventer, Wolters Kluwer, 1990) 101.

Member States (eg in Hungary, Ireland, Poland and Portugal), the Central Authority has to contact specific authorities which will provide the necessary data. In view of accelerating the processing of maintenance cases a direct electronic access to the relevant data seems to be an appropriate solution. Nevertheless, safeguard mechanisms are required in order to prevent any misuse of data.

ii. Obtaining Information on the Debtor's Income

In the majority of Member States, information concerning the debtor's income can be obtained through Social Security Registers, the Land Registers[155] and with the help of other public authorities such as the Road Traffic Department or the Register of Enterprises.[156] Due to particularities of the Member States' internal law, problems may arise when requesting information on the debtor's bank account since this information can only be disclosed on the basis of a court order.[157] The Portuguese Central Authority has no legitimacy to take the necessary measures directly, so it depends on cooperation with other authorities holding the relevant data. Some Central Authorities have direct electronic access to certain registries, for example, the land registry or taxation databases.[158] In one Member State (Estonia) this matter falls within the competence of the bailiffs. Other Member States make use of a system of intermediaries to be contacted by the Central Authority. For example, in Finland, assistance is provided by the Social Welfare Authorities, which can access several national registers.[159]

iii. Encouraging Amicable Solutions

There are different practices in the Member States with regard to encouraging amicable solutions. In some Member States (eg in Austria, Estonia and Poland) amicable solutions are promoted by courts or by legal representatives (as is the case in Ireland). Conversely, in other Member States the Central Authority plays a decisive role by addressing the debtor, either directly or through intermediary bodies, and calling for voluntary payments.[160] In Finland, for example, the Central Authority requests the Social Welfare Authorities which are able to reach an agreement between the parties with similar force and effect as a judicial decision.

iv. Assistance in Establishing Parentage

It has to be pointed out that in many Member States there is no or very little experience in dealing with requests for assistance in establishing parentage.[161] Only one Member State (UK—England and Wales) has already dealt with numerous requests in this regard. Again, the strategies in the Member States are manifold. There are Member States in which the

[155] Eg in Austria and Cyprus.

[156] Latvia.

[157] Problem reported by Cyprus.

[158] Czech Republic and Lithuania.

[159] In Greece, the Central Authority can communicate with taxation services through the competent Public Prosecutor's Office. In Hungary, the Central Authority requires data from the National Chamber of Bailiffs. The territorially competent bailiff will collect the requested data from several databases.

[160] Inter alia in the Czech Republic, Finland, Germany, Hungary, Italy, Luxembourg, Malta, the Netherlands, Portugal, Slovak Republic, Slovenia, and England and Wales.

[161] Cyprus, Ireland, Italy, Latvia, Luxembourg, Poland and Slovakia.

Central Authority tries to achieve a voluntary acknowledgement of paternity with the help of other authorities such as the Social Welfare Board.[162] Other forms of assistance consist in providing legal information or providing the applicant with the necessary contact details of laboratories.[163] In other Member States the Central Authority does not provide such assistance, since this matter is dealt with by the court.[164]

v. Power of Attorney (Article 52 of the Maintenance Regulation)

Regarding the power of attorney the Member States' experiences are diverse. Some Central Authorities do not represent the applicant in judicial proceedings[165] or do not have any practical experience until now.[166] In other Member States (eg in the Czech Republic, Germany and Luxembourg) the Central Authority has experience in acting on behalf of the applicants or at least certain categories of applicants such as creditors under the age of 21 or those with limited means. In Finland, it depends on the type of claim whether the applicant is represented by the Central Authority or not. In cases regarding recognition and enforcement the Central Authority acts on behalf of the applicant whereas in cases concerning the establishment of maintenance the applicant is represented by a lawyer. According to the German implementing act, the Central Authority shall be deemed to be authorised to represent the applicant in judicial and extrajudicial proceedings.[167]

D. Identified Problems

The problems identified by the Central Authorities operating under the Maintenance Regulation in the first year of its application are categorised below. Given the limited experience of some Central Authorities[168] and the limited number of court cases in the first year of the Regulation's application[169] the categorisation may not be complete.

i. General Problems of Cooperation

In general, cooperation between Central Authorities seems to meet expectations. Only one Member State[170] reported that no improvement or change in the work of Central Authorities could be noticed in comparison to acting only as a Receiving and Transmitting Agency under the New York Convention 1956. It has also been noted that some Member States are not yet familiar with the Regulation.[171]

162 This is the case in Finland.
163 Eg in Romania.
164 Eg in Austria, Ireland and Portugal.
165 Eg in Austria, Cyprus, Estonia and Ireland. In Portugal the Central Authority only represents applicants in the time before judicial proceedings.
166 Eg Malta, Poland, Romania, Slovakia, Slovenia and Sweden.
167 s 5(4) AUG 2011.
168 The lack of experience was emphasised by Greece, Hungary, Ireland, Lithuania, Luxembourg, Malta, Slovakia and Slovenia.
169 Only two Member States (Estonia and Germany) have reported any case law.
170 Czech Republic.
171 Reported by the Netherlands.

One general problem relates to language barriers which might cause misinterpretation.[172] Therefore, it would be helpful to agree upon one common working language to facilitate and accelerate cross-border communications. Moreover, indicating the language skills of the Central Authority employees on the European Judicial Atlas's website could improve cooperative efforts, building on the website of the Hague Conference, which partly indicates the respective language skills.

ii. Specific Problems of Cooperation

In relation to the federal system of Germany one Central Authority has encountered difficulties, since the German Central Authority can only handle applications if the applicant provides information on the federal state of the debtor's habitual residence.[173]

a. Forms

Several Member States pointed out that the forms annexed to the Regulation have caused operational problems. First, the wording of the forms appears to be unclear (eg in Annex VI, correlation between point 6.1 and 6.2).[174] Second, there are some technical problems since it is impossible to print the standard forms in the language first used as well as in the translated language. Since the form in Annex VI cannot be completed electronically both by the transmitting court and the Central Authority, it has been suggested that the form be split into Part A and Part B. The user-friendliness of the existing forms could also be improved, for example by a facility that allows the names and contact details of the Central Authority[175] to be supplied automatically or providing forms in a format different from HTML.[176]

Moreover, a few Member States (especially Austria and Germany) have suggested creating an additional standard form for the statement of arrears. A working group has been set up in the framework of the Central Authority meetings whose purpose is to develop such a form. As regards the forms, one Member State[177] has also recognised that not using Annexes VI and VII has caused delays.

b. Lack of Information

Another problem that has arisen consists in applications submitted on the basis of vague or insufficient information, especially regarding the debtor's whereabouts.[178] Cooperation by preliminary inquiries in accordance with Article 53(1) of the Maintenance Regulation could improve the situation and accelerate the recovery of maintenance.[179]

Some Member States have stated that requests for specific measures according to Article 53 of the Maintenance Regulation are often lacking substantive grounds.[180] In their view,

[172] Raised by Finland.
[173] This problem was encountered by the Latvian Central Authority.
[174] Problem raised by Austria.
[175] An example is the forms under Directive 2003/8/EC.
[176] Suggestion by England and Wales.
[177] England and Wales.
[178] Problem raised by Cyprus and Portugal.
[179] Proposed by Kurucz (n 124) 104.
[180] Problem reported by the Italian Central Authority.

it is not sufficient to state that the debtor is not paying maintenance to his or her child. Consequently, it could be useful to agree on minimum grounds to be presented.

c. Unclear Provisions of the Regulation

There are several provisions of the Regulation which have been misinterpreted. In particular, difficulties arose concerning the interpretation of the transitional provisions.[181] According to the original wording of Article 75(2)(a) of the Maintenance Regulation maintenance decisions issued in a Member State which has recently joined the European Union could have been recognised and enforced under the Maintenance Regulation though not falling within the scope of the Brussels I Regulation. The unclear wording of Article 75(2) of the Maintenance Regulation has now been resolved by means of a corrigendum procedure.[182] In addition, Article 75(3) of the Maintenance Regulation has caused difficulties insofar as it is unclear which time is decisive.[183]

Other provisions which have caused problems are Articles 20 and 28 of the Maintenance Regulation relating to the necessary documentation. Due to the particularities of some Member States' internal law, Article 51 of the Maintenance Regulation might also cause difficulties. For example, in Cyprus information as to a party's bank account can only be obtained by means of a court order. Moreover, Member States reported facing problems with regard to the provisions on legal aid as the scope of legal aid is more restrictive in some Member States and Central Authorities are not willing to provide legal aid to creditors over the age of 21.[184] The relationship between Article 53 and Article 56 of the Maintenance Regulation seems to be unsettled. It is unclear whether requests for specific measures are only admissible if no application under Article 56 of the Maintenance Regulation has been made.[185] The Polish Central Authorities have encountered difficulties in the interpretation of Article 62(2) of the Maintenance Regulation, namely as to whether the courts are only entitled to use the information obtained from Central Authorities internally or whether they can forward information to other national public authorities in order to facilitate the recovery of maintenance claims.[186]

d. Delegation of Certain Functions to Public Bodies

Some Member States have faced difficulties relating to the delegation of certain functions to public bodies in accordance with Article 51(3) of the Maintenance Regulation where such delegation has led to a complicated or unclear distribution of responsibilities.[187] Cooperation with Poland has been complicated since Poland has delegated certain Central

[181] Difficulties with transitional provisions were encountered by Estonia, Finland, Ireland, Italy, Portugal and Romania.

[182] Corrigendum to Council Regulation (EC) No 4/2009 of 18 December 2008 on jurisdiction, applicable law, recognition and enforcement of decisions and cooperation in matters relating to maintenance obligations [2013] OJ L 8/19.

[183] Problem raised by Hungary.

[184] Mentioned by the Czech Republic.

[185] Problematic relation identified by the German Central Authority. According to M Andrae, in T Rauscher (ed), *Europäisches Zivilprozess- und Kollisionsrecht-EuZPR/EuIPR* (Munich, Sellier, 2010) Art 53 para 1 the answer should be affirmative.

[186] Note from the Polish delegation to the Working Party on Civil Law Matters, Doc No 10966/12, available at www.register.consilium.europa.eu/pdf/en/12/st10/st10966.en12.pdf (accessed December 2013).

[187] Problem mentioned by Finland and Italy.

Authority functions to its 45 regional courts.[188] The absence of one single interlocutor has caused delays in handling maintenance cases with Poland.

E. Suggested Improvements

Although the system of cooperation through Central Authorities within the Maintenance Regulation seems to be the right way forward, it is a long way from solving all existing problems. Against the backdrop that each Central Authority is still embedded in its national legal context, national legal obstacles in the daily work of Central Authorities looks set to remain an unresolved issue. Any uniform operation in a European Union of 28 Member States is a very ambitious goal. However, it is very important to improve understanding of the Regulation's provisions by means of training, guidelines, manuals for good practice and bilateral or multilateral exchanges of experience.[189] It would also be useful to establish guidelines for completing the forms annexed to the Regulation. The guidance notes developed by the Austrian[190] and English[191] Central Authorities concerning the forms referred to in Annex VI might serve as examples.

A second major issue concerns information policy. Regularly updated information on national procedures and legislation in force contributes to a better mutual understanding. This information should be made available online through the website of the European Judicial Atlas. It would also speed up maintenance cases if information technology such as the iSupport system and electronic databases were used. Moreover, the employment of multilingual electronic databases would overcome language barriers and facilitate communication between Central Authorities.

[188] Mentioned by England and Wales.

[189] Suggested by Finland, Portugal and England and Wales. See also Walker (n 141) 174.

[190] Guidance in relation to the forms in Annexes II, IV, V and VI, available at www.justiz.gv.at/web2013/file/2c94848525f84a630130466991fa4435.de.0/unterhaltsverordnung.muster.kommentiert.pdf (accessed December 2013).

[191] Guidance notes for completing the form in Annex VI, available at www.justice.gov.uk/downloads/forms/ospt/remo-7-application-form-guidance.pdf (accessed December 2013) and guidance notes for completing the form in Annex VII, available at www.justice.gov.uk/downloads/forms/ospt/remo-8-application-form-guidance.pdf (accessed December 2013).

23

Love and Money: Problems of Characterisation in Matrimonial Property and Maintenance Matters in the European Union

CSONGOR ISTVÁN NAGY

I. Introduction

The chapter analyses, from an applicable law perspective, the property issues connected to the dissolution of marriage, in the context of the European Union (EU) Maintenance Regulation and the European Commission's Draft Regulation on the conflict of laws of matrimonial property. It examines the problems emerging from the differences between Member State laws in terms of thinking and conceptualisation, and analyses how these impact on matrimonial and maintenance matters. The chapter points out that the EU Maintenance Regulation and the Draft Matrimonial Property Regulation fail to appropriately settle the problems of characterisation entailed by the differences between civil law and common law legal systems.

In the EU, approximately 13 per cent of marriages are international.[1] In 2007, the EU saw the dissolution (through divorce or death) of approximately 500,000 international marriages. This figure is alarming, not (only) because it shows that everything that has a beginning has an end but because it calls for a comprehensive regulatory framework at the EU level. Different issues emerge in connection to the dissolution of marriage: for example, divorce, matrimonial property, maintenance, placement of the child, custody rights. Experience shows that today matrimonial property and maintenance are the most important driving forces in international matrimonial matters[2] and they are also

[1] Commission Staff Working Document Impact Assessment. Accompanying document to the Communication of the Commission 'Bringing legal clarity to property rights for international couples', Proposal for a Council Regulation on jurisdiction, applicable law and the recognition and enforcement of decisions in matters of matrimonial property regimes and the Proposal for a Council Regulation on jurisdiction, applicable law and the recognition and enforcement of decisions regarding the property consequences of registered partnerships, SEC (2011) 327 final, 8.

[2] TMC Asser Institute, 'Practical problems resulting from the non-harmonization of choice of law rules in divorce matters JAI/A3/2001/04, Final report' (The Hague, December 2002) 46–47, available at www.ec.europa.eu/civiljustice/publications/docs/divorce_matters_en.pdf (accessed January 2014).

powerful inducements for forum shopping. Although the question of divorce was also a very important inducement for several decades, as the marriage can be dissolved in all EU Member States,[3] this aspect of marriage law may appear to have lost much of its significance,[4] although there are still considerable differences between Member State laws (in certain countries some years of domiciliary separation is needed, while in others quick divorces are possible).

This chapter deals with the problem of characterisation in EU conflict of laws of the property issues related to marriage (or rather: divorce), in the context of the EU Maintenance Regulation,[5] the Commission's Draft Regulation on Matrimonial Property[6] and the EU Succession Regulation.[7] It analyses the questions induced by the diversity of Member State laws and makes some proposals.[8]

The first part of the chapter explores the problems of characterisation and the problem of context (interrelation) attached to matrimonial property, maintenance and succession. The second part deals with how party autonomy can obviate the problem of characterisation. The third part contains a summary and some proposals.

It is submitted that in the domain of family law EU conflicts instruments essentially ignore characterisation and interrelation problems emerging from the conceptual differences between civil law and common law. On the one hand, they disregard that common law matrimonial concepts cannot be pumped into civil law categories, thus leading to unresolvable issues when the matter has a connection to a common law jurisdiction; and four out of 28 Member States have a common law regime (Cyprus, England and Wales and Northern Ireland in the UK, Malta and the Republic of Ireland). On the other hand, EU instruments also fail to take into account that the rules on matrimonial property, maintenance and, to some extent, those on inheritance law are interrelated (ie they are shaped with reference to each other); thus, pulling these rules out of their context and applying them in a mixed manner may lead to over- or under-compensation. This problem is not tackled at all in EU private international law, although for conflicts lawyers it is certainly nothing new. Nevertheless, EU rules on spousal maintenance (the Hague Protocol of 23 November 2007 on the law applicable to maintenance obligations (the 2007 Hague Protocol)), through an escape clause,[9] enable the judge to adjudicate the question of maintenance on the basis of the law that was applied to matrimonial property. Although this escape clause was not adapted to the future rules on matrimonial property, it is hoped that courts will properly utilise it for tackling the problem of interrelation between matrimonial property and maintenance.

[3] The last Member State to introduce the possibility of divorce was Malta; on 28 May 2011, in a referendum a slight majority of the Maltese people voted for the legalisation of divorce.

[4] TMC Asser Institute (n 2) 44.

[5] Regulation 4/2009 of 18 December 2008 on jurisdiction, applicable law, recognition and enforcement of decisions and cooperation in matters relating to maintenance obligations [2009] OJ L 7/1.

[6] Proposal for a Council Regulation on jurisdiction, applicable law and the recognition and enforcement of decisions in matters of matrimonial property regimes COM (2011) 126 final.

[7] Regulation (EU) No 650/2012 of the European Parliament and of the Council of 4 July 2012 on jurisdiction, applicable law, recognition and enforcement of decisions and acceptance and enforcement of authentic instruments in matters of succession and on the creation of a European Certificate of Succession [2012] OJ L 201/107.

[8] See CI Nagy, 'El derecho aplicable a los aspectos patrimoniales del matrimonio: la ley rectora del matrimonio empieza donde el amor acaba' (2010) *Anuario Español de Derecho Internacional Privado* 511–29 (the paper was translated from English to Spanish by Professor Clara Isabel Cordero Álvarez).

[9] Art 5 of the 2007 Hague Protocol.

II. Problems of Characterisation and the Problem of Context

How much? 30! What is 30? What is how much?

Matrimonial matters contain a repository of problems of characterisation and context. The problems that emerge here are not new at all. It does not come as a surprise that most problems of characterisation emerge in the context of marriage and succession.

Since private international law deals with legal notions and not real life cases, it determines the law applicable to a legal question (matrimonial property, validity of the will, etc) and not to a real life matter. Hence, the matter at stake and the legal question are to be connected to each other; and this is the point where the problem of characterisation comes into the picture: legal systems have different structures and the same issue may come under different categories in the individual legal systems.

Furthermore, the individual rules of a legal system interact with each other; legal institutions are created in the context of a given legal system, taking into account the contextual legal notions. In terms of practice, the law of a country may be very generous in the field of spousal maintenance because it follows the principle of separation in the field of matrimonial property. Here, maintenance serves the purpose of compensating one of the spouses for the loss of the matrimonial status, while in community of property systems there is normally nothing to be compensated for, since assets are usually split between both spouses. Moreover, inheritance rules may also be shaped by considerations driven by matrimonial property: by way of example, the surviving spouse may inherit one part of the legacy simply because of the principle of separation of property; while the system of community of matrimonial property may warrant that the widow does not inherit ownership but some kind of life interest (usufruct). If the rules of different legal systems are taken out of their context and mixed in their application, this could lead to over- or under-compensation: although under most substantive laws there is no rose without thorns, conflicts law may lead to situations where the spouse gets only the roses or only the thorns.

A. Problems of Characterisation

The trouble with the institution of matrimonial property is that this is a civil law conceptual category and is unknown for common law.[10] Under civil law, the property questions related to the dissolution of the marriage are mainly two-fold: matrimonial property and maintenance.[11] While divorce relates to the dissolution of the marital bond, property issues are tackled under the heads of matrimonial property and maintenance. Matrimonial property is, in principle, an objective category where the property is divided in accordance with neu-

[10] See the Response of the Law Society of England & Wales and the Society of Trust & Estate Practitioners to the European Commission's Green Paper on Conflict of Laws in Matrimonial Property Regimes, 1. See also M Harding, 'The Harmonisation of Private International Law in Europe: Taking the Character out of Family Law' (2011) *Journal of Private International Law* 1, 5–7.

[11] Of course, other adjacent issues may arise, such as eg, placement of the child and child maintenance.

tral rules;[12] maintenance is based on the needs of the maintenance creditor. The 'financial provision orders' of the English judge do not fit this black and white world: they tackle both problems (ie matrimonial property and maintenance) but they are neither matrimonial property nor maintenance decisions. The raison d'être of this regime is that English law follows the separation of property approach,[13] hence, the breadwinner ends the marriage with a more considerable fortune than the spouse who kept the house warm (including doing the housework and bringing up the children). This unfairness was counter-balanced by the English judge by awarding generous maintenance and subsequently,[14] as a surrogate, by allotting one part of the husband's property to the wife.[15] Such judicial arrangements are normally much more generous than continental maintenance decisions because they are also meant to make up the 'loss' the spouse suffers on the matrimonial property side.

The civil law characterisation of common law matrimonial property arrangements is like the characterisation of mules; an obstinate question: are mules horses or donkeys? This question cannot be answered. Mules are half horse and half donkey. Hence, they are, at the same time, both horses and donkeys; and neither horses, nor donkeys.

The Court of Justice of the European Union (CJEU) faced this problem of characterisation in *Antonius van den Boogaard v Paula Laumen*[16] under the Brussels I Regulation.[17] An alleged maintenance creditor sought the recognition and enforcement of an English judgment that transferred one part of the husband's property to the wife. While maintenance came under the scope of the Brussels I Regulation and, hence, maintenance decisions were to be recognised and enforced accordingly,[18] matrimonial property was (and is) completely excluded from its purview.[19] The CJEU held that English 'money after divorce' judgments are mixtures of matrimonial property and maintenance; but the language of the judgment suggests that they are rather maintenance (at least this was the case in the matter at stake).

If so, the question emerged: are these claims left out of the future Regulation on Matrimonial Property? Although the UK is very unlikely to opt-in to the Regulation,[20] this will very probably have universal application;[21] accordingly, the civil law judge may face the above questions of characterisation when the provisions of the Regulation happen to point to, for example, English or Irish law.

[12] European civil law jurisdictions normally follow the pattern of community property. See B Rešetar, 'Matrimonial Property in Europe: A Link between Sociology and Family Law' (2008) *Electronic Journal of Comparative Law* 1 and 4–9, available at www.ejcl.org (accessed January 2014).

[13] Ibid 1, 3.

[14] See S Cretney, 'Trusting the Judges: Money After Divorce' (1999) *Current Legal Problems* 286, 288–89 and 293.

[15] Matrimonial Causes Act 1963. See Cretney (n 14) 286, 290.

[16] Case C-220/95 *Antonius van den Boogaard v Paula Laumen* [1997] ECR I-1147.

[17] Regulation (EC) 44/2001 of 22 December 2000 on jurisdiction and the recognition and enforcement of judgments in civil and commercial matters [2001] OJ L 12/1.

[18] Art 5(2) of the Brussels I Regulation.

[19] Ibid Art 1(2)(a).

[20] See Arts 1 and 2 of the Protocol on the position of the UK and Ireland in respect of the area of freedom, security and justice annexed to the Treaty on European Union (TEU) and to the Treaty on the Functioning of the European Union (TFEU).

[21] Art 21 of the Draft Regulation on Matrimonial Property.

B. Problems of Interrelation

The absence of a *lingua franca* in the field of the marriage's property questions also raises problems of interrelation, which leads us to the problem of substantive justice. Matrimonial property, maintenance and inheritance law are interrelated and shaped with reference to each other. One field may try to do away with the skimping of the other.

In civil law systems, maintenance provisions are normally less generous, because the spouses are expected to halve the property they earned during the marriage; likewise, the surviving spouse may not inherit after the other spouse, although usufruct and special arrangements may apply. For instance, in Hungarian law,[22] there is a community of property (or rather: community of gains) system, supplemented by tight-fisted maintenance and inheritance rules. The spouse receives maintenance only in case of need (the ex-spouse cannot support him or herself and this is not his or her fault).[23] Under succession law, the widow does not inherit anything if the deceased left issue; nevertheless, she acquires a widow's usufruct, which terminates if she passes away or gets married again.[24]

The rather tight-fisted English rules on matrimonial property are counter-balanced by generous financial orders and similarly bountiful inheritance provisions: the surviving spouse inherits the chattels, a statutory legacy of £250,000 (when the deceased left issue; failing this, the statutory legacy is £450,000)[25] and a life interest in half of what remains.[26]

The above phenomenon of interrelation may lead both to over-compensation and under-compensation. It is questionable whether a spouse who has received half of the matrimonial property under Hungarian, German, etc law can claim 'maintenance' on the basis of English law. Likewise, may the widow (who has acquired half of the common gains under Hungarian or German matrimonial property law) inherit under English law, where he or she also inherits the chattels and the rest up to £250,000 or £450,000?

C. Does EU Private International Law Tackle Problems of Characterisation and Interrelation?

Unfortunately, the Draft Regulation on Matrimonial Property settles neither the issue of characterisation, nor the problems of interrelation. The Draft Regulation is applicable to matrimonial property regimes[27] with the express exclusion of maintenance matters.[28] Article 2 defines the term 'matrimonial property regime' as 'a set of rules concerning the property relationships of spouses, between the spouses and in respect of third parties'.[29] This definition certainly covers common law financial arrangements without giving any

[22] In this paper, references to Hungarian Law refer to the status before the entry into force of the new Hungarian Civil Code on 15 March 2014.

[23] s 21 of the Hungarian Family Law Code.

[24] s 615 of the Hungarian Civil Code.

[25] s 46(1) of the Administration of Estates Act 1925; Family Provision (Intestate Succession) Order 2009 (SI 2009/135).

[26] See R Probert, *Family and Succession Law, England and Wales—International Encyclopaedia of Laws* (The Hague, Kluwer Law International, 2008) 199–200.

[27] Art 1(1).

[28] Art 1(3)(b).

[29] Art 2(a).

indication as to how to split common law 'financial provision orders' into matrimonial property and maintenance. Accordingly, one has to proceed from the hints in the ruling of the CJEU in *Antonius van den Boogaard v Paula Laumen*; this is, however, a shaky crutch.

Furthermore, the Draft Regulation does not even address the issue of interrelation. Although the judge might be granted some possibilities under the applicable substantive law (or laws) to exclude material injustice (ie under- or over-compensation), it seems to be an objectionable plight to force judges to resort to substantive law escape clauses to cure conflicts law imperfections. The civil law judge may use his or her discretion in respect of awarding and determining maintenance in order to counter-balance the tight-fisted or generous attitude of the matrimonial property regime. Nevertheless, this flexibility embedded in substantive law is far from being sufficient and it is certainly not meant to counteract problems caused by private international law. On the other hand, the 2007 Hague Protocol contains a feeble but viable escape clause that may be used for this purpose (see below).

Problems of characterisation and interrelation may be easily overcome by employing the same connecting factor to both questions; in such cases the conceptual dilemma loses its practical significance. This approach is followed, by way of example, by Hungarian private international law. Section 39 of the Hungarian Act on Private International Law treats the personal and property law relationships between the spouses as one unit and subjects them to the same connecting factors. Until the Maintenance Regulation's entry into force, the category of 'personal and property law relationships' embraced both matrimonial property and spousal maintenance.

If the two questions are not regulated uniformly, a further regulatory tool ensuring consistency is escape clauses. Though not dealing with family matters, the treatment of concurrent liability under the Rome II Regulation on Non-Contractual Obligations[30] provides a good example in this respect. If A causes damages to B and there is a pre-existing contract between them, B may have both a contractual and a delictual claim against A, provided the conditions of the two heads of damages are met (concurrent liability). Different laws approach this phenomenon differently: some laws enable the plaintiff to choose the form of liability he or she bases his or her claim on, others provide that the existence of a contract excludes the possibility of basing the claim on delictual liability. Accordingly, in French and Belgian law the plaintiff cannot found his or her case on delictual liability, if there is a pre-existing contract between the parties.[31] On the other hand, in Austrian, German and Hungarian law the plaintiff has the option of choosing his or her statement of claim's cause of action, with the obvious exclusion of double recovery.[32] In English tort law such a choice is, in principle, also possible, with some provisos.[33] The Rome II Regulation tackles the

[30] Regulation 864/2007 of 11 July 2007 on the law applicable to non-contractual obligations (Rome II) [2007] OJ L 199/40.

[31] C von Bar and U Drobnig et al, *Study on Property Law and Non-contractual Liability Law as they Relate to Contract Law* (SANCO B5-1000/02/000574, 2003) 205, available at www.ec.europa.eu/consumers/cons_int/safe_shop/fair_bus_pract/cont_law/study.pdf (accessed January 2014).

[32] For Austrian and German law, see ibid 206–07. For German law see also K Larenz and M Wolf, *Allgemeiner Teil des Bürgerlichen Rechts* (Munich, CH Beck, 1997) 355. For Hungarian law see G Eörsi, *Elhatárolási problémák az anyagi felelősség körében* (Budapest, KJK, 1962). However, the new Hungarian Civil Code effective as from 15 March 2014 provides in s 6:146 that compensation for damages caused during the execution of the contract can be claimed on the basis of the rules applicable to contractual liability.

[33] See *Hedley Byrne v Heller* [1964] AC 465; *Esso Petroleum Co Ltd v Mardon* [1976] QB 801; *Batty v Metropolitan Realisations Ltd* [1978] QB 554; *Midland Bank Trust Co Ltd v Hett Stubs & Kemp* [1979] Ch 384; *Henderson v Merrett Syndicates Ltd* [1994] 3 All ER 506. See also von Bar and Drobnig (n 31) 209–11.

problem of concurrent liability through inserting an escape clause in Article 4(3): '[w]here it is clear from all the circumstances of the case that the tort/delict is manifestly more closely connected with a[nother] country ..., the law of that other country shall apply'. Article 4(3) expressly refers to the problem of concurrent liability and enables the court to subject the delictual claim to the law governing the contract:[34] '[a] manifestly closer connection with another country might be based in particular on a pre-existing relationship between the parties, such as a contract, that is closely connected with the tort/delict in question'.[35]

In the field of family law, EU private international law employs none of the above tools, although a timid escape clause is provided for in respect to maintenance, which is, nevertheless, not adapted to the Draft Regulation on Matrimonial Property.

The EU legislator decided against treating matrimonial property and maintenance jointly. A special piece of legislation (the Maintenance Regulation) deals with all maintenance matters, including spousal maintenance, while this issue is expressly excluded from the scope of the Draft Regulation on Matrimonial Property.[36] Accordingly, different laws may be applicable to the question of matrimonial property and to that of maintenance.

As noted above, the Maintenance Regulation contains an escape clause, albeit no express reference is made to the problem of interrelation. The Draft Regulation on Matrimonial Property contains no such provision; this seems to be reasonable taking into account that in civil law systems matrimonial property is governed by 'objective' rules where the court has no discretion as to how to divide the spouses' community of property (albeit discretion certainly exists concerning the interpretation of these 'objective' rules). The Maintenance Regulation deals with the determination of the applicable law in Article 15, and refers to the 2007 Hague Protocol.[37] The 2007 Hague Protocol, in Article 3, provides that maintenance obligations, in principle, are governed by the law of the State where the maintenance creditor has his or her habitual residence, and in case the habitual residence changes, the law of the State of the new habitual residence shall be applied from the moment of the change. Article 5 contains an escape clause that enables the court to apply a law different from the maintenance creditor's habitual residence; the scope of this provision is broad: it applies to divorce and annulment cases equally.[38] Article 5 provides that

> in the case of a maintenance obligation between spouses, ex-spouses or parties to a marriage which has been annulled, Article 3 shall not apply if one of the parties objects and the law of another

[34] See Recital 14 of the Rome II Regulation.

[35] Art 4(3) of the Rome II Regulation. See CI Nagy, 'The Rome II Regulation And Traffic Accidents: Uniform Conflict Rules with Some Room for Forum Shopping—How So?' (2010) *Journal of Private International Law* 93, 102–03.

[36] Art 1(3)(b).

[37] The EU declared that it would apply the rules of the Protocol provisionally from the Maintenance Regulation's entry into force (18 June 2011) if the Protocol would not have entered into force by that date. Note that the 2007 Hague Protocol is not applicable in Denmark or the UK.

[38] Although the language of the Protocol does not exclude all uncertainty when it refers to the 'maintenance obligation between spouses, ex-spouses or parties to a marriage which has been annulled', as this could be interpreted also as if the terms 'spouses, ex-spouses or parties' all referred to the element of annulled marriage, the Protocol's Explanatory Report makes it unequivocal that the scope of Art 5 is broad. A Bonomi, 'Explanatory Report of the Protocol of 23 November 2007 on the Law Applicable to Maintenance Obligations' (The Hague, Permanent Bureau, 2009), 24. '[T]his provision of the Protocol is meant to be applicable not only to obligations between divorced or separated spouses, or spouses whose marriage has been annulled or declared void, but also to maintenance obligations between spouses during their marriage', ibid 24.

> State, in particular the State of their last common habitual residence, has a closer connection with the marriage. In such a case the law of that other State shall apply.

The above provision is capable of tackling the problem of interrelation but it is hardly perfect. First, it presumes that the parties are knowledgeable: it applies only 'if one of the parties objects'. In matrimonial matters this may not always be the case. Second, and more importantly, although the law of any State that has a closer connection with the marriage can be applied, the example given refers to 'the State of last common habitual residence'; a connecting factor that was abandoned by the Draft Regulation on Matrimonial Property. In one word, this provision was not adapted to the Draft Regulation; this, of course, would have been an impossible mission: the Draft Regulation was only a thought when the 2007 Hague Protocol was born.

In sum, the judge is granted the power to apply the same law to matrimonial property and maintenance in cases where the problem of interrelation warrants this and the claim for maintenance emerges simultaneous with or subsequent to the division of matrimonial property. Nevertheless, the two instruments are not fully adapted to each other: the Draft Regulation on Matrimonial Property favours the connecting factor of first common habitual residence (in the absence of party choice), while the 2007 Hague Protocol's escape clause mentions the connecting factor of last common habitual residence, albeit the power of the judge is not restricted in this regard and he or she may apply the law of any country that is more closely connected to the marriage.

The spouses may use their freedom under party autonomy to make the same law applicable to these questions. The 2007 Hague Protocol's and the Draft Regulation's provisions on party autonomy are in accord with each other; Article 8 of the 2007 Hague Protocol provides that the parties may subject the question of maintenance to 'the law designated by the parties as applicable, or the law in fact applied, to their property regime'. Furthermore, the laws that can be chosen by the spouses under the Draft Regulation on Matrimonial Property and under the 2007 Hague Protocol converge. This is relevant in the unlikely case where an agreement on maintenance is concluded before reaching a compromise on matrimonial property. Under Article 16 of the Draft Regulation on Matrimonial Property, the spouses may choose one of the following laws: law of the common habitual residence, law of the habitual residence of one of the spouses, or the law of the nationality of one of the spouses. Under Article 8 of the 2007 Hague Protocol, the maintenance creditor and debtor may stipulate one of the following laws: law of the habitual residence of one of the spouses, the law of the nationality of one of the spouses, or the law governing the matrimonial property, divorce or legal separation.[39]

All in all, it seems that the problems of context cannot be solved in general but they may warrant the discretion of the judge. It is also to be taken into account that the decisions on the above issues (division of matrimonial property and maintenance) are often not rendered in the same procedure. In certain legal systems, the spouse may claim maintenance both before and after the dissolution of the marriage and the division of the matrimonial property. All these problems suggest that the property relations between the spouses should be subjected to the same law, thus ensuring a coherent approach and avoiding under- and

[39] Note that Art 7 of the 2007 Hague Protocol deals with the designation of the law applicable for the purpose of a particular proceeding.

over-compensation. On the other hand, the achievement of this goal seems not to be realistic; hence, the second best solution is to enable the judge, through escape clauses, to subject matrimonial property and maintenance to the same law in cases where this is justified.

Currently, EU private international law, through a feeble escape clause, enables courts to take the problem of interrelation properly into account; nevertheless, this provision is not adapted to the Draft Regulation on Matrimonial Property. Furthermore, the parties can tackle this problem by the help of party autonomy (the provisions of the Draft Regulation on Matrimonial Property and the 2007 Hague Protocol enable this), although this seems to be far from sufficient, taking into account that European couples utilise this possibility only rarely.

III. Party Autonomy: Does it Help to Overcome the Problems of Characterisation and Interrelation?

> I promise to be true to you in good times and in bad, in sickness and in health. I will love you and honour you all the days of my life ... By the way: under which law shall we divorce?

Party autonomy is a universal panacea in conflicts law.[40] It ensures legal certainty and triggers the assumption that the law freely chosen by the parties is the proper law, which has the closest connection to the matter; otherwise, why would the parties (it is assumed that they act rationally) agree to the application of a law that does not meet this requirement?

Party autonomy is crucial to marriage contracts.[41] If the parties cannot choose the law applicable to the marriage contract, they run the risk that the agreement would be void or unenforceable under a law that may (suddenly and surprisingly) turn out to be applicable at the end of the day. The following case gives an insight into the uncertainties faced by international marriage contracts.

A court in Hungary had to adjudicate the legal effects of a marriage contract concluded in Switzerland.[42] The parties, both Hungarian citizens, married in Switzerland and subsequently concluded a marriage contract. The contract provided that the spouses chose the separation of property regime ('Gütertrennung') on the basis of section 247 (and subsequent sections) of the Swiss Civil Code (ZGB).

Under Swiss marriage law the general regime is community of gains ('Errungenschaftsbeteiligung'); briefly, the earnings acquired during the marriage are common property, while the assets that belonged to one of the spouses before the contraction of the marriage remain individual property; roughly speaking, this is the system followed by Hungarian law as well.[43] Nevertheless, the spouses may opt for other property regimes: community of property and separation of property. Under the community of

[40] On the functions of party autonomy in international family and succession law see CI Nagy, 'What Functions may Party Autonomy have in International Family and Succession Law? An EU Perspective' (2012) *Nederlands Internationaal Privaatrecht* 576, available at SSRN: www.ssrn.com/abstract=2232192 (accessed January 2014).

[41] On party autonomy in international family and succession law, see ibid 576.

[42] Case No 1-H-PJ-2009-732. See CI Nagy, *Private International Law in Hungary* (The Hague, Kluwer Law International, 2012) 110–11.

[43] ss 196–220 ZGB.

property regime ('Gütergemeinschaft') the marriage, in principle, unites the property of the spouses.[44] Under the separation of property regime ('Gütertrennung') the properties of the spouses are completely separated.[45]

The Hungarian court had to adjudicate the legal consequences of the above marriage contract concluded in Switzerland. The Court of Appeal held that the contract was formally valid, since it was prepared by a notary and as such it was to be recognised in Hungary as a public deed on the basis of the Apostille Convention.[46] The Court also established that Hungarian law was applicable as the law of the spouses' common citizenship.

When examining the marriage contract's substantive validity, the Court of Appeal came to the conclusion that it was void; it established that

> those agreements meet the substantive requirements of martial property contracts [in Hungarian: 'házassági vagyonjogi szerződés'], which, besides referring to the general principles, rules of the property regime chosen by the spouses, settle their property relations with complete elaboration. … The agreement between the deceased and the defendant … does not meet this requirement because it states only in general and as a principle that the spouses manage, use and dispose of their properties themselves; it does not contain concrete provisions on property relations departing from the Code on Family Law. Accordingly, the agreement does not amount to a marital property contract in accordance with Section 27(2) of the Code on Family Law; thereby, it is not capable of arranging the property relations of the spouses differently from the provisions of the Code on Family Law.

Hence, the Court applied the rules of the Hungarian Code on Family Law on matrimonial property, which provide that the spouses' community of property, in principle, covers what they acquired during the marriage; the assets antedating the marriage remain individual property. The Court refused to follow some kind of 'choice in a substantive sense' approach (in German: 'materiellrechtliche Rechtswahl'), that is, to apply the rules of the foreign law as if they were contractual provisions, thus incorporating them into the agreement.

The limits of party autonomy relate to the external effects of the matrimonial relationship (third parties). Since matrimonial property normally entails *in rem* effects, the relevance of third party interests is comparable to property law; here, the external projections (the protection of the rights of third parties) can mainly be reduced to two aspects: public notice and the effect of the change of the applicable regime on third parties. Contrary to conflicts rules containing objective connecting factors (which are applicable irrespective of the parties' will), the parties' choice may remain secret and trigger surprise effects. Likewise, the change of the applicable law (either via a new agreement on the applicable law or due to the change of the circumstances) could be detrimental to the creditor's interests, especially if these possibilities are abused by the debtor.

The Draft Regulation on Matrimonial Property ensures the parties' right to choose the applicable law both prior to and during the marriage. At first glance it may seem that the parties' options to choose the applicable law during the marriage are more limited than before it. Article 16 provides that the spouses may choose from the following laws: (a) the law of common habitual residence, (b) the law of the habitual residence of one of the spouses, (c) the law of the nationality of one of the spouses. The relevant moment is the time when the choice is made. Although the Regulation mentions this criterion solely in points (b) and

[44] Ibid ss 221–246.
[45] Ibid ss 247–251.
[46] Hague Convention Abolishing the Requirement of Legalisation for Foreign Public Documents 1961.

(c) ('at the time this choice is made'), it can reasonably be assumed that this is also applicable to point (a). Article 18 deals with the case when the spouses make a choice subsequent to the conclusion of the marriage: the spouses may make a choice during the marriage both where they concluded no ante-nuptial agreement and where they did (ie they may choose a law different from the one initially chosen). At this stage, the spouses may opt either for (a) the law of the habitual residence of one of the spouses, or (b) the law of the nationality of one of the spouses (at the time this choice is made). Although the spouses' common habitual residence is not mentioned at this point, it is covered by point (a). If the spouses have a common habitual residence, this serves, *per definitionem*, also as the individual habitual residence of each spouse. As a corollary, Articles 16 and 18, as a matter of practice, apply the same connecting factors.

The Draft Regulation on Matrimonial Property effectively tackles the troubles attached to the retrospective effects of the change of the applicable law by the parties. If the spouses agree to subject their matrimonial relations to a law different from the one that has been applicable, this change during the marriage applies, in principle, only for the future, though the spouses may provide otherwise. Nevertheless, if the spouses take advantage of the latter freedom, 'the retrospective effect may not affect the validity of previous transactions entered into under the law applicable hitherto or the rights of third parties deriving from the law previously applicable'.[47]

Unlike retrospective effects, the Draft Regulation does not tackle the problem of public notice on the law applicable to matrimonial property. If the spouses do not reveal their choice, potential creditors may run the risk of surprise effects. Although the introduction of a common registrar of marriage contracts emerged in the Commission's initial plans,[48] this was dropped midway. It is, nonetheless, to be added that even in the absence of party choice potential creditors may not be aware of the applicable law if not enquiring about the circumstances of the spouses. For instance, if the spouses change their common habitual residence and move from England to Hungary where they are seeking credit from a bank, the latter may not be aware of the fact that the spouses' first common habitual residence was in England and, thus, their matrimonial property is governed by English law.[49]

Although, at first glance, this may seem to be merely a technical question, formal requirements lie at the heart of the rules on party autonomy; they may complicate easy matters. Hence, the introduction of uniform rules in this question would have been beneficial. In the absence of uniform rules the court or other authority in charge of deciding on the property of the spouses may not be spared the burden and cost of identifying the applicable law and

[47] Art 18.

[48] Green Paper on conflict of laws in matters concerning matrimonial property regimes, including the question of jurisdiction and mutual recognition COM (2006) 400 final, 4 and 9.

[49] Art 17(1) of the Draft Regulation on Matrimonial Property. It is to be noted that Art 35 of the Draft Regulation addresses effects in respect of third parties:

> 1. The effects of the matrimonial property regime on a legal relationship between a spouse and a third party are governed by the law applicable to matrimonial property regimes under the terms of this Regulation. 2. However, the law of a Member State may provide that the law applicable to the matrimonial property regime may not be relied on by a spouse in dealings with a third party if one or other has their habitual residence in the territory of that Member State and the conditions of disclosure or registration provided for in the law of that State are not satisfied, unless the third party was aware of or ought to have been aware of the law applicable to the matrimonial property regime. 3. The law of the Member State in which immovable property is located may provide for a similar rule to that laid down in paragraph 2 in respect of the legal relationship between a spouse and a third party in respect of that property.

controlling whether the marriage contract complies with this potentially foreign law. On the other hand, uniform formal requirements would be expedient because of creating a clear-cut situation, while such provisions are neither lengthy, nor politically sensitive.

Article 20 of the Draft Regulation deals with formal requirements applicable to the marriage contract (the formal requirements applicable to the parties' choice are covered by Article 19). Although Article 20 does not contain uniform rules as to formality, in Article 20(2) it establishes minimum standards: irrespective of the applicable law, 'the marriage contract must at least be set out in a document dated and signed by both spouses'. Accordingly, the agreement is to be made in writing and, contrary to normal contractual practice, cannot be concluded through the exchange of one-sided declarations: the agreement has to take the form of a single deed.

Apart from the above minimum requirements, the Draft Regulation does not introduce provisions as to the form of marriage contract but establishes rules on the applicable law.

> 1. The form of the marriage contract shall be that prescribed by the law applicable to the matrimonial property regime or by the law of the State where the contract is drawn up.
>
> …
>
> 3. If the law of the Member State in which the spouses have their common habitual residence at the time the marriage contract is concluded provides for additional formal requirements for that contract, these requirements must be complied with.

Accordingly, the law of the spouses' common habitual residence applies to the form of the marriage contract; the law governing matrimonial property (ie the law chosen by the spouses) and the place of the act come into picture only if their rules on formality are stricter. Furthermore, the language of Article 20 suggests that these two connecting factors are to be applied disjunctively: the contract is formally valid if it complies either with the *lex pro voluntate* or with the *lex loci actus*. Accordingly, the Draft Regulation does not enable the law enforcer (judge or administrative authority) to skip the learning of the foreign law or laws applicable to the form of the marriage contract and save related costs and time.

IV. Conclusions

Some conceptual aspects of the Maintenance Regulation and the Draft Regulation on Matrimonial Property were analysed above. The provisions have the virtue of introducing (with some exceptions) uniform provisions throughout the EU but fail to create a path through Europe's notional jungle: they do not address the issues of characterisation and interrelation.

Common law does not recognise the concept of matrimonial property; on the other hand, the judicial arrangements handling the property issues at the dissolution of the marriage settle jointly all the questions that in civil law jurisdictions are separated to matrimonial property and spousal maintenance. Furthermore, matrimonial property, maintenance and inheritance regimes are interrelated—a rule just in its domestic context may lead to over- or under-compensation when applied jointly with a foreign provision. By way of example, English maintenance law is said to compensate the spouse for what it lost under the matrimonial property heading (note that English matrimonial law follows the separation of property approach); on the other hand, there is no need for such counterbalancing in civil law, which normally follows the community of property approach and, thus, usually leaves the spouses with half of the gains made during the marriage. It may lead to overcompensation if the community of property rules of civil law are applied in combination with English rules on maintenance. Likewise, it may lead to under-compensation if the English separation of property approach is applied in combination with the tight-fisted maintenance rules of civil law: the spouse does not get half of the gains because he or she is expected to be entitled to maintenance, while he or she receives moderate maintenance because he or she is expected to be entitled to half of the gains.

The easiest way to solve the above problems would be to subject matrimonial property and maintenance to the same law; this would deprive the problems of characterisation and interrelation of their practical significance. Nonetheless, EU private international law opted for separating the conflicts regulation of these two issues and employs diverging connecting factors in this regard. The second best solution is the insertion of escape clauses. These are not clear-cut rules but vest in the judge the discretion of correcting unwelcome outcomes: the judge should be granted the right to apply the same law to matrimonial property and maintenance. Although the Draft Regulation on Matrimonial Property contains no such escape clause, the Maintenance Regulation (through the 2007 Hague Protocol) does contain such a way of escape, which is, nevertheless, not fully adapted to the Draft Regulation: the Draft Regulation (in the absence of party choice) points to the law of the first common habitual residence, while the 2007 Hague Protocol provides that the law of the country that is more closely connected to the marriage may be applied, 'in particular the State of the … [spouses'] last common habitual residence'. It can only be hoped that courts will use this escape clause to bring the decision on maintenance in line with the applicable matrimonial property regime. Furthermore, the spouses may utilise the possibilities derived from the freedom of party autonomy in order to subject matrimonial property and maintenance to the same law.

The Draft Regulation favours party autonomy and effectively protects the interests of third parties; nonetheless, it contains no provisions on providing public notice about the law applicable to matrimonial property. Furthermore, it would be expedient to establish uniform rules for the form of marriage contracts due to their high practical relevance and low political sensitivity.

Although party autonomy seems to be a perfect solution, in Europe it does not amount to settled practice. European couples seem not to care about matrimonial property while the marriage is working; and once it stops working it is normally too late to reach a compromise. Normally, this is the first point where, in practical terms, matrimonial law comes into the picture. This is not a surprise: we all know that the law of marriage starts where love ends.

24

Drawing a Demarcating Line between Spousal Maintenance Obligations and Matrimonial Property in the Context of the New Instruments of European Union Private International Law

MAARJA TORGA

I. Introduction

The need to characterise 'spousal maintenance obligations' as something different from 'matrimonial matters' has been an issue in European Union (EU) private international law since the 1968 Brussels Convention,[1] which applied to maintenance claims, but excluded claims concerning matrimonial property from its substantive scope of application.[2] The distinction introduced by the Brussels Convention has remained intact in the subsequent Community legislation as the rights in property arising out of matrimonial relationships have been excluded from the scope of application of the Brussels I[3] and the Maintenance Regulation,[4] and, according to Article 1(3)(b) of the Commission's proposal for an EU Regulation on matrimonial property regimes (the Proposal for Matrimonial Property Regulation),[5] maintenance obligations will be excluded from the scope of application of the future Matrimonial Property Regulation. However, it might not be so easy to draw a clear line between spousal maintenance questions on one hand and matrimonial property issues on the other when applying the EU private international law regulations. This is due to the fact that under the law of some Member States (England and Ireland) there is no legal concept equivalent to rights in property arising out of the marital relationship, which

[1] 1968 Brussels Convention on jurisdiction and the enforcement of judgments in civil and commercial matters [1972] OJ L299/32.

[2] See Arts 5(2) and 1(1) of the Brussels Convention.

[3] Council Regulation (EC) No 44/2001 of 22 December 2000 on jurisdiction and the recognition and enforcement of judgments in civil and commercial matters [2001] OJ L 12/1.

[4] Council Regulation (EC) 4/2009 of 18 December on jurisdiction, applicable law, recognition and enforcement of decisions and cooperation in matters relating to maintenance obligations [2009] OJ L 7/1.

[5] Proposal for a Council Regulation on jurisdiction, applicable law and the recognition and enforcement of decisions in matters of matrimonial property regimes, COM (2011) 126 final.

means that the distinction between matrimonial property and maintenance issues is not so easy to draw as might seem at first glance.[6]

The purpose of the present chapter is to give an overview of the possible methods of solving the characterisation problem of distinguishing between the matrimonial property issues and issues of maintenance in the context of the newer EU private international law instruments. More precisely, the Maintenance Regulation and the Proposal for Matrimonial Property Regulation are used as the main examples of competing legal rules dealing with similar issues in the most recent Union legislation. The chapter focuses only on spousal maintenance issues, although similar characterisation problems might arise in connection with the claims between partners of registered partnerships. It should be noted, however, that at the same time when the proposal on matrimonial property regimes was presented, the European Commission also presented a similar proposal for registered partnerships—the Proposal for a Council Regulation on jurisdiction, applicable law and the recognition and enforcement of decisions regarding the property consequences of registered partnerships.[7] Similarly with the Proposal for Matrimonial Property Regulation, all maintenance obligations are excluded from the scope of application of the future Regulation on registered partnerships. This may give rise to analogous characterisation problems in disputes involving registered partners in the future.

II. Autonomous Nature of the Terms 'Spousal Maintenance Obligation' and 'Matrimonial Property'

According to the case law of the Court of Justice of the European Union (CJEU), the provisions of EU law (including the provisions of the private international law regulations) must be given an autonomous and uniform interpretation, having regard to the context of these provisions and the objective pursued by the legislation in question, except if the provisions in question make express reference to the law of the Member States for the purpose of determining their meaning and scope.[8] Abiding by this principle, the CJEU has in several of its judgments interpreted autonomously the terms contained in the EU private international law instruments. This has, for example, been done in order to give meaning to the terms 'civil and commercial matters',[9] 'tort, delict or quasi delict'[10] and 'matters

[6] For an introduction to this problem, see further Máire ní Shúilleabháin, *Cross-Border Divorce Law Brussels II bis* (Oxford, Oxford University Press, 2010) 173–74; T Sverdrup, 'Maintenance as a Separate Issue—The Relationship between Maintenance and Matrimonial Property' in K Boele-Woelki (ed), *Common Core and Better Family Law in European Family Law* (Antwerp et al, Intersentia, 2005) 119–22.

[7] Proposal for a Council Regulation on jurisdiction, applicable law and the recognition and enforcement of decisions regarding the property consequences of registered partnerships, COM (2011) 127 final.

[8] Case C-116/11 *Bank Handlowy v Warszawie SA, PPHU 'ADAX'/Ryszard Adamiak v Christianapol sp.z o.o.*, judgment of 22 November 2012, para 49; Case C-396/09 *Interedil Srl, in liquidation v Fallimento Interedil Srl and Intesa Gestione Crediti SpA* [2011] ECR I-9915, para 42.

[9] See, eg, Case 29-76 *LTU Lufttransportunternehmen GmbH & Co KG v Eurocontrol* [1976] ECR 1541; Case 814/79 *Netherlands State v Reinhold Rüffer* [1980] ECR 3807; Case C-266/01 *Préservatrice foncière TIARD SA v Staat der Nederlanden* [2003] ECR I-4867.

[10] See, eg, Case 189/87 *Athanasios Kalfelis v Bankhaus Schröder, Münchmeyer, Hengst and Co et al* [1988] ECR 5565; Case C-167/00 *Verein für Konsumenteninformation v Karl Heinz Henkel* [2002] ECR I-8111; Case C-228/11 *Melzer v MF Global UK Ltd*, judgment of 16 May 2013.

relating to a contract'[11] as found in various provisions of the Brussels I Regulation and the old Brussels Convention.

No express reference to the national law of the Member States has been made in the relevant provisions of the EU private international law instruments in order to give meaning to the terms 'maintenance obligations' or 'matrimonial property'. Hence, the terms 'maintenance obligations'[12] and 'matrimonial property'[13] as used in the European private international law instruments should also be treated as autonomous concepts in order to achieve predictability and harmony of judgments between the courts of different Member States. In addition, the autonomous nature of the term 'maintenance obligation' has explicitly been stressed by Recital 11 of the Maintenance Regulation which provides a general definition for maintenance obligations covering obligations arising from 'family relationship, parentage, marriage or affinity'. Although Article 1(3)(b) of the Proposal for the Matrimonial Property Regulation excludes all 'maintenance obligations' from the scope of the Proposal, Recital 12 of the Proposal specifically refers to 'maintenance obligations between spouses'. Thus, the term 'spousal maintenance obligations' should also be regarded as a separate (autonomous) concept compared to a more general category of 'maintenance obligations' in the context of the European private international law instruments. No reference to the autonomous nature of the term 'matrimonial property' has been given in the text of the Proposal for Matrimonial Property Regulation itself, but as stressed in the Commission's explanatory memorandum accompanying the text of the proposal: 'the notion of "matrimonial property regime" must be given an autonomous interpretation and embrace considerations of both the spouses' daily management of their property and the liquidation of the property regime as a result of the couple's separation or the death of one of the partners'.[14]

In order to give meaning to autonomous concepts found in EU private international law instruments, the starting point should be the CJEU case law. Although the CJEU is yet to distinguish between matrimonial property issues on one hand and questions of maintenance on the other in the context of the EU Maintenance Regulation and the future Matrimonial Property Regulation, the existing case law of the CJEU can still be used in order to predict how these autonomous terms found in these instruments would be defined by the CJEU. The relevant case law of the CJEU to be taken into account at this point is the case law made under the old Brussels Convention.

[11] See, eg, Case 34/82 *Martin Peters Bauunternehmung GmbH v Zuid Nederlandse Aannemers Vereniging* [1983] ECR 987; Case 9/87 *SPRL Arcado v SA Haviland* [1988] ECR 1539; Case C-26/91 *Jakob Handte & Co GmbH v Traitements Mécano-chimiques des Surfaces SA* [1992] ECR I-3967; Case C-265/02 *Frahuil SA v Assitalia SpA* [2004] ECR-1543; Case C-419/11 *Česká spořitelna, a.s. v Gerald Feichter*, judgment of 14 March 2013.

[12] See Art 1(1) of the Maintenance Regulation; Recital 11 and Art 1(3)(b) of the Proposal for Matrimonial Property Regulation; Art 5(2) of the Brussels Convention; Art 5(2) of the Brussels I Regulation (note that, according to Art 68(1) of the Maintenance Regulation, this provision has been replaced by the provisions of the Maintenance Regulation).

[13] See Art 1(1) of the Proposal for a Matrimonial Property Regulation. See also Art 1(2)(a) of the Brussels I Regulation and Art 1(1) of the Brussels Convention, which both refer to 'rights in property arising out of a matrimonial relationship'.

[14] See (n 5) 6.

III. Case Law of the CJEU on the Concepts of 'Maintenance Obligations' and 'Matrimonial Property'

The CJEU has so far shed light on the meaning of the autonomous terms of 'matters of maintenance' and 'matrimonial property' only in the context of the old Brussels Convention. The first time this was done was back in 1979 in *de Cavel v de Cavel (No 1)*,[15] but this case was shortly followed by *de Cavel v de Cavel (No 2)*[16] and later by *Van den Boogaard v Laumen*.[17]

In *de Cavel v de Cavel (No 1)* a husband had applied for a divorce in a French court, which had authorised, as a protective measure, a freezing order covering the wife's assets located in Germany. The husband had then applied in Germany for the declaration of enforcement of the French decision. Since the German Bundesgerichtshof was not sure whether the matter fell within the substantive scope of the Brussels Convention, that is, whether the French freezing order related to the 'rights in property arising out of a matrimonial relationship' (which would have been excluded from the scope of the Brussels Convention by its Article 1(1)), it decided to ask for a preliminary ruling from the CJEU. The CJEU confirmed that judicial decisions authorising provisional or protective measures in the course of proceedings for divorce fall under the exception found in Article 1(1) of the Brussels Convention if those measures concern or are closely connected with either questions of the status of the persons involved in the divorce proceedings or proprietary legal relations resulting directly from the matrimonial relationship or the dissolution thereof. Although *de Cavel v de Cavel (No 1)* was not instrumental in developing any precise criteria for distinguishing between 'maintenance obligations' and 'matrimonial matters' in the context of EU private international law instruments, it is important that in that case the CJEU gave, for the first time, an autonomous meaning to the term 'rights in property arising out of a matrimonial relationship' as used in the old Brussels Convention. The CJEU did so by giving a definition, independent from any reference in the relevant national laws, to the property arrangements, which could fall under the matters dealing with 'rights in property arising out of a matrimonial relationship'.[18] This autonomous interpretation should similarly be applied when interpreting the corresponding terms found in the EU Maintenance Regulation and the future Matrimonial Property Regulation.

The second case where the CJEU paid any thought to the concepts of 'maintenance obligations' and 'matrimonial property' was *de Cavel v de Cavel (No 2)*. In that case, the French court had awarded the wife an interim maintenance allowance pending divorce. The wife had then sought to enforce the French decision in Germany. However, since the Bundesgerichtshof was again not sure whether the matter fell within the substantive scope of the Brussels Convention, it asked for a preliminary ruling from the CJEU. More precisely, the CJEU was invited to answer whether an ancillary order of maintenance could fall

[15] Case 143/78 *de Cavel v de Cavel (No 1)* [1979] ECR 1055.

[16] Case 120/79 *de Cavel v de Cavel (No 2)* [1980] ECR 731.

[17] Case C-220/95 *Van den Boogaard v Laumen* [1997] ECR I-1147.

[18] According to the CJEU, the term 'rights in property arising out of a matrimonial relationship' includes not only property arrangements specifically and exclusively envisaged by certain national legal systems in the case of marriage but also any proprietary relationships resulting directly from the matrimonial relationship or the dissolution thereof, see Case 143/78 *de Cavel v de Cavel (No 1)* [1979] ECR 1055, para 7.

under the scope of the Brussels Convention if the primary issue in dispute (divorce) fell outside the scope of that Convention. The CJEU held that, for the purposes of the Brussels Convention, the ancillary claim of maintenance comes under its scope even when the primary dispute (granting a divorce) relates to the status of persons, which under Article 1(1) of the Brussels Convention would fall outside the scope of the said Convention.[19] This conclusion is of course again not very helpful in distinguishing between the two ancillary claims to divorce—those of the maintenance and division of property. What is more important, however, is that, as a side issue, the CJEU, in *de Cavel v de Cavel (No 2)*, gave a definition of the rules on maintenance. Namely, the CJEU held, based on the relevant rule at issue in that case,[20] that such rules are: 'concerned with the financial obligations between the former spouses after divorce, are fixed on the basis of their respective needs and resources and are in the nature of maintenance'. Looking at this definition it seems that the needs and resources of the spouses are the relevant criteria for deciding whether a particular rule should be characterised as having the nature of maintenance as opposed to a rule relating to matrimonial property. This can be concluded based on the wording 'fixed on the basis of their respective needs and resources' as used by the CJEU in this definition. Naturally, one might want to conclude that the same criteria should be used in order to distinguish not only between the 'rules' on maintenance and the 'rules' on matrimonial property, but also between the relevant 'matters' and 'obligations'.

In *de Cavel v de Cavel (No 1)* and *de Cavel v de Cavel (No 2)* the relevant national rules in the background of the case were the national rules of Germany and France. These are both civil law jurisdictions, where the problem of distinguishing between the matrimonial property issues and maintenance issues is much clearer compared to England and Ireland.[21] In contrast, in *Van den Boogaard v Laumen* the CJEU was finally faced with a legal system where the distinction between matters of maintenance and matters relating to rights in property arising out of a matrimonial relationship was less clear.[22]

In *Van den Boogaard v Laumen* the CJEU had to give general guidelines on how to decide whether an English financial order should be characterised as the order of maintenance as opposed to the order for the division of property. It was held that an order for a lump sum and transfer of ownership comes under the scope of maintenance as long as the purpose of the award is to ensure the former spouse's maintenance.[23] As explained by the CJEU, on divorce, an English court may, by the same decision, regulate both the matrimonial property relationships of the parties and matters of maintenance. In order to decide whether the order is in its essence a maintenance order, the distinction between those aspects of the decision which relate to rights in property arising out of a matrimonial relationship and

[19] Case 120/79 *de Cavel v de Cavel (No 2)* [1980] ECR 731, paras 9 and 12.

[20] The case concerned Art 271 of the French Civil Code providing for certain 'compensatory payments' for the spouse, ibid para 5.

[21] It should be noted that some civil law states (France, Spain) seem to be aiming at a 'clean break' on divorce as well and therefore provide payments which also have a compensatory and redistributive function. For an overview of the relevant maintenance rules in different Member States, see R Fucik, 'Unterhaltsanprüche in der Europäischen Union—Eine tabellarische Übersicht' (2007) *Interdisziplinäre Zeitschrift für Familienrecht* 97; see also D Martiny, 'Current Developments in the National Laws of Maintenance: A Comparative Analysis' (2012) *European Journal of Law Reform* 65.

[22] On the problem of characterising 'maintenance orders' in English private international law, see J Fawcett, J Carruthers and Sir Peter North, *Cheshire, North & Fawcett Private International Law* 14th edn (Oxford, Oxford University Press, 2008) 1056–57.

[23] Case C-220/95 *Van den Boogaard v Laumen* [1997] ECR I-1147, para 27.

those which relate to maintenance should be made, having regard in each particular case to the specific aim of the decision rendered.[24] According to the CJEU, the aim of each decision should be deduced from the reasoning of the decision—if the reasoning of the decision shows that a provision (sum) awarded is designed to enable the spouse to provide for him or herself or if the needs and resources of each spouse are taken into consideration in the determination of the amount, the decision will solely be concerned with maintenance.[25] Basing the characterisation of the judgment only on its reasoning is somehow contradictory, since in divorce proceedings the needs and resources of each spouse could be taken into consideration even when making orders for the division of matrimonial property. For example, where both parties are earning well, an order awarding a lump sum will frequently be intended as a division of assets rather than maintenance and should be characterised accordingly.[26] Whether the maintenance was awarded as a lump sum or as a periodic payment is irrelevant according to the CJEU, since the choice of method of payment by the original court cannot alter the nature of the aim pursued by the decision.[27] Likewise, the fact that the decision, of which enforcement is sought, also orders ownership in certain property to be transferred between the former spouses cannot call into question the nature of that decision as an order for the provision of maintenance—the aim is still to make provision, by means of a capital sum, for the maintenance of one of the former spouses.[28] Hence, the CJEU seems to suggest that the prevailing nature of the claim (or decision) is that which should be decisive from the point of view of characterising claims as relating to maintenance as opposed to matrimonial property.

In conclusion, although general in its nature, the criteria developed by the CJEU seem to make the needs and resources of the spouses the core issue in maintenance matters and the distributive function of the property rules as the main aim in the matrimonial property cases. These conclusions can be supported further when analysing the general objectives of the relevant rules in question.

IV. General Objectives of EU Private International Law Rules on Maintenance and Matrimonial Property

In order to characterise certain legal relationships between the spouses as falling under the autonomous concept of 'spousal maintenance obligations', a functional approach as a generally accepted method of characterisation in EU private international law should be

[24] Ibid para 21.

[25] Ibid para 22. However, the distinction might be hard to draw in practice due to the intermingling of matrimonial property and maintenance on one hand and multi-purposiveness in substantive law on the other. See U Magnus and P Mankowski (eds), *Brussels I Regulation* (Munich, Sellier, 2007) 162.

[26] Case C-220/95 *Van den Boogaard v Laumen* [1997] ECR I-1147, Opinion of Advocate General Jacobs, para 80.

[27] Ibid para 24. Although the judge deciding upon the recognition or enforcement of the judgment should in principle always have the right to inspect whether a matter comes under the scope of the relevant instrument (Brussels Convention, Brussels I Regulation, Maintenance Regulation), the CJEU puts the actual burden on the original judge who resolved the case on its merits and possibly also resolved the jurisdictional dispute under the relevant European instrument, since the reasoning of this judge will be decisive for the latter conclusion on whether the decision falls under the scope of the relevant instrument.

[28] Ibid para 25.

adopted.[29] The CJEU itself has traditionally adopted a systematic and functional approach in order to give meaning to autonomous concepts contained in EU private international law instruments.[30] As stressed by the CJEU, in order to interpret the terms found in the EU instruments autonomously, regard should be had to the context of the provision and the objective pursued by the legislation in question.[31] The same principle should be applied when giving meaning to the rules referring to (spousal) 'maintenance obligations' or 'matrimonial property' as used in the various provisions of the EU Maintenance Regulation and the Proposal for a Matrimonial Property Regulation.

A. General Objectives of the EU Rules on Maintenance

As is the case with all the other EU private international law instruments, the general objective of the Maintenance Regulation is to promote the aims which the EU has set for itself in the field of private international law.[32] This means that the primary objective of the Maintenance Regulation is maintaining and developing an area of freedom, security and justice, in which the free movement of persons is ensured. The original Proposal for the Maintenance Regulation explains more specifically what the Maintenance Regulation seeks to achieve—according to the Proposal, the main objective of the Regulation is to eliminate all obstacles which prevent the recovery of maintenance within the EU.[33] This in turn entails that the free circulation of judgments should be the primary concern of the Regulation, which can be best illustrated by the abolition of *exequatur* provisions that the Regulation contains in its Article 17. Abolition of *exequatur* in maintenance cases means first, that the decisions awarded in the Member States bound by the 2007 Hague Protocol[34] (ie all Member States, except Denmark[35] and the UK)[36] are recognised in other Member States without any

[29] On characterisation according to the functional approach in the context of European private international law, see R Baratta, 'The Process of Characterisation in the EC Conflict of Laws: Suggesting a Flexible Approach' (2004) *Yearbook of Private International Law* 155. Baratta argues that the decisive element in characterisation is to take into account the function of each conflict of law rule to be characterised and that the characterisation should rely on common legal concepts and values expressed in the uniform general principles shared by the Member States, taking into account the principal objectives of the EC conflict of laws. See ibid 158 and 168.

[30] See, eg, Case 150/77 *Bertrand v Paul Ott KG* [1978] ECR 1431, paras 14–16; Case C-26/91 *Jakob Handte & Co GmbH v Traitements Mécano-chimiques des Surfaces* SA [1992] ECR I-3967, para 10; Case C-89/91 *Shearson Lehmann Hutton Inc v TVB Treuhandgesellschaft für Vermögensverwaltung und Beteilligungen mbH* [1993] ECR I-139, para 13.

[31] Case C-396/09 *Interedil Srl v Fallimento Interedil Srl, Intesa Gestione Crediti SpA* [2011] ECR I-9915, para 42.

[32] Based on Art 81(1) TFEU, judicial cooperation in civil matters having cross-border implications is based on the mutual recognition of judgments and of decisions in extrajudicial cases. See the Treaty on the Functioning of the European Union (Consolidated Version) [2012] OJ C 326/1.

[33] Proposal for a Council Regulation on jurisdiction, applicable law, recognition and enforcement of decisions and cooperation in matters relating to maintenance obligations, COM (2005) 649 final 3.

[34] Hague Protocol of 23 November 2007 on the Law Applicable to Maintenance Obligations www.hcch.net/index_en.php?act=conventions.text&cid=133 (accessed January 2014).

[35] Note that Denmark has notified the Commission of its decision to implement the contents of the Maintenance Regulation to the extent that this Regulation amends Brussels I Regulation. See the Agreement between the European Community and the Kingdom of Denmark on jurisdiction and the recognition and enforcement of judgments in civil and commercial matters [2009] OJ L 149/80.

[36] On 8 April 2010 the European Community declared that its Member States shall be bound by the Hague Protocol by virtue of its conclusion by the European Community. For the purpose of the declaration, the term 'European Community' does not include Denmark and the UK. Ireland has chosen to take part in the adoption of the decision to be bound by the Hague Protocol. See the Council Decision of 30 November 2009 on the conclusion by the European Community of the Hague Protocol of 23 November 2007 on the Law Applicable to Maintenance Obligations [2009] OJ L 331/17.

special procedure being required and without any possibility of opposing their recognition; and secondly, that such decisions are enforced in the other Member States without the need for a declaration of enforceability as opposed to the previous regime found in the Brussels I Regulation, which preceded the Maintenance Regulation.

The objective of achieving mutual recognition and enforcement of maintenance decisions and the effective step that the Maintenance Regulation takes for securing such aim by abolishing the *exequatur* proceedings should be borne in mind when reaching any conclusions as to the scope of the Maintenance Regulation. Securing the free flow of judgments means that the burden on the Member States to provide for maintenance creditors is lightened. When maintenance creditors are able to effectively claim maintenance from maintenance debtors, the burden on Member States to offer social benefits to maintenance creditors is lessened, which is a consideration that should be taken into account when interpreting the relevant rules in question.[37] Thus, there is, at least from an economic point of view, a good case for interpreting the scope of the Maintenance Regulation as widely as possible in cases where the judgment creditor is in need. Hence, it can be argued that the autonomous concept of 'maintenance obligations' should also be construed widely.

At this point one might of course argue that the economic considerations should not play a crucial role when deciding upon the recognition and enforcement of foreign judgments within the EU as it is true that in judicial proceedings other concerns, such as the rights and interests of the parties (and more specifically the rights of maintenance debtors in maintenance cases), should outweigh purely economic considerations. However, interpreting the scope of the Maintenance Regulation widely would not in itself automatically mean that the interests of creditors or the economic interests of the Member States would somehow be unfairly preferred to the interests of the maintenance debtors for the following reasons.

First, maintenance is awarded by the courts of the Member States under the substantive national rules, which although not yet harmonised,[38] generally take into account the rights and interests of maintenance debtors. For example, the courts of the Member States will often be applying a law that does not award maintenance beyond an amount that would

[37] Eg in the context of the negotiations for the Hague Maintenance Convention of 23 November 2007 the United States supported a policy of rather generous legal assistance provisions for maintenance creditors. One of the reasons for this policy was the belief that the state benefits in the long run if maintenance creditors are helped to secure maintenance from the maintenance debtors as this reduces the need for the state to support the child (the usual maintenance creditor). See P Beaumont, 'International Family Law in Europe—The Maintenance Project, the Hague Conference and the EC: A Triumph of Reverse Subsidiarity' (2009) *Rabels Zeitschrift für ausländisches und internationales Privatrecht* 509, 517. For the Maintenance Convention, see the Hague Conference on Private International Law, 'Convention of 23 November 2007 on the International Recovery of Child Support and Other Forms of Family Maintenance' www.hcch.net/index_en.php?act=conventions.text&cid=131 (accessed January 2014).

[38] As with most other fields of private law in Europe, the harmonisation of substantive rules on maintenance has so far not occurred and will probably not occur in the near future, as the EU has chosen to harmonise the private international law rules instead of substantive rules. However, it is worth mentioning a positive initiative made by the Commission on European Family Law (CEFL). The Commission has published non-binding principles on maintenance law, which, although not meant to be considered as a model law, aim to bestow the most suitable means for the harmonisation of family law within Europe, see K Boele-Woelki et al, *Principles of European Family Law Regarding Divorce and Maintenance Between Former Spouses* (Antwerp, Intersentia, 2004) 3.

leave the debtor below his or her subsistence level.[39] If, on the other hand, the applicable foreign substantive law to be applied in a maintenance dispute in the courts of a Member State deprives the debtor of his or her subsistence, the public policy defence as applicable in the Member States[40] by Article 13 of the Hague Protocol would probably bar the application of such law to the extent that it reduced the debtor to an impoverished level. In addition, the other choice-of-law rules in the Hague Protocol provide for certain protection for the creditor as well. For example, under Article 4(3) of the Hague Protocol, if the maintenance creditor has seized the competent authority of the State where the debtor has his or her habitual residence, the law of the forum shall apply. In addition, under Article 5 of the Hague Protocol either of the spouses can request the court that the law of another State, in particular the State of the last common habitual residence, be applied if that State has a closer connection with the marriage. These rules are intended to protect both parties from unfairness. Thus, the protection of maintenance debtors is an issue which does not necessarily have to be addressed in the context of the recognition and enforcement provisions in the Maintenance Regulation, but can instead be left to be dealt with as a matter of substantive justice or choice of law justice.

Secondly, the Maintenance Regulation itself contains safeguards for maintenance debtors, which balance any preference for maintenance creditors that the wide interpretation of the 'maintenance obligations' might entail. Such safeguards are found in Article 19 of the Maintenance Regulation under which a defendant who did not enter an appearance in the Member State of origin of the decision has the right to apply for a review of the decision before the competent court of that Member State if he or she was not served with the document instituting the proceedings or an equivalent document in sufficient time and in such a way as to enable him or her to arrange for his or her defence or he or she was prevented from contesting the maintenance claim by reason of *force majeure* or due to extraordinary circumstances without any fault on his or her part; provided that he or she has not failed to challenge the decision when it was possible for him or her to do so. Thus, the argument for interpreting the scope of the Maintenance Regulation as widely as possible in favour of maintenance creditors is not rebutted by the need to protect the interests of maintenance debtors since the interests of the debtors have already been taken into account by the substantive rules in the phase where the decision was awarded and by private international law rules in the possible review proceedings of the maintenance decisions. Hence, there is an argument in favour of interpreting the scope of the Maintenance Regulation more widely as covering also those spousal obligations, which lie on the borderline of maintenance and matrimonial property issues, provided that one of the spouses would lack the necessary means if the relevant decision would not be enforced.

From a purely formalistic point of view one might of course ask why the economic status of parties should play any role in giving meaning to the terms found in the EU

[39] According to the report by the CEFL this is the case in eg Austria, Bulgaria, Denmark, England and Wales, Finland, France, Germany, Ireland, Portugal, Spain and Sweden. For a general overview of Member State practices in calculating maintenance and on the right of the debtor to retain a certain amount for his or her own subsistence, see the CEFL publication on the matter by K Boele-Woelki, B Braat and I Sumner (eds), *European Family Law in Action vol II: Maintenance Between Former Spouses* (Antwerp, Intersentia, 2003) 261–326.

[40] As explained earlier, only Denmark and the UK are not bound by the Hague Protocol. They both apply the *lex fori* to maintenance cases and thereby ensure appropriate protection for the debtor.

Regulations. Although private international law rules may favour certain litigants as a group (eg children in parental responsibility disputes[41] or maintenance creditors[42] who are generally considered as being in a weaker position and therefore deserving extra protection) no preference should be given to particular litigants depending on their economic or social status as private international law rules, like any other legislation, should be neutral towards the interests of particular litigants. Thus, while the objective of releasing States from the burden of supporting maintenance creditors is relevant when deciding whether certain groups of persons (spouses, children, vulnerable adults) should be covered by the Maintenance Regulation, the characteristics of specific litigants should not be decisive in order to determine whether a dispute falls under the scope of the Maintenance Regulation. This in turn means that there must be some other criterion which determines when the Maintenance Regulation is applicable to a particular spousal dispute and that looking only at the general objectives of the Maintenance Regulation does not help to solve the question of how to distinguish between (spousal) 'maintenance obligations' and 'matrimonial property' in borderline cases in the context of the Maintenance Regulation and the proposed Matrimonial Property Regulation.

B. General Objectives of the Proposed EU Rules on Matrimonial Property Regimes

Similar to the Maintenance Regulation, the general objective of the proposed Regulation on matrimonial property regimes is to guarantee the mutual recognition of decisions rendered in the Member States.[43] It could be argued that if the spouse is awarded a fair proportion of the marital property, the State would not be required to provide subsistence for the spouse and thus the scope of the proposed Matrimonial Property Regulation should, similarly to the Maintenance Regulation, be interpreted widely in order to bring more cases within the scope of application of the proposed Regulation and its provisions on the mutual recognition and enforcement of decisions. However, there are two counter-arguments against this proposition.

First, the Proposal for Matrimonial Property Regulation does not, contrary to the Maintenance Regulation, foresee any abolition of *exequatur*, which means that the rules

[41] The Brussels IIa Regulation jurisdiction rules on parental responsibility matters (Arts 8–15) constitute an example of how the European legislator has chosen to rely on the interests of children when choosing appropriate connecting factors (such as the child's habitual residence) for parental responsibility cases. See the Council Regulation (EC) 2201/2003 of 27 November 2003 concerning jurisdiction and the recognition and enforcement of judgments in matrimonial matters and the matters of parental responsibility, repealing Regulation (EC) 1347/2000, [2003] OJ L338/1.

[42] Eg the EU private international rules of jurisdiction have generally chosen to prefer maintenance creditors by allowing them to sue, among other places, in the courts of the place where the maintenance creditor is domiciled (Art 5(2) of the Brussels I Regulation) or habitually resident (Art 5(2) of the Brussels I Regulation, Art 3(b) of the Maintenance Regulation). Similarly, the Hague Protocol has chosen to protect maintenance creditors by providing a general conflict of laws rule in favour of the law of the State of the habitual residence of the maintenance creditor (Art 3(1) of the Hague Protocol), which presumably is the law which is most familiar to the maintenance creditor. For a critical assessment of these preferences, see GE Schmidt, 'Equal Treatment of the Parties in International Maintenance Cases' in J Basedow et al (eds), *Private Law in the International Arena From National Conflict Rules Towards Harmonization and Unification, Liber Amicorum Kurt Siehr* (The Hague, TMC Asser Press, 2000) 657–60.

[43] Commission, Proposal on Matrimonial Property Regimes (n 5) Recital 27.

on recognition and enforcement of decisions would be less beneficial for creditors than the relevant rules contained in the Maintenance Regulation. Thus, it would be better for creditors at least to treat the borderline decisions as relating to the (spousal) 'maintenance obligations' rather than to 'matrimonial property' in order to release the Member States from the possible duties of providing for the spouses who cannot have their decisions enforced in the other Member States.

Secondly, while in maintenance cases the maintenance creditor cannot manage without the relevant financial support from the maintenance debtor or failing that, from the state, in matrimonial property matters, neither of the spouses is necessarily in a weaker position. According to Article 2(a) of the Proposal for Matrimonial Property Regulation, the term 'matrimonial property regime' refers to the set of rules concerning the property relationships of spouse, between the spouses and in respect of third parties. Although the term 'property relationship' has been left undefined, it is apparent that it focuses on the property rights of the spouse instead of the economic and social needs of the spouse.[44] While the purpose of maintenance as a legal and social concept is to provide for the party who lacks the necessary financial means to get by in his or her everyday life, the purpose of the division of matrimonial property is to uphold the ownership rights of the spouse or to compensate him or her for the contributions that he or she has made during the marriage in relation to the matrimonial property.[45] Thus, cases falling within the scope of the proposed Matrimonial Property Regulation lack the social urgency that maintenance cases present and, at least from the economic point of view, there is no need to interpret the scope of the proposed Matrimonial Property Regulation as widely as the scope of the Maintenance Regulation.

However, as was the case with the Maintenance Regulation, analysing the general aim of the Proposal for the Matrimonial Property Regulation does not entirely solve the question of how borderline cases should be characterised. Therefore, guidance has to be sought elsewhere. Since a comparative approach is often used in EU private international law in order to solve characterisation problems,[46] it is worth looking at how the concepts of 'maintenance' and 'matrimonial property' are treated in different Member States. At this point two jurisdictions (Germany and England) will be used as providing the most distinctive examples on how the questions of maintenance and marital property have been addressed in different Member States, which have different legal traditions and approaches

[44] For a comparison (according to the Schlosser Report the 'rights in property' in the meaning of the Brussels Convention include all rights of administration and disposal—whether by marriage contract or statute) of property belonging to the spouses, see the Report on the Convention on the Accession of the Kingdom of Denmark, Ireland and the United Kingdom of Great Britain and Northern Ireland to the Convention on jurisdiction and the enforcement of judgments in civil and commercial matters and to the Protocol on its interpretation by the Court of Justice [1979] OJ C 59/71, 89.

[45] According to Sverdrup the main purpose of the marital property rules is distributive and the main purpose of the maintenance rules is supportive. However, both sets of rules interact on a general level—they are both aimed at allocating property on divorce and providing for the future needs of the spouses. See Sverdrup (n 6) 119, 120. Similarly, Martiny refers to the concepts of support, sanction, solidarity and compensation for losses as the main aims of the maintenance rules in D Martiny, 'Divorce and Maintenance Between Former Spouses—Initial Results of the Commission on European Family Law' in K Boele-Woelki (ed), *Perspectives for the Unification and Harmonisation of Family Law in Europe* (Antwerp, Intersentia, 2003) 545–46.

[46] Eg the CJEU has often stressed the need to take into account the general principles stemming from the corpus of national legal systems when giving meaning to various autonomous terms in the EU regulations. See Case C-420/97 *Meletis Apostolides v David Charles Orams and Linda Elizabeth Orams* [2009] ECR I-3571, para 41; Case C-172/91 *Volker Sonntag v Hans Waidmann, Elisabeth Waidmann and Stefan Waidmann* [1993] ECR I-1963.

to the institutions of marital property and maintenance. These jurisdictions are also chosen since they represent different schemes of enforcement of judgments. Namely, Article 17 of the Maintenance Regulation contains a rule on the abolition of *exequatur* which does not apply to the English maintenance orders, but does apply to German maintenance orders. Whether this difference should play a role in the characterisation of the common autonomous term (spousal) 'maintenance obligations', should become clearer if the institutions of maintenance and matrimonial property are compared in the legal systems of which only the first one is bound by the Hague Protocol (and the concurrent abolition of *exequatur* provisions).

V. Distinction between Spousal Maintenance and Matrimonial Property Issues in German Law

Germany is bound to apply the Maintenance Regulation, which means that the German courts will need to turn to the Maintenance Regulation and the concurrent Hague Protocol in order to resolve the questions of jurisdiction, applicable law and recognition and enforcement of judgments in international spousal maintenance disputes. The German courts of course should not proceed from their own national law in order to characterise the terms found in these instruments as these rules contain autonomous definitions independent from the *lex fori*. However, if not decisive, the treatment of maintenance and matrimonial issues in German domestic law would at least be a logical starting point for a German judge in order to give meaning to the autonomous concept of (spousal) 'maintenance obligations' or 'matrimonial property' as referred to in the new Maintenance Regulation and the proposed Matrimonial Property Regulation.

The term 'maintenance' is not expressly defined in German substantive family law. Section 1360a (1) of the German Civil Code (Bürgerliches Gesetzbuch (BGB))[47] creates the spouses' general obligation to maintain each other during the marriage as, according to this provision, the reasonable maintenance of the family includes everything that is necessary, depending on the circumstances of the spouses, to pay the costs of the household and to satisfy the personal needs of the spouses and the necessities of life of the children of the family entitled to maintenance. The word 'necessary' used in this provision should not be read as focusing on the level of subsistence of the spouse claiming maintenance,[48] but instead the purpose of the rule is to ensure that both spouses make contributions in order to attain the living standard which is deemed appropriate for the family in each particular case. However, awarding maintenance depends nevertheless on the needs of the particular spouse even if such needs are higher than the minimum level of subsistence. Similarly, other specific maintenance provisions found in BGB proceed from the presumption that

[47] German Civil Code (Bürgerliches Gesetzbuch (BGB)) 1896 (Federal Republic of Germany).

[48] For the purposes of s 1360(a)(1) the entitled spouse does not have to be 'needy' (bedürftig), see B Weber-Monecke, in F Säcker and R Rixecker (eds), *Münchener Kommentar zum Bürgerlichen Gesetzbuch*, 6th edn (Munich, CH Beck, 2013) § 1360 para 6. Family maintenance under s 1360 is usually paid in kind and not owed in cash. Instead of the term 'neediness' (Bedürftigkeit), the term 'requirement' (Bedürfnis) or 'necessity' (Erforderlichkeit) is used in order to describe the precondition upon which the maintenance is owed, see B Heiß and W Born (eds), *Unterhaltsrecht Ein Handbuch für die Praxis*, 39th edn (Munich, CH Beck, 2011) ch 11 para 6.

the awarding of maintenance depends on the specific needs of the creditor, like the need for insurance for old age and for reduced earning capacity[49] or (in the case of post-divorce maintenance) for old age[50] or illness or infirmity,[51] which all make it impossible for the maintenance creditor to earn the necessary allowance by him or herself. The main purpose of the German post-divorce spousal maintenance rules is to enable the spouse to live independently from the other spouse.[52] Thus, the main criterion for deciding whether a spouse has a right to maintenance before or after the divorce is the necessity of the said spouse. Therefore, the German maintenance rules serve supportive rather than distributive or compensatory functions.

In contrast, German substantive rules on matrimonial property do not proceed from the necessity of the spouse as a relevant criterion when resolving the marital property dispute. Under the German statutory property regime the spouses live under the property regime of accrued gains,[53] unless they opt for the community of property regime upon which the property of the spouses would become the joint property of both spouses.[54] The statutory property regime of accrued gains means that the property of the spouses does not become the common property of the spouses. The same applies to the property that one of the spouses acquires after the marriage. However, the accrued gains that the spouses acquire during the marriage are equalised between the parties if the community of accrued gains ends.[55] Thus, the German rules on matrimonial property serve distributive[56] and compensatory[57] functions allowing the spouse who has stayed at home to care for the children to get his or her share from the income that the other spouse has earned during the marriage. In addition, since the equalisation of the accrued gains also depends on the behaviour of the spouses during the marriage, the rules on matrimonial property also serve a retributive function. For example, in order to determine the extent of the final assets of the spouse the following is taken into account: whether the spouse, after the beginning of the property regime made gratuitous dispositions by which he or she was not fulfilling a

[49] Eg if divorce proceedings are pending between the spouses, who are living apart, then maintenance, from the date when the proceedings are pending, also includes the costs of appropriate insurance for old age and for reduced earning capacity, s 1361(1) of the German Civil Code.

[50] Ibid s 1571.

[51] Ibid s 1572.

[52] See P Wendl and S Staudigl (eds), *Das Unterhaltsrecht in der familienrichterlichen Praxis. Die neuere Rechtsprechung des Bundesgerichtshofs und die Leitlinien der Oberlandesgerichte zum Unterhaltsrecht und zum Verfahren in Unterhaltsprozessen*, 7th edn (Munich, CH Beck, 2008) § 3 para 1.

[53] 'Accrued gains' means the amount of the property by which the final assets of the spouse exceed the initial assets. The term 'initial assets' refers to the assets which belong to the spouse at the beginning of the property regime after the deduction of liabilities. Assets which the spouse acquires after the beginning of the property regime as a result of death or with regard to a future right of succession, by donation or as advancements, are added to the initial assets after the deduction of the liabilities, to the extent that in the circumstances they are not to be seen as income. The term 'final assets' refer to the assets which belong to the spouse at the end of the property regime after the deduction of the liabilities. See ss 1373–1375 of the German Civil Code.

[54] Ibid s 1416(1).

[55] Ibid s 1363(2).

[56] The justification of an accrued gains regime is that in a marriage, which is based on the division of labour, the spouse who, in the interests of the family is not working full time and enabling to other spouse to work full time, should be entitled to fully participate in the division of the profit earned by the other, see E Koch's preliminary remark to § 1363 para 8, in F Säcker and R Rixecker (eds), *Münchener Kommentar zum Bürgerlichen Gesetzbuch*, 6th edn (Munich, CH Beck, 2013).

[57] Due to the distribution of roles in the family the spouse who stays at home is entitled to compensation for waiving his or her opportunity to work. See HG Bamberger and H Roth (eds), *Beck'scher Online-Kommentar BGB*, 20th edn (Munich, CH Beck, 2011) § 1363 para 12.

moral duty or showing regard for decency or whether he or she squandered property or performed acts with the intention of disadvantaging the other spouse.[58] Thus, the matrimonial property rules in German law serve rather different aims to the maintenance rules which are primarily supportive rather than distributive or compensatory. This means that the rules on matrimonial property are not based on the concept of the necessity of the spouse. Hence, there is a clear difference between the functions of the maintenance and matrimonial property rules in German substantive law and between the relevant criteria that these rules take into account in order to characterise financial claims that one of the spouses is making against the other.

The distinction in German substantive law between the functions of maintenance and matrimonial property rules has also been reflected by the German case law on the Brussels I Regulation. Article 5(2) of the Brussels I Regulation uses the term 'matters relating to maintenance', which was interpreted by the German Supreme Court (Bundesgerichtshof) in 2009 in a case[59] concerning a decision made by the English High Court in a spousal dispute. The English Court had (among other things) ordered the transfer of the rights under a life insurance policy as a security for the maintenance of one of the spouses, the payment of £213,055 as a lump sum and periodic payment of £24,600 per year for the maintenance of the spouse. Deciding upon the enforcement of the decision in Germany, the Bundesgerichtshof explicitly relied on the case law of the CJEU[60] and found that the English decision could not have been enforced under the Brussels I Regulation concerning the ordering of the lump sum of £213,055. According to the Bundesgerichtshof this was the issue, which dealt with the division of matrimonial property of the spouses and thus fell outside the scope of the Brussels I Regulation.[61] The Bundesgerichtshof proceeded to give guidelines on how the distinction between the maintenance and matrimonial property issues should be made. According to the Bundesgerichtshof, a maintenance duty is established when the performance that is granted by the decision secures the sustenance of the spouse or when the needs and means of both spouses are considered when awarding the maintenance.[62] In contrast, if the decision's purpose is to distribute the financial assets of spouses then the decision concerns the division of matrimonial property and not maintenance and cannot therefore be enforced under the Brussels I Regulation. Furthermore, the Bundesgerichtshof noted that characterising a decision as an award of maintenance is not questioned simply because part of the property is transferred from one of the spouses to the other. Such a decision can also be about the accumulation of capital, the purpose of which is to secure the sustenance of the other spouse. However, a clean break[63] between the

[58] s 1375(2) of the German Civil Code.

[59] Decision of the German Supreme Court (2009) *Familie Partnerschaft Recht* 541. The Bundesgerichtshof has been criticised for not asking for a preliminary ruling on the matter from the CJEU. See the case analysis by B Heiderhoff, 'Wann ist ein "Clean Break" unterhaltsrechtlich zu qualifizieren?' (2011) *Praxis des Internationalen Privat- und Verfahrensrechts* 156.

[60] See the case law described in 'C' of the present part.

[61] Art 1(2)(a) of the Brussels I Regulation.

[62] The Court had already reached similar conclusions in 2007, see the Decision of the German Supreme Court from 17 October 2007 BGH XII ZR 146/05.

[63] A 'clean-break' option means that the court orders the division of assets of the parties so that one spouse cannot be subject to any further claim by the other spouse. The benefits of such orders include the finality of decisions and financial certainty of the spouses. However, clean-break orders may be criticised for addressing only the events up to the time of the divorce, whereas the disadvantages to the spouses may be much more long lasting. On the advantages and disadvantages of clean-break orders as opposed to periodic payment orders of maintenance, see G Shannon, 'Clean-Break or Long-Term Payment of Maintenance' in K Boele-Woelki (ed), *Common Core and Better Family Law in European Family Law* (Antwerp, Intersentia, 2005) 103–17.

spouses, according to which all the financial matters are resolved between the spouses with one decision, goes beyond maintenance. Although the Bundesgerichtshof based its conclusions on how to characterise the term 'matters relating to maintenance' on the case law of the CJEU, the solution of the Bundesgerichtshof reflects the distinction found in German substantive law according to which the rules on maintenance and matrimonial property serve different functions with the rules of maintenance bearing a supportive function and the rules on matrimonial property bearing a distributive function.

VI. Distinction between Spousal Maintenance and Matrimonial Property Issues in English Law

Contrary to German law, English substantive law does not formally distinguish between property division and maintenance on divorce. In addition, the policies that English law follows when dealing with pre- and post-divorce maintenance vary from German law. Under the English domestic rules there are several procedures available for making financial orders while a marriage is still subsisting.[64] For example, under the Matrimonial Causes Act 1973[65] a spouse may apply to the court for a maintenance order on the ground that the other spouse has failed to provide reasonable maintenance for him or her during the marriage. There are several factors which the English courts must take into account when awarding such maintenance orders.[66] Among these are the financial needs, obligations and responsibilities which each spouse has or is likely to have for the foreseeable future, the standard of living enjoyed by the family before the breakdown of the marriage, the contributions which each spouse has made or is likely in the foreseeable future to make to the welfare of the family, including any contribution made by looking after the home or caring for the family and the conduct of each spouse, if that conduct is such that it would in the opinion of the court be inequitable to disregard it. Thus, the English rules regulating spousal maintenance prior to the divorce do not focus merely on the need of the maintenance creditor. On the contrary, the need of the spouse is only one factor amongst many to be taken into account when awarding maintenance.

The redistribution of property upon divorce has even more functions and underlying policies in English law compared to the provisions regulating the provision of maintenance during the marriage. The statutory powers of the courts to make financial orders[67] in divorce proceedings and the factors that the courts consider when making such orders are remarkably wide.[68] It has been stated that the general principles to be taken into account by the English courts when making financial awards are the 'need' of the spouse, 'compensation'

[64] For a general overview of these procedures, see J Masson, R Bailey-Harris and R Probert, *Cretney Principles of Family Law,* 8th edn (London, Sweet & Maxwell, 2008) 99–103; N Lowe and G Douglas, *Bromley's Family Law,* 10th edn (Oxford, Oxford University Press, 2007) 956–66.

[65] Matrimonial Causes Act 1973 (United Kingdom), s 27(a).

[66] Ibid s 25(2)(a)–(h).

[67] Under the Matrimonial Causes Act 1973 such orders may be made against the spouse and may include: unsecured periodical payments to the other spouse, secured periodical payments to the other spouse, lump sum payments to the other spouse, transfer of property to the other spouse or for the benefit of any child of the family etc. For a general overview of the powers of the court to award such orders, see Lowe and Douglas (n 64) 983–85 and 991–1018.

[68] Masson, Bailey-Harris and Probert (n 64) 340.

and 'sharing'.[69] In addition, other policies that English law seeks to protect in the redistribution of property upon divorce include the aim of supporting the spouse and the children, upholding respect for the marriage contract, upholding respect for the partnership of the parties, securing equality between the spouses and their equal opportunities after the divorce, and upholding the general interests of the State, such as saving public money.[70] Thus, unlike the German courts, the English courts enjoy wide discretion to take into account various policies and purposes when awarding financial orders upon divorce and there exists no clear cut divide between the issues of maintenance and matrimonial property found in German law when deciding upon the financial relations between the spouses upon divorce.[71]

The lack of a clear distinction between maintenance and matrimonial property orders in English domestic law has not stopped English courts from interpreting the autonomous terms 'maintenance' and 'matrimonial matters' in the context of EU private international law instruments. In the significant case of *Moore v Moore*[72] the Court of Appeal was faced with the need to distinguish between the issues of 'maintenance' and 'matrimonial property'.

Moore v Moore concerned an English couple who, after their move to Spain, had divorced in Spain. The (former) wife had then applied to the High Court of Justice in England for an order for financial relief against which the husband had submitted a counter application requesting that the English court refuse the wife's application on the basis that the proceedings on maintenance were already underway in Spain. The English High Court of Justice decided to grant the financial order requested by the wife, on the basis that the object of the husband's claim in the Spanish proceedings was not that of the claim for maintenance. The husband appealed and the Court of Appeal gave guidelines on how to distinguish between 'maintenance' and 'matrimonial property' issues.

Not surprisingly, the Court of Appeal based its reasoning on the case law of the CJEU. Based on this case law, the Court of Appeal began by stressing the autonomous nature of the term 'maintenance'.[73] The Court of Appeal then went on to clarify how to distinguish between maintenance and matrimonial property orders. First, the Court of Appeal stressed that the question of whether a payment of a lump sum or transfer of property may be in the nature of maintenance depended on whether it was intended to ensure the support of a spouse. Secondly, the payment of a lump sum or transfer of property which serves only the purpose of a division of property or compensation for non-material damage is not in the nature of maintenance. Thirdly, a payment or transfer of property intended as a division of assets will concern 'rights in property arising out of a matrimonial relationship'. Fourthly, whether a claim relates to maintenance or not will depend on its purpose, and in particular whether it is designed to enable one spouse to provide for him or herself or if the needs and resources of each spouse are taken into consideration in the determination

[69] *Miller v Miller* [2006] UKHL 24, [2006] 2 AC 618, paras 138–41.

[70] These objectives have been pointed out by J Herring, *Family Law*, 4th edn (Harlow, Pearson Education Limited, 2009) 208–14.

[71] Which has led Lord Denning to aptly compare the flexibility of the courts to make financial orders with taking small pieces from a mixed bag and handing them to the spouses without 'paying any too nice a regard to their legal or equitable rights but simply according to what is the fairest provision for the future, for mother and father and the children'. *Hanlon v The Law Society* [1981] AC 124, 146.

[72] *Moore v Moore* [2007] EWCA Civ 361.

[73] See ibid paras 80 and 86.

of its amount, or where the capital sum set is designed to ensure a predetermined level of income, and lastly, if the provision is solely concerned with dividing property between the spouses, the decision will be concerned with rights in property arising out of a matrimonial relationship.[74]

The Court of Appeal decided that since the essential object of the husband in the Spanish proceedings was to achieve sharing of the property on his terms rather than an order based on financial needs, the application was not for maintenance but for the division of the wealth or assets to which the couple had a claim. In order to verify the exact objective of the claim, the wording of the application was taken as a starting point for shedding the light on the purpose of the application. The Court of Appeal stressed that 'in order to determine whether the application relates to maintenance it is necessary to consider the terms of the application in so far as it sheds light on the purpose of the application'.[75]

Two criteria can be derived from *Moore v Moore* for deciding whether a particular dispute should be characterised as a maintenance or matrimonial property case in the English legal doctrine. First, the objective of the application should be the claim for maintenance. Secondly, the order of maintenance sought should be based on enabling the applicant to provide for him or herself, or if the needs and resources of each of the spouses are taken into consideration in the determination of its amount, or where the capital sum that is set is designed to ensure a predetermined level of income. The controversial part of this is the extent to which transferring a capital sum from one spouse to generate a predetermined income for the other spouse falls wholly within maintenance or could fall partly within maintenance and partly within matrimonial property.

VII. Conclusions

The problem of how to distinguish between the issues of 'maintenance' and the issues of 'matrimonial property' can arise in very different phases of proceedings when applying the EU Maintenance Regulation and the future Matrimonial Property Regulation. On one hand the court might need to characterise a particular factual dispute as relating to 'maintenance' when it is invited to resolve a dispute between the spouses and thus determines jurisdiction or applicable law. On the other hand, the characterisation of a foreign judgment as dealing with 'matrimonial property' or 'maintenance obligations' may be required during the phase of recognition and enforcement. In both of these phases the autonomous terms (spousal) 'maintenance' and 'matrimonial property' should, however, be understood in the same way.

In general, based on the case law division found in the national legal systems and the evaluation of the functions of the relevant norms, it could be said that 'spousal maintenance' is concerned with the subsistence and needs of the spouses while the issues of 'matrimonial property' are concerned with the division of assets. This general conclusion is too simplistic and of course not very helpful in dealing with the borderline cases. Even the CJEU refers to the 'resources' of both spouses as well as their 'needs' and this has been picked up

[74] Ibid para 80.
[75] Ibid para 86.

by the English courts as a reason to justify quite substantial lump sum payments that are designed to give a predetermined income to one spouse as being 'maintenance' rather than 'matrimonial property' for the purposes of EU law. One should, however, bear in mind that the existing case law reflects specific factual and legal backgrounds which were taken into account when these judgments were made. Thus, the guidelines given by the case law should be complemented by assessing the functions of the relevant legal rules and by taking into account the different enforcement schemes which the newer instruments of EU private international law provide for—a consideration which might not have played any role when the case law on the Brussels I Regulation and the Brussels Convention was made.

The EU Maintenance Regulation provides for two types of enforcement schemes by allowing the judgments of the Member States bound by the Hague Protocol to circulate more freely than the judgments of the Member States not bound by the Hague Protocol, such as the UK. This means that there might be an incentive to interpret the concept of 'maintenance' more widely, depending on the place where the main proceedings took place or where the maintenance judgment would be enforced, in order to let more judgments benefit from the abolition of *exequatur*. Whether this consideration plays any role in practice will be shown by the future case law.

25

Characterisation within Private International Law: Maintenance or Succession?

JAYNE HOLLIDAY

I. Introduction

This chapter discusses the issue of characterisation within private international law. Focussing on the relationship between maintenance and the laws on succession, it will argue that where a dependent is able to make a claim for financial provision from the estate of the deceased, at least where any award is to meet the needs of the applicant, that the character is one of maintenance. The laws of England and Wales will be used as an example.[1]

The chapter will also consider whether for the effective international recovery of family maintenance, the EU Maintenance Regulation and the 2007 Hague Child Support Convention should be read to include maintenance claims of this type.

In contrast to civil law systems, freedom of testamentary disposition, the ability to choose who receives our property after we die, is an established right within the law of England and Wales.[2] Part of the right of ownership of private property,[3] testamentary freedom is accepted in England as an inherent part of the common law and protected by statute.[4] If the deceased has not made a will or the will is not valid or only covers part of the estate of the deceased, then the law of intestacy will apply.[5] The law of intestacy lists the family members to whom the property is to pass.[6] Where the outcome of a will or the rules of intestacy lead to severe financial hardship of family members or people who were dependent on the deceased, then testamentary freedom is potentially limited by the Inheritance (Provision for Family and Dependents) Act 1975 (the 1975 Act). (Note that all section references in the footnotes are to the 1975 Act, unless stated otherwise.) Under the 1975 Act the court is able

[1] The Law of England and Wales will be known as English law for the purpose of this chapter.

[2] The Wills Act 1837, s 3. Although note that there is no requirement in English law that a will must nominate an 'heir', see R Kerridge, 'Testamentary Formalities in England and Wales' in KGC Reid, MJ De Waal and R Zimmermann (Eds), *Testamentary Formalities, Comparative Succession Law*, vol 1 (Oxford, Oxford University Press, 2011) 317.

[3] See Kerridge (n 2) 308 for a historical account of the development of property law on death within England.

[4] The Wills Act 1837.

[5] Law Commission, *Intestacy and Family Provision Claims on Death* (Law Com No 331, 2011).

[6] Administration of Estates Act, s 46.

to limit the deceased's ability to make inadequate provision for his surviving dependents.[7] This is a discretionary approach to maintaining dependents of the deceased as opposed to the concept of forced heirship, which is common within civil law systems.[8] It should be noted that the Act is only triggered when an application for financial provision is made by a dependent and therefore testamentary freedom is only limited in successful cases.[9] One policy motivation behind this limitation of testamentary freedom is to minimise the cost to the State of maintaining the dependents.[10]

The 1975 Act is generally regarded as forming part of the private international law of succession within England and Wales.[11] It requires the deceased to have been domiciled in England and Wales.[12] It allows for spouses[13] and former spouses,[14] those who were living in the same household of the deceased or living as the deceased's husband or wife,[15] children,[16] those whom the deceased treated as a child of the family,[17] and those whom the deceased 'maintained either wholly or partly'[18] to apply for reasonable financial provision from the estate of the deceased. Spouses are able to apply for financial provision that is reasonable in all the circumstances[19] whereas the other dependents are limited to the award of maintenance.[20]

The question that this chapter seeks to address is whether there is evidence to support the proposal that part of the 1975 Act should be characterised as maintenance for the purposes of private international law. The element that this chapter will focus upon is the group of dependents found within section 1(1)(e) of the 1975 Act who would not ordinarily inherit under the law of succession.[21] It will be argued that the nature of the application for financial provision from the deceased's estate by this group of dependents clearly falls within the character of maintenance, meaning that the 1975 Act is a hybrid of both maintenance and succession law. It will therefore be recommended that the application for financial provision by a section 1(1)(e) dependent should be characterised as maintenance and not succession and that the law should be changed to allow the habitual residence of the dependent within England and Wales to be a connecting factor. This would allow habitually resident dependents to make claims for financial provision on the estate of the

[7] L Collins (ed), *Dicey, Morris and Collins: The Conflict of Laws*, 15th edn (London, Sweet and Maxwell, 2012) 1429, 27-051. 'In contrast to England, the testator is bound to leave a certain proportion of his estate to his wife or civil partner or children under the laws of Scotland, France and many Continental countries.' (P Beaumont and P McEleavy, *Anton's Private International Law*, 3rd edn (Edinburgh, W Green, 2011) 1029, paras 24.12–24.29 discusses the legal rights available to the spouse, civil partner and children of the deceased in Scotland; see also s 8 of the Succession (Scotland) Act 1964.) The French Civil Code, Arts 721 and 912 lay out the reserved portion of the estate for the deceased's descendants and spouse.

[8] Law Commission (n 5) 1.21.

[9] Ibid 1.63.

[10] J Dainow, 'Limitations on Testamentary Freedom' (1939–40) *Cornell Law Quarterly* 337 www.heinonline.org/HOL/Page?handle=hein.journals/clqv25&div=27&g_sent=1&collection=journals (accessed February 2013).

[11] Dicey, Morris and Collins (n 7) 1429, 27-051.

[12] s 1(1).

[13] s 1(1)(a).

[14] s 1(1)(b).

[15] s 1(1)(ba).

[16] s 1(1)(c).

[17] s 1(1)(d).

[18] s 1(1)(e).

[19] s 1(2)(a).

[20] s 1(2)(b).

[21] The spouse and children of the deceased are the usual heirs to an estate within the law of succession.

deceased where the deceased has assets within England and Wales, regardless of where the deceased is domiciled. Successful applications would reduce the burden on the State to maintain these dependents.

This chapter will be structured as follows. Section II will explain the process of the administration of estates within England and Wales and how it relates to the 1975 Act. In particular the separation of the duty to pay debts from the duty to pay the beneficiaries will be considered. Section III will consider the nature of maintenance under English law and whether section 1(1)(e) of the 1975 Act falls within its scope. Section IV will discuss the connecting factor of domicile under the 1975 Act and assess whether there is a more appropriate approach. Section V will consider law reform and will recommend the use of habitual residence as an additional connecting factor to domicile. Section VI will consider whether, for the effective international recovery of family maintenance, the EU Maintenance Regulation and the 2007 Hague Child Support Convention should be read to include maintenance claims of this type. Section VII will conclude that there is sufficient evidence to suggest that section 1(1)(e) should be characterised as maintenance for the purpose of private international law.[22]

II. The Administration of Estates within England and Wales

When someone dies in England their estate has to be administered.[23] In contrast to some civil law systems the process of administration in England has never been the duty of the heir.[24] The administration is carried out by a personal representative of the deceased, either an executor or an administrator,[25] who gains authority to deal with the estate by obtaining a grant of representation from the court.[26] This procedure for administering property after the death of its owner is fundamentally different from the civil law approach where it is common for the property of the deceased to pass directly to the heirs on death.[27]

In England the personal representative has two clearly separate duties to perform. The first is that they must clear the estate of liabilities by paying funeral expenses and debts, including taxes.[28] Having dealt with the debts, the second duty is that they must distribute the remainder of the estate amongst the beneficiaries according to the applicable law.[29]

22 An example of where a claim by a cohabitant on the estate of the deceased is considered to be one of maintenance and not succession is found within Art 2020 of the Portuguese Civil Code, which allows a cohabitant to claim maintenance rights from the estate of the deceased. Council of Europe, 'Social Policy and Family Law: Marriage and Divorces and Parenthood' www.coe.int/t/dg3/familypolicy/Source/4_1_ii%20Legislation%20on%20cohabitation.pdf (accessed May 2013). Thanks to Raquel Correia for confirmation of this.

23 Kerridge (n 2) 318.

24 Ibid.

25 J Fawcett and J Carruthers, *Cheshire, North and Fawcett, Private International Law*, 14th edn (Oxford, Oxford University Press, 2008) 1253. An executor is the person specifically identified in the will to deal with the estate. An administrator is the person who is given authority to deal with the estate but who was not mentioned by name in the will, or the deceased died intestate.

26 Dicey, Morris and Collins (n 7) 1393, 26-002.

27 Ibid.

28 Ibid 1393, 26-002.

29 Kerridge (n 2) 318.

The general rule in English law is that every question relating to the first duty or the questions relating to administration of the estate is to be determined in accordance with the *lex fori*.[30] The deceased's domicile is irrelevant at this point.[31] The English law governs the priority of the debts and their extinction through lapse of time.[32] It is also irrelevant whether the creditor is English or foreign.[33] It is possible for an English personal representative to deal solely with the assets within England and Wales for a deceased who died domiciled outside of England.[34] In this case they still apply the *lex fori* and have a duty to pay the creditors following the order prescribed by English law.[35] If there is insufficient money then they pay the creditors pro rata.

The personal representative may also have responsibility for the whole estate, in which case they will gather the deceased's estate from outside of the UK. If the deceased died domiciled in England and Wales all of the assets, both immoveable and moveable, need to be collected in order to pay the debts and only then will the law of succession be applied to divide the assets between the beneficiaries.

The duty to pay a maintenance debt, where a dependent is owed maintenance by the deceased is dealt with under the first duty under administration of estates and not under succession law. As long as the personal representative is made aware of the debt within the first six months of the death of the deceased then the debt must be treated as any other and paid according to the priority set out in law.

III. The Nature of the Claim for Financial Provision under Section 1(1)(e) of the 1975 Act

A. Character of Maintenance

The duty to consider applications for future maintenance or financial provision for dependents after the death of the deceased is currently dealt with under the law of succession.[36] This is in line with the general conflict of laws rules that do not include claims of this kind in the law of maintenance, as the basis of the relationship is not one that gives a claimant a right of maintenance within the framework of family law.[37] It is argued that it is only on the death of the person that the needs of the dependents appear and the courts usually endeavour to sufficiently protect this group through the law of succession.[38] However there is a strong relationship between succession and maintenance. Referring to prior rights

[30] Dicey, Morris and Collins (n 7) 1405, 26-032.

[31] Ibid.

[32] Cheshire, North and Fawcett (n 25) 1258.

[33] Dicey, Morris and Collins (n 7) 1405, 26-032.

[34] Ibid 1405, 26-033.

[35] Ibid.

[36] Although Dicey, Morris and Collins (n 7) 1406, 26-035 states that the payment of maintenance out of the estate to infant beneficiaries has been held to be a matter of administration, see *Re Nanton Estate* [1948] 2 WWR 113 (Man).

[37] D Martiny, 'Maintenance Obligations in the Conflict of Laws' (1994) 247 *Hague Academy Collected Courses* 131, 220.

[38] Ibid.

under French succession law Jean Carbonnier described them as 'an extension beyond death of the duty to maintain'.[39] In England there is no forced heirship, but the discretionary approach found within the 1975 Act is demonstrably a duty to maintain dependents beyond death.

The concept of the duty to maintain varies greatly within Europe. The difference can be attributed to variable cultural expectations as to how the family is expected to support itself as opposed to relying on state support.[40] France for example has a higher expectation of intra-familial maintenance as a result of the expectation of family solidarity.[41] However this is currently in decline with state support on the increase.[42] In contrast the extent of maintenance in England is that there is a common law duty for the husband to maintain the wife[43] and a statutory duty for the spouses and civil partners to maintain each other and their children.[44] There is no requirement to maintain the wider family, which is considered to be the duty of the State.[45] Therefore it should be noted that there is no legal duty to maintain the dependents within section 1(1)(e) of the 1975 Act during life. When this group are maintained it is by voluntary arrangement between the parties.

The definition of maintenance awarded to the dependents within section 1(1)(e) is found within English case law. In *Re Dennis* it was explained that maintenance 'connotes only payments which directly or indirectly enable the applicant in the future to discharge the cost of his daily living at whatever standard of living is appropriate to him.'[46] In *Re Coventry*[47] it was added that:

> On the one hand … one must not put too limited a meaning on it; it does not mean just enough to enable a person to get by; on the other hand it does not mean only which may be regarded reasonably desirable for his general benefit and welfare.

The case of *Moore v Moore*[48] noted the guidance from the Court of Justice of the European Union (CJEU) in *Van den Boogaard*[49] that

> First, whether a claim is for maintenance depends upon an autonomous interpretation of the term, and the label given to the claim by national law is not decisive; secondly payment of a lump sum or transfer of a property may be in the nature of maintenance if it is intended to ensure the support of the spouse; thirdly payment of a lump sum or transfer which serves only the purpose of a division of property or compensation for non material damage is not in the nature of maintenance; fourthly a payment of transfer of property intended as a division of assets will concern rights in property arising out of a matrimonial relationship; fifthly whether a claim relates to maintenance will depend on whether it is designed to enable one spouse to provide for himself or herself or the needs and resources of each of the spouses are taken into consideration in the determination

[39] J Carbonnier, *Droit Civil*, Tome II, La Famille, 16th edn (Paris, Presses Universitaires de France, 1998) 79.

[40] M Oldham, 'Financial Obligations Within the Family—Aspects of Intergenerational Maintenance and Succession in England and France' (2001) *Cambridge Law Journal* 5.

[41] Ibid.

[42] Ibid.

[43] *Price v Price* [1951] P. 413 (CA).

[44] Matrimonial Causes Act 1973, s 27(1); Civil Partnership Act 2004, Sch 5; Marriage (Same Sex Couples) Act 2013.

[45] Oldham (n 40).

[46] *Re Dennis* [1981] 2 All ER 140, 145.

[47] *Re Coventry* [1980] Ch 461, 485.

[48] *Moore v Moore* [2007] EWCA Civ 361.

[49] Case C-220/95 *Antonius van den Boogaard v Paula Laumen* [1997] ECR I-1147.

of the amount, or where the capital sum is designed to ensure a predetermined level of income; sixthly where the provision is solely concerned with dividing the property between the spouses the decision will concern the rights in property arising out of a matrimonial relationship and will not be enforceable under Brussels I.[50]

B. Statutory Interpretation

The wording within the 1975 Act speaks clearly of maintenance. The precondition for a successful claim of financial provision by the dependent in section 1(1)(e) is that immediately before the death of the deceased they were 'being maintained, either wholly or partly'.[51] The definition of 'being maintained' is that the deceased was making a substantial contribution in money or money's worth towards the reasonable needs of that person.[52] If their application is successful then the award that they are entitled to is 'financial provision as it would be reasonable in all of the circumstances of the case for the applicant to receive for his maintenance'. Reasonable financial provision under the 1975 Act does not mean that the award cannot be substantial.[53]

The 1975 Act allows a dependent to apply for an interim order.[54] This is a solution for when the applicant is in immediate need of financial assistance. In this situation the court is able to pay the applicant out of the net estate of the deceased such sum or sums at such intervals as the court thinks reasonable until such a date as the actual order for financial provision under section 2 of the 1975 Act has been agreed.[55] Although it is not essential that maintenance be in the form of sums paid at intervals, the nature of the interim order falls within the scope of maintenance in that they are for the purpose of covering the fundamental needs of the dependent to survive.[56]

Under the 1975 Act the courts have the powers to make a variety of awards.[57] If the court accepts that there has been inadequate financial provision for the dependent either by the disposition of the will or the law of intestacy or a combination of the two then they have various remedies available to them. These orders can take the form of periodical payments,[58] lump sum awards,[59] property transfers[60] or property sales.[61] These awards are appropriate for maintenance in England.[62] The 1975 Act also allows the court to vary both

[50] *Moore v Moore* [2007] EWCA Civ 361 [80]. The reference to Brussels I should now be read as referring to the EU Maintenance Regulation.

[51] s 1(3).

[52] Ibid.

[53] *Musa v Holliday* [2012] EWCA Civ 1268. The maintenance award in this case was calculated at the not insubstantial sum of £60,000 per annum.

[54] s 5.

[55] s 5(1).

[56] Case 120/79 *de Cavel v de Cavel (No 2)* [1980] ECR 731 [3].

[57] s 2.

[58] s 2(1)(a).

[59] s 2(1)(b).

[60] s 2(1)(c).

[61] s 2(1)(e).

[62] In civil law systems matrimonial property and maintenance are treated as separate issues whereas in England they are considered as a whole. This chapter will not discuss this area as the dependent within the meaning of s 1(1)(e) is not the spouse of the deceased.

pre-nuptial and post-nuptial agreements.[63] This essentially means that under the 1975 Act if the deceased died domiciled in England and there are sufficient assets in England it is impossible to leave a valid dependent in severe financial hardship.

When determining the level of the award the court is able to refer to the guidelines within the 1975 Act.[64] The court has to take into account the financial resources and needs of the applicant,[65] the financial resources and needs of any other applicant,[66] the financial resources and needs of any beneficiary,[67] the obligations and responsibilities which the deceased had to any applicant or beneficiary,[68] the size and nature of the net estate of the deceased,[69] any physical or mental disability of the applicant or beneficiary[70] and any other matter which the court may consider relevant such as conduct of the applicant.[71] For the purpose of determining the award for a section 1(1)(e) dependent the court must consider the extent to which the deceased had assumed responsibility for the application of maintenance.[72]

As we can see, the 1975 Act is primarily concerned with the concept of 'need'. The aim is to determine what is necessary for maintenance and does not award sums that would reward the applicant by improving their standard of living beyond that which they experienced during the deceased's life.

C. Is it a Succession Right?

Traditionally the financial provision under section 1(1)(e) is characterised as a succession right within private international law. Clearly if a dependent falls within the named beneficiaries under the laws of intestacy or is named within the will this would be a succession right. Yet the dependent in section 1(1)(e) is not commonly protected under the law of succession. Therefore there is an argument that where a dependent was being maintained by the deceased immediately prior to death this creates a right for maintenance to be continued after death, a voluntary arrangement becoming an obligation to maintain, at the discretion of the court.

These dependents are not beneficiaries of the estate as understood in succession law. The 1975 Act makes a clear distinction in the chosen vocabulary when discussing the guidelines between those who are dependents and those who are beneficiaries of the estate, supporting the argument against the application for financial provision by section 1(1)(e) dependents being characterised as a succession issue.

63 s 2(1)(f).
64 s 3.
65 s 3(1)(a).
66 s 3(1)(b).
67 s 3(1)(c).
68 s 3(1)(d).
69 s 3(1)(e).
70 s 3(1)(f).
71 s 3(1)(g).
72 s 3(4).

IV. The 1975 Act and the Appropriate Connecting Factor

The purpose of characterising the nature of a legal issue in private international law is to identify the appropriate jurisdiction or applicable law.[73] The question that needs to be asked in this case is whether the claim concerns administration of estates or rights of succession or maintenance. If it involves the administration of estates then under the private international law of England the *lex fori* is applied as the law where the administration is taking place.[74] If the claim concerns the rights of succession then the connecting factors that should be considered are *lex situs* for immoveable property[75] and *lex domicilii* for moveable property.[76] The 1975 Act uses the condition for its application that the deceased has to die domiciled within England and Wales which is the same as the connecting factor for the law applicable to succession in relation to moveable property. The 1975 Act does not take into account the law applicable to succession in relation to immoveable property. The condition for application of the 1975 Act is therefore not the same as the conditions for application of the English private international law of succession.[77]

The requirement that the deceased has to be domiciled in England and Wales for the Act to apply is a self-limiting statutory rule.[78] This means that when a foreign court is applying English law it can only apply the 1975 Act if the deceased died domiciled in England and Wales.

If, however, the relevant part of the 1975 Act is characterised as a maintenance obligation under English private international law then the law of the forum applies and the EU Maintenance Regulation applies to questions of jurisdiction.

A. Domicile as a Connecting Factor and the Section 1(1)(e) Dependent

Domicile is a notoriously difficult connecting factor. The legal relationship between a person and the legal system of the territory, which invokes his personal law, is based on a combination of residence and intention.[79] Everybody has a domicile of origin, which can be replaced, if that person has capacity, by a domicile of choice.[80] However the point at which a person loses the domicile of origin and acquires a domicile of choice is extremely opaque. The acquisition of domicile of choice considers the intention to remain in the new country and can be weakened by evidence of the person's intention to return to their domicile of origin to retire or to be buried.[81] In law this 'day dreaming' in some cases can

[73] Cheshire, North and Fawcett (n 25) 41.

[74] Dicey, Morris and Collins (n 7) 1405, 26-032.

[75] Ibid 1414, 27R-017.

[76] Ibid 1414, 27R-010.

[77] See Dicey, Morris and Collins (n 7) 1417, 27-018 for discussion that *lex situs* has outlived its usefulness in succession law and should be abandoned in favour of *lex domicilii*.

[78] K Lipstein, 'Inherent Limitations in Statutes and the Conflict of Laws' (1977) *International and Comparative Law Quarterly* 884.

[79] *Bell v Kennedy* (1866–69) LR 1 Sc 307.

[80] Anton (n 7) 166, para 7.40.

[81] *Fuld (Deceased)(No. 3)* [1968] P.675, 685.

be sufficient to conclude that the person has not lost their domicile of origin as it satisfies the legal requirement for the parties' state of mind for intending to return.[82]

Where a deceased is found to be not domiciled in England and Wales for the purpose of the 1975 Act it means that even though they may have been resident in England for many decades and have assets in England and Wales their dependents will be unable to apply for financial provision under the 1975 Act. The problem of domicile as a connecting factor for the purpose of the 1975 Act will be illustrated by means of the following case-law examples.

Agulian & Anr v Cygnik *[2006] EWCA Civ 129*

This appeal case concerned a preliminary question about whether the deceased Mr Andreas Nathanael (Andreas) died domiciled in England and Wales for the purpose of the 1975 Act. Andreas had been born in Cyprus but had moved to England when he was 19 years old.[83] He had lived in England for 43 years.[84] He had built up a property business but had not lost his Greek/Cypriot connections. He met the applicant Renata Cygnik (Renata) and formed a relationship with her, intending to marry her in the UK. He left her a legacy of £50,000 in his will.[85]

It was held that when attempting to determine Andreas's domicile the deputy judge had placed too much importance on the facts that he intended to marry in the UK and had left Renata a legacy. The crucial question that should have been addressed was whether the deceased had formed an intention to live in England, thereby abandoning the domicile of origin for a domicile of choice. It was noted that marriage by a man with a domicile of origin in one country to a woman domiciled in another with the intention to live in the wife's domicile was not conclusive of his loss of domicile of origin.[86] It was also noted that the deputy judge had concentrated on the latter years of the deceased's residence in England whereas the whole of his lifetime should have been taken into account.[87] The appeal court held that the deceased was not domiciled in England and Wales and therefore his partner's application under the 1975 Act had to be dismissed.

The harsh reality of this case is that there was a dependent who had been maintained by the deceased immediately prior to his death and who was now unable to apply for financial provision from the estate of the deceased due to the complex nature of domicile. Andreas had lived in England for 43 years, from the age of 19 to his death at the age of 63.[88] His net estate within England and Wales had been valued at £6,527,362.[89] He was without doubt habitually resident in England and Wales yet this was insufficient for the purpose of the 1975 Act. In an obiter comment, Lord Justice Longmore spoke quite candidly about the outcome of this case stating:

> Now that many family matters are decided by reference to habitual residence, there may, perhaps, be something to be said for reconsidering the terms of section 1 of the Inheritance (Provision for

[82] Ibid.
[83] *Agulian & Anr v Cygnik* [2006] EWCA Civ 129 [3].
[84] Ibid.
[85] Ibid [4].
[86] Ibid [46].
[87] Ibid [49].
[88] Ibid [4].
[89] Ibid.

Family and Dependents) Act 1975. As Dr JHC Morris observed of the concept of domicile in the last (3rd) edition of the *Conflict of Laws* (1984), which he wrote before he died,

> 'Originally it was a good idea; but the once simple concept has been so overloaded by a multitude of cases that it has been transmuted into something further and further removed from the practicalities of life.'[90]

Holliday v Musa *[2010] EWCA Civ 335*

This appeal case also concerned a preliminary question about whether the deceased died domiciled in England and Wales for the purpose of the 1975 Act in order to allow an application for financial provision under section 1(1)(e) of the 1975 Act to go ahead. The applicants for financial provision were Diane Holliday (Diane) the partner of the deceased and her adult son by a former marriage, Kevin Holliday (Kevin). The deceased Ramadan Houssein Guney (Ramadan) had been born in Cyprus to parents of Turkish descent. He had left Cyprus in the 1950s and come to live in England. He married in England but his first wife subsequently died. Ramadan had six children, now adults, from his first marriage. He met and commenced a relationship with Diane whom he lived with for six years prior to his death.[91] They had a son Houssein Guney (Houssein). They lived together in the UK. He died intestate.

The reasoning behind the court's decision as to the deceased's domicile was rather strained. The court upheld the decision that the deceased had lost his domicile of origin and was domiciled in England and Wales for the purpose of the 1975 Act. Yet Ramadan was a self-declared non-domicile for tax purposes.[92] He had property in both England and Cyprus.[93] He held bank accounts in both England and Cyprus. His assets in the UK were valued at £1 million. He spent substantial periods of time in Cyprus towards the end of his life.[94] He even stood for election in Cyprus in 1998.[95] But none of this was thought to be sufficient to support the idea that he had retained his domicile of origin in Cyprus.

The appeal court stated that the correct question to ask in order to identify Ramadan's domicile would have been whether it was right to infer that at any stage of his residence in England prior to his death he had formed the intention to settle in the UK indefinitely and abandon his domicile of origin. The original rationale had looked to whether there was an intention to return to his domicile of origin. Both questions returned the answer that he was domiciled in England.[96]

In this case the dependents were able to apply for financial provision under the 1975 Act. However it took three years from the point at which Ramadan died for a final decision as to the deceased's domicile to be made in the appeal court. Once again the need to consider the preliminary question of domicile in the courts meant that both substantial amounts of time and expense were spent on the issue. If a dependent could apply for maintenance

[90] Ibid [58].
[91] *Holliday v Musa* [2010] EWCA Civ 335 [1].
[92] Ibid [40].
[93] Ibid.
[94] Number of days Ramadan spent in Cyprus: 1997—66 days, 1998—180 days, 1999—31 days, 2000—82 days, 2001—38 days, 2002—32 days, 2003—61 days, 2005—120 days, 2006—89 days.
[95] *Holliday v Musa* [2010] EWCA Civ 335 [46].
[96] Ibid [3].

under the 1975 Act based on their own habitual residence within England it would avoid both of these issues.

Musa v Holliday *[2012] EWCA Civ 1268*

This appeal case concerned the recommendation for the financial provision for Diane. As mentioned above, Ramadan owned property both in England and Wales and in Northern Cyprus and the courts had decided that he was domiciled in England and Wales for the purpose of the 1975 Act.

Diane's needs were assessed by the court and the judge decided that a figure of £60,000 per annum was an appropriate starting point.[97] It was decided that she needed accommodation and sufficient income to maintain herself and her son Houssein until he had finished university at the same standard of living they had experienced when Ramadan was alive.[98] The rationale behind the judge's decision as to what Diane and Houssein should be awarded was one of maintenance. The judge looked to what was reasonable and looked to Diane's needs.[99]

Kevin's needs were not contested. He was awarded financial provision from the estate to cover payment of tuition fees, enrolment fees and maintenance expenses to support him while he qualified as a lawyer.[100]

Diane's original application for financial provision under section 2 of the 1975 Act as a section 1(1)(e) dependent was made in 2007. The final appeal was settled in 2012. It took three years to get a decision from the court with regards to the deceased's domicile and a further two to settle the issues surrounding the financial provision. The judge's decision, although undoubtedly providing the fairest outcome for the dependents in the circumstances, was certainly strained by the deceased's written declaration that he was not domiciled within England and Wales albeit for tax purposes and the time he spent in Cyprus.

If the claim for financial provision by a section 1(1)(e) dependent was regarded as maintenance and habitual residence was used as the appropriate connecting factor, this case would not have had to endure three years in the courts with all the associated costs to determine the domicile of the deceased. Diane and her sons would have been able to demonstrate that they were habitually resident within England and Wales. Although the concept of habitual residence is not without its own problems of definition,[101] there is evidence to show that the dependents had lived with Ramadan in the UK for the six years prior to his death. Houssein went to school in the UK. Before Ramadan's death Diane had worked for the family firm. This would have been sufficient to demonstrate habitual residence within England and Wales.

[97] *Musa v Holliday* [2012] EWCA Civ 1268 [16].

[98] Ibid.

[99] Ibid [47].

[100] Ibid [48].

[101] Dicey, Morris and Collins (n 7) 117, para 6-123. A lack of definition for the term habitual residence has created inconsistencies in the interpretation between different legal systems. There are also problems caused by a person having no habitual residence (para 6-136), or dual habitual residence (para 6-137). Anton (n 7) paras 7.60–7.127 discusses the issues surrounding habitual residence such as that it may be lost in a day, but also may not be acquired in a day and that a person may have no habitual residence.

V. Recommendation for Law Reform

The Law Commission has made it clear that the precondition in the 1975 Act that the deceased be domiciled in England and Wales should be removed.[102] Habitual residence of the deceased within England and Wales was put forward as a possible alternative to domicile. However there is a strong argument against this as habitual residence as it is also difficult to prove on occasion and would therefore also lead to lengthy and expensive court cases. Other suggestions included using a deemed domicile test as used in the inheritance tax legislation[103] or a combination of domicile and residence.[104] Obviously none of these options resolve the unfairness for the section 1(1)(e) dependent if the deceased is found not to be domiciled or habitually resident in England and Wales.

In October 2012, the House of Lords passed the second reading of the Inheritance (Cohabitants) Bill [HL]. This Bill recognised the financial hardship that may be experienced by a cohabitant at the time of their partner's death and sought to redress this by amending the Administration of Estates Act 1925 to place a qualifying cohabitant in the same position as a spouse or civil partner so that they would 'benefit by default under the intestacy rules'.[105] In order to be a qualifying cohabitant the dependant had to have lived with the deceased as spouse or civil partner in the same household for a period of five years prior to the death.[106] If the couple had children together this time period would be reduced to two years.[107] This would have meant that a cohabitant would be able to inherit under the laws of intestacy without the need for litigation, which is necessary for an application for maintenance under the 1975 Act. However due to the controversial nature of this Bill, the Government decided not to proceed with it during the 2012/13 Parliament.[108]

However, even if this had been implemented it would not resolve the matter for all section 1(1)(e) dependents. Not all cohabitants will meet the qualifying criteria and therefore their only option is to apply for maintenance under the 1975 Act. Also it should be noted that not all section 1(1)(e) dependents are cohabitants, for example the deceased may have maintained a disabled person who falls outside of the succession rules. For a dependent needing to rely on the 1975 Act for their future maintenance, the rule requiring the deceased to have been domiciled in England and Wales can produce harsh and unfair results. Only by widening the scope to include habitual residence of the dependent in England and Wales as a connecting factor can we hope to bring fairness to these cases.

For a maintenance creditor, habitual residence is the accepted connecting factor within private international law.[109] The evidence put forward within this chapter supports the

[102] Law Commission (n 5) para 7.15.

[103] Ibid para 7.26.

[104] Ibid para 7.27.

[105] HL Deb (Inheritance (Cohabitants) Bill [HL]) 19 October 2012, col 1657.

[106] Inheritance (Cohabitants) Bill 2012 s 1(6).

[107] Ibid s 1(7).

[108] Law Commission, Intestacy and Family Provision Claims on Death, available at www.lawcommission.justice.gov.uk/areas/intestacy-and-family-provision-claims-on-death.htm (accessed January 2014).

[109] Dicey, Morris and Collins (n 7) 187, para 6-146: 'Habitual residence plays a key role in European Union private international law and is the primary connecting factor in instruments dealing with family law matters'; Anton (n 7) 175, para 7.61: 'Today, habitual residence is the connecting factor of choice, in issues of choice of law as well as jurisdiction, for family law and related matters, not only in initiatives of the Hague Conference, but also in EU private international law instruments'. Council Regulation (EC) No 4/2009, Art 3(b) states that the court of

proposal that the claim made by this group of dependents is more accurately characterised as maintenance rather than succession. Dependents within section 1(1)(e) of the 1975 Act who are habitually resident in England and Wales, would benefit from this connecting factor as they would be able to make claims on the estates of the deceased where the deceased was not domiciled within England and Wales. This would in turn reduce the economic burden on the State.

Is it reasonable to use the dependent's habitual residence in England and Wales as a connecting factor for the purpose of section 1(1)(e) if the deceased is domiciled outside of England and Wales? It is arguable that it is indeed fair to ask for financial provision from the estate of the deceased in these circumstances. The deceased was knowingly maintaining the dependent in England and Wales before death and therefore was aware that the person was dependent on them. Therefore it is not unreasonable to suggest that this should continue after the deceased's death.

As it is both beneficial and reasonable to use the habitual residence of the dependent applying for maintenance under section 1(1)(e) it is recommended that the 1975 Act should be amended accordingly.

VI. The EU Maintenance Regulation and the Hague Child Support Convention: Should they be Read to Include Maintenance Claims of this Type?

A. The EU Maintenance Regulation

If a claim by the section 1(1)(e) dependent is characterised as one of maintenance then the EU Maintenance Regulation can be applied. The scope of the Maintenance Regulation can be read to include claims by section 1(1)(e) dependents due to the fact that the term 'maintenance obligation' has an 'autonomous interpretation'.[110]

In order for the section 1(1)(e) dependents to fit within the meaning of Article 1(1) of the Maintenance Regulation it is necessary for them to be recognised as falling within the definition of 'family relationship'. The term 'family relationship' is not defined within the Maintenance Regulation. The CJEU would normally give an autonomous definition to the term 'family relationship' given that the term is used in the Regulation. However, the Member States were anxious to ensure that the private international law rules on family relationships were not harmonised by the back door through an autonomous interpretation

the habitual residence of the creditor will have jurisdiction. Art 3(1) of the Hague Protocol on the Law Applicable to Maintenance Obligations states that maintenance obligations shall be governed by the law of the State of the habitual residence of the creditor, save where this Protocol provides otherwise.

[110] Recital 11 of Council Regulation (EC) No 4/2009 on jurisdiction, applicable law, recognition and enforcement of decisions and cooperation in matters relating to maintenance obligations [2009] OJ L7/1. See Case C-220/95 *Antonius van den Boogaard v Paula Laumen* [1997] ECR I-1147 for an analysis by the CJEU of the meaning of 'maintenance obligation'. The maintenance obligations described in the 1975 Act fall within the scope of the requirements found within this case as demonstrated in the analysis of the characterisation of maintenance above.

of this concept by the CJEU.[111] Therefore the Regulation expressly states that it remains a matter for the national law of the Member States, including their private international law rules, to establish a family relationship on which the maintenance obligation is based.[112] Recognition of a decision relating to maintenance from Member State X by Member State Y does not imply that Member State Y recognises the family relationship out of which the obligation arose, but that Member State Y recognises the obligation for maintenance.[113] It is therefore argued that this does not constitute a problem if 'family relationship' is given a broad construction within Member States. It is also argued that the CJEU should not attempt to place an outer limit on the meaning of 'family relationship' in terms of the scope of the EU Maintenance Regulation but rather recognise that the interests of debtors are protected by the application of the Hague Protocol in States party to that instrument and by the *exequatur* process in relation to judgments coming from Member States that are not party to the Hague Protocol, such as the UK.

It should also be noted that although the EU[114] and the CJEU have historically taken a strict approach to the term family relationship to mean direct blood or legal link, the European Court of Human Rights (ECtHR) has been willing to apply a reality test to de facto relationships in light of the increase in non-traditional families.[115]

If, however, the CJEU were to decide that the section 1(1)(e) 1975 Act dependents were not in a family relationship with the deceased, an English judgment under that Act could not be enforced in another EU State under the Maintenance Regulation and would instead fall within the current Brussels I Regulation. Under the existing Brussels I Regulation if their maintenance claim was characterised as maintenance then, as it is a civil and commercial matter, it could be enforced. However if the claim is characterised as succession then Article 1(2)(a) would exclude it from the Brussels I Regulation. However, once the Brussels I Recast applies in 2015 their claim would be excluded, as the Recast does not apply to maintenance obligations arising from a family relationship[116] nor maintenance obligations arising by reason of death.[117] In practice it may be difficult to see cases where recognition and enforcement of an English order under the 1975 Act will need to be enforced in another EU State but one example might be where the English assets were insufficient to meet the claim and assets belonging to the deceased existed in another Member State.

[111] P Beaumont, 'International Family Law in Europe—The Maintenance Project, the Hague Conference and the EC: A Triumph in Reverse Subsidiarity' (2009) *Rabels Zeitschrift für ausländisches und Internationales Privatrecht* 509, 528. Beaumont notes that the broad scope at EU level was the same as that achieved at global level in Art 1(1) of the Hague Protocol 'Recital 11 of the Regulation adds these important words after repeating the words in Art 1(1) "in order to guarantee equal treatment for all maintenance creditors"'. See also the Proposal for a Council Regulation on jurisdiction, applicable law, recognition and enforcement of decisions and cooperation in matters relating to maintenance obligations, COM(2005) 649 final 1.2.2.

[112] See the Council Regulation (EC) No 4/2009 on jurisdiction, applicable law, recognition and enforcement of decisions and cooperation in matters relating to maintenance obligations, Recital 21.

[113] Ibid, Recital 25.

[114] J Borg-Barthet, 'The Principled Imperative to Recognise Same-Sex Unions in the EU' (2012) *Journal of Private International Law* 359, 362: 'Only the traditional nuclear family is guaranteed recognition throughout the Union'.

[115] H Stalford 'Concepts of Family under EU Law—Lessons from the ECHR' (2002) *International Journal of Law, Policy and the Family* 410, 429.

[116] Art 1(1)(e) of Regulation (EU) No 1215/2012 of the European Parliament and of the Council of 12 December 2012 on jurisdiction and the recognition and enforcement of judgments in civil and commercial matters (recast) [2012] OJ L351/1.

[117] Ibid Art 1(1)(f).

However if the claims are characterised as maintenance and fall within the meaning of 'arising from a family relationship' then Article 3(b) of the EU Maintenance Regulation gives jurisdiction based on the habitual residence of the creditor, which would support a section 1(1)(e) of the 1975 Act dependent claim. With regards to applicable law, the Protocol on the Law Applicable to Maintenance Obligations does not apply in England and Wales. An English and Welsh judgment based on the 1975 Act would be recognised and enforced using the simplified *exequatur*, however public policy concerns could arise if there were clashes between fulfilling the rights of beneficiaries under succession law and fulfilling the claim by the dependents under the law of maintenance.

As previously mentioned, an example of where claims of this type are already defined as maintenance can be found in Portugal where a cohabitant is able to apply for maintenance from their deceased partner's estate under Article 2020 of the Civil Code. As the character is one of maintenance and not succession, these claims should fall within the scope of the EU Maintenance Regulation.

B. The Hague Convention

The Hague Convention on the International Recovery of Child Support and Other Forms of Family Maintenance (2007) concerns applications for establishment of 'family maintenance' decisions and a process for recognition and enforcement of maintenance decisions.[118] Claims of the kind discussed in this chapter would only come under the core of the Convention if the dependent is treated for the purposes of the Convention as being in a 'parent-child relationship' with the deceased and is under the age of 21 or, in certain circumstances, if the dependent's application is treated as one for 'spousal support' under the Convention.[119] As it was the European Union that concluded the Convention on behalf of its Member States,[120] it will ultimately be for the CJEU to interpret the meaning of 'parent-child relationship' and 'spousal support' in this context. The Union has chosen not to extend the scope of the Convention beyond the core except by allowing spousal support applications however brought always to fall within the scope of the Convention.[121] It is clear that the EU does not intend to apply the Convention with as broad a scope as the Regulation because it has not made the declaration under Article 3(2) of the Convention to extend its application to 'any maintenance obligation arising from a family relationship, parentage, marriage or affinity' even though this is the scope of the Regulation. It is therefore certain that some

[118] Hague Convention on the International Recovery of Child Support and Other Forms of Family Maintenance (2007), Arts 1 and 10.

[119] Ibid Art 2(1). An application for recognition and enforcement of spousal support is within the core but only gets the assistance of Central Authorities if it is combined with a claim for child support.

[120] Council Decision of 9 June 2011 on the approval, on behalf of the European Union, of the Hague Convention of 23 November 2007 on the International Recovery of Child Support and other forms of Family Maintenance [2011] OJ L192/39.

[121] This power to declare a wider scope of the Convention is provided for by Art 2(3) of the Convention and the limited exercise of this declaration, only in relation to spousal support, can be found in Art 4(1) of the Council Decision. The consequence of the declaration is that the EU will allow its Central Authorities to be used for all applications to establish spousal support and for independent applications for recognition and enforcement of a spousal support decision not linked to a child support application. However, this extension requires a reciprocal declaration by the other Contracting State concerned giving the same or greater extension of the core scope of the Convention.

dependents who may benefit from a claim under section 1(1)(e) of the 1975 Act will not fall within the scope of the Maintenance Convention as it applies in the EU (eg an adult disabled person who is over the age of 21 who is not a cohabitant of the deceased)[122] and will therefore not be able to utilise the Convention to get their 'maintenance' decision under the 1975 Act recognised and enforced in a non-EU Contracting State to the Convention because of the principle of reciprocity in relation to the declarations extending the scope of the Convention.[123] On the other hand it is possible that a cohabiting person making a claim under section 1(1)(e) of the 1975 Act might be treated as a spouse by the CJEU for the purposes of the Maintenance Convention and therefore could benefit from recognition and enforcement of the decision in a non-EU Contracting State to the Convention that takes a similarly liberal approach to the concept of 'spousal support'.

VII. Conclusion

The current situation in England and Wales would appear to be that a voluntary decision to maintain someone during life becomes an involuntary obligation to maintain at the point of death through the application of section 1(1)(e) of the 1975 Act. At present this claim is categorised as a succession issue. Yet the use of the deceased's domicile as the sole connecting factor is leaving dependents habitually resident in England and Wales unable to make a claim on the estate of the deceased where the courts decide that the deceased was not domiciled in England and Wales, even though the deceased may have substantial assets there.

By characterising the claim for financial provision under section 1(1)(e) of the 1975 Act as one of maintenance, it would allow this group of dependents who are habitually resident in England and Wales, who are not ordinarily protected under the law of succession, to make a claim on the estate of the deceased, regardless of where the deceased was domiciled. This would in turn support the initial reasoning behind the Act to reduce the overall burden on the State.

The characterisation of claims under section 1(1)(e) of the 1975 Act as maintenance has the potential benefit of enabling English and Welsh court decisions arising from these claims to be enforced in other EU Member States, against the deceased's assets situated there, under the EU Maintenance Regulation 2009. In certain circumstances it would also enable such decisions to be enforced in non-EU Contracting States to the Hague Maintenance Convention 2007.

[122] Unless the decision was granted while the person was under 21 and has continuing effect thereafter and recognition and enforcement is being sought after the person is over 21 (see Art 37(3) of the Convention).

[123] See Art 2(3) of the Convention for the requirement of reciprocity: 'Any such declaration shall give rise to obligations between two Contracting States only in so far as their declarations cover the same maintenance obligations and parts of the Convention'.

26

Choice of Court in Matters Relating to Maintenance Obligations

MATTHIAS ABENDROTH

I. Introduction

In today's increasingly globalised world and closely knit European Union, the number of cross-border maintenance cases has increased.[1] Besides the familiar 'difficulties' of the various national maintenance laws, legal practitioners must also overcome additional obstacles.[2] Cross-border differences in substantive law must be managed and the range of issues relating to international civil procedure must be addressed.[3] In particular, legal practitioners are regularly required to clarify international jurisdiction, legal aid, international service of process as well as recognition, enforceability and enforcement of decisions.[4] The complexity of the international, European and national sources of law has made this a real challenge in the past.[5]

The European Union legislator intended to simplify the legal complexity of cross-border maintenance disputes and to accelerate their settlement with the adoption of the Maintenance Regulation.[6] In particular, the Regulation contains separate rules of jurisdiction including a provision for choice of court agreements. In international commercial transactions, choice

[1] K Eschenbruch, F Klinkhammer and H Dörner (eds), *Der Unterhaltsprozess*, 5th edn (Cologne, Luchterhand, 2009) ch 7, para 1; H Dörner, 'Der Vorschlag für eine europäische Verordnung zum Internationalen Unterhalts- und Unterhaltsverfahrensrecht' in B Großfeld, K Yamauchi, D Ehlers and T Ishikawa (eds), *Probleme des deutschen, europäischen und japanischen Rechts: Festschrift aus Anlass des 20-jährigen Bestehens der Partnerschaft der Westfälischen Wilhelms-Universität Münster und der Chuo-Universität Tokio auf dem Gebiet der Rechtswissenschaft* (Berlin, Duncker & Humblot, 2006) 81; N Conti, *Grenzüberschreitende Durchsetzung von Unterhaltsansprüchen in Europa* (Munich, Sellier European Law Publishers, 2011) 1.

[2] Dörner (n 1) 81; B Hess, *Europäisches Zivilprozessrecht* (Heidelberg, CF Müller, 2010) § 7 para 96.

[3] D Looschelders and S Boos, 'Das grenzüberschreitende Unterhaltsrecht in der internationalen und europäischen Entwicklung' (2006) *Zeitschrift für das gesamte Familienrecht* 374.

[4] D Martiny, 'Grenzüberschreitende Unterhaltsdurchsetzung nach europäischem und internationalem Recht' (2008) *Zeitschrift für das gesamte Familienrecht* 1681, 1682.

[5] Ibid 1682; Hess (n 2) § 7 para 96.

[6] Council Regulation (EC) No 4/2009 of 18 December 2008 on jurisdiction, applicable law, recognition and enforcement of decisions and cooperation in matters relating to maintenance obligations [2009] OJ EU L7/1. In particular, see Recitals 4 and 9 to the EU Maintenance Regulation; U Gruber, 'Die neue EG-Unterhaltsverordnung' (2010) *Praxis des Internationalen Privat- und Verfahrensrechts* 128, 129; D Coester-Waltjen, 'Einführung' in D Coester-Waltjen, V Lipp, E Schumann and B Veit (eds), *Europäisches Unterhaltsrecht* (Göttingen, Universitätsverlag Göttingen, 2010) 1, 2.

of court agreements have gained practical importance in European civil practice and the relevant provisions have often been the subject of the rulings of the Court of Justice of the European Union (CJEU) accompanied by heated debates in the literature.[7]

The purpose of this chapter is to explain the fundamental innovations of the EU Maintenance Regulation in relation to choice of court agreements in cross-border maintenance disputes. It particularly aims to provide guidance for legal practitioners involved in contract drafting, counselling and decision-making; who must consider whether to conclude a choice of court agreement and judge its effectiveness, especially in connection with marriage contracts, divorce agreements and maintenance agreements.[8] For this purpose, the requirements for and the effects of a choice of court agreement according to the new Regulation will be illustrated.

II. Choice of Court Agreements in European Maintenance Law

A. The Existing Legal Framework of the Brussels I Regulation

Until the EU Maintenance Regulation entered into force, choice of court agreements in cross-border maintenance disputes were subject to the provisions of the Brussels I Regulation.[9] Therefore, the requirements for a choice of court agreement were regulated comprehensively and conclusively by Article 23(1) of the Brussels I Regulation. According to this Article, parties, of which one or more is domiciled in a Member State, could agree that a court or the courts of a Member State have jurisdiction to settle any disputes which have arisen or which may arise in connection with a particular legal relationship. Hence, choice of court agreements were not subject to extensive restrictions, but were permitted in principle.[10] The protection of the weaker party was not a concept unknown to the Brussels I Regulation, as illustrated by the parties' limited autonomy to determine jurisdiction in relation to insurance, consumer contracts and employment. However choice of court agreements relating to maintenance disputes were permitted in a surprisingly generous manner, despite the significance of a maintenance obligation.[11]

[7] A Layton and H Mercer (eds), *European Civil Practice*, vol 1, 2nd edn (London, Sweet & Maxwell, 2004) para 20.002; U Magnus, in U Magnus and P Mankowski (eds), *European Commentaries on Private International Law: Brussels I Regulation*, 2nd edn (Munich, Sellier European Law Publishers, 2012) Art 23 Brussels I Regulation para 5.

[8] M Andrae, in T Rauscher (ed), *Kommentar zum Europäischen Zivilprozess- und Kollisionsrecht - EuZPR/EuIPR* (Munich, Sellier European Law Publishers, 2010) Art 4 EG-UntVO para 2.

[9] Council Regulation (EC) No 44/2001 of 22 December 2000 on jurisdiction and the recognition and enforcement of judgments in civil and commercial matters [2001] OJ EU L12/1.

[10] R Geimer, in R Geimer and R Schütze (eds), *Kommentar zum Europäischen Zivilverfahrensrecht*, 3rd edn (Munich, CH Beck, 2010) Art 23 EuGVVO paras 11, 12.

[11] R Süß, 'Europäisierung des Familienrechts—Handlungsempfehlungen für den Notar zum status quo' (2011) *Zeitschrift für Notarpraxis* 282; J Kropholler and J von Hein (eds), *Kommentar zum Europäischen Zivilprozessrecht*, 9th edn (Frankfurt am Main, Verlag Recht und Wirtschaft, 2011) Art 23 EuGVO para 79; but see B Hess, 'Die Verordnung Nr. 4/2009/EG zum Unterhaltsrecht (EU-Unterhaltsverordnung)', in C Schmidt (ed), *Internationale Unterhaltsrealisierung—Rechtsgrundlagen und praktische Anwendung* (Baden-Baden, Nomos, 2011) 27, 31.

Choice of court agreements related to maintenance disputes are now exclusively regulated by Article 4 of the EU Maintenance Regulation which, in contrast to the generosity of the previous legal framework, contains several restrictions. Pursuant to Article 67 of the Brussels I Regulation, the application of provisions of the Maintenance Regulation, which are based on specific values of the European legislator for matters relating to maintenance obligations, shall not be prejudiced by the Brussels I Regulation. Although the relationship between the two Regulations seems to be solved through this provision, Article 68(1) of the Maintenance Regulation stipulates that the maintenance obligation provisions of the Brussels I Regulation are to be replaced by the relevant provisions of the Maintenance Regulation. However, as a consequence of the recent reform of the Brussels I Regulation, maintenance obligations arising from a family relationship, parentage, marriage or affinity will fall outside the material scope of the Brussels I Regulation.[12] Therefore, the existing competition between the Maintenance Regulation and the Brussels I Regulation will soon be eradicated.

B. The Fundamental Innovations of the EU Maintenance Regulation

i. Written Form Requirement

The restrictive impact of the Maintenance Regulation on the generous legal framework for choice of court agreements in the Brussels I Regulation is first evidenced by the strict requirements of formality laid down in Article 4(2). Now, in accordance with this Article, choice of court agreements must be expressed primarily and almost exclusively in writing. However, a communication by electronic means, which provides a durable record of the agreement, is also sufficient. Accordingly, Article 4(2) of the Maintenance Regulation renounces the alternative formal elements of Article 23(1) of the Brussels I Regulation, which probably would not have played a role in the legal practice of maintenance disputes anyway.[13] The application of this clearly formulated requirement provokes the question of which specific requirements are thereby imposed, and how they ought to be interpreted by legal practitioners.

In order to answer these questions, one can refer to the settled case law of the CJEU on the provisions of the Brussels I Regulation. The legal term in question must therefore be regarded as 'an independent concept and must be interpreted by referring first, to the objectives and scheme of the Regulation and, second, to the general principles which stem from the corpus of the national legal systems'.[14] The CJEU thereby seeks to ensure that the

[12] Art 1(2)(e) of Regulation (EU) No 1215/2012 of the European Parliament and of the Council of 12 December 2012 on jurisdiction and the recognition and enforcement of judgments in civil and commercial matters (recast) [2012] OJ L351/1.

[13] P Gottwald, 'Prozessuale Zweifelsfragen der geplanten EU-Verordnung in Unterhaltssachen' in W Hau and H Schmidt (eds), *Facetten des Verfahrensrechts: Liber Amicorum Walter F. Lindacher* (Cologne, Heymanns Verlag, 2007) 13, 15.

[14] Case C-292/05 *Lechouritou* [2007] ECR I-1519, para 29; Case C-167/08 *Draka NK Cables* [2009] ECR I-3477, para 19; Case C-372/07 *Hassett and Doherty* [2008] ECR I-7403, para 17; Case C-464/01 *Gruber* [2005] ECR I-439, para 31; Case C-167/00 *Henkel* [2002] ECR I-8111, para 35; Case C-269/95 *Benincasa* [1997] ECR I-3767, para 12.

rights and obligations arising from the Brussels I Regulation have uniform application in all Member States.[15]

Nevertheless, the classic criteria of interpretation can be utilised for independent interpretations, taking into account certain EU particularities.[16] In this respect, the questions raised could not be answered satisfactorily by a grammatical interpretation focused on the wording of the provision because Article 4 of the Maintenance Regulation does not elaborate on the meaning of written form. In particular, the Maintenance Regulation does not contain a definition of 'in writing'. Basing an interpretation of such a legal term merely on national conceptions is forbidden, since it is the EU legal meaning of the term that must be determined. From a German perspective, therefore, section 126 of the German Civil Code cannot simply be automatically applied.[17] Instead the remaining criteria for interpretation have to be used and the objectives and scheme of the Maintenance Regulation have to be taken into consideration. The Recitals to the Maintenance Regulation provide useful guidance in this respect.[18]

As evidenced by Recital 15, the European Union legislator sought to adapt the rules on jurisdiction in the Brussels I Regulation to those in the Maintenance Regulation. Since choice of court agreements are related to the rules on jurisdiction, the same interpretation of 'in writing' as for Article 23(1) of the Brussels I Regulation is suggested for systematic reasons by this Recital.[19] Hence, written form just requires a declaration, which clearly expresses the intention of the relevant party to conclude a choice of court agreement.[20] Further requirements such as a signature or a uniform contractual document are consequently unnecessary, although advisable for purposes of evidence.[21] This systematic interpretation is also confirmed by Recital 44, which expressly underlines the intention of the European legislator that the provisions of the Brussels I Regulation are to be replaced by the provisions of the Maintenance Regulation.[22]

By contrast to the aforementioned systematic interpretation of writing, Recital 8 provides that the Hague Convention on the International Recovery of Child Support and Other Forms of Family Maintenance (the Hague Convention 2007)[23] should also be taken into account in the Maintenance Regulation. In contrast to the interpretation of writing in the Brussels I Regulation, Article 3(d) of the Hague Convention 2007 explicitly defines the legal term 'in writing' and implies that the written agreement must be recorded in a

[15] Case C-292/05 (n 14) para 29; Case C-125/92 *Mulox IBC* [1993] ECR I-4075, para 11.

[16] Instructive: B Hess, 'Methoden der Rechtsfindung im Europäischen Zivilprozessrecht' (2006) *Praxis des Internationalen Privat- und Verfahrensrechts* 348, 351; J Kropholler, 'Die Auslegung von EG-Verordnungen zum Internationalen Privat- und Verfahrensrecht' in J Basedow, U Drobnig, R Ellger, K Hopt, H Kötz, R Kulms and E Mestmäcker (eds), *Aufbruch nach Europa: 75 Jahre Max-Planck-Institut für Privatrecht* (Tübingen, Mohr Siebeck, 2001) 583, 588; Kropholler and von Hein (n 11) Einl EuGVO paras 68 et seq.

[17] Kropholler (n 16) 583 and 590; Hess (n 16) 353.

[18] Hess (n 16) 354.

[19] V Lipp, in T Rauscher (ed), *Münchener Kommentar zum FamFG*, 2nd edn (Munich, CH Beck, 2013) Art 4 EG-UntVO para 13; Andrae (n 8) Art 4 EG-UntVO para 14.

[20] Kropholler and von Hein (n 11) Art 23 EuGVO para 33; Andrae (n 8) Art 4 EG-UntVO para 15.

[21] Geimer (n 10) Art 23 EuGVVO para 104; G Wagner, in F Stein and M Jonas (eds), *Kommentar zur Zivilprozessordnung*, vol 10, 22nd edn (Tübingen, Mohr Siebeck, 2011) Art 23 EuGVVO para 57; P Mankowski, in T Rauscher (ed), *Kommentar zum Europäischen Zivilprozess- und Kollisionsrecht - EuZPR/EuIPR* (Munich, Sellier European Law Publishers, 2011) Art 23 Brüssel I-VO para 15.

[22] Lipp (n 19) Art 4 EG-UntVO para 13 fn 27.

[23] Hague Convention on the International Recovery of Child Support and Other Forms of Family Maintenance (Concluded 23 November 2007) [2011] OJ L192/51.

uniform document. However, the wording of Article 4(2) of the Maintenance Regulation does not impose such a requirement in the context of the legal term 'in writing'.[24] Since the European Union legislator refrained from establishing such a definition of 'in writing' within the Maintenance Regulation, even though it knew about the specification in the Hague Convention 2007, Article 4 of the Maintenance Regulation should be deemed to be 'eloquently silent' on further formal requirements, which are deliberately not included in its scope.

Against this background, only an analysis of the objectives of the Maintenance Regulation could enable the imposition of further requirements of formality. Recital 19 states the intention of the European Union legislator regarding choice of court agreements. Hereafter, legal certainty, predictability and party autonomy should be increased by choice of court agreements under the Maintenance Regulation. Furthermore, the weaker party should be protected. In respect of this protection the written form requirement ensures that the parties involved are warned of the consequences of their actions, informed of the scope of their rights and duties and that the content of the agreement is clearly evidenced. These functions are already satisfied to a certain extent in the aforementioned systematic interpretation of writing, because this makes certain that there is a real consensus between the parties, and avoids the risk of jurisdiction clauses being incorporated unilaterally by one party and going unnoticed by the other contracting party.[25] In addition, deriving further demands such as a uniform contractual document or signatures of both does not seem convincing given the European Union legislator's intention to safeguard the autonomy of the parties.[26] Further demands of formality may be desirable, but they are not required by the objectives of the Maintenance Regulation.[27]

In conclusion, the written form requirement in the European Maintenance Regulation should be interpreted in accordance with Article 23(1) of the Brussels I Regulation. The requirement is therefore satisfied by a declaration that clearly expresses the intention of the relevant party to conclude a choice of court agreement. Consequently, only the cancellation of the alternative formal elements of Article 23(1) of the Brussels I Regulation can be regarded as a fundamental innovation.

ii. Real Consensus between the Parties

In addition to the requirements of form, it is necessary for the parties to reach a consensus on the conclusion of a choice of court agreement. Like Article 23(1) of the Brussels I Regulation, Article 4(1) of the Maintenance Regulation only refers to the term 'agree'. Since the wording of the Maintenance Regulation corresponds to the wording of the Brussels I Regulation, the exisiting interpretation of 'agree' from the Brussels I Regulation can be applied.[28] According to this interpretation, the existence of a consensus has to be determined

[24] Andrae (n 8) Art 4 EG-UntVO para 14; Lipp (n 19) Art 4 EG-UntVO para 13.

[25] Case C-159/97 *Castelletti* [1999] ECR I-1597, para 19; Case C-71/83 *Russ* [1984] ECR 2417, para 24; Case C-24/76 *Estasis Saloti di Colzani* [1976] ECR 1831, para 9; Hess (n 2) § 6 para 138.

[26] V Lipp, 'Parteiautonomie im Internationalen Unterhaltsrecht', in A Verbeke, J Scherpe, C Declerck, T Helms and P Senaeve (eds), *Confronting the Frontiers of Family and Succession Law—Liber Amicorum Walter Pintens*, vol 1 (Cambridge, Intersentia, 2012) 847, 860.

[27] However, the German 'Bundesrat' criticised the formality of writing due to the lack of legal assistance and thus recommended the formality of notarial certification, 'Bundesrat' decision of 19 May 2006, BR-Drucks 30/06, 7.

[28] Lipp (n 19) Art 4 EG-UntVO para 14; Andrae (n 8) Art 4 EG-UntVO para 20.

independently and, in principle, without recourse to the national law of the court seised (*lex fori*).[29] The leading source of evidence of consensus between the parties is the meeting of formal requirements because these are specified to ensure that an agreement between the parties is in fact established.[30] According to the jurisprudence of the CJEU, the fulfilment of the formal requirements is a strong indication of a real consensus between the parties.[31] If, however, the requirements of form do not demonstrate the establishment of a mutual agreement, recourse can be had to the national law of the court seised.[32] This law may play an especially important role in questions of legal capacity, representation and the avoidance of an agreement.

In relation to the consensual element of the agreement, the recent reform of the Brussels I Regulation significantly changes the balance between these two Regulations. In line with the Hague Convention on Choice of Court Agreements (Hague Convention 2005),[33] the revision of the Brussels I Regulation provides a harmonised conflict of laws rule on the substantive validity of choice of court agreements.[34] This aims particularly to ensure a similar outcome on this matter whichever court is seised.[35] The extent to which the entry into force of this reform to the Brussels I Regulation can extend this goal of the European Union legislator to the Maintenance Regulation is highly questionable, given the unambiguous wording of Article 4 of the Maintenance Regulation and the jurisprudence of the CJEU to date. As long as the Maintenance Regulation is not reformed accordingly, the continuance of the current interpretation appears more likely than an extension of the conflict of laws rule in the Brussels I Regulation to the Maintenance Regulation.

iii. Restriction on the Free Choice of Jurisdiction

In contrast to Article 23 of the Brussels I Regulation, Article 4 of the Maintenance Regulation contains several requirements for the content of the agreement. In particular, the parties involved are no longer able to nominate the jurisdiction of any court in the Member States.[36] Rather, this free choice is considerably restricted by Article 4(1)(a) to (c) of the Maintenance Regulation. According to these restrictions, the parties may merely choose a court of a Member State in which one of them is habitually resident or of which one of them has the nationality. In the case of matrimonial maintenance obligations, the court of the Member State that has jurisdiction to settle matrimonial disputes or the court(s) of the Member State, which was the spouses' last common habitual residence for a period of at least one year, can be chosen by the parties.

[29] Kropholler and von Hein (n 11) Art 23 EuGVO para 23; Geimer (n 10) Art 23 EuGVVO para 75; Mankowski (n 21) Art 23 Brüssel I-VO para 39.

[30] Case C-387/98 *Coreck* [2000] ECR I-9337, para 13; Case C-106/95 *MSG* [1997] ECR I-911, para 15; Case C-24/76 (n 25) para 7.

[31] Case C-159/97 *Castelletti* [1999] ECR I-1597, para 20; Case C-106/95 (n 30) para 19.

[32] Mankowski (n 21) Art 23 Brüssel I-VO para 41; Lipp (n 26) 863; Kropholler and von Hein (n 11) Art 23 EuGVO para 28.

[33] Hague Convention on Choice of Court Agreements (Concluded 30 June 2005) [2009] OJ L133/3.

[34] Art 25(1) sentence 1 of the revised Brussels I Regulation.

[35] Proposal for a Regulation of the European Parliament and of the Council on jurisdiction and the recognition and enforcement of judgments in civil and commercial matters (recast) 14 December 2010, COM (2010) 748 final, 9.

[36] Lipp (n 26) 863.

a. Objective of the Restriction

Although the restriction on the free choice of jurisdiction causes a fundamental change in the existing legislation, the European Union legislator did not disclose the motivation behind this, neither in the Recitals to the Regulation nor in other legislative materials. Even the draft of the Regulation still provided for a free choice of jurisdiction.[37] Consequently, the objective pursued by the European Union legislator in restricting the free choice of jurisdiction can and must be questioned.[38] In this regard, various opinions exist on the possible motivation of the legislator.

It is often claimed that the restriction intends to ensure a proximity between the chosen court and the facts of the case.[39] This interpretation can be supported by the connecting factors of 'habitual residence' and the 'matrimonial court'. In fact, these particular courts are either best placed to evaluate the living conditions when answering the needs of the dependant and the capabilities of the debtor, or are able to take on maintenance disputes and all the connected disputes.[40] However, with regard to the connecting factor of 'nationality', a justification of the restriction based on proximity becomes questionable, since in maintenance matters 'nationality' often does not express a particularly close link between the persons involved and the Member State.[41] Above all, the relevant time for assessing whether the conditions of the agreement have been met is contrary to this interpretation, as even the connecting factors that imply the proximity may have elapsed long before the time that the maintenance proceedings are initiated.[42]

Additionally, it is repeatedly assumed that the European Union legislator intends in the future to make choice of court agreements in maintenance matters subject to criteria which are relevant for jurisdiction in order to ensure reasonable justification in matters of fact and, in particular, to avoid abuse.[43] The substantial proximity of the court would accordingly be far less relevant than the vulnerability of the dependant, who relies significantly on maintenance and who is therefore in a disadvantaged situation.[44] Not least in light of the long demanded but largely rejected general control of abuse in choice of court agreements in European civil procedure law, this interpretation appears convincing.[45]

[37] Proposal for a Council Regulation on jurisdiction, applicable law, recognition and enforcement of decisions and cooperation in matters relating to maintenance obligations, 15 December 2005, COM (2005) 649 final, 16; Andrae (n 8) Art 4 EG-UntVO para 27; Conti (n 1) 96.

[38] Lipp (n 26) 863.

[39] Andrae (n 8) Art 4 EG-UntVO paras 3 and 28; M Andrae, '§ 13 Familiensachen mit Auslandsberührung', in R Garbe and C Ullrich (eds), *Verfahren in Familiensachen*, 3rd edn (Baden-Baden, Nomos, 2012) § 13 para 159; P Reuß, in R Geimer and R Schütze (eds), *Internationaler Rechtsverkehr in Zivil- und Handelssachen*, 43rd edn (Munich, CH Beck, 2012) Art 4 EuUntVO para 6; M Heger, 'Haager Unterhaltsübereinkommen und UnterhaltsVO der Europäischen Union' in D Coester-Waltjen, V Lipp, E Schumann and B Veit (eds), *Europäisches Unterhaltsrecht* (Göttingen, Universitätsverlag Göttingen, 2010) 5, 10; P Finger, 'Verordnung EG Nr. 4/2009 des Rates (EuUnterhaltsVO)' (2011) *Familie und Recht* 254, 260.

[40] Andrae (n 8) Art 4 EG-UntVO para 28.

[41] Ibid para 29; Lipp (n 26) 864; Lipp (n 19) Art 4 EG-UntVO para 22.

[42] Lipp (n 26) 864; Lipp (n 19) Art 4 EG-UntVO para 22; Conti (n 1) 96.

[43] Lipp (n 26) 864; Conti (n 1) 97.

[44] Conti (n 1) 97; Lipp (n 19) Art 4 EG-UntVO para 3.

[45] Conti (n 1) 98; control of abuse in general Mankowski (n 21) Art 23 Brüssel I-VO para 12e; Kropholler and von Hein (n 11) Art 23 EuGVO para 86; Wagner (n 21) Art 23 EuGVVO para 38; E Gottschalk and S Breßler, 'Missbrauchskontrolle von Gerichtsstandsvereinbarungen im europäischen Zivilprozessrecht' (2007) *Zeitschrift für Europäisches Privatrecht* 56, 65; N Horn, 'Einwand des Rechtsmissbrauchs gegen eine Gerichtsstandsvereinbarung i.S.d. Art. 23 EuGVO?' (2007) *Praxis des Internationalen Privat- und Verfahrensrechts* 2.

In the sensitive area of maintenance disputes, this restriction thus could be interpreted as an institutionalised control of abuse. Moreover, this would conform to the legislation applicable to other vulnerable persons, such as insured persons, consumers and employees, in which the choice of jurisdiction is also restricted for the benefit of the vulnerable person. Consequently, this interpretation can explain both the suitability of 'nationality' as a connecting factor and also why the conditions have to be met either at the time the choice of court agreement is concluded or at the time the court is seised.[46]

b. Connecting Factors

'Habitual residence' as a connecting factor is the first restriction on the choice of jurisdiction (Article 4(1)(a) of the Maintenance Regulation). Although 'habitual residence' is the most important connecting factor for establishing international jurisdiction within the Maintenance Regulation, the term is not defined in the Regulation.[47] However, Recital 32 to the Regulation indicates that 'habitual residence' should be stricter than 'residence' and 'residence' is more than just mere 'presence'. In order to derive a uniform interpretation of 'habitual residence' from the Brussels IIa Regulation,[48] the Hague Convention 2007 and the Maintenance Regulation, 'habitual residence' should be interpreted as the main place of residence and ascertained on the basis of objective criteria such as length and permanence of residence, as well as family, professional and social ties.[49]

'Nationality' is another connecting factor (Article 4(1)(b) of the Maintenance Regulation). The legal term 'nationality' is self-explanatory, although it is tied up in the fundamental concerns about primary law surrounding Article 18 TFEU.[50] In cases of dual nationality, both nationalities could be applied.[51] Regarding this connecting factor, Article 2(3) of the Maintenance Regulation is also worth mentioning because it takes a specific characteristic of the *common law* into account, since it deems 'domicile' to be the relevant connecting factor in matrimonial matters instead of 'nationaliy'.[52] The legal term 'domicile' characterises the legal relationship of a person to a particular territory and thus to a particular legal system.[53]

In the case of maintenance obligations between spouses or former spouses, the 'court which has jurisdiction in matrimonial matters' and the 'last common habitual residence' are named as connecting factors, the latter of which must be maintained for a period of at least one year (Article 4(1)(c) of the Maintenance Regulation). In this regard, it is questionable whether this restricts the choice of court agreement for maintenance obligations in matrimonial matters further or whether this connecting factor extends the scope

[46] Lipp (n 26) 864; Lipp (n 19) Art 4 EG-UntVO para 23.

[47] Andrae (n 8) Art 3 EG-UntVO para 23; Lipp (n 19) Art 2 EG-UntVO para 18.

[48] Council Regulation (EC) No 2201/2003 of 27 November 2003 concerning jurisdiction and the recognition and enforcement of judgments in matrimonial matters and the matters of parental responsibility, repealing Regulation (EC) No 1347/2000 [2003] OJ EU L338/1.

[49] Lipp (n 19) Art 2 EG-UntVO para 20; Andrae (n 8) Art 4 EG-UntVO para 27.

[50] The Treaty on the Functioning of the European Union (Consolidated Version) [2008] OJ C115/47; W Hau, 'Das Zuständigkeitssystem der Europäischen Unterhaltsverordnung—Überlegungen aus der Perspektive des deutschen Rechts' in D Coester-Waltjen, V Lipp, E Schumann and B Veit (eds), *Europäisches Unterhaltsrecht* (Göttingen, Universitätsverlag Göttingen, 2010) 58, 64; Lipp (n 19) Art 4 para 22.

[51] Reuß (n 39) Art 4 EuUntVO para 23; Andrae (n 8) Art 4 EG-UntVO para 38.

[52] Lipp (n 19) Art 2 EG-UntVO para 15; Reuß (n 39) Art 4 EuUntVO para 23.

[53] Andrae (n 8) Art 2 EG-UntVO para 22.

of the choice. Although the wording of Article 4(1)(c) of the Maintenance Regulation is conclusively formulated, a restrictive interpretation thereof is largely and rightly rejected.[54] Otherwise the EU legislator would have restricted the choice of jurisdiction in the most practically relevant field of application to the greatest extent possible without any further explanation, namely nuptial and post-nuptial maintenance.[55] Moreover, the reinforcement of the autonomy of the parties intended by the EU legislator and proclaimed in Recital 19 contradicts a restrictive interpretation of this wording.[56]

c. Exercise of Choice

By virtue of the wording of Article 4(1) of the Maintenance Regulation, the choice of court agreement does not require the parties to explicitly refer to the relevant connecting factor. The mere declaration of a specific court that meets the conditions at the relevant time is sufficient.[57] Consequently, the mere declaration of the relevant connecting factor in the agreement is also sufficient, without any further specification as to the court.

However, an idiosyncrasy exists with respect to the connecting factor of the 'court which has jurisdiction in matrimonial matters'. In these cases, the parties must clearly express the link between the chosen court and the court in matrimonial matters.[58] The current legal situation in matrimonial matters does not enable a prior choice of court agreement, but only allows a prorogation of jurisdiction under the restrictive conditions of Article 12 of the Brussels IIa Regulation. Accordingly, the connecting factor of the court in matrimonial matters could be considered to be of relevance only in pending or concluded disputes relating to matrimonial matters, not least because of the measure of certainty required for a choice of court agreement.[59]

iv. Exclusion Relating to Maintenance Obligations towards a Minor

Article 4(3) of the Maintenance Regulation contains an exception to the generally approved, albeit significantly restricted, conclusion of choice of court agreements. Consequently, Article 4 does not give effect to a choice of court agreement in relation to a maintenance obligation towards a child under the age of 18. The European Union legislator aims to intensify the protection of the minor as the weaker party.[60] For this reason, the claimant in such a maintenance dispute is only able to choose between the competent courts that fall within Article 3 of the Maintenance Regulation. In particular, the court appointed by Article 3(b) of the Maintenance Regulation, which is beneficial for the dependant, can no longer be waived by a choice of court agreement.[61]

[54] Reuß (n 39) Art 4 EuUntVO para 26; Andrae (n 8) Art 4 EG-UntVO para 40; Gruber (n 6) 133.
[55] Andrae (n 8) Art 4 EG-UntVO para 42.
[56] Reuß (n 39) Art 4 EuUntVO para 26.
[57] Andrae (n 8) Art 4 EG-UntVO para 31.
[58] Ibid para 43.
[59] Ibid paras 44 et seq.
[60] Recital 19 to the Maintenance Regulation and Communication from the Commission to the Council and the European Parliament, 12 May 2006, COM (2006) 206 final, 3; critical, Hau (n 50) 64; Gottwald (n 13) 15; B Hess and M Mack, 'Der Verordnungsvorschlag der EG-Kommission zum Unterhaltsrecht' (2007) *Das Jugendamt* 229, 230; S Motzer, 'Anwendungsbeginn der EU-Unterhaltsverordnung' (2011) *Der Familienrechtsberater International* 56, 58.
[61] J Heinig, *Grenzen von Gerichtsstandsvereinbarungen im Europäischen Zivilprozessrecht* (Jena, Jenaer Wissenschaftliche Verlagsgesellschaft, 2010) 531; Reuß (n 39) Art 4 EuUntVO para 28; Andrae (n 8) Art 4 EG-UntVO para 50.

Moreover, the exclusion of the autonomy of the parties can be justified by the fact that a child cannot participate in the agreement as he or she is a minor, even though the child bears the legal consequences of the agreement.[62] According to the clear wording of Article 4(3) of the Maintenance Regulation, the exclusion only relates to maintenance obligations towards a child under the age of 18. Therefore, agreements relating to the maintenance of older children and vulnerable adults are not excluded.[63] An application of this exclusion by analogy in cases of vulnerable adults was contemplated but ultimately rejected on the basis of legislative history.[64]

In determining whether a choice of court agreement is covered by the exclusion in Article 4(3) of the Maintenance Regulation, the subject matter of the particular agreement is crucial because the Article does not regulate legal capacity, rather it excludes certain maintenance obligations from the autonomy of the parties.[65] The particular content of a choice of court agreement is determined by interpretation. Within the context of the interpretation, the parties involved and the time of the conclusion of the agreement can be relevant, although these criteria are not essential to the subject matter of the agreement.[66] If the interpretation leads to the conclusion that the choice of court agreement relates to a maintenance obligation towards a child under the age of 18, then the choice of court agreement is legally void in the EU due to Article 4(3) of the Maintenance Regulation.

If, however, the interpretation of an agreement leads to the conclusion that the general maintenance of a child is covered by the agreement, that is, that the maintenance of a child under and above the age of 18 is covered, problems arise regarding the application of Article 4(3) of the Maintenance Regulation. On the one hand, the solution for this special situation could be seen in the invalidity of the entire choice of court agreement.[67] On the other hand, a partial invalidity relating to the maintenance towards a child under the age of 18 could be considered the better solution.[68] Since the aim of this Article is the protection of the minor, which at first sight does not seem to require the invalidity of the entire agreement, partial invalidity would appear favourable.[69] However, potential risks for the vulnerable dependant are inherent in the use of an incomplete or imprecise agreement, since the dependant could, in reliance on the validity of the agreement, appear before a court, the selection of which was at least partially invalid. Pursuant to Article 5 of the Maintenance Regulation, if the jurisdiction of the court is not contested, the court becomes unreservedly competent, as this Article also applies in the face of the Article 4(3) exclusion.[70] Furthermore, courts are not legally obligated to inform vulnerable persons about the consequences of appearing before them without contesting their jurisidiction, although such

[62] Andrae (n 8) Art 4 EG-UntVO para 50.

[63] Lipp (n 19) Art 4 EG-UntVO para 9.

[64] Gruber (n 6) 133; W Hau, in H Prütting and T Helms (eds), *Kommentar zum FamFG*, 3rd edn (Cologne, Schmidt, 2013) § 110 para 50; Reuß (n 39) Art 4 EuUntVO para 31.

[65] Lipp (n 19) Art 4 EG-UntVO paras 10 et seq; Lipp (n 26) 861; Andrae (n 8) Art 4 EG-UntVO para 49; against Reuß (n 39) Art 4 EuUntVO para 30.

[66] Lipp (n 19) Art 4 EG-UntVO para 10; Andrae (n 8) Art 4 EG-UntVO para 49.

[67] Andrae (n 8) Art 4 EG-UntVO para 51.

[68] Lipp (n 19) Art 4 EG-UntVO para 11; Lipp (n 26) 861ff.

[69] Lipp (n 26) 862; Lipp (n 19) Art 4 EG-UntVO para 11.

[70] T Rauscher, 'Gerichtsstandsvereinbarungen in Unterhaltssachen mit Auslandsberührung' (2013) *Familienrecht und Familienverfahrensrecht* 25, 29; Reuß (n 39) Art 5 para 3; Lipp (n 19) Art 5 EG-UntVO para 6; critical, Andrae (n 8) Art 5 EG-UntVO para 1.

an instruction is not prohibited by law.[71] Consequently comprehensive protection of the minor dependant requires the invalidity of the entire agreement, which strengthens the significance of a precise choice of court agreement as well.

C. Effect of the Choice of Court Agreement

A valid choice of court agreement is binding on the parties involved and the court seised.[72] Therefore, the court seised must generally examine the validity of the choice of court agreement and ensure its efficacy (Article 10 of the Maintenance Regulation).[73] This obligation does not apply only if the dependant appears before a court without contesting its jurisdiction (Article 5 of the Maintenance Regulation). In a manner entirely consistent with the autonomy of the parties, the specific effects of the choice of court agreement depend on the intentions of the parties involved.[74] Accordingly, a variety of possibilities exist in favour of the parties, however, the wording of which must be sufficiently clear in the agreement. In particular, the parties may exclusively nominate a court or appoint it alongside other courts, or exclude certain courts, and confer international as well as local jurisdiction.[75] Hence, it is the content of the agreement that is decisive and which must be interpreted when necessary.[76]

In cases of doubt, Article 4(1) of the Maintenance Regulation presumes that the jurisdiction conferred by the agreement is exclusive in order to increase legal certainty and predictability.[77] Furthermore, choice of court agreements that confer exclusive jurisdiction on a third-country court are assessed in relation to Article 4 of the Maintenance Regulation when, but for the choice of court agreement, a court of a Member State would have had jurisdiction.[78]

Finally, one must also note that according to the current legal situation the *lis pendens* rule retains the strict priority, even in the event of an exclusive choice of court agreement.[79] At least within the scope of the Brussels I Regulation, the legal situation will change when its revised version enters into force. 'In order to enhance the effectiveness of exclusive choice of court agreements and to avoid abusive litigation tactics', Article 31(2) of the revised Brussels I Regulation prioritises courts which have been conferred exclusive jurisdiction by the parties.[80] However, it is doubtful whether the Maintenance Regulation will

[71] Case C-111/09 *Bilas* [2010] ECR I-4545, para 32; Hau (n 64) § 110 para 54; Wagner (n 21) Art 24 EuGVVO para 39.

[72] Reuß (n 39) Art 4 EuUntVO para 36; Lipp (n 19) Art 4 EG-UntVO para 31.

[73] Lipp (n 19) Art 4 EG-UntVO para 31.

[74] Case C-22/85 *Anterist* [1986] ECR 1951, para 14.

[75] Andrae (n 8) Art 4 EG-UntVO paras 10 and 57; Lipp (n 19) Art 4 EG-UntVO para 27.

[76] Conti (n 1) 106; Reuß (n 39) Art 4 EuUntVO para 13; Lipp (n 19) Art 4 EG-UntVO para 27.

[77] Kropholler and von Hein (n 11) Art 23 EuGVO para 90.

[78] Lipp (n 19) Art 4 EG-UntVO para 31; Hau (n 50), 68; Reuß (n 39) Art 4 EuUntVO para 16; pro application by analogy Andrae (n 8) Art 4 EG-UntVO para 70.

[79] Art 27(1) of the Brussels I Regulation and Art 12(1) of the Maintenance Regulation.

[80] Recital 22 to the revised Brussels I Regulation. See U Magnus, 'Gerichtsstandsvereinbarungen im Vorschlag zur Reform der EuGVO' in H Kronke and K Thorn (eds) *Grenzen überwinden—Prinzipien bewahren: Festschrift für Bernd von Hoffmann* (Bielefeld, Gieseking, 2011) 664, 675; B Hess, 'Die Reform der EuGVVO und die Zukunft des Europäischen Zivilprozessrechts' (2011) *Praxis des Internationalen Privat- und Verfahrensrechts* 125, 129.

be changed accordingly in the foreseeable future, since the abusive litigation tactic of a so-called *torpedo action* is still widely unknown in maintenance disputes.[81]

D. Need for a Cross-Border Implication?

The material scope of the Maintenance Regulation merely covers maintenance obligations arising from a family relationship (Article 1(1)). Although the Maintenance Regulation neither expressly requires a cross-border element, nor defines it, the material scope additionally requires that the dispute has a cross-border element, thus a choice of court agreement is excluded for purely domestic cases anyway.[82] This result already emerges from the numerous Recitals to the Maintenance Regulation.[83] Moreover, the European Union legislator does not have the competence to regulate a purely domestic case. The competence under Article 65 of the EC Treaty or under Article 81 TFEU is limited to civil matters with cross-border implications.[84]

However, it remains questionable how one is to examine the requirement of a cross-border implication. Two possibilities exist: either the cross-border element is considered as a positive condition for applying the Maintenance Regulation,[85] or the material scope of particular provisions of the Maintenance Regulation is reduced on teleological grounds in purely domestic cases.[86] At least in relation to choice of court agreements, there are several good reasons for the scope of Article 4 of the Maintenance Regulation to be reduced on teleological grounds. First, the wording of the Regulation does not explicitly require that the dispute contains a cross-border element, which per se renders a teleogical reduction more appropriate. Furthermore, the opponents of the teleogical reduction are faced with the challenge of defining the requirement of a cross-border implication exactly, which is very difficult, if not impossible. By contrast, the proponents of the teleogical reduction merely have to determine that the case is not purely domestic. Moreover, one must keep in mind the situation of the parties involved in a choice of court agreement. By concluding a choice of court agreement, the parties strive to increase legal certainty and predictability. In particular, they seek to prevent future ambiguities. Often it is hard to predict whether a cross-border element will exist. Therefore, a general assumption of validity of a choice of court agreement and teleological reduction in a purely domestic case would comply better with the legal reality.

III. Conclusion

The EU Maintenance Regulation contains several innovations that are of practical relevance for choice of court agreements in maintenance matters. Admittedly legal practitioners can often rely on their existing knowledge of choice of court agreements, since the provisions

[81] Andrae (n 8) Art 12 EG-UntVO para 9.
[82] Conti (n 1) 90; R Hüßtege, in H Thomas and H Putzo (eds), *Kommentar zur Zivilprozessordnung*, 34th edn (Munich, CH Beck, 2013) Vorbem Art 1 EuUnterhaltVO para 17; Hau (n 50), 60; Gruber (n 6) 132.
[83] Lipp (n 19) Art 1 EG-UntVO para 72.
[84] Gruber (n 6) 132; Andrae (n 8) Art 4 EG-UntVO para 8; Reuß (n 39) Art 1 EuUntVO para 7.
[85] Reuß (n 39) Art 1 EuUntVO para 7; Hüßtege (n 82) Vorbem Art 1 EuUnterhaltVO para 17.
[86] Lipp (n 19) Art 1 EG-UntVO para 73; Hau (n 64) § 110 para 14; Gruber (n 6) 133.

of the Maintenance Regulation governing the choice of court agreements principally follow on from the Brussels I Regulation. Nevertheless, the existing generous framework for choice of court agreements in the Brussels I Regulation is significantly restricted by the Maintenance Regulation. First, the requirements of formality were significantly increased by the reduction of the alternatives to written form. Secondly, the possible content of a choice of court agreement has been significantly restricted. Consequently, the contracting parties no longer enjoy the same autonomy in their choice of jurisdiction. In order to avoid abuse, they have instead to make their choice on the basis of connecting factors. In relation to a maintenance obligation towards a child under the age of 18, the possibility of concluding a choice of court agreement and thus the autonomy of the parties is completely excluded.

In view of the vulnerability of the maintenance dependant, the innovations made by the Maintenance Regulation appear, on the whole, to be welcome. In particular, they provide increased protection for maintenance creditors more in line with that given to other weaker parties, such as the insured, consumers and employees, in European Union civil procedure law. In light of the most recent reforms in this area generally and more particularly in the Brussels I Regulation, the current legal position of choice of court agreements in maintenance matters will remain the subject of further academic and political debate. Therefore, additional fundamental innovations are likely to occur. However, the Maintenance Regulation could also strongly influence reform discussions and potentially become the model for other Union legislation within European civil procedure law, since it contains an institutionalised control of abuse in its reduction of the parties' choice of jurisdiction.

27

The Enforcement of Maintenance Decisions in the EU: *Requiem* for Public Policy?

Family Relationships and the (Partial) Abolition of *Exequatur*

ILARIA VIARENGO

I. Introduction

This chapter deals with some aspects of the public policy defence by focusing on the relationship between the recognition of foreign maintenance decisions and the problem of the underlying family relationship. It analyses the (partial) abolition of *exequatur* for maintenance decisions in the European Union (section II). Consequently it examines whether public policy is actually weakening, despite the need for safeguarding domestic values, mirrored in the most recent Regulations in family matters (sections III and IV). In view of the increasing divergence of modern families from the traditional family archetype the overall objective of this chapter is to show how the most traditional Member States cope with the issue of the enforcement of maintenance decisions founded on unknown family patterns (sections V and VI).

II. Setting the Scene

A. The Abolition of the *Exequatur* in the Maintenance Regulation

Regulation (EC) No 4/2009 of 18 December 2008 on jurisdiction, applicable law, recognition and enforcement of decisions and cooperation in matters relating to maintenance obligations (the Maintenance Regulation) abolishes the *exequatur* for decisions given in a Member State bound by the Hague Protocol of 23 November 2007 on the Law Applicable to Maintenance Obligations (the Protocol).[1] This means that judgments, which are enforceable in the State of origin, will be enforceable in other Member States by mere

[1] Art 17 of the Maintenance Regulation [2009] OJ L7/1.

operation of law and without any procedure being necessary. By contrast, an *exequatur* is still necessary for decisions given in a Member State not bound by the Protocol, namely, the UK and Denmark.[2] For these decisions, the Maintenance Regulation provides a separate track, effectively similar to the already applicable Brussels I provisions,[3] but with reduction of the time terms, and limitations on the execution formalities (Articles 23 to 38).[4]

The reason is clear and is stated in Recital 24. The mutual recognition of decisions finds its justification in the guarantee of the application of the same substantive Regulation to the same matter, by means of uniform, conflict of laws provisions.[5] As is well known, the Maintenance Regulation does not provide rules on conflict of laws in respect of maintenance obligations, but Article 15 refers to those set out in the Protocol. After waiting for the results of the negotiations on the Protocol and the long discussions on possible solutions on the relationship between the two instruments,[6] the European Union legislator abandoned the initial draft of a complete system of conflict rules, as proposed by the Commission.[7] Therefore the Protocol has been adopted by the EU, with the exception of the UK and Denmark.[8]

The complete abolition of the *exequatur* is the final objective of judicial cooperation in civil matters and it is founded on the principle of mutual recognition, the cornerstone of the European Union. This approach has begun with the political programme of the Tampere summit in October 1999, which envisages in certain suggested areas, including maintenance claims, the removal of the 'grounds for refusal of enforcement'.[9] In this

[2] See the Council Decision of 30 November 2009 on the conclusion by the European Community of the Hague Protocol of 23 November 2007 on the Law Applicable to Maintenance Obligations (2009/941/EC) [2009] OJ L 331/17. On the Protocol see, eg, A Bonomi, 'The Hague Protocol of 23 November 2007 on the Law Applicable to Maintenance Obligations' (2008) *Yearbook of Private International Law* 339.

[3] Council Regulation (EC) No 44/2001 of 22 December 2000 on jurisdiction and the recognition and enforcement of judgments in civil and commercial matters [2001] OJ L12/1 (Brussels I).

[4] See in particular Arts 30 (30 days for the decision of enforceability) and 34(2) (90 days from the date the court was seised, except for exceptional circumstances, for the refusal or revocation of a declaration of enforceability).

[5] For a critique see C Kohler, 'Elliptiques variations sur un theme connu: competence judiciaire, conflits de lois et reconnaissance de décisions en matière alimentaire d'après le Règlement (CE) No 4/2009 du Conseil' in K Boele-Woelki, T Einhorn, D Girsberger and S Symeonides (eds), *Convergence and Divergence in Private International Law—Liber Amicorum Kurt Siehr* (The Hague, Eleven International Publishing, 2010) 277, 285. He affirms that uniform conflict of laws rules are not sufficient to provide justifications for abolishing *exequatur* and public policy together. The coherence between the new regime established by the Protocol and the Maintenance Regulation has also been criticised by S Arnold, 'Entscheidungseinklang und Harmonisierung im internationalen Unterhaltsrecht' (2012) *Praxis des Internationalen Privat- und Verfahrensrechts* 311. On the unification of conflict of laws rules as a tool for facilitating recognition of foreign judgments in matrimonial matters see also S Marinai, 'Matrimonial Matters and the Harmonization of Conflict of Laws: A Way to Reduce the Role of Public Policy as a Ground for Non-Recognition of Judgments' (2011) *Yearbook of Private International Law* 255, 262–72.

[6] See Interinstitutional File 2005/0259 CNS of 7 February 2008 'Discussion paper on the relationship between the draft Regulation on jurisdiction, applicable law, recognition and enforcement of decisions and cooperation in matters relating to maintenance obligations, and the 2007 Hague Protocol on the Law Applicable to Maintenance Obligations'.

[7] Arts 12–21 of the Proposal for a Council Regulation on jurisdiction, applicable law, recognition and enforcement of decisions and cooperation in matters relating to maintenance obligations, COM (2005) 649 final.

[8] For the reasons why the UK did not opt into the Decision of the Council to ratify the Protocol and therefore opted not to be bound by the applicable law rules see P Beaumont, 'International Family Law in Europe. The Maintenance Project, the Hague Conference and the EC: A Triumph of Reverse Subsidiarity' (2009) *Rabels Zeitschrift für ausländisches und internationales Privatrecht* 509, 514.

[9] Presidency Conclusions, Tampere European Council of 15 and 16 October 1999, paras 33–34, www.consilium.europa.eu/uedocs/cms_data/docs/pressdata/en/ec/00200-r1.en9.htm (accessed January 2014).

respect, several new legal instruments have abolished the *exequatur* proceedings, such as Regulations regarding the European Enforcement Order, the European Payment Order, and the European Small Claims Procedure.[10]

All of these Regulations, which could also affect maintenance claims, have abolished the public policy defence and established instead minimum procedural standards in the Member States. The Maintenance Regulation has gone further. It does not require that the authorities of the State of origin issue a certificate that attests that specific procedural requirements have been respected, as, for example, provided for in Articles 5 and 6 of the European Enforcement Order Regulation.[11] It does not even provide, as suggested in the Commission Proposal of 15 December 2005, a minimum harmonisation of procedural measures, in order to guarantee *ab origine* the respect of the fair trial. The claimant must only provide the competent enforcement authorities with the documents listed in Article 20.

Therefore, the only protection of the debtor is the right to apply for a review according to Article 19 regarding procedural mistakes in the original proceedings. However, this represents an exception, since the review, subject to strict time restrictions, is possible only if a defendant has not entered an appearance due to not having been properly served, or has been prevented from contesting the maintenance claim by reason of *force majeure* or other extraordinary circumstances without fault on his or her own part.

Moreover, grounds to refuse or suspend enforcement under the law of the Member State of enforcement must be as limited as possible. These grounds can be applied insofar as they are compatible with the very strict reasons listed in Article 21; the enforcement must be refused if the right to enforce the decision of the court of origin is extinguished. The enforcement must also be refused if the decision is irreconcilable with decisions in the Member State of enforcement, in other Member States, or in third States. These

[10] Regulation (EC) No 805/2004 of the European Parliament and of the Council of 21 April 2004 creating a European Enforcement Order for uncontested claims [2004] OJ L 143/15; Regulation (EC) No 861/2007 of the European Parliament and of the Council of 11 July 2007 establishing a European Small Claims Procedure [2007] OJ L 199/1; Regulation (EC) No 1896/2006 of the European Parliament and of the Council of 12 December 2006 creating a European Order for payment procedure [2006] OJ L 399/1.

[11] A certificate is also requested by Regulation 2201/2003 (EC) on jurisdiction and the recognition and enforcement of judgments in matrimonial matters and matters of parental responsibility, repealing Regulation 1347/2000 EC [2003] OJ L338 (Brussels IIa), in cases concerning rights of access and relating to the return of an abducted child (Art 42). The declaration of enforceability is replaced, to a certain extent, by a certificate which must accompany the judgment in such cases. By that certificate, the court giving judgment provides evidence that the requirements laid down by the Regulation have been complied with, in particular that the child has had the opportunity to be heard. Consequently, the issue of the certificate in the Member State of origin, referred to in Art 42(1) of the Regulation, is to be recognised and is to be automatically enforceable in another Member State, there being no possibility of opposing its recognition. The CJEU stated that the court of origin retains the sole power of review, even if in the view of the court of enforcement there have been 'serious infringements of fundamental rights', as the child's right to be heard: Case C-491/10 PPU *Aguirre Zarraga v Pelz* [2010] ECR I-14247, para 48. For a critique of *Zarraga* see L Walker and P Beaumont, 'Shifting the Balance Achieved by the Abduction Convention: The Contrasting Approaches of the European Court of Human Rights and the European Court of Justice' (2011) *Journal of Private International Law* 231, 239–49. Even more recently the abolition of *exequatur* and the guarantee system of human rights provided in Brussels IIa were not considered 'dysfunctional' by the European Court of Human Rights in *Povse v Austria* App No 3890/11 (ECtHR, 18 June 2013) available at the HUDOC internet page www.hudoc.echr.coe.int/sites/eng/Pages/search.aspx (HUDOC), para 87. The case concerned a dispute relating to the custody of a child who had been taken to Austria by its mother after leaving the child's father with whom she had been living in Italy. A return order was issued by an Italian court, as the court of the child's pre-abduction residence under Art 11(8) of Brussels IIa. As Brussels IIa has abolished *exequatur* with respect to return orders, the issue was whether the Austrian court was compelled to enforce the Italian decision despite the allegation that the return of the child would have entailed a grave risk for its well-being.

decisions must fulfil the conditions necessary for their recognition in the Member State of enforcement. As a result only the violation of very fundamental principles of the fair trial may be invoked against recognition and enforcement of a decision coming from a Member State that is bound by the Protocol.

Substantive public policy is no longer available in order to refuse recognition.[12]

B. The Survival of the *Exequatur* for Maintenance Decisions

Conversely, an *exequatur* is still necessary for decisions from those Member States not bound by the Protocol, as mentioned above, as well as for decisions given in a third State which is party to the 2007 Hague Convention on the International Recovery of Child Support and Other Forms of Family Maintenance (the Hague Recovery Convention).[13] The Hague Recovery Convention provides a more rapid, two-step procedure for recognition and enforcement modelled on Brussels I, as well as an alternative one-step procedure that applies in the States which make a declaration to that effect. In both procedures, a prominent ground for non-recognition is public policy.

As a result, EU Member States may rely on the public policy defence in order not to recognise decisions from the UK or Denmark where the Protocol does not apply, or from a third State, party or not to the Hague Recovery Convention. In the family field, unlike in civil and commercial matters, there are still fundamental differences between the legal systems of the Member States that could trigger the application of substantive public policy. The practical need for a public policy defence is particularly strong in those States that have a strong objection to same-sex relationships (ie registered partnership and same-sex marriages). The public policy defence allows these States to refuse to enforce a maintenance decision obtained by one same-sex partner against another.

The possibility of resorting to public policy for this purpose survives in another legal context. In this respect, it is worth recalling the interplay between Brussels I and the Maintenance Regulation. The new Brussels I Regulation, adopted following recasting negotiations

[12] On the distinction between procedural and substantive public policy in EU private international and procedural law see B Hess and T Pfeiffer, *The Interpretation of the Public Policy Exception as referred to in EU Instruments of Private International and Procedural Law* (Brussels, European Parliament, 2011) 29 available at www.europarl.europa.eu/committees/en/juri/studiesdownload.html?languageDocument=EN&file=40891 (accessed January 2014). One may wonder whether in the Maintenance Regulation the minimum procedural protection of the debtor is sufficiently guaranteed. This chapter does not deal with the several procedural issues to which public policy could be referred. However one cannot help but quote the very famous case of the German Federal Court of 26 August 2009, concerning paternity proceedings (BGH, 26 August 2009, XII ZR 169/07, BGHZ 182, 188; (2009) *Neue Juristische Wochenschrift* 3306; (2009) *Zeitschrift für das gesamte Familienrecht* 1816). The defendant was declared the father of the minor claimant by a Polish court and was ordered to pay maintenance. During the paternity proceedings the defendant had requested a medical expert opinion in order to prove that he was not the father. The Polish court, however, ignored this request and based its judgment exclusively on the examination of the grandmother of the child that testified that her daughter, the child's mother, had told her that the defendant was the child's father. The Federal Court refused enforcement on the basis of the violation of procedural public policy. Suffice it to note here that under the Maintenance Regulation it would have been hopeless for the claimant to seek withdrawal of the foreign judgment.

[13] The Hague Recovery Convention is in force between Albania, Bosnia and Herzegovina, Norway and Ukraine. It has been signed by the EU, and the Decision has been taken by the EU to ratify it [2011] OJ L 93/9, and it has been signed by Burkina Faso and the United States, but not yet ratified. See www.hcch.net/index_en.php?act=conventions.status&cid=131 (accessed January 2014).

during 2011 and 2012 on the Regulation presently in force,[14] formally acknowledges the exclusion from its scope of the 'maintenance obligations arising from a family relationship, parentage, marriage, or affinity'.[15] Since 18 June 2011, they have already been subject to the Maintenance Regulation.[16] The definition of maintenance obligations does not raise any doubts, thanks to the autonomous notion of the Court of Justice of the European Union (CJEU) in interpreting Article 5(2) of the Brussels Convention (and therefore of Brussels I).[17] The Maintenance Regulation, even if it does not explicitly provide a definition of maintenance obligations, highlights the necessity to give it such an autonomous interpretation, in order to avoid discrimination in similar situations and to facilitate the recovery of maintenance claims (Recital 11).

On the contrary, EU law is still lacking a common notion of 'family relationship'. It is obvious that such a notion would be appropriate to determine the limits of application of both Regulations, such as the positive limits of the Maintenance Regulation and the negative limits of Brussels I. In fact, this latest Regulation does not exclude all maintenance obligations.

But in the absence of an autonomous definition of family relationship, this notion is necessarily left to Member States. The Maintenance Regulation did not follow the extension included in the Commission's Proposal to maintenance obligations deriving from 'relationships deemed by the law applicable to such relationships as having comparable effects'.[18] This form has been dropped in order to coordinate with the Protocol, which determines its own substantive scope of application in the same terms, but also guarantees coherence with the content of Recitals 21 and 25 and of Article 22 of the Maintenance Regulation, regarding the non-application of the Regulation to the preliminary questions related to family status.[19]

However, maintenance claims based on family patterns that differ from the traditional ones, such as the different forms of same-sex relationships, cannot be considered excluded from the Maintenance Regulation. The above-mentioned relationships are to be determined under the *lex fori*. Therefore, Member States that recognise these relationships will be able to consider them as possible sources of maintenance obligations, according to the Maintenance Regulation. On the contrary, States such as Italy,[20] in which these relationships

[14] The new Regulation, Regulation (EU) No 1215/2012 of the European Parliament and of the Council of 12 December 2012 on jurisdiction and the recognition and enforcement of judgments in civil and commercial matters [2012] OJ L 351/1 (New Brussels I), shall apply from 10 January 2015. On the New Brussels I, for the first commentaries, see H Gaudemet-Tallon and C Kessedjian, 'La refonte du règlement Bruxelles I' (2013) *Revue Trimestrielle de Droit Europeen* 1; P Hay, 'Notes on the European Union's Brussels-I "Recast" Regulation' (2013) *The European Legal Forum* 1; PA Nielsen, 'The New Brussels I Regulation' (2013) *CMLR* 503.

[15] Art 1(2)(e).

[16] The Maintenance Regulation (and accordingly the Protocol adopted by the EU with the exception of the UK and Denmark) is applied to proceedings instituted after 18 June 2011, and to decisions following proceedings commenced before that date, insofar as they fall within the scope of Brussels I. On the other hand, Brussels I shall continue to apply to procedures for recognition and enforcement that are already underway on the date that the Maintenance Regulation is applied (Art 75).

[17] Case C-220/95 *van den Boogaard v Laumen* [1997] ECR I-1147.

[18] Art 1(1) of the Proposal.

[19] Art 22 provides that the recognition and enforcement of a decision on maintenance shall not in any way imply the recognition of the family relationship, parentage, marriage, or affinity underlying the maintenance obligation which gave rise to the decision.

[20] Currently the discipline of marriage, as interpreted by the Italian Constitutional Court (Judgment No 138, 14 April 2010; see also Order No 4, 16 December 2010, www.cortecostituzionale.it/actionPronuncia.do), excludes from the Italian notion of marriage, registered partnerships, as well as marriages and unions between persons of the same sex.

are not recognised, could apply Brussels I, at least if the maintenance obligations are specified in an agreement. Actually contractual maintenance claims will continue to be governed by Brussels I. The New Brussels I has abolished the *exequatur*, but substantive public policy, according to Article 45, maintains a role as grounds to refuse enforcement of a judgment. In fact, the Commission's Proposal to abolish any substantive public policy control, providing just the respect for the procedural aspects of public policy,[21] has not been followed. The abolition of the *exequatur* procedure was one of the most difficult questions discussed during the recast negotiations. Intense discussions took place in particular on whether or not to retain all the grounds of non-recognition contained in Brussels I. The proposed abolition of substantive public policy was deemed to be too radical by a large number of Member States.[22] So, while *exequatur* was abolished, the grounds retained in the end correspond to those of Brussels I.

III. *Requiem* for Public Policy?

In this context one may wonder whether a weakening of the limits of public policy is effectively consolidating vis-à-vis the opposite need for safeguarding the domestic values. Family law has undergone a radical change over the last twenty years or so. The recent decades have seen the rise of new protections to couples outside traditional marriage (eg registered partnerships and same-sex marriages) as well as to the new frontiers of the establishment of parenthood (eg surrogacy, adoption by an unmarried person and second-parent adoptions). As a result, the landscape of family law in Europe is extremely diverse.[23]

And in Europe there are different views as to the notion and application of public policy, and a contrast between a more liberal approach and, on the contrary, a more rigid approach. This contrast is mirrored in the most recent Regulations where other mechanisms aimed at preserving States' core values in addition to public policy can be found.

[21] Proposal for a Regulation of the European Parliament and of the Council on jurisdiction and the recognition of judgments in civil and commercial matters, COM (2010) 748 final, Brussels, 14 December 2010.

[22] For a treatment of this issue during the recast see, among others, R Arenas Gárcia, 'Abolition of *Exequatur*: Problems and Solutions—Mutual Recognition, Mutual Trust and Recognition of Foreign Judgments: Too Many Words in the Sea' (2010) *Yearbook of Private International Law* 351; P Beaumont and E Johnston, 'Abolition of the Exequatur in Brussels I: Is a Public Policy Defence Necessary for the Protection of Human Rights?' (2010) *Praxis des Internationalen Privat- und Verfahrensrechts* 105; P Schlosser, 'The Abolition of Exequatur Proceedings—Including Public Policy Review?' (2010) *Praxis des Internationalen Privat- und Verfahrensrechts* 101; P Oberhammer, 'The Abolition of Exequatur' (2010) *Praxis des Internationalen Privat- und Verfahrensrechts* 197; G Cuniberti and I Rueda, 'Abolition of *Exequatur*—Addressing the EU Commission's Concerns' (2011) *Rabels Zeitschrift für ausländisches und internationales Privatrecht* 286; B Hess, 'The Brussels I Regulation: Recent case-law of the Court of Justice and the Commission's proposed recast' (2012) *CMLR* 1075; E Lein (ed), *The Brussels I Review Proposal Uncovered* (London, BIICL, 2012); F Pocar, I Viarengo and FC Villata (eds), *Recasting Brussels I* (Padua, Cedam, 2012).

[23] See generally K Boele-Woelki and A Fuchs (eds), *Legal Recognition of Same-Sex Relationships in Europe*, 2nd edn (Cambridge, Intersentia, 2012). The same conclusion applies worldwide. In this respect one cannot help but quote the recent and historic judgment of the US Supreme Court of 26 June 2013 in *United States v Windsor* 570 US___ (2013). The Supreme Court struck down s 3 of the Defense of Marriage Act (DOMA), that defines the term 'marriage' for all purposes under federal law, including the provision of federal benefits, as 'only a legal union between one man and one woman as husband and wife', ruling that s 3 DOMA is unconstitutional as it violates the Fifth Amendment's guarantee of equal protection of the laws, as applied to persons of the same sex who are legally married under the laws of their State.

Regarding maintenance, it is true that the Maintenance Regulation abolishes the *exequatur* for the decisions given in a Member State bound by the Protocol. However, the claim of maintenance may sometimes be rejected under Article 6 of the Protocol, which allows for a 'special defence' against maintenance claims between same-sex partners.

This provision confers on the debtor of the maintenance obligation the possibility to contest a claim from the creditor on the ground that there is no such obligation under either the law of the State of the habitual residence of the debtor or the law of the State of the common nationality of the parties, if there is one. This defence, although it is not the same mechanism as public policy, as it is obviously raised by the defendant, is meant to pursue the same goal.[24] For example, a debtor residing in Italy, who has made a civil partnership in Germany, could contest the maintenance claim of his or her partner residing in Germany, before the German judge, due to the lack of this institution in the Italian system. This may be possible even if the applicable law (in this case the German law) has been chosen in advance by the parties, according to the Protocol which allows such an agreement.[25]

Paradoxically, it could be easier for the creditor to recover maintenance obligations when the decision is given in a Member State not bound by the Protocol. It is true that public policy still plays a role, but it is also true that Article 37 of the Maintenance Regulation provides for the partial enforceability of the decision. The declaration of enforceability could be limited to the part of the decision regarding the maintenance obligations, even if based on the recognition of an unknown family relationship in the requested State.

IV. Trend towards a Laissez-faire Approach

The same logic informed Article 13 of Rome III,[26] according to which the judicial authorities of Member States party to the Regulation, and whose law does not deem the marriage valid for the purposes of divorce, may abstain from ruling on divorce. For instance, as a result of the fact that they do not recognise the validity of same-sex marriages, Italian courts are not compelled to render a decision on divorce between same-sex spouses. Likewise, those States that do not characterise registered partnerships as marriages are not compelled to pronounce their dissolution.[27] To safeguard fundamental national values,

[24] Kohler (n 5) 286, speaks of a 'privatisation' of public policy.

[25] Art 8.

[26] Council Regulation (EU) 1259/2010 implementing enhanced cooperation in the area of the law applicable to divorce and legal separation [2010] OJ L 343/10 (Rome III). On Art 13 see especially K Boele-Woelki, 'For Better or for Worse: The Europeanization of International Divorce Law' (2010) *Yearbook of Private International Law* 1, 22; P Hammje, 'Le nouveau règlement (UE) No 1259/2010 du Conseil du 20 décembre 2010 mettant en œuvre une cooperation renforcée dans le domaine de la loi applicable au divorce et à la séparation de corps' (2011) *Revue Critique du Droit International Privé* 291, 337f; M Fallon, 'Le nouveau droit du divorce international selon le règlement Rome III: une evolution tranquille' (2012) *Revue trimestrielle de droit familial* 291, 308.

[27] This issue is currently disputed in Member States which only provide for registered partnership but not for same-sex marriage. eg in Germany it is held that the effect of a homosexual marriage concluded abroad cannot exceed the effects of a registered partnership concluded under German law. Therefore, a homosexual marriage is 'downgraded' and converted into a registered partnership also with regard to the effects of its dissolution. See P Mankowski and F Hoffmann, 'Scheidung ausländischer gleichgeschlechtlicher Ehen in Deutschland?' (2011) *Praxis des Internationalen Privat- und Verfahrensrechts* 247. Critical, UP Gruber, 'Le mariage homosexuel et le

Article 13 introduces a substantive provision which reinforces public policy limitations and entails the exclusion of the application of a foreign law when that law clashes with such fundamental values.[28]

We can find the same attitude of the European legislator—this laissez-faire approach—when family status is important as a preliminary question. In this respect, as already mentioned, the Maintenance Regulation provides that the recognition and enforcement of a decision on maintenance shall not in any way imply the recognition of the family relationship, parentage, marriage or affinity underlying the maintenance obligation which gave rise to the decision.[29] Along the same lines, Brussels IIa expressly excludes from the scope of its rules 'the establishment of parenthood'.[30] Brussels IIa includes then, among the reasons for non-recognition of judgments, a double and generic incompatibility with other decisions matching the characteristics outlined in Article 22(c) and (d). Finally, albeit with different wording and subject to different interpretations, Article 1(2)(a) (b) (f) of Rome III, Article 1(3)(a) of the two Proposals on matrimonial property regimes, and on property consequences of registered partnerships,[31] and Article 1(2)(a) of the Succession Regulation,[32] exclude family status from their scope.

A different solution is provided by the Protocol, according to which the *lex causae* 'shall determine inter alia a) whether, to what extent and from whom the creditor may claim maintenance'.[33] But decisions issued pursuant to the Protocol shall not affect the existence of a family relationship, such as parentage, marriage or affinity whereby that obligation is owed.[34]

droit international privé' (2013) *Revue critique du droit international privé* 65, 71. For further references to other Member States see P Wautelet, 'Private International Law Aspects of Same-Sex Marriages and Partnerships in Europe—Divided We Stand?' in K Boele-Woelki and A Fuchs (eds), *Legal Recognition of Same-Sex Relationships in Europe*, 2nd edn (Cambridge, Intersentia, 2012) 143, 165.

[28] It is worth noting that this provision ensures an effect opposite to another provision, bearing the same title, provided in Brussels IIa. Art 25 of Brussels IIa narrows down the relevance of public policy, providing that the divergence between national laws, that is to say the different prerequisites and conditions whose existence is the ground in the different legal orders for the dissolution of marriage, does not constitute per se an obstacle to recognition.

[29] See (n 19).

[30] Recital 10, Art 1(3)(a).

[31] Proposal for a Council Regulation on jurisdiction, applicable law and the recognition and enforcement of decisions in matters of matrimonial property regimes (COM (2011) 126 final) and Proposal for a Council Regulation on jurisdiction, applicable law and the recognition and enforcement of decisions regarding the property consequences of registered partnerships (COM (2011) 127 final) both of 16 March 2011. See, among others, C González Beilfuss, 'The Proposal for a Council Regulation on the Property Consequences of Registered Partnerships' (2011) *Yearbook of Private International Law* 183 and I Viarengo, 'The EU Proposal on Matrimonial Property Regimes' (2011) *Yearbook of Private International Law* 199. On 10 September 2013 the European Parliament adopted many amendments to the Proposal regarding the property consequences of registered partnerships, particularly stressing that the recognition of a decision in a Member State has the sole object to allow the enforcement of the property consequences determined in that decision, without implying recognition by that Member State of the underlying partnership and without any influence in Member States where the institution of a registered partnership does not exist (Recital 8a and Art 21(1) European Parliament legislative resolution of 10 September 2013 on the proposal for a Council Regulation on jurisdiction, applicable law and the recognition and enforcement of decisions regarding the property consequences of registered partnerships, COM(2011)0127–C7-0094/2011–2011/0060(CNS)).

[32] Regulation (EU) No 650/2012 of the European Parliament and of the Council of 4 July 2012 on jurisdiction, applicable law, recognition and enforcement of decisions and acceptance and enforcement of authentic instruments in matters of succession and on the creation of a European Certificate of Succession (Succession Regulation). See, eg, P Lagarde, 'Les principes de base du nouveau règlement européen sur les successions' (2012) *Revue Critique de Droit International Privé* 713.

[33] Art 11.

[34] Art 1.

These provisions reflect the effort of the European Union to affirm the principle of mutual recognition, even in the presence of different family institutions in Member States. In this respect, the relationship between the protection and the circulation of family status and the mechanism of recognition of foreign measures—whose outcome remains unclear—is crucial. As a matter of fact, any obstacle to the recognition of a personal status may undermine the free movement of persons.

V. The Role of European Public Policy

The current legal framework in EU family law allows conflicting principles to co-exist, but also allows escape from systems that are viewed as being too progressive. It is true that, if a maintenance decision also includes a decision on the establishment of status, the decision on family status would not necessarily have to be recognised and enforced. In fact, as already mentioned, Article 37 of the Maintenance Regulation provides for the partial enforceability of a decision. This means that it is possible to recognise and enforce only the part of the decision that deals with the maintenance payment without giving effect to the establishment of parentage per se.[35]

But it is also true that where public policy survives, the judicial authorities of an 'objecting' State may refuse the recognition and enforcement of foreign judgments. Actually, their behaviour is difficult to foresee, especially in those States that have strong objections to the recognition of different family patterns and in particular if there are strong connections, such as citizenship, between the parties and the State of enforcement.

The increasing mobility of people emphasises the need to reconcile such differences into one framework that protects individuals and eliminates obstacles to their possible movements from one State to another.

One may wonder whether the application of a possible common concept of European public policy[36] would play a role in this regard. This raises the question of whether the concept of public policy, as determined by national law and aiming primarily at the preservation of certain family models, is compatible with a growing Europeanisation of the public policy exception, which focuses on safeguarding individual rights and on the prohibition of discrimination. With regard to procedural public policy, national public policy has been largely replaced by standards of European Union law. Since the landmark decisions in the *Krombach*, *Maxicar* and *Gambazzi* cases,[37] the CJEU has positively determined the content of the public policy exception by referring to Article 6 of the European Convention on Human Rights (ECHR) and to the pertinent case law of the European Court of Human Rights (ECtHR). Consequently, in most EU Member States, judicial practice is currently shifting from national procedural guarantees to European standards.[38] One wonders whether a uniform notion of substantive public policy is also developing in family matters.

[35] The same rule is provided in Art 19(2) of the Hague Recovery Convention and already in Art 3 of the 1973 Hague 1973 Maintenance Enforcement Convention.

[36] On this concept see generally J Kramberger Škerl, 'European Public Policy (with an Emphasis on Exequatur Proceedings)' (2011) *Journal of Private International Law* 461, also for further references.

[37] Case C-7/98 *Krombach v Bamberski* [2000] ECR I-1935; Case C-38/98 *Renault v Maxicar* [2000] ECR I-2973; Case C-394/07 *Marco Gambazzi v DaimlerChrysler Canada Inc, CIBC Mellon Trust Company* [2009] ECR I-2563.

[38] Hess and Pfeiffer (n 12) 157.

Such a common notion has been evoked in the latest EU Regulations, with reference both to the role of fundamental rights and to the consolidation of common principles.[39]

Common standards leading to a European public policy in family matters are beginning to appear. Recently signals of a possible extension of the notion of family are emerging both in the ECtHR and, although more timidly, in the CJEU case law.[40]

For example, the ECtHR, in the landmark judgment of *Schalk and Kopf v Austria*, declared that cohabiting same-sex couples living in a stable relationship constitutes 'family life' just as the relationship of a different-sex couple in the same situation would.[41]

With regards to new forms of establishing parenthood it is worth recalling the well-known case of *Wagner and JMWL v Luxembourg*, dealing with 'full adoption' by a single person, which was not possible in Luxembourg. The Court convicted Luxembourg of violating Article 8 ECHR, because it refused to recognise, on the basis of national rules of private international law, a judicial decision adopted pursuant to foreign legal rules that were different from those of Luxembourg.[42]

In the cases of *Gas and Dubois v France*[43]and *X and others v Austria*,[44] the ECtHR was requested to express its views on the exclusion of the second-parent adoption in a same-sex couple. The cases had similar facts, but the judgments went in opposite directions. In *Gas and Dubois*, the Court found that there had been no difference of treatment based on sexual orientation between an unmarried, different-sex couple and a same-sex couple because under French law, second-parent adoption was not open to either type of relationship. Thus, the Court concluded that there was no violation of the prohibition against discrimination and of the right to respect for private and family life. On the contrary, in *X and Others v Austria*, there had been a violation because Austria allows this type of adoption in an unmarried, different-sex couple.

[39] In Recitals 30 of Rome III and 81 of the Succession Regulation there is a reference to the fundamental rights and principles recognised by the Charter of Fundamental Rights of the European Union, and in particular by Art 21 thereof, which prohibits all forms of discrimination, such as those based on sex or sexual orientation. Both Regulations should be applied by the competent authorities in Member States in observance of those rights and principles. Furthermore, Recitals 25 of Rome III and 58 of the Succession Regulation point out that the public policy exception cannot be applied in contrast to the Charter of Fundamental Rights of the European Union, and in particular Art 21 thereof. Finally, Art 10 of Rome III can be traced back to the general framework of the common values of public policy, in that it provides for the applicability of the *lex fori* where the foreign applicable law 'does not grant one of the spouses equal access to divorce or legal separation on grounds of their sex'. With such a provision, the Regulation aims to ensure respect for the principle of non-discrimination between a man and a woman in its specific enforcement of substantive and procedural equality before the law, and thus removes any doubts in all the Member States bound by it.

[40] Overtures to the general applicability of the fundamental right to non-discrimination can be found in the CJEU in Case C-267/06 *Tadao Maruko v Versorgungsanstalt der deutschen Bühnen* [2008] ECR I-1757, and Case C-147/08 *Römer v Freie und Hansestadt Hamburg* [2011] ECR I-3591, para 28. In these cases the CJEU ruled in favour of the comparability between a registered partnership (for persons of the same sex) and marriage (solely open to persons of different sex) under German law in order to obtain, in the first case, a survivor's pension and, in the second, a supplementary retirement pension. However, although the Court held that the refusal of these employment benefits constituted direct discrimination on the ground of sexual orientation, it pointed out that the two situations are comparable in the light of the broad provisions of the German law in which the same obligations are incumbent on both registered life partners and married spouses (*Römer*, paras 43, 52). It is highly questionable whether from this case law a more general obligation to eliminate any discrimination can be determined. See also J Borg-Barthet, 'The Principled Imperative to Recognise Same-Sex Unions in the EU' (2012) *Journal of Private International Law* 359, 381.

[41] *Schalk and Kopf v Austria* App No 30141/04 (ECtHR, 24 June 2010) HUDOC, para 94.

[42] *Wagner and JMWL v Luxembourg* App No 76240/01 (ECtHR, 28 June 2007) HUDOC. See also *EB v France* App No 43546/02 (ECtHR, 22 January 2008) HUDOC.

[43] *Gas and Dubois v France* App No 25951/07 (ECtHR, 15 March 2012) HUDOC.

[44] *X and Others v Austria* App No 19010/07 (ECtHR, 19 February 2013) HUDOC.

As mentioned before, some signals of a possible extension of the notion of family are emerging in the case law.[45] However, the ECtHR is still rather cautious. In all these judgments, the Court has reiterated that the ECHR does not impose either an obligation on Member States to grant same-sex couples access to marriage, or to extend the right to second-parent adoption to unmarried couples, or to give full adoption rights to a single person. In the Court's words 'this area should still be regarded as one of evolving rights with no established consensus, where States enjoy a margin of appreciation'.[46]

The use of the margin of appreciation by the ECtHR is reminiscent, mutatis mutandis, of the use of public policy by the European legislator. Both seem reluctant to move too far beyond the consensus position between the ECHR and EU Member States.

Be that as it may, one can see the first effects of this case law on a State such as Italy, which still maintains the most traditional notion of marriage at the European level. Some recent Italian decisions reveal a more open approach.

The Italian Supreme Court (Corte di Cassazione), following the *Schalk and Kopf* judgment, has stated that a same-sex couple living in a stable relationship holds the right to family life, and may, in specific situations, sue to claim a consistent treatment as regards to married couples.[47] This decision marks a fundamental change of direction in the treatment of same-sex couples in the Italian legal system. The Supreme Court rejected the lower court's reasoning, which had denied the registration in the public records of the same-sex marriage at stake on public policy grounds.[48] Instead, the Corte di Cassazione refused recognition of the marriage as well, but for the technical reason that the marriage is unable to produce legal effects in the Italian legal system, rather than under the public policy exception. Consequently, it seems prepared to recognise some of the consequences of a same-sex marriage validly concluded abroad.

Following this approach, very recently, a court of first instance ordered the registration in the public records of a marriage celebrated in New York between two Italian men. The couple took the municipality to court after its registrar refused to register their marriage.[49] This ruling is historical because for the first time an Italian court has recognized a same-sex couple as legally married.[50]

[45] Following this trend see *Vallianatos and others v Greece* App Nos 29381/09 and 32684/09 (ECtHR, 7 November 2013) HUDOC, regarding the application of the principle of non-discrimination between different-sex couples and same-sex couples entering in registered partnerships. The ECHR, on February 21, 2014 has decided to consider some cases regarding same-sex unions in Italy (*Orlandi and others v. Italy; Oliari and Longhi v Italy*). In all cases the applicants complain that they are being discriminated against, in the enjoyment of their rights protected by the Convention, on the basis of their sexual orientation. In the *Orlandi* case they complain specifically about the authorities' refusal to register their marriage contracted abroad and in the *Oliari* case that the Italian legislation did not allow them to get married or enter into any other type of civil union. Moreover, it is still pending the case *Taddeucci and McCall v Italy* which concerns the refusal to issue a residence permit to the non-EU citizen, unmarried, same-sex partner of an Italian citizen.

[46] *Schalk and Kopf v Austria* (n 41) para 105.

[47] Cass civ 15 March 2012 No 4184 (2012) *Rivista di diritto internazionale privato e processuale* 747.

[48] Trib Latina 10 June 2005 (2005) *Rivista di diritto internazionale privato e processuale* 1095, upheld by the Court of Appeal (App Roma 13 July 2006 (2007) *Rivista di diritto internazionale privato e processuale* 426), concerning a request to recognise a marriage celebrated in the Netherlands between two Italian men.

[49] Trib Grosseto, 3 April 2014, not published yet.

[50] Until now the most progressive ruling was a judgment of Trib Reggio Emilia, 13 February 2012 (2012) *Rivista di diritto internazionale privato e processuale* 457. In this case the court has ruled in favour of a request for family unification claimed by an Italian citizen for his Peruvian spouse of the same sex, married in Spain. In particular, it has been considered that the status of spouse acquired, and registered, in another EU country imposes the enjoyment of freedom of movement under Directive 2004/38/EC [2004] OJ L158/77, irrespective of any conflict of laws rules, even for public policy purposes.

The same trend also emerges with regard to surrogacy.[51] An Italian Court of Appeal in 2009 recognised two British orders giving effect to a surrogacy arrangement, stating that it was not in contrast with public policy, in the light of the international principle of 'the child's best interests'.[52]

VI. Conclusion

With regard to family matters, the national approaches to the application of public policy still differ from one Member State to another, which might endanger the objective of mutual recognition of decisions. EU legislation tends to adopt a neutral approach. Similarly, the CJEUand ECtHR case law is still rather cautious. Nevertheless, concerning maintenance, with the abolition of the *exequatur* in the Maintenance Regulation, States have proved to be prepared to abandon the public policy defence. With respect to decisions from States not bound by the Protocol, or third States, given the most recent European case law, it is getting more and more difficult to refuse recognition to maintenance decisions, even if the family relationship on which they are based cannot be recognised (eg *de facto* and same-sex relationships, and registered partnerships). And this becomes rather impossible if the decision concerns children, where the principle of 'the child's best interests' is itself a public policy principle.

Take the example of Italy, undoubtedly one of the most objecting States in Europe. The Italian Supreme Court has endorsed the concept of 'family life' expressed in the ECtHR case law, thus beginning to recognise the effects of stable, same-sex relationships. However, stating that such an overture concerns all the effects of these relationships is too bold a move at this stage. For example, concerning property, the need not to prejudice the rights of third parties plays a role and can justify the invocation of public policy. But maintenance involves the welfare, and even the survival, of the members of the family and this is the only need that should be taken in account. In practice, it means that a decision concerning both, maintenance and sharing, could be automatically recognised for the part relating to maintenance, but be faced with the obstacle of public policy on the part relating to sharing. Such a result is not desirable, but seems inevitable at this stage and even for the two future Regulations on matrimonial property regimes and the property consequences of registered partnerships, which maintain the *exequatur* procedure.

These divergences and difficulties will be overcome only if, and when, in the long run, the CJEU adopts an autonomous notion of 'family relationship'. At that point, it will not even be necessary to call upon the substantive public policy notion and there will be no room for its application.

Therefore, *requiem* for public policy indeed.

[51] On the issue of cross-border surrogacy see generally K Trimmings and P Beaumont, 'International Surrogacy Arrangements: An Urgent Need for Legal Regulation at the International Level' (2011) *Journal of Private International Law* 627.

[52] App Bari 13 February 2009 (2010) *Rivista di diritto internazionale privato e processuale* 699. See especially C Campiglio, 'Lo stato di figlio nato da contratto internazionale di maternità' (2010) *Rivista di diritto internazionale privato e processuale* 589.

28

Jurisdiction, Recognition and Enforcement in Cases of Reimbursement Claims by Public Bodies

DIETER MARTINY

I. Cross-border Recovery of Maintenance by Public Bodies

In maintenance cases it is common for public bodies to be called upon to provide benefits in place of a maintenance debtor, or support the individual seeking maintenance by other means.[1] Article 64 of the EU Maintenance Regulation of 2009[2] and Article 36 of the Hague Maintenance Convention of 2007[3] deal with such public bodies as applicants. Article 10 of

[1] D Martiny, 'Current Developments in the National Laws of Maintenance' (2012) *European Journal of Law Reform* 64, 81; D Martiny, *Unterhaltsrang und -rückgriff II* (Tübingen, Mohr Siebeck, 2000) 1076, 1130.

[2] Art 64 Public bodies as applicants

1. For the purposes of an application for recognition and declaration of enforceability of decisions or for the purposes of enforcement of decisions, the term 'creditor' shall include a public body acting in place of an individual to whom maintenance is owed or one to which reimbursement is owed for benefits provided in place of maintenance.
2. The right of a public body to act in place of an individual to whom maintenance is owed or to seek reimbursement of benefits provided to the creditor in place of maintenance shall be governed by the law to which the body is subject.
3. A public body may seek recognition and a declaration of enforceability or claim enforcement of: (a) a decision given against a debtor on the application of a public body which claims payment of benefits provided in place of maintenance; (b) a decision given between a creditor and a debtor to the extent of the benefits provided to the creditor in place of maintenance.
4. The public body seeking recognition and a declaration of enforceability or claiming enforcement of a decision shall upon request provide any document necessary to establish its right under paragraph 2 and to establish that benefits have been provided to the creditor.

(Council Regulation (EC) No 4/2009 of 18 December 2008 on jurisdiction, applicable law, recognition and enforcement of decisions and cooperation in matters relating to maintenance obligations [2009] OJ L 7/1).

[3] Art 36 Public bodies as applicants

(1) For the purposes of applications for recognition and enforcement under Article 10(1) a) and b) and cases covered by Article 20(4), 'creditor' includes a public body acting in place of an individual to whom maintenance is owed or one to which reimbursement is owed for benefits provided in place of maintenance.

(2) The right of a public body to act in place of an individual to whom maintenance is owed or to seek reimbursement of benefits provided to the creditor in place of maintenance shall be governed by the law to which the body is subject.

(3) A public body may seek recognition or claim enforcement of—

the Hague Maintenance Protocol of 2007 provides that reimbursement claims by public bodies are governed by the domestic law to which that body is subject.[4]

What do these new rules mean for jurisdiction, recognition and enforcement in cross-border recovery of maintenance?

Public bodies that support maintenance creditors or pay benefits to them, are, according to the EU and international rules, entitled to the same services and the same legal aid as if they were an individual maintenance creditor.[5] The Regulation, as well as the Convention, contains an extensive chapter on cooperation between central authorities.[6] Public bodies are, however, only placed on equal footing with individual creditors for the purposes of recognition and enforcement.

II. Involvement of Public Bodies

Maintenance obligations primarily arise to benefit minor children. Apart from the provision of maintenance for children, if and to what extent maintenance obligations arise in other circumstances varies significantly between the domestic laws of the various jurisdictions.[7] Likewise, significant variation is also seen in the area of social welfare law.[8]

There is no precise definition of 'public body' in the Regulation or the Convention. However, the term should be interpreted in the same way in both provisions. A public body can be a public authority or another organisation.[9] There are two ways required of a public body by the Regulation and the Convention. The first possibility is that the public body acts

a) a decision rendered against a debtor on the application of a public body which claims payment of benefits provided in place of maintenance;
b) a decision rendered between a creditor and debtor to the extent of the benefits provided to the creditor in place of maintenance.
(4) The public body seeking recognition or claiming enforcement of a decision shall upon request furnish any document necessary to establish its right under paragraph 2 and that benefits have been provided to the creditor.

(Convention of 23 November 2007 on the International Recovery of Child Support and Other Forms of Family Maintenance, see www.hcch.net). *Cf* A Borrás and J Degeling, 'Explanatory Report on the Convention on the International Recovery of Child Support and Other Forms of Family Maintenance' (2009) paras 586–98. See www.hcch.net (accessed March 2014).

[4] Art 10 Public bodies
The right of a public body to seek reimbursement of a benefit provided to the creditor in place of maintenance shall be governed by the law to which that body is subject.
(Protocol of 23 November 2007 on the Law Applicable to Maintenance Obligations [2009] OJ L 331/19).

[5] Recital 14. See also Arts 44 and 64(1) of the EU Maintenance Regulation of 2009; Arts 15 and 36 of the Hague Maintenance Convention of 2007. *Cf* Borrás and Degeling (n 3) para 590.

[6] Arts 49–63 of the EU Maintenance Regulation of 2009; Arts 4–13 of the Hague Maintenance Convention of 2007.

[7] See in more detail, P Wendl and H-J Dose, *Das Unterhaltsrecht in der familienrichterlichen Praxis*, 8th edn (Munich, CH Beck, 2011) para 100–599. *Cf* also D Martiny, 'Maintenance Obligations in the Conflict of Laws' (1995) *Hague Academy Collected Courses* 131, 144ff; Martiny, 'Current Developments in the National Laws of Maintenance' (n 1) 190.

[8] See in more detail Martiny, *Unterhaltsrang und -rückgriff* (n 1) 1099.

[9] M Andrae, 'Verordnung (EG) Nr 4/2009 des Rates vom 18. Dezember 2008 über die Zuständigkeit, das anwendbare Recht, die Anerkennung und Vollstreckung von Entscheidungen und die Zusammenarbeit in Unterhaltssachen', in T Rauscher (ed), *Brüssel IIa-VO, EG-UntVO, EG-ErbVO-E, HUntStProt 2007* (Munich, Sellier, 2010) Art 64 EG-UntVO para 1.

in place of an individual to whom maintenance is owed,[10] for example, the Dutch National Bureau Collection of Maintenance.[11] The second alternative is where the public body itself provides benefits in place of maintenance.[12] This encompasses social security benefits by social welfare authorities, advance maintenance payments by maintenance advance payment offices or by guarantee funds. By way of example, this includes the Finnish social welfare authorities,[13] German welfare authorities or the German State.[14]

III. Recovery of Maintenance by Public Bodies

A. Applicability of the Maintenance Regulation and Maintenance Convention 2007 to Maintenance Claims

The Maintenance Regulation and the Maintenance Convention are applicable to maintenance claims. The recovery of maintenance by public bodies is treated in principle like the handling of maintenance claims.[15] This is in line with the case law of the Court of Justice of the European Union (CJEU)[16] on the application of the Brussels Convention.[17] The Court decided that reimbursement claims by public bodies are covered as a 'civil matter' by the Convention. The cases concerned recovery for Dutch social assistance[18] and for a scholarship granted by German authorities.[19]

[10] Art 64(1) of the first alternative EU Maintenance Regulation; Art 36 of the first alternative Hague Maintenance Convention of 2007.

[11] *Landelijk Bureau Inning Onderhoudsbijdragen; LBIO. Cf* M Jonker, 'Enforcement of Child Maintenance in the Netherlands' in I Curry-Sumner and C Skinner (eds), *Persistent Problems, Finding Solutions: Child Maintenance in The Netherlands and the UK* (Nijmegen, Wolf Legal Publishers, 2009) 83.

[12] Art 64(1) of the second alternative EU Maintenance Regulation of 2009; Art 36 of the second alternative Hague Maintenance Convention of 2007.

[13] See 'Maintenance claims—Finland' no 12, in European Judicial Network, Maintenance claims, Finland, www.ec.europa.eu/civiljustice/maintenance_claim/maintenance_claim_fin_en.htm (accessed January 2014).

[14] See 'Maintenance claims—Germany' no 13, in European Judicial Network, Maintenance claims, Germany, www.ec.europa.eu/civiljustice/maintenance_claim/maintenance_claim_ger_en.htm (accessed January 2014). For the British Child Support Agency see M Barnes and D Hammond, *International Child Maintenance* (Bristol, Jordans Family Law, 2013) para 4.14.

[15] P Reuß, 'Unterhaltsregress revisited: die internationale gerichtliche Zuständigkeit für Unterhaltsregressklagen nach der EuUntVO' in T Garber, Reinhold Geimer and RA Schütze (eds), *Europäische und internationale Dimension des Rechts—Festschrift für Daphne-Ariane Simotta* (Vienna, LexisNexis ARD Orac, 2012) 483, 484.

[16] *Cf* Case C-271/00 *Gemeente Steenbergen v Baten* [2002] ECR I-10489; (2004) *Praxis des Internationalen Privat- und Verfahrensrechts* 237 annotation D Martiny, 195; P Trenk-Hinterberger, 'Recourse to Maintenance in European Procedural Law' (2003) *The European Legal Forum* 87, www.simons-law.com/library/pdf/e/388.pdf (accessed January 2014); P Trenk-Hinterberger, 'Der Unterhaltsregress von Sozialleistungsträgern in der Rechtsprechung des Europäischen Gerichtshofs', in S Hofer, D Klippel and U Walter Schütze (eds), *Perspektiven des Familienrechts: Festschrift Schwab* (Bielefeld, Gieseking, 2005) 1081.

[17] Convention of 27 September 1968 on Jurisdiction and Enforcement of Judgments in Civil and Commercial Matters [1972] OJ L 299 (English version [1978] OJ L 304). A consolidated version of the Brussels Convention was published in [1998] OJ C 27/1.

[18] Case C-271/00 *Gemeente Steenbergen v Baten* [2002] ECR I-10489.

[19] Case C-433/01 *Freistaat Bayern v Blijdenstein* [2004] ECR I-981; (2004) *Praxis des Internationalen Privat- und Verfahrensrechts* 240 annotation D Martiny, 195.

Under the Maintenance Regulation and the Maintenance Convention the term 'creditor' means any individual to whom maintenance is owed or is alleged to be owed.[20] Under both instruments there is at least partial equality in the treatment of individual maintenance creditors and public bodies seeking to recover. This is an improvement because under the New York Convention on the Recovery Abroad of Maintenance of 1956[21] it remains contested if a public body can be a maintenance creditor for the purposes of that Convention.[22]

B. Support of Creditor

As already mentioned, support of a creditor may take different forms under the Maintenance Regulation and the Maintenance Convention. In the first category the public body acts on behalf of a maintenance creditor for enforcement purposes. In the second, the public body provides benefits in place of maintenance. It is mainly in these cases that the question of reimbursement arises.

C. Different Kinds of Reimbursement

i. Legal Subrogation (cessio legis)

There are different statutory mechanisms that provide recourse against a person owing maintenance. Often—as for example in Germany and Switzerland[23]—there is a legal subrogation of the maintenance claim, which means that the public institution may rely on the maintenance claim for the purpose of recovery.[24] In these cases, recovery claims are based on special provisions of public law and maintenance law. The maintenance claim against the maintenance debtor passes to the public body as a consequence of its providing maintenance and/or other benefits. This is, for example, the case in Germany for basic social security benefits,[25] social assistance[26] advance maintenance payments[27] and some

[20] Art 2(10).

[21] New York Convention of 20 June 1956 on the Recovery Abroad of Maintenance, see www.hcch.net.

[22] According to Art 1(1) the purpose of the Convention is to facilitate the recovery of maintenance to which a 'person' claims to be entitled.

[23] See the general provision in Art 289 of the Swiss Civil Code (*Zivilgesetzbuch*):

(1) The right to maintenance contributions is that of the child and, so long as he or she is a minor, is fulfilled by payment to the child's legal representative or to the person with custody of the child.

(2) However, where the state authority assumes the cost of maintaining the child, such claim and all attendant rights pass to the state authority.

(Translation by the Swiss Federal Office of Justice, www.admin.ch/ch/e/rs/2/210.en.pdf (accessed January 2014)).

[24] See in more detail: D Martiny, 'Unterhaltsrückgriff durch öffentliche Träger im europäischen internationalen Privat- und Verfahrensrecht' (2004) *Praxis des Internationalen Privat- und Verfahrensrechts* 195, 197; Martiny, *Unterhaltsrang und -rückgriff* (n 1) 1080.

[25] s 33(1) of the German Social Security Act II (Sozialgesetzbuch [SGB], Zweites Buch [II], Grundsicherung für Arbeitsuchende) of 24 December 2003, Federal Gazette (Bundesgesetzblatt; BGBl) [2003] I 2954 as amended.

[26] s 94(1) of the Social Security Act XII (Sozialgesetzbuch [SGB], Zwölftes Buch [XII], Sozialhilfe) of 27 December 2003 [2003] BGBl I 3022 as amended.

[27] s 7(1) of the Maintenance Advancements Act (Gesetz zur Sicherung des Unterhalts von Kindern alleinstehender Mütter und Väter durch Unterhaltsvorschüsse oder -ausfallleistungen [Unterhaltsvorschussgesetz] of 17 July 2007 [2007] BGBl I 1446, as amended).

scholarships paid under the Federal Training Assistance Act.[28] In the case of the scholarships a federal State subrogates to the maintenance claim of the student. Such claims are maintenance cases in the sense of the Maintenance Regulation.[29] It is also possible for a claim to be transferred to the public body by way of an administrative decision and a notification of assignment.

ii. Separate Reimbursement Claims

Separate claims for reimbursement of benefits paid in place of maintenance are also covered by the Regulation and Convention and treated like maintenance claims. The CJEU decided along these lines in a reimbursement claim of a Dutch municipality for social assistance payments.[30] In that decision, the claim was subject to the then Brussels Convention of 1968.

D. Separate Claims for Reimbursement of Costs

On the other hand, a separate claim by the State for reimbursement of costs (eg for institutional care) is not a maintenance claim.[31] It is, however, difficult to determine exactly when such claims are excluded from the Regulation. This is because, despite the fact that the Maintenance Regulation does not expressly mention a requirement of a 'civil matter' for its applicability, it has been argued that there is such a requirement.[32] On the other hand, the CJEU did not hesitate to classify measures for the protection of children, which are of a public law nature, as being covered by the Brussels IIa Regulation.[33] For the Brussels Convention, the CJEU argued for the exclusion of claims where there is a competence of the State to enforce the claim in exercise of public powers.[34] Another argument relates to the nature of the claim. If such a claim only amounts to a claim for compensation by the State, then its purpose is not a substitute for maintenance of an individual.[35]

E. Re-transferred Maintenance Claims

A specific reimbursement technique under German law is the 're-transfer' of maintenance claims. Where a claim has been the subject of a statutory transfer to a public body, that claim can, by way of a voluntary assignment, be transferred back to the individual creditor

[28] s 37(1) of the Federal Training Assistance Act (Bundesgesetz über individuelle Förderung der Ausbildung; Bundesausbildungsförderungsgesetz; BAföG) of 7 December 2010 [2010] BGBl I 1952, as amended.

[29] Reuß (n 15) 484; Andrae (n 9) Art 1 EG-UntVO paras 33 and 38; R Hausmann, *Internationales und Europäisches Ehescheidungsrecht* (Munich, CH Beck, 2013) ch C no 60. Contra DC Bittmann, 'Europäische Unterhaltsverordnung (EuUntVO)' in M Gebauer and T Wiedmann (eds), *Zivilrecht unter europäischem Einfluss*, 2nd edn (Stuttgart, Boorberg, 2010) ch 36 no 16; U Gruber, 'Die neue EG-Unterhaltsverordnung' (2010) *Praxis des Internationalen Privat- und Verfahrensrechts* 128, 137.

[30] Case C-271/00 *Gemeente Steenbergen v Baten* [2002] ECR I-10489.

[31] Hausmann (n 29) ch C no 59.

[32] See Andrae (n 9) Art 1 EG-UntVO para 44; Hausmann (n 29) ch C no 59.

[33] Case C-92/12 *PPU Health Service Executive* judgment of 26 April 2012; (2012) *Zeitschrift für das gesamte Familienrecht* 1466.

[34] *Cf* Martiny (n 24) 200.

[35] Ibid 197; Hausmann (n 29) ch C no 59.

who may then pursue it in a fiduciary capacity (eg this is possible under section 94(5)(1) of the German Social Security Act XII and section 7(4)(2) of the Maintenance Advancements Act). In cross-border enforcement proceedings, this technique secures the same privileged treatment for the re-transferred claim that the original maintenance claim enjoyed.[36] However, critics argue that it is only a reimbursement claim.[37] The consequence would be a treatment like reimbursement claims of public bodies.

IV. Jurisdiction

A. Grounds for Jurisdiction under the EU Maintenance Regulation

Contrary to the Hague Maintenance Convention 2007, which provides only indirect jurisdiction for recognition purposes (see Article 20), the Maintenance Regulation contains rules on the direct jurisdiction of courts and other authorities in maintenance matters (Articles 3 to 8).[38] This encompasses a general jurisdiction based on habitual residence and an ancillary jurisdiction in connection with status proceedings. A choice of court is also possible and there are some additional cases of special jurisdiction. However, it is necessary to examine which of these grounds for jurisdiction can be relied upon by a public body.

B. General Jurisdiction

i. Habitual Residence of the Debtor (Article 3(a) of the Maintenance Regulation)

First, in the alternative jurisdictional fora, is the jurisdiction based on habitual residence. Jurisdiction lies with the court in the place where the defendant is habitually resident (Article 3(a) of the Maintenance Regulation). A claim of a public body may also be based on this jurisdiction.[39]

ii. Habitual Residence of the Creditor (Article 3(b) of the Maintenance Regulation)?

For an individual seeking maintenance there is also jurisdiction of the court in the place where the creditor is habitually resident (Article 3(b) Maintenance Regulation). Such a rule also exists in the Brussels I Regulation. It also applies where the defendant is habitually resident in a third State.[40] However, the Regulation only mentions that for the purposes of an application for the recognition and enforcement of a decision relating to maintenance

[36] Local Court (Amtsgericht) Stuttgart 4 September 2013 (2014) *Praxis des Internationalen Privat- und Verfahrensrechts* 280, annotation P Mankowski, 249. *Cf* N Hartig and I Jäger-Maillet, 'Durchsetzung übergegangener Unterhaltsansprüche im Ausland' in C Schmidt (ed), *Internationale Unterhaltsrealisierung* (Baden-Baden, Nomos, 2011) 115, 122.

[37] M Andrae, 'Der Unterhaltsregress öffentlicher Einrichtungen nach der EuUntVO, dem HUÜ 2007 und dem HUP' (2013) *Familie Partnerschaft Recht* 38.

[38] For more detail, see Andrae (n 9) Art 3 EG-UntVO para 43.

[39] Reuß (n 15) 489.

[40] Recitals 15–17. *Cf* Barnes and Hammond (n 14) para 4.12.

obligations the term 'creditor' includes public bodies (Article 64(1)). The literal meaning of this provision seems to be that a public body cannot use the jurisdictional base of habitual residence of a maintenance creditor.

Such an interpretation is in line with the case law of the CJEU. In a reimbursement case arising under the Brussels Convention, the public body—the Freistaat Bayern, a German federal State—could not take advantage of the more favourable jurisdictional rules provided for maintenance creditors.[41] The Court said that the Convention must be interpreted independently, by reference to its system and objectives. The general principle in the system of the Brussels Convention is that the courts of the Contracting State in which the defendant is domiciled are to have jurisdiction (Article 2).[42] Article 5(2) of the Convention enables the maintenance creditor to sue the defendant before the courts of the Contracting State in which the applicant is domiciled. This is a rule of jurisdiction which derogates from the general principle of the Convention. However, other than in the cases expressly provided for, the Brussels Convention appears hostile towards the attribution of jurisdiction to the courts of the applicant's domicile. Article 5(2) does not contain any indication as to the party who may be the applicant and has to be interpreted narrowly. A public body which brings an action for recovery against a maintenance debtor is not in an inferior position with regard to the latter. Moreover, the maintenance creditor, whose maintenance has been covered by the payments of the public body, is no longer in a precarious financial position. It follows that, since the maintenance creditor has benefited from the grant to which he or she could lay claim, there is no need to deny the maintenance debtor the protection offered by Article 2 of the Convention, particularly as the courts of the defendant are better placed to determine the latter's resources. Therefore there was no need to grant public institutions, not being the weaker party, the benefit of this jurisdictional basis.[43]

The dominant view follows the approach that Article 3(b) of the Maintenance Regulation is not available for public bodies.[44] However, critics argue that the system of jurisdiction is different in the new Regulation.[45] Under Article 3(b) there is no longer a restrictedly interpreted and exceptional forum but alternative fora. The argument by the Court that a public body itself is not in need is not very convincing because an effective collection of maintenance is one of the purposes of the Regulation. Whether the payer is an

[41] Case C-433/01 *Freistaat Bayern v Blijdenstein* [2004] ECR I-981.

[42] Case C-433/01 *Freistaat Bayern v Blijdenstein* [2004] ECR I-981, paras 24, 25.

[43] Ibid para 30.

[44] Bittmann (n 29) ch 36 no 33; W Hau, 'Die Zuständigkeitsgründe der Europäischen Unterhaltsverordnung' (2010) *Zeitschrift für das gesamte Familienrecht* 516, 519; B Hess, 'Die Verordnung Nr. 4/2009/EG zum Unterhaltsrecht' in C Schmidt (ed), *Internationale Unterhaltsrealisierung* (Baden-Baden, Nomos, 2011) 27, 30; M Kuntze, 'Unterhaltsrückgriff nach dem SGB II mit Auslandsbezug durch die Jobcenter und Optionskommunen' (2011) *Familie Partnerschaft Recht* 166, 170; R Fucik, 'VO (EG) Nr. 4/2009 des Rates vom 18.12.2008 über die Zuständigkeit, das anwendbare Recht, die Anerkennung und Vollstreckung von Entscheidungen und die Zusammenarbeit in Unterhaltssachen', in HW Fasching and A Konecny (eds), *Kommentar zu den Zivilprozeßgesetzen*, Vol 5/2, 2nd edn (Vienna, Manz, 2010) Art 3 EuUVO no 4.

[45] M Weber, 'Die Zuständigkeitstatbestände des Art 3 EU-Unterhaltsverordnung' (2012) *Zeitschrift für Ehe- und Familienrecht* 13, 17; Andrae (n 37) 38; Reuß (n 15) 489; Hausmann (n 29) ch C no 95; P Reuß, 'VO (EG) Nr. 4/2009 des Rates vom 18.12.2008 über die Zuständigkeit, das anwendbare Recht, die Anerkennung und Vollstreckung von Entscheidungen und die Zusammenarbeit in Unterhaltssachen' in R Geimer and R Schütze (eds), *Internationaler Rechtsverkehr in Zivil- und Handelssachen*, 42nd edn (Munich, CH Beck, 2011) Art 1 VO No 4/2009 para 32, Art 3 VO No 4/2009 para 28; V Lipp, 'Verordnung (EG) Nr. 4/2009 des Rates über die Zuständigkeit, das anwendbare Recht, die Anerkennung und Vollstreckung von Entscheidungen und die Zusammenarbeit in Unterhaltssachen (EGUntVO)', in T Rauscher (ed), *Münchener Kommentar zum FamFG*, 2nd edn (Munich, CH Beck, 2013) vor Art 3 EG-UntVO para 29.

individual or a public body should not alter the primary responsibility of the maintenance debtor. The public body should therefore be able to use the jurisdiction at the habitual residence of the claimant.[46] There is also an argument based on a provision in the Hague Maintenance Convention which obliges a State which has made a restricting reservation against the recognition of judgments rendered at the place of habitual residence of the maintenance creditor to undertake all necessary steps for the establishment of a reimbursement decision (see Article 36(1) in conjunction with Article 20(4)).[47] This is, however, not a very convincing argument because the Hague Convention 2007 deals with a very specific situation with no parallel in the EU Regulation. Above all such an argument based on indirect jurisdiction is not strong enough to create a non-existent direct jurisdictional base in the framework of the EU Regulation. However, there remains the main argument against a broad interpretation, the wording of the Maintenance Regulation. The public body is expressly mentioned in Article 64(1). If this provision only stipulates an equal treatment for recognition and enforcement why should there be also equal treatment for jurisdiction which is not mentioned?

iii. No Ancillary Jurisdiction

In certain cases the courts have jurisdiction to address the issue of maintenance when it is ancillary to proceedings on the status of a person (Article 3(c) of the Maintenance Regulation). Examples of this are divorce and paternity proceedings. However, since these cases arise purely from personal matters, a public body cannot use this jurisdictional basis, not to mention the lack of any statutory basis for doing so.[48] The same applies for proceedings concerning parental responsibility (Article 3(d) of the Maintenance Regulation).[49]

C. Other Grounds for Jurisdiction

The Regulation enables the parties to choose the competent court by agreement, on the grounds of there being specific connecting factors (*cf* Article 4).[50] However, such choice of court agreements (unlikely to be used by public bodies) are not possible where a dispute relates to a maintenance obligation towards a child under the age of 18. A subsidiary jurisdiction based on the common nationality of the parties is excluded (Article 6).[51] Furthermore, where no court of a Member State has jurisdiction pursuant to Articles 3 to 6 the courts of a Member State may, on an exceptional basis, hear the case (Article 7). It is doubtful if this *forum necessitatis* is available to public bodies.[52]

[46] Andrae (n 37) 38; Reuß (n 15) 489; Hausmann (n 29) ch C no 95; Reuß, 'VO (EG) Nr. 4/2009' (n 45) Art 1 VO No 4/2009 para 32, Art 3 VO No 4/2009 para 28.

[47] Andrae (n 37) 38.

[48] Reuß, 'VO (EG) Nr. 4/2009' (n 45) Art 3 VO No 4/2009 para 30.

[49] Ibid para 33.

[50] Reuß (n 15) 491.

[51] Ibid 491.

[52] For rare cases only, see ibid 492.

V. Recognition, Declaration of Enforceability and Enforcement

A. Different Situations

There is no single solution for recognition and enforcement. Thus, several tracks and scenarios have to be distinguished:

- Recognition and enforcement of foreign decisions between Contracting States of the *Hague Convention 2007*.[53]
- Recognition and enforcement of foreign decisions *without* exequatur *coming from EU Hague Protocol States* (Article 17ff of the Maintenance Regulation).[54] Under this system the decision is automatically enforceable in another Member State without further formalities.
- Exequatur *procedure for decisions from EU non-Protocol States* (Article 23ff of the Maintenance Regulation).[55]
- *National procedural law* applies for the enforcement as such.[56]

B. Recognition and Enforcement

For the purposes of an application for recognition and declaration of enforceability of foreign decisions or for the purposes of enforcement of decisions, the term 'creditor' includes a public body (Article 64(1) of the Maintenance Regulation and Article 36(1) of the Maintenance Convention 2007). The public body is entitled to the same services and the same legal aid as a creditor.[57] However, a public body is excluded from the Maintenance Convention and from support by the Central Authorities where the public body applies

[53] German implementing provisions in ss 57 and 60a of the Foreign Maintenance Act (*Gesetz zur Geltendmachung von Unterhaltsansprüchen im Verkehr mit ausländischen Staaten [Auslandsunterhaltsgesetz;* AUG] of 23 May 2011, [2011] BGBl I 898). Amended by Act on the Implementation of the Hague Convention of 2007, the amendment of provisions in the field of international maintenance law and on the amendment of substantive maintenance law of 20 February 2013 (*Gesetz zur Durchführung des Haager Übereinkommens vom 23. November 2007 über die internationale Geltendmachung der Unterhaltsansprüche von Kindern und anderen Familienangehörigen sowie zur Änderung von Vorschriften auf dem Gebiet des internationalen Unterhaltsverfahrensrechts und des materiellen Unterhaltsrechts*), [2013] BGBl I 273. After its ratification the Hague Convention 2007 will be covered by the Foreign Maintenance Act (see s 1(1) no 2(a) of the Foreign Maintenance Act as amended. For the Hague Convention of 1973, implementing provisions are found in ss 57 and 61 of the Foreign Maintenance Act. For more detail, see Hausmann (n 29) ch K no 581.

[54] German implementing provisions in s 30 of the Foreign Maintenance Act. See in more detail Hausmann (n 29) ch K no 500.

[55] German implementing provisions in s 36 of the Foreign Maintenance Act. For more detail see Hausmann (n 29) ch K no 526.

[56] For the enforcement of foreign maintenance decisions, s 120(1) of the Family Proceedings Act (Familienverfahrensgesetz) is applicable. According to this provision enforcement in matrimonial and contentious family proceedings follows the provisions of the Code of Civil Proceedings (CCP; *Zivilprozessordnung*; ZPO).

[57] Recital 14.

for a maintenance decision in another Contracting State (but see Article 20(4) of the Maintenance Convention).[58]

C. Decision for the Public Body

There are different categories of foreign decisions. The first category concerns recognition of decisions and declarations of enforceability, as well as enforcement of decisions made against maintenance debtors on the application of public bodies claiming payments of benefits provided in place of maintenance (Article 64(3)(a) of the Maintenance Regulation and Article 36(3)(a) of the Maintenance Convention 2007). Here there is equality of treatment between creditor and public body; the public body is entitled to the same services and the same legal aid as a creditor.

D. Decision for the Original Maintenance Creditor

The second category of decisions concerns recognition of decisions and declarations of enforceability, as well as claims for enforcement of decisions in proceedings between creditors and debtors (Article 64(3)(b) of the Maintenance Regulation and Article 36(3)(b) of the Maintenance Convention 2007). If there has been a later transfer of the claim to the public body then the original maintenance creditor is no longer the real creditor. If the original maintenance creditor nevertheless applies for enforcement of the foreign decision then his or her position in the enforcement proceedings must be determined.[59]

i. Position of the Maintenance Creditor after a Transfer of the Claim

a. Recognition and Enforcement under the Hague Convention

If recognition and enforcement is sought according to the Hague Convention, then under the national procedural framework for declarations of enforceability, it can be taken into account that there is now a new creditor. Under German procedural law the debtor has an objection based on substantive law against the claim to be enforced.[60] This is possible already against the declaration of enforceability.

[58] See Borrás and Degeling (n 3) para 590.

[59] K Hilbig-Lugani, 'Forderungsübergang als materielle Einwendung im Exequaturverfahren' (2012) *Praxis des Internationalen Privat- und Verfahrensrechts* 333.

[60] According to s 120(1) of the Family Proceedings Act enforcement in matrimonial and contentious family proceedings follows the provisions of the CCP. Therefore s 767 CCP on the action raising an objection to the claim being enforced (*Vollstreckungsgegenklage*) is applicable.

s 767 CCP Action raising an objection to the claim being enforced

(1) Debtors are to assert objections that concern the claim itself as established by the judgment by filing a corresponding action with the court of first instance hearing the case.

(2) Such objections by way of an action may admissibly be asserted only insofar as the grounds on which they are based arose only after the close of the hearing that was the last opportunity, pursuant to the stipulations of the present Code, for objections to be asserted, and thus can no longer be asserted by entering a protest.

(3) In the action that he is to file, the debtor must assert all objections that he was able to assert at the time at which he filed the action.

(Translation provided for the Federal Ministry of Justice, available at www.gesetze-im-internet.de/englisch_zpo/englisch_zpo.html (accessed January 2014)).

A recent decision of the German Federal Supreme Court concerned a complaint against a declaration of enforceability pronounced for a Swiss judgment under the Hague Recognition Convention of 2 October 1973 under the Act Implementing Recognition and Enforcement (*Anerkennungs- und Vollstreckungsausführungsgesetz, AVAG*) of 19 February 2001[61] (the pertinent provision is now found in the Foreign Maintenance Act).[62] The case raised the questions of whether the court deciding on enforceability could take into account defences of the debtor based on a modification of the judgment, on partial performance of the maintenance obligation and on reasons to modify the judgment. But it particularly dealt with the effect of a legal subrogation of the maintenance claim to the public authority which has provided the maintenance creditor with subsidiary social security benefits. The Federal Supreme Court held that this qualified as a defence to be taken into account in the *exequatur* decision.[63] The court seems to limit its statements to those defences which are undisputed or which are based on circumstances having acquired the force of *res judicata*. One has to assume that the treatment of the claim's transfer should be the same under the new German enforcement provisions in the Foreign Maintenance Act for the Hague Maintenance Conventions.[64]

b. Recognition and Enforcement under EU Procedural Rules

If recognition and an application for declaration of enforceability are made under EU procedural rules, the CJEU has held that the *exequatur* courts of the State addressed have no competence to decide on objections such as having already paid the ordered judgment debt.[65] It is primarily the task of the courts in the first State to make a decision. This has been decided for the Brussels I Regulation but has to be respected also under the Maintenance Regulation.[66] Therefore the former national German provision in section 44 of the Foreign Maintenance Act allowing such objections conflicted with European Union law and has been repealed.[67] However, such an objection can nevertheless be raised in the

[61] See s 12 of the Act Implementing Recognition and Enforcement (AVAG). This provision is not applicable in proceedings covered by the Brussels I Regulation (s 55(1) AVAG).

[62] See s 66(2) of the Foreign Maintenance Act. For more detail see Hausmann (n 29) ch K no 595a.

[63] See for the Hague Convention of 1973: German Federal Supreme Court 2 March 2011 (2011) *Zeitschrift für das gesamte Familienrecht* 802; (2012) *Praxis des internationalen Verfahrensrechts* 360 annotation Hilbig-Lugani, 333.

[64] Hilbig-Lugani (n 59) 335. For the *exequatur* proceedings, s 59a of the Foreign Maintenance Act applies, according to which objections against the claim may be raised in the appeal proceedings. At the enforcement stage objections against the claim may be raised according to s 66(2) of the Foreign Maintenance Act.

[65] Case C-139/10 *Prism Investments* [2011] ECR I-9511; (2011) *Neue Juristische Wochenschrift* 3506; (2013) *Praxis des internationalen Privat- und Verfahrensrechts* 357 annotation Rolf Wagner, 326 (enforcing courts may not deny *exequatur* to foreign judgments on the ground that they were already paid by way of set-off).

[66] R Wagner, 'Vollstreckbarerklärungsverfahren nach der EuGVVO und Erfüllungseinwand' (2012) *Praxis des internationalen Privat- und Verfahrensrechts* 326, 333; Hausmann (n 29) ch K no 553.

[67] See Art 1(1)(a) of the Act on the Implementation of the Hague Convention of 2007, the amendment of provisions in the field of international maintenance law and on the amendment of substantive maintenance law of 20 February 2013 (*Gesetz zur Durchführung des Haager Übereinkommens vom 23. November 2007 über die internationale Geltendmachung der Unterhaltsansprüche von Kindern und anderen Familienangehörigen sowie zur Änderung von Vorschriften auf dem Gebiet des internationalen Unterhaltsverfahrensrechts und des materiellen Unterhaltsrechts*), [2013] BGBl I 273. s 44 AUG was the equivalent of s 12 AVAG. For more detail see K Hilbig-Lugani, 'Die Änderungen im AUG und AVAG durch das Durchführungsgesetz zum Haager Unterhaltsübereinkommen 2007' (2013) *Familien-Rechts-Berater International* 74, 76; Hausmann (n 29) ch K no 553.

enforcement proceedings in the State addressed. This has been clarified in an amended provision of the Foreign Maintenance Act.[68]

c. Recognition and Enforcement between EU Protocol States

There is no requirement for an *exequatur* if an enforcement proceeding is based on a maintenance decision coming from an EU Protocol State (Article 17 of the EU Maintenance Regulation). There is no European legal provision stipulating how such an objection based on substantive law against the claim has to be dealt with. It is clear that the competent court for the actual enforcement proceedings has to decide the issue. In Germany there was uncertainty as to which specific provision should be applied.[69] However, it seems that also in this case the amended section 66(1) of the Foreign Maintenance Act in conjunction with section 767 CCP will be applied.

ii. Position of the Public Body after a Transfer of the Claim

In the case of a foreign decision in favour of an individual creditor *under the* exequatur *procedure*, the change in creditor can be taken into account. A declaration of enforceability in favour of the public body is possible (section 39 of the Foreign Maintenance Act).[70] For decisions on maintenance obligations given in an EU Member State not bound by the 2007 Hague Protocol, there is a procedure for recognition and declaration of enforceability in the Regulation (Articles 23 to 38). It is, however, not totally clear if such a change of creditor can be taken into account in these proceedings.

In cases of enforcement of a foreign decision without *exequatur* from an EU State bound by the Hague Protocol, such a change can be taken into account in the enforcement proceedings. However, an amendment according to the general provision of section 727 CCP seems to be unlikely.[71]

VI. Conclusion

Under the new Maintenance Regulation and the Hague Convention there have been major improvements for cross-border recovery of maintenance claims and enforcement. However, equality in the treatment of individual maintenance creditors and of public bodies exists only with respect to the recognition and enforcement of decisions. For public bodies the available bases of jurisdiction are restricted. The fact that there are different recognition schemes and many questions of delineation between EU and international rules on the one hand and national procedural law on the other hand will, in the future, give rise to many more questions and undoubtedly lead to some complicated problems for the application of the EU rules but also of the rules integrating them into national legal orders.

[68] See s 66(1) of the Foreign Maintenance Act as amended. See further Hilbig-Lugani (n 67) 77; Hausmann (n 29) ch K no 594. For s 767 CCP, see Andrae (n 37) 45.

[69] For proceedings according to s 66 of the Foreign Maintenance Act in conjunction with s 767 CCP (action to oppose enforcement), see Hilbig-Lugani (n 59) 336. For an analogous application of s 767 CCP only, see Andrae (n 37) 45.

[70] The public body is the legal successor, Andrae (n 37) 44; Hausmann (n 29) ch K no 536.

[71] See Andrae (n 37) 44.

INDEX

Page numbers in *italics* refer to figures and those in **bold** refer to information in tables.

Lightning Source UK Ltd.
Milton Keynes UK
UKOW04f1456220916

283564UK00008B/204/P

9 781509 909285